TO STAND WITH PALESTINE

To Stand with Palestine

TRANSNATIONAL RESISTANCE
AND POLITICAL EVOLUTION
IN THE UNITED STATES

Karam Dana

Columbia University Press
New York

Columbia University Press
Publishers Since 1893
New York   Chichester, West Sussex

Copyright © 2025 Columbia University Press
All rights reserved

Library of Congress Cataloging-in-Publication Data

Names: Daʿnā, Karam, author.
Title: To stand with Palestine : transnational resistance and political evolution in the United States / Karam Dana.
Other titles: Transnational resistance and political evolution in the United States
Description: New York, NY : Columbia University Press, [2024] | Includes bibliographical references and index.
Identifiers: LCCN 2023058652 (print) | LCCN 2023058653 (ebook) | ISBN 9780231186162 (hardback) | ISBN 9780231186179 (trade paperback) | ISBN 9780231546522 (ebook)
Subjects: LCSH: Palestinian Arabs—United States x Public opinion. | Palestinian Americans—Political activity. | Palestine question (1948–)—Public opinion. | National characteristics, Palestinian. Palestinian Americans—Ethnic identity. | United States—Ethnic relations. | Palestinian Arabs—United States. | Palestinian diaspora.
Classification: LCC E184.P33 D36 2024 (print) | LCC E184.P33 (ebook) | DDC 305.89274073—dc23/eng/20240214

Cover design: Elliott S. Cairns
Cover illustration: tanshy / Shutterstock

*To my mother Um Gharib, my partner Sharon,
and our kids Serene and Nadeem.*

CONTENTS

ACKNOWLEDGMENTS ix

PREFACE xi

Introduction
The Evolving Palestine Question 1

Chapter One
Palestinians in the American Imagination 25

Chapter Two
Structural Transformations in Culture, Society,
and Politics in the United States 80

Chapter Three
Social Change and Sound Bites:
The Fight Intensifies in American Culture 114

Chapter Four
The Intensification of Political and Legal Battles
in the United States and Beyond 185

Chapter Five
The Fight for Solidarity and Legitimacy 235

Conclusion 277

NOTES 287

BIBLIOGRAPHY 341

INDEX 379

ACKNOWLEDGMENTS

I extend my deepest gratitude to those who have supported me throughout the journey of writing this book. The book is a product of the unwavering encouragement, guidance, and support of so many.

First, I would like to thank my family. You have provided me with endless encouragement, and I am eternally indebted and grateful to be part of the family. My sincere gratitude goes to my mother, Um Gharib, who has always been very supportive of everything I do and continues to be an inspiration. My mother has inspired me to be empathetic and taught me that the key to everything is acquiring more knowledge.

I am grateful to my loving wife, partner, and companion, Sharon. You have made my life wonderful, even during hardships. I am lucky to have and to raise our two lovely children with you. To Serene and Nadeem, I express my infinite love. Being your parent is one of the most important (and difficult) roles I hold. Thank you for understanding the significance of my work and giving me space and time to do my research. I am proud of you, now and always, for being who you are without any hesitation, and for being proud of your identities as Palestinian. You are the next generation of Palestinians living transnationally.

To my siblings, who have been my pillars of strength and sources of inspiration, thank you for your unwavering belief in me ever since I was born. Gharib, Arwa, Adli, Majdi, Jihan, Ramzi, and Rana, you have always

ACKNOWLEDGMENTS

been there for me, and I am blessed to have you by my side. I love you all, and I am lucky to be the youngest to receive your wisdom and advice (including unsolicited!).

The list of colleagues and friends who have been influential in my intellectual development is long. First, I thank Sara Roy, who has been a true friend and supportive mentor for more than twenty years. Scott Kurashige was one of the earliest friends who encouraged me to write this book. He pointed out the void in this area, encouraged me to do it. This set me on a path of deep reflection that led to this book.

I thank Matt Barreto, Nubar Hovsepian, George Bisharat, Alwyn Rouyer, Gary Segura, and Hannah Walker for their long-lasting friendship and support. At UW Bothell and Seattle, I have worked with truly amazing individuals. My deep gratitude goes to Jody Early, Dan Berger, Maryam Griffin, Allison Hintz, Shauna Carlisle, Janelle Silva, Ron Krabill, Wadiya Udell, Jin-Kyu Jung, Paola Rodriguez Hidalgo, Alexes Harris, Rachel Chapman, Juliana Villegas, Wolf Yeigh, and others. Your friendship has shaped the process of my personal and intellectual development.

I have made long-lasting friendships with my former research assistants whose help was instrumental in making this book and other research projects come to light. I particularly would like to single out Reem Sabha for working on the early research stages of the book. I am greatly indebted to you for your efforts. I also would like to thank Brieanna Smith for her tremendous help in pushing this project forward. I also thank Kelly Berg, Raeanne Hutchins, and Hannah Ravani. My gratitude goes to my editor Caelyn Cobb for working with me after the book was long overdue, and to the rest of the staff at Columbia University Press.

I want to single out one individual. Alyson McGregor was truly influential in making history with a financial gift to create the first ever named professorship at UW Bothell, the Alyson McGregor Distinguished Professorship of Excellence and Transformative Research, which I have held since 2021. The professorship shows that philanthropy can indeed make a difference. I have come to cherish my friendship with Alyson McGregor and Mark Olson.

Finally, I would like to express my deep appreciation and love for the people of Palestine, both in historical Palestine and outside its borders. Their efforts at decolonization and their very existence are the driving forces that inspire and forge the very meanings of global social justice of resilience.

PREFACE

At the very center of it, settler colonialism is a zero-sum game. It's either the colonizer's account or that of the indigenous inhabitants. They can never coexist. The continuous colonial effort of Zionism to delegitimize the indigenous Palestinian narrative is best described by the fact that colonialism is a process with twists and turns, not a one-time event. The Palestinian experience of colonization continues. The *Nakba* is ongoing. Lifeless Palestinian bodies have crowded social media platforms in recent years. Palestinian lives seem to be worth a lot less than others.

From the calamity, however, many opportunities have emerged. The very existence of Palestinians, whether under occupation or outside of Palestine, has itself become a source of power. The transnational Palestinian presence has created new frontiers for Palestinian resistance against Israel, in places and spaces beyond its control.

As I write this preface, the war and genocide against Gaza have been raging for 249 days. Although the vast majority of this work does not directly address the events that took place on October 7, 2023, and the subsequent genocidal war against Gaza, the analyses presented contextualize the current historical moment and provide explanations for and descriptions of the shifts that are taking place with regard to the question of Palestine. I have been able to include some updates of the events that have occurred since then, but they are not critical to the analyses and arguments of this book.

In fact, the situation since October 7th has reinforced the arguments of this book.

The amount of death and destruction has been astonishing, but more so has been the Western world's ambivalence to the deaths and suffering of Palestinians. The United States has supplied Israel with weapons multiple times during these past few months. The world has witnessed the endless barrage of bombs falling on homes, schools, and hospitals.

Although Palestine has long been central to American politics, many people are just discovering it. The two major political parties might disagree on a number of issues, but they have long been in agreement over Israel and Palestine. Whether progressive or not, the Palestinian cause has been perceived and depicted as illegitimate in the halls of power, a phenomenon dubbed as "progressive except Palestine." The shift in U.S. public opinion, however, is ushering a new era that seemed impossible just two decades ago.

Since January 2024 the International Court of Justice has described Israel's action as genocide on multiple occasions. The war brought unprecedented levels of violence and destruction, resulting in tens of thousands of Palestinian civilians killed, with daily death rates breaking records of any other major twenty-first-century conflicts, according to Oxfam. The Committee to Protect Journalists has said the death toll of more than one hundred and fifty journalists has exceeded the total number of journalists killed during the entire period of World War II and the Vietnam War.

The images of genocide, death, and destruction in Gaza have contributed to an intensifying change in how Palestine and Palestinians are viewed. This change is noticeable globally, but particularly in the United States. What we are witnessing in Palestine and the reactions to violence around the world reflects a changing sociopolitical landscape on the question of Palestine. The current moment in history is critical, not only for Palestine, but also for social movements that center equity in their quest for justice. As the genocidal war against Palestinians rages and intensifies, so are the opposing forces calling for a permanent ceasefire, an end to Israeli apartheid, and holding Israel accountable for its actions. Countries around the world are viewed as enabling this genocide, and political costs are rising when defending the unprecedented levels of destruction and death. The United States is the first of these countries where a noticeable shift is taking place at college campuses, city halls, and in congress.

Palestine has become the true test of intersectionality and of solidarity politics. It has become central in how Jewish Americans see themselves in relation to Israel and practices of settler colonialism. It is the true test of people's power against the established status quo.

Palestine has become the true test of one's very own humanity.

TO STAND WITH PALESTINE

INTRODUCTION

The Evolving Palestine Question

The Palestinian people trace their lineage back through the farthest reaches of history, through different dynasties and empires. It was on this land and in its vibrant society, filled with cities, ports, and villages, where people lived, worked, and raised their families.[1] In keeping with colonial traditions, it seems, inside a conference room in Europe, the seeds of a decades-long struggle were planted when the United Nations legitimized the colonization of Palestine by approving the Partition Plan (UN Resolution 181) in 1947. Although the paths to colonization had been paved over decades earlier, in 1948 the land of Palestine was colonized, leading to the newly created state of Israel. The violence of settler colonial practices has since largely been overlooked, tolerated, and ignored with almost absolute impunity and effectively viewed as legitimate. The newly established state in 1948 was meant to solve the problem of the Jewish people, escaping the abuse and violence they suffered at the hands of Europeans. The remainder of Palestine (i.e., the West Bank and the Gaza Strip, which comprised less than a quarter of Palestine's geography) was left for the native indigenous Palestinians, whose very own existence has since been challenged over decades of evolving battles around the legitimacy of their identity as a people and claims to their homes and lands. Since 1948, forcibly removed from their homes or fleeing the advance of an army that has been continuously funded by the United States and Europe, indigenous Palestinians became subject to their own diaspora. Violence dominated Palestinian daily existence and erupted again and again as Israel conquered more Palestinian lands, and the Palestinians attempted to fight back to claim their freedom from an oppression that has long gone unchecked by the global community. The displacement of close to one million Palestinians created the longest refugee crisis in modern times. That event marked the Palestinian *Nakba* (Catastrophe), referring to the Palestinian calamity of displacement and destruction that began in 1948. For more than seventy-six years the struggle has been evolving, and, as the war on Gaza that started in October 2023 has shown, it has become more violent and deadly, with civilian casualties in the tens of thousands and no long-term resolution in sight.

In today's political landscape, a new type of fight is taking place around Palestine. The struggle has moved into new fronts and expanded beyond land and physical warfare and into transnational spaces. The struggle for justice dominated the hearts and minds of generations of Palestinians in diaspora and has shifted to include more non-Palestinians, who have begun to understand their plight and stand alongside them. Although many people around the world have discussed and sympathized with Palestine for as long as Zionist colonial ambition has existed, the struggle around Palestine has increased in intensity over the past two decades or so. Today, the fight is happening on social media, on the internet, in the mission statements of grass-roots organizations as part of the vision of other oppressed groups, in laws enacted in the United States, in resolutions passed in student government bodies, and in professional academic organizations. This book provides an explanatory framework to describe the current Palestinian condition both in Palestine and transnationally. It examines two structural phenomena: the way Westerners in general and Americans in particular have viewed Palestinians with disdain and distrust, and the societal transformation that has allowed this view to shift. This societal transformation has created new solidarity and organizing spaces for Palestinian voices to be heard in new ways and has challenged the traditional view of Palestinians primarily in the United States. These new, more accurate, fact-based understandings have led to an intensification of the fight for Palestinian legitimacy in society and policy, specifically by challenging the stereotypes that have traditionally caused the vilification of Palestine and Palestinians.

INTRODUCTION

The noticeable transformation of American public opinion since October 2023 was inevitable. It is an intensification of the fight between the pro-Palestine voices, and those wanting to preserve the status quo of occupation and pro-Israel stance in society and politics around the world. In the United States particularly, sympathy toward the Palestinian struggle has been becoming more common. Israel's violence against Palestinians and ethnic cleansing in the Gaza Strip has been met with global outrage, reaching new levels of condemnation and calls to hold Israel accountable for its actions. These voices are becoming louder. The largely one-sided reporting of the October 2023 war on Gaza favoring Israel and the continued U.S. support for Israel despite growing dissent among the American public have furthered solidarities and helped catalyze many protests in favor of Palestinian rights.

American public opinion toward Palestinians has long favored Israel, but this has been changing. For example, two recent polls that were conducted a month apart highlight a drastic change in public support for Israel. One survey was conducted a few days after October 7, 2023, and the second a month later. In the October poll, 41 percent of Americans agreed with the statement that "the US should support Israel." This number dropped to 32 percent in the November 2023 poll.[2]

The shift has been taking place over time, but it is accelerating. Before the genocidal campaign against Palestinians in the Gaza Strip that started in October 2023, earlier examples have signaled a change. The backlash against the May 2021 physical expulsion of Palestinian inhabitants from the Sheikh Jarrah neighborhood in Jerusalem is an example. Although this event was a classic expression of the settler colonialism against Palestinians that had happened countless times previously, this time it was different. Whether in the Occupied Palestinian Territories (OPT), in Israel, or globally, many human rights organizations have issued reports of blatant violations committed against Palestinians since Israel's independence and the resulting ongoing Nakba. Some of these organizations, such as Human Rights Watch and Amnesty International, have labeled Israel an apartheid state. Even former U.S. president Jimmy Carter used the term "Apartheid" to refer to the realities of Palestinian daily life under Israeli occupation in 2005.[3] Global outcry over the Sheikh Jarrah events in May 2021 highlighted that in addition to the physical battle in Palestine and colonization of land, there has also been an intensifying fight outside of the geography of Palestine.

For as long as the colonization of Palestine has existed, Palestinians and their supporters around the world have had limited agency in their ongoing attempts to change the status quo around global support for Israel and its crimes. Palestinians have long been perceived as illegitimate, not only in regard to their claims on the lands to which they are indigenous, but also in regard to the nature of oppression they face at the hands of their colonizer, Israel. Crimes committed by Israel against Palestinians have also been justified as necessary actions, despite substantial and overwhelming contrary evidence. Today, in the midst of a changing world, these attempts are given more weight. There is a global shift occurring in attitudes toward marginalized groups, evidenced by movements such as the Arab Spring, Occupy Wall Street, and Black Lives Matter and the response to those movements generally. The shifts in perspective and the changing acceptance of the legitimacy of the Palestinian story are a critical case study of this global shift.

This book examines a wide array of primary and secondary sources to provide a broad, comprehensive, and systematic analysis of existing literature and expert observations. Drawing on academic literature, biographies, interviews, news reports, legal documents, statistical data, and social media posts, I trace multiple processes in answering four interconnected questions. The first question is transnational in nature: What is the current condition of Palestinian identity, given that their diaspora status gives them a national identity that resides transnationally, and what is the role of the Palestinian diaspora in resisting Israeli policy around the world?

The second question is a genuine attempt to provide an explanation as to why Palestine and Palestinians have been vilified, and how their struggle has been characterized as illegitimate. Why do Westerners, primarily Americans, support Israel and accept that their tax dollars are used to fund the Israeli war machine against Palestinians? Why is the humanity of Palestinians secondary at best and their suffering perceived as illegitimate?

The third inquiry involves examining a number of structural changes that have taken place globally over the past two decades. These changes have created more space for Palestinian narratives to be heard and accepted and have allowed the emergence of new arenas to communicate and disseminate the Palestinian story, which has long been vilified.

The fourth and last question considers how the fight over Palestine has intensified between the traditionally dominant voices that support Israel's policies, right or wrong, and the newly emergent progressive voices challenging the status quo position on Palestine and Israel.

TRANSNATIONAL IDENTITY AND ITS ROLE IN RESISTING ISRAEL

To understand the plight of Palestinians, their continuing dispossession, and the demonization that legitimizes the crimes committed against them, we must accept basic historical facts about the establishment of Israel. The story of Palestine is one of continued colonization, fragmentation, and social dismemberment, on the one hand, and a never-ending anticolonial struggle, on the other. Israel's intentional and violent separation of the Palestinian people from their lands created a scattered Palestinian society around the world. Although territoriality is central to the question of Palestine, its people, no matter where they reside, continue to identify around their shared cultural and historical experiences as Palestinians. This creates a unique identity that is influenced by the forced condition of transnationalism. As Ted Swedenburg suggested, "Palestinians, who have not yet won formal national independence, must produce their history and memory in a space that is more like a bomb shelter under continuous shelling rather than a railway station."[4]

The loss of homeland was devastating to the Palestinian people. Ismat Zaidan relays the feelings of Palestinians, writing:

> With such [a] hard situation and the bitter feeling towards their lost land, the Palestinians managed to form a kind of resistance from exile to transcend the state of dispossession, denial and statelessness. . . . Generations who were born in exile have become familiar [with] their lost homes and towns through vivid descriptions of memories [shared] by their parents and grandparents. For members of the generations [born in diaspora], their relationship to, and familiarity with, the homeland has been passed on for the most part through "acts of memory." . . . Such memories began to be tangible in the minds of the younger generations where they could give detailed descriptions of how their homes looked like with minute details.[5]

Struggle sustains this connection, and in some ways struggle is part of the Palestinian identity.[6] The shared cognizance of oppression, injustice, and loss of homeland binds Palestinians together across the world in appreciation of their identity. Paolo Boccagni notes that this shared cognizance is common among migrants, who often have "a strong homeward attachment—whether in nostalgic or patriotic terms—[that] is a source of personal and group consistency against the typical hardships of everyday life overseas, including external categorizations 'by defect' as immigrants, rather than full-blown citizens."[7]

More than half the Palestinians in the world now live outside of Mandatory Palestine. They are holding the memory of a place, a people, a culture, and a nation and keeping them alive without an independent nation-state. This unique situation has affected the agency of the Palestinian people, and the transnational characteristic of their existence in the global sociopolitical and economic landscape has given them new opportunities to create solidarity and a strong shared national identity. Studying Palestine through a transnational lens captures the nature of processes that affect Palestinians and are affected by them, and it provides us with insights into the role of the scattered diaspora that itself has become the reference point for identity, social norms, and Palestinian nationalism and perseverance. Any analysis of Palestinians should take these issues into account as fundamental, given the nature of their struggle. The question of Palestine is no longer geography-bound but rather a global phenomenon.

The experience of exile, while agonizing, has helped reshape a Palestinian identity inspired by Palestine, the place, and also by views on justice, resistance, and resilience. Exploring the internalized, involuntary condition of exile serves as a useful concept in thinking about the collective global Palestinian condition. The story of Palestine and Palestinians is one that transcends borders, lands, and oceans. It is a story found in most societies in the world today, diversely represented by the Palestinians who are now living outside of Palestine. The stories of and around Palestine and Palestinians have created identities, often challenged and contested, and often pragmatically negotiated through interactions with others in different host societies, some of which are friendlier than others. Palestinian identity, a product of forced diaspora, constantly evolves and takes on new meanings within the contexts of each particular society.

INTRODUCTION

INTRODUCTION

Living as refugees with forced immobility, physically and politically, has confined the Palestinian diaspora to reside in exile in host countries while belonging to no internationally recognized state. The transnational Palestinian identity is reinforced through the shared experiences of discrimination and exclusion experienced by the Palestinian diaspora and is strengthened through the diaspora communicating and sharing in the borderless world of the internet. Palestinians in the United States face their own unique set of discrimination and exclusion politically and socially but maintain their transnational identity and community ties. The transnational Palestinian identity has become that which ties together Palestinians living in various host countries, with the same wish felt by every Palestinian in diaspora: for political change in their homeland, an end to the discrimination against and exclusion of their community, and shared feelings of place and belonging to their ancestral land of Palestine.

Akhil Gupta and James Ferguson write this about production of identity through formation of community:

> "Community" is never simply the recognition of cultural similarity or social contiguity but a categorical identity that is premised on various forms of exclusion and constructions of otherness. This fact is absolutely central to the question of... identities..., for it is through processes of exclusion and othering that both collective and individual identities are formed. With respect to locality as well, at issue is not simply that one is located in a certain place but that the particular place is set apart from and opposed to other places. The "global" relations that we have argued are constitutive of locality are therefore centrally involved in the production of "local" identities too.[8]

Gupta and Ferguson argue that community identity, applied here to transnational Palestinian identity, is unified by how other groups and states interact with such communities, and what type of "othering" process they may endure.

In basic terms, an individual is Palestinian if something affecting Palestinians elsewhere affects that individual, whether directly or indirectly. For Palestinians, nationality replaces ethnicity in the construction of identity. To be a Palestinian is to hold a conceptualization of Palestinian nationality; the role of ethnicity is minimized. Palestinian identity is therefore a "wandering identity," yet one that capitalizes on shared nationalistic goals.[9] Palestinian identity from its roots was not based on nationally recognized borders, but rather on its own community and the physical land on which generations of families had lived. Despite being driven away from their homeland and spread across the world, "feelings of Palestinian patriotism and Arab nationalism exist to a large extent among the Palestinians, especially those who are recent immigrants. They talk about being from a certain village or city in Palestine even when they have never been to that particular village or city in their lives and do not speak any Arabic."[10]

Two complicating factors are the identity of Palestinians within the modern state of Israel and in Mandatory Palestine, and the identity of Palestinians claiming other Arab lineage. Palestinians residing in Tel Aviv, for example, who may even be Israeli citizens, still possess identities marked by isolation, exile, and diaspora. These Palestinians may have resisted being driven from their homeland, but their homeland no longer exists on *their* terms. "Palestine" has been replaced by "Israel," and the Palestinian political, social, and cultural ways of life are being replaced by Israeli political, social, and cultural ways of life. Palestinians within Israel are uniquely exiled within the boundaries of their former homeland.

Palestinian identity may be masked by individuals of Palestinian descent who claim an association with other Arab groups, often out of convenience. Knowledge of Palestine, and of the Palestinian people, is lacking to varying degrees in the non–Middle Eastern or regional population. To claim a Palestinian identity is often to be met with blank stares or contradiction. Individuals may also refrain from claiming Palestinian descent because of stereotypes and negative connotations associated with that label; they may fear repercussions if they outwardly and explicitly label themselves as "Palestinian," either in their personal or their professional lives.

Despite this complexity, there is a global sense of unity among Palestinians that inspires them to solidarity with the Palestinian cause and liberation. Together, they feel a responsibility to resist Israeli oppression. Diasporic Palestinians are more able than ever to engage in the fight, as it is no longer a geographical war but one around ideas, legitimacy, equality, and privilege. The actions of Palestinians both in Palestine and around the world are often constrained due to social, political, or professional pressure, and the struggle continues to intensify. The irony is that this phenomenon is a product of the intentional and forceful expulsion and dismemberment of Palestinian society. Israel's intention to control the territory by expelling its inhabitants led to the impossibility of controlling the fate of the Palestinians.

RACIAL IDENTITY IN THE UNITED STATES

The experience of Palestinian transnationalism is best epitomized by the community's presence in the United States, a place where race and cultural dominance are persistent structures. Historically, U.S. citizenship was predicated on whether a person fit into the white category. Early Arabic-speaking immigrants from Greater Syria made arguments to acquire U.S. citizenship based on their Christianity, suggesting that this would distinguish them from others in the Middle East.[11] They had to distinguish themselves as distant from the concept of "Black Asian" in order to be considered for U.S. citizenship. The historical process by which Arabs acquired the "white" category is in itself racist and a reflection of how the United States has engaged in systematic discrimination around dominant cultural values, like Christianity and whiteness. Scholarly work reflecting this cultural paradigm places Arab Americans in terms of race as "'not-quite white,' 'not-quite people of color,' or 'between Arab and white.'"[12]

Palestinian immigrants to the United States are documented as quickly adapting to the local norms of society while successfully maintaining their own ethnic identity and alertness to Palestinian politics. Thea Renda Abu El-Haj notes:

> On the one hand, through everyday discourse and practices inside their schools and communities, Palestinian youth experience their positioning as outside the "imagined community" of the U.S. nation, framing them as "enemies within." As a result, they struggle to feel a sense of belonging to a nation in which they hold citizenship. On the other hand, these Palestinian American youth view their U.S. citizenship positively in terms of legal and political rights and economic access. Yet they tie their national identities—their sense of where they belong—to a Palestinian homeland.[13]

A dual sense of community and citizenship arises for the Palestinian diaspora, especially those living inside the United States, but only serves to strengthen the transnational Palestinian identity. Abu El-Haj writes, "These youth acknowledged that their U.S. citizenship was legally important, but they identified as being Palestinian, as belonging to an imagined community that is engaged in a struggle for liberty and an independent nation-state."[14]

Living in diaspora abroad, and specifically in the United States, has given Palestinians a set of shared experiences as refugees and reinforced their ties to their homeland, creating a sense of duality in, as well as strengthening, the transnational Palestinian identity and its political agency in its homeland. Halleh Ghorashi says that "most studies of transnationalism take the approach that migrants experience a duality between place of origin and place of residence. In that kind of approach, transnationalism refers to a sense of in-betweenness caused by this duality."[15] This identity is kept alive by every Palestinian in diaspora who feels a connection to their historical heritage and land, and it is reinforced by the navigation of one's heritage through a set of shared experiences as a community living in diaspora.

Faida Abu-Ghazaleh notes that Palestinians in the United States are proud of their heritage and have attempted to be part of American society while maintaining their Palestinian identity, effectively living what feels like two lives. This is especially the case for second- and third-generation Palestinian Americans, who work to keep a strong Palestinian identity and connection to their homeland while becoming more in sync with American society than their parents. It is the situation of Palestinians to live in a foreign place and continue to identify as Palestinian as generations pass while facing scrutiny for being a Palestinian. According to Abu-Ghazaleh, Christison,

> a former political analyst with the CIA, broadly researched the Palestinian population in the United States. Investigating assimilation of the first and second generation of Palestinians immigrants to America, Christison found that Palestinians still face ethnic intolerance and have been the object of terrorist attacks, but have never been the perpetrators of those types of attacks in the United States. Palestinians have reacted to these incidents with considerable self-control and self-confidence. In spite of their hardships, "Palestinian-Americans" generally have a remarkably healthy attitude, and are relatively optimistic, always searching for home.[16]

INTRODUCTION

The forcible removal of Palestinians from their homes, and the less-than-magnanimous welcome they have received globally and particularly in the United States, has nurtured an identity of fierce loyalty to Palestine. Thus the psychological manifestations of exile will urge collective action on the part of global Palestinians to remedy the decades-long injustice faced by several generations of Palestinians. Today's Palestinians, armed with this inner sense of justice, are now able to join the fight for their homeland in ways that were impossible a few decades ago. Their fight is not with weapons, but over airwaves and on websites. As they and their allies rise up, the allies of Israel also take to the conflict, feeding an increasingly global struggle over the future of Palestine. Abu-Ghazaleh notes that "the unfair treatment of the American government toward the Palestinian people in Palestine, the unlimited support of Israel and the one-sided way the American media views the conflict only serves to reinforce the Palestinian-American's sense of being Palestinian as they know they are the only ones, without international help, who could defend their rights and identity from being taken away."[17]

Today's Palestinian diaspora community is significant in resisting Israeli occupation of Palestine. Contemporary Palestinian identity politics (and, by proxy, global Palestinian politics) is marked by willful resistance to the violent erasures of settler colonial mythology that efface histories of ethnic cleansing by forcibly carving names of places off of maps. Palestinians are a people with a legitimate cause. Their suffering embodies the search for social and political justice, and they have spoken out about their cause despite all attempts to silence them. The diasporic and transnational elements contained within Palestinian identity are not at odds with nationalism in the homeland. Palestinian identity is based on the premise of exile, and the resolution of this physical condition is at the core of resolving the sense of exile within individuals.

The continuously changing sociopolitical landscape has allowed the Palestinian anticolonial struggle to take on previously unseen shapes and forms. Different sociopolitical contexts have themselves transformed to allow for the emergence of new solidarities toward the Palestinian plight. In a unique and representative survey conducted in the Palestinian Territories in 2013 to correspond with the twentieth anniversary of the signing of the Oslo Accords, respondents were asked about their views about the most effective approaches to resisting Israeli occupation. There were strong views on lobbying for the Palestinian cause in Western nations and resisting Israeli occupation through the international campaign of Boycott, Divestment, and Sanctions (BDS) (see tables 0.1 and 0.2).[18] These results show that Palestinians understand that part, if not most, of the solution to their colonization is to communicate the cause of Palestinians to other peoples and to articulate their suffering through methods and arguments that create sympathy for their struggle against colonization.

Palestinians are more likely to adopt a non-geography-bound approach to challenge Israeli occupation and to confront the discriminatory policies that have resulted in the disappearing geography, intensifying violence, and deteriorating living conditions of Palestinians. To be clear, this is not to say that Palestinians had not engaged in transnational solidarity. On the contrary, there are countless situations where the Palestinian cause was fought

TABLE 0.1
Perceived effectiveness of lobbying in Western societies in resisting Israeli occupation (0–5 scale)

	Number of observations	**Percent**
0 (least effective)	51	6.1
1	49	5.9
2	67	8.1
3	237	28.5
4	264	31.7
5 (most effective)	164	19.7
Total	832	100.0

Note: Scale ranges from 0 (least effective) to 5 (most effective).

TABLE 0.2
Perceived effectiveness of Boycott, Divestment, and Sanctions (BDS) in resisting Israeli occupation (0–5 scale)

	Number of observations	**Percent**
0 (least effective)	60	7.2
1	47	5.6
2	59	7.1
3	240	28.8
4	275	33.1
5 (most effective)	151	18.1
Total	832	100.0

Note: Scale ranges from 0 (least effective) to 5 (most effective).

alongside non-Palestinians, especially in terms of how leftist and Marxist Palestinian factions viewed their struggle against imperialism as global.

José de Jesus Lopez Almejo, in writing about the lobbying power of diasporic communities, notes that "the U.S. political system has created structures where politicians pay more attention to demands made by the local constituencies, than to those made by foreign actors. Due to this, diasporas become key allies for the governments of their countries of origin to push combined interests. Therefore, grassroots mobilization is important."[19]

PALESTINE IN THE AMERICAN IMAGINATION

In the American imagination, the struggling underdog is usually the hero. In a culture that idolizes the self-made person, the rags-to-riches story, the pulling of oneself up by one's bootstraps, it might be assumed that a scrappy, scattered band of people fighting against their unjust removal from their homeland would be lauded. This has not been the case for Palestinians, who have been vilified and whose struggle has been characterized as illegitimate in the United States. This is due to their orientalization and marginalization as well as to extremely high levels of support for Israel, financially, politically, militarily, and socially. Even those who tend to side with the minority have generally not backed Palestine.

Despite their efforts to adapt and integrate into American society, Palestinians in the United States face discrimination and misunderstanding on a regular basis. This is due to the conflation of Asian and Middle Eastern cultures and nationalities through Orientalism, a prominent feature of U.S. culture. *Orientalism*, a term coined by Edward Said, defines the process by which those of Asian, Arab, and Middle Eastern descent are mischaracterized as a single group and stereotyped as shifty, cunning, dishonest, and violent.[20] Orientalism serves as a mechanism to achieve hegemony. Hegemony, as introduced and explained by Antonio Gramsci, is achieved through a mechanism of establishing superiority.[21] Exaggerated, out-of-context, inaccurate, and often fabricated representations can establish this superiority and are often politically motivated and reflective of colonial and imperial power relations. Strains of Orientalism can be seen in movies and television, with the typecasting of "Arab-looking" people as greedy and sly, and in the way news reports portray Middle Eastern peoples as violent. It also appears in American Christianity, where Islam is seen as the enemy of

Christianity. It can be seen in the immigration policies of the U.S. government, which instituted quotas in 1924 that limited immigration from the twenty-two Arabic-speaking countries and encouraged immigration from Northern and Western Europe. Although the quotas were dropped in the 1960s, suspicion remained rampant. After 9/11 the U.S. government "began to require male Muslims over the age of 16 who had recently immigrated from certain Arab countries to submit to annual photographs and fingerprinting, making many Arab Americans feel unwelcome in the country." In 2017 President Donald Trump signed an executive order banning immigration from seven primarily Muslim countries in the Middle East.[22]

Arab, *Muslim*, and *Palestinian* are terms that refer to distinct groups of people, but they are often indistinguishable in an American context. Arab as an identity is religion-neutral and language-based, whereas Muslims are those who hold Islam as part of their identity. It should be noted that this does not necessarily imply the level of an individual's religiosity: Muslims can be practicing or nonpracticing. Palestinians can hold all three of these identities, but many do not. Each designator individually and separately plays a role in the ways the other two are constructed.

This dominant cultural paradigm lends itself to hasty, erroneous, and often intentionally prejudiced conclusions that force Arab Americans into socially constructed categories without their input. Popular culture, pundits, and sometimes academics determine the societal understanding of how Arabs act and interact. Along with the embedded distrust that comes with being a minority, Arabs are faced with the suggestion that they are capable of terrorism even when no evidence is present. Arabs themselves vary in terms of how they react to these realities. Some have contributed to the complicity, yet others have found pockets of solidarity around the United States, both among themselves and through connecting with other people of color. Today, Palestinians, Arabs, and Muslims fall into these structures that make up the core of the dominant American "cultural citizenship."[23] The culturally accepted prejudice against Arabs in general and Palestinians in particular has blinded the general public to the plight of Palestinians, even among those who hold progressive ideals for most minority groups.

Some scholars have explored the reasons progressives in the United States have limited sympathy for Palestinians. Marc Lamont Hill and Mitchell Plitnick, in their book *Except for Palestine*, examine the fact that progressives in the United States, who typically oppose repression when it comes

INTRODUCTION

to immigration, racial and gender politics, and other issues, often fail to extend their liberal philosophy to Palestinians.[24] In *Tolerance Is a Wasteland*, Saree Makdisi considers how Israel is embraced by American and European society as a tolerant, democratic, forward-thinking country despite evidence of oppression, racial segregation, and human rights abuses within its borders.[25] Keith Feldman examines the historical relationship between the United States and Israel, and how cultural forces have shaped the current political relationships between them and in regard to Palestine. His book *A Shadow Over Palestine* analyzes the connection between American democracy and Palestinian oppression.[26] John Collins examines in *Global Palestine* the way the struggle for Palestinian rights is a reflection of greater global issues such as colonization, occupation, and securitization.[27] These analyses are important in examining the next stages of the Palestinian plight, but a number of unanswered questions remain. This book provides a comprehensive analysis of the Palestinian narrative that Americans have put forth over the past few decades, along with the more recent transformations within that image in the Western world generally and the United States specifically.

As previously discussed, minorities in the United States tend to experience harsh treatment and suspicion the farther they seem to be from an ideal of whiteness. Palestinians are no exception. In the United States they experience discrimination in schools, in the media, and when interacting with domestic and foreign politics. This directly affects their quality of life and their treatment. Abu El-Haj discusses her research on Palestinian students in U.S. schools, citing how such students "negotiate their way through a school environment in which they are frequently framed by pervasive and pernicious public discourses and practices that render their communities invisible, save for one dominating image—that of a 'terrorist.'" She goes on to describe the experience of having authorities, such as classroom teachers, deny Palestine's existence to Palestinian students. Such denials outrage those students, she says, highlighting their unified hope of having an independent state of Palestine one day: "It signals their sense of belonging to a national community that exists beyond the borders of a recognized nation-state."[28]

Discrimination against Palestinians is seen in multiple arenas. It is found in the way they are portrayed on television and in movies, news sources report on their struggle, and school curriculum erases their history. It appears in antiboycott laws and referendums in state and local legislatures. And it is not due to Palestinian's minority status alone. There are additional layers to the negative view of Palestinians, primarily based on the close U.S. relationship with Israel. This aspect of the prejudice Palestinians face is seen in the federal government's unfettered political and military support of Israel and its refusal to vote, along with many countries in the United Nations, to condemn human rights violations perpetrated by Israel. To validate the experience of Palestinians, one must face the realities of Israel's actions, and this means dealing with the violence perpetrated by America's ally, something the United States is loath to do.

In addition, the United States takes political steps to deny cultural and heritage rights to Palestinians and block other foreign powers from intervening on behalf of Palestinians. As a permanent seat holder in United Nations Security Council, the United States holds veto power, and it has been cited numerous times as blocking international action that would penalize Israel for war crimes and/or would support the Palestinian political agenda. U.S. government actions exacerbate the exclusion and denial of Palestinians everywhere, reinforcing the common experience of being denied political and social equality at home and as refugees abroad. The transnational identity of Palestinians is further unified each time another state or institution engages in such detrimental political and social discourse that affects Palestinians living in the Occupied Palestinian Territories and in countries such as the United States.

Western colonialism operates by replacing one narrative with another that is deemed to be "friendlier," even if that is inaccurate. The Zionist Israeli narrative of a "land without a people for a people without a land" and of Israel as a democratic country and a just society flourishing in the Middle East is far more palatable than the narrative of Palestinian displacement and state-sanctioned violence. For Israel to be the "good guy," Palestine must either cease to exist or become the "bad guy." This dichotomous, short-sighted approach of "good" versus "bad" is aimed at legitimizing an engineered narrative at the expense of erasing a factual one. It further intensifies the clash between those speaking against Israeli settler colonial violence and occupation, on the one hand, and those who vigorously contest any existence of a Palestine or even a Palestinian people, on the other. The perception of Palestinians in the United States has largely been constructed by Israel, and the public awareness of the question of Palestine has morally

INTRODUCTION

favored Israel in its framing, narrative, and implications. The dominant opinions found in the United States regarding Palestinians are a function of the Israeli narrative. Because of this, Palestinians have an additional struggle for legitimacy compared with other Orientalized peoples, be they Muslims or Arabs.

A great deal of effort is applied to maintaining the superiority of Israel in the minds of the American public and the institutions of the state.[29] Zionist narratives revolve around and are about Palestine, emphasizing the Western identity and character of Israel and the inferiority of Arab and Muslim societies. An example from recent years is the series of advertisements paid for by a Zionist, pro-Israel organization that read, "In any war between the civilized man and the savage, support the civilized man. Support Israel. Defeat Jihad." The ads appeared first on buses in San Francisco and subsequently were installed in New York subway stations, metro stations in Washington, D.C., and light-rail trains in Portland, Oregon.[30] In each city the ads provoked a backlash, but Pamela Geller, the conservative blogger behind them, won a lawsuit that allowed their placement.[31] The connections between Palestine and terrorism are often greatly exaggerated and manufactured to allow for an easy moral association to influence and manipulate public opinion. Palestinians living in the United States are living in a country that essentially supports Israel's occupation of, and illegal expansion into, the Occupied Palestinian Territories, and the politics that made refugees out of the Palestinian population in the first place.

Theodore Sasson writes about Jewish Americans and their relationship with Israel. While he notes that in the past Jewish Americans relied on lobbying efforts to manage their interests, they increasingly "relate to Israel directly, by advocating their own political views, funding favorite causes, visiting frequently or living there part time, consuming Israeli news and entertainment, and expressing a distinctly 'realistic' rather than idealistic orientation toward the Jewish state."[32] This change contributes to the intensification of feelings and actions on both sides of the Palestine and Israel discussion.

What is lacking in this narrative is the Palestinian narrative itself, where voices *from* Palestine *about* Palestine are brought to the forefront of the conversation. Palestinians themselves rarely get the chance to share their stories, and speaking the truth about Palestine and the practices of Israel against the Palestinian people has had severe consequences. Those who speak out on behalf of Palestine face punitive measures, accusations of anti-Semitism, and comparisons to Nazi Germany. Many countries have introduced laws equating critique of Israeli human rights violations to anti-Semitism.[33] Again, such conditions reinforce the power of the transnational Palestinian identity. Oppression experienced by Palestinians in the United States further unifies all Palestinians and their connection to one another and their homeland. Stories of Palestinian persecution are increasingly easy to find and easy to relate to. Israel spends an enormous amount of time and money silencing Palestinian stories. Though they may be seen as peripheral, Palestinians have used and continue to use their voices, regardless of how much they have been silenced.

STRUCTURAL CHANGE

Since the early 2000s, a series of social, political, and technological transformations have played a significant role in changing the traditional formula of power relations and structures. These changes include a social revolution that has led to a gain in rights and representation for marginalized groups. New technological advancements have transformed the sociopolitical landscape, allowing larger spaces for ignored voices. Together, these changes mean that minority voices are more represented in politics and in the minds of the public. This increase has led to pushback in policy, society, and policing, which in turn leads to more activism. The tension between traditional power structures and progressive movements continues to grow, and it is changing the conversations around Palestine.

In the United States there have been major shifts in the social fabric and in rights of the traditionally marginalized, including the legalization of gay marriage and the rise and continued support of the Black Lives Matter movement. These markers are indicative of a change in the moral and cultural landscape of American society. Polls show an increase in acceptance of minority and alternative lifestyles and cultures. This foundational shift, especially in younger generations, has led to a greater willingness to go against the status quo and reconsider the validity of established narratives. This in turn has led to greater acceptance of Palestinians by the general public as well as established solidarity with other minority groups. Palestinians are now seen as worthy of compassion. I emphasize "Palestinians" here, and not the Palestinian Authority or the Palestine Liberation Organization.

INTRODUCTION

Palestinians have essentially led a globally focused social movement that found multiple outlets to tell an alternative story about Palestine and provided a model to other oppressed people to change public opinion globally to increase pressures against oppressive regimes and governments.

Technology today allows for more voices to be heard in what is known as the democratization of media, breaking the past hold of elites on news coverage. Anyone with a cell phone can now film events as they occur and broadcast them via social media to a global audience. Atrocities and violence committed by the Israeli military are now recorded and reported by Palestinians, allowing their perspective to be shared with concrete evidence. The internet has opened a new world of possibility for activists, and Palestinians are capitalizing on it. It allows them to connect with one another and with allies around the world, to raise money and awareness, and to create a sense of unity. Social media has changed the way people relate to one another, the way news is consumed, and the speed at which narratives and information can be dispersed. Young people, savvy consumers of this new form of media, are also the demographic most likely to hold progressive views of the Israel/Palestine situation, and to share their views with their peers via platforms such as Instagram, TikTok, and Snapchat.

In the United States, changes in church attendance and religious allegiance have lessened the degree of automatic affiliation with Israel that many American Christians hold. Traditionally, Christian churches have felt at least some degree of solidarity with Israel due to their historic connection to ancient Judaism and the fact that their Holy Land exists in Palestine. The past fifty years have seen a sharp drop in both church attendance and religious affiliation, both of which have loosened that cultural connection to Israel. This has opened the door for the consideration of the Palestinian cause for many Americans.

Some of the Americans who are beginning to view the Palestinian narrative as legitimate are Jewish. Several groups have been formed by Jewish Americans who view the oppression of Palestinians as antithetical to their Jewish beliefs and values. These individuals and groups are evidence that support for Jewish people does not automatically mean unwavering support for the Israeli government. Jewish Voice for Peace (JVP), for example, is a nonprofit that sees the Palestinian struggle for self-determination as a point of solidarity based on the Jewish struggle for the same. Their view is that "Zionism was a false and failed answer to the desperately real question many of our ancestors faced of how to protect Jewish lives from murderous antisemitism in Europe." Groups like JVP prove that "Judaism beyond Zionism is possible."[34]

In some arenas, the increasingly hostile nature of the occupation has led to more physical violence. The terror attacks of 9/11 led to the introduction of the Global War on Terror, which provided opportunities for oppressive regimes to unleash violence under the justification of antiterrorism. In the West Bank and the Gaza Strip, the early 2000s witnessed unprecedented levels of violence in the Occupied Palestinian Territories. Most Palestinians around the world watched in shock and disbelief as pundits rationalized the indiscriminate Israeli military brutal violence against Palestinians. Images of the slain child Muhammad al-Durra, killed with Israeli bullets, circulated the globe, yet they were portrayed as justified, or it was claimed that the bullet was fired by Palestinians. The very humanity of Palestinians had been stolen from them.

Yet the nature of the violence and the ability to broadcast it around the world, in color and with immediacy, were themselves factors in the societal transformation that began around that time. The increased securitization of the United States has many citizens concerned. Those who may have defended the necessity of the government to use force against its citizens are far less likely to do so when they feel that force is being used against innocent people. American citizens dislike being surveilled and are less trustful and supportive of a government that increasingly watches them.

AN INTENSIFYING FIGHT

In light of these structural changes, the battle over the rightful place of the Palestinian narrative has been intensifying. Not a week goes by without references to a policy debate related to Israel or Palestine in the halls of political power around the world. Today, it is not uncommon to read about members of Congress having to explain where they stand on Palestine, and on Israel's long record of human rights violations. Although the question of Palestine and Israel has been part of global political debate at least since the end of World War II, more recent debates are centered on rights and legitimate claims that have long been ignored. The availability of technology and an interconnected world through the internet is providing the necessary platforms to reach a global critical mass. In addition, social movements that reflect dissatisfaction with economic conditions or long-standing oppressive policies around the world, like Occupy Wall Street, the Arab Revolts, and Black Lives Matter, among others, are gaining widespread acceptance and support.

The genocide and War on Gaza, which the International Court of Justice has characterized as genocide in its ruling on the case brought by the Government of South Africa in January 2024, has been met with global condemnation. Global views of Palestine and Israel have shifted to the point where the International Criminal Court issued arrest warrants for Israeli officials, to include prime minister Benjamin Netanyahu in May 2024 for their crimes against Palestinians in the Gaza Strip. The forced eviction of Palestinians in Sheikh Jarrah, Silwan, and other neighborhoods in Jerusalem in May 2021 was met with much stronger public condemnation than previous events of the same magnitude had been. Israeli brutality, especially with its bombing and airstrike campaigns in Gaza and the murder of tens of thousands of Palestinian civilians, is seen as less legitimate and is criticized globally. Although the official line of the U.S. government remains the same, stating that Israel is an ally no matter what, the American public sees things differently, knowing that their tax dollars are paying for this destruction. Things are shifting for Palestine.

As the global community becomes more accepting of Palestinians and their plight, Palestinians themselves are becoming more connected and less afraid of identifying with their homeland. Gabriel Sheffer notes the desire of the Palestinian diaspora to keep their transnational identity strong, writing that

> despite their intra-diasporic social, political, and economic heterogeneity, core members of such entities continuously maintain or revive their original ethno-national identity, and these days they are not very ashamed or afraid to identify as such. An important element that contributes to the maintenance of their ethno-national identity and their willingness to identify as such is their fairly regular contacts with their homelands, whether or not these are independent states. These contacts can be and are performed as a result of a number of strategic decisions by diasporic individuals, groups, and organizations. These contacts are carried out by a voluntary return to their homeland, by regular visits to the homeland, by remittances and investments there, by political and diplomatic support to the homeland, by

participation in activities organized by the representatives of their homelands in their countries of residence, etc.[35]

Technological advances contribute to this transformation. Sheffer discusses the building of the trans-state network, noting that diasporic communities, like the Palestinians, use "means of communication, such as mail, telephones, internet, the media, and various means of transportation ... [to] enable and encourage multiple exchanges of cultural features, social thoughts, political ideas, and economic cooperation with their homelands and with other segments of the Diaspora wherever these reside. These are, of course, significant means for potentially influencing what is happening in their homelands." Indeed, the online world has allowed means of communications for the Palestinian diaspora, keeping the Palestinian identity active as well as giving force to political movements in the homeland.

Miriyam Aouragh notes, "Far from 'dis-embedding' national identities, the technologies comprising the internet revive national sentiments and past or present dreams of becoming united again, and incite the struggles related to such dreams."[36] Such modes of communication are the means through which the Palestinian diaspora can communicate in a borderless world, and where organizing for political impacts can come to fruition. Sheffer argues that it is the development and activities of diasporic organizations, rather than individuals, that ultimately impacts the diaspora's relations with their host lands and homeland. The ability to organize and facilitate discussion and political action as a transnational identity living in diaspora has been provided through the platform of the online world. It is due to the internet that the Palestinian diaspora can connect as individuals as well as create organizations that can support the transnational Palestinian political agenda. Sheffer suggests that it is in cases where diasporic communities are stateless, such as the Palestinians, that they become the most involved in effecting political change in their homeland: "Quite often there is a strong wish to help the people in the homeland to achieve independence and sovereignty. In most cases, these Diasporans are committed to help their relatives and associates to achieve that independence in order to free the ethno-national group from the rule of another ethno-national group and liberate their homeland."[37] The will of the transnational Palestinian community is active in wishing to achieve political change in their homeland, and the means for organizing themselves in a way that can help effect such a change has arisen with the use of the internet.

As Noura Erekat has said,

> Everything that we know we have been given permission by somebody to know. . . . If we do not pursue alternative ideas, antihegemonic ideas. Ideas that have been buried. If we don't lift up histories that don't exist, histories of the defeated and the conquered, other epistemologies, other forms of life, other forms of faith, and engagement with the world, then we are merely reproducing power over and over again. So I think that the pursuit, not of merely ideas, but really of knowledge and the creation of new knowledge is necessary in order for us to be able to have the courage and the vision to create new futures.[38]

Today's Palestinians are sharing that new knowledge, and today's global community is increasingly willing to hear it.

These interconnected issues are examined thematically in the chapters that follow. Chapter 1 explains how and why Palestine and Palestinians have traditionally been viewed in American society and politics in the ways they have. Chapter 2 identifies and examines the five different processes that have created sociopolitical spaces that allowed for Palestinians and their supporters to amplify their voices against injustice. Chapter 3 underlines and explains the ongoing social change in American society around Palestine, and the backlash that these movements have experienced. Similarly, chapter 4 explores how the battle around Palestine is taking place within the world of the law, legal structures, and U.S. policy at all levels. Chapter 5 examines how solidarities toward Palestinians are strengthening but also challenged by traditional narratives.

This book provides an alternative lens through which the question of Palestine is best conceptualized and studied that accommodates the Palestinian diaspora communities around the world in contemporary times. It redefines Palestinian identity as a global, transnational identity that is defined and framed by historical events, has transformed due to forced migrations, and has evolved due to interactions with the socioeconomic and political contexts in host societies. It further shows how that transnational identity has allowed the fight for Palestine to break free from the geographical boundaries of Palestine and emerge in the social and cultural values of the global community, and how structural changes in the United States are allowing old stereotypes to fall away and be replaced by new, more accurate understandings of the Palestinian struggle. This book further explains the intensification of the fight for Palestine and the ways in which the momentum is shifting, moving toward a global fight not on a battlefield but in hearts and minds, on the internet, in media and school curriculum, in popular culture, academia, and politics. It tells a story of persistence and resilience, of persecution and hope, and of the violent occupation and tenacious beauty of an imperishable Palestine.

Chapter One

PALESTINIANS IN THE AMERICAN IMAGINATION

Americans hold strong opinions about Palestine. It elicits strong reactions, even among those without accurate knowledge about Palestinian history or culture. Unfortunately, these passionate opinions are generally based on a combination of ignorance, misinformation, and intentional disinformation. It is critical to understand that American perceptions of Palestine are almost entirely informed by the American relationship with Israel and the perceived cultural connectedness around religion. The United States and Israel are so interconnected in the minds of Americans that they cannot be easily separated. The U.S. government is intensely sympathetic to Israel, inevitably putting it at odds with anything positive about Palestine, to the point that uttering the word "Palestine" seems to border on blasphemy. American media portrayals of Palestinians are almost universally negative. The American news media is predictable in how it renders Palestine: almost always a one-sided portrayal of events, withholding information and context critical to the accuracy of the story.

Americans' understanding of Palestine is frequently based on half-truths, outright deceptions, and decontextualized events. These opinions are framed as support for either one or the other. In other words, you are supportive of either Israeli self-determination or Palestinian, and this opinion is connected to how the suffering of the Jewish people around the world can be eliminated only if one supports Jewish people's self-determination, manifested in the shape of the Israeli state, even if the cost is the displacement of the vast majority of Palestinians from their homeland. This narrow view is dangerous and has had severe consequences. Americans simply do not have the opportunity to evaluate all the information and formulate an unbiased, objective opinion when a moral dilemma is presented at the core of any opinion influenced by mainstream media and policy formulations related to Palestine and Israel.

A nationally representative public opinion survey 1,200 of Americans conducted in 2022 was designed uniquely to examine and measure American views concerning a variety of socioeconomic and political issues, with a focus on views and opinions about Muslims, Arabs, and Middle Easterners. The study was meant to correspond with the twentieth anniversary of 9/11 and the subsequent invasion of Afghanistan. Through a feeling thermometer measure (scale of 0–100, with 100 being the warmest and most positive feelings), respondents were asked to share their feelings toward different groups and peoples. The feelings show a mean of 45.49 toward Palestinians, and 54.70 toward Israelis, a significant difference between how the two peoples are viewed. In addition, the mean toward Jewish people was 59.52, but toward Muslims it was 45.63 (table 1.1).

One cannot help but notice that American feelings about Muslims and Palestinians are somewhat similar in this survey. They are part of the process of Orientalism that will be discussed later in this chapter. Meanwhile, American feelings toward Israel and the Jewish people are far warmer, nearing the highest marks given to any other group, including the British, who in contemporary times are typically seen in the United States through a positive lens.[1]

TABLE 1.1
American views toward different groups
(feelings thermometer, 1-100 scale, n = 1,200)

Feelings toward Israelis	54.70
Feelings toward Jewish people	59.52
Feelings toward Palestinians	45.49
Feelings toward Muslims	45.63
Feelings toward British (highest)	61.02
Feelings toward Afghans (lowest)	43.45

Source: Karam Dana, "Survey of American Views Toward Foreign Policy and International Affairs Twenty Years Post 9/11," 2022.

PALESTINIANS IN THE AMERICAN IMAGINATION

The United States has long had a sympathetic political relationship with modern Israel, and political messaging has reflected this alliance. In addition, the public school system, which has the responsibility of educating young Americans, regularly fails at teaching social studies, social justice, and global issues in a holistic and accurate way, especially surrounding Palestine. Misinformation has led Americans to hold negative and inaccurate views toward Palestine, a surprising stance given the perceived American ideal of supporting the "little guy." Lending a helping hand to the underdog is commonly seen as the right thing to do, yet failure to see that Palestinians are deserving of sympathy runs deep. The dominant Orientalist discourse around Palestinians lumps them together with all Muslims and Arabs and reduces them to prepackaged tropes. They become dehumanized, racialized, and criminalized in public discourse. The verdict around Palestine and Palestinians has already been determined, without any meaningful opportunity for Palestinians to present their case.

This chapter will examine the development of Palestine in the American imagination and the ways it has been manipulated by politics, the media, and churches, and how the school system has failed to combat prejudiced views of Palestine, despite the promise of a level playing field for all.

ARABS AND PALESTINIANS IN THE UNITED STATES

To understand American perceptions of Palestine and Palestinians, I explore the larger sociopolitical contexts in which these communities find themselves. The idea of an Arab American identity started to coalesce as World War II was ending and a wave of independence movements rocked the Arab World. Then, in 1967, Israel's conquest in the Six-Day War spurred the movement on. Although Arabs are separated by country-specific nationality and, within that, religion, a pan-Arab identity began to solidify. The post-1967 era saw the creation of pan-ethnic organizations like the Arab-American University Graduates (AAUG), the National Association of Arab Americans, the Arab-American Anti-Discrimination Committee (ADC), and the Arab American Institute (AAI). Arab Americans sought to create a place for themselves, an identity that could be respected and accepted within American culture, and a voice that might be heard and understood. As this group gained cohesion and a modicum of power, they were met with fear and derision by the established culture and political elites. Arab Americans joined forces to make their political opinions heard, and they found the term "Arab" being distorted by those in power. Arab Americans felt erased from the political process. Helen Samhan of the Arab American Institute Foundation calls this exclusion "political racism," a system of anti-Arab attitudes and behavior that is not rooted in "the traditional motives of structurally excluding a group perceived as inferior, but in politics."[2]

Keith Feldman, in his book *A Shadow Over Palestine: The Imperial Life of Race in America*, extends the idea of political racism, tying it to U.S. imperialistic motives abroad. He argues that "the competing meanings given the 'special relationships' between the United States, Israel, and Palestine are compellingly clarified by the analytical concept of U.S. *imperial culture*. U.S. imperial culture names the crucible within which an enduring U.S. national ideology of territorial expansion and its attendant regimes of racial domination and war-making have been codified, reified, naturalized, and contested."[3] A group that could not acquiesce to this imperial culture could not find a place in the politics of the United States.

This imperial culture is the reason behind the whitewashing of American history and the disappearance of native peoples in the story of the expansion of the United States. Sana Saeed succinctly explains this concept in an episode of *Backspace*, a video-based reporting service:

> There is an assumption of virtue, of a greater good, in America's official history that has been consciously reproduced by Israel's advocates for a large part of the last century in an attempt to Americanize the Israeli project. And so when the curtain is pulled away to reveal the violence that upholds Israel's existence, there is an understanding from the United States of the necessity of this violence because Israeli violence is necessary to protect Israel from threats to its exceptional existence, just as American violence is necessary to protect the United States from threats to its exceptional existence.[4]

Sunaina Maira observes that "to speak of the question of Palestine in the U.S. public sphere is to note that the public sphere, by definition and in debates about its constitution, is marked by relations of power. Silencing and exclusion are built into the structure of who and what can and cannot legitimately be a part of the public sphere and what can and cannot be spoken."[5] Maira found that Palestinian voices were dismissed and silenced through allegations of anti-Semitism and the question of the "national security" of the state of Israel. Feldman notes that the racial liberal frameworks of the United States change a racial "critique of Zionism into an argument about a viral anti-Semitism" and frame "its ideological contours within a Cold War lexicon of a shared U.S. and Israeli exceptionalism." This notion of a shared U.S.-Israeli exceptionalism sanctions the use of violence to defend national borders, even as these national borders are undefined and constantly shifting.[6]

Political erasure, historical whitewashing, and the defense of Israeli violence as a right have combined to create barriers to Palestinians who have long been prevented from presenting their own stories in meaningful ways. When they are given a platform, their contributions are limited, often serving purposes other than the genuine inclusion of the Palestinian story. This omission serves as a mechanism to reinforce stereotypes that encourage people to reach predetermined conclusions. There is a constant repetition of the Orientalist discourse, a trope that creates a dichotomy between the greatness and exceptionalism of the "Occident" and the immorality and suspicious character of the "Orient." This discourse is consistently used to further the invented illegitimacy of Palestinian claims to their lands. Although there are ample Palestinian accounts available in a variety of scholarly works, these accounts are not readily available to people who do not specialize in research. Because of this, unintentionally misinformed opinions circulate and spread, as has been the case for decades. Edward Said wrote in *The Question of Palestine* in 1979, "What we must again see is this issue involving representation, an issue always lurking near the issue of Palestine."[7] More viciously, Americans are victims of intentional disinformation, whereby deliberate obfuscation of facts and truths leads to widely held inaccurate opinions and beliefs. To interrogate these two processes further, I will examine all the ways through which Americans are exposed to information and knowledge about Palestine and Palestinians.

The failure of Americans to understand the legitimate claims of Palestinians has long been perplexing, especially to those well-versed in the factual history of the region. This confusion is compounded by the fact that Americans are generally fully and vehemently sympathetic to and supportive of other countries and peoples in similar scenarios. What causes this stark disparity of opinion? Do Americans form their opinions about Palestine through their biblical knowledge? Is their knowledge a product of how Palestinians are represented in the media, entertainment, and popular culture? Or do they hold opinions inspired by the official position of the U.S. government in relation to Palestine and Palestinians?

The ways in which American society views Palestine, Palestinians, Arabic-speaking peoples, Islam, the modern State of Israel, and Judaism are interconnected. Discussions of one of these concepts have implications for how the other concepts are viewed. For example, a discussion of Israel that intentionally omits Palestine is part of a strategy of identity erasure that affects how Palestine and Palestinians are viewed in the immediate and long term. Not only do opinions about Israel influence opinions about Palestine and Palestinians, but they are also connected as the flip side of a coin.

There are four intertwined factors that influence American perceptions and knowledge about Palestine. The first is around how the Orientalist views of "Eastern" peoples have dominated public discourse in the United States. The conflation of different identities to fit a racist mold has been powerful in creating the conditions of persistent demonization. The second factor centers on American Christianity and its influence on perceptions of Israel and, by extension, perceptions of Palestine and Palestinians, even if Palestinian Christians are at the receiving end of Israeli violence, a critical piece of information that tends to be ignored. Sympathy toward Israel in the American (Christian) mind is a fulfillment of a belief that does not extend to Palestinian and Arab Christians. The third factor is the culmination of political advocacy groups' efforts that engage in strengthening social and political ties between Israel and the United States. This has direct social and political implications at all levels—city, state, and federal. The fourth and final factor that contributes to American perceptions of Palestine and Israel is around the nature and content of education in the United States in general, but particularly with regard to Palestine, Israel, the Middle East, Islam, and other global issues.

As Peter Beinart notes, ideas about Israel and Palestine are deeply embedded in American culture. "These things are very much bound up to one another, and so I think that American exceptionalism and an exceptionalist view of Israel, which is that Israel is also inherently virtuous, are very deeply intertwined."[8] The following section will interrogate each of these factors to paint a comprehensive picture of the various issues that contribute to the American understanding of Palestine and its people.

ORIENTALIST REPRESENTATION

The first factor, Orientalism, is the conflation of peoples and cultures located in what Europeans call the "Middle East" as a single, monolithic group. First described by Edward Said in his book *Orientalism*, it is "a way of seeing that imagines, emphasizes, exaggerates and distorts differences of Arab peoples and cultures as compared to that of Europe and the U.S. It often involves seeing Arab culture as exotic, backward, uncivilized, and at times dangerous."[9] This view creates a false dichotomy between the Eastern "Orient" and the Western "Occident" and stereotypes non-Westerners as immoral, backward, and inherently in opposition to the values of Europe and the United States. This perception creates fertile ground in which misinformation and disinformation grow and spread.

In the United States, "Palestinian" is almost synonymous with "terrorist." Palestinian resistance to the British mandate authority in the 1920s and 1930s, and to the Zionist colonialism of the 1930s and onward, has largely been nonviolent in nature.[10] Despite this, Palestinians are seen as terrorists and their claims to their lands as illegitimate due to what are perceived as violent and bloody tactics that only target defenseless civilians. In most situations where violence and acts of sabotage are used against colonizers, for example in America's own history of rebellion against the British, Americans respond favorably to such action, but not in the case of Palestine. There are countless movies with underdog heroes fighting in anticolonial wars, or even in imaginative anti-extraterrestrial colonization and organizing. In these examples, the heroes have white, European, familiar faces. When the rebels are Arabs, Americans have difficulty sympathizing. To Americans, all Palestinians are Sirhan Sirhan, who assassinated the presidential hopeful Robert F. Kennedy for his staunch support of Israel in 1968.

Palestinians are represented through an Orientalist lens, a misguided stereotype that conflates myriad groups of people into a monolithic whole in which mistaken representations of Muslims, Arabs, and Palestinians feed into one another and reinforce biases. Perceived identities are based on half-truths and half-imagined ideas that come together to create authoritative and dominant definitions.[11] Orientalism produces a Palestinian who is also an Arab, who is also a Muslim. Even though these three identities refer to different groups of people and are distinct in terms of their definitions (one is based on language, another on religion, and the third refers to a national identity), they are conflated and lumped together. These attitudes are not new. In his book *Islam and the West*, Norman Daniel convincingly demonstrates that the negative depictions of Islam date back to early Christian exegesis and are therefore deeply embedded in Western culture.[12]

There is recognition in contemporary American culture that stereotypes are harmful, and that all racial and ethnic groups are composed of individuals who should not be discriminated against for their race or ethnicity. As Janice Terry writes, "Similar sweeping generalizations have, properly, long been unacceptable when applied to other religions, racial or ethnic groups." Yet the stereotypes of Palestinians, and all Arabs and Muslims, are so commonplace that "it was not surprising that in the immediate aftermath of the 1995 Oklahoma City bombing, the media and public, primed to expect the worst from Arabs and Muslims, concluded—wrongly—that Arabs or Muslims were responsible. Only after it became abundantly clear that neither Muslims nor Arabs were responsible did some op-ed pieces, ambivalently headlined 'Media jump to conclusion: Muslims did it,' appear. Yet no headlines proclaimed that Timothy McVeigh was a 'Christian terrorist.'"[13]

RACE, ETHNICITY, AND RELIGION IN AMERICAN SOCIETY

It should come as no surprise that politicians and the media persistently characterize individuals of Arab and Muslim descent as the "Other": different and incompatible with Western values and ways of life. This characterization is labeled "selective racialization" by John Tehranian, and it manifests itself in the emphasis on infamous individuals of Arab or Muslim origins. These "bad agents," so to speak, are reduced to their regional, ethnic, and religious identities as explanations for why they digress from established, Western social values. Meanwhile, individuals holding these identities who contribute positively to society have their identities downplayed or ignored completely; these "good agents" become whitewashed.[14]

Palestinian American racialization is tied to a shifting definition of race that hinges on notions of empire. Kristine Ajrouch and Amaney Jamal discuss racial identity as an

> interactionally accomplished category, enacted through the multiple ways that individuals and groups negotiate identities as they encounter others on

either micro or macro levels. Race categories are, therefore, unstable and fluctuating. White identity arises from ideological and cultural premises as well as physical appearance. Ethnic traits, including those of descent (immigrant status and national origin) as well as culture (religion and expressions of Arab Americanness), may indicate to what extent immigrants and succeeding generations are likely to announce a white racial identity.[15]

In other words, a Palestinian may pass or present as "white" due to appearance, clothing, mannerisms, and language. This white-passing Palestinian may avoid the racialized stereotypes their co-nationalists face. Meanwhile, "Arab-looking" and -speaking peoples will find it difficult to avoid prejudice, no matter how much they may consider themselves patriotic Americans.

In the context of Palestine, selective racialization manifests itself in the characterization of Palestinians as terrorists, tools of terrorists, or anti-Semitic bigots. The humanity of Palestinians is repeatedly reduced through the automatic application of these associations, and this phenomenon is not limited to conservatives or right-leaning individuals. People on the left, those who label themselves progressives, also entrench selective racialization.[16] A critical ramification of selective racialization is that the sheer normalcy of the vast majority of individuals of Arab or Muslim descent from the region known as the Middle East are overshadowed by the actions of an extremely tiny few. All Palestinian Americans are assumed to be extremist because the media grants the few violent individuals a disproportionate amount of coverage. The actions and opinions of a few become what is most strongly associated with all individuals who are connected, however tenuously, to that group. Selective racialization is thus a self-feeding cycle, growing in intensity over time.

Keith Feldman advances this theory of race by linking racialization to domestic and foreign policies, noting:

> Race is where orders of exploitation and elimination are codified, where domains of subjectivity and consciousness are fashioned and refashioned. Even as it is routinely encountered and addressed through national rubric—indeed, even as it shapes the affective, geopolitical, and legal contours of the national—race's freighted transnational legacies and wrenching spatial transformations reveal the porosity of the domestic and the foreign.

Investigations of race open up those historical and social fields saturated by differential regimes of value, wherein, as Lisa Cacho incisively argues, "the production and ascription of human value are both violent and relational."[17]

Amina Zarrugh echoes Feldman's linkage of politics and racialization, writing that "race is an essentially unstable 'complex of social meanings' attached to human bodies":[18]

These meanings, which are manifested in social structures and central to cultural representations, are constantly in flux and subject to variation as a consequence of political struggles and group mobilization. Racial categories are deliberately managed and transformed by political elites and by the public. This vacillating process that creates and reconstitutes race is conceptualized as "racial formation," a "sociohistorical process by which racial categories are created, inhabited, transformed, and destroyed." Arab Americans epitomize category variations; they have been regarded intermittently as "white," "non-white," and "Asian" in the United States.[19]

The volatile classification of Arab Americans in the racial hierarchy of the United States demonstrates how this system is fraught with inconsistencies yet simultaneously critically influential in the ways that Palestinian Americans and issues surrounding the Palestinian American community are viewed. In the first half of the twentieth century, Arab migration to the United States did not pose a significant perceived threat to white America, because the volume of migration was low and most of these migrants were Christian.[20] Important distinctions in the classification of "white" persons arose during this time, however, manifested in two naturalization cases.

In the first, Costa George Najour, a Syrian immigrant who arrived in the United States in 1906, was granted naturalization on the grounds that he was white enough. The judge presiding over his case ruled that he considered "the Syrians as belonging to what we now recognize and what the world recognizes, as the white race," and commented that Najour "is not particularly dark, and has none of the characteristics or appearance of the Mongolian race, but so far as I can see and judge, has the appearance and characteristics of the Caucasian race."[21] Najour's acceptance as an American was predicated on his ability to fit the mold of whiteness, as manifested by phenotypic characteristics. Yet in 1914 George Dow, another Syrian immigrant, was denied naturalization. This time a judge ruled that while "Syrians might be free white persons," they were "not that particular free white person to whom the act of congress had donated the privilege of citizenship."[22] In this instance, race was defined not in terms of physical characteristics, language, or even ethnicity, but in terms of geography; since Syria was in Asia, not in Europe, this judge did not perceive Syrians as being in the same class of whiteness as European immigrants.

These early cases underscore how whiteness relies on privilege, power, and the construction of an "other." Whiteness becomes a litmus test to gauge inclusion within the group that is granted all the privileges that are associated with citizenship. Whiteness, as Ajrouch and Jamal note, "is a privileged status that does not require contemplation or reflection."[23] With whiteness comes a lack of repercussions. White people can freely discuss their political opinions without being seen as holding anti-American views. Arab and Palestinian Americans have not enjoyed this privilege.

Since Muslim and Arab Americans do not fit neatly into one racial category according to the U.S. legal system, their religion has been used to create their racialized identity. The conflation of Muslim and Arab identities leads to what Nadine Naber terms the "racialization of religion."[24] For Arabs, religion has taken the place of race in their racialization. Religious identity becomes the sliding scale used to determine Arab "otherness." This concept explains why Christian and Muslim Arabs and Arab Americans have vastly different experiences. The plight of Christian Arabs elicits more empathy from Western media sources compared to Muslim Arabs; the common religious tradition humanizes Christian Arabs more so than Muslim Arabs from a Western perspective.

The characterization of Palestinian Americans as "other" creates the potential for conflict, which Volha Charnysh, Christopher Lucas, and Prerna Singh observed "is rooted in the existence of boundaries that separate an ingroup, which elicits preferential attitudes and behavior on the part of members, from an outgroup, which could be a target for discrimination or hostility."[25] In the United States, this conflict is rooted in political ideology and the discourse of dissent: Palestinian Americans, characterized as an "outgroup" by the nature of their identities, find themselves increasingly suspect if they voice dissent with U.S. foreign policy toward the Israeli-Palestinian conflict. Going against the status quo of U.S. foreign policy further entrenches the notion of the Palestinian American as "other" and opposed to "Western ideals" of democracy.

The idea that dissent is un-American calls into question the values that underlie American identity. If finding fault with the status quo is considered grounds for racialization and otherization, then every group advocating for some sort of change could be considered un-American or unpatriotic. While "patriotism is not easily separated from nationalism, ... nationalism needs to be evaluated in light of shared principles," such as diversity. Instead of basing American national identification on agreement with the status quo, the definition of "Americanness" should leave room for the politics of dissent.[26] Pushback against racialization and the notion that dissent is unpatriotic has steadily gained momentum, especially in the age of social media. Prominent Palestinian Americans have begun to embrace their Palestinian identities, writing and posting on social media about their unique experiences as "hyphenated" Americans. The experiences of these Palestinian Americans emphasize the diversity of Palestinian American identity and directly challenge media tropes of Palestinian identity. The way Palestinian Americans are understood in terms of their sociopolitical struggle for visibility and a change in U.S. foreign policy relates to how they are racialized as "the other," and how Palestinian American identity became inextricably entwined with political events unfolding in Palestine. As members of a group mostly opposed to the way the United States conducts foreign policy in the Middle East, Palestinian Americans continuously mark themselves as outsiders to the political status quo through their political dissent, accentuating the notion that they are racially separate from the white status quo, which in turn feeds into their grievances not being viewed as legitimate.

As explained by Edward Said, even the most "progressive" thinkers of the twentieth century have little to no sympathy when it comes to Palestine and, more broadly, the Arabic-speaking world and Muslim-majority countries. Said was invited to a conference in Paris in 1998, "the first time that the so-called 'new' Israeli historians and their Palestinian counterparts" held an academic meeting on Palestine, since even progressives struggled to understand the situation from the Palestinian perspective. Said later remarked that "the Israeli participants . . . often spoke of the need for detachment, critical distance, and reflective calm as important for historical study, the Palestinian side was much more urgent, more severe and even emotional in its insistence on the need for new history." He spoke of "the profound contradiction, bordering on schizophrenia" of the Israelis who insisted that "although it was morally wrong to expel Palestinians, it was necessary to do so."[27] It was clear that even these forward-thinking historians could not quite ascribe dignity and humanity to the Palestinians.

This is an example of the attitude that Marc Lamont Hill and Mitchell Plitnick wrote about in their book, *Except for Palestine*. They describe the way "the American political left has normalized a world in which it is acceptable, through words and policies, to embrace the ethical and political contradiction of being 'progressive except for Palestine.'"[28] It's hardly the only example. A clear instance of Hill and Plitnick's thesis came during the run-up to the 2016 elections. Actor George Clooney and his wife, lawyer and activist Amal Clooney, held a fundraising dinner for candidate Hillary Clinton. The dinner, which cost $34,000 to attend, was hosted at the Clooney mansion, jointly with Israeli American mogul Haim Saban. Saban has described himself as a "protector of Israel" and once said, "I'm not suggesting we put Muslims through some kind of a torture room to get them to admit that they are or they're not terrorists, but I am saying we should have more scrutiny." Amal Clooney, who is known for her work on behalf of refugees in Syria and many United Nations–based human rights cases, "turned down a position on the panel to investigate Israeli and Hamas war crimes during the 2014 assault on Gaza." The Clooneys are known for their support of progressive causes like LGBTQ rights, climate change, and conflict victims but have chosen not to speak out on behalf of Palestinians. For her part, Hillary Clinton "criticized . . . Donald Trump and Ted Cruz for calling for increased surveillance of Muslim Americans" but was happy to take more than $6 million from Saban, despite his having the same point of view.[29]

Another example of this attitude is the interview of Benjamin Netanyahu by Bill Maher in October 2022. Maher is a comedian and political commentator and a self-described liberal who frequently interviews high-profile politicians and public figures. In his interview with Netanyahu, however, he asked no difficult questions and, in fact, gave him a platform to promote himself and his version of Israel. The Israeli activist and author Miko Peled writes, "The actual questions Maher posed to Netanyahu made a mockery of the grave reality in which Palestinians live. Rather than holding him accountable for the killing and destruction that Palestinians experience every day, Maher gave Netanyahu a platform in which to spew lies and repeat outrageous accusations against them."[30] Peled was far from the only voice criticizing Maher's handling of the interview. Marlow Stern, writing for the *Daily Beast*, said, "While I'm not under any illusion that Maher is anywhere close to a journalist, if he's going to continue masquerading as some sort of *tell it like it is* cultural authority, then he should at least exercise a degree of social responsibility."[31]

Instead, Maher lobbed softball questions to Netanyahu and almost sarcastically asked him if Israel was inflicting genocide on Palestinians. Netanyahu, to Maher's large audience, replied, "No, no, and no. I mean, these are ridiculous charges against the one democracy in the Middle East. The one democracy that upholds human rights, that defends freedom, and is America's best ally. So, I think these people should wake up to reality, but I think that's far too great a hope."[32] When the message going out to the American people is this one-sided, it should come as no surprise that the general position of most U.S. citizens is support for Israel.

This type of one-sided message is common, as has been proven by multiple empirical studies to either demonize or altogether ignore Palestinian viewpoints. In 2018 a Canadian research center, 416Lab, analyzed more than 100,000 headlines related to Palestine and Israel. Their findings suggest that major newspapers are 4 times more likely to present the Israeli government's perspective than a Palestinian perspective and 2.5 times more likely to cite Israeli sources than Palestinian.[33] Similarly, a more recent study that analyzed more than thirty-three thousand *New York Times* articles found that there is "a historical bias against Palestine in a newspaper of international importance—the *New York Times*—during the First and Second Palestinian Intifadas."[34] As Maha Nassar concluded, even as opinion pieces on Palestine, the absolute vast majority are written by non-Palestinians, which suggests that Palestinians are not needed to tell their own story.[35]

MEDIA PORTRAYALS OF PALESTINIANS

These Orientalist views, and the idea that Palestinians are anti-American because of their critique of some aspects of U.S. foreign policy, do not emerge fully formed in the minds of Americans. Their views are shaped by their exposure to various sources, one prominent one being the media. Palestinian Americans, like other Arab and Muslim Americans, are heavily stereotyped by the media in television, movies, and news broadcasting. These negative depictions affect not only how they are portrayed by larger American society, but also how they themselves relate to their American identity. While Palestinian American media stereotypes are similar in many respects to media biases against other Arab and Muslim Americans, the media bias against Palestinian Americans is also framed and influenced by the narratives around Israel. These portrayals assume the unquestioned legitimacy of Israel and the illegitimate, manufactured claims of Palestinians. The cultivation of an image of Palestinians as terrorists and backward nomad Bedouins limits the ability of Palestinians and, by extension, Palestinian Americans to express themselves and tell their own stories. Their narratives are not viewed as legitimate or deserving of empathy, or even a platform, but rather their problems are seen as consequences of their innately problematic characters.

Persistent media bias against Arabs has been quite prevalent historically.[36] Jack Shaheen, author of *Reel Bad Arabs*, wrote about the "dangerously consistent pattern of hateful Arab stereotypes" in film, especially when it comes to women.[37] Media biases against Arabs are compounded by the scores of biases against Muslims. One of these stereotypes is that all Arabs are Muslims, and vice versa. The media biases against Muslims are a key element in the stereotyping of Palestinians and Palestinian Americans. By situating Islam and, by proxy, Arabs as mutually opposed to Western values, the lived experiences of Palestinians and Palestinian Americans cannot be understood. Matt Duss, former president of the Foundation for Middle East Peace, remembers one salient example from his childhood: "The Libyans in *Back to the Future*, you know, one of the most absolutely absurd . . . riding around in their Volkswagen van waving their Kalashnikovs out the [window]. It's like the Reaganite nightmare."[38]

In the news, it is very common for the Western media to take sides against the Palestinians as a function of the perceived idea of a shared "Judeo-Christian" heritage with the state of Israel. Thus the racialization of Palestinians becomes inextricably intertwined with the racialization of Muslims as a highly suspect outgroup at odds with Western civilization. James North, an independent writer based in New York who has been an international correspondent for over forty years, has compiled evidence of the *New York Times*'s biased reporting of Israel-Palestinian issues. In a presentation in 2019, he explained that "there's a way of doing business at *The Times* in which they try and minimize Israel's culpability on what goes on and try and maximize Palestinians'. I don't even think, half the time, they're even aware of this."[39]

This may be due to the fact that Israeli bias in media reporting is almost as old as the state of Israel itself. In 1947 the Jewish Agency, a socialist Jewish group formed to promote Zionism, gave a $50,000 grant to the magazine the *Nation*. Its editor, Freda Kirchwey, proceeded to use the magazine as an engine for promoting the Zionist Israeli cause. The magazine's publisher produced twelve widely circulated reports promoting Jewish migration to Palestine, and Kirchwey wrote a 133-page memorandum for the United Nations urging it to support Zionism and comparing Arab Palestinians to Nazis, a falsehood that "became a mainstay of liberal arguments against Palestinian self-determination."[40] Kirchwey was highly influential, corresponding with President Truman over the issue and taking credit for his administration's acceptance of the state of Israel.

Edward Said, writing to his fellow Jewish Americans in an unpublished open letter in 1989, said:

> You have *The New York Review*, *The New York Times*, *New Republic*, *Atlantic Monthly*, and nearly every major newspaper, weekly, and quarterly open to you; each of the networks consults you 150 times to the once they consult Arab Americans. When a film such as *Days of Rage* displeases you, you can prevent it from being shown, you can have stations surround the film with pro-Israeli material, you can stack any panel. All of this to maintain Palestinians as ragtag terrorists, thereby to keep their torture and killing a matter of swatting flies or stepping on roaches. All of this to permit Israel in the name of the Jewish people to go on with the repression.[41]

His calls for ethical media portrayals have in general gone unanswered.

In film, Palestinians are frequently depicted as terrorists, limiting sympathy for their plight. Jack Shaheen notes the works of two Israeli producers, Menaham Golan and Yorum Globus, as instrumental in the negative portrayal of Palestinians in Western media. In a period of twenty years, Golan and Globus's American-based film company, Canon, released thirty films laden with anti-Arab and anti-Palestinian tropes and themes. These films created a baseline impression of Palestinians as evil and diametrically opposed to "the American way of life," cementing the notion that America ought to support Israel financially, culturally, and militarily.

PALESTINIANS IN THE AMERICAN IMAGINATION

Golan and Globus's films affected not only American views of Palestine and Israel abroad, but also how Palestinian Americans relate to the Palestinian struggle and express their identities domestically. Scholar and author Steven Salaita observes that "by virtue of America's unilateral support for Israel, Palestine necessarily transformed Arab Americans from a rapidly acculturating immigrant group into a radical, anti-mainstream community."[42] Not only was disapproval of the American alliance with Israel considered radical and antimainstream, *being* Palestinian itself became an instant mark of otherness, a politicized identity automatically attached to a host of inaccurate assumptions regarding Palestinians. Countless popular culture references demonize them, making "Palestinians" and "Palestine" terms that refer to the foreign, the violent, the untrustworthy, the suspect. While culture in the modern age is getting progressively better at inclusivity and the positive portrayal of minorities, Palestinians are frequently still either absent or portrayed negatively, and often their representations become political.

These racialized characterizations are not relegated to the past. Marvel created controversy with its decision in 2022 to bring comic-book character Sabra into its universe. Sabra, an Israeli operative with mutant powers, was introduced in *The Incredible Hulk* in 1980 and has been criticized as a negative, stereotyped image of Palestinians. The comic features a young "Arab" boy named Sahad, who is "illiterate, steals, and lies to tourists for money."[43] The only other Palestinians portrayed are terrorists. Sabra's backstory includes the fact that "her son, Jacob, was killed by Palestinian terrorists who attacked a school bus full of Israeli children."[44] The announcement was met with outrage and calls on social media by Palestinian allies to boycott Marvel and Disney.[45]

Pro-Israel groups, on the other hand, saw the inclusion of Sabra as a victory. "It's the 'TikTok' way, the 'cartoon' way of talking to the new generation. They'll learn the word 'Mossad,'" said Avner Avraham, "a former intelligence officer and founder of the Spy Legends agency, which advises on films and TV shows featuring Israeli spies." "According to him, such exposure can even help the Israeli secret service to recruit sources in other countries.... Israeli cartoonist Uri Fink, who created the character," is more concerned about progressive Marvel executives not giving "the most accurate portrayal of the Israeli-Palestinian conflict.... 'I suggest that Shira (Haas) [the actress playing Sabra] read the script carefully, and make sure that the character is not portrayed too problematically,'" Fink said.[46] Furthering the controversy was the date of the announcement, just days before the fortieth anniversary of the Sabra and Shatila massacre of three thousand Palestinian civilians, many of them children, in Lebanon by Israeli-backed Christian militias. While the character was not named for the massacre, victims' families were appalled by the lack of sensitivity on Marvel's part in timing their announcement.

RACIALIZED PALESTINIAN IDENTITY

These examples of ingroup and outgroup status and of media representation can help us understand how Palestinians are viewed in the United States, but how do they see themselves? Laura Wray-Lake and colleagues have discussed the implications of media stereotyping on Arab American identity, noting that Arab Americans do not see themselves reflected in the paradigm of what it means to be an American due to this media bias.[47] By extension, the categorization of Palestinian as *other* by the media, bolstered by a suite of foreign policy directives, creates a situation where Palestinian Americans find their American identities called into question simply by the existence of their "hyphenated" identities. Edward Said has written extensively about Palestine from an academic perspective, but also from a personal one. He speaks of the 1948 Nakba as a "natural tragedy," one that caused those he knew to forever be "lined with the cares of exile and homelessness."[48]

Najla Said, who happens to be the late Edward Said's daughter, is an actor and playwright who writes about Palestinian identity in her memoir, *Looking for Palestine*. Although she grew up in an affluent family in New York, Najla's childhood was filled with confusion over her identity as a Palestinian Lebanese American. She describes her search for acceptance in a culture where the only depictions of Arabs were either hyper-American, like radio host Casey Kasem and singer Tiffany, or exotically ethnic, like Cleopatra and Aladdin: "I constantly questioned everything about who I was and where I fit in the world, constantly judged my own worthiness and compared myself to others, and I struggled desperately to find a way to reconcile the beautiful, comforting, loving world of my home, culture, and family with the supposed 'barbaric' and 'backward' place and society others perceived it to be."[49]

Karmah Elmusa, a Palestinian American journalist, shared her own experience with *Elle* magazine, writing from the perspective of one who "live[s] with the guilt that we are here, not there. The guilt that we can come and go as we please while Palestinians in the West Bank and Gaza are barricaded into their homes, neighborhoods, or cities." In this essay, Elmusa directly confronts the double standard the racialization of Palestinian Americans creates, observing that her light complexion means she "can seamlessly blend into a culturally white world," while her "Palestinian cousins with darker skin are given dirty looks on planes." Elmusa's essay elicited such divisive comments that the editors of *Elle* were obliged to issue the following statement: "In light of the reactions this piece has elicited, the editors of *Elle.com* and *Elle* magazine would like to underscore that this piece reflects one woman's personal perspective on the Israeli-Palestinian conflict. This piece does not reflect the opinions of the editors or *Elle* magazine."[50]

There is a commonality to these experiences that is applicable to the Palestinian experience worldwide: the persistent sense of dispossession and loss, and the feeling of belonging neither here nor there, forever outsiders in whatever society they find themselves in. In his memoir, *Out of Place*, Edward Said describes living with an "overriding sensation . . . of being out of place," and of needing "fifty years to become accustomed to, or, more exactly, to feel less uncomfortable with, 'Edward,' a foolishly English name yoked forcibly to an unmistakably Arabic family name Said."[51]

The identity crisis Palestinian Americans find themselves in, that of being neither here nor there, is echoed in the sentiments of Dean Obeidallah, a lawyer, comedian, and radio host. In an op-ed addressing the question "Do Palestinians Really Exist?" Obeidallah admits that being Palestinian is "not just an ethnicity, it's a conversation starter," as many people try to deny the existence of Palestine.[52] Obeidallah also touches on another important aspect of Palestinian identity: its transnational nature. He asks his father, a Palestinian refugee, where Palestine is, since many people do not recognize its official existence. The senior Obeidallah touches his heart and says that Palestine is in there. In another op-ed, Obeidallah pushes back against the conflation of anti-Zionism and anti-Semitism, calling out anti-Semites as "morally repugnant" and "hurting my family and the millions of other Palestinians struggling for basic human rights." He is blunt: "We don't want the Palestinian cause to be defined by your hate."[53]

In addition to these observations, a host of young Palestinian Americans have taken to social media and other digital outlets to discuss their Palestinian identities. YouTube personality Subhi Taha, who rose to fame through his comedic interpretations of life in an Arab American household, wrote in an Instagram post liked over twenty-nine thousand times: "ya'll . . . i [sic] made it home." It included a picture of himself in front of the Dome of the Rock Mosque. In another post, viewed over sixty-nine thousand times, Taha features a video of dabka dancers with the caption, "israelis took the land but deeefinitely [sic] didn't take the culture," with the hashtag #alnakba.

Two other prominent Palestinian Americans with public identities are Gigi and Bella Hadid, international models who are half-Palestinian. The Hadids rose to fame through their prolific modeling careers and have since leveraged their platforms to discuss their identities as Palestinian Americans. Celebrating the launch of the first *Vogue Arabia*, Gigi Hadid posted on Instagram that "being half-Palestinian, it means the world to me to be on the first-ever cover(s) of @voguearabia." The post has been liked over a million times. In another post, she writes that she is "half Palestinian and proud of it."[54]

In the wake of the Trump administration's recognition of Jerusalem as Israel's capital, Bella Hadid wrote: "a very very sad day. Watching the news and seeing the pain of the Palestinian people makes me cry for the many many generations of Palestine. Seeing the sadness of my father, cousins, and Palestinian family that are feeling for our Palestinian ancestors makes this even harder to write."[55] The Hadids' openness about their Palestinian American identity is especially salient as they have amassed a huge, loyal follower base through which they are able to humanize the experiences of Palestinian Americans.

Of course, for some people, the plight of Palestinians means very little because Palestinians do not exist, per se. In an interview with Jewish Channel in 2011, Newt Gingrich referred to "an invented Palestinian people, who are in fact Arabs and were historically part of the Arab community" as justification for his pro-Israel stance.[56] Gingrich is not wrong; Palestinians *are* Arabs, but claiming that they are indistinguishable from other Arabs is much like saying that the French and the Germans are one and the same because they are both European.

Gingrich's statement echoes earlier assertions made by Rabbi Meir Kahane, who argues that there is no such thing as a Palestinian, just

Arabs of Israel. Kahane defends Israel as "the one and only land that we have, whereas the Arab of Eretz Yisrael can find a home in any one of more than the twenty lands of his 100 million fellow Arabs."[57] Kahane falsely lumps all Arabs together, erasing the differences in culture. He also assumes that other Arab nations will gladly take in the "Arabs of Eretz Yisrael," disregarding the reality that most Arab nations do not extend the same rights and privileges to Palestinian refugees as they do to their own people. Kahane's solution for the Palestinian-Israeli conflict, incidentally, is far from peaceful. He advocates for the complete separation of Arabs and Jews, stating: "For Jews and Arabs in Israel there is only one answer—separation. Jews in their land, Arabs in theirs. Separation. Only separation."[58]

Another argument often brought forth to justify the claim that Palestinians have no right to the land they have historically occupied is that what is currently Israel was formerly barren land, and that the invented Palestinians started overrunning it only *after* Israel's creation. Proponents of this argument will grasp at any pretense of evidence to bolster this claim, no matter how tenuous—even satirical literature like Mark Twain's *The Innocents Abroad*. In this travel book, which is meant to be interpreted as witty humor, Twain writes: "Come to Galilee for . . . these unpeopled deserts, these rusty mounds of barrenness, that never, never, never do shake the glare from their harsh outlines," and "Palestine sits in sackcloth and ashes. . . . Palestine is desolate and unlovely."[59]

Twain's statements are directly refuted by every scholarly analysis of the demographics of Palestine during the time he was writing, yet they were used in the U.S. Senate by Senator James M. Inhofe in 2002 "as one of the seven reasons why the State of Israel was entitled to the land."[60] Incidentally, the following comments also appear in *The Innocents Abroad*, about the same stretch of land described earlier:

> Here were evidences of cultivation . . . an acre or two of rich soil studded with last season's dead cornstalks of the thickness of your thumb and very wide apart. . . . it was a thrilling spectacle. . . . The view presented from its highest peak was almost beautiful. Below, was the broad, level plain of Esdraelon, checkered with fields like a chessboard, and full as smooth and level, seemingly; dotted about its borders with white, compact villages, and faintly penciled, far and near, with the curving lines of roads and trails.[61]

Far from being an "invented people," Palestinians have existed for centuries. Haim Gerber, a Jewish Israeli scholar at the Hebrew University of Jerusalem, has demonstrated that "embryonic territorial awareness" existed among Palestinians at least since the seventeenth century, and that this awareness went beyond simply a name.[62]

The erasure of Palestinian identity isn't limited to Congress or television pundits; it begins in childhood. *Rah! Rah! Mujadara!* is a twelve-page board book for children ages one to four. The book uses the term "Israeli Arabs" to refer to Palestinians with Israeli citizenship and identifies hummus and falafel as Israeli. Both foods are traditionally Palestinian, a fact that Jewish Israeli cooks have acknowledged.[63] Nora Esther Murad notes that the publisher of *Rah! Rah! Mujadara!*, Kar-Ben Publishing, "either [chose] to ignore it or intentionally intend to steer readers towards the Israeli narrative—by hiding the Palestinian one." Furthermore, there is no mention or illustration of Palestinians despite their making up 20 percent of the citizens of Israel and 50 percent of the population under Israeli control. There is only one illustration that might be a Muslim Arab girl, "despite the inauthentic way her headscarf allows her bangs to show."[64]

Israel ABCs: A Book About the People and Places of Israel, by Holly Schroeder, includes a page titled "B is for Bedouin" and reads "Bedouins are Arab people who come from Israel's deserts." As Murad notes, Bedouins have lived on the "land that is now the State of Israel for hundreds of years" and are the original inhabitants. Since the formation of the State of Israel, they "have been systematically discriminated against," a fact the book ignores.[65]

Two books about Israel for children ages seven to eleven, *All Around the World Israel* by Kristine Spanier and *Travel to Israel* by Matt Doeden, feature cover images of East Jerusalem, despite the fact that, legally, it is part of Palestine. Murad comments that "Israel has used every possible administrative and military tool available to make East Jerusalem unlivable for Palestinians, in an effort to get them to leave so their land can be repurposed for Jewish use. These cover photos not only fail to acknowledge the reality of life for Palestinian Jerusalemites, they deceptively cover it up."[66]

Welcome to Israel with Sesame Street by Christy Peterson includes a map of Israel in which the West Bank and the Gaza Strip, while outlined, are unlabeled and colored the same shade of yellow as Israel of 1948. This effectively erases the Occupied Palestinian Territories. It also includes pictures of Muslim girls under a caption stating that Jerusalem is "special to people of many religions" and giving the word for "hello" in Hebrew and Arabic.[67] While this might appear inclusive at first glance, it is a common tactic used by Israel to deny Palestinian identity, instead making Palestinians just an Israeli minority.

Books that do show Palestine can be kept out of the hands of children by powerful pro-Israel groups. *P Is for Palestine*, a children's alphabet book, was taken off the shelves of the New York bookstore Book Culture after advocates for Israel "complained about the use of the word "Palestine" in the book's title. "The Stephen Wise Free Synagogue also opposed the use of the word *intifada* to illustrate the letter I, threatening to ban Book Culture from a book fair if it did not denounce the book. The book states: 'Intifada is Arabic for rising up for what's right, if you are a kid or a grown up!' and depicts a Palestinian girl on her father's back raising peace signs behind barbed wire." "The author, Golbarg Bashi, received messages threatening to report her to the Department of Homeland Security and deport her to Guantanamo, along with pornographic messages and calls for her book to be banned or burned." The owners of the store were forced to put out a statement "denouncing boycotts for Palestinian rights."[68]

The erasure of Palestine from children's books is an effective way to erase Palestine itself from collective memory. When children are taught that there is only Israel, they, being impressionable, will believe it and may grow up to be adults who deny the existence of a Palestinian people.

HOSTILITY, INTIMIDATION, AND VIOLENCE

When Palestinians do assert their identities, there are often consequences. The experiences of two Palestinian Americans, and one Palestinian's experience in the United States, illustrate the hostility that emerges when Palestinian Americans speak out about political issues that affect their identities. Those who speak out about Palestine or the Arab American experience are often accused of sympathizing with terrorists or being anti-Semitic. The messages that Palestinian American activists attempt to convey are lost in this sea of accusations.

Linda Sarsour is a case in point. Sarsour, a Brooklynite of Palestinian heritage, has worked tirelessly in New York and nationwide on a variety of social justice causes. She organized the successful campaign to have New

York public schools recognize Muslim holidays as school-sanctioned days off.[69] She also helped partly dismantle the New York Police Department program that was spying on Muslim neighborhoods post-9/11.[70] On March 6, 2018, she was arrested outside Speaker Paul Ryan's office for protesting the Trump administration's stance on DACA.[71] Sarsour is known for speaking up for Muslim or Palestinian causes, but also for "women, gays, prison inmates, victims of racial profiling—facing the problems that concern her."[72] Despite the positive contributions Sarsour routinely makes to society, conservative media sources such as Breitbart, Fox News, and Conservative Review describe her using terms such as "terrorist" and "Islamic radical."[73]

The application of the term "terrorist" to Palestinians who advocate for the Palestinian cause is not new. It reflects the way that Palestinian self-determination and even self-worth are completely disregarded by allies of Israel. A striking example of how Palestinians who advocate for Palestinian causes are dismissed and subject to humiliation is the treatment of Yasser Arafat by Rudy Giuliani. In 1995 Giuliani, then mayor of New York City, kicked Arafat out of a concert for world leaders held at the Lincoln Center. He did this despite Arafat being recognized by both the United States and Israel as a part of the peace-brokering process. In a *New York Times* article the next day, Giuliani defended his decision, calling Arafat a murderer and a terrorist. The White House quickly distanced itself from Giuliani's actions, calling them "an embarrassment to everyone associated with diplomacy," yet Giuliani has never apologized for his treatment of Arafat.[74]

No Palestinian American has paid as steep a price for advocating for Palestinian causes as Alex Odeh. Odeh was a Christian Palestinian American who was the regional director of the Arab-American Anti-Discrimination Committee (ADC). In his work, Odeh advocated for building interfaith unity. On the day of his assassination, Odeh was slated to speak at a synagogue in Fountain Valley, California. The night before, he had appeared on a late-night talk show condemning the killing of Leon Klinghoffer by Palestinian gunmen aboard the *Achille Lauro* cruise ship. During this interview, he "repeated his oft-stated belief that peace and cooperation between Palestinians and Israelis was not only necessary, it was possible." On October 11, 1985, as Odeh walked into his office in Santa Ana, a powerful bomb went off, killing him. The three men suspected by the FBI of carrying out the assassination, Robert Manning, Keith Fuchs, and Andy Green, fled to Israel. Manning was later extradited and charged for another bombing, but Fuchs and Green remain in Israel. Speaking at a memorial service for Odeh, Jack Shaheen, author of *Reel Bad Arabs*, observed that "the tragedy of Alex's assassination shows that the life of an American civil rights advocate with Palestinian roots is not valued by our government or media as much as the lives of other Americans."[75]

Odeh was among the first, but not the last, of those who paid with their lives after supporting the Palestinian cause. In Palestine, Rachel Corrie and Shireen Abu Akleh, American women who had traveled or lived in the country, were killed by the Israel Defense Forces twenty years apart. Corrie was an American college student who traveled to Rafah in 2003 to initiate a Sister City program between Rafah and her hometown of Olympia, Washington. While there, she participated in nonviolent protests intended to stop the IDF from tearing down homes of Palestinians to make way for Israeli settlements. During a protest, she was crushed to death by a Caterpillar bulldozer driven by an IDF soldier.[76] Eyewitnesses claimed the soldier had run her over deliberately, but an investigation by the Israeli military found Israel held no responsibility for her death. Subsequent lawsuits were filed, with organizations such as B'Tselem and Human Rights Watch criticizing the investigation. In 2012 the Israeli Supreme Court upheld the earlier verdict, exonerating the Israel Defense Forces. Amnesty International said "the verdict continues the pattern of impunity for Israeli military violations against civilians and human rights defenders in the Occupied Palestinian Territories."[77] Civil suits against Caterpillar and the Israeli government by the Corrie family were likewise dismissed.[78]

While in Palestine, Rachel expressed her reasons for aligning herself with the Palestinian cause: "When I come back from Palestine, I probably will have nightmares and constantly feel guilty for not being here, but I can channel that into more work. Coming here is one of the better things I've ever done. So when I sound crazy, or if the Israeli military should break with their racist tendency not to injure white people, please pin the reason squarely on the fact that I am in the midst of a genocide that I am also indirectly supporting, and for which my government is largely responsible."[79]

In 2022 Shireen Abu Akleh, a Palestinian American journalist, was shot to death in the West Bank while reporting on the conflict. Despite wearing a "PRESS" insignia that was clearly visible, Abu Akleh was shot several times by IDF soldiers. A civilian who tried to render aid was shot at as well. Multiple investigations, including those by the Associated Press (AP) and the UN, found that an Israeli soldier deliberately targeted her and two other journalists who were with her. The Israeli government offered to perform a joint investigation with the Palestinian Authority, but the latter declined, saying Israel "cannot be trusted to investigate itself." Israel's own investigation ultimately absolved itself of all responsibility and at one point suggested that the gunfire may have come from Palestinian militants.[80] A forensic report by Palestinian human rights group Al-Haq and the UK-based research agency Forensic Architecture released in September 2022 was "literally the last nail in the coffin of what the army is arguing," according to a Forensic Architecture spokesman. That report determined the shooting was "fully intentional." In a statement to press, Susan Power, Al-Haq's head of legal research and advocacy said, "Israel's failure to carry out an effective investigation into the killing of Shireen amounts to a shielding of perpetrators and highlights the need for the Prosecutor of the International Criminal Court to expedite the investigation in the situation in Palestine."[81] Despite the evidence, it appeared unlikely that the Israeli military will be held accountable for Shireen's death. However, in November 2022 the Federal Bureau of Investigation opened an investigation into the incident, suggesting things might be changing for the IDF and its carelessness with human rights.[82]

AMERICAN CHRISTIANITY AND ITS PERCEPTIONS: CHRISTIAN ZIONISM AND THE ROLE OF CHURCH IN POLITICS

Religious institutions in the United States have enormous influence on American understanding of politics and the world at large and play a significant role in civic engagement and political participation. In every tradition and denomination, these institutions are integral to the formation of cultural understanding around political issues and inform the views of congregants regarding other people's religious and political beliefs. The church's influence varies in different social, economic, and geographic contexts, but the existence of a strong and clear connection between the Jewish tradition and the Christian tradition in the United States is undeniable. Christian Zionism is a product of religious belief and is spread by religious elites to intentionally forge a connection between Israel and American

Christianity. Although there are churches and denominations that view the issue of Palestine differently, and more accurately, these voices are limited in terms of creating a countercommunity. Ideas about the eventual culture clash between the manufactured Orient, on the one hand, and the "Christian" West on the other, are deeply entrenched.

American Christian culture and Israel

American culture is centered on Christian themes and messages. While this is understandable given the historical prevalence of the Christian religion in the United States, it creates a nearly invisible but ever-present underlying assumption of Christianity as normal and non-Christian faiths as "other." An example of this is a memory relayed by Matt Duss, former president of the Foundation for Middle East Peace and former foreign policy advisor to Bernie Sanders:

> When I was growing up in Sunday school, I played Noah in a play, I played Joshua in the play . . . I never played, you know, "Hussein" or other characters from the history of Islam. I played characters from the Old Testament and the New Testaments. We are inclined to recognize and identify with this history in a way we are simply not with Islam. It's not a question of good will or bad will, it is simply that we know this story, and not the other story. We were raised and inculcated in this from the time we were little in Sunday school in a way that makes us kind of more instinctively sympathetic to one narrative over another.[83]

The ways in which Americans perceive Israel and Palestine are deeply affected by these messages. Duss, describing his childhood, says, "I first came to be interested in Israel/Palestine just from growing up in the evangelical church. That was my first (time) learning about Israel, learning about the history, the Old Testament and then the New Testament, the biblical history, the story of the Jewish people, the Hebrews, the land of Canaan. My family was fairly devout, going to church two, sometimes three times a week, even on Wednesday. Those stories (are) just part of our family. . . . I mean this was part of our faith, our culture."

American Christianity is distinct from global Christianity, primarily due to the prevalence of White Evangelicalism, a strain of fundamentalism that has been gaining in popularity and political prominence in the United States for at least five decades. This strain of Christianity embraces alignment with Israel due to its importance to end-times theology and promotes that unity even above solidarity with Christians around the world. Peter Beinart describes it in this way: "There are certain powerful narratives or tropes that influence a lot of people; one of them is Christianity and especially Christianity since 9/11. American Christian identity is often defined [as] against Islam, so the notion of Palestinians as Muslims and therefore Israel as America's ally... and even America as the tip of the spear of the West and of the Judeo Christian world in a struggle against Islam was just very natural for a lot of people, in the way it brings together Christianity and American nationalism."[84] If it were as simple as Christians taking other Christians' side, there would be no question as to whether American Christians would take the side of Palestinian Christians and advocate for their self-determination. Self-determination is, after all, an idea that is uniquely American, especially the way it has been defined since World War I. In addition to this, Christianity and colonialism have played an intertwining role in matters relating to predominantly Muslim societies. The majority of Palestinians are Muslim, and thus they are seen as part of the larger Orientalist discourse that demonizes Islam and Muslims and defines the greatness and glory of the West in contrast to the Islamic world.

While the strength of the Israel/US connection varies from one Christian denomination to another and from one church to another, many interpretations of Christian theology in the West hold Judaism at their core.[85] This connection creates a sense of cultural proximity between the United States and Israel, since these churches feel aligned with the biblical Israel. This connection cannot be ignored in explaining the way Americans see contemporary Israel and Palestine, especially because some Christian traditions in the United States read and interpret the scripture in a literal fashion. This literalist interpretation fails to take into account the two millennia of history that have transpired between the biblical accounts and the modern state of Israel and ignores the movement and migration of people and the introduction and transformation of ideas and technologies.[86] This collapse of history creates a false sense of continuity from the past into contemporary times. It means that many Christians in America hold views and vote for candidates that presage Israel and its Jewish population over Palestinian Christians. Even in instances when this solidarity does not subsume

Christian allegiance, evangelicals are not welcoming of Arabs and Muslims. When Jeb Bush was running for president in 2015, he said he would allow Syrian refugees into the country under certain conditions. "'At a minimum we ought to be bringing in people that have—orphans or people that clearly aren't going to be terrorists. Or Christians,' Bush said during a campaign stop in South Carolina. 'There are no Christian terrorists in the Middle East, they're persecuted.'"[87] His plan, however, would not include Muslim refugees.

A rapidly growing trend called "Jewish affinity" combines Protestant Christian beliefs with elements of Judaism. Hillary Kaell, an anthropologist at McGill University who specializes in North American Christianity, notes that these "Jewish affinity" Christians are either drawn to Judaism to engage more literally with scripture (including the Torah) or are "drawn to Hebraic rituals as an access point for God's blessings."[88] Jewish affinity differs from Christian Zionism, which includes support for Israel as part of its theology, but the two are often linked. Jewish affinity Christians tend to be strong supporters of Israel. Kaell has referred to the integration of Jewish elements into Christianity as the "Hebraic style." She notes that this Hebraic style goes back to the latter half of the nineteenth century, when some Protestants viewed Jewish settlement in Palestine as a necessary precondition for bringing about Jesus's return. Christian Zionism, Kaell notes, was popularized in 1967 after the "reunification" of Jerusalem. The Hebraic style believes in "the binding relevance of the entire Bible," leading to political support for Israel. As a whole, "through the Hebraic style, Christians around the world find potent ways to entwine their fate with the Biblical nation of Israel."[89]

This affiliation with Israel is widespread since, for some, church attendance in the United States is part of the American experience. Church is often where Americans acquire political and social views about the world. The way in which Israel is presented during a Sunday sermon influences the way it is viewed, discussed, and debated in contemporary issues. There is no space for Palestinians in this equation, except for the reference to the Philistines, who, as the historical enemies of the Israelites, are painted in the most negative light in the biblical narrative. Islam, too, is portrayed as hostile, a "false" religion that draws people away from the "true God" and must be resisted. Christian Zionists often hold anti-Arab and Orientalist perspectives, and a view that "the two nations of America and Israel, like

Siamese twins, are perceived to be pitted against an evil world dominated by Islam."[90] Church attendees are exposed to these ideas and internalize them as norms. There is great political power in this portrayal of Muslims and Palestinians as antithetical to Christians and Israelites, and to the modern Israelis who are seen as the inheritors of the biblical promises. Demonizing Palestinians becomes quite acceptable and natural.

One highly influential facet of the shared history discourse is the evangelical production and promotion of a God-ordained America that is intended as a Christian nation. This idea can be traced to the late 1970s, when several influential history books were published by conservative Christian publishing houses. As Diana Butler Bass writes, the most notable came in 1977 when "a book appeared that would wind up being one of the most influential histories of the late twentieth century: *The Light and the Glory (God's Plan for America), 1492–1793* by Peter Marshall and David Manuel." This book "was the first in a three-volume set that told American history 'from God's point of view,' and revealed the nation to be divine in conception, guidance, and mission—telling the story in dramatic and compelling fashion without complexity and with moral certainty. The series also came in a children's version, and was used in churches and Christian schools (often as the required textbook for high school students) across the nation." These books were then picked up by Texas youth pastor David Barton, who repackaged them into videos that pastors used to educate their congregations. His organization, WallBuilders, "influenced the entirety of contemporary evangelicalism."[91] Its descriptions of a Christian nation ordained by God complement and support the idea of Israel as a Jewish nation ordained by God.

American Christianity and Zionism

Christian Zionism is the belief that a return of biblical Israel is necessary and part of a divine plan, but it is not the only form of Zionism. Ummayah Cable writes about compulsory Zionism, a form of support for Israel that has changed over time. Cable describes the way it was used early in the twentieth century by anti-Semites eager to rid their countries of Jewish people. Cable cites Gisela Lebzelter, who "uses the phrase to describe precisely the kind of political anti-Semitism prevalent during the interwar period in England, wherein 'compulsory Zionism was advocated as a peaceful "final solution"' at a time when the British fascist movement supported the establishment of a Jewish national homeland to justify the expulsion of Jews from England." In other words, the idea of compulsion was conceptualized as compelling the Jewish people to leave Europe. Over time, however, that conception changed. After the horrors of World War II, more people held sympathetic views regarding the Jewish people and began to conceive of a Jewish state as a way to keep them safe from violence. "For the non-Jewish European and U.S. public and politicians, the creation of the State of Israel represented a politically benevolent solution to the problem of Nazi imperialism," and the term began to represent an idealistic moral necessity. Zionism was "refashioned for the era of decolonization, and compulsory Zionism went from politically abhorrent to politically correct." Over time, the term's meaning shifted again. Today, "compulsory Zionism manifests as a hegemonic discourse—the unwavering support for Israel and unwillingness to critique Zionism that have dominated U.S. culture and politics for decades."[92]

Compulsory Zionism, however it is defined, has been a political ideology. Christian Zionism similarly believes in the necessity of a Jewish state, but for theological reasons. Those who adhere to Christian Zionism believe that God will reveal Himself in stages, and that some of those stages have already passed. This belief, called dispensationalism, sees historical and political events as part of this progression. The establishment of the state of Israel is viewed as the literal fulfillment of biblical prophecy, and the 1967 war "provided more conclusive evidence of the dispensationalist predictions of...'end of time events.'"[93] Zionist Christians believe the Israeli victory in the war was evidence of God's acting on their behalf and blessing them with more land. Carlo Aldrovandi of the University of Dublin has studied the Christian Zionist movement. He notes that the events of 1948 and 1967 provided proof for Christian Zionists and Jewish religious Zionists of God's intervention and the fulfillment of biblical prophecy.[94] In *The New Christian Zionism*, Craig Blaising writes: "Common among various forms of Christian Zionism are two points: (1) there is an ethnic, national, territorial Israel in the consummate plan of God, and (2) what we are witnessing today in the nation of Israel is a preconsummate work of God in continuity with the divine plan for Israel and the nations."[95] Note how no mention is given of the Palestinians residing within Israel, even as an afterthought.

The development of Christian Zionism can be traced back to England as early as the sixteenth century. Ronald Stockton, retired professor of political science at the University of Michigan-Dearborn, notes that Christian Zionism has historical roots in West European Protestant challenges to Catholic authority in the sixteenth century.[96] The Catholic St. Augustine viewed the concept of a return to Israel as a metaphorical return of individuals to the fold of God (the church), while Protestants interpreted this return to be literal. According to the Reverend Naim Ateek, a Palestinian Anglican, "British Anglicans as early as the 16th century promoted the belief that the Jewish people must be restored to the Promised Land of Palestine to fulfill a biblical prophecy before the Second Coming of Christ."[97] This idea of the Second Coming was developed by Irish Anglican priest Rev. John Nelson Darby, who coined the phrase "dispensationalism."[98]

During the nineteenth century, the British Society for the Propagation of the Gospel Amongst the Jews and the Anglican London Society for Promoting Christianity, in conjunction with the Church of Scotland, sent missionaries to the Holy Land.[99] At the same time, Anthony Ashley Cooper, the seventh Earl of Shaftesbury, connected the biblical interest in the Jews and their ancient homeland with national foreign policy. He proposed the resettlement of Jews in Palestine in 1838.[100] Victoria Clark observes that "Shaftesbury can take the credit for briefly making 'the English madness' of Restorationism part and parcel of England's answer to the endlessly plaguing Eastern Question" (i.e., the Ottoman Empire). Of course, as Clark notes, "never having set foot in Palestine, he was ignoring the region's majority of Arab inhabitants, of whose existence he must have been aware via his London Jews' Society contacts. Perhaps he was not well informed enough to know that Palestinian Arabs were not the same people as the Ottoman Turks."[101] Later, the Anglican Rev. William Henry Hechler attended the first Zionist Congress in Switzerland in 1897. He was the only non-Jewish person in attendance.[102]

In the United States, support for Christian Zionism is sometimes traced back to 1809, when President John Adams promoted Jewish settlement in Palestine to create a homeland and "civilize" the existing population, saying, "I will insist that the Hebrews have done more to civilize men than any other nation. If I were an atheist and believed in blind eternal fate, I should still believe that fate had ordained the Jews to be the most essential instrument for civilizing the nations."[103] In the early twentieth century, President Woodrow Wilson supported the Balfour Declaration, a British statement of support for the establishment of a national home for the Jewish people in Palestine.[104] Various Protestant groups supported the restoration of Jews to Palestine as a result of ongoing persecution in Russia. Ronald Stockton notes that the idea of Israel also appealed to the American myth of national origin, of a barren land tamed and populated by successive generations of Americans.[105] Furthermore, Christian Zionists hold a covenant view of America's existence, a covenant that is extended toward the promise of the reestablishment of the biblical kingdom of Israel. British and later American efforts to colonize historic Palestine were also aided by travelogues from European travelers, who commented that the area was uninhabited. Writer E. L. Mitford, "a member of the Ceylon Civil Service, who had lived some years in Morocco and the Levant and knew the Jewish population there, came forward with a proposal for the 'reestablishment of the Jewish nation in Palestine, under British protection.'" He wrote, "Palestine, though now barren and desolate, requires only an active and industrious population, so abundant are its natural advantages of soil and climate, to restore its original fertility."[106] It was a false claim, but Europeans and Americans who had never traveled to the region had no way of knowing that.

Paul Merkley writes of Emanuel Neumann as one of the orchestrators of the Zionist movement in twentieth-century America, and perhaps the inspiration for those who sought to bring Christians over to the Zionist cause. "Of all the official Zionists, Emanuel Neumann seems to have been the most constant in his belief that there was such a thing as a Christian conscience, and he certainly made the most conscientious efforts to study and understand it, so that he could recruit it on behalf of the cause of Zionism."[107] Born in Latvia, Neumann immigrated to the United States as an infant and was heavily involved in Zionism from a very young age. His father required the family to speak only Hebrew while at home; Neumann continued this tradition with his own family, as did his children. He started a Hebrew school in Brooklyn, served as president of the American Zionist Organization in 1947, and died in Tel Aviv. And he understood how Zionists could influence politics. In August 1931 Neumann wrote to Selig Brodetsky, who managed the "Political Affairs" portfolio within the World Zionist Organization:

> The political situation here [in the United States] presents a certain opportunity. The Republican Administration is in a cold sweat about the national elections in 1932.... The State in turn cannot normally carry a Republican Presidential candidate without strong support in the City of New York where Jews constitute almost one-third of the electorate. Under these circumstances... the Republican leaders would think twice before refusing us some reasonable requests. In the circumstances it may be advisable for me to endeavor to initiate political action in Washington with the help of our friends.[108]

Thus began a long history of Zionist influence on American politics.

In the United States, Christian Zionism has manifested in a growing number of pro-Israel organizations, the two largest of which are Christians United for Israel (CUFI) and Christians' Israel Public Action Campaign (CIPAC). These groups have their roots in the 1940s, under the sway of Jewish leaders such as Neumann and their own horror at the treatment of Jewish people at the hands of the Nazi Party in Germany. During and after the horrific events of World War II, liberal Christians supported Jewish migration to Palestine as a way of assuaging American and European guilt over the Holocaust. In 1942 the Christian Council on Palestine (CCP) was established to advocate for the right of the Jews to establish their own state, to atone for the genocide that European Jews were experiencing.[109] The CCP later merged with the American Palestine Committee to form the American Christian Palestine Committee (ACPC). In 1945 the ACPC sent a letter to the White House demanding recognition of unrestricted Jewish immigration and colonization to the Holy Land. President Truman's Protestant heritage was crucial to his administration's quick recognition of Israel. Truman viewed the formation of Israel as a biblical mandate for God's chosen people and conferred de facto recognition of Israel within minutes of its declaration of independence.[110] Elizabeth Edwards Spalding of Claremont McKenna College argues that Truman "identified a legitimate Jewish right to Palestine that preceded the horrors of WWII and the Balfour Declaration,"[111] and he went out of his way to recognize the newly declared state against the advice of officials at the State Department and his secretary of defense. Later administrations took various positions on Israel, with Jimmy Carter playing more of a statesman role in attempting to find compromise between the Palestinians and Israelis, and Ronald Reagan staking his claim as a Christian Zionist. George W. Bush was an even stronger Zionist. He endorsed Christians United for Israel's grand launch and allowed CUFI leaders to hold off-the-record meetings with White House officials.[112] A discussion of how Zionist beliefs influenced government policy and presidential power can be found in chapter 4.

During the 1970s Evangelical strains of Christianity rapidly grew while other mainstream Protestant and Roman Catholic denominations experienced a steep decline. During this decade, American Evangelist Hal Lindsey published his bestseller *The Late Great Planet Earth*, which linked current events to end-of-time prophecies and "did for Christian Zionism what the invention of the printing press did for the Bible."[113] In the 1980s the Christian Right, which was composed of Evangelical Dispensationalists and American Jewish pressure groups and Israeli politicians, formed a key voting bloc for the Republican Party. More recently, a LifeWay poll in 2018 found that 80 percent of Evangelicals believed that "the creation of Israel in 1948 was a fulfillment of biblical prophecy that would bring about Christ's return."[114] The growing influence and importance of Christian Zionists was not lost on Prime Minister Menachem Begin of Israel, who appointed Harry Hurwitz as special envoy liaison for Evangelical Christians.[115]

The prevalence of pro-Zionist views among Evangelical Christians is largely due to the work of influential Evangelical figures. John Hagee, Pat Robertson, Ralph Reed, Franklin Graham, and Jerry Falwell are five Evangelicals who amassed millions of zealous followers and are outspoken in their support of the state of Israel. Hagee was the founder of the aforementioned Christians United for Israel, which he built "by weaving Christian End Times theology with nationalistic pro-Israel organizations."[116] In return for support from Jerry Falwell and the American Evangelicals, Begin "was willing to record a broadcast for Falwell's television program on the Camp David agreement and happy to issue residence visas to Evangelicals 'beyond the customary quotas which allowed for the building of new congregations.'" Falwell's support of Begin was rooted in his belief that the restoration of Israel was God's plan, and that in supporting it, he was doing God's will. Falwell worked on Begin's behalf to silence criticism from other Christian groups and to implore the Reagan White House "not to press Israel to make concessions on the West Bank, and that, instead, there should be 'total military and financial support for Israel.'"[117]

It is important to note that within his dispensationalist framework, war is not something to be avoided, but welcomed. Hagee has advocated for a U.S.-initiated war with Iran and "welcomes the current situation in the Middle East as portending the End Times and Second Coming." He cites Matthew 24:8: "All these are the beginning of birth pains." Hagee explains the passage in this way: "The world and Israel are now having contractions (wars, rumors of wars, acts of terrorism, bloodshed, and violence around the globe) that will produce a new Messianic Era. The increasing rapidity and intensifying of these birth pains can be seen on the newscasts every evening. We are racing toward the end of the age. Messiah is coming much sooner than you think!"[118] Many under Hagee's influence share this rather gleeful approach to a potential war in the Middle East.

As Yaakov Ariel, professor of religious studies at UNC Chapel Hill, summarizes, "In no other case have members of one religious community considered members of another religious tradition to hold a special role in God's plans for human redemption and to be God's first nation." Ariel observes that "Christian Zionists have, at times, been more enthusiastic than Jews over the prospect of a Jewish state."[119] A case in point: the establishment of the International Christian Embassy in Jerusalem (ICEJ) in 1980 to promote support for Israel among Evangelicals and support philanthropic programs in Israel. A Pew Research study found that Jews who believe in God are less likely than Evangelicals to believe that God gave Israel to the Jewish people (55 percent vs. 82 percent). White Evangelicals are also more likely than Jews to favor stronger U.S. support for Israel and are less optimistic than Jews about the prospects for a two-state solution. A full 50 percent of white Evangelicals believe that an independent Palestine cannot coexist with Israel.[120]

The implications of Christian Zionism on the politics of Palestine are quite striking. Because of the belief that the creation of Israel fulfills a biblical prophecy, any withdrawal from "Judea/Samaria" (the biblical terms for what is now known as the West Bank) is considered to be an act against divine will. According to Christian Zionism, the Second Coming of Christ cannot occur without an "End of Days" cataclysm occurring in the Middle East. Bringing about peace in Israel/Palestine is therefore viewed as going against God's predefined plans. Christian Zionists view the application of the promises concerning ancient tribes of Israel to the modern Zionist state quite literally; modern Israel and Eretz Ysrael of Genesis 15:18 are seen as one and the same.[121] As Victoria Clark observes in *Allies for Armageddon*, "where Bible scholars have traditionally regarded the prophetic parts of the Bible, including the New Testament's Book of Revelation, as relating to the era and political context in which they were written and as therefore to be understood metaphorically or in a mythical sense," many in Evangelical denominations "believe that those ancient Middle Eastern forecasts accurately and literally describe present and future events."[122]

It is important to understand that a biblical basis for friendship with Israel and an understanding of the resurrection of a Jewish state as crucial to a world-ending war requires an enemy. That enemy, as taught by fundamentalists, is Islam. "Bible teachers became increasingly attentive to the perils they saw in Islam after the oil crisis of 1973," explains Stephen Spector in his book *Evangelicals and Israel: The Story of Christian Zionism*. For example, Spector writes, "John F. Walvoord expressed this concern in *Armageddon, Oil, and the Middle East*, which sold 750,000 copies."[123] According to many fundamentalist teachers, the end of the world and the second coming of Christ can only occur when all the Jews of the world are back in Jerusalem. Satan, attempting to thwart this plan, is therefore attempting to influence mankind to prevent that return (the root of anti-Semitism). "Many Christian Zionists take this to the next logical step, declaring that Muslims have become Satan's army in this ancient struggle," writes Spector.[124] Televangelist Benny Hinn has called the Israel/Palestine conflict "a war between God and the devil," while pastor Jack Hayford says that "Arab animosity is driven by 'spiritual powers that will not be satisfied until Israel ceases to exist.' . . . These forces are just as hostile to Christian believers as to Israel and they cannot be overthrown politically; . . . the only way to break them is by intercessory prayer."[125] While many Christians take the position of Hayford, seeing this as a spiritual battle to be dealt with by prayer, far more see their role as an active one, taking part in politics, giving money, and voicing concerns. This makes Christian Zionism particularly dangerous to Muslims in particular and, due to Orientalism, Arabs in general.

Elizabeth Phillips's ethnography of a Christian Zionist congregation in Colorado led her to conclude that Christian Zionists "have an utter certitude that they are cooperating with God in the fruition of God's ultimate intention for human history."[126] Part of Christian Zionist belief is Restorationism, the belief that the Christian church should actively assist Jewish people in gathering to Eretz Ysrael as a means to fulfill biblical prophecy. More militant interpretations of Christian Zionism view the expansion of

Israel into parts of Egypt, Lebanon, and Jordan as part of the biblical prophecy. Despite the synergy between Christian Zionism and Jewish Zionism, there has been a tension between Christian Zionists' emphasis on premillennialist theology (the Second Coming of Christ) and Christian Zionists' disappointment by the secular character of the early Zionist movement. However, Zionist leaders were willing to overlook Christian Zionists' emphasis on the End of Times narrative for the sake of political and cultural support.

Not all denominations of Christians espouse Christian Zionism. Anglican Reverend Naim Ateek has noted that while Anglicans were key "in developing the doctrine of Christian Zionism," they should now actively work to curb its influence. Ateek's objection to Christian Zionism rests in part on its unquestioning acceptance of "a tribalism evident in some parts of the Old Testament that is based on racial exclusivity."[127] Wes Michaelson, former general secretary of the Reformed Church in America, condemns the idea that "God has a vested interest in the amount of real estate controlled by the state of Israel," further noting that Christian Zionism sanctifies "contemporary Israeli nationalism and aggrandizement with spurious interpretations of Old Testament 'prophecy.'"[128] Tom Driver, a professor at the Union Theological Seminary, notes that "'it is also a great and frightening thing' that 'the most pro-Israeli group in American Christianity is also the most antisemitic,'" calling out the strange paradox of those who hold both anti-Semitic and pro-Israel views.[129]

As Matt Duss puts it:

> As Christians, we need to think more deeply about what we are supporting and how we understand this issue because for Christians, our model is Jesus Christ and his way of living is through kindness and care for all of our brothers and sisters and all of our neighbors. And who is our neighbor? Everyone is your neighbor. And that means Israelis and Palestinians, and there's simply no way to square this just kind of lock step support for the Israeli government. There's no way to support settlement building and expulsion and home demolition and the humiliation of one people by another with the message of Jesus Christ.[130]

Palestinian Christians themselves "consider Christian Zionist views as a negation of the teachings of Jesus on justice and compassion for all of humanity," and as a tool in the whitewashing of Israel's harsh politics toward Palestinians, both Muslim and Christian, report Daniel Siryoti and Gideon Allon.[131] Mitri Raheb, in "Palestinian Christian Reflections on Christian Zionism" writes, "This movement doesn't care what the human rights charter is stating, because the divine rights supersede all other rights. International laws are not important because the Divine laws are to be followed."[132] For Stephen Robert Sizer, former vicar of Christ Church, Christian Zionist hostility to Arabs, especially Palestinians, "is difficult to square with the New Testament ethic. The followers of Jesus Christ are called to be peacemakers . . . , to love their enemies . . . and seek reconciliation."[133]

Zionist influence on politics

> Very few people search to find the truth that they would never get from the media or from the mouths of politicians, for some of whom we are "invented people." Evangelicals are also abusing the Holy Scriptures by using the word of God for political reasons. They confuse the metaphoric, spiritual Israel with the State of Israel as a political entity founded on the Land of Palestine in 1948.
> —GEORGE MAKHLOUF, 2016

While public opinion is only one factor in policy formulations, these ideas influence the ways in which people vote and the politicians they vote for. As Matt Duss explained, "U.S. policy is made by Americans, it is a product of American culture. The American culture is pretty much a Christian culture and if we are not religiously devout, our literature, our media reflects this dominant culture. AIPAC, when they're lobbying, they say they're pushing on an open door. I take that to mean that the pro-Israel lobby says [to Americans] 'listen . . . this is our shared history.' That is part of why it is much easier to sell this pro-Israel story, and not a pro-Palestinian or even a story suggesting that there are two narratives."[134]

Christians, particularly conservative and fundamentalist believers, have shown they support in great numbers politicians who share their religious views toward Israel. When politicians who write and vote on foreign policy share the view that Israel has a divine right to occupy the land due to a biblical connection, Palestinians and their rightful claims against the settler-colonial Zionist movement are categorically rejected. This rejection occurs not because Palestinian claims are illegitimate, although this argument is prevalent in Congress and in public discourse around Palestine and Israel. It occurs because of ingrained ideas about Christianity, Jews, Israel, Islam, Arabs, and the Palestinians as an extension of the biblical Philistines. This perspective effectively whitewashes Zionist settler-colonialism as legitimate.

Despite the purported separation of church and state, religion plays a large and often fundamental role in legislation, especially around "moral" issues such as same-sex marriage and abortion. Congress emerged as a battlefield for cultural conflicts such as women's suffrage, prohibition, and civil rights during the twentieth century. During the 1970s and 1980s, religious traditionalists framed social agendas as the work of God, thus implying that opponents of such agendas were immoral or against God. These religious traditionalists, according to Elizabeth Oldmixon, vice provost at James Madison University, embraced "a vision of society in which individual decisions are made with an eye toward divinely ordained social relationships."[135]

It is interesting to note that, while religion plays an important role in policymaking, the 117th Congress looked "quite different from Americans overall," as the Pew Research Center noted, with almost nine in ten Congress members identifying as Christian, compared with two-thirds of the general public. According to Pew, Congress is both more heavily Protestant (55 percent versus 43 percent) and more heavily Catholic (30 percent versus 20 percent) than the U.S. adult population overall.[136] Jewish members of Congress make up a slightly larger share than their percentage in the general public, while the percentage of Buddhists, Muslims, Hindus, and Unitarians more closely match their percentages in the general public. According to William D'Antonio and his colleagues at the Catholic University of America, the First Congress (which comprised sixty-six members) had representatives from the Christian Reformed, Catholic, Quaker, Episcopalian, Congregational, and Presbyterian denominations.[137] Since then there has been a decline in Mainline (non-Evangelical) Protestants in both the House of Representatives and the Senate, and an increase in Catholic and Jewish members of Congress. Between the 83rd Congress (1953–1955) and the 103rd Congress (1993–1995), the percentage of Mainline Protestants in the U.S. House of Representatives decreased from 68.6 percent to 49.4 percent, while white Evangelicals more than doubled, from 6.9 percent to 15.2 percent. These statistics show that American politicians, who decide on policy both at home and abroad, are more religious than their constituents. This disparity leads to policies that may not reflect the true opinions of Americans by and large.

The interplay between religion and policymaking, of course, depends on a host of factors, including religious denomination, party affiliation, and partisanship. When Congress is evaluated specifically on the matter of support for Israel as based on Senate sponsorship and cosponsorship of bills between 1993 and 2002, ideology, partisanship, and religion appear to matter more than constituency factors, that is, more than the makeup and opinions of a Senate member's actual constituents. One exception is the Jewish population in senators' home states. Notably, the strongest supporters of pro-Israel bills were Jewish, conservative, Republican, or Evangelical. Some have interpreted Republican leadership on matters relating to Israel as an effort to drive American Jews away from the Democratic Party, although this has been relatively unsuccessful. Oldmixon noted that "legislative policy on Israel is largely *elite*-driven; Senators are influenced by their *own* values and personal group affiliations and loyalties, and ... perhaps by party leaders' electoral strategies." She and her coauthors conclude that "the significance of elite religious identification (but not constituent religious identification) suggests that there is more at work than simply elites taking positions for religious communities at the state level. Rather, some aspect of religious identification—whether it is doctrinal beliefs or communal association—shapes how many senators have responded to changing events in the Middle East.[138]

Oldmixon and colleagues examined votes and cosponsorship decisions in the House of Representatives between 1997 and 2002, which revealed schisms based on religion, race, party, and ideology. They found that "when Congress considers innocuous resolutions of support for Israel, support is consensual and nonpartisan." However, as violence escalated between Israelis and Palestinians during the Second Intifada, schisms emerged. Democrats, liberals, and African American members of the House began to identify with the Palestinians, while religious and ideological conservatives, as well as Republicans, doubled down on their support for Israel. Ethnoreligious forces appeared to be a salient reason for support for Israel. "Jewish legislators and legislators with large Jewish constituencies are some of Israel's strongest supporters." Conservative and Republican support for Israel was based on the premise of a state under attack from individuals outside of the Judeo-Christian religious tradition. Oldmixon cautioned, however, against the perception of Evangelical support for Israel as permanent and unconditional, noting that "Evangelicals may support Jews and the state of Israel in the foreign policy arena, but express antipathy for Jews in other areas" and that Evangelical support for Israel is "rooted in interpretation of the Bible rather than in recognition of Israel's importance as a democratic state, or in recognition of Israel's significance to the Jewish people in the light of the Holocaust, or in any other secularly based rationale for supporting Israel."[139]

It isn't just Congress that is predominantly religious. The alliance of Christians and Zionists can be partly explained by the dominance of Christians in the Oval Office. According to the Pew Research Center, nearly every U.S. president has been Protestant Christian.[140] The author of the report notes that Lincoln and Jefferson were the only two presidents without a formal Christian affiliation, although given their ethnic backgrounds, it is highly unlikely that this was not an issue for either president. Long before the creation of Israel in 1948, U.S. presidents expressed support for a Jewish national homeland, often couching their support in religious language. John Adams, in a letter to Mordecai Manuel Noah in 1819, wrote: "for I really wish the Jews again in Judea an independent nation."[141] Woodrow Wilson, reacting to the Balfour Declaration, stated that "the allied nations with the fullest concurrence of our government and people are agreed that in Palestine shall be laid the foundations of a Jewish Commonwealth."[142] Dwight Eisenhower noted that his support for Israel was due to how "the people of Israel, like those of the United States, are imbued with a religious faith and a sense of moral values."[143] Lyndon Johnson observed that his "Christian faith sprang from yours . . . the Bible stories are woven into my childhood memories as the gallant struggle of modern Jews to be free of persecution is also woven into our souls."[144]

While it is undoubtedly important to have the support of the highest U.S. government figures, the real power of Christian Zionism springs from the masses, the millions of individuals who consider themselves part of the Christian Right and who have thrown their political support wholeheartedly behind Israel. Professor Stephen Zunes of the University of San Francisco attributes the vast financial, military and diplomatic support in the United States to the Christian Right's support for Israel, observing that "American aid to Israel goes well beyond protecting Israel's security needs within its internationally recognized borders." Zunes disproves

U.S. policymakers' claims that increasing aid to Israel is purely due to "security interests," writing:

> Were Israel's security interests paramount in the eyes of American policymakers, U.S. aid to Israel would have been highest in the early years of the existence of the Jewish state, when its democratic institutions were strongest and its strategic situation most vulnerable.... Instead, the trend has been in just the opposite direction: major U.S. military and economic aid did not begin until after the 1967 war. Indeed, 99% of U.S. military assistance to Israel since its establishment came only after Israel proved itself to be far stronger than any combination of Arab armies and after Israeli occupation forces became the rulers of a large Palestinian population.[145]

The irony of Christian Zionism is that the support American Evangelicals extend toward Israel comes at the expense of Christian Palestinians, whose lives have been made difficult by Israel. In Bethlehem, Palestinian Christians have difficulty accessing clean water and maintaining basic infrastructure; education and economic opportunities are scarce. Christian Palestinians in Bethlehem must apply for permits and wait at checkpoints to travel between Bethlehem's Church of the Nativity and Jerusalem's Church of the Holy Sepulcher. Munther Isaac, a Palestinian Christian, writes about his life in Palestine in his *The Other Side of the Wall*. He documents the hardships he endures as a Palestinian, hardships that his fellow Christians around the world don't seem to grasp. He tells of a childhood interrupted by demonstrations, curfews, and the closure of schools by the Israeli military, of the identification he must carry at all times that identifies him as a Palestinian and restricts his movement in and around Jerusalem, and of his struggle to understand, as a Christian, how his God could intend for him to live this way. He lives behind a wall constructed by the Israeli government to separate the Palestinians and Israelis and writes that "in the same way in which we are almost invisible on the other side of the wall for the millions of pilgrims who visit the Holy Land every year, we have been invisible when it comes to Western Christian attitudes toward our land."[146]

In an open letter to American Christians, Isaac writes, "Many years from today, when our descendants look back on the long misery of the Palestinians, they will not judge kindly the willful neglect of the global church. We

Palestinian Christians will not let you pretend that you did not know. You will either take a stand to end the oppression of the Palestinian people or continue to be part of the matrix that allows it."[147] Palestinian Christians often feel abandoned by their Western coreligionists. Isaac's wife, Rudaina, "believes that American evangelicals who form a vital base of support for hard-line Israeli policies—and helped propel President Donald Trump to power—have made the local Palestinian Christian community's suffering more acute. 'If we are sisters and brothers in Christ—they should understand,' she says. 'They want Jews to control this land, but Christ came for all the nations.'"[148]

The Evangelical-supported influx of Jewish people into Israel has had the perhaps unintended consequence of creating an atmosphere that is borderline hostile to native Christians. Rev. Ramzi Sidawi, who was born in Jerusalem and is a theology professor and Roman Catholic Church official, is determined to stay and maintain the Christian faith. "Here we have our roots," he said, "we have our faith that started exactly in this place, and our mission is to maintain our roots alive in order to keep the whole tree alive." Sidawi explains that Palestinian Christians are subject to land seizure, detention, and collective punishment by the Israeli government. "Evangelical Christians can make life difficult for Christians living in Israel and the West Bank. 'Sometimes when they make some declarations pro-the-state-of-Israel, it becomes difficult for the Christians among the Palestinians,' adding that such comments make some Muslims assume that 'all Christians are pro-Israel.'"[149]

NBC News reports that the number of Christians in Israel and Jerusalem, the birthplace of Jesus, has declined sharply since the inception of the state of Israel. "In and around Bethlehem, Christians have gone from around 80 percent of the population just after the establishment of the state of Israel in 1950, to around 12 percent today. Jewish settlements have eaten up Arab land—some of it originally owned by Christians—in areas that Palestinians hope to be a future state. In Israel itself, Christians have gone from some 21 percent of the Arab population to around 8 percent today. Overall, they now number just 2 percent of the Israeli population." These departures are supported by some American Christians. Pastor Robert Jeffress has said of Palestinian Christians, "If they do not want to continue to live under that arrangement, perhaps some need to go someplace else." Bethlehem pastor Munther Isaac "has heard this sort of talk before. 'We are secondary to

Christians in America,' he says. 'These Christians do not think about or care about us.'"[150]

This is a core problem with Zionism. It is exclusionary to the Jewish people and oppressive to any who do not fit that demographic. Native Palestinians are forced out of their homes and towns and refused reentry. A Jewish person from another country can request citizenship and room will be made for them; a Palestinian will not be permitted. This segregation belies centuries of religious tolerance in the region, and even today. Palestinians, like Noura Erakat, do not want to deny Jewish people the right to live in the area. As Erakat says:

> Had Jews merely wanted to live in Palestine, this would not have been a problem. In fact, Jews, Muslims and Christians had coexisted for centuries throughout the Middle East. But Zionists sought sovereignty over a land where other people lived. Their ambitions required not only the dispossession and removal of Palestinians in 1948 but also their forced exile, juridical erasure and denial that they ever existed. So, during Israel's establishment, some 750,000 Palestinians were driven from their homes to make way for a Jewish majority state.... This is why Palestinians have been resisting for more than seven decades: They are fighting to remain on their lands with dignity. They have valiantly resisted their colonial erasure.... This resistance is not about returning to the 1947 borders or some notion of the past, but about laying claim to a better future in which Palestinians and their children can live in freedom and equality, rather than being subjugated as second-class citizens or worse.[151]

Zionist impact on Palestinian Americans

The alliance of Christian Zionists and elected public officials creates a difficult situation for Palestinian Americans. The pro-Israel slant of U.S. foreign policy makes it impossible for Palestinian Americans to *not* dissent, and their dissent is used as evidence that they do not belong in American society. Dissenting from the status quo of American foreign policy is characterized by Christian Zionists as unpatriotic, and Palestinian Americans' views on Israel and Palestine are leveraged by the Christian Right as proof that they are un-American and a threat to Western ideals. Foreign policy becomes the litmus test by which Christian Zionists characterize ethnic groups as being "with us or against us." Because they almost always oppose U.S. foreign policy interventions in the Palestinian-Israeli conflict, they are labeled as being "against us."

Yet dissent is not universally unpatriotic. Several scholars have unpacked the associations between dissent and patriotism and concluded that the portrayal of dissent as unpatriotic often serves as justification for military intervention. Historian Howard Zinn observes that the association between patriotism and supporting one's government "ignores the founding principles of the country expressed in the Declaration of Independence. That is: the Declaration of Independence makes it clear that governments are artificial creations set up to achieve certain ends—equality, life, liberty, the pursuit of happiness—and when governments become destructive of those ends it is the right of the people, in the words of the Declaration, to alter or abolish the government."[152] Furthermore, Zinn notes, governments often invoke national security considerations as justification for not allowing dissent on foreign policy matters. By creating an artificial relationship between patriotism and support for policy, it is easy for members of society to police each other on behalf of the state. Zinn is not the only academic to raise objections to the implied relationship between government support and patriotism. Johnathan Hansen, author of *The Lost Promise of Patriotism: Debating American Identity 1920–1980*, views the relationship between patriotism and government support to be an artificial construction. He observes that "America was born in an act of defiance; the American republican experiment can be declared dead once political minorities lose the right to dissent publicly. Social and political progress depends on dissent. Those who would *quash* dissent are inherently reactionary and self-serving—indeed, unpatriotic."[153]

Another mechanism Christian Zionists employ to delegitimize the Palestinian American experience is to associate them with negative, stereotypical Orientalist connotations of the Middle East. Brigitte Gabriel, a Lebanese Christian turned anti-Islam activist, has been especially successful at linking Palestinian American identity to radicalism. She founded ACT! for America in 2007 to "inform, educate, and mobilize Americans regarding the multiple threats of radical Islam." Other notable ACT! figures include Guy Rodgers, a consultant to the John McCain campaign in 2008, and Chris Slick, regional field director for Mitt Romney in 2008. Gabriel has stated that the difference between Arabs/

Muslims and Israelis is "barbarism versus civilization. It's democracy versus dictatorship. It's goodness versus evil."[154] Statements like Gabriel's are problematic for many reasons. The first is that it oversimplifies the Palestinian-Israeli conflict by painting it as a religious/ethnic struggle as opposed to a political struggle. Gabriel implies that the Palestinian-Israeli conflict pits Muslim Arabs against Israeli Jews, when the reality is that Christian and Jewish Arabs in what was formerly Palestine are also affected by Zionist Israeli policies. The core of the Palestinian-Israeli conflict is political: it is a question of whether Zionism is a legitimate justification for Israel's annexation of Palestinian land. By situating the Palestinian plight as an ethnic or religious one, Gabriel implies that Palestinian and Palestinian American grievances against Israel are based on discrimination against Jews.

Gabriel's statement is also problematic in the sense that it racializes Palestinian Americans simply for having a different perspective. Being pro-Palestinian becomes associated with "barbarism" in Christian Zionist terminology, and that opens the floodgates for other negative, Orientalist descriptors. Gabriel's statement echoes the sentiments expressed in Bernard Lewis's controversial and incorrect opinion piece "The Roots of Muslim Rage."[155] Both imply that Palestinian Americans are "other," not like "normal" Americans, and even go so far as to dehumanize them through the rationale that because they are not "like us," their experiences do not matter.

AMERICAN POLITICAL SOLIDARITY WITH ISRAEL

The third factor, the political relationship between Israel and the United States, is multifaceted. American politicians' policy positions are influenced by pro-Israel feelings as well as specific interest groups advocating for Israel as a necessary sovereign state. These special interest groups enhance the image of Israel, distorting events in an effort to create a structure favorable to Israel. This is done by creating connections to the church and Zionism, and through the Israeli government making direct contact with governors and state legislators, mayors and city council members, or members of the House of Representatives and the Senate. In addition, specific lobbying organizations like the American Israel Public Affairs Committee (AIPAC) have influenced policy formulations that shield Israel from accountability in regard to human rights violations and create a foreign policy favorable to Israel. Organizations around the United States have engaged in practices that silence critique of Israel and its occupation and discrimination against Palestinians. Whether well-known and influential national groups like the Anti-Defamation League (ADL), which describes itself as a civil rights group working to curb anti-Semitism in the United States, or smaller regional groups like StandWithUs, Canary Mission, Campus Watch, and AMCHA Initiative, these groups have worked to discredit legitimate critique of Israeli policy and discriminatory practices by conflating critique of Israel with anti-Semitism.

As discussed earlier, American solidarity with Israel extends back almost to the founding of the country. The title of Amy Kaplan's book, *Our American Israel: The Story of an Entangled Alliance*, originates from "a Puritan expression of colonial American exceptionalism." According to Kaplan, in 1799 a Massachusetts minister preached a Thanksgiving sermon about the resemblance between Americans and ancient Israelites. In the sermon, the minister, Abiel Abbot, remarked: "It has been often remarked that the people of the United States come nearer to a parallel with Ancient Israel, than any other nation upon the globe. Hence, 'our American Israel' is a term frequently used; and common consent allows it apt and proper."[156] By linking the newly fledged United States to a biblical mythology, the United States gained a mythologized legitimacy. In turn, the comparison of modern Israel to the United States legitimizes the new state and gives it a shared exceptionality with America.

Since World War II, this analogy between the United States and Israel has been used to muster support for Zionism and the newly established state of Israel. An editorial from the *Congressional Record* in 1956 likened "the courage and stamina of the Israelis to that of the courageous Americans who declared their Independence in 1776." Israel's tenth anniversary was even celebrated at the Independence Hall in Philadelphia, where the Declaration of Independence had been signed.[157] In 1967 Hearst Metrotone News released a newsreel that called David Ben-Gurion "the George Washington of Israel."[158] Thus the parallels between the United States and Israel, first articulated through a mythologized biblical narrative, were later built on as shared struggles against colonial powers, glossing over the fact that the founding of both nations was achieved through the ethnic cleansing and genocide of its native inhabitants. Out of this view of Israel's creation as a struggle for independence arose a "liberal consensus... around a narrative of two peoples fighting over one land, and a belief that only mutual recognition could resolve the conflict between them."[159] This narrative failed to acknowledge the colonizer/colonized nature of the relationship between Israeli Jews and the Palestinians who were displaced or placed under occupation, and it attempted to "both sides" the conflict.

American presidential candidates have contributed to the idea of "our American Israel" by relating images of Israel to ideas of American exceptionalism. According to Kaplan, Barack Obama emphasized Israel's multiethnic origins, which "reflected America's noble commitment to social amelioration and renewal." For Trump, Israel's dedication to security was an ideal to which to aspire.[160] This simplified characterization of Israel as a beacon of hope and stability in an otherwise volatile region has been leveraged to emphasize American exceptionalism and to articulate an idealized version of America's future, the result of which is to further tie these two nations together in a special relationship.

It is no secret that the United States considers Israel to be a strategic ally in the Middle East. In 1962, after signing the first arms agreement with Israel, President Kennedy reiterated that the United States had a "special relationship with Israel in the Middle East, comparable only to that which it has with Britain over a wide range of world affairs."[161] The United States has provided more support politically and financially to Israel than to any other nation. In 2016 the United States and Israel signed an agreement granting Israel $38 billion in military aid over the following ten years. It was the largest aid package in U.S. history.

Occasionally, the United States will call out Israel for its harm of Palestinians, but censure tends to be extremely mild and short lived. In 2001 the Bush administration pressed Israel to cease building settlements in the Occupied Territories and called for the creation of a Palestinian state. These developments immediately raised alarm within the circle of Israeli leaders, who feared "that Washington might 'sell out' the Jewish state to win favor with the Arabs." In late March 2002 a Palestinian suicide bomber killed thirty Israelis during Passover; the Israelis responded by launching Operation Defense Shield and reoccupying the West Bank. The Bush administration, fearing that this action would worsen American relations with the Arab world, demanded that Prime Minister Ariel Sharon's government stop the incursions into the West Bank "without delay." Condoleezza Rice is quoted as having told reporters "'without delay' means without delay. It means now." Just one week later the Bush administration backed down, with Bush reportedly telling his press secretary Ari Fleischer "that [Ariel] Sharon was 'a man of peace.'"[162]

What happened? Immediately after Bush demanded that Sharon withdraw the Israel Defense Force from the West Bank, pro-Israel lobbyists descended on the administration. Pro-Israel supporters in Vice President Cheney's office and the Pentagon pushed Bush and Rice to abandon attempts to restrain Israel. Neoconservative pundits criticized Powell's efforts to negotiate a cease-fire as hurting U.S. "moral clarity." Christian Evangelical and Jewish groups lobbied Bush's office, demanding that he stop putting pressure on Sharon to withdraw from the West Bank. Reverend Jerry Falwell inspired so many of his followers to email and call the Executive Office on behalf of the Israeli cause that the next day, "senior presidential aides phoned Falwell to reassure him that Bush stood behind Sharon."[163]

The high level of support Israel enjoys in the American government is based on key similarities between the United States and Israel, as many politicians and the pro-Israel lobbyists who fund them are quick to point out. One of these key similarities is the fact that both nations are governed under a democratic system. However, there are fundamental differences between American and Israeli democracy that illustrate the precarious nature of the latter. Mearsheimer and Walt observe that while "the United States is a liberal democracy where people of any race, religion, or ethnicity are supposed to enjoy equal rights," Israel "was explicitly founded as a Jewish State, and whether a citizen is regarded as Jewish ordinarily depends on kinship (verifiable Jewish ancestry)." Israel does not treat its Jewish and non-Jewish citizens equally, and this is reflected in the Basic Law on Human Dignity and Liberty, which is the Israeli equivalent of the U.S. Bill of Rights. The initial draft of the Basic Law "contained language that promised equality for all Israelis.... Ultimately, however, a Knesset committee removed the clause from the final version that became law in 1992."[164]

The "special relationship" with Israel means that the United States often turns a blind eye when Israel breaks international law or engages in human rights violations. For instance, the United States has failed to enforce article 49 of the Geneva Convention, the international statute that states that "the Occupying power shall not deport or transfer parts of its own civilian population into the territory it occupies." This statute should prevent Israelis from occupying illegally taken land, yet between 1967 and 2009, Israel established 121 settlements in the West Bank.[165] U.S. military assistance to Israel contributes to this illegal settlement building. Israel receives its entire aid package at the beginning of the year, in contrast to other aid packages that are paid out quarterly, and is allowed to spend a quarter of this military aid to subsidize its own military industry. Furthermore, Israel does not have to account for how its aid is spent, which, as John Mearsheimer and Stephen Walt point out, "makes it virtually impossible to prevent the money from being used for purposes the United States opposes, like building settlements in the West Bank."[166]

At the onset of the War in Gaza, politicians in the United States were quick to voice support for Israel. Senate Majority Leader Chuck Schumer said, "October 7, 2023, will go down as a day of infamy and . . . as long as there is a United States of America, the people of Israel will never stand alone."[167] An October Senate resolution affirming "support for Israel, its right to self-defense, and condemning Hamas's attacks on civilians" passed 97–0. This bipartisan support transcended party and ideology. Senator John Fetterman, a Democrat from Pennsylvania, faced backlash on social media after posting his support, saying, "If not for the horrific attacks by Hamas terrorists, thousands of innocent Israelis and Palestinians would still be alive today. Now is not the time to talk about a ceasefire." Fetterman's remarks illustrate the concept of being progressive except for Palestine. He has faced pressure from supporters and former staffers to call for a ceasefire, but so far he has refused. "Cecily Harwitt, an organizing consultant who attended a protest at Fetterman's Philadelphia office, said activists have taken aim at him 'because his entire brand and persona is standing up for oppressed people.'" Fetterman's chief of staff says that those who are surprised at his unyielding support for Israel "weren't really paying attention when he staked out his strong support of Israel during the campaign."[168]

The U.S. alliance with Israel, which is often touted as a necessary alliance to defeat terrorism in the region, paradoxically fuels terrorism. Mearsheimer and Walt observe that while "U.S. support for Israel is hardly the only source of anti-American terrorism," it is a significant factor, as "there is no question, for example, that many al-Qaeda leaders, including Osama bin Laden, are motivated in part by Israel's presence in Jerusalem and the plight of the Palestinians. According to the U.S. 9/11 Commission,

Bin Laden explicitly sought to punish the United States for its policies in the Middle East, including its support for Israel."[169] Even Israeli leaders understood that the creation of Israel violated the human rights of Palestinians. David Ben-Gurion, first prime minister of Israel, is said to have told Nahum Goldmann, president of the World Jewish Congress, "If I was an Arab leader, I would never make terms with Israel. That is natural: we have taken their country. Sure, God promised it to us, but what does that matter to them? Our God is not theirs. We come from Israel, it's true, but two thousand years ago, and what is that to them? There has been antisemitism, the Nazis, Hitler, Auschwitz, but was that their fault? They only see one thing: we have come here and stolen their country. Why should they accept that?"[170] Despite such frank statements from Israeli leaders, the United States repeatedly ignores human rights abuses when it comes to Israel, selectively taking the moral high road when it is in U.S. interests. And since the pro-Israel lobby makes up the backbone of U.S. politics, it is almost never in the interests of the United States to enforce human rights principles in the Israeli-Palestinian conflict.

The U.S.-Israel alliance places Palestinian Americans in a difficult situation domestically. Immigrant groups and their descendants are often considered to be biased because of their cultural connections to their homelands, and criticism of U.S. foreign policy, as has been noted, is considered unpatriotic. Kathleen Christison, author of *The Wound of Dispossession: Telling the Story of Palestine*, notes: "America often demands more of its immigrants than it does of its native-born citizens. Unlike native-born Americans, immigrants must eschew criticism of any aspect of the American system, or risk being thought ungrateful, and they must submerge interest in foreign causes or risk being regarded as of questionable loyalty."[171] The threat of having one's loyalty questioned because of political stances on foreign policy is not limited to immigrants. Their descendants, native-born citizens, face inquiries into their loyalty simply for being "ethnic." As Hasan Minhaj, the *Daily Show* correspondent, jokes in his comedy special *Homecoming King*, "brown and beige people are constantly having to 'audition' to prove their loyalty to America."[172]

For Palestinian Americans, separating the personal from the political is nearly impossible.[173] Just as many Jewish Americans view support for Israel as part of their personal politics, advocating for Palestinian rights and self-determination are core aspects of Palestinian American identity.

Christison observes that "for the very reason that there is no sovereign Palestinian state, Palestinian Americans tend to be acutely conscious of the Palestinian problem in all its aspects, and it is virtually impossible to be a Palestinian in America without also being political about it." She cites the example of Hisham D., a Los Angeles liquor store owner. While he is too "cautious about his security to take active part in Arab-American politics, he can cite the dates, circumstances, and outcomes of every Arab-Israeli war and every Palestinian massacre over the last forty years."[174]

Palestinian Americans who run for elected office face scrutiny due to their Palestinian identity. Opponents will point to that identity as a reason the individual is not worthy of the office. For example, in California's 50th Congressional District, a young Palestinian Latino American Democrat by the name of Ammar Campa-Najjar ran against the Republican incumbent Duncan Hunter in the 2020 congressional election. Campa-Najjar was vocal about his Palestinian and Latino American heritage; for a few years, he and his family lived in Gaza. Even though he considers himself to be Christian (his father is Muslim; his mother, Protestant), he has had to defend himself against accusations of being anti-Israel, given his family's background on his father's side.

Campa-Najjar's paternal grandfather, Muhammad Yusuf al-Najjar, was involved in the Palestinian political organization Fatah.[175] Although Campa-Najjar had never met his grandfather, his family history was used as an argument against his candidacy. Two rabbis came to Campa-Najjar's defense, citing conversations they had with him in which he discussed the importance of honoring both Israel's security and Palestinian human rights.[176] The Palestinian-Israeli conflict became an issue in Campa-Najjar's campaign because outside parties decided that his half-Palestinian background was an issue, and that as such he could not possibly have an unbiased opinion on Israel and Palestine. His campaign, incidentally, was focused on domestic issues, and a stance on the Palestinian-Israeli conflict was not part of his platform. He ultimately lost his bid for Congress, at least in part due to this issue. This form of racialization is a common experience amongst many immigrant groups, but it is an especially poignant one for Palestinian Americans, whose "Palestinianness" is constantly called into question even when an unrelated issue is being discussed.

Americans tend to think poorly of Arabs in general and Palestinians in particular. They are viewed, due to media portrayals, as dark, violent, and untrustworthy, as described earlier. Their culture is seen as strange; their customs, as barbaric. Their language is never one of the choices heard over the airport loudspeaker: Spanish, French, Chinese, but never Arabic. Federal policy never favors them, and multiple wars have been fought against them. Religious leaders see them as, at best, potential converts in need of missionary influence, or, at worst, the enemy. In an "America first" culture, anything non-Western, noncapitalist, and non-Christian is seen as unwanted. This view is deeply entrenched in American values and culture.

But perhaps the tide is turning. While historically the American government and public have strongly supported Israel and had difficulty finding empathy for Palestinians, there may be hope for the future. A shift in discourse on Israel/Palestine as a result of social movements in the United States, as well as increased knowledge of the cruelty of Israel's treatment of Palestinians, is becoming apparent in American culture, especially after the Israeli war on Gaza, with tens of thousands of Palestinian civilians killed. Sara Leah Whitson, the former director of Human Rights Watch's Middle East and North Africa Division, wrote in a tweet on May 18, 2021, in the wake of an Israeli attack on Gaza, that "the conversation has shifted far, far away from the regurgitated, stale defenses of 'Israel's right to exist,' 'terrorists,' and 'anti-Semitism' to a new recognition of Palestinian rights. Protesters are bringing words to the fore like 'apartheid,' 'land theft,' and 'ethnic cleansing.'" Whitson notes that American think tanks and analysts have also shifted away from the idea of a two-state solution and are now recommending a focus on equal rights and freedom for Palestinians and Israelis in a one-state reality.[177] Shibley Telhami concurs, noting that there is "a significant increase in support of the one state solution."[178] This shift, says Whitson, is inextricably tied to the movement for racial justice occurring in the United States, spearheaded by the Black Lives Matter movement: "The bottom line is it's just really hard, in an American society so focused on racial justice, to justify support for an ethno-national state that privileges one racial group over another in a diverse, mixed-race and -religion society. It's become impossible to keep mouthing that human rights are for all humans—except Palestinians."[179]

Matt Duss sees the tide shifting:

> I will say there's a lot of reasons for [the increase in support for Palestine]. I think new tools of activism are important. Democratizing media. I don't

want to overstate the impact of say Twitter, or Facebook, or video, or the internet, but that's important. There aren't just a few major newspapers deciding what gets covered and who gets quoted. Palestinians, to use the familiar term, have given themselves permission to narrate; they are featuring a way to build [their] own voices and get their voices out there.[180]

This ability to tell both sides of the story has lifted some of the fog from the eyes of Americans, helping them see the Palestinian people in a clearer light. Duss continues, "I mean you understand, yes, there are things about this that are complicated, but there are things about it that are fairly simple on the domination of one people by another. A military occupation where some people have complete freedom of movement and freedom generally and others face a set of daily onerous and humiliating restrictions on their most basic needs."

It is worth mentioning that since the Hamas attack on October 7, 2023, and the subsequent war against Gaza, political support for Israel has become less popular among the American public. Journalist Asma Khalid noted that "some Democrats on the left want Biden to show more sympathy for Palestinians. . . . [F]or much of Biden's career, criticism of Israel was political suicide. But the generational politics on this issue are changing."[181]

"You know the saying," Duss says. "It's apocryphal but it's attributed to Gandhi, 'First they ignore you, then they laugh at you, then they fight you, then you win.' We're very much in the 'then they fight you' phase of it."[182] As the tide shifts, the backlash signals a challenge that is feared by the status quo. The Palestinians and their stories are gaining traction and increasingly being heard and understood within American society. Israeli human rights violations committed against Palestinians, and traditional ways through which Palestine and Israel have long been portrayed, are being confronted at multiple levels. How Palestine is discussed and talked about in the American sociopolitical landscape is changing, and a turning point is on the horizon.

Chapter Two

STRUCTURAL TRANSFORMATIONS IN CULTURE, SOCIETY, AND POLITICS IN THE UNITED STATES

The past two decades in the United States have seen an increasing trend of structural transformation in culture, society, and politics that has deeply affected the way Americans perceive the ongoing question of Palestine. These foundational shifts have led to an increase in receptivity to the Palestinian cause, but this positive change has in turn resulted in stronger resistance and further anti-Palestinian action. The rise of internet use over the past thirty years and the decline of traditional media with its truncated representation of the issue mean that everyday Americans have access to Palestinian voices and a better understanding of the complex issues surrounding Israel and Palestine. The broad landscape of religious belief in America has been undergoing a seismic shift since the mid-twentieth century, and regular church attendance has become less of a cultural matter. Church membership, no longer the key to societal and political power, is falling out of fashion, and the Evangelical movement, the mass exodus of members from the most conservative and pro-Israel branches of Christianity, means that fewer and fewer Americans are taking their cues from Sunday pulpits. Many Jewish American and Israeli voices are speaking out for the rights of Palestinians as the desire for Jewish self-determination has given way to a more universalist belief in self-determination for all. Further, Israelis and Jewish people around the world are recognizing credible accusations of human rights violations perpetrated by Israel, and many are showing tremendous courage in standing up against them.

BLACK LIVES MATTER AND THE CHANGING LANDSCAPE OF FREEDOM FIGHTING

The current state of the Palestinian cause in America would not be what it is without the influence on American politics and culture of the Black Lives Matter (BLM) movement. The rise of BLM has fundamentally changed the way Americans understand race and prejudice, not just in regard to the African American population, but in the way all people relate to one another. As Frank Leon Roberts notes, "Black Lives Matter has always been more of a human rights movement rather than a civil rights movement. BLM's focus has been less about changing specific laws and more about fighting for a fundamental reordering of society wherein Black lives are free from systematic dehumanization."[1] This push for broad, nondiscriminatory human rights has changed the fabric of American race relations and the way people view acts of oppression. "The conversation around race didn't exist in a vast capacity until we saw the BLM movement, this surge," says T. Sheri Amore Dickerson, executive director and core organizer of BLM Oklahoma City. "Now difficult conversations, honest conversations, and even some discourse, have become part of the daily discussion here in Oklahoma, and I think that goes nationwide in many different factions. It's also become more intergenerational."[2]

Cultural impacts of BLM

This change in the perception of race and human rights has been profound. A YouGov poll released in April 2015 showed that "over a period of about four months, the percentage of white Americans likely to characterize the death of a Black man at the hands of the police as an 'isolated incident' plunged by 20 percentage points."[3] Americans, including privileged white Americans, are beginning to see racial violence as a systemic problem, and that change is coming at a rapid rate. Journalist Zeeshan Aleem, writing for the online magazine *Mic*, explains that

The speed with which white perception of police homicides changed seems unlikely to be attributable to an uptick in deaths, which have been a constant feature of black life for years. It's much more likely to be the product of the sustained debate about systemic racism in policing and criminal justice that was forced into the national consciousness by the raucous Black Lives Matter movement, which garnered enormous media attention during those months. The sum effect [of] all this is that Americans are now reporting that they're more concerned about racism than they have been in more than 20 years. The last time it ranked so high in the polls was in 1992, when the beating of Rodney King by police officers sparked a national debate over the state of American race relations.[4]

It isn't just race relations that are being affected by this cultural shift. Rights for underrepresented groups and communities have become part of a conversation feeding into a larger narrative that advocates all forms of rights that have long been neglected. All human rights are worth fighting for. Roberts says, "As we reflect on five years of BLM, we would do well to consider the myriad ways that #blacklivesmatter has influenced our contemporary moment and given us a framework for imagining what democracy in action really looks like. Whether it be transforming how we talk about police violence or transforming how we talk about 'abolitionism,' the BLM movement has succeeded in transforming how Americans talk about, think about, and organize for freedom."[5] That influence extends to the issue of Palestinian oppression and human rights violations at the hands of Israel's government. No longer is the American public willing to turn a blind eye, or to assume that any force used against Palestinians must be justified. Instead, many are beginning to ask questions and even criticize incidents that violate the freedoms Americans hold dear. Noura Erakat and Marc Lamont Hill cite the concurrent attacks on Gaza and occupation of Ferguson, Missouri, in 2014 as a point of renewal of the solidarity between Black Americans and Palestinians.[6]

A salient point of solidarity between the two movements is the way they are treated by police. This is not a coincidence: the police exchange program between the United States and Israel is a concerted effort to share tactics in policing to suppress dissent. Deadly Exchange, a group that fights against police exchanges, explains it this way:

STRUCTURAL TRANSFORMATIONS IN U.S. CULTURE

Both the U.S. and Israeli governments perpetuate the deadly falsehood that violence against some communities will create security for others. The exchanges programs bring together police, ICE, border patrol, and FBI from the U.S. with soldiers, police, border agents, etc. from Israel. In these programs, "worst practices" are shared to promote and extend discriminatory and repressive policing practices that already exist in both countries, including racial profiling, massive spying and surveillance, deportation and detention, and attacks on human rights defenders.[7]

This union of police forces has created a common experience for Black Americans and Palestinians. Both groups were under the oppressive, military-style control of governments that did not respect them or their rights, and the global nature of the modern world gave them a way to communicate that solidarity.

Social justice in the digital space

Beyond the shifting of attitudes, the BLM movement changed the way inequality is reported on and made accessible to the public. Much like the open casket of Emmett Till in 1955 energized a generation, the use of cell phone videos and social media is animating today's human rights movement. A new generation of activists, armed with personal recording devices and the means to disseminate them, are capturing events from the point of view of the oppressed. The aforementioned democratization of media was the foundation on which this citizen journalism was built, and it was also driven by home videos that receive massive engagement online. Adeshina Emmanuel describes how, with the gatekeepers of media out of the way, stories are being told from multiple points of view:

> A new coverage dynamic is emerging. Outlets are crowdsourcing video investigations of police use of force, centering accounts from demonstrators and police violence victims rather than police accounts and concerns about property damage. Newsrooms are taking an interdisciplinary approach to reporting, scrutinizing, for example, the relationship between tech corporations and police monitoring activists' social media feeds. And reporters are telling more in-depth stories about victims of police violence, without

fixating on the killing or digging into the victim's past to highlight criminality.[8]

In tandem with the success of BLM in the digital space, young Palestinians are taking to the internet with their own videos. Khaled Abu Aker, director of Amin, one of Palestine's first news websites, told *Al-Monitor* that for the first time, Palestinians no longer need traditional media. He said, "During the first and second intifada, we used to get calls asking the media to come and cover events. Today, the youth are doing the broadcasting themselves."[9] This shift means the narrative is no longer controlled by the powerful but is in the hands of the oppressed. "During the aerial bombardments of 2008–9 and 2012," this was not the case, Rebecca Stein reports, as "most Palestinians in Gaza lacked widespread access to mobile digital technologies and reliable internet connectivity, a condition rooted in extreme economic deprivation and Israeli restrictions on electricity and broadband. Coupled with the Israeli state-imposed blockade on the entry of journalists into the Gaza Strip, and a growing military presence on social media, Israel had effectively maintained control of the wartime visual message." In recent years, however "smartphone witnessing had become a regularized part of Palestinian political practice across the occupied territories."[10]

The spread of these homegrown videos influenced network news sources as well. Sheikh Jarrah Jerusalem resident and activist Mohammed el-Kurd recounted the response of news outlets to the May 2021 Gaza offensive: "Newspapers ran articles about Israeli war crimes . . . and plastered photos of murdered Palestinian children on their front pages. TV channels showed the Israeli military dropping bombs that reduced residential and media towers to rubble. Social media networks exploded with images of Palestinians—dead and alive—pulled from under the wreck. And, to a certain degree, Palestinian voices steered the global conversation."[11]

In response, "Israeli television commentators and military analysts warned live audiences about the torrent of 'bad images' coming out of Gaza, shot on the smartphones of Gazans under fire."[12] A public relations campaign designed to delegitimize photos and videos that showed the Israel Defense Forces (IDF) in a bad light was largely unsuccessful, and government officials admitted that they could not do much to minimize the effect of footage of civilians being mistreated. While they may be losing ground journalistically, the IDF is taking advantage of increasingly sophisticated technology

STRUCTURAL TRANSFORMATIONS IN U.S. CULTURE

by ramping up surveillance of Palestinians inside and outside the borders of Palestine/Israel. A *Washington Post* investigation "demonstrated that Israel has been systematically increasing surveillance on Palestinians in the West Bank by building a database that integrates facial recognition." The government is also encouraging citizen's media participation of its own. Avner Gvaryahu, executive director of Breaking the Silence, "was surprised at how widespread and accessible these technologies were to everyday soldiers and even Israeli citizens. In fact, the Israeli government and certain universities provided extra credit to students to monitor Palestinian social media, while also encouraging Israeli citizens to take pictures of Palestinian adults, children and the elderly."[13]

THE ROLE OF SOCIAL MEDIA IN MASS MOBILIZATION

The protest formula and mobilization has transformed and intensified over the years. The Arab Revolts that were sparked in 2010 in Tunisia and then in Egypt showed that social media has played a pivotal supportive role for protest and mobilization. In recent years, the critical U.S.-based mass mobilization around the BLM movement further revolutionized the use of social media as a mass mobilization tool. Frank Roberts says that

> BLM will forever be remembered as the movement responsible for popularizing what has now become an indispensable tool in 21st-century organizing efforts: the phenomenon that scholars refer to as "mediated mobilization." By using the tools of social media, BLM was the first U.S. social movement in history to successfully use the internet as a mass mobilization device. The recent successes of movements, such as #MeToo, #NeverAgain, and #TimesUp, would be inconceivable had it not been for the groundwork that #BlackLivesMatter laid.[14]

Palestinians are also taking up the tools of social media to spread their message, and the reception of those posts is far more open due to the successful BLM use of social media. TikTok, with over seven hundred million active monthly users, is a favorite platform for Palestinian activists, and its use has been referred to as the "TikTok Intifada."[15] A post showing Palestinian citizens fleeing an Israeli air assault garnered forty-four million views, and a post by Sabrina Abukhdeir "shows crying Palestinian kids and the destruction of a high-rise block enclave. 'You guys know what to do,' she wrote, urging people to share the clip."[16]

BLM altered the American understanding of racial justice, human rights, and the fight for freedom, revolutionized the use of social media for organizing, and pioneered citizen journalism in telling the stories to the point that traditional newsrooms took notice and made changes to the way they reported. The inroads BLM carved into the minds and hearts of Americans laid the groundwork for other groups to follow, including those fighting for freedom in Palestine. The work of BLM made possible much of the progress that has been seen in the fight for a new conception of the question of Palestine.

Decline of traditional media and emergence of new forms of news dissemination

This new way of using media was necessitated by the historical way information has been monopolized by a handful of channels (first radio and print, then TV), which limited both the amount of content and commentary on such content. Traditional media acted as a gatekeeper, editing the narrative before disseminating it to the people. During the creation of Israel in 1948 and the subsequent forced removal of hundreds of thousands of Palestinians from over four hundred villages in the decades that followed, news was primarily attained through newspapers. While these papers were offering a truncated version of events, they were at least relatively diverse, with local and state papers running their own stories. It is certainly true that Palestinians, along with other marginalized groups, had no voice in these white-dominated organizations, but the bottleneck of information was about to grow even narrower.

The decline of traditional media was inevitable. Thomas E. Patterson reported in 2007 that "by the 1980's, the boomer boost had run its course and a new threat to newspapers had emerged: 24-hour cable news. Newspaper circulation edged slowly downward, falling by 10 percent overall in the 1980's and 1990's. In the past few years the drop has accelerated, fueled in part by the growing audience for Internet-based news."[17] Journalistic standards dropped in concert with newspaper circulation, as cable TV and internet-based news sources relied on advertisers as a revenue source. These marketing dollars don't follow accurate reporting, they follow views and clicks, which are generated by crises and breaking stories. In-depth reporting and nuanced representations thus were increasingly replaced by opinion segments designed to stir up emotions in viewers. In 2005 a "617-page study by the Project for Excellence in Journalism confirm[ed] what many people have been saying for a long time: FOX News journalists . . . are better at voicing personal opinion than they are at reporting the facts. According to the study, 73 percent of FOX's coverage on the conflict in Iraq was based on the opinions of the cable news channel's anchors or journalists."[18]

As newspaper circulation fell and cable news viewership rose, single-perspective, visceral reporting became the new normal. This change was instrumental in the polarization of American culture, as pro-Israel perspectives in line with governmental policy and typical cultural opinion found backing and promotion on conservative news channels. This polarization, however, also brought about an increase in support for the Palestinian cause. As news reporting became more siloed, those with different views, or who questioned the national narrative, sought out other sources of information. They found those sources by accessing the other great innovation of the late twentieth century: the internet and the democratized media that flowed from it. More news was suddenly available, good and bad, accurate and inaccurate; more space was accessible for people to write about the issue than they had in the past. People had always written about Palestine, but the work being put out was subject to scrutiny. The internet democratized the news.

Media democratization and new participation spaces

Nico Carpentier and colleagues identify two main waves of media democratization. The first, post–World War II, centered on the creation of alternative, independent, participatory media outlets. These new outlets challenged the monopolization of information previously enjoyed by the large media networks and gave access to new and underrepresented voices. Media democratization continued at an unprecedented pace via the internet, which was a boon for direct democracy.[19] While such democratization certainly raises the potential for misinformation and disinformation and may direct consumers to highly partisan news that confirm their biases, media proliferation does have some positive impacts on democracy. Jimmy Chan and Daniel Stone demonstrate that even for voters who prefer highly partisan news sources, media proliferation creates conditions whereby these voters are more likely to obtain informative news.[20] In the context of Palestine, alternative media sources such as Electronic Intifada, Mondoweiss and +972 allow consumers across the world to understand the on-the-ground realities facing Palestinians. The global reach of the internet, coupled with the rise of 24/7 cable news networks, allowed Americans to see Israel's brutal treatment of Palestinians in occupation and Israel's assault on Lebanon in 2006.[21]

Younger generations, in particular, are likely to access news through these nontraditional channels. Per PBS NewsHour and Common Sense Media, "78 percent of teens ages 13 to 17 say it's important for them to follow current events. About 70 percent of those polled also believe news reported by news organizations 'generally gets the facts straight.' However, teens are more likely to get their news from social media and YouTube than traditional news outlets. . . . 54 percent of teens get news from social media, 50 percent get news from YouTube and fewer than half—41 percent—get news from news organizations, at least a few times a week."[22] While disinformation is rampant on these channels, they are also accessible to those who don't have access to traditional media. Palestinians have turned to outlets such as TikTok to spread their stories and were particularly successful after the May 2021 bombings in Gaza and the assault on Sheikh Jarrah. Izz ad-Din al-Akhras, a social media researcher for the Quds News Network, reported that

> "the events of Sheikh Jarrah marked users' first effective use of TikTok to support the Palestinian cause," adding that "Palestinians were able to attract support from international figures such as Greta Thunberg, Naomi Klein, Bella Hadid and Roger Waters, who have publicly expressed their support for the Palestinian cause. Akhras pointed out that the Palestinians used TikTok to report the news as it happened, with Palestinians inside the cities of Ramla and Lod covering the clashes between the Palestinians and the Israeli army. . . ."Palestine has definitely won the war on TikTok because [Palestinians] support a just cause and present direct content, leading to millions expressing solidarity with it," Akhras noted.[23]

Social media sites and the universality of cell phones with high-quality cameras have made photographs and video evidence of atrocities readily available and easily dispersed. Consider this example, as relayed by Saree Makdisi: "You may spend a minute watching that video—widely circulated in May 2021—of Jewish vigilantes trying to break into a Palestinian family home, the father and son desperately trying to barricade the front door while the younger children scream in terror from the kitchen. The result is the same: the hideous spectacle of a once apparently formidable state project unraveling into the elementary racial violence out of which it was born."[24] This kind of evidence was not possible for the first six decades of the Palestinian occupation, and its arrival and accessibility have changed the way these incidents are reported and perceived.

The expansion of the internet has also allowed Palestinians to declare their own narrative through online news sources. *Electronic Intifada* is "an independent online news publication and educational resource focusing on Palestine, its people, politics, culture and place in the world."[25] It was founded in 2001 and receives all financial support from donations from individuals and foundations. *Electronic Intifada* has received accolades for its reporting. During the 2006 war on Lebanon, the mainstream Dutch newspaper *NRC Handelsblad* recommended the publication to its readers, noting that "*Electronic Intifada (EI)*, a news site in English, reports from a Palestinian perspective, but as impartial as possible. *EI* is often faster than the established media."[26] The *Palestine Chronicle* is an online news source founded in September 1999, with a mission to "educate the general public by providing a forum that strives to highlight issues of relevance to human rights, national struggles, freedom and democracy in the form of daily news, commentary, features, book reviews, photos, art, and more." The site enjoys a "high" rating for factual reporting by MediaBias/FactCheck and is available in both English and French. According to the website, it has "grown in its importance and scope of coverage mostly because of the support it received from socially conscious and progressive scholars, writers, activists, readers and communities around the world."[27]

CULTURAL SHIFTS IN AMERICAN SOCIETY AND POLITICS

Since the country's inception, the American people have had a strange and complicated relationship with the idea of "justice for all." Despite the primacy of those words in the country's founding documents, justice has rarely been truly for every American, let alone every person living in the United

States. Marginalized communities and groups, particularly indigenous peoples, people of color, and women have protested their unjust treatment since the country was founded and have been opposed by white, male elites. Their struggles and victories have helped reshape the American idea of justice, stretching it to include marginalized people in a clash of moral and political values. This conflict intensified during the Civil Rights movement, and the definition of justice has continued to expand to include every group that is unjustly treated. The recent Black Lives Matter movement and the rioting and protesting surrounding police violence in the last ten years have pushed the issue to the forefront of American thought.

I argue that some of the motivations of these social justice movements are in response to the militarization of police in America and the increase in surveillance under which the average citizen lives. These policies were in turn a response to the World Trade Organization (WTO) protests in Seattle in 1999 and the attacks of September 11, 2001. Taken together, these events mark a considerable shift in attitudes toward the American government and global power differentials, particularly in the United States. This same process also has ramifications on Israeli society. This shift has caused a surge in support and advocacy for the Palestinian cause and a willingness to consider critically the way Israel and the United States wield their power. In turn, the Democratic Party has experienced incremental shifts toward the left, increasingly embracing ideas of equity and action on the part of the oppressed that were much less popular a few decades ago.

Americans are waking up to the fact that their tax dollars finance the displacement of Palestinians and continued oppression of defenseless populations. They are becoming more aware of the oppression perpetrated by their government over the course of its history and are less inclined to believe the whitewashed version of history they have been fed. They are becoming emboldened to speak out against injustice and take action to support marginalized groups of all kinds, including Palestinians. Jewish Americans and Israelis, as well, are becoming aware of the offenses perpetrated by the Israeli government in an attempt to solidify Israeli power in the region, and some are taking action against it. Yet for every step forward, there is a reciprocal pushback by pro-Israel advocates to further the Israeli cause. This section examines the structural transformations that have led to an intensification of the fight between Israel and Palestine, not on the ground with guns and tanks, but in the minds, politics, and values of U.S. citizens.

There have been a series of critical sociopolitical and cultural shifts in the United States. American culture, society, and politics have undergone significant changes over the past three decades. From acceptance and legalization of same-sex marriage, to the legalization of marijuana, to an increased attention to and visibility of the plight of underrepresented groups and minorities, the social and political landscape and terrain have changed. There have been shifts in political parties as well, as both dominant political parties have moved along the political spectrum farther from center. Today's cultural landscape is simultaneously more open and sympathetic to the plight of underserved and underrepresented groups and communities, and deeply entrenched in traditionally conservative values. These paradigm shifts have led to action on both sides of the debate.

Increased militarization and surveillance and their effects

As in all societies, there is a constant discontent between American society and the state. The police, as an institution of state power, are at the center of this clash. While confrontations between police and protestors were common during the Civil Rights movement, they had become much less prevalent as a permanent fixture and a defining characteristic of American society during the 1980s and 1990s. Events like the Rodney King riots were powerful in their transformation of society, but they were rare. Toward the end of the century, this started to change. On November 30, 1999, thousands of protestors blocked the entrances to the Seattle Convention Center, where the World Trade Organization (WTO) was scheduled to meet. With concerns ranging from labor rights to the environment and other social justice issues, activists were determined to make a stand against the slogan of "Free Trade" by advocating for "Fair Trade," and to have their voices heard by the representatives of the 135 member nations convening in Seattle. The protests were met with an intense police response: tear gas and rubber bullets were used to make the crowds disperse, and "the mayor declared a downtown curfew and no-protest zone—restrictions not seen in Seattle since World War II." The protest was a turning point for U.S. activists, as "some still credit the protest with restoring a sense that mass demonstrations and civil disobedience can effect change."[28]

The WTO event was also a turning point for police, whose response to protests and activism steadily increased in militarization and force. Two years later, the attacks of September 11, 2001, in New York instantly changed the temperature in America in regard to combating terror. The intensity of emotion from the American public, unaccustomed to attacks like the one on the World Trade Center, and the threat of further violence led to swift action by the president and Congress. Along with a focus on finding and punishing terrorists from overseas, the federal government began an intense push to find and punish domestic terrorists. This initiative included the passage of the Patriot Act, which allowed for enhanced law enforcement investigatory tools. These tools were frequently used against Arab and Muslim American citizens, revealing and fanning the flames of Orientalism and racism at home while military action against Arab and Muslim countries abroad reinforced that narrative. Initially, many Americans felt safer after handing over additional power to law enforcement agencies. They believed that the terrorists would be caught and their lives would regain the normalcy and safety of the pre-9/11 world.

This attitude shifted over time. The Patriot Act appeared more and more oppressive and invasive, militarized police departments spent huge sums on tactical gear that was used, not on domestic terrorists, but on American citizens, and the "Arab threat" failed to materialize. The 1033 program, which allowed police departments to 'borrow' unused military equipment, had been in place since the 1990s, but participation increased steeply after 9/11. Before the attacks, $27 million in military equipment had been transferred to law enforcement agencies. Numbers are difficult to come by, but since the attacks somewhere between $1.6 and $7.4 billion worth of equipment have changed hands. This equipment includes weapons, tactical gear, and armored vehicles. The effects of this increase are visible "on city streets during protests in the form of MRAPs, or mine-resistant ambush protected armored vehicles."[29] "Police militarization also involves agencies changing themselves to follow the principles of the military model," Scott Phillips reports.[30] These tactics are unnecessary and inappropriate in the context of civilian peacekeeping.

The result of these actions has been an increasingly frenetic spiral. Citizens protest unfair laws and oppression, and the police respond with even more brutal tactics and outright violence, leading to further anger and unrest, which is met with stronger shows of force, and so on. The protestors of the Civil Rights era organized sit-ins and were met with dogs and firehoses; today's protestors organize global boycotts, broadcast video to millions of viewers, and are met with militarized police and laws that stifle their efforts.

Changes in the Democratic and Republican parties

This intensification and polarization have been felt on the political front as well. While some Americans remained confident in the power of their military and the belief that Middle Easterners were terrorists threatening democracy, many became disillusioned with the surveillance and militarization they were becoming subjected to. Furthermore, the voices of Arabs and Muslims were becoming more accessible through an increase in alternative media. Together, these influences changed the minds of many, creating a level of discontent with the status quo and an increasing comfort in questioning the traditional narrative.

It should be noted that in the election in 2000, for the first time in history, Muslim and Arab Americans organized to vote in favor of the Republican Party candidate, George W. Bush. Bush's opponent, Al Gore, had chosen Joseph Lieberman as his running mate. Lieberman had been a staunch supporter of Israel in the Senate. After 9/11, when the Republicans passed the Patriot Act and alienated their Arab American constituents through racialized portrayals of terrorists, these two communities felt abandoned. They left the Republican Party but didn't move toward the Democrats. Instead, they found themselves politically disenfranchised.[31] By the 2004 election, "many viewed the Muslim bloc vote for Bush as a mistake, given the restrictive policies facing Muslims both domestically and abroad including the War on Terror and military conflicts against Muslims around the world."[32] Frequently, American Muslims didn't identify with any political party because they saw the American political system as rejecting them. Seeing the chance to capitalize on this population without a political party, some Democrats began to be more inclusive of minority groups, including Muslim and Arab Americans. These voices gave rise to the progressive movement in the Democratic Party.

This cultural shift paved the way for the presidential election of Barack Obama. The previous two decades had seen Republicans and a "tough on crime" Democrat elected. Now, progressive Americans wanted something new. Obama, who ran primarily on the universally welcome issues of an economic platform and a promise to provide universal healthcare, also held more progressive ideas than his Democratic predecessors. Many perceived him—the first nonwhite president, a former community organizer, and a left-leaning Democrat with environmentalist tendencies—as being likely to create real change and reform the system they felt had grown too powerful.

While the Obama administration came through on many of its promises, including that of providing a national healthcare system, it also led to further division in the country. Republicans felt Obama was too soft on terror, that his healthcare plan was socialist, and that he wasn't an "America first" president. The Tea Party, birthed out of a reactionary movement against the progressive swing in the United States, married racism, Orientalism, and conservative values in its disdain for Obama. Christopher Parker and Matt Barreto examine this phenomenon in their book *Change They Can't Believe In*. They quote Tea Party activist Laurie Roth, who spoke to a Tea Party event, "comparing Obama to the Democrats who preceded him in the Oval Office: 'This was not a shift to the Left like Jimmy Carter or Bill Clinton. This is a worldview clash. We are seeing a worldview clash in our White House. A man who is a closet seculartype Muslim, but he's still a Muslim. He's no Christian. We're seeing a man who's a socialist communist in the White House, pretending to be an American. . . . he wasn't even born here.'"[33] Obama announced that he was not a Muslim but a Christian and, despite claims that he was not American, was in fact born in the United States. These tropes were brought out to discredit him, as though one's religion could make one unfit for office.

Because this occurred concurrently with the rise of the internet, cable opinion news, and alternative media, their dissatisfaction was shared and amplified in what turned into internet echo chambers: Facebook groups and Twitter algorithms that fed the narrative that the Democratic Party was all that was wrong with America. This led to a shift to the right in Republican politics and the eventual nomination of Donald Trump for president. Wendy Hall and colleagues have worked with data from social media sites leading up to the 2016 election and "observed an uneven distribution of content being produced by several key actors in the network. As a consequence of the small number of highly active actors, there were several . . . strongly connected clusters of actors who are producing more than 60 percent of the network content (excluding retweets)."[34] In other words, a few very popular individuals produced content that was circulated widely and had great influence, drowning out other voices, which could not gain the same kind of traction due to algorithmic preferences.

Meanwhile, Palestinian Americans were disheartened at President Obama's lack of support. He had made remarks before his inauguration about his stance on the Palestinian situation, saying "the loss of civilian life in Gaza and in Israel is a source of deep concern" and that he would "have plenty more to say about the issue" after his January 20 inauguration.[35] Despite these remarks, little in this vein was accomplished during his tenure. The Democratic Party, in response to the Republicans, had been growing more progressive. The intensified fight between individuals and states was increasing, with more protests occurring around the world and in the United States. The securitization of the public sphere and emergence of a stronger police state in response to this created a long-term pushback against oppressive policies. People began seeing themselves as separate from the state, and feeling that the state was not working for them. Some people viewed socialism as less problematic than previously. The antiwar, prosocialist part of the Democratic Party had been slowly gathering momentum. Democrats had their own digital space for siloed thinking. This leftward shift in the party led to the surprisingly popular presidential bid of Bernie Sanders. Michael Corcoran noted that "the self-described 'democratic socialist' has tapped into some of the country's populist outrage and is raising issues like single-payer health care, tuition-free college and Wall Street's sinister influence on the political process."[36] The American left was ripe for his message. In the presidential primary of 2020, he won 26.6 percent of the vote and carried seven states.[37]

The polarization of American politics, led in part by the emergence of the automation of the internet that furthered the natural skew of people's opinions, was not limited to opinions on economics and healthcare. It spread to ideas on race and race relations, violence, and relative deprivation. The far right of the Republican Party became increasingly entrenched in ideas of primacy and conservatism, leading to strongly held convictions that it was white, Christian patriots who were under attack in America from leftists and foreigners. This view led to the election of Donald Trump, whose policies on immigration and Israel codified fears that Hispanics and Arabs were a threat to affluence and democracy, respectively. The structural, cultural shift toward American exceptionalism, on the one hand, and social activism and calls for justice, on the other, intensified the existing disagreements over the Palestine/Israel issue. The right solidified its backing of Israel under Donald Trump, who promoted several pro-Israel policies, moved the U.S. Embassy from Tel Aviv to Jerusalem, and officially recognized the Golan Heights, Syrian territory captured by Israel in 1967, as part of the occupier's territory. The left, in concert with Black Lives Matter and other social movement organizations, stood more and more behind the Palestinians. Within this group, it became acceptable to talk about injustice for all and to push for initiatives to remedy it. The messages Palestinians had been sending for decades were falling on the ears of Americans in new ways.

"The fact that there is something called Democrats for Israel suggests that there is a need for it from the perspective of those creating this organization," Matt Duss has said.[38] His observation is acute. While ebbs and flows in politics are a natural part of the democratic process, there has been a sustained shift in the Democratic Party toward universal justice that includes the voices of Palestinians, and pro-Israel PACs are firmly against it. Branco Marcetic reports that "the pro-Israel group Democratic Majority for Israel infamously intervened in [Nina] Turner's 2021 race [for Ohio's 11th District seat], rapidly dissolving her massive polling lead with a blitz of negative advertising that painted the longtime Democrat as insufficiently loyal to the party, part of the pro-Israel lobby's emerging strategy to make criticism of Israel a congressional nonstarter."[39] The Democratic Majority for Israel political action committee spent nearly $2 million on ads attacking Turner and supporting her opponent, Shonel Brown, and AIPAC gave Brown's campaign more than half a million dollars.[40]

Democrats for Israel have reason to worry. The Democratic Socialists of America (DSA), a generally small part of the Democratic Party, have been gaining momentum within the cultural shift of American politics in past decades, and the group is the only American political party to fully support Boycott, Divestment, and Sanctions (BDS). Sam Adler-Bell, a DSA New York delegate in 2018, observed in the fall of 2020:

> DSA [had] doubled in size, from 45,000 members to over 90,000. [Julia] Salazar won [the state Senate seat for North Brooklyn] and helped shepherd landmark tenants' rights legislation through the statehouse. [Alexandria

Ocasio-Cortez] upset Joe Crowley in the Democratic primary for New York's 14th Congressional District and became, well, *AOC*. Middle school principal Jamaal Bowman replaced thirty-one-year incumbent Eliot Engel in New York's 16th District. The organization did endorse Bernie again (surprise!) in 2019 and contributed thousands of volunteer hours to his campaign. In 2020, NYC-DSA sent its entire slate of five socialists to Albany. In 2021, two more were elected to the New York City Council.[41]

By the November 2022 elections, the DSA had gained still more support. The DSA November Dispatch reported that 68 percent of its thirty-seven nationally endorsed candidates had won their elections, and five DSA-supported ballot initiatives had passed. There are currently six members of the DSA in Congress: Alexandria Ocasio-Cortez, Rashida Tlaib, Ilhan Omar, Ayanna Pressley, Cori Bush, and Jamaal Bowman. They represent the largest number of socialist representatives in Congress in U.S. history, breaking 2020's record of four.

As an example of the shifts occurring in American politics, Democrat Summer Lee, a progressive and former community organizer, won a congressional seat in Pennsylvania in November 2022. Lee is the first Black woman to be voted into Congress in Pennsylvania and has expressed support for Palestinian rights. She embodies the intersection of BLM and Palestine, having said during the attacks on Gaza in spring 2021, "I was seeing, as a black woman, somebody who has also experienced oppression—we as black folks have experienced global oppression—and really looking at the parallels and being startled." Her election is even more surprising given the $4 million dollar campaign against her that was funded by AIPAC.[42] It shows a shift in American culture: marginalized groups who support Palestine are gaining political power thanks to a changing American voting public.

The pro-Palestine arm of the Democratic Party is poised to continue its rise. It's true that there had been some dissent. Jamaal Bowman voted "to fund Israel's Iron Dome missile defense system and then traveled to Israel/Palestine on a trip organized by J Street, a liberal Zionist organization. Both actions violated DSA's 2017 endorsement of the Boycott, Divestment, and Sanctions (BDS) movement."[43] Some smaller chapters of DSA, and the BDS Working Group, wanted to expel Bowman from the party for the violation, but the National Policy Committee declined to do so. When "the working group continued its campaign to demonize the congressman ... the NPC voted to de-charter the BDS Working Group, saying that it had violated DSA's code of conduct."[44] It was a stark reminder that neither BDS nor the DSA has enough power to take on the institutionalized power structures of the Democratic Party, and that to retain the power they held, it was sometimes necessary to make compromises.

Still, support for BDS is strong and growing in multiple arenas, including the labor movement, which has shown enormous support for Palestine. The Young Democratic Socialists of America are well aware of BDS and its growing support. When "student workers at Grinnell College won the first wall-to-wall undergraduate labor union, representing all student workers, the YDSA National Labor Committee [which] worked ... with five undergraduate labor unions to coordinate labor activity and support new organizing drives," hoped they would join YDSA. "But the leaders of the Grinnell union, the largest undergraduate union in the country, have declined to join YDSA because of their frustration at the dissolution of the DSA BDS working group." At Dartmouth College, "YDSA leaders first started organizing around Palestinian liberation. In an essay for the *Dartmouth Radical*, Kaya Çolakoğlu explains how the YDSA chapter formed following the gathering of hundreds of people for demonstrations at Dartmouth last May in protest of Israel's murder of hundreds of Palestinians."[45]

There are certain issues all politicians have to take a stand on. Abortion, gun rights, and Israel have historically fallen in this category. Any politician who wanted to be elected had to be clear on these things. WithinOurLifetime, a pro-Palestinian group based in New York, has called Palestine the "litmus test" for politicians wishing to be elected in their state and released information about each candidate's stand on Palestine ahead of the most recent election.[46] It appears Palestine has joined the short list of all-important electoral issues.

THE CHANGING LANDSCAPE OF CHRISTIANITY: DECLINING U.S. CHURCH ATTENDANCE AND PARTICIPATION

I have discussed how American Christianity has defined its relationship to Israel and how such a relationship operates to include various belief structures that fundamentally affect how Palestine and Palestinians are seen. To varying degrees, the majority of Christian denominations in the United

States see Israel as a fulfillment of Christian belief and prophecy. This belief is connected to an ongoing political crisis, and the interpretation of the biblical text informs Christians' decisions regarding it. Yet the landscape of Christianity in the United States is changing drastically. According to a Gallup poll, "U.S. church membership was 73% when Gallup first measured it in 1937 and remained near 70% for the next six decades, before beginning a steady decline around the turn of the 21st century."[47]

This change is most significant among millennials, those born between 1981 and 1996. This demographic, which is becoming increasingly prominent in leadership in the United States as their parents and grandparents age out of positions of power, is very different from their conservative elders, who tended to side with Israel out of political and religious affiliation. According to Pew Research, "they are the most ethnically and racially diverse cohort of youth in the nation's history," "the most politically progressive age group in modern history," and "the least religiously observant youths since survey research began charting religious behavior."[48] According to Pew Research data from 2019, 59 percent of millennials who were born with a religious affiliation tend to unplug from their church, only two of ten millennials consider church attendance as important, and 35 percent of millennials think that the church does more harm than good.[49]

The shift in church attendance and religious affiliation informs and coincides with the change in support for Palestine seen in American society. As fewer people sit under weekly teachings that describe Muslims as "other" and "enemy," and fewer Americans are under the influence of pastors and leaders who promote a Zionist, pro-Israel agenda, they are more likely to be open to hearing Palestinian stories and to be moved by the plight of those being oppressed. The Evangelical church, which holds to fundamentalist views of the Bible, is experiencing the most rapid decline. Martyn Whittock of *Christianity Today* reported on the decline in 2021, saying that "this is becoming particularly apparent within the US white evangelical community":

> In July 2021 the Public Religion Research Institute (PRRI) published new data, as part of its "2020 Census of American Religion," that is very revealing. The PRRI data reveals what can only be described as an extraordinary decline in the number of white Americans who now identify as "evangelical Christians." As the PRRI report concludes: "Since 2006, white evangelical

Protestants have experienced the most precipitous drop in affiliation, shrinking from 23% of Americans in 2006 to 14% in 2020.

Not only this, but the PRRI research reveals that these white evangelicals constitute the oldest age-profile of any identifiable group of religious Americans. They have an average age of 56. In short, white U.S. evangelicalism is both shrinking in size and failing to attract younger members. Or, as importantly, it is shedding its younger members who no longer wish to be classified as part of this group. If the current rate of decline continues, we could expect the number of U.S. white evangelicals, as a percentage of the U.S. adult population, to be in single figures by 2030. And they will also be old.[50]

Terry Johnson, a senior minister of Independent Presbyterian Church in Savannah, Georgia, in a profoundly self-aware op-ed for the *Evangelical Times*, writes, "Most alarming, evangelicals as a percentage of the population have sharply declined since the 1990s. What has happened? No doubt causes for evangelical decline are complex and reasons multi-faceted. Nevertheless, the roots of decline are in evangelicalism itself, and specifically in whatever is left of its public ministry."[51]

Christian support for Palestinians

While this may be bad news for Evangelicals, it tends to be good news for Palestinians, who face constant oppression from an Israel that is backed by a U.S. government under primarily white Evangelical sway. As Terry Johnson explains in *Evangelical Times*, these Evangelical leaders, who hold great political power

> are almost fanatical in their pro-Israel stance. One TV evangelist leader, in particular, John Hagee of the Cornerstone Church in San Antonio, Texas, is especially vehement. Hagee avers, "Supporting Israel is not a political issue. It is a biblical issue ... the 'Battle of Jerusalem.'" His support is overwhelming, according to a Justice News Flash Report (JNFR). He recently declared, "Whenever Jesus returns, Israel will become the dominant country in the world." ... This perspective leaves little room for compassion, much less tolerance, of the Palestinians. Hagee's words, almost too difficult to quote, pronounce that "The Jews are God's chosen people and have become the legal owners of the entire Palestine through a 'blood alliance.'"[52]

STRUCTURAL TRANSFORMATIONS IN U.S. CULTURE

Even within its declining population, a change is appearing in the composition of Evangelicals in the U.S. According to *Arab America*,

> a glimmer of hope is breaking through this dismal picture. It does so in the attitudes of some younger American evangelicals. Some polls taken show a portion of a younger, 18–29-year-olds, more diverse population of evangelicals with a more sympathetic view of Palestinians. They espouse a less rigid form of Zionist theology. One such younger evangelical, a pastor, cited by JNFR, rejects a strong Christian Zionism. Conversely, he supports a more compassionate view of the Israel-Palestine conflict. The pastor says that Christian Zionism "was flawed in theology" and did not adhere to the teachings of Jesus and the Jewish tradition. Furthermore, he suggested, "Those who take the Bible seriously cannot use the Bible as an excuse to be unfair to others."[53]

Outside the Evangelical world, churches are beginning to embrace the Palestinian cause:

> One recent campaign for such rights, labeled "Churches are Standing Up," was sponsored by a coalition of U.S. churches. It is under the banner of the U.S. Campaign for Palestinian Rights. That campaign reported on ten churches that had recently united in sanctioning Israel. These ten denominations meet periodically to discuss issues of the day, among other recurring topics of faith. The ten participating members, according to Washington Report on Middle East Affairs (WRMEA), are the Alliance of Baptists; Church of the United Brethren in Christ; Religious Society of Friends (Quakers); Mennonite Church USA; Presbyterian Church (USA); Roman Catholic Church; Unitarian Universalist Association; United Church of Christ; United Methodist Church; and the World Communion of Reformed Churches. High on the list of the ten churches' concerns is Palestinian rights.[54]

JEWISH AMERICAN AND ISRAELI VOICES FOR PALESTINE

The opinions of Jewish Americans are becoming more and more open to the idea that being critical of some Israeli governmental policies can be compatible with a general sense of being pro-Israel. A November 2022 survey of Jewish Americans found that "only 4% of Jewish voters said that Israel was one of the their top two issues in deciding who they vote for Congress, 89% of Jewish voters agreed that 'someone can be critical of Israeli government policies and still be pro-Israel,' and 72% of Jewish voters disapproved of AIPAC endorsing and raising money for Members of Congress who support Israel but voted against certifying the 2020 Presidential election."[55] This shift has been precipitated by the writings of Jewish Americans who are unafraid of sharing the brutality of the occupation and, in fact, see the struggle of Palestinians in light of their own history of oppression.

Much like the younger generation of American Christians is beginning to question the presumed narrative surrounding Israel and the U.S. involvement in it, young Jewish Americans are beginning to question the stories they are being told. Birthright Israel has sent 750,000 young Jewish Americans to Israel on free trips since 1999.[56] The trips are designed to encourage Jewish American solidarity with Israel and appreciation for Israeli national heritage. However, several participants have walked off their Birthright trips, or simply come home with negative views of the Israeli occupation of Palestine. In a cell phone video released to NowThis Politics, a birthright participant is seen questioning his tour guide about maps that are handed out, which show no reference to Palestine. The guide explains that Israel sees the West Bank as part of Israel and reflects that view on the maps they distribute. The young Jewish man states that, "It feels like the equivalent of going to the Jim Crow south." He challenges the tour guide, noting that Palestinians in the West Bank are not part of Israel by any international agreement, they can't vote, and their water and roads are controlled by the Israeli government. The guide's response? "It's free. You didn't pay (to come here) and there's no such thing as a free lunch."[57]

Risa Nagel, a Jewish woman from New York, wrote of her Birthright experience for the *Huffington Post*. She believed that she was going on the trip to experience her heritage, but "it became clear that Birthright was advancing a political agenda, both hiding and supporting Israel's military occupation of Palestinians." She and some of the other participants contacted IfNotNow and decided to leave the trip. The organization put them in touch with Israeli and Palestinian anti-occupation leaders, who introduced them to Palestinians living under occupation. Nagel was able to meet their families and talk to them about their experience living under military control. She describes visiting the village of Umm Al-Khair, where "the Civil Administration controls almost every aspect of life for

Palestinians living under occupation: demolishing buildings, cutting off electricity and limiting Umm Al-Khair's water supply to only seven hours of running water a week. The Community Center, which doubles as a summer camp for children, has been demolished and rebuilt twice already—once in the middle of the night." She returned with a message for her fellow Jewish Americans: "It's a moral failure for the largest organization that educates American Jews about Israel to tell a false narrative that obscures the truth about the occupation and its effects on Palestinians."[58]

The pushback against Israeli treatment of Palestinians is not only found in college students. Miko Peled is an Israeli writer and former IDF soldier whose family was instrumental in the creation of the Israeli state. His grandfather, Avraham Katznelson, signed the Israeli Declaration of Independence, and his father, Matti Peled, was a general in the Israeli Army. In 1997 Miko's niece, Smadar, was killed in a suicide bombing in Jerusalem. While some in his position would have turned wholeheartedly against the Palestinians after this tragedy, Peled decided to discover what was driving them to commit such crimes. This journey led him to write his first book, *The General's Son, Journey of an Israeli in Palestine*. He has become a sought-after speaker and author of several books criticizing the Israeli occupation of Palestine and the U.S. government's role in it.

Amira Hass is an Israeli journalist who writes for *Haaretz*. She has lived in the Occupied Palestinian Territories since 1993, first in Gaza City and then in Ramallah, and reports on daily life for Palestinians. In 2002 the *Los Angeles Times* reported that Hass "is the only Israeli Jew known to be living under Palestinian rule and one of a handful of Jewish reporters who still cross enemy lines for the Israeli media." In May 2009 "she was detained by Israeli police on her return from a four-month stay in Gaza 'for violating a military order' (which forbids entry into Gaza) and 'for staying illegally in an enemy state.' She had also been detained in December 2008 by Israeli police on her return to Ramallah for violating the same military order."[59] Yet Hass is undeterred. In 2010 Reporters Without Borders awarded her a "Press Freedom" prize for "independent and outspoken reporting."[60] She is also the recipient of the World Press Freedom Hero award from the International Press Institute, the Bruno Kreisky Human Rights Award in 2002, and the UNESCO/Guillermo Cano World Press Freedom Prize in 2003, among others. Her published works include *Drinking the Sea at Gaza* and *Reporting from Ramallah: An Israeli Journalist in an Occupied Land*.

Jeff Halper is an Israeli American anthropologist who has worked as a peace and human rights activist since the 1960s. Halper emigrated to Israel in 1973, where he taught anthropology at Haifa and Ben-Gurion Universities. He served in the Israeli military but "refused to bear arms or serve in the occupied Palestinian territories."[61] In 1997, Halper cofounded the Israeli Committee Against Home Demolitions (ICAHD), which led the American Friends Service Committee to nominate him alongside Palestinian activist Ghassan Andoni for the Nobel Peace Prize in 2006. Halper has also been a member of the steering committee of the UN Conference on the Exercise of the Inalienable Rights of the Palestinian People. "We think, as Israelis, that Jews and Arabs should live together," Halper told journalist Iwasaki Atsuko of *Counterpunch* Magazine. "Palestinians have rights of self-determination just like we have. We have to fight also for their rights. One of our slogans is 'we refuse to be their enemies.'"[62] Halper's most recent book, *Decolonizing Israel, Liberating Palestine: Zionism, Settler Colonialism, and the Case for One Democratic State*, has been described as "an extremely convincing and persuasive argument that the only conceivable future for justice and peace necessitates a process of decolonization and equal rights for all."[63]

Leah Tzemel is an Israeli attorney and advocate who has dedicated her career to assisting Palestinians in their struggle against Israeli oppressors. Born in Haifa, Tzemel has spent five decades defending Palestinians in their legal battles, a career that was documented in the film *Advocate* by Rachel Lee Jones and Phillippe Bellaiche in 2019. The film "attests to the wrongs of occupation but also to the faults of those who try to resist it, the failings of those who try to defend them, and the fundamental flaws of a legal system that purports to serve justice but in fact serves the powers that be."[64] It won multiple awards, including Best Documentary at the UK Jewish Film Festival and the News and Documentary Emmy for Best Documentary.[65] Tzemel herself has won several awards, including the Prix des Droits de l'Homme, France's highest humanitarian award, in 1996.[66]

Taken together, the work of these Jewish Americans and Israelis is evidence that within the Jewish community there are voices against Palestinian oppression. One might get the impression that there is universal acceptance of Israeli policy across the American Jewish community. For example, the majority of synagogues display Israeli flags. However, critique of Israeli policy has existed as long as the idea of establishing a nation-state on Palestinian lands. More recently, some synagogues have officially designated themselves at anti-Zionist, such as Tzedek Chicago, under the leadership of Rabbi Brant Rosen.

Emerging critiques by Israeli historians and prominent Jewish voices

Almost all critiques of Israeli policies against Palestinians are met with accusations of anti-Semitism. When these critiques are coming from prominent Israeli and Jewish scholars, they start carrying a heavier weight, especially when coming from children and grandchildren of Holocaust survivors. This is changing. Academia is being affected by newly pro-Palestinian voices as well. The "New Historians" movement can be traced back as far as 1988, when Benny Morris, a Jewish Israeli journalist, published his book *The Birth of the Palestinian Refugee Problem, 1947–1949*. In it he made public information he had learned about the origins of the Palestinian internal refugee issue while working at the *Jerusalem Post*. Having gone through government documents, "he found evidence that there had been a lot of expulsions and atrocities committed by Jewish soldiers."[67]

Ilan Greilsammer writes about the New Historian phenomenon and gives several structural reasons for its appearance. The first was the Ramadan/Yom Kippur War in 1973. The aftermath of the war left Israelis "in a state of total shock and of extreme anger. It discovered that the whole leadership of the country had lied when it affirmed that *Tsahal* [Israeli military] was ready to face any attack and that, anyway, the Arab countries would never dare to attack Israel."[68] This led common Israelis to consider whether other "sacred and untouchable" stories about its government might be lies. The perceived incompetence of the military also caused some questioning of its behavior during the 1948 war. Another cause was the opening of government archives containing information about the events in 1948 surrounding the establishment of Israel. The records had been sealed after the war but were gradually released to Israeli researchers.

Greilsammer also points out that Israel "was already a forty years old State, not a new country of the Third World. It was no more in real danger, it had the strongest army in the Middle East, a strong police, a strong economy, so … the well-known Israeli warning: 'Be careful, caution, we are weak, we are in a state of danger, the Arabs want to kill us, so be quiet, don't publish things which could harm the security of the State, etc.,' such a warning began to be obsolete and irrelevant." He also refers to the appearance of "a new generation of first-rate young social scientists, historians, anthropologists, economists, etc., which took their professional work very seriously and decided not to surrender to any ideological constraints, from the right as from the left."[69] Those "first-rate young social scientists" are today producing excellent scholarship despite immense criticism from Zionists and pro-Israel voices, including Ilan Pappé, Avi Shlaim, Hillel Cohen, Neve Gordon, and Tom Segev.

Jewish American voices were also very important. Sara Roy is a Jewish American academic who is an associate and a senior research scholar at the Center for Middle Eastern Studies at Harvard. She is the author of a number of books on the political, economic, and social conditions in Gaza, including *Hamas and Civil Society in Gaza: Engaging the Islamist Social Sector* and *The Gaza Strip: The Political Economy of De-development*. She has been called the leading researcher and most widely respected academic authority on Gaza today.[70] The child of Holocaust survivors, Roy writes that "'it was perhaps inevitable that I would follow a path that would lead me to the Arab-Israeli issue,' providing certain, carefully articulated parallels between the Nazi treatment of Jews and Israeli soldiers' treatment of Palestinians which, in her opinion, 'were absolutely equivalent in principle, intent, and impact: to humiliate and dehumanize.'"[71]

Peter Beinart is a prominent Jewish American journalist and political commentator who was educated at Yale and Oxford and has written for *Time*, the *New York Times*, the *Atlantic*, *Haaretz*, and the *Forward*, among other publications, as well as authoring several books. He has been outspoken in his critique of Israel. In 2010 he wrote a lengthy essay in the *New York Review of Books* titled "The Failure of the American Jewish Establishment," which critiqued the relationship of the Jewish American community with Israel:

> American Zionism is in a downward spiral. If the leaders of groups like AIPAC and the Conference of Presidents of Major American Jewish Organizations do not change course, they will wake up one day to find a younger, Orthodox-dominated, Zionist leadership whose naked hostility to Arabs and Palestinians scares even them, and a mass of secular American Jews who range from apathetic to appalled. Saving liberal Zionism in the United

States—so that American Jews can help save liberal Zionism in Israel—is the great American Jewish challenge of our age."[72]

Beinart has faith in his fellow Jews and their humanity. In the same article, he said that "it's time to envision a Jewish home that is a Palestinian home, too."

Commenting on Beinart's shift to becoming one of the most recognized Jewish American voices against Israeli occupation, Jeffrey Goldberg, editor-in-chief of *Atlantic* magazine, wrote that "if Israelis believe that the vast majority of American Jews—their most important supporters in the entire world—are going to sit idly by and watch Israel permanently disenfranchise a permanently-occupied minority population, they're deluding themselves. A non-democratic Israel will not survive in this world."[73]

In a *New York Times* piece in 2020, Beinart wrote, "Now liberal Zionists must make our decision, too. It's time to abandon the traditional two-state solution and embrace the goal of equal rights for Jews and Palestinians."[74] Beinart is an observant Jew, who keeps kosher and sends his children to Jewish school, but this has not protected him from attacks by his coreligionists, who have called him "the Pope of liberal Zionism" and accused him of "fabricating Israeli crimes, overstating Palestinian desire for peace, trivializing Palestinian terrorism against Jews, and throwing in schmaltzy, cringeworthy matzo-ball Jew-talk by which he seeks to legitimize his extremist anti-Israel views."[75] Despite this pushback, Beinart continues to write and speak on the need for Palestinians to be viewed as human beings with rights.

Dr. Gabor Maté, a Holocaust survivor whose grandparents died in Auschwitz, is now a physician. He has strong family ties to the Likud Party in Israel and as a young man was a Zionist who dreamed of a place of safety and freedom for the Jewish people. He found, however, that to make the Jewish dream a reality, one had to "visit a nightmare on the local population. . . . There was no land without a people. There was [sic] people living there who had been living there for hundreds of years or even longer." In a video interview with Russell Brand, he promotes the new Israeli historians who have proven that the settling of Jewish people in Israel required the expulsion of Palestinians and describes his visit to Occupied Palestine during the first Intifada, during which he cried over the treatment of Palestinians at the hand of Israelis.[76]

ISRAELI AND JEWISH ORGANIZATIONS

A number of organizations have emerged in attempts to present a different narrative than the dominant, official view of the Israeli government, and to assist Palestinians living under oppression. Many of them are Israeli and Jewish-led. Progressive Jewish Americans and Israelis, aware of the disparities in the way Israel presents the Palestinian situation, are deeply sympathetic to the suffering of Palestinians.

B'Tselem, the Israeli Information Center for Human Rights in the Occupied Territories, for example, is deeply committed to the cause of justice for Palestinians. Created in 1989, B'Tselem stated on its website: "The essence of the apartheid regime in place between the Jordan River and the Mediterranean Sea is to promote and perpetuate the supremacy of one group over another. B'Tselem works to change this reality, recognizing that this is the only way to realize a future in which human rights, liberty and equality are guaranteed to all human beings living here, Palestinians and Jews alike." The organization focuses on "documenting, researching and publishing statistics, testimonies, video footage, position papers and reports on human rights violations committed by Israel in the Occupied Territories."[77]

Peace Now is an Israeli organization with roots in the late 1970s bids for peace between Israel and all its Arab neighbors. Although Peace Now favors a two-state solution that led to apartheid-like governance, it pushed against the systemic demonization of Arabs and Palestinians. Peace Now believes that Israeli settlements are driving the conflict. It has created a monitoring program called "settlement watch," reporting to the U.S. government and the world the new settlements being built in Occupied Palestine. It has a sister organization in the United States, called Americans for Peace Now (APN). APN's mission is to "educate and persuade the American public and its leadership to support and adopt policies that will lead to comprehensive, durable, Israeli-Palestinian and Israeli-Arab peace, based on a two-state solution, guaranteeing both peoples' security, and consistent with U.S. national interests."[78] Although its stance remains pro-Israel and pro-America, Peace Now is more willing than most organizations to listen to the Palestinian point of view.

Combatants for Peace is a joint Israeli/Palestinian organization made up of former militants who have decided to lay down arms and take a stand for peace. They prefer a two-state solution but would support "any

STRUCTURAL TRANSFORMATIONS IN U.S. CULTURE

other just solution agreed upon in negotiations."[79] The group was formed in 2006 and offers binational tours of the West Bank for Israelis to see the reality of life on the Palestinian side of the wall. As its focus is on nonviolent means of achieving peace, the group holds rallies, meetings, and marches and uses theater to draw both Israelis and Palestinians into communion.

The Israeli Committee Against House Demolitions was founded by the aforementioned Jeff Halper and has existed since 1997. Originally a non-profit organization dedicated to ending the conflict, ICAHD now exists to promote the idea of a one-state solution:

> Over time it became clear that this was not a conflict; there were never two equal parties. Now we refer to ending Israel's apartheid policies and the settler colonial goal that the state of Israel has over the Palestinian people. ICAHD has always called for there to be a just resolution to this issue. For a few years we referred to a two-state solution however with each year that passed, and with growing understanding of Israel's Matrix of Control over the Palestinian people we could see that the only just way forward is for there to be a one democratic state over all of historic Palestine. With mobilization now happening amongst Palestinians who are calling for one state, we as critical Jews are able to stand with them as together, we go forward.[80]

ICAHD is active in working to prevent home demolition and settlement building and has partner organizations around the world that support the political and activist agenda of the organization and engage in fundraising, events to raise awareness, and lobbying.

IfNotNow is a Jewish American organization dedicated to freedom for Palestinians. Its mission is rooted in its Jewish values and history of oppression, which it feels cannot be stood for, no matter whom it affects. Its website states:

> So long as we teach our children that our safety can only come through oppressing Palestinians, we will remain severed from our partners in justice. It is long past time for the American Jewish community to confront our role, alongside the U.S. government, in the systemic displacement of the Palestinian people. We acknowledge with compassion the circumstances that

Jewish refugees faced over the past century, leading many to settle in what is now Israel-Palestine. Nevertheless, we must face what these actions led to: apartheid, a system of inequality and displacement that oppresses Palestinians throughout the entire land.[81]

IfNotNow collaborates with local Israeli organizations that work to create more livable and equitable conditions for Palestinians, from those that defend freedom of movement, like Gisha, to those that document human rights violations, like Yesh Din.[82]

Breaking the Silence is an organization of former Israeli soldiers who witnessed and experienced the inhumane treatment of Palestinians. Journalist Dena Takruri interviewed soldiers involved with Breaking the Silence for a series of YouTube videos.[83] These videos, available to stream for free anywhere in the world with an internet connection, are examples of the kinds of systemic changes that have occurred over the past twenty or so years.

One of the most visible and influential organizations on this front is Jewish Voice for Peace, a Jewish American organization started in 1996 by students at UC Berkeley. JVP opposes the Israeli occupation of Palestine and insists that criticism of Zionist policies is not anti-Semitic. Its website states: "We represent a growing portion of Jewish Americans. Israel claims to be acting in the name of the Jewish people, so we are compelled to make sure the world knows that many Jews are opposed to their actions. There are often attempts to silence critics of Israel by conflating legitimate criticism with anti-Semitism. Israel is a state, not a person. Everyone has the right to criticize the unjust actions of a state."[84] JVP is incredibly active in the United States, with more than sixty chapters, and "was the first major Jewish peace group to demand that American military aid be withheld until Israel ends its occupation." It is "the only major Jewish group to support the Palestinian civil society call for boycott, divestment and sanctions."[85]

Into this new surge of Jewish and Israeli support for Palestine have entered celebrities whose Jewish heritage and visibility in American pop culture give them a platform for speaking on the issue. During his tenure as host of the *Daily Show*, Jewish American Jon Stewart spoke out repeatedly on Israel and Palestine. The show was, and continues to be, popular among young Americans. His segments in support of Palestinians showed both the change in culture that allowed him to speak out in such a way without cancellation (though he certainly experienced backlash and censorship) and the effect of celebrity voices on the opinions of the general public. Other celebrities have spoken out as well, including Seth Rogan, who has said that as a young person he was "fed a huge amount of lies about Israel" and would never live in Israel, and, perhaps most famously, Natalie Portman, who declined a major Israeli award over her negative opinion of some of Israel's actions toward Palestinians.[86]

Gideon Levy was the spokesman for Israeli president Shimon Peres and is now "one of the most outspoken journalists in Israel, someone who . . . is a true dissident in Israeli society, and the voice of the voiceless in Israel." In an interview with Max Blumenthal, he criticized the role of the United States in Israel's oppression of Palestinians:

> The U.S. is the big financer of the Zionist project and the big financer of the settlement project. Without the U.S. there is no occupation. And the U.S. carries responsibility for any of Israel's deeds and crimes, because without the U.S. Israel couldn't do it, very clearly. . . . Doesn't America see that it pays a hell of a price for this automatic and blind support of Israel and of the occupation project? Is it reasonable that in the 21st century, the United States will finance an apartheid regime in the occupied territories? All those questions should be raised, but I'm not sure anyone has an answer.[87]

Jewish Americans and Israelis are becoming less blind to the injustices happening at the behest of the Israeli government, and a growing number are appalled by the treatment of Palestinians, leading them to push against Israeli apartheid and its supporters.

In the early 2000s Palestinians seemed to have lost positive global public opinion, their lands, and their livelihoods. The American global War on Terror poured resources into Israel, it became clear that Palestinian hopes for self-determination were further away than ever, and resistance needed to evolve. The fight would have to be taken elsewhere, externally, and to be globalized in order to gain the kind of support needed to make progress. It also became clear, through the work of Omar Wasow and others, that nonviolent protest was the most effective means of changing society. This understanding, coinciding with the rise of the internet and easy access to it through smartphones, gave rise to BDS, the externalization of the conflict through lawsuits in international court, and an increasing use of social media and citizen journalism to garner support around the world. Palestinians in Palestine began to feel a renewed and increased connection to Palestinians abroad.

Gabriel Sanchez and Edward Vargas write that "scholars interested in the political implications of group identity have applied the concept of group consciousness to many political outcomes over time, finding evidence that the concept leads to increased political engagement for racial and ethnic groups."[88] This was certainly true for Palestinians, who feel a strong link to Palestine whether they live there or in diaspora. This feeling of "linked fate" has been studied in the United States, where, according to Kiana Cox, "U.S. adults say that what happens to their own racial or ethnic group affects them the most."[89] Palestinians around the world were deeply affected by stories and images of the treatment of Palestinians under Israeli control that were being made available to them. This group identity led to political action in the form of participation in BDS, the sharing of personal narratives, and making their voices heard through voting.

During the same time period, the United States underwent structural changes in its politics, media, and social systems that allowed for the acceptance of alternative narratives. This new, fertile ground for civil unrest helped BDS and other criticism of Israel to gain traction. More like the American Civil Rights movement than a passing protest, BDS has been around long enough to be the subject of lawsuits, studies, and books like *The Case for Sanctions Against Israel*.[90] The world has begun to see Palestinians in exile and in Israel as people with agency. Their voices matter, and while they have little power on the ground, they can effect change in other ways.

Another process is at play. As time passes, the crimes of Israel grow steadily worse, and the treatment of Palestinians degrades. This intensification is tied to a rise of fascism in Israel, as noted by Levy: "American liberals should know all this. They should know that they are supporting the first sign of fascism in Israel." He describes an Israel that is "becoming less and less tolerant, and the standing of democracy is minimal and many times very twisted."[91] Fascism in Israel is not new. In 1980 the *Journal of Palestine Studies* published an article that began, "Liberal circles in Israel are concerned about the increasing aggressivity of Israel's extreme right and the support it is getting from official personalities. The trend towards fascism is taking place in a climate of public indifference to the fate of Israeli 'democracy.'"[92] Recently, however, Israel's self-identification has become more arrogant, and its actions more blatant. Ahmad Tibi, a Palestinian living within Israel and an Israeli parliamentarian, said in a November 2022 interview that "the Palestinian people are facing the 'most fascist' and 'most extreme' government in Israel's history. . . .'Fascism has become a central current in the government. The rise of this fascism in Israel does not mean that the former governments were moderate, but the upcoming one is the most fascist after the rise of the Zionist religious parties.'"[93] The rise of fascism is disconcerting, and the increasing light shed on Israeli human rights violations in Gaza, the West Bank, and Palestinian populations inside Israel is garnering global attention toward action that for many decades Palestinians have been calling for.

Norman Finkelstein describes the recent visibility this way:

> It is often alleged that the Israel-Palestine conflict is so complex that a knowledge on the order of rocket science is needed to penetrate its mysteries. Its roots are alleged to reach back to the hoary past, or it is said to be grounded in a cosmic clash of religions, cultures, and civilizations. This mystification of a conflict that, judging by the documentary record, is relatively straightforward serves a dual function. First, it rationalizes suspending ordinary moral and legal standards, which supposedly can't be applied because of the singularity of the conflict. Thus, when Robert Malley, an American negotiator at the failed 2000 Camp David summit, was publicly challenged as to why U.S. aid to Israel continued to flow despite egregious Israeli violations of international law, he replied: "This is really a truly unique conflict." End of discussion. A second, related purpose of this mystification is to preempt the making of obvious analogies—for example, between the fate of Native Americans at the hands of European settlers and Palestinians at the hands of Zionist settlers, and between Apartheid in South Africa and Israeli policy in the Occupied Palestinian Territory.[94]

But now, the simple truth is coming out: Palestine is oppressed, and Israel is its oppressor.

Chapter Three

SOCIAL CHANGE AND SOUND BITES
The Fight Intensifies in American Culture

The intensification of the fight between the pro-Israel forces and the growing countercommunity in the United States is clearly visible in the American public sphere. From education to pop culture, from debates on social media platforms to shifting journalism narratives, the traditional way of understanding the Palestinian question is no longer the only way. Palestine has become one of the central social justice issues in the United States. This is due in part to the structural changes and the impact of other social movements, such as the Boycott, Divestment and Sanctions movement. Influential groups, from Black Lives Matter to Native Americans to LGBTQ+ allies and environmentalists, are joining the global voices speaking out for Palestine. Celebrities, from actors and singers to athletes, are joining the fight, often using social media to voice their opinions or boycotting Israel as a way of taking a stand. Social media platforms have become sites of these daily fights for justice, but not without backlash. Lobbyists and special interest groups are putting pressure on the American educational system, from K-12 public schools, where curriculum is scrutinized and rewritten, to college campuses, where new pro-Palestine groups are forming and formerly entrenched pro-Israel groups are pushing back. This chapter will examine the ways in which these cultural changes reflect the intensifying confrontation between Israel and Palestine in its many forms.

SOCIAL CHANGE AND SOUND BITES

PROTESTS AND BOYCOTTS

> Just as the struggle to end South African apartheid was embraced by people all over the world and was incorporated into many social justice agendas, solidarity with Palestine must likewise be taken up by organizations and movements involved in progressive causes all over the world. The tendency has been to consider Palestine a separate—and unfortunately too often marginal—issue. This is precisely the moment to encourage everyone who believes in equality and justice to join the call for a free Palestine.
>
> —ANGELA DAVIS, 2016

The BDS movement, which launched in July 2005, is a global, peaceful protest of the treatment of Palestinians by the Israeli government. The movement's stated goals are "the end of Israel's occupation and colonisation of Arab lands, dismantling the security wall, full equality for Palestinian-Arab citizens of Israel, and recognition of the right of return for Palestinian refugees."[1] Supporters view the movement as synonymous with other boycotts of the past, including the South African apartheid boycott and the Civil Rights movement in the United States, and see it as a nonviolent way to promote human rights and oppose racialized inequalities. The movement has been steadily gaining support in the United States, leading to clashes between consumers and businesses, activists and celebrities, and even the courts.

Economic and commercial boycotts

Since the inception of the BDS movement, an increasing number of individuals and organizations have been made aware of the issue and have chosen to take a stand. The movement, which mimics the boycotts launched against apartheid South Africa, is a global phenomenon aimed at defeating oppression by harnessing social, political, and consumer power.

Much of the boycotting is done against Israeli companies and their products. This can look like personal refusals to purchase products from Israeli companies, calls for widespread boycotts of the same, or divestment from those companies by individuals and groups. A number of Christian denominations in the United States have chosen to stop investing in Israeli companies and in investment funds that do. These choices are frequently met with derision, accusations antibiblicalism, and occasionally lawsuits. The increasing frequency of actions taken by individuals and groups to support BDS and Palestine more generally, and the increasingly vitriolic responses to those actions from those with power and the general public, are signs of the rising intensity in the fight against Israeli oppression. What follows is a symbolic but hardly exhaustive list of examples of such interactions.

One of the first companies to be marked for boycott was the construction equipment company Caterpillar, which has been under scrutiny for more than two decades over its sale of machinery to Israel. These machines are used to demolish Palestinian homes, roads, and olive groves. It was a Caterpillar bulldozer driven by an Israeli soldier that crushed and killed American student and peace activist Rachel Corrie in 2003 while she was protesting such a demolition. The boycott is backed by over twenty organizations around the world, and Caterpillar is on the BDS list of companies to avoid.[2] The company has suffered very little, however. Its official statement is that it "appreciates the concerns raised over unrest in the Middle East" but trusts its purchasers to use products in an ethical manner.[3]

In October 2010 a boycott was launched against hummus company Sabra for its complicity in the Palestinian occupation. Sabra is co-owned by Pepsi and the Israeli company Strauss, which supports the Israeli Defense Forces and the Golani and Givati Brigades, which have been accused of human rights abuses against Palestinians. Activist Susan Landau noted that "the IDF implements Israel's policies of discrimination against Palestinians at checkpoints, through home demolitions, curfews, detentions, targeted assassinations, control over freedom of movement. Corporate complicity is exactly the point of the boycott of best-seller Sabra, the pride of Strauss."[4] Sabra hummus is popular in the United States, and the response, especially on college campuses, was strong. Several universities considered removing Sabra products, including Harvard, where student group Harvard Out of Occupied Palestine held a rally in Harvard Yard demanding the university stop serving the hummus on campus.[5] Bans on the sale of the hummus were passed at Dickinson College and the University of Manchester.[6] At the University of California, Riverside, a student association voted to ban the product but was overruled by administrators.[7]

Another company marked for boycott is Hewlett-Packard, the sole provider of computers to the Israeli military and the servers used by the Israeli government for its population registry, which is used when issuing identification. "IDs issued based on this registry determine one's level of rights," with Jewish citizens receiving more rights than others.[8] Their servers are also used in Israeli prisons, where Palestinians are frequently imprisoned without any form of due process, by military decree, indefinitely in some cases. In 2017 human rights organizations in nine countries sent a petition to Hewlett-Packard asking them to cease business in Israel and citing HP's own internal documents, which claim that "respect for human rights is essential to the way we do business and approach our value chain."[9] BDS has called for a boycott of the company's products.

In some cases, founders of companies have little power over the distribution of the products made by their family companies and are fighting their own boards over the ethics of doing business in Israel. Members of the Pillsbury family announced in 2020 that they would boycott their own family's products after learning that General Mills, which acquired Pillsbury in 2000, had opened and was operating a Pillsbury factory in Occupied Palestinian Territory. In an op-ed in the *Minnesota Star-Tribune*, the family, represented by Charlie Pillsbury, wrote that "as people of conscience, we have no choice but to join this boycott of the very brand our family worked so hard to build." He cited "the enormous costs of a brutal occupation" and "General Mills . . . profiting from Israel's war crimes" as reasons for the boycott.[10] The Pillsbury plant is located in the Atarot Industrial Zone, a settlement that Israel occupied during the 1967 war and then illegally annexed. Noam Perry, of the American Friends Service Committee, explains that "the factory is exploiting land, water, and other resources that were captured by force from their legal Palestinian owners, in violation of international law—and General Mills is directly profiting from the illegal occupation of Palestinian territory."[11]

On July 19, 2021, Ben & Jerry's announced that it would no longer sell its products in the Occupied Palestinian Territory, stating that to do so would be inconsistent with their values.[12] Their intention was to not renew their license agreement at its expiration and to find a new licensee within Israel. However, Unilever, the umbrella corporation that owns Ben & Jerry's, "sold its license to operate the . . . brand within Israel to an Israeli company without consulting with the Ben & Jerry's board . . . and went against the merger agreement" they had made with the original founders of the company that gave them "the ability to protect the founder's values and reputation." U.S. District Judge Andrew Carter of New York ruled against the company founders, stating that the "company must allow its ice cream to be sold in the illegal Israeli colonies, . . . that the company's claim that such sales violate its core values is 'too speculative,'" and that the company "did not show it would suffer irreparable harm, or that customers would be confused."[13] Unilever continues to sell Ben and Jerry's ice cream in settlements in the West Bank.

Some companies that have come under fire sell experiences rather than products. Vacation rental platform Airbnb has come under scrutiny for listing properties in settlements in Occupied Palestinian Territory. It is reported that these properties are listed as "being inside the state of Israel, raising questions about the technology platform's legal position in profiting from rentals on the land."[14] The company agreed to remove those listings, but after pressure from the Israeli government they were restored. It has promised to donate any profits off properties in occupied land to "non-profits focused on humanitarian aid in different parts of the world."[15] Palestinians, feeling that this was insufficient, called for a boycott of the company on May 15, 2019, stating that "by doing business in these settlements, Airbnb and other international companies are contributing to the economic viability of settlements and are normalizing Israeli annexation of Palestinian land."[16] In September 2022 hotel website Booking.com announced it would add a warning to listings for properties inside illegal Israeli settlements in the West Bank. The warning, which the site says will be posted on all properties in conflict zones around the world, will inform tourists that "visiting the area may be accompanied by an increased risk to safety and human rights or other risks to the local community and visitors" and may include the word "occupied" to describe the area.[17]

A similar story can be told of the Psagot Winery. Psagot operates on eighty dunams of stolen land in Palestine; thus the issue is not the product being manufactured and sold, but the fact that its existence is due to the forced expulsion of Palestinians and the theft of their land. Psagot labels its wine as a "Product of Israel," a claim that France has disputed. The dispute ended in a ruling by the European Court, which stated that "foodstuffs originating in the territories occupied by the State of Israel must bear the indication of their territory of origin, accompanied, where those foodstuffs come from an Israeli settlement within that territory, by the indication of that provenance." In layman's terms, Psagot wines must be labeled as "Product of Palestine" based on this court ruling. In a press release, the Court of Justice of the European Union stated that "the Court first of all underlined that the settlements established in some of the territories occupied by the state of Israel are characterised by the fact that they give concrete expression to a policy of population transfer conducted by that state outside its territory, in violation of the rules of general international humanitarian law." The court ruled that the mislabeling might mislead consumers.[18]

Furthermore, Psagot Winery is owned by the Falic family, which also owns the Duty Free stores found in American airports. The Falics, who sell Psagot wines in these stores, contributed $5.6 million to Israeli settlement groups between 2009 and 2019. In essence, the money made from wine produced on occupied land pays for additional occupation.[19] Along with legal censure for their less than honest practices, the company is facing increased social pressure and boycotts related to its involvement with Israeli settlements.

The story of SodaStream, a company that manufactures a home appliance that turns water into flavored, carbonated beverages, sheds light on the complex ways the occupation of Palestine harms Palestinians. SodaStream built a factory in the Mishor Adummim industrial zone in the West Bank, in one of the largest settlements east of Jerusalem. This settlement is considered "one of the largest expropriations of private Palestinian land during the occupation."[20] Because it does business in the West Bank, the company's taxes help fund the settlement. BDS called for a boycott of the company, which gained support around the world, particularly in the United States, where local groups in New York, Seattle, Portland, Boston, and Washington, D.C., campaigned for it.[21] The movement was successful in tarnishing the SodaStream image, causing the stock price to fall, and finally prompting a relocation of the factory into Israel proper.[22] However, even as it removed itself from Palestinian land, there were repercussions to Palestinians who had found work in the factory. Five hundred Palestinian workers were laid off after the Israeli government refused to give them permits to work after the factory had moved. The government issued only seventy-four work permits, and those allowed to work had to endure two-hour commutes to the factory and scrutiny at Israeli checkpoints on their way to and from their jobs. Even those seventy-four permits were not renewed by the Israeli government. Work permit requirements are often arbitrary and very prohibitive in themselves; in order to receive one, Palestinians must be at least twenty-two years old and married, among other requirements.[23]

Social pressure has also affected the choices of the Oakland Roots, a professional soccer team. Fans made it clear they would not support the team's relationship with Puma after it was announced that the latter would provide the team's uniforms. The Oakland Roots Radicals, a primary fan group, released a statement that read, "PUMA is the main sponsor of the Israel Football Association, which includes teams in illegal Israeli settlements.... The injustice Palestinian people suffer as they are displaced by illegal settlements is in direct opposition to the values of the Oakland community, and the values espoused by the Roots that make us so proud to support them. We are calling on the Roots to stand up and confront injustice, by severing ties to Puma until they end their support for Israel's regime of apartheid and military occupation."[24] The team ceased its relationship with Puma a few months later, although they would not give a reason for the departure.[25]

Not all protests come from consumers: they can also come from organizations and legal entities. In October 2022 Adidas and Balenciaga dropped Kanye West as a spokesperson after he made anti-Semitic remarks on social media that were widely decried. Not long after, both companies hired Palestinian American model Bella Hadid in his place. That decision, however, was met with backlash. Arsen Ostrovsky, CEO of the International Legal Forum, "said the decision to hire Hadid was 'the height of hypocrisy.... They have simply just replaced one antisemite for another, only underscoring it was never about values or tackling racial hatred for these brands, but only about profits.... The fact that Kanye's antisemitism was directed at Jews as individuals, while Hadid relentlessly vilifies Israel and supports Palestinian terror, should make no difference. Hatred is hatred is hatred, and we need to call it out regardless, as well as all those who enable it and profit from it.'"[26] Ostrovsky's conflation of disagreement with Israeli policies of oppression and anti-Semitism is a common and harmful one.

At times, protestors have chosen to take more extreme action when refusal to engage in commerce isn't an option. In May 2021, while Israeli bombs rained down on Gaza, pro-Palestinian activists in the United Kingdom seized control of a building owned by weapons manufacturer Elbit Systems. The group Palestine Action "occupied Elbit's factory, UAV Tactical Systems, in Leicester and chained the gates shut, disrupting the company's production of arms and military technology. Activists have taken direct action in response to Elbit's funneling of arms to the Israeli occupation force, which the group said are committing war crimes in Gaza."[27] Needless to say, the action did not lead to a reduction in arms production for Israeli forces.

While street demonstrations in support of Palestine are rare in the United States, they are not uncommon in the rest of the world. In May 2021 several thousand protestors convened in Dublin in a show of solidarity, waving Palestinian flags in front of the Israeli Embassy. Similar events were held in London, Sydney, Melbourne, and Athens, where "Greek police fired tear gas and water cannon to disperse pro-Palestinian demonstrators."[28]

American labor union boycotts

Unions have also participated by refusing to work with Israeli companies, or by collectively choosing to participate in the BDS boycotts. On June 4, 2021, workers belonging to the International Longshore and Warehouse Union in Oakland, California, refused to unload cargo from the ship *Volans*, which is operated by the Israeli company ZIM. "An injury to one is an injury to all. Just as ILWU Local 10 workers refused to unload cargo from apartheid South Africa in the 1980s, we honored community pickets asking us not to unload cargo from Israeli ZIM vessels," said Jimmy Salamy, a Palestinian member of the union. Workers in South Africa and Italy have also refused to unload Israeli ZIM vessels.[29] When members of L'Unione Sindacale di Base, an Italian trade union of port workers, discovered that an arms shipment passing through their port was headed for Israel, they refused to unload it, saying, "the port of Livorno will not be an accomplice in the massacre of the Palestinian people."[30] In 2010 protestors in Oakland blocked the unloading of a ZIM ship by longshoremen in response to the treatment of Palestinians in Gaza by the Israeli government.[31] Later that week, Swedish longshoremen announced a week-long boycott of all Israeli vessels in solidarity.[32]

The San Francisco Teacher's Union, which is an affiliate of national labor union AFL-CIO, passed a resolution in May 2021 in support of BDS. The resolution "denounces Israel's 'forced displacement and home demolitions' of Palestinians and accuses the Jewish state of being 'a regime of legalized racial discrimination.'" Tyler Gregory, executive director of the Jewish Community Relations Council, called the legislation "factually inaccurate" and "inflammatory."[33] The decision does not appear to have been condoned by the AFL-CIO, however, and some months later, another affiliate, the San Francisco Labor Council (SFLC), was blocked from debating a proposal to endorse BDS. In its memo to the SFLC, the AFL-CIO cited the precedent that international policy is decided at the national level, but the decision is a departure from historic decisions by the union, such as its allowing affiliates in 1977 to boycott South Africa, though a national consensus was not reached until 1984.[34] In a statement signed by multiple union leaders in 2007, the AFL-CIO officially opposed BDS, saying that "any just and fair resolution of the Israeli-Palestinian conflict must be brought about through meaningful negotiations between their elected representatives."[35] In 2009, Richard Trumka, then the president of the AFL-CIO, "explicitly called anti-Zionism antisemitic." The official memo sent to the SFLC stated that it "may not hold a vote on [the] resolution . . . and thus any debate is not germane at your meeting." According to Frank Lara, vice president of the San Francisco Teachers Union, "the memo contravenes basic union principles. 'I want to believe that unions are one of the most democratic institutions. . . . To suddenly see a labor organization trump the membership? That's problematic to say the least.'"[36]

The Seattle Education Association, a union representing about 5,500 teachers who work for Seattle Public Schools, voted in 2021 to pass a resolution in solidarity with the Palestinian people. A statement from the union read:

> In response to the ongoing Israeli colonization, occupation, and bombardment of Gaza, the West Bank, and East Jerusalem, rooted in principles of justice, human rights, and equality, Seattle Education Association (SEA) representatives passed a resolution in solidarity with the people of Palestine. The resolution endorses the Palestinian call to boycott, divest, and sanction (BDS) Israel. Furthermore, the resolution endorses End the Deadly Exchange Seattle, a coalition of individuals and organizations demanding the end to exchanges and collaboration between the Seattle Police Department and the Israeli military and police. The recommendation overwhelmingly passed by a vote of 90 percent.[37]

The resolution was reportedly inspired by and based on a similar resolution passed by the San Francisco Teachers Union in May 2021. Greg McGarry, one high school teacher in the San Francisco caucus that wrote their union's resolution, explained the importance of their stance to the *San Francisco Independent Journal*:

> Organized labor must put its weight behind the Palestinian cause and support the BDS movement. Real, material labor solidarity actions helped to end South African Apartheid, and they are the most effective way to end the ethnic cleansing and occupation of Palestine. Now begins the hard work of making sure our leadership follows through and that the movement spreads throughout organized labor. The U.S. government and the U.N. won't defund the Israeli war machine, so the international workers must do it, until all of Palestine is free.[38]

Religious organizations and solidarity with Palestine

Religious organizations have also taken note of the Palestinian issue, and sometimes taken action. Quaker investment fund Friends Fiduciary Corporation chose to drop both French company Veolia Environment and U.S.-based Caterpillar in 2012 over concerns regarding those companies' involvement with the Israeli military. Caterpillar, in particular, "would neither confirm nor deny the extent or type of modifications to equipment sold to the Israeli military" when asked for clarification by the denomination.[39]

The Presbyterian Church (USA) (PCUSA) voted in 2014 to sell stock it held in Motorola Solutions, Hewlett-Packard, and Caterpillar over their dealings with Israel. "'We as a church cannot profit from the destruction of homes and lives,' the Rev. Gradye Parsons, Director of Operations of Office of the General Assembly, said in a statement. 'We continue to invest in many businesses involved in peaceful pursuits in Israel.'"[40] The amendment specifically stated that the "action of divestment is not to be construed or represented by any organization of the PCUSA as divestment from the State of Israel, or an alignment with or endorsement of the global BDS (Boycott, Divest and Sanctions) movement," and that the denomination recognized "Israel's right to exist as a sovereign nation within secure and internationally recognized borders."[41] Despite this, the move incited a wave of criticism and was quickly denounced by several groups, including the Anti-Defamation League, which said that the PCUSA had fostered "an atmosphere of open hostility to Israel within the church, promoted a one-sided presentation of the complex realities of the Middle East, and permitted the presentation of a grossly distorted image of the views of the Jewish community," and that the sale "sends a painful message to American Jews."[42] The Southern Baptists called the decision "tragic," while Mitch Glaser, president of the Jewish evangelism and discipleship organization Chosen People Ministries, asserted that "the PCUSA seems to be leaving its biblical moorings."[43] American Jewish leaders reacted with "anger and disbelief" and accused the Presbyterians of delegitimizing Israel under "the guise of helping Palestinians."[44] The Jewish News Syndicate suggested that the denomination's declining numbers were due to its refusal to take a pro-Israel stance. David Brog, executive director of CUFI, "sees a link between the growing radical anti-Israel agenda within PCUSA and a steady decline in the church's membership over the last decade, leading some PCUSA members to cross denominational boundaries and seek support from pro-Israel evangelical Christian groups."[45]

A year later, the United Church of Christ passed a resolution calling "for the church to divest from the Israeli occupation, to boycott Israeli settlement products, to persist in pressuring Congress to end unconditional U.S. military aid to Israel, and to study the Kairos Palestine document produced by prominent Palestinian Christians, which calls on Christians around the world to take action to support the basic human rights of the Palestinian people." The resolution was introduced by members of the United Church of Christ Palestine Israel Network and supported by Reverend Desmond Tutu, who wrote, "I affirm your resolution's condemnation of all violence and your uncompromising commitment to the path of non-violence and inter-religious dialogue. And I commend the resolution's call for accountability from your own, United States, government over its annual $3.1 billion in military aid to Israel."[46] The divestment was expected to "have political consequences in the United States, since the Trinity United Church of Christ in Chicago is the congregation where Barack Obama has worshiped for two decades and he and his children were baptized." The church was accused of being "another powerful Christian group ... waging a war" against the Jews amid claims that "the new Christians' economic warfare is a return to the church of anti-Semitism."[47]

The United Methodist General Board of Pension and Health Benefits sold "its stock in the U.K.-based G4S, which provides equipment and services for Israeli prisons, checkpoints and settlements in the West Bank."

David Wildman, executive secretary for human rights and racial justice at the church's General Board of Global Ministries, said this was the first time they had "included human rights violations related to Israel's illegal settlements and military occupation in a decision to divest from a company" and noted that the move was "part of our efforts at examining how we are approaching human rights issues and the longstanding Israeli occupation and settlements."[48] The board later sold stock in five Israeli banks after deciding to remove its investments from "high risk" areas, including North Korea, Saudi Arabia, Somalia, and Sudan, that "demonstrate[d] a prolonged and systematic pattern of human rights abuses," according to the pension board's website. Despite the broad impact of the decision, Methodist pastor Derek Johnson called the move "unbiblical."[49]

Boycotting and divesting from Israel carry consequences that are not seen in any other justice-oriented stance. The fact that a church's decision not to invest in certain funds can be met with national political repercussions and accusations of a departure from the faith shows how connected the issue of Israel/Palestine is to American culture.

Academic boycotts

Not all boycotts are related to commerce. Stephen Hawking's refusal to attend the Israeli president's conference in 2013 was widely applauded by both academia and the general public. Hawking made it clear that his "refusal was made because of requests from Palestinian academics" in support of the Palestinians harmed by Israel's policies.[50] While Hawking's voice may be the most well-known, his refusal was part of an academic boycott of Israel that was launched by the Palestinian Academic and Cultural Boycott of Israel in 2004 and found support from academics in several countries, including the United Kingdom, France, Australia, Canada, Italy, Ireland, and South Africa. The academic boycott began as a response to "Israel's practice of infringing upon the right to education coincid[ing] with the founding of the first Palestinian university, Birzeit, in 1975."[51]

Marcy Jane Knopf-Newman writes about educational discrimination in Palestine and explains the types of oppression educators face:

> In addition to curricular materials being subjected to Israeli censors—both in terms of intellectual production within Palestine and what sorts of

academic materials may be imported—Palestinian students, faculty, and academic institutions have been under siege. In the West Bank, this began when Birzeit's founding president, Dr. Hanna Nasir, was arrested and deported to Lebanon in 1974. It continued with the closing of all Palestinian universities, schools, and kindergartens during the first intifada in 1987.... Between 1988 and 1992, all universities remained closed, and Palestinian education was pushed underground into people's homes, mosques, churches, and community centers, which were repeatedly raided and during which people were arrested. Since 1992 when Birzeit and other universities were allowed to reopen, Palestinians still found themselves struggling to arrive at their educational institutions as a result of curfews, closures, checkpoints, and Jewish-only roads throughout the West Bank. More recently, since the start of the second intifada, Palestinian academic institutions have become military targets as "eight universities and over three hundred schools have been shelled, shot at or raided by the Israeli Army."[52]

The boycott had little effect in the United States at its inception but, as with many facets of the Palestinian issue, gained traction over time. In 2009, for the first time, a group of professors announced its embrace of the boycott. The U.S. Campaign for the Academic & Cultural Boycott of Israel released a statement that read, "As educators of conscience, we have been unable to stand by and watch in silence Israel's indiscriminate assault on the Gaza Strip and its educational institutions."[53] In 2013 both the Association for Asian American Studies and the American Studies Association (ASA) voted to participate; at the time "more than 200 American universities and six major U.S. academic organizations [had] announced their opposition to the boycott." The move was not without pushback. Sixty-nine Democrats and sixty-five Republicans from the U.S. House of Representatives signed a letter to the president of the ASA, denouncing the ban and stating that they "cannot tolerate these ignorant smear campaigns to isolate Israel and deteriorate the historic U.S.-Israel relationship," calling it "thinly veiled bigotry and bias against the Jewish state."[54]

Not long after, the Native American and Indigenous Studies Association voted unanimously to support a boycott of Israeli academic institutions. Its council released a statement stressing that "the boycott is directed against 'the Israeli state, not at Israeli individuals,'" and urging members "to boycott Israeli academic institutions because they are imbricated with the

Israeli state, and we wish to place pressure on that state to change its policies."⁵⁵ At an annual business meeting, members of the American Anthropological Association (AAA) also voted in favor of a resolution calling on the group to boycott Israeli academic institutions. The group had recently "defeated an alternative, antiboycott resolution pushed by a group of Israeli and North American academics that calls itself Anthropologists for Dialogue on Israel/Palestine. The text of that resolution ... called for an end to the occupation while also rejecting boycott in favor of strengthened 'anthropological engagement with Palestine and Israel.'"⁵⁶ However, the resolution was narrowly defeated the following June at the AAA general meeting. Despite this, the organization planned to issue a statement of censure of the Israeli treatment of Palestinians, write to the U.S. government, and work to actively support Palestinian and Israeli academics. "The consensus within the AAA remains and that is that there are serious human rights problems that exist in Israel/Palestine as a result of Israeli state policy, practices and the occupation and that AAA must take a course of action," said a spokesperson.⁵⁷

Members of the Middle East Studies Association (MESA) voted in early 2022 to ratify a resolution endorsing BDS. MESA is the largest Middle East academic body in North America. Its members voted 768–167 to ratify the resolution, and MESA president Eve Troutt Powell issued a statement saying, "Our members have cast a clear vote to answer the call for solidarity from Palestinian scholars and students experiencing violations of their right to education and other human rights. MESA's Board will work to honor the will of its members and ensure that the call for an academic boycott is upheld without undermining our commitment to the free exchange of ideas and scholarship."⁵⁸ This vote was unsurprising given the opinions of scholars in the association. In March 2021 the University of Maryland conducted its "Middle East Scholars Barometer" survey and found that 60 percent of academics surveyed use the word "apartheid" to describe the situation in Mandatory Palestine.⁵⁹

Many academic organizations have resisted participation in the academic boycott, including some with histories of solidarity with causes that are similar. In 2013 David Lloyd of UC Riverside and Malini Johar Schueller of the University of Florida wrote an open letter to the American Association of University Professors, which was published in the association's journal. In it they demanded to know why the AAUP had not endorsed the campaign, citing its boycott of South Africa during the apartheid years. They noted that "public officials and academics who have critiqued Israel have faced campaigns of distortion, intimidation, threats of termination, and denial or loss of tenure. While Norman Finkelstein's may be the best-known academic case, campaigns have also targeted scholars like Nadia Abu El Haj, Sami Al-Arian, David Shorter, and David Klein, in direct attempts to restrict their freedom of speech." This in itself is a form of boycott, of those who support Palestine. Lloyd and Schueller ended their letter with a passionate plea: "If academic freedom is, indeed, a universal value, not one restricted to a few who are privileged by geography and colonial histories, then the Palestinian call for an academic and cultural boycott of Israel becomes, as South Africa was in the 1980s, a test case for our intellectual and moral consistency. If we or the AAUP refuse to endorse that call, then the commitment to academic freedom becomes vacuous and meaningless, an assertion of privilege and entitlement, not of fundamental values."[60]

Boycott organizers emphasize that the censure is to be directed at institutions, not individuals, but detractors claim bigotry and prejudice. Some go so far as to invoke patently false motives for the movement. Martin Kramer, for example, argued in his essay "The Unspoken Purpose of the Academic Boycott" in 2021 that the boycott "is actually meant to isolate and stigmatise Jewish academics in America. It serves the aim of pushing Jewish academics out of shrinking disciplines, where Jews are believed to be 'over-represented.'"[61]

This conflation of Judaism and the state of Israel is a common rebuttal against BDS and those who choose to boycott Israel academically, culturally, or in the marketplace. It is important to understand that the purpose of the boycott is not to minimize the contributions of Jewish academics, or to undermine Jewish safety and security. It is to increase knowledge of the Palestinian struggle and to encourage support for equal rights and treatment of Palestinians living in Occupied Palestine and within the state of Israel. While the majority of Israelis are Jewish, and Israel is considered a Jewish state, these are mere coincidences. It is not Judaism that is protested, but the treatment of Palestinians by a government that has power over them.

Another objection to BDS was raised by Evan Gerstmann, a professor at Loyola Marymount University, who claimed that the boycott was hypocritical. His essay is specifically about California's Pitzer College, where faculty voted to suspend a study-abroad program in Israel. Stunningly,

Gerstmann does not deny that Israel occupies Palestine. In fact he writes, "It is certainly true that Israel occupies the West Bank." He then goes on to compare the occupation of the West Bank with Chinese occupation of Tibet, quoting the Dalai Lama as saying "that the Chinese occupation of Tibet has produced a 'Hell on Earth.'" His claim is that if Pitzer College is going to boycott Israel, it ought to boycott China as well, since the two countries are engaged in the same activities. He does not seem to recognize that his comparison is an open acknowledgment of the atrocities carried out against Palestinians by the Israeli government. Instead, he deflects, pointing out other countries that also violate human rights and claiming that Israel ought to get a pass. "A boycott of Israel while maintaining [study abroad programs] in other nations with poor human rights records . . . is a clear statement that Israel is the worst of the worst, despite the fact that this is obviously not true."[62]

Cultural boycotts

Hawking is not the only prominent figure to turn down invitations to visit Israel, nor are the educators who joined the boycott the first to be reprimanded or publicly called out for their participation. Multiple celebrities have chosen to take part in a cultural boycott of the country and not perform there. Examples include Elvis Costello, Roger Waters, Brian Eno, Annie Lennox, and Mike Leigh.[63] Popular singer Lorde canceled a planned show in Tel Aviv in June 2017, saying, "I have done a lot of reading and sought a lot of opinions before deciding to book a show in Tel Aviv, but I'm not proud to admit I didn't make the right call on this one." In response, Rabbi Shmuley Boteach took out a full-page ad in the *Washington Post* criticizing Lorde.[64] It reads, in part, "21 is young to become a bigot,"[65] and continues, "let's boycott the boycotters and tell Lorde and her fellow bigots that Jew-hatred has no place in the twenty-first century."[66] Boteach also used her boycott, and the activism of Roger Waters, in an end-of-year campaign in 2017 to raise money for his nonprofit, the World Values Network, an organization "committed to advancing a vision of Judaism as a light to the nations and ensuring that America benefits from the core values of the Jewish people."[67] The campaign raised over $27,000 but also drew negative comments, such as, "stop acting like savages and start acting like human beings and there wouldn't be a boycott. . . . You just want free money, this is ridiculous and you truly are nauseating," and "could you be any more disgusting occupying another people's land, committing mass murder and you attack people for finally taking a stand, you colonists are deluded."[68] This interaction between a singer, a rabbi, a newspaper, and the public encapsulates the high tension and rising emotions surrounding the Israel/Palestine debate.

It is also an early example of the lengths to which Israel will go to discourage dissent and solidify its own position. Lorde's decision to withdraw was due in part to a letter sent to her by Jewish New Zealander Justine Sachs and Palestinian New Zealander Nadia Abu-Shanab, asking her not to perform. The women wrote, "Our part in movements for justice and equality shouldn't just be a memory that gathers dust. We can play an important role in challenging injustice today."[69] A month after the announcement, three Israeli Lorde fans sued Sachs and Abu-Shanab, seeking 45,000 shekels ($13,000) in damages for the "terrible disappointment from the cancellation of the appearance" that they say was caused by the activists' inciting of Lorde. While this may seem like a frivolous lawsuit, it carried larger implications. The fans were represented by Shurat Hadin, a right-wing legal organization. Darshan Leitner, who heads the organization, sued Sachs and Abu-Shanab for violating Israel's Boycott Law, passed in 2011. The suit was the "first time tort liability will be imposed on someone who called to boycott the State of Israel," she said. "We are representing the girls with the aim of battling those who call to boycott the State of Israel and to deter those who seek to do so in the future."[70] In October 2018 Judge Mirit Fohrer ruled in favor of Leitner and the three teenaged fans, ordering the New Zealand women to pay damages, citing the girls' "artistic welfare."[71] This was the first effective use of the Israeli law that allows civil lawsuits of anyone who encourages a boycott of Israel.

Palestinian cultural groups called for the boycott of the 2019 edition of international singing contest Eurovision, which was held in Tel Aviv because the 2018 winner, singer Netta, is Israeli. In an open letter, thirty art, culture, and theater groups asked "for people of conscience around the world to heed our call for boycott, divestment and sanctions of Apartheid Israel just as they did to help bring down Apartheid in South Africa." They also announced plans to host "Gazavision, a festival of Palestinian songs and music held while surrounded by the most brutal and well-equipped army in the Middle East. Even when Israel bombs us, imprisons our men, women and children, kills and maims thousands of Palestinian protesters on the Great Return March and does everything to silence our voices, we will continue to sing."[72] The Palestinians were supported by 141 artists from around the world who stated in an open letter: "We, the undersigned artists from Europe and beyond, support the heartfelt appeal from Palestinian artists to boycott the Eurovision Song Contest 2019 hosted by Israel. Until Palestinians can enjoy freedom, justice and equal rights, there should be no business-as-usual with the state that is denying them their basic rights."[73]

Some artists agreed and boycotted the show. Others expressed their solidarity in other ways. Heavy metal band Hatari was Iceland's entry to the competition. They chose to perform but held up a Palestinian flag during their appearance on the show. Madonna also performed, and two of her dancers, one with an Israeli and one with a Palestinian flag on their backs, walked off the stage arm in arm. "Let's never underestimate the power of music to bring people together," she remarked.[74] The European Broadcasting Union (EBU) chastised both groups, saying, "The Eurovision Song Contest is a non-political event and this directly contradicts the contest rules."[75] While Madonna's act went unpunished, the Icelandic Broadcasting Union was fined 5,000 euros for Hatari's actions, and the EBU described the group as an "anti-capitalist, BDSM, techno-dystopian, performance art collective."[76] Hatari also received criticism from the Palestinian Campaign for the Academic and Cultural Boycott of Israel, who said, "Palestinian civil society overwhelmingly rejects fig-leaf gestures of solidarity from international artists crossing our peaceful picket line."[77]

Singer Lana Del Rey pulled out of another multi-artist event, a music festival held on a kibbutz in northern Israel in September 2018. She cited the fact that most Palestinians would not be allowed to attend as her reason for not attending. The Palestine Campaign for the Academic and Cultural Boycott of Israel applauded her decision in a tweet.[78] Other artists felt their presence did not equal support for Israel and insisted that their performing did not mean they endorse the Israeli government. Radiohead front man Thom Yorke defended his decision to perform in Tel Aviv, saying, "Playing in a country isn't the same as endorsing its government. . . . We don't endorse Netanyahu any more than Trump, but we still play in America."[79]

The seventieth Miss Universe Pageant was held in Eilat, Israel, in 2021, despite calls for a boycott. Miss Universe president Paula Shugart "has said

Israel has been on the shortlist of host countries 'due to its rich history, beautiful landscapes, myriad of cultures and appeal as a global tourist destination.'"[80] That this "rich history" includes four thousand years of Arab and Palestinian culture, art, technology, and religion was not mentioned. Andrea Meza, chosen Miss Universe in 2020, agreed with the decision to hold the contest in Israel and stated that the pageant shouldn't be politicized, insisting that the contest was about multiculturalism and supporting women. Some countries, however, saw the decision as supportive of an oppressive regime. Notably, the South African government withdrew its support for their national Miss Universe contest due to its decision to send a contestant, saying, "The atrocities committed by Israel against Palestinians are well documented," and adding that it "refuses to associate itself with the 70th annual Miss Universe pageant."[81] Malaysia also declined to participate, though it cited concerns regarding COVID. Both countries have been supportive of Palestine.

The Burning Man Project, which serves as the umbrella organization for events around the world, recently called for organizers of a similar event in Occupied Palestine to cancel their planned festivities. While Burning Man does have an affiliate, Midburn, that has hosted events in the Naqab (Negev) desert, it is not officially affiliated with Dead Sea Burn, the group that organized the festival in question. Yaron Ben-Shoshan, the organizer of Dead Sea Burn, is a member of the Burning Man community and planned to follow the ten principles that encapsulate the community's code. He claims that he sees a "world with borders, with(out) lines between people," but his choice to host the event in Jericho, which is under Israeli occupation, is not in line with Burning Man's policy of "radical inclusion." Because of this, the Burning Man community has taken steps to distance themselves from the event and urged participants to boycott it. Their actions forced the project to be renamed Dead Sea Reborn.[82]

By May 2021 six hundred American musicians, including Rage Against the Machine, Julian Casablancas, the lead singer and primary songwriter of rock band The Strokes, members of Cypress Hill, Patti Smith, and Serj Tankian, had signed an open letter pledging to support BDS by not performing in Israel. The effort was part of a campaign called Musicians for Palestine. "As musicians, we cannot be silent. Today it is essential that we stand with Palestine. We are calling on our peers to publicly assert their solidarity with the Palestinian people. Complicity with Israeli war crimes is found in silence, and today silence is not an option," the letter reads. At the same time, more than a thousand Canadian artists "put out an open statement and asked the Ottawa government to impose military and economic sanctions on Israel and 'to end its complicity in the oppression of Palestinians.'" Rehab Nazzal, a pro-Palestinian activist, said that supporters of the statement came from many different art fields including "curators; media and visual artists; filmmakers; workers in art organizations and artist-run centers; independent artists; musicians; researchers and art scholars; and other cultural workers."[83]

Protests and boycotts after October 2023

The climate surrounding pro-Palestinian activism and protest has fundamentally changed since October 7, 2023, and pro-Palestinian activism has increased around the world. Since the beginning of Israel's war against Gazans, thousands of demonstrators have gathered around the world. Outside the White House, demonstrators held signs that read "No votes for Genocide Joe" and "Let Gaza live." In London, "Little Amal," an 11.5-foot-tall puppet made to represent a refugee child, marched through the streets, accompanying protestors. The puppet was created in 2001 to highlight the plight of Syrian refugees and has become a human rights emblem. Additional marches and protests were held in Paris, Rome, Milan, and Dublin.[84] Some 1,400 Finnish musicians signed a petition requesting that Eurovision, a televised European music festival, exclude Israel from the 2024 competition. The petition further urges organizers to withdraw Finland from the competition if Israel remains part of it.[85] The U.S. Embassy in Kuala Lumpur, Malaysia, was the site of another gathering, following action taken by Malaysia's government to prevent Israeli-owned ships from docking in Malaysian ports. Similar events were held outside the U.S. Embassy in Jakarta and the U.S. Consulate in Johannesburg.[86] On January 2, 2024, pro-Palestine protesters briefly interfered with the Rose Bowl Parade route in Pasadena, California, and blocked a road to JFK airport in New York.[87] On January 8 more than a thousand people stopped traffic over several New York bridges during rush hour traffic as the death toll in Gaza reached more than twenty-two thousand.[88] These are only a few examples of the activism that has been rising across the globe.

Calls for boycotting companies that support Israel without taking an even-handed position have also grown. Immediately following the attacks of October 7, Starbucks Workers United, the union representing employees at 350 of the coffee house chain's 9,300 stores, posted its support of Palestine on social media. The tweet was not authorized by the leadership and was quickly taken down, but it sparked protests, boycotts, and a lawsuit filed by Starbucks claiming trademark infringement by the union.[89] The increasingly visible solidarity shown by workers unions for Palestine and the increasingly strong reactions to that stance are examples of the rise in awareness and concern over the issue of Palestine globally and in the United States specifically. McDonald's was also boycotted globally after its Israeli locations reportedly gave away "thousands of free meals to members of the Israeli military."[90] McDonald's corporate office put out a statement denying its support for "any governments involved in the Middle East crisis," which did little to dispel disapproval of the brand.[91]

In November 2023 "hundreds of protestors . . . succeeded in blocking the International Longshore and Warehouse Union, or ILWU, from loading weapons onto a ship" in Tacoma, Washington.[92] The weapons were believed to be bound for Israel. A similar protest in Oakland, California, blocked the loading of weapons onto ships; in this instance longshore workers refused to load the weapons.[93]

Fashion retailer Zara was heavily criticized for its December ad campaign featuring mannequins wrapped in white cloth and white powder sprinkled on the floor, images that brought to mind dead Palestinians and phosphorus powder. While the campaign was developed and photographed before the onset of the war, its release in December was seen as insensitive and sparked protests at stores as far from Gaza as Tunisia and Germany. The company pulled the ads, apologizing that "some customers felt offended" by the visuals.[94] In 2021 the company was tied to the conflict when it was forced to condemn Vanessa Perilman, one of its head designers, for sending a public social media post to a Palestinian model, which read in part "maybe if your people were educated then they wouldn't blow up hospitals and schools."[95]

While historically most activism on behalf of Palestinians has been confined to minority communities, universities, and a few politicians, current and growing Palestinian solidarity, among young people particularly, in response to the violence in Gaza has pushed the issue to the forefront. During the first days after the October 7 Hamas attack, most protests were in support of Israel, but as time went on, sympathy for the Palestinian cause has grown. According to the Crowd Counting Consortium, as of

November 28, 2023, there had been 1,869 protests in the United States on behalf of Palestinians, with hundreds of thousands of participants.[96] *Haaretz* reported on December 5 that more than one million Americans had participated in protests and vigils in response to the war.[97] Corey Robin, a political scientist from Brooklyn College, noted the change in the willingness of individuals who are not Jewish or Arab to engage in protest.[98]

The rise in activism is not mirrored by political representatives. While one in four pro-Israel demonstrations have been attended by an elected official, only 1 percent of Palestinian protests have. Instead, some leaders have criticized pro-Palestinian protests as anti-Semitic and have tried to create unity around support of Israel, but, as Robin noted, "the opposition and discontent is just that much greater." The issue was significant enough that it became an early concern for President Biden's 2024 re-election campaign. In January 2024, Kenichi Serino at PBS NewsHour reported that "79 percent of Democrats approve of the job Biden is doing as president in general," but "that number drops to 60 percent when asked about his role in the war between Israel and Hamas."[99] During a campaign speech at a South Carolina church that was the site of a shooting in 2015, Biden was interrupted by protestors who insisted, "If you really care about the lives lost here, then you should honor the lives and call for a cease-fire in Palestine."[100] Frustration with President Biden's reaction to the violence rose among Muslim Americans, who tended to support Biden in the 2020 election. Hammad Chaudhry, a second-generation Pakistani American who has organized several pro-Palestinian demonstrations, told the *Washington Post* in December 2023 that he saw Muslim support for Biden wane during the war. "I think young Muslims ideally would want to vote for Biden, but they feel like Biden isn't hearing what they have to say and it's kind of wearing them down," Chaudhry explained to reporters Tim Craig and Clara Ence Morse. "So, they feel they have no option but to withdraw their support."[101]

During the War on Gaza, Arab American democratic leaders Michigan urged a vote of "uncommitted" in the Michigan primaries to send a message to the Biden administration over its support of Israel and for not supporting a ceasefire as the death doll of Palestinians reached tens of thousands, despite declining of support for his policies.[102]

Chaudhry helped organize demonstrations at Appalachian State University in North Carolina, and is one of many Muslims in rural areas and small towns who have become more politically active about Palestine.

Asmmaa Zaitar, a student at the University of Alabama, is another. "People now know there is a Palestinian voice in this city," she told Craig and Morse. "Everyone has a voice and can say whatever feels right and fight back using our voice." The rise of these voices, which "Muslim scholars said would have been unthinkable just a decade or so ago," has been made possible by the spread of Muslims throughout the United States, and the rise of a new generation of Muslims who feel more confident in both their Muslim and American identities.[103]

New York mayor Eric Adams condemned the protests, saying "I have been extremely clear—it gives us all pain to see innocent lives being lost right now. We need to do everything that is possible to end anything that is going to take the lives of innocent people. But Hamas must be destroyed. They are a terrorist organization. Their barbaric act on October 7 should not be ignored."[104]

Although many protesters said they do not support Hamas but "do not believe Israel's response has been proportional and argue their demonstrations are designed to showcase how Palestinian civilians are now swept up in the conflict," their activism has been met on many occasions with accusations of anti-Semitism and "hate-filled heckling." At the University of Alabama, vehicles circled the demonstrators, who were called rapists.[105] After an early demonstration in New York City, *Newsweek* reported that "New York Democratic Rep. Ritchie Torres wrote on X . . . that the protest was glorifying Hamas violence against Israel. 'The NYC-DSA [New York City Democratic Socialists of America] is revealing itself for what it truly is: an antisemitic stain on the soul of America's largest city. There is a special place in hell for those who glorify the cold-blooded murder of civilians and children.'"[106] The conflation of support for Palestine and approval of Hamas has been ubiquitous.

Supporters of Palestine face other repercussions as well. After a number of Harvard student organizations signed their support for an open letter that began, "Today's events did not occur in a vacuum" and outlined the wider circumstances in Palestine to highlight the origin of the conflict, calls were made on social media for the names of students involved to be released. The advocacy group Palestine Legal and lawyers at the Council on American-Islamic Relations have noticed steep increases in the number of reports of firings over political speech. In one high-profile example, Ryna Workman, the former president of the Student Bar Association at the NYU

School of Law, had a job offer rescinded after expressing solidarity with the Palestinian people. Law students at Harvard and Columbia also reported having their employment offers revoked after signing statements of solidarity. More than 150 corporations have put out statements of solidarity with Israel, a sign that pro-Palestinian speech or activism may be seen as in opposition to company values, creating an environment in which, as employment lawyer Peter Goselin told journalist Angelina Chapin of *The Cut*, "a difference of opinion is somehow being coded as hate speech." Amr Shabaik, the legal and policy director at CAIR's L.A. office, explained to Chapin that "antisemitism is a very real thing that should be condemned and called out," but also cautioned that "there is a very real and palpable environment of fear and intimidation when it comes to speaking up about Palestine in the workplace."[107]

PALESTINIAN SOLIDARITY IN POPULAR CULTURE

As the BDS movement gains traction among church leadership, academics, and celebrities, it becomes more visible to the general public. This results in both more support by those receiving new information and more pushback from those interested in maintaining the status quo. It also influences the ways in which Palestinians and Israelis are portrayed. Pop culture has an enormous influence on public perception, and recent years have seen a surge in activism from celebrities, both in support of Israel and in support of Palestine, yet it is frequently those standing up for Palestinians who are censured.

Imagine a well-known Jewish actress dressed up as Hitler and posing for a photo in which she is seen taking a tray of people-shaped cookies out of an oven. One would think that such an occurrence would draw the ire of media commentators around the world for its blatant racist, anti-Semitic, and anti-Arab representation, yet this was not the case. That actress is not hypothetical: the incident took place in 2009, when Roseanne Barr, who identifies as Jewish, posed for the offensive photos for *Heeb* magazine (the original article and photos were subsequently taken down). In an *ABC Nightline* interview in 2011, Barr is quoted saying that the cookies were not symbolic of Jews, but of Palestinians.[108] It is unclear how this clarification made the situation better, but it was certainly in line with public perception. Despite the photos, and despite the "clarifying" comments made in the interview, Barr suffered no consequences career-wise. ABC rewarded her with a reboot of *Roseanne* in 2017—a reboot that was ultimately canceled after she tweeted Islamophobic and racist language about a former Obama aide.

Barr is not the first nor the last individual to exhibit anti-Arab, and specifically anti-Palestinian, racism in such a public context. Such forms of racism are routinely expressed by politicians and reiterated by the media, with little to no consequences for the people who express those discriminatory sentiments. Being anti-Arab, especially anti-Palestinian, is one of the few forms of racism that does not draw immediate outrage and scorn—partly because Arabs, and Palestinians especially, have become so racialized and dehumanized by rhetoric that they are viewed as less deserving of basic empathy.

While Barr may not have suffered consequences for denigrating Palestinians, plenty of celebrities and organizations have faced repercussions for supporting them. Actress and director Natalie Portman, who was born in Israel and speaks fluent Hebrew, turned down the prestigious Israeli Genesis Prize in 2018. Her refusal to accept the award was a strong statement against the Israeli treatment of Palestinians, especially given her vocal support of Israel in the past. Her statement that "the mistreatment of those suffering from today's atrocities is simply not in line with my Jewish values" is an example of the way that younger Jewish people are more critical of Israel's actions than their parents' generation. Portman received backlash over her remarks from many, including Israeli Parliament member Oren Hazan, who called for her citizenship to be stripped, and Energy Minister Yuval Steinitz, who said her remarks had "elements of anti-Semitism." The controversy is not a minor one; instead, as *Vox* journalist Zach Beauchamp wrote, it can be understood as a "leading indicator of the rising tensions between liberal American Jewry and the increasingly right-wing Israeli government."[109]

Pink Floyd front man Roger Waters has been outspoken in his support for Palestine and has drawn criticism for it. Pro-Israel protestors held signs outside Madison Square Garden in New York on a warm August night in 2022 to protest his political opinions, urging concert-goers not to attend. Waters, who has condemned the violence perpetrated against the Palestinian people, did not engage with the protestors or even speak much during the concert, preferring to spread his message through his music and the

SOCIAL CHANGE AND SOUND BITES

multimedia presentation of the concert itself. At one point, the name of slain journalist Shireen Abu Akleh was projected on enormous screens behind the band. The names of other victims of violence, including Eric Garner, Philando Castile, and George Floyd, were also displayed as Waters made the connection between the treatment of Palestinians and the treatment of African Americans in the United States.[110] Waters is undeterred by criticism. He was the narrator for the documentary film *Occupation of the American Mind* in 2016 and has criticized Britain's Labour Party, saying, "Fifty years people have been in the labour party defending the working class and defending human rights all over the world irrespective of people's race, religion, nationality. Are they allowed to defend the Palestinians? No no. That's where we draw the line."[111]

Jewish American comedian and longtime *Daily Show* host Jon Stewart is known for standing up to stereotypical messaging regarding Israel and Palestine. Palestinian American comedian Amer Zahr wrote that Stewart had "become a bit of a hero to us Palestinians over the years."[112] Stewart often used his platform as a popular late-night show to highlight the way American media portrayed the issue and to express compassion for Palestinians, leading to criticism from some. His segment on Israel's bombing of Gaza in 2014 received a response from *Times of Israel* journalist David Horovitz, who said Stewart had misrepresented Israel. "But hey, it is funny," he said, "and all those millions of Americans who watched it on Monday know that it's just satire, don't they?"[113] Radio host Mark Levin went on the Sean Hannity show and called Stewart "a clown" and his criticism of Israel "putrid."[114] Stewart, who generally takes criticism in stride, including accusations of being a self-hating Jew, was quoted as saying, "I've made a living for sixteen years criticizing certain policies that I think are not good for America. That doesn't make me anti-American. And if I do the same with Israel, that doesn't make me anti-Israel."[115] Trevor Noah, who took over the *Daily Show* when Stewart retired, continued to make the Israel/Palestine issue a subject of discussion. On an episode filmed in May 2021, he compared Israel and Palestine to a teenager fighting a child, saying, "If you are in a fight where the other person cannot beat you, how hard should you retaliate when they try to hurt you?" That remark, along with others he made about the complexities of the conflict, was written up in *Vanity Fair*.[116]

Other celebrities may have been encouraged by Stewart to express their feelings regarding the crisis. Comedian Dean Obeidallah wrote in

2017 that he sees Stewart's influence "in the reactions of certain celebrities and in an increasing number of college students."[117] The actor John Cusack has tweeted in support of Palestinian rights regularly since the 2014 Gaza War.[118] That same year, pop star Rihanna and NBA player Dwight Howard both tweeted "Free Palestine."[119] The New York Knicks' Amare Stoudemire, who holds Jewish heritage, tweeted a photo that read: "Pray for Palestine."[120] All three eventually deleted those tweets, perhaps bowing to popular pressure. Actress and singer Selena Gomez did not delete her 2014 Instagram post that read "It's About Humanity: Pray for Gaza" with the caption, "Please pray for those families and babies today. Please always remember what's important in life. It's not any of this. We are here to help, inspire and love. Be that change."[121] This seemingly innocuous post drew the ire of Israel supporters and inspired *TMZ* to claim that Gomez was "either directly or indirectly supporting Hamas in the Middle-East conflict."[122]

Activism and its repercussions are not limited to actors and musicians. In 2016 the Union for European Football Associations (UEFA) fined the team Celtic 8,616 British pounds after their fans flew Palestinian flags before and after a match against Hapoel Be'er Sheva in a Champions League qualifier. The team had previously been fined eight times in five seasons for similar "offenses." After the fine was levied, fans of the club launched an online fundraising campaign that raised $100,000 for pro-Palestinian causes.[123] UEFA did not, however, fine players or fans for flying the flag of Ukraine at several matches during the 2022 season. The reason given was that UEFA rules prohibit the display of "provocative" banners, and the Ukrainian flag was not seen as provocative, while the Palestinian flag was. UEFA has ruled previously that certain "banners," such as a rainbow flag for LGBTQ rights, were allowed because they promote "good causes." This leaves UEFA "open to the charge of being subjective with their use of football 'good causes'" one of which, it has apparently decided, the Palestinian cause is not.[124]

Social media activists called for the wearing of armbands with Palestinian colors ahead of the 2022 FIFA World Cup, to be held in Qatar. The call was in response to both the actions by FIFA to limit the wearing of Palestinian flags and emblems and its support of players who wear Ukrainian armbands in response to the Russian invasion of Ukraine. FIFA appeared to sanction Russia "after Moscow's military operation in Ukraine as, during many games, banners were held to condemn Russia." The double standard FIFA has shown in which political stances it considers unacceptable

SOCIAL CHANGE AND SOUND BITES

is being called out by those sharing an Arabic hashtag that translates as "the captain's armband is Palestinian."[125]

Support for Palestinian causes is evident on social media, where accounts that post pro-Palestine content amass huge followings. Africa 4 Palestine is a human rights organization founded in 2009 under the name "BDS Africa" that provides support for Palestinians and their allies and education regarding the occupation of Palestine. Working out of its base in Johannesburg, it is the most active pro-Palestinian organization in the world.[126] It maintains an Instagram profile with more than forty-five thousand followers,[127] and it had a TikTok account with well over one million views before being dismantled. A video shared on the organization's Instagram account was a recording of Vanessa Redgrave's Oscar speech after her win for the movie *Julia* in 1978. In it, she praised the Palestinian people and decried all forms of anti-Semitism and fascism. The post received nearly two thousand likes in its first day.[128] Incidentally, Redgrave also produced and starred in the controversial film *The Palestinian* in 1977 and remains an activist to this day.[129]

The Israeli government has taken an active role in influencing the way celebrities talk about the Palestine and Israel. The Face of Israel, a "nongovernmental public diplomacy firm," was established in 2013 and exists to form relationships with influential people around the world and "better acquaint them with Israel" through trips and other means. Chanan Elias, who directs the organization's North American branch, said the organization was growing quickly and had "hosted 40 groups in its first year and 98.9% of the time, they walk away with a great impression."[130] The organization receives funding from the Foreign Ministry and private donors and works closely with the Tourism Ministry. One of the tools the organization uses to foster these relationships is free trips to Israel. One such trip in 2014 included celebrities Steve Byrne, Jamie Chung, Bryan Greenburg, and Bobby Lee. In 2022 a video surfaced of Lee being interviewed about the trip. He described being approached by representatives of Israel and invited on a free, first-class trip to see the country. "But it wasn't free," he said. "You have to every day tweet positive things about Israel" and tag the Israeli government in the posts. Lee admitted feeling uneasy over the requirement given the ongoing violations of Palestinian rights. "I wish I hadn't gone, really."[131]

"[Israel's message] must be repeated ad infinitum until the people get it."[132] This was the message sent by lawyer and producer Glenn D. Feig in an email to a group of Hollywood executives in 2014. The email was one of multiple documents published by WikiLeaks exposing the active role some in Hollywood have taken to spread pro-Israel messaging. Around the same time, producer Ron Rotholz called out Penelope Cruz and Javier Bardem for their condemnation of the bombing of Gaza in 2014 that prompted the email. "Change must start from the top down. It should be unheard of and unacceptable for any Academy Award–winning actor to call the legitimate armed defense of one's territory . . . genocide," he wrote, before expressing his concern over increased participation in BDS in the United States. Ryan Kavanaugh, CEO of Relativity Media, and Ben Silverman, former cochair of NBC Entertainment and Universal Media Studios, called for a boycott of director Ken Loach, who was nominated for a Palme d'Or, and the entire Cannes Film Festival after Loach "publicly called for a cultural and sporting boycott of the apartheid state." "It is no surprise, because apologists for Israel's oppression of the Palestinians will go to any length to prevent the people opposing them," Loach said. "We shouldn't underestimate the hatred of those who cannot tolerate the idea that Palestinians have human rights, that Palestine is a state; and they have their country."[133] Further leaked emails show Hollywood elites communicating with a retired commander in the Israeli Army and planning a documentary to counter *Boycott*, a film about the BDS movement.

Boycott has created controversy in other circles, as well. The film documents three individuals negatively affected by anti-BDS legislation: Bahia Amawi, who lost her job as a school speech pathologist; Mik Jordahl, an Arizona lawyer who had to sign a loyalty pledge in order to remain at his job; and Alan Leveritt, publisher of the *Arkansas Times*, who was told his paper would be "blocked from running any state university advertisements unless they sign an oath to Israel." In the film, Leveritt asserts that he's not even a supporter of the BDS movement but is "concerned about the chilling impact of such laws on the First Amendment." Lawmakers in Arizona from both parties urged their colleagues not to attend a screening of the documentary at the capitol. The memo urged lawmakers not to attend as they were "likely to be documented by anti-Israel and anti-Semitic groups." Democratic state representative Alma Hernandez tweeted, "Don't be fooled. #BDS is a hate movement aimed at demonizing #Israel, asking our colleagues to say no to hate & not attend!"[134]

The film itself is "not terribly political" but includes interviews with lawmakers who voted for anti-BDS legislation. One, Republican Bart Hester, admits in the film that he doesn't understand the bill's implications but "feel[s] like Jewish people are God's chosen people" and "felt an obligation to do anything within my control or power to support them or protect them." In the film, Hester also admits that he didn't consult with "any local Jewish leaders about the bill because they don't agree with him." Journalist Michael Arria reported that Democrat Greg Leding, who voted in favor of the law, told filmmakers, "I regret not knowing more about the issue when I voted and now. After hearing from my constituents, I probably would have voted against it."[135]

Palestinian actors and filmmakers are pushing back. Cherien Dabis, a Palestinian American writer, director, and film-maker, experienced firsthand the discrimination that is endemic for Arab Americans. During the first Gulf War, when she was fourteen, her family received death threats and a Secret Service visit to determine whether her seventeen-year-old sister was planning to kill the president. "I began to study the ways in which we Arabs were dangerously misrepresented, portrayed as villains, terrorists and jihadists—and that's if we were represented at all. There was a complete dearth of any remotely authentic portrayal. I vowed to change that," she said. Her hard work has paid off. Her first feature, *Amreeka*, "was the first Arab American film to get major theatrical distribution, and the most-screened Arab-directed film in U.S. cinema history." Her second feature, *May in the Summer*, "attempted to go even more mainstream, with a romantic comedy that transported audiences to Jordan and shattered stereotypes about Arab and Arab American women."[136] In 2022 she was nominated for an Emmy for her work on *Only Murders in the Building*.[137] Her work has helped break down stereotypes and has given Palestinian Americans a nuanced and positive representation in film.

CULTURAL PRODUCTION, INTELLECTUAL ICONS, AND PALESTINIAN SOLIDARITY

Authors have also taken sides. Bestselling author Sally Rooney declined to sell the rights to her latest novel, *Beautiful World, Where Are You?*, to the Israeli publishing house that did the translations of her first two books, citing her "'solidarity with the Palestinian people' and support of the Boycott, Divestments and Sanctions movement."[138] Rooney also signed the online "Letter Against Apartheid" that calls for "an immediate and unconditional cessation of Israeli violence against Palestinians."[139] Rooney is not the first author to make such a stand: there is a long history of solidarity between the Irish and Palestinians. Pulitzer Prize–winning novelist Alice Walker, who served on a 2011 tribunal in South Africa to consider the situation in Palestine, "refused to allow an Israeli edition of her classic novel *The Color Purple* to be published" in 2012. Walker spoke of the testimony she heard during the tribunal as her reasoning, stating that the situation in Israel was worse than the one she grew up in in segregated America and that many South Africans "felt the Israeli version of these crimes is worse even than what they suffered under the white supremacist regimes that dominated South Africa."[140]

Ta-Nehisi Coates is an author who became widely known in popular culture for his contributions to major publications like the *Atlantic* and his book *Between the World and Me*. He was criticized for saying the state of Israel was given as reparations for the Jewish people and comparing this to his ideas about reparations for Black Americans. In an *Atlantic* article in 2014, Coates pointed to the $7 billion (in today's dollars) that West Germany paid to the nascent state of Israel from 1953 to 1963, a payment that provided the nation with "two-thirds of [its] merchant fleet" and "nearly half of its investment in its railways," as well as allowing it to triple its electrical capacity.[141] Coates points to this act of reparations as paving the way for the Jewish people to regain what had been lost through the actions of the Germans and as having a positive effect on the German people, who were faced to reckon with the damage that had been inflicted on their Jewish population. What Coates missed was the fact that it was the Palestinians who were forced to sacrifice their homes and land for Jewish reparations, and that German money funded that usurpation. Despite this obvious error, Coates's essay was widely lauded and "helped propel him into the national spotlight as a MacArthur Foundation 'genius' and a best-selling author read, among others, by President Barack Obama."[142]

Coates's views on Israel and Palestine have changed since then. He went on a trip in the summer of 2023 to the West Bank and saw the practices of Israeli occupation against Palestinians in the city of al-Khalil (Hebron). In an interview with Democracy Now, he shares that "the most shocking thing about my time over there was how uncomplicated it actually is.... There's no way for me, as an African American, to come back and stand before you, to witness segregation and not say anything about it."[143]

Social media platforms

While social media is frequently used as a way of spreading information and opinions about Israel and Palestine, the platform operators also play a role in the intensification of the cultural conflict, and technology companies often find themselves caught in political conflicts due to their user-based content. Social media and peer-to-peer payment sites have policies and automated reactions in place to curb misinformation and stop terrorism and lawbreaking, but these policies often appear prejudiced against the Palestinian cause. Following violence in Gaza in May 2021, pro-Palestinian users on Facebook and Twitter found their accounts blocked and posts removed. Facebook CEO Mark Zuckerberg sent a top policy executive to meet with Israeli and Palestinian leadership over the issue as Palestinians rallied to leave one-star reviews on app stores in order to damage the company. According to internal documents, Facebook executives designated the incident as "severity 1" and reached out to Apple, Google, and Microsoft to have the bad reviews taken down. Both Twitter and Facebook blamed the censorship on accidents and artificial intelligence and said that accounts and posts were reinstated as soon as the problem was detected, but the Arab Center for the Advancement of Social Media noted that 170 Instagram posts remained offline. 7amleh, Access Now, and other digital rights organizations have spent the past ten years tracking the ways in which the social media presence of Palestinians and those who support them is limited by tech companies.[144]

One way in which social media limits the freedom of Palestinians to post is the automatic blocking of certain hashtags, even when they are not terrorist-aligned. One example is the hashtag #savesheikhjarrah, a reference to the Palestinian neighborhood of Sheikh Jarrah, which, at the time of the hashtag's popularity, was under review by the Israeli Supreme Court for colonization. Both Twitter (now known as X) and Facebook have deactivated the accounts of journalists and, at one point, the Palestinian Quds News Network, then later reactivated them, stating the bans were "accidental." A Palestinian using the term "Zionist" in a post will see that post automatically censored as it is assumed to be anti-Semitic.¹⁴⁵ The name of the al-Aqsa mosque, one of Islam's holiest sites, was also banned when it was mistakenly given the designation Facebook uses for terrorist organizations. The ban drew criticism even from Facebook employees, one of whom noted that "the external perception is the FBI is timely silencing political speech and apologizing later."¹⁴⁶ Employees filed internal complaints. Speaking with Ryan Mac for *Buzzfeed News*, the former head of Facebook policy for the Middle East and North Africa, Ashraf Zeitoon, noted that

> the company employed some of the top terrorism experts in the world who could surely distinguish mentions of Al-Aqsa from the Al-Aqsa Martyrs' Brigades. "For them to go and identify one word of a two-word name as associated with a terrorist organization is a lame excuse," he said, noting that he was involved in drafting policies on how the company designated terrorist groups and their content. "They are more qualified than this and more competent than this." Zeitoon cited an internal fear at Facebook of upsetting Israeli interests and overreporting of the content as potential reasons why the Al-Aqsa videos and images were removed.¹⁴⁷

Bella Hadid, the Palestinian American model, spoke out after Instagram deleted a picture she posted of her father's Palestinian passport in 2020; the platform "said it violated 'community guidelines on harassment or bullying' and noted the platform doesn't allow 'hate speech.'"¹⁴⁸ "Are we not allowed to be Palestinian on Instagram?" Hadid responded. The social media platform claimed they do not allow images that contain sensitive or identifying information, but Hadid stated the passport number in the photo was blurred, which places it in compliance with guidelines. Around the same time, an Instagram search by the reporter Arwa Mahdawi for *The Guardian* found "multiple posts that should, according to the guidelines, have been removed." Instagram maintains the deletion was an error.

Facebook is also under scrutiny for its relationship with the Israeli government after they "agreed to work together to determine how to tackle incitement on the social media network." The announcement came after Facebook officials met with government ministers in Israel to discuss legislation the government was bringing forward to curb "content that Israel says incites violence." Interior Minister Gilad Erdan and Justice Minister Ayelet Shaked "proposed legislation that seeks to force social networks to remove content that Israel considers to be incitement." The law may have been unnecessary, given the relationship between the Israeli government and the social media company which, according to Shaked, granted some 95 percent of the requests made by the government to remove material.[149]

In September 2022 a report that Meta had commissioned to determine whether its platforms had been discriminatory was released. The report found that "Meta's actions in May 2021 appear to have had an adverse human rights impact . . . on the rights of Palestinian users to freedom of expression, freedom of assembly, political participation, and non-discrimination, and therefore on the ability of Palestinians to share information and insights about their experiences as they occurred." The report indicates that Meta did not intentionally discriminate against Arab users but suffers from a lack of manpower, with few employees who speak the Palestinian dialect or understand the culture. This, and the machine-learning programs used to flag and block posts, lead to unintentional bias, the result of cultural ignorance and apathy. However, Meta depends on "an 'Arabic hostile speech classifier' that uses machine learning to flag potential policy violations and has no Hebrew equivalent" and utilizes a list of "Dangerous Organizations and Individuals" that "focuses mostly on Muslim and Middle Eastern entities."[150]

Social media sites are not the only ones involving themselves in political determination. Google has been accused of not updating maps of Gaza and the West Bank with current, high-resolution images. These images would show the destruction of Palestinian neighborhoods after Israeli airstrikes. When asked to comment on the delay, Google declined to give a reason. Payment app Venmo at one point suspended transactions of humanitarian aid to Palestinians. The company said it was trying to comply with U.S. sanctions and had resolved the issue.[151] Amazon came under fire for offering free shipping to Israeli addresses but charging up to $24 to ship to addresses within Palestine.[152]

When social media posts about Palestine are allowed to remain, Palestinians are able to creatively share their experiences. One example is a parody tourist ad put out by In Context in November 2022. The ad sarcastically touted Israel as a world-class tourist destination, offering stays in illegal Israeli settlements and Jeep tours through "the largest open air prison in the world." It concludes with the tagline, "Visit Israel, the last apartheid on earth!"[153]

JOURNALISM AND PALESTINE

It doesn't sound like propaganda. It just sounds like news.

—SUT JHALLY, IN *THE OCCUPATION OF THE AMERICAN MIND*

The state of Israel has, since the 1960s, established an incredibly powerful and effective information campaign to manage the way the world, and particularly the United States, sees it and interprets its actions. It seeks to reframe the way the Palestine/Israel is spoken of, with all Palestinian resistance framed as terrorism and all Israeli violence framed as defense, a tactic that has been successful particularly in the American media. Americans, whose government has had a vested interest in the success of Israel since 1967 as part of the American cold-war interest, are more likely than anyone else to stand in solidarity with Israelis, seeing them as the "good guys" and Arabs and Palestinians as "bad guys," a concept already discussed at length in this book. Benjamin Netanyahu himself speaks to this framework when he says, "I think Americans largely get it. They know who the good guys are and who the bad guys are."[154] For decades, Israel has insisted that all its actions are for defense, including its occupation and settlement of the West Bank and Gaza. As American journalist Norman Solomon notes, "The conventional wisdom is that continuing the occupation makes Israel more secure. And if you buy that argument, then it's a license to occupy indefinitely."[155]

Then, in 1982, the Israeli government attacked members of the Palestinian Liberation Organization living in Lebanon, sending their military fifty miles north of the border of Lebanon and Israel, in an obvious act of aggression. Where up to this point Israel had claimed all its military endeavors were efforts at self-defense, the attacks in Lebanon that left seventeen thousand Lebanese and Palestinians, mostly civilians, dead were seen as antagonistic by world powers. Then, in September of the same year, a militia of one of the Lebanese factions slaughtered as many as thirty-five hundred Lebanese civilians and Palestinian refugees in the Sabra neighborhood and adjacent Shatila Palestinian refugee camp, both of which were under the control of the Israeli military and the command of Ariel Sharon. Though informed of the atrocities being committed, the Israeli military allowed the slaughter to take place and took no action to stop the militia. The military was later found to be responsible for the massacre under international law.[156]

SOCIAL CHANGE AND SOUND BITES

These events challenged the narrative that Israeli violence was always in self-defense and assumed to be justified, while Palestinian violence was assumed to be aggressive. In response to growing international criticism, the Israeli government embarked on a public relations operation to manage its image. Two years after the Lebanon invasion, the American Jewish Council convened a conference in Jerusalem to deal with the problem. As one attendee noted, "News doesn't just jump into a camera. It's directed, it's managed. It's made accessible."[157] The government hired advertising executive Carl Spielvogel to manage the campaign and called it *hasbara* or explanation. Israeli advertising executive Martin Fenton took issue with the term, saying, "I am bothered by the use of the word 'hasbara.' Propaganda is not a dirty word and it is what we are talking about. Face it, we are in the game of changing people's minds, of making them think differently. To accomplish that we need propaganda."[158]

Spielvogel understood his American audience, and the campaign was very successful. As part of the reframing, efforts were made to consistently link the modern state of Israel as democratic and modern, and Arabs as backward, primitive, and aggressive. Israeli leaders like Netanyahu and Morton Klein of the Zionist Organization of America have compared Hamas to ISIS, al-Qaeda, and the Nazi regime.[159]

Following in the footsteps of Spielvogel, the Committee for Accuracy in Middle East Reporting in America (CAMERA) works to undermine reporting that is critical of Israel. As John Mearsheimer and Stephen Walt note in their book, *The Israel Lobby and U.S. Foreign Policy*,

> [CAMERA] has been especially critical of National Public Radio, which it sometimes refers to as "National Palestine Radio." In addition to maintaining a website to publicize alleged examples of media bias, CAMERA organized demonstrations outside National Public Radio stations in thirty-three cities in May 2003, and it tried to convince contributors to withhold support from NPR until its Middle East coverage became more sympathetic to Israel. One of Boston's public radio stations, WBUR, reportedly lost more than $1 million in contributions as a result of these efforts. In 2006, CAMERA ran expensive full-page advertisements in the *New York Times* and *New York Sun* criticizing Jimmy Carter's book *Palestine: Peace Not Apartheid*, ads that included the publisher's phone number and encouraged readers to call and complain.[160]

The consolidation of media into large conglomerates also plays a role in the whitewashing of Israel's actions. Janice Terry, author of *U.S. Foreign Policy in the Middle East*, argues that

> because a handful of individuals or international corporations now own and control media communications, including cable and large television networks, motion pictures, radio stations, magazines and newspapers, a near 'unanimity of view' has emerged in the presentation of all issues, not only those dealing with the Middle East. In addition, some analysts have argued that corporate ownership of most media sources has made the media more conservative and prone to support the established and powerful elite. Debate on the Middle East in the media is increasingly limited to a small group of commentators, often from Washington based pro-Israeli think tanks, who perform as "talking heads" and write high profile opinion and/or editorial pieces.[161]

Radio and television hosts frequently parrot talking points handed to them by producers, presenting a seemingly unanimous understanding of the crisis that ignores Palestinian voices.

As an example, during coverage of the bombardment of Gaza in 2008, Rachel Maddow presented four segments to her audience about the violence that was occurring but never mentioned the Israeli blockade of the Gaza Strip or the U.S. financial and military support for Israel.[162] A study of U.S. newspapers in 2017 found that those examined had "foreground Israeli agency in achieving a ceasefire, whereby Israeli actors are predominantly assigned activated roles. By contrast, the four newspapers foreground Palestinian agency in refusing ceasefire through assigning activated roles. The findings of this study suggest that news reports on the Gaza war of 2008–2009 are influenced by the political orientations of the newspapers and also their liberal and conservative ideological stances."[163] These reports frequently show Israel as the peace-seeker and Palestine as the war-seeker, without mentioning the occupation of Palestinian land by Israel. A keyword search on global research website LexisNexis "reveals the use of "rockets raining down" more than 6,900 times compared to the fewer than 800 references to Israel's "siege" or "blockade" of Gaza."[164]

Robert Friedman explains that "the U.S. press often treats Israel with kid gloves." Media outlets whitewash stories coming out of Israel and simply do not publish unsettling stories. According to Friedman, "Americans have very little idea about how severely troubled Israel is, or how critical many Israelis are of their own government's policies.... And some prominent U.S. editors and publishers who have dropped all pretense of objectivity to become public relations advisors for the Israeli government hope to keep it that way." The American press is often more careful in its reporting of and criticism of Israel than even Israeli papers. "Unflattering stories about Israel that are routinely covered by Israel's own press are often buried or overlooked by the U.S. mainstream media. 'It is a very strange experience to read the newspapers from Israel, even those of right-wing orientation, alongside the pro-Israel publications in the United States,' Arthur Hertzberg, the former president of the American Jewish Congress, has noted. 'What everyone in Israel knows as a matter of course is often denounced as false and subversive when quoted in America,... Israel is loved and defended in the United States.'"[165]

Journalists have been ostracized for challenging the narrative on Israel, or even for presenting events as they happen without the gloss of pro-Israel reporting. An example of this going back to the 1950s is Mike Wallace, who grilled Ambassador Abba Eban over Israel's annexation of Palestinian land. Although Wallace was a well-respected journalist known for asking difficult questions of his famous interviewees, he received backlash for his questioning of Eben. Conservative television and radio news talk show host Debbie Schlussel wrote a scathing review of his work after his death in 2012, saying, "He was no journalist. Just a smug, arrogant, agenda-driven fraud who said he admired mass-murderer Yasser Arafat and went out of his way to defame Israel and American patriots who served our country."[166]

In the summer of 2014, the award-winning journalist Ayman Mohyeldin was removed from Gaza by his employer, NBC, after reporting on the deaths of four Palestinian boys who had been playing soccer on a beach when they were killed by an Israeli airstrike. While the network claimed his removal was due to security reasons, many saw it as a "way of ensuring that the coverage isn't seen as too sympathetic towards the Palestinians."[167] Glenn Greenwald wrote, "Over the last two weeks, Mohyeldin's reporting has been far more balanced and even-handed than the standard pro-Israel coverage that dominates establishment American press coverage; his reports have provided context to the ongoing occupation that is missing from most American reports and he avoids adopting Israeli government talking points as truth. As a result, neocon and 'pro-Israel' websites have repeatedly attacked him as a 'Hamas spokesman' and spouting 'pro-Hamas rants.'"[168] Mohyeldin's removal from reporting sparked a trending hashtag, #LetAymanReport, a protest at the London offices of the BBC, and an online petition signed by forty-five thousand people calling for unbiased reporting in the region. The petition stated it "would like to remind the BBC that Gaza is under Israeli occupation and siege [and] that Israel is bombing a refugee population."[169] Under pressure, NBC sent Mohyeldin back to Gaza at the end of July.

In the same month, British correspondent Jon Snow spent five days in Gaza and returned to film a segment that was broadcast on the British Channel 4 YouTube channel, though not on television. In the three-minute video, Snow highlights the level of civilian casualties and injuries, particularly those of children, and calls for peace in the region. It was met with massive viewer support but criticism from media executives. John Hardie, chief executive of ITN News, said he would not have aired the segment. "That would never constitute anything we'd put on broadcast news. We don't open up television broadcast news to that kind of sentimental expression." BBC News deputy chief Fran Unsworth agreed, saying, "If one of our presenters had done something like that in a private capacity on YouTube, I'd have had to have said, this isn't really appropriate in terms of your public role as an impartial presenter of BBC news programmes. We take it very seriously." Sky News chief John Riley suggested he may have aired the video, with the proper caveats that it was not news, but a reporter's opinion. "We expect broadcasters as fellow human beings to neuter and cauterise their own emotion to what they see . . . we should respect that emotion."[170] Despite this pushback, Snow then had Israeli Spokesman Mark Regev on his show to question him about the civilian casualties in Gaza. Unlike American broadcasters, Snow was able to ask difficult questions during the eight-minute video, which Regev deflected by pointing to Hamas as the aggressor.[171]

The desire to re-examine the settler-colonial practices of Israel from a more intersectional lens is echoed by a rather unlikely individual—Geraldo Rivera, the lawyer turned political commentator who regularly appeared on Fox News opinion segments. On an edition of the Fox News segment *The Five* in 2018, Rivera expressed regret over not backing the Palestinians during the Second Intifada. He noted that despite witnessing direct violations of human rights by the IDF, he chose to stay silent instead of "adding my voice as a Jew, adding my voice to those counseling a two-state solution." Rivera added that it is easy to ignore the Palestinian plight because of the way Palestinians are portrayed as terrorists.[172]

In 2012 journalist Bob Simon reported on the living conditions of a Christian family living in Palestine. Before the segment even aired, he was confronted by Israeli ambassador Dr. Michael Oren, who came on air to express his concerns. Oren was unable to articulate those concerns, however, saying on camera, "It's just . . . that's an extraordinary move for me to complain about something. When I heard that you were going to do a story about Christians in the Holy Land and my assum . . . and . . . and had, I believe, information about the nature of it, and it's been confirmed by this interview today." Simon's response was that "nothing's been confirmed by the interview, because you don't know what's going to be put on air."[173] Once it had aired, Simon's piece was criticized in the *Jerusalem Post* for being one-sided.[174] The segment also drew criticism from CAMERA, the pro-Israel watchdog group, which sent a letter to CBS "enumerating errors in the Bob Simon segment." When the letter went unanswered, CAMERA sent representatives to a CBS shareholders meeting where "Edward Schwartz also complained to CBS shareholders, executives and board members of inaccuracies in the segment that he said are so egregious, they could be interpreted as anti-Semitic."[175] After his death, Simon received harsh criticism from some on the right, including columnist Debbie Schlussel, who wrote, "So, liberal, elitist, anti-American, anti-Israel, self-hating Jew and professional propagandist Bob Simon is dead. No tears from me."[176]

Photojournalist Hosam Salem, who spent four years covering the situation in Gaza, was dismissed from the *New York Times* in September 2022. He released a statement on Twitter detailing his dismissal, which occurred after a Dutch editor who had obtained Israeli citizenship published an article highlighting Salem's work, especially social media posts in which he was supportive of Palestinians. Salem's statement said, "The editor later wrote an article stating that he had succeeded in sacking three Palestinian journalists working for the New York Times in the Gaza Strip, on the basis of us being 'anti-Semitic.' . . . What is taking place is a continuous and systematic effort to distort the image of Palestinian journalists as being incapable of trustworthiness and integrity, simply because we cover the human rights violations that the Palestinian people undergo on a daily basis at the hand of the Israeli army."[177]

Jewish American journalist Katie Halper was fired from the *Hill* in 2022 after producing a video monologue in which she criticized the state of Israel. Halper included a quote from Michigan congresswoman Rashida Tlaib, who said, "I want you all to know that among progressives, it becomes clear that you cannot claim to hold progressive values yet back Israel's apartheid government." Halper also shared the international definition of apartheid, quotations from B'Tselem, Human Rights Watch, and Amnesty International accusing Israel of committing the crime of apartheid, as well as "a quote from former Israeli Prime Minister Ehud Barak who said that Israel could become an apartheid state if it didn't change course."[178] The monologue was produced in response to criticism and censure Tlaib received for her remarks, and it resulted in Halper receiving the same.

Academic and author Marc Lamont Hill has consistently spoken out against the injustice endured by Palestinians on a daily basis, and he frequently shares that justice in Palestine is deeply important to other struggles. In a speech to the United Nations in 2018, Hill spoke of justice in Palestine "from the river to the sea." The phrase, which had been used to refer to historic Palestine, was taken to mean the destruction of Israel and the takeover of all the land between the Jordan River and the Mediterranean by Palestine, rather than an antiracist governance providing equal rights to the inhabitants on the area between the two bodies of water. The response to Hill's speech was immediate and harsh. Hill later apologized, saying, "Rather than hearing a political solution, many heard a dog-whistle that conjured a long and deep history of violence against Jewish people. Although this was the furthest thing from my intent, those particular words clearly caused confusion, anger, fear, and other forms of harm. For that, I am deeply sorry."[179] He was fired from CNN the next day. Three years later he published the best-selling book *Except for Palestine: The Limits of Progressive Politics* with Mitchell Piltnick. The book received criticism from pro-Israel voices but was widely viewed as necessary and enlightening. Hill and Plitnick continue to speak out on the subject, appearing on YouTube and Instagram, where their interviews receive tens of thousands of views.[180] The phrase that led to Hill's firing made a comeback in protests calling for an end to the genocide in Gaza after the outbreak of the 2023 War on Gaza in an effort to highlight demands for justice and equality.[181]

On May 15, 2021, the Israeli airforce destroyed a building that housed the Associated Press (AP) headquarters in Gaza. Shortly thereafter, Emily Wilder, a recent Stanford graduate and an employee of the AP, was targeted by the Stanford College Republicans, Senator Tom Cotton, and right-wing commentator Ben Shapiro. Wilder had been a member of student organizations Students for Justice in Palestine and Jewish Voice for Peace. Although the AP assured Wilder that it would not take action against her for her past activism and social media activity, the AP fired her in late May. The AP refused to reconsider this action, even though Wilder's termination was met with outrage and support for the young journalist.[182]

As historian and professor Rashid Khalidi noted, "It's almost impossible to get any view that isn't one way or another shaped by an Israeli perspective, almost impossible. It cannot get in without facing a firestorm of pit-bull attacks to make sure that the line is followed."[183] Take the exchange between talk-show host Bill Maher and *New York Times* opinion writer Bari Weiss over the violence that erupted during the U.S. Embassy's move from Tel Aviv to Jerusalem. Palestinians protesting the movement of the embassy (a movement criticized by other nations as flying in the face of peace process attempts) were met by Israeli military gunfire; dozens were killed or injured, including a twenty-one-year-old medic who rushed to help injured protesters.[184] Weiss and Maher concluded that the only responsible parties in the ensuing bloodbath were the Palestinians. Weiss implored the audience to "not fall for a trap that is being set by a theocratic, authoritarian group that are sending women and children to be human shields." The theocratic, authoritarian group she is referring to is Hamas, which Amnesty International has repeatedly exonerated on the allegations of using civilians as human shields.[185]

Maher agreed with Weiss. He added that he thought Palestinians were "the bigots when they just assume that if something goes on in this part of the world, there's gonna be riots, and you can't organize your foreign policy around, 'What is Mohamed Atta gonna do?'"[186] Mohamad Atta, one of the 9/11 hijackers, is not even Palestinian; he is Egyptian. Aside from Maher automatically drawing the connection between Palestinians and terrorism, his statement is noteworthy in that it reveals a strongly held belief that

Palestinians are not entitled to protest the political, social, or economic constraints placed on them. If Israel is truly a democracy, then why shouldn't they be entitled to exercise this right?

Maher's and Weiss's statements are part of a long and broad pattern of shifting the blame for Palestinians' plight onto Palestinians themselves. The arguments typically go as follows: if the Palestinians weren't so violent / if they rejected Hamas / if they accepted Israel's existence, then things wouldn't be so bad for them. This line of thought dramatically oversimplifies issues surrounding Palestine/Israel and places the blame only on Palestinians, despite the mounting evidence that proves Israel has committed human rights abuses in the Palestinian territories, and despite the fact that Israeli officials have resoundingly rejected several peace agreements.

In an opinion piece published in the *New York Times* after the embassy-related violence in Gaza, author Schmuel Rosner explains why Palestinians protested the moving of the U.S. Embassy as follows:

> They marched because they are desperate and frustrated. Because living in Gaza is not much better than living in hell. They marched against Israel because they dislike Israel, and because they cannot march against anyone else. Israel puts Gaza under siege, bombs it occasionally, and is still remembered as an occupying power and as the country whose establishment made many Palestinians consider themselves refugees to this day. They marched to Israel because the alternative to marching against Israel would be to march against Hamas, a regime whose actions and policies make Gaza suffer. But if people had dared to do that, their government would no doubt have killed scores of them without much hesitation.[187]

Rosner correctly notes that Palestinians are "frustrated" and "desperate" given their circumstances but places the blame for this frustration and desperation on Hamas, despite observing that Israel itself puts Gaza under siege and bombs it. Furthermore, the author explains Palestinians' qualms with Israel as a simple "dislike" of Israel, which glosses over the scores of sociopolitical and economic ways that Israel has consistently made life difficult for Palestinians. This simplified and one-sided viewpoint was the one being broadcast by journalists and celebrities without question, while those who pushed back against injustices in the region received censure. As Matt

SOCIAL CHANGE AND SOUND BITES

Duss said, "Tell me, if Palestinians are not allowed to go to the UN, if they're not allowed to use violence, they're not allowed to use legal means, they're not allowed to use boycotts, what are their options?"[188]

Newspapers play a part in the centering and promotion of pro-Israel discourse in their choice of editorials and columnists. The most-read papers in the country tend to employ writers whose views line up with Israel. The *Washington Post* gives platforms to columnists such as Jim Hoagland, Robert Kagan, Charles Krauthammer, and George Will, all of whom have consistently supported Israel. William Kristol, who supports the more extreme Likud Party, has a column in *Time*. Neither organization "employs any full-time commentator who consistently favors the Arab or Palestinian side," according to Mearsheimer and Walt. The *Los Angeles Times* doesn't employ any columnists that are critical of Israel, much less pro-Palestinian, but has three columnists who are pro-Israel: Max Boot, Jonathan Chait, and Jonah Goldberg. Robert Bartley, the late editor of the *Wall Street Journal*, once remarked, "Shamir, Sharon, Bibi—whatever those guys want is pretty much fine by me."[189]

As Mearsheimer and Walt point out, the *Wall Street Journal*, the *Chicago Sun-Times*, the *New York Sun*, and the *Washington Times* "regularly [run] editorials that read as if they were written by the Israeli prime minister's press office." *New York Times* editorials do sometimes offer criticism of Israeli policies, and the *Times* "recognizes that the Palestinians have legitimate grievances and a right to have their own state." This has not always been the case, however. Former executive editor Max Frankel wrote in his memoir that he "was much more deeply devoted to Israel than I dared to assert.... Fortified by my knowledge of Israel and my friendships there, I myself wrote most of our Middle East commentaries. As more Arab than Jewish readers recognized, I wrote them from a pro-Israel perspective." According to Mearsheimer and Walt's assessment, periodicals such as *Commentary*, the *New Republic*, and the *Weekly Standard* are similarly fervently committed to defending and justifying Israeli actions.[190]

Peter Beinart highlights the untouchable quality of Israel in his explanation of the difference between Ukraine and Israel. He focuses on the assassination of Daria Dugan, a Russian politician's daughter, by Ukrainian forces and suggests that we are allowed to criticize this event without the assumption that we are not supportive of Ukraine and its struggle on a fundamental level. "We should be able to understand that . . . if there are acts of Palestinian violence, they have to be contextualized within the larger system of the violence of oppression." It's "not a way of excusing things one opposes," but a way of talking about "a larger system of violence." Ukrainians aren't going to stop being violent toward Russia as long as they are being attacked. Palestinians aren't going to stop being violent against Israel as long as they are under oppression. All people are deserving of human rights and self-determination. People in the West have deep empathy toward the Ukrainians, so perhaps this will be an opening toward our understanding of Palestinians. We can "channel that empathy towards other people who also suffer from . . . domination, from subjugation . . . and be able to have the same kind of have empathy" for those people even when "they take actions with which we disagree."[191]

PALESTINE IN PUBLIC EDUCATION

Education as a moral force

Views on Israel and Palestine are established long before an American is old enough to read the *New Yorker* or turn on *Fox News*. It starts with public education, which in the United States has never been objective. Puritans in the sixteenth century were the first to provide town schools for elementary-aged children; the required subjects were reading, writing, and religion.[192] In the late 1700s, standardized textbooks were introduced "to help unify the nation after the Revolutionary War." The purpose of these books was "to standardize spelling and pronunciation and to instill patriotism and religious beliefs in students." Because these textbooks reflected the cultural preconceptions of their white, largely Protestant writers, they also portrayed Indigenous communities in dehumanizing and disparaging ways. In idealizing white, Protestant culture, education became a vehicle for the creation and reinforcement of prejudice and discrimination against other groups. Education at this point was still primarily for males, and only upper-class families could afford the tuition. By the mid-nineteenth century, many Americans supported free, compulsory education as a way to educate and "patriotize" young citizens. The purpose of this free education was as much to instill "American" values as it was to teach reading and

SOCIAL CHANGE AND SOUND BITES

writing. By the end of the nineteenth century, compulsory education became widespread.[193]

The provision of free, legally required education was "an important development, as children from all social classes could now receive a free, formal education" that would prepare them for the workforce and ensure a homogeneous culture. "Compulsory schooling began in part to prevent immigrants' values from corrupting American values" and to teach poor workers the skills they needed to participate in the emerging industrial economy.[194] It also promoted cultural unity and patriotism, with daily pledges to the American flag and pictures of the president in classrooms. While unity and patriotism can be necessary and beneficial, the promotion of American values often came at the expense and belittling of other cultures and perspectives. Critics argue that, rather than educating poor citizens, particularly immigrants, this new compulsory education kept them trapped in low-paying, back-breaking jobs while erasing their cultural identities. Howard Zinn, historian and author of *A People's History of the United States*, spent much of his career pushing back against the American educational system and its biased teaching of history. As Zinn explained, "What struck me as I began to study history was how nationalist fervor inculcated from childhood on by pledges of allegiance, national anthems, flags waving and rhetoric blowing permeated the educational systems of all countries, including our own."[195] Zinn's response was to write his own history book, one that told the story of American history from the point of view of the people rather than the government. It has sold over two million copies.[196]

Whitewashing history and glorifying empire

In addition to politicians and religious leaders' narratives binding Israel and the United States together, the American educational system emphasizes this connection and contributes to the erasure and dehumanization of Palestinians. Marcy Jane Knopf-Newman's book *The Politics of Teaching Palestine* provides an in-depth discussion of the ways in which the United States–Israel alliance is cemented at the expense of Palestinians. It identifies several overarching themes in the discussion of Palestine and Israel that form a one-sided narrative that too few Americans ever question. The first theme is the sidelining of historical reality, which has the effect of keeping Americans "complicit in our silence over the U.S. role in expanding colonization in Palestine." The creation of an ahistorical reality in American curriculum chills empathy with the oppressed (in this context, Palestinians) and conveniently removes context from the liberation struggles of oppressed groups. Knopf-Newman, reflecting on her education as a Jewish American, says teachers and curricula "instilled an early and irrational fear of Arabs." She goes on to state that "information about elaborate plans by Zionist leaders, including David Ben-Gurion, to ethnically cleanse Palestine, known as Plan Dalet, devised before United Nations Resolution 181 partitioning Palestine, is suppressed" in these curricula.[197]

The removal of context is one mechanism through which the one-sided narrative on Israel/Palestine is maintained. The other way is by altering historical reality and constructing parallel alternatives. For instance, in one American high school history textbook, "Palestinians' expulsion is represented, but as a response to a defensive war in which Zionists represent David and Palestinians Goliath. This narrative presents Jewish children with Zionist dogma; Palestinians left their homes with no indication of Zionist culpability."[198] In this narrative, they simply chose to leave. This framing deliberately misconstrues reality, as multiple historians, including Israeli historian Benny Morris, have found ample evidence of premeditated efforts to drive Palestinians out of their homes in order to clear the area for Jewish settlement.

Another key theme in Knopf-Newman's analysis is the glorification of empire, which also serves to elide historical facts and erase Indigenous peoples from the narrative. Knopf-Newman compares Zionist curricula to anti-immigrant legislation in Arizona, which conveniently omitted the fact that Arizona was once part of Mexico. A similar erasure occurred in Israel, when the government of Ariel Sharon "initiated the systematic removal of any textbook of school syllabus that referred to the *Nakbah*, even marginally" (Pappé, quoted in Knopf-Newman). This erasure contributes directly to policy. The wall along the U.S.-Mexico border, constructed in part by an Israeli company, has been compared to the wall Israel erected along, and within, the West Bank border. As Knopf-Newman notes, "Both walls protect imperial interests, not people who become separated from their lands, their livelihoods, and their communities."[199]

Pro-Israel advocacy in education

Recent years have seen an increase in activism from schools, parents, and publishers of curriculum for elementary, middle, and high schools working to frame the way the Israel/Palestine issue is presented in schools, and the ways in which Palestinian students are treated and come to understand their identities. Across the country, parents, publishers, and pro-Israel organizations have acted to control the way Israel and Palestine are taught. When those preferences are ignored, some fight back. For example, Israeli American parents filed a lawsuit against Newton Public Schools in Massachusetts after they objected to texts and teacher-training materials about Palestine. "After several years of costly litigation and strong pushback by the American Civil Liberties Union (ACLU), the plaintiffs finally abandoned their lawsuit," the *Washington Report on Middle East Affairs* reported in 2020.[200]

In California, Dr. Samia Shoman of the Advisory Committee to the California Ethnic Studies Curriculum said that she was monitored in the classroom after a rabbi learned of what he thought was an unwarranted discussion of the situation in Palestine.[201] In 2020 Arab Americans were intentionally dropped from the Ethnic Studies Model Curriculum of the State of California, based on lobbying by Israel-advocacy groups that specifically targeted Palestine and Palestinians, which were subsequently wiped out of the curriculum; the words *Palestine* and *Palestinians* were entirely eliminated. The original authors of the curriculum were so enraged by the edits that all twenty of them removed their names from the draft. Dr. Allyson Tintiangco-Cubales, professor of Asian American studies at San Francisco State University and a founding cochair of the Ethnic Studies Model Curriculum Advisory Committee that wrote and advised on the curriculum, was "outraged that some of the loudest voices being heard and making decisions about what ethnic studies should or should not be in California have never even taken an ethnic studies class. Many of them are not even educators, and they are making decisions about what we are allowed to learn."[202]

The Institute for Curriculum Services (ICS) is "a nonprofit organization founded in 2005 dedicated to improving the quality of K-12 education on Jews, Judaism and Israel."[203] ICS has trained more than six thousand teachers in more than ninety cities and worked with textbook publishers to ensure Israel is portrayed in a positive light. While it claims to be an educational nonprofit, it is actually a public affairs and advocacy group operating under the umbrella of the Jewish Community Relations Council (JCRC) of San Francisco, an organization that is committed to promoting positive views about Israel. ICS also receives financial backing from the Schusterman Family Foundation, a group that takes all freshmen congressional representatives to Israel.

In reviewing history curriculum for the state of Virginia, ICS proposed hundreds of edits. In one, the original text read "ongoing conflict over Israeli occupied territories." The words "occupied territories" are crossed out and the proposed change reads, "ongoing conflict over Israeli control over the West Bank and Gaza." The ICS comments say that the term "occupied territories" is "politicized and inappropriate" for a public school text. "Settlements" become "communities." The wall becomes a security fence. Maps are relabeled, and Palestine becomes "Mandatory Palestine." The proposed edits were sent to the Department of Education along with thanks for the adoption of past ICS edits. They state, "In particular, we'd like to thank Pearson and McGraw Hill for the many improvements made to their textbooks based on earlier ICS recommendations."[204] Pearson and McGraw Hill combined control roughly 60 percent of the textbook market.[205]

Jeanne Trabulsi is a retired educator who taught for sixteen years in Arlington County, Virginia. She now works as an advocate, leading the Education Committee at the Virginia Coalition for Human Rights (VCHR). The coalition has been working to stop pro-Israel groups from rewriting curriculum to remove Palestine from the classrooms of American children. Trabulsi sent the ICS edits and the textbooks to academics for review and reported that they were "just astounded. They had no idea this was going on. It sort of made sense because when freshmen come to their classes in college, they know nothing about the Middle East. They know that there's a kind of a desert area, that there are two peoples, one Palestinian and one Israeli. The students think that the Palestinians are trying to take away Israeli land. I mean that's how ignorant they are because of the textbooks that they have encountered in high school."[206] Trabulsi and the VCHR are not the only ones with concerns. Across the Atlantic, scholars at the British Committee for the Universities of Palestine opposed two Pearson textbooks, forcing the publisher to withdraw them after their content was determined to include "dangerously misleading pro-Israel bias."[207]

SOCIAL CHANGE AND SOUND BITES

Another pro-Israel organization that is deeply involved in the school system is the Anti-Defamation League (ADL). The ADL claims to "work in partnership with schools, organizations and communities to design and deliver anti-bias education, both online and in person." The ADL offers education in three areas: antibias, antibullying, and anti-Semitism and Holocaust education.[208] While antibias and antibullying are mentioned, they don't seem to take priority. The ADL curriculum in truth serves to promote the state of Israel at the expense of an understanding of the Arab point of view. Its emphasis on anti-Semitism is problematic for a number of reasons. One is its repeated support of and approval for actual anti-Semites. When Donald Trump peppered a speech in 2015 with anti-Semitic tropes, "a number of prominent Jewish Republican commentators immediately derided Trump's comments." The ADL, however, defended him. CEO Jonathan Greenblatt said, "After having carefully reviewed the speech, we do not believe that it was Donald Trump's intention to evoke anti-Semitic stereotypes," and that "context is everything."[209] The ADL regularly gives awards to right-wing politicians and public figures, often for supporting Israel. Recipients of awards include Rupert Murdoch of Fox News and Cardinal Bernard Law, who resigned from the Catholic Church for his role covering up sexual abuse of children.[210]

Second, the ADL is active in promoting stereotyped images of Arab and Muslim Americans, and in policing them when they attempt to make their voices heard in the civil rights space. The website DropTheADL argues that "virtually all of the ADL's projects have contributed to normalizing Islamophobia/anti-Muslim racism & anti-Arab racism."[211] The ADL helped to fund anti-Islamic propaganda films like *Obsession* and *The Third Jihad: Radical Islam's Plan for America*, which "ignited a firestorm of criticism from Muslim, civil rights and other groups" for its blatant and dishonest anti-Muslim bias.[212] Despite this clear prejudice and the implicitly (and in some cases, explicitly) problematic nature of the organization's curriculum, the ADL is active in K-12 school across the country, bringing pro-Israel, anti-Arab teachings directly into classrooms.

Anti-Palestinian prejudice in schools

Thea Renda Abu El-Haj, whose research was mentioned in the introduction, highlights the complexities of having to negotiate one's own identity as Palestinian in the United States against the erasure of that identity, "render[ing] their communities invisible" except for "terrorist." She explains how erasure and denial of identity in schools and classrooms creates a unified hope having an independent state of Palestine one day.[213] This idea reinforces the power of the transnational Palestinian identity, where varied oppressions experienced by Palestinians in the United States further unify all Palestinians and their identity and connection to one another other as well as to their homeland.

When Palestinians are portrayed in sympathetic ways in school curricula, the pushback is often fierce and immediate. As one example, school officials in Washington removed "an assignment from a school curriculum which was what they called a 'clear example of implicit bias' concerning the Israeli-Palestinian conflict." The lesson was on the American Revolution and its effect on the Indigenous population of what is now the United States. The Israel/Palestine conflict was suggested as a contemporary connection, and the assignment proposed critical-thinking exercises: "Why do the Palestinians want to be free from Israeli dominance? Have their sacred homelands returned to them?"[214] These questions were seen as taking sides with the Palestinians, an error considered so egregious that the lesson was pulled from the classroom. The Jewish News Syndicate celebrated the removal, claiming that the lesson was political manipulation and that "misappropriating history to attack Israel is unacceptable in public schools."[215] Historically speaking, the removal of Indigenous peoples to make way for European settlers is remarkably similar to the removal of Palestinians to make way for Jewish Israeli citizens. The lessons came to public attention after action by the Committee for Accuracy in Middle East Reporting and Analysis.[216]

In this way, American public schools, policed by pro-Israel groups, are rewarded for teaching that is supportive of Israel and punished for teaching that is sympathetic to Palestinians, as Palestinian students deal with erasure and prejudice.

Higher education

The experience of bias against Palestinians continues in college settings. Clashes over anti-Palestinian discrimination are intensifying in number and in intensity. In 2021 Palestinian student Ahmad Daraldik filed a civil rights complaint against Florida State University. Palestine Legal, an organization committed to protecting the rights of individuals in the United States to speak about Palestine, notes that "the 22-page complaint, the first of its kind alleging a violation of Title VI of the Civil Rights Act of 1964 on the basis of Palestinian national origin, described the severe and pervasive anti-Palestinian hostile environment Ahmad faced after he was elected student senate president in 2020." Despite legal action, the Department of Education had not responded to the complaint after nineteen months of silence, a delay that "exceeds the Office for Civil Rights' (OCR) internal benchmark to resolve a complaint within 180 days of receipt by a factor of three."[217] At the time of this writing, the complaint had not been resolved.

Universities have long been heralded as the epicenter of debate and intellectual engagement. They are places where students go not only to learn, but also to engage in discussions about highly nuanced and multifaceted issues. For many academics, the point of a university education is not to train students for a particular job, but to teach them how to learn and how to engage critically with ideas presented to them.

Despite the lofty ambitions of universities to produce open-minded and engaged learners, actions taken by colleges across the nation have stifled free speech on campus and made pariahs out of students and academics who dare to criticize Israel's policies toward Palestinians. Universities have failed to protect students and academics who voice anti-Zionist opinions and in some cases have directly intimidated and harassed said students and academics. As a result of such intimidation, many students are left wondering, if they can't express their opinions on a college campus, where can they? As Dima Khalidi, director of Palestine Legal, states, "When you look at the very framework of universities and what their policies are and their mission statements, everything says this is about free inquiry, and this is where you'll come to this as an academic where you can do your work freely, as a student where you will experience new ideas, etc. And so the very purpose of higher education is at stake."[218]

It is important to emphasize that universities stifle pro-Palestine, anti-Zionist speech on the grounds that such speech is discriminatory and anti-Semitic. It's often tied to the broader discussion over the limits of free speech, but in many ways this is a separate issue. Universities attempt to silence pro-Palestine and anti-Zionist opinions on campus by labeling such speech as "hate speech," despite the growing consensus among academics, including

Jewish academics, that such speech is *not* hate speech. The instances in which academia stifles pro-Palestine, anti-Zionist speech are numerous and increasing in scope and frequency. As Kahlidi explains, Zionists

> have really attached themselves to that broader agenda, they have aligned themselves with those right wing forces that are trying to dictate what can and cannot be done on a campus, what can and cannot be taught, what students can and cannot say. They are trying to police the discourse on campuses. Take the Title VI arguments. They're basically alleging discrimination on the part of universities because of their tolerance of Palestine organizing. The Department of Education has repeatedly said, this is not discrimination, this is not a hostile environment, this is political speech. Just because you're offended by something doesn't mean you're being discriminated against.[219]

The censorship of pro-Palestine and anti-Zionist speech is accomplished through a multilayered mechanism of racialization, which paints those who speak out against Israeli policies as uncivilized, undemocratic, and anti-Semitic. Many academics have expressed concern with the U.S. State Department's broad definition of anti-Semitism, which includes provisions for the demonization and delegitimization of Israel. Simona Sharoni, a professor of gender and women's studies at SUNY Plattsburgh, points out that these provisions "are so vague, that they could be, and have been, construed to silence any criticism of Israeli policies."[220] In 2016 the Anti-Semitism Awareness Act was introduced in the Senate; the proposed legislation used the extraordinarily broad State Department definition of anti-Semitism as a litmus test to determine if speech on campus constituted anti-Semitic harassment. The issue with this act, as the *Los Angeles Times* pointed out, is that it "unfairly conflates anti-Israel speech with anti-Semitic speech, in a way that, if enforced, would violate the free speech rights of students and professors."[221]

Critics of pro-Palestine, anti-Zionist speech argue that it's discriminatory, likening it to extreme-right-wing speech against left-wing notions of gender, race, and culture. By classifying pro-Palestine speech in the same category as speech that vilifies feminists and extols white supremacy, pro-Israel groups can make the argument that such speech is hate speech and therefore should not be protected or tolerated by universities. Critics of this comparison point out that opinions on Israel and Palestine are "political, not racist, positions, shared by a significant number of Jews, and qualify as protected speech under the First Amendment of the Constitution."[222] In addition, the way the suppression of speech has played out in each situation (right-wing speech versus pro-Palestine speech) differs markedly. In the former, charges of speech suppression are leveled against students who protest such speech as offensive. In the latter, "state-funded bureaucracies and government officials have been involved in stifling speech on an issue directly related to American foreign policy."[223]

Punishing students for Palestinian activism

Palestine Legal reported that in 2014, of the 152 campus incidents it responded to, half "involved accusations of anti-Semitism 'based solely on speech critical of Israeli policy.'"[224] The report also noted how pro-Israel groups and university donors employ false accusations of support for terrorism, and threats of criminal investigations, to silence speech critical of Israel. Simona Sharoni, who is Jewish and Israeli herself, concedes that anti-Semitism is a real issue at universities, but that parties targeted by groups such as StandWithUs "are not anti-Semitic, but critics of Israel. Pro-Israel groups seem intent on conflating the two, displaying any critique of Israel as a threat to Jewishness itself."[225] The result, as noted by Steven Salaita, a tenured professor fired by the University of Illinois-Urbana Champaign due to a series of tweets in which he criticized Israeli crimes against Palestinians, is that "graduate students and young scholars are fearful of speaking out on this issue because of the potential career implications of being perceived as a critic of Israel. It's an example of the compromises to our freedoms that an unthinking commitment to a foreign country can produce. Even if we disagree with people politically, it's a bad idea to voluntarily confer more power to a hierarchy that can silence people just because we don't like what they say."[226]

Dima Khalidi, Palestine Legal's director, has commented on the rise in persecution. "There are definitely trends towards more repression," she says, "and this is also partly a result of the trend of the privatization and corporatization of universities. [Universities] are more responsive to donors, to politicians who hold the purse strings as well. And to private pressure from organizations. They're also very responsive to the media.... We're seeing also the insertion of the Israeli Government itself in policy arenas and in mobilizing opposition to not only academics, but student activism and other things."[227]

Campus Watch, a web-based organization launched in 2002, "reviews and critiques Middle East studies in North America, with an aim to improve them." The group claims that Middle East studies are of particular importance in American higher education due to their political nature and focuses on "analytical failures, the mixing of politics with scholarship, intolerance of alternative views, apologetics, and the abuse of power over students."[228] In practice, the site gathers and publishes news articles, encourages students to report on professors and curriculum, and keeps records of statements and actions by professors it deems to be biased. This practice is controversial. After a list of professors was published for their views on Palestinian rights and political Islam, "100 outraged professors nationwide—Jewish and non-Jewish, English professors and Middle East specialists—have responded to the site by asking to be added to the list."[229] Academics claimed the site was stifling free speech and engaging in McCarthyesque silencing tactics. Daniel Pipes, the original director of Campus Watch, insists this is not the case. The organization's website states that the group "fully respects the freedom of speech of those it debates while insisting on its own freedom to comment on their words and deeds." The site remains active, posting weekly updates and maintaining lists of "Recommended Professors" and "Professors to Avoid" as well as a "Howler of the Month," who they say "demonstrate the moral obtuseness, politicized outlook, and rank absurdity in the field of Middle East studies."[230]

Similarly, Canary Mission, a website launched in 2014, "documents people and groups that promote hatred of the USA, Israel and Jews." The site keeps a list of students, professors, and professionals it deems to be "promoting hatred." This promotion can take the form of participation in groups such as Students for Justice in Palestine, Jewish Voice for Peace, and the Anti-War Committee and conflates all criticism of Israel with anti-Semitism and hate speech. The site posts personal information about students and professors, such as social media handles, job titles, and majors.[231]

In 2015 billionaire casino-owner Sheldon Adelson founded Maccabee Task Force to combat BDS on college campuses.[232] The organization funds pro-Israel events on campuses, sends groups of students on trips to Israel, and works to defeat BDS causes while urging colleges to adopt the International Holocaust Remembrance Alliance definition of anti-Semitism, which includes "the targeting of the state of Israel," "accusing Jewish citizens of being more loyal to Israel, or to the alleged priorities of Jews worldwide, than to the interests of their own nations," and "denying the Jewish people their right to self-determination, e.g., by claiming that the existence of a State of Israel is a racist endeavor."[233] The Maccabee Task Force describes itself in this way: "We maintain that BDS is an Antisemitic movement that crosses the line from legitimate criticism of Israel into the dangerous demonization of Israel and its supporters. We are determined to help students combat this hate by bringing them the strategies and resources they need to tell the truth about Israel. These attacks on Israel and its supporters won't be going away any time soon. Neither will we."[234]

Despite the well-organized and well-funded efforts to stifle pro-Palestinian speech and action on college campuses, more and more universities are becoming open to including Palestinian voices. Students are organizing, joining BDS, and calling on their schools to do the same. These actions are rarely without consequences but are increasing nonetheless. Portland State University's student senate passed a resolution in 2016 that was brought forward by Students United for Palestinian Equal Rights. The resolution called on the university "to divest from Israeli apartheid by an overwhelming vote of 22–2."[235] Other examples can be found on campuses around the country.

The University of California system has had several intensifying incidents of conflict regarding opinions and activism on the Palestine issue. In 2011 ten students at the University of California, Irvine, disrupted a speech by Israeli ambassador Michael Oren by shouting him down. University administrators disciplined the students and suspended the Muslim Student Union, of which some of the students were members, for a quarter. This seemed sufficient recourse, but criminal charges were also brought against the students, and a year later they were found guilty and "sentenced to three years of probation, fifty-six hours of community service, and fines." The district attorney likened the student's actions to "thuggery." Erwin Chemerinsky, then dean of the UC Irvine School of Law, agreed with the university's punishment but felt that criminal charges went too far. Some called the case "political grandstanding" that "stoked the flames of a controversy that seemed to have died." "It's unnecessary and it's harmful. It's unnecessarily divisive," Chemerinsky said. The "Irvine 11" became a cultural flashpoint for pro-Palestinian voices.[236]

Five years later, students belonging to the Students for Justice in Palestine, Jewish Voice for Peace, and the Black Student Union at UC Irvine protested the film *Beneath the Helmet*, a documentary about recruits in the Israeli Defense Forces which was being shown on campus. The students felt the film was pro-Israel propaganda and were also upset over the presence of "several IDF representatives who were holding a panel discussion at the screening." The next day they were informed by the university that their actions were being referred to the district attorney, who would determine whether criminal charges would be filed. Students also faced expulsion from campus. Daniel Carnie of Jewish Voice for Peace spoke to reporters after the event, saying, "We held our protest in a way that reflected university guidelines; we didn't use amplified sound and we didn't restrict anyone's freedom of access to the event." Palestine Legal and the Center for Constitutional Rights responded to the incident in a report on free speech on university campuses, saying that it and cases like it "undermin[e] the traditional role of universities in promoting the free expression of unpopular ideas and encouraging challenges to the orthodoxies prevalent in official political discourse."[237]

Despite pushback, student support for Palestine grew, and in August 2022 nine student organizations at the University of California Berkeley Law School adopted a pro-Palestine bylaw that states they "will not" invite speakers who support Zionism or "the apartheid state of Israel." Dean Chemerinsky pushed back against the students, saying that "taken literally, this would mean that I could not be invited to speak because I support the existence of Israel, though I condemn many of its policies."[238] The Jewish Student Association also decried the bylaw, asserting that they "are troubled that this by-law creates an environment in which only one viewpoint is acceptable."[239] As of this writing, the conversation is ongoing.

At Harvard University, the student-run newspaper the *Crimson* published several articles in 2013 asserting that pro-Palestine activism on campus is anti-Semitic. In the wake of a conference the Palestine Solidarity Committee (PSC) hosted at the Harvard Kennedy School, the paper "published a piece labeling the conference as 'deeply wrong' before the conference had even taken place." Hannah Schafer, an MPP candidate at Harvard and member of PSC, stated that "as the daughter of a Rabbi who previously fought in the Israeli military, I am deeply offended that *The Crimson* keeps publishing pieces that label our PSC activism on campus as anti-Semitic. This is defamatory, and they should be ashamed of themselves."[240] In a stunning reversal, however, in April 2022 the Crimson Editorial Board published an editorial in support of BDS and a Free Palestine, saying, "This editorial board is broadly and proudly supportive of (the Palestine Solidarity Committee's) mission and activism." It went on to insist that its pro-Palestinian stance was in no way anti-Semitic, asserting that "Jewish people, like every people, including Palestinians, deserve nothing but life, peace, and security."[241]

Harvard has been the subject of other recent protests as well. In October 2022, student protesters disrupted a public policy class being taught by Kennedy School professor Meghan O'Sullivan. O'Sullivan served the Bush administration as deputy national security advisor for Iraq and Afghanistan and currently sits on the board of directors for Raytheon Technologies, a weapons manufacturing firm. The protest was co-organized by Resist and Abolish the Military Industrial Complex and anti-imperialist organization United Against War and Militarism. "We want to expose the fact that Harvard Kennedy—in spite of the image it's putting forward—is employing someone who profits every time bombs or missiles are dropped or launched at Palestine and Yemen," a spokesperson for the protestors told *The Harvard Crimson*. The *Crimson* also reported that protestors chanted, "'Meghan O'Sullivan, you can't hide, we can see your war crimes' and 'When missiles fly, people die, and O'Sullivan's profits multiply,' while holding up a banner critical of O'Sullivan in front of the class."[242] Campus police were called, and the protesters left peacefully, with no arrests occurring. The protest may have already sparked honest conversation, as O'Sullivan reportedly did not continue with her planned material but opened a classroom discussion about her time in the Bush administration and the conflicts in the Middle East.

In 2022 Princeton University students put forth a referendum calling for a boycott of Caterpillar in line with BDS. The referendum became the focus of scrutiny on campus and nationally and was labeled as being "rooted within a bigoted global movement."[243] Reid Zlotsky, student leader of the opposition to the referendum, wrote that the decline to debate by supporters of the bill indicated "they know their campaign could not withstand the rigorous scrutiny of the student body."[244] The referendum did not pass, as it needed a majority to do so. It received 44 percent of the vote, the opposition received 40 percent, and 16 percent of voting students abstained.[245]

After the referendum failed, the *Jerusalem Post* printed an article stating, "For too long, tertiary institutions have remained complacent amidst the blatant Jew-hatred of the BDS movement. At Princeton, we demonstrated how students can successfully fight back. Now it's time to continue the charge."[246] The topic has always engendered strong emotions. In 2015, when a similar referendum was considered, "the University recorded a marked rise in anti-Semitic sentiments and activity on Princeton's campus."[247]

In one case, "students at Northeastern University . . . attempted to introduce a divestment referendum asking the university's board of trustees to divest from companies that aid and abet human rights violations in the West Bank. In response . . . the student government released two legal memos that argued that the student body could not even discuss this matter because doing so would create a hostile environment for Jewish students." In another example, "Omar Shakir . . . discussed the case of Prof. Steven Salaita of the University of Illinois at Urbana-Champaign, who was removed from his post after tweets critical of Israel during its 2014 assault on Gaza. Shakir and the CCR filed a lawsuit on Salaita's behalf, and in the ensuing months the chancellor of the university was forced to resign."[248] Ramie Abounaja, a student at George Washington University, was written up by campus police for hanging a Palestinian flag outside of his dorm room window. The student cited that he had seen other students hanging flags with which they identified their heritage, but that he was the only one asked to take down his flag and given a write-up by George Washington University. While it was determined the flag was in violation of a fire code, students decried the punishment as selective enforcement, pointing out multiple other flags positioned in the same way as Abounaja's.[249]

Suhaib Khan and Rina Abd El Rahman also discuss forms of discrimination and penalization for those who identify as Palestinian or support "Palestinian issues" in the United States, describing the false accusations of terrorism and anti-Semitism that are given by institutions as a result. Attorney Radhika Sainath mentioned "students at Northeastern University who attempted to introduce a divestment referendum asking the university's board of trustees to divest from companies that aid and abet human rights violations in the West Bank"; in response, "the student government released two legal memos that argued that the student body could not even discuss this matter because doing so would create a hostile environment for Jewish students."250 Such examples give light to the fact that Palestinians in the United States are limited in their ability to speak their truths when it comes to Israel and Palestine and are often penalized for it. Identifying as Palestinian warrants scrutiny not just in the scenario of activism, but also in simply expressing pride in Palestinian heritage. The narrative emerging in such social discourse in the United States is that identifying as Palestinian is problematic, that Palestinians are a problem. Such a message is transferred through institutional mechanisms of denial, exclusion, and direct penalty. Faida Abu-Ghazaleh describes the difficulties faced for Palestinians in the United States due to the media as well, saying that "for Palestinians, being a Palestinian in a Western community is difficult due to the general image of Palestinians in the media. . . . Palestinians are often viewed by the media as Arab refugees or terrorists."251

Organizations have also been caught up in the melee. In 2018 the Modern Language Association passed Resolution 2017-1, which takes a firm stance against the Palestinian Campaign for the Academic and Cultural Boycott of Israel. Eleven former presidents of the association had expressed concern over the resolution, and the current president, Margaret Ferguson, resigned after it passed, citing that "the resolution misrepresents the MLA's purpose in its opening clause, leaving out the Association's long-standing efforts to advocate for humanities educators' rights; and because the resolution prohibits future discussion of an issue of public concern." She went on to say that "the MLA has taken an extreme and ethically untenable position by endorsing the idea, promoted by a group of members who were openly 'assisted' by outside groups, that it is illegitimate for professional groups to protest Israel's policies towards its Palestinian subjects."252

In 2006 the Union of Progressive Zionists (UPZ) sponsored campus appearances by Breaking the Silence, an organization of former Israeli soldiers that is critical of IDF operations in the Occupied Territories. The Zionist Organization of America (ZOA) denounced UPZ and demanded that it be expelled from the Israel on Campus Coalition (ICC), a network of pro-Israel groups. Morton Klein, president of ZOA, said that sponsoring groups that are critical of Israel "is not the mission of the ICC."253

An incident at UC Berkeley Law School in 2022 may be the best example of how the debates raging over anti-Semitism and free speech on college campuses become a social force in and of themselves. On September 22 the *Jewish Journal* published an op-ed titled "Berkeley Develops Jewish-Free

Zones." The article reported on the adoption of bylaws by nine student groups that prevented them from inviting pro-Israel or Zionist individuals to speak at campus events and stated that "anti-Zionism is flatly anti-Semitic." Law School dean Chemerinsky pushed back on the accusation in a letter that, to its credit, the *Jewish Journal* printed under the original article, explaining that there were absolutely no "Jewish-free zones" at Berkeley and that, in fact, "the Law School has an 'all-comers' policy, which means that every student group must allow any student to join and all student organized events must be open to all students," and that he knew "of no instance in which this has been violated or there has been any discrimination against Jews."[254]

Furthermore, Berkeley has become a leader in campus inclusion and the prevention of anti-Semitism, taking steps to ensure that Jewish students feel safe and included on its campus. Its Chancellor's Advisory Committee on Jewish Student Life and Campus Climate "meets regularly with senior campus leaders to address challenges for students on the Berkeley campus, continue to bolster the infrastructure of Jewish student life, and increase awareness about the dangers of anti-Semitism."[255] The college is also home to the Berkeley Anti-Semitism Education Initiative (AEI), which "carries out regular programs and trainings for Berkeley students, staff and faculty, and has created multimedia presentations, including a widely praised anti-bias training film."[256]

Despite the immediate condemnation of the *Jewish Journal* article by the university, social media quickly caught the article and ran with it. Christians United for Israel retweeted the headline and first paragraph to its ten million followers. Rob Eshman reports that "the *Jerusalem Post*, JTA, and *Times of Israel* soon featured a story and op-eds about the issue." This media focus fed into a phenomenon that has been recently studied of fears of anti-Semitism fomenting legislation against it even when it doesn't exist. Eshman notes that "in her 2022 doctoral study of Jewish students at three different universities, Sara Fredman Aeder found that the students' fear of antisemitism was far greater than their actual experience of it. 'Their fear of anti-Semitism was informed not by their own experiences, but by what they read online and on social media,' Aeder concluded. 'Online messaging is causing students to hide even in environments where their identity is accepted and celebrated.'"[257]

This is not to say that anti-Semitism does not exist or should not be confronted when it is identified and encountered. It is an example of the kind of culture we find ourselves in, where minor issues with attention-grabbing headlines become major problems and the media has the power to shape narratives and influence attitudes without carrying the burden of proving its accusations.

These views are not new. Jean-Paul Sartre, a staunch defender of the Algerians in their anticolonial struggle against the French, notably did not extend the same logic to the plight of Palestinians. Edward Said, attending a conference hosted by Sartre in Paris, observed:

> For reasons that we still cannot know for certain, Sartre did indeed remain constant in his fundamental pro-Zionism. Whether that was because he was afraid of seeming anti-Semitic, or because he felt guilt about the Holocaust, or because he allowed himself no deep appreciation of the Palestinians as victims of and fighters against Israel's injustice, or for some other reason, I shall never know. All I do know is that as a very old man he seemed pretty much the same as he had been when somewhat younger: a bitter disappointment to every (non-Algerian) Arab who admired him.[258]

Repercussions and punishments for Palestinian activism in higher education

Students are not the only ones affected by such policies, though at times universities are constrained by law. For example, in 2019 former president Trump signed executive order 13899, which is centered on combating anti-Semitism and requires federal agencies to "consider the International Holocaust Remembrance Alliance's (IHRA) working definition of anti-Semitism and the IHRA's contemporary examples of anti-Semitism in enforcing Title VI."[259] States have similar laws aimed at criticism of Israel. In accordance with Arizona law, Arizona State University requires speakers invited to campus to sign a contract that includes a statement that the speaker "is not currently engaged in a boycott of Israel and will not engage in a boycott of Israel during the term of this Contract." The university is facing a lawsuit filed by the Council on American-Islamic Relations (CAIR) on behalf of the student group American Muslims for Palestine, who were unable to host Hatem Bazian, slated to talk about Palestine and the BDS movement.[260]

Professors and academics are also under fire. There is a cost to criticizing Israel in U.S. academic institutions. In 2006, the Departments of

History and Sociology at Yale University voted to extend an offer of appointment to Juan Cole, a renowned historian of the Middle East from the University of Michigan. Cole, who is well-known in his field and edits *Informed Comment*, had critiqued various Israeli policies throughout his career—much like most scholars who study the Middle East. The decision to hire Cole was criticized by columnists from the *Wall Street Journal* and the *Washington Times*. According to *Jewish Week*, notable Yale donors opposed Cole's appointment, which was eventually reversed.[261]

Steven Salaita, who was mentioned earlier, was a tenured professor at the University of Illinois Urbana-Champaign; he was fired from his position after posting a series of anti-Israel tweets during the bombing of Gaza in 2014. It is notable that Christopher Kennedy was the chair of the university's board of trustees at the time of Salaita's firing.[262] Kennedy's father was the late Robert F. Kennedy, who was assassinated by Sirhan Sirhan, a Palestinian Jordanian man, in 1968. Whether this connection affected the board's decision to fire Salaita is unknown. What is known is that the board of trustees was influenced by donors who threatened to cut funding for the university should Salaita remain on staff. This is one example of the ways in which boards of trustees have power and influence while also being subject to outside pressure.

In November 2015, Salaita won a lawsuit against the university and was awarded a settlement of $875,000. The victory came after intense backlash against the university, including "student walkouts; the cancellation of more than three dozen scheduled talks and conferences at the school; further pledges to boycott UIUC by more than 5,000 academics; a vote of no confidence in the university administration by 16 UIUC academic departments; and public condemnation by prominent academic organizations."[263] Salaita recently announced that he was leaving academia, writing, "Whatever I end up doing, I will maintain the spirit of noncompliance that defined my time in academe. If you take any lesson from my ouster, please don't let it be fear or caution. Docility is a gift to those who profit from oppression. Academe can no longer afford this luxury."[264]

Norman Finkelstein, a Jewish American academic whose parents were in Auschwitz and Majdanek concentration camps, has been openly critical of Israel's anti-Palestinian policies. His book *The Holocaust Industry: Reflections on the Exploitation of Jewish Suffering*, published in 2000, details the ways in which the memory of the Holocaust is misused to give the state of

Israel legitimacy and to expunge it of responsibility for its humanitarian offenses. The book received critical acclaim as well as criticism, and Finkelstein was labeled as anti-Semitic and a "self-hating Jew." A few years later, he publicly criticized Alan Dershowitz's book *The Case for Israel*, accusing him of plagiarism. The accusation boiled down to a disagreement over citations, but Dershowitz campaigned against Finkelstein's being granted tenure at DePaul University, where he was teaching. His campaign was successful, and Finkelstein, whose political science department voted nine to three in favor of his tenure, was denied tenure by DePaul's Board on Promotion and Tenure.[265] In May 2008 Finkelstein was denied entry to Israel for a period of ten years.[266] In 2009 he was the subject of the documentary *American Radical: The Life of Norman Finkelstein*. Critics panned the film, with one saying that "Finkelstein comes off as sad, disturbed, strange, and pathetic."[267]

In 2017, S. Bruce Duthu, a leading scholar of Native American law, faced a campaign opposing his appointment as Dartmouth's dean of the faculty of arts and sciences, initiated by another Dartmouth professor, Alan Gustman. Gustman brought to light a 2013 statement from the council of the Native American and Indigenous Studies Association (NAISA)—an organization for which Duthu was then treasurer—which called for an academic boycott of Israel, saying, "we strongly protest the illegal occupation of Palestinian lands and the legal structures of the Israeli state that systematically discriminate against Palestinians and other Indigenous peoples." Gustman argued that this statement constituted support for the BDS movement. Duthu attempted to defend himself in an email to school faculty, but did not capitalize the word "state" in his assertion of support for the State of Israel, which led to accusations of anti-Semitism and refusal to acknowledge Israel as a state. Gustman sent his letter opposing Duthu's prospective deanship to Dartmouth's faculty and to David Horowitz, who runs the right-wing website Frontpage, leading to online outrage. Eventually, Duthu declined the deanship, saying that "this matter has been and will likely continue to be a significant distraction for me professionally and a source of considerable pain and frustration for me personally."[268]

Simona Sharoni, a professor of gender and women's studies at SUNY Plattsburgh, has been publicly critical of Israel on a number of occasions and was accustomed to receiving pushback. After an interview in 2016 in which she connected feminism and gender studies with the Palestinian cause, however, she received more than just idle criticism. Articles calling her an anti-Semite or a "shill" appeared online, and she received death and rape threats. Nineteen Freedom of Information requests were filed, including one by StandWithUs, a pro-Israel group, which asked for seventeen different kinds of information, including lists of events, rallies, talks, and faculty meetings she had attended and "every email about any of the seventeen different forms of records ever sent by any member of SUNY Plattsburgh's staff and faculty," more than ten thousand pages of documents. Administrators "admitted the public records requests seemed designed to intimidate the administration into taking action against Sharoni" but took little action apart from an internal email supporting free speech but not mentioning Sharoni, who experienced high levels of anxiety during the attacks.[269]

Jasbir Puar, a professor of women and gender studies at Rutgers University, was targeted by several groups after she gave a talk at Vassar College in 2016. An op-ed in the *Wall Street Journal* called her out as anti-Semitic and suggested her talk, along with other events, had "transformed a prestigious institution into a parody ripe for ridicule."[270] She received numerous threats, one of which police decided was serious enough to potentially lead to violence, and she was alerted that her home address was being searched online.

Purdue University American studies professor Bill Mullen was also targeted for his criticism of Israel and his work with Purdue's pro-Palestine student group, Students for Justice in Palestine. Three websites appeared online in April 2015 criticizing his achievements, accusing him of not supporting his university's administration, and suggesting he had a track record of sexual harassment. These claims were baseless, and an investigation revealed that each of the three websites was "purchased through the same hosting provider and its creator(s) share an IP address."[271]

The October 2023 War on Gaza brought questions around academic freedom and the role of academic institutions in American society. University of Pennsylvania president Liz Magill resigned after pressure from donors due to her testimony at a congressional hearing around anti-Semitism on U.S. campuses. Harvard president Claudine Gay was forced to resign after her comments regarding the discipline of students involved in pro-Palestine protests on campus. Dr. Gay had expressed that she "found calls for genocide of Jews personally abhorrent" but would need to understand the context and specificity of those remarks to determine whether they violated Harvard's code of conduct. More than seven hundred faculty members signed a petition calling for Harvard to "resist political pressures that are at odds with Harvard's commitment to academic freedom, including calls for the removal of President Claudine Gay." However, more than seventy members of Congress called for her resignation, and a major donor withdrew a $100 million grant, precipitating her exit.[272] While hers was the highest-profile case, universities have been at the center of the newest wave of intensifying protest and support regarding Israel and Palestine. Shortly after the onset of the war, more than one hundred university presidents signed a declaration of solidarity with Israel. Several high-profile donors to major universities weighed in, threatening to halt endowments if universities did not clamp down on what they see as anti-Israel demonstrations by students. Seth Klarman, a significant donor to Harvard University, remarked that "heads of all colleges and universities should step into the shoes of what it's like to be in Israel right now."[273] At the same time, pro-Palestinian protests and events have been increasing on college campuses.[274]

University campuses as shifting landscapes for justice on Palestine

The American educational system from kindergarten to college is culturally and academically disposed to supporting and protecting a status quo that includes validating the Israeli narrative and invalidating that of Palestinians. Its failure to properly educate students in history and critical thinking creates fertile soil for the dismissal of Palestinian voices; interference from pro-Israel groups pushes curriculum in favor of Israel; and prejudicial policies make Palestinian students feel marginalized. This is the atmosphere in which American students are brought up. By the time they are adults, they are predisposed to accept the political and media narratives that replace schools in educating and informing the populace about important issues.

Despite the massive pushback on college campuses, there is evidence that the environment is improving for Palestinians as the fight intensifies. As Sara Roy noted, "The university has opened up dramatically since my undergraduate days when one couldn't even use the word 'Palestine' or 'Palestinian' in a classroom as far as I know. When I attended Harvard in the 1970s, it was not possible to say anything critical of Israel. Nobody told us that explicitly, it was simply understood. There was no acceptable context for criticizing Israel."[275]

In an example that showcases the multifaceted nature of the issue, the University of Washington in 2022 returned a five-million-dollar endowment after the donor expressed disagreement with how the scholarship and activities generated from the gift stood against her staunch pro-Israel position. Becky Benaroya, a Seattle philanthropist, gave the gift for the creation of an endowed chair and lecture series for Israel studies. Liora Halperin, a professor of history, Jewish, and International studies, was appointed as the inaugural Benaroya Chair but soon realized there were "donor expectations that were not and could not legally have been stated in the endowment agreement.... It became clear... that the holder of the Benaroya chair was expected to refrain from making 'certain political statements.'" When Halperin signed a statement, along with hundreds of other Jewish and Israeli scholars, denouncing the May 2021 violence perpetrated by the state of Israel against residents of Sheikh Jarrah, Benaroya responded in anger. She requested meetings with the university, bringing Randy Kessler, executive director of the Northwest chapter of StandWithUs, to the meetings with her. "Despite multiple efforts to repair the discord, Halperin was informed that ultimately, Benaroya wanted her money back."[276]

While Benaroya's actions regarding the endowment highlight the increase in agitation and hostility on the pro-Israel side of the debate, the actions of the university reflect the ways in which institutions and individuals are less and less likely to bow to such pressure. University president Ana Mari Cauce agreed that the money should be returned but did not disband the endowed chair. Instead, the university agreed to pay half of Halperin's salary out of its general fund, using money that remained in the endowment from interest and other gifts to cover the rest. It was also reported that "the university is also working on clarifying language for future donor agreements," and that "it was not in their interest to get into a tussle with a major donor over a minor donation and a small program."[277] This is a major departure from prior attitudes that might have induced the university to bow to the wishes of pro-Israel donors so as to avoid political issues. Instead, the school found a way to maintain the program while cutting ties to the donor.

Many students, and Halperin herself, did not feel the university's response went far enough and spoke out against the unethical practice of catering to donor's preferences instead of pursuing free speech and academic integrity. They felt the endowment should not have been returned. Professor Halperin said that "the potential professional and material consequences of the university's decision were so dangerous to academic freedom that their explanation, defending that freedom, did not ring true." As she noted, "I didn't express the political views the donors wanted, and then a bunch of money went away." Graduate students in the Israel Studies Program "condemned the return of the endowment and were very concerned with the threat to academic free speech, the possibility of future self-censorship, and the potential loss of professional opportunities and grants for graduate level research."[278] This incident highlights how Palestine is now more central to academic freedom on college campuses than it had been before.

In August 2023 Amichai Chikli, Israel's minister of diaspora affairs and combatting anti-Semitism, sent a request to Princeton University president Christopher L. Eisgruber regarding a book assigned by a professor. Satyel Larson, an assistant professor in the Department of Near Eastern Studies, was teaching a course called "The Healing Humanities: Decolonizing Trauma Studies from the Global South" and had assigned the book *The Right to Maim: Debility, Capacity, Disability*, by Rutgers professor Jasbir Puar. The Israeli minister called for the withdrawal of the book, citing defamatory accusations against Israeli soldiers. Others went further. As reported in the *National Review*, "Ronald Lauder, president of the World Jewish Congress, called for canceling the course and terminating the professor. 'Princeton University is not only sanctioning hate speech, but establishing fertile ground for a new generation of antisemitic thought leaders,' Lauder tweeted. 'I am calling on Princeton University to cancel the course in question immediately, fire its professor, Satyel Larson, and issue a public apology to its students, the global Israeli community, and Jews all over the world.'"[279] Other professors noted that challenging material was sometimes assigned as a way to inform students about worldviews without condoning them and asserted that the text may be used to teach about the evils of anti-Semitism. Apart from the potential risk of violating the free speech rights of professors and students at Princeton, it is alarming that another nation's minister might have an influence on the types of texts deemed appropriate at an American university.

In 2023 Harvard University blocked a fellowship appointment at the Carr Center at the Harvard Kennedy School of Government of the longtime director of Human Rights Watch, Kenneth Roth. Roth was dubbed as the "godfather of human rights" in an article published in the *Nation*, in which Michael Massing reports that the reason the appointment was blocked was Roth's "anti-Israel bias."[280] The School of Government's dean later reversed the decision after widespread criticism of the decision about Roth, but not necessarily around free speech on Palestine.[281]

In January 2024 University of Wisconsin-Milwaukee students demanded that Golda Meir's name be taken off a campus library. Meir was the prime minister of Israel from 1969 to 1974 and graduated from the University of Wisconsin-Milwaukee in 1917.[282] Protests are also occurring on fronts other than universities. In November 2023 Josh Paul, a State Department official, resigned from his role due to the U.S. government's unconditional support for Israel.[283] Tariq Habash, a Biden appointee in the Department of Education, resigned in January 2024, citing the feeling that his humanity as a Palestinian American was undervalued by the administration.[284] The texture of support on college campuses and in the educational system itself is shifting, becoming more open and nuanced.

> I think that part of BDS is the fact that you have more and more American-born Palestinian-Americans and also our Muslim Americans who naturally speak the language of the American left. That's who they are, and people of color, too. I think perhaps some of that would have happened, even without the BDS movement simply because of those people who now exist, and who Jewish students will meet on a college campus in a way that their parents would not have.
> —PETER BEINART, APRIL 19, 2021

The landscape of the American understanding of the Israel/Palestine relationship is changing. The advent of the BDS movement and its increasing prevalence and acceptance in the American public has opened the minds of many to allow the stories of Palestinians a place on the stage of national discourse. As more and more people support the commercial, academic, and cultural boycotts of Israel, the message is spread farther and farther. Pro-Palestinian voices have taken to social media to share their stories, and the censorship they experience is being brought to light and brought to court. Journalists are more willing to report in a way that is more balanced. Educators are becoming more aware, and college students are using their passion for justice to speak out for the cause. Yet forward progress also means stronger resistance. As with all social movements, as one side increases in intensity, a fervor will rise on the other side to meet it.

A poignant example of the struggle is a story told by Sara Roy, describing her early research. Her experience of being dismissed and reviled yet continuing to follow the inner compass gifted her by her parents is a seed of the movement growing today. "I remember when I first went to the West Bank and Gaza as a doctoral student doing fieldwork in 1985," she says.

> After I returned, I was invited by various institutions to give talks on my research. In those early days of my work, I was asked to speak to Jewish groups. I welcomed the opportunity. I was well-trained in research methods at Harvard, armed with hard data, analyses, and personal experiences. What I soon learned was that none of it mattered; facts did not matter if they contradicted what people wanted and needed to believe. This was one of my earliest lessons in working on the Israeli-Palestinian crisis—for many people, evidence was irrelevant. Looking back to those early days, I did not fully appreciate that I was entering a field that was radioactive, particularly as a Jew and as a child of survivors.

Yet that understanding of how "radioactive" the work was did not deter her.

> Doing the work I was doing was always consistent with my family history. It was informed and shaped by that history. Speaking out against injustice was a deeply embedded value with which I was brought up. It was consistent with my parents' experience during the war. But for many people in the Jewish American community—which admittedly is not homogenous—including for the community of survivors among whom I grew up, I was considered a traitor. I can't say this was true for everyone but it was certainly true for many, probably most. Again, in the early days of my writing and lecturing, people would attack me verbally and viciously, and even throw things at me. On occasion, I would get a death threat. I had one man calling me from Israel weekly, screaming at me. This was in 1986 or 1987.

Almost forty years later she is still in the fight, and her experience sheds light on the increasing intensity and globalization of the movement. "There is an inverse relationship," Roy says, between deteriorating conditions in Palestine and widening activism here. The situation has become so much worse in Israel, the West Bank, Gaza, Jerusalem, and beyond. Because of this and coupled with access to information that did not exist when I began my work, increasing numbers of Jews and Israelis are now speaking out against the occupation and Israeli settler colonialism, which emanates from a growing disillusionment with Zionism. The future is staring all of us in the face and it's a dark future in the absence of real change. There is a recognition that there is more than one way to think about this tragic conflict, and more than one set of questions that must be asked. And, either one has the courage to ask those questions and to seek the answers, or one does not.[285]

Chapter Four

THE INTENSIFICATION OF POLITICAL AND LEGAL BATTLES IN THE UNITED STATES AND BEYOND

In the spring of 2021 Israel undertook a massive COVID-19 vaccination program that was lauded internationally. Israelis, including settlers in the Occupied Palestinian Territories, received vaccines quickly and efficiently. Yet the four million Palestinians living under the control of the Israeli government did not receive vaccinations, despite international law holding Israel accountable for their welfare.[1] This should have garnered some level of media coverage and chastisement by the world's leadership as a global effort to vaccinate was underway. It did not. Apathy toward Israel's prejudiced treatment of Palestinians within its nebulous borders is one example of the way the American government accepts actions that are antithetical to its own values and the values Israel claims it holds.

It is no secret that the United States considers Israel to be a strategic ally in the Middle East. In 1962, after signing the first arms agreement with Israel, President John F. Kennedy reiterated that the United States had a "special relationship with Israel in the Middle East, comparable only to that which it has with Britain over a wide range of world affairs."[2] Since Israel's inception in 1948, the United States has provided more financial and political support for Israel than for any other country in the world. In 2016 the United States and Israel signed an agreement granting the latter $38 billion in military aid over the next ten years—the largest aid package to any country in U.S. history.[3]

Israel is embraced by American liberal society and politicians from both sides of the aisle as a progressive country that embodies "tolerance, plurality, inclusivity, and democracy" and "can be passionately defended for its lofty ideals."[4] The relationship between the United States and Israel is supposed to be based on the shared values of democracy and personal freedom, yet, as Saree Makdisi notes, "Israel was founded through a process of ethnic cleansing and the subsequent colonization of forcibly occupied land. It maintains and enforces not only a decades-old military occupation but also a stark system of ethnic and racial distinction and separation across all the territory it has seized since 1948." Well-documented evidence suggests that Israel

> has a system of government characterized by what the instruments of international law specifically identify as apartheid. It systematically demolishes homes belonging . . . to Palestinian Arabs—whether they are citizens of the state or not—while equally systematically building homes for . . . Israeli Jews in the service of a stark logic of racial exclusion. Similarly, it selectively restricts health care, access to education, access to water, freedom of movement, and other basic rights—including access to sufficient nutrition—to one racial group while granting extraordinary privileges to the other.[5]

As Keith Peter Keily writes in *U.S. Foreign Policy Discourse and the Israel Lobby*, "The global leadership of the United States was premised on and deeply connected to the representation of universally applicable 'progressive and enlightened ideals' which directly informed that subjects [have] special responsibilities and duties. This form of leadership again echoes major themes of American exceptionalism, as well as the core oppositions of Progressive/Backward and Good/Evil."[6] This is why U.S. policy toward Israel is far more complex than simple foreign policy, the kind employed toward other nations. Israel is supposed to embody a certain American ideal; the United States and Israel are intertwined and interconnected on issues that go beyond foreign policy. A striking example of this is found in Keith Feldman's book *A Shadow Over Palestine*, as described by Rawan Arar: "Feldman begins with the passage of Resolution 3379 by the United Nations General Assembly in November of 1975. The resolution states, 'Zionism is a form of racism and racial discrimination.' The passage of the resolution sparked protest in the United States as '. . . support for Israel was an expression of U.S. patriotism.' Tens of thousands of Americans demonstrated and both chambers of congress condemned the resolution."[7]

Israel's relationship with Palestine echoes the historic relationship between white and Black people in America. Palestine, then, is at the heart of U.S. sociopolitical definitions of privilege and social hierarchy. The way the United States speaks of its treatment of minorities is mirrored in the way Israel speaks of its treatment of Palestinians. That defenders of Israel would deny its violations of international law and humanitarian policy would be one thing, but when it comes to the Jewish state, we see something even more entrenched: the denial that there has been any denial—not, as Makdisi puts it, "merely ignorance (readily facilitated in any case by the mainstream media in the United States and Europe), not merely the denial of Palestinian history, Palestinian dispossession, and Palestinian rights, but the denial that they have been denied in the first place."[8] This denial eerily mimics the acts of the United States in its repression of information regarding its treatment of indigenous populations and Native Americans, and its refusal to acknowledge either that the abuses occurred or that it has covered them up. In this way, the United States is an ally to Israel not because of a mutual love of democracy and freedom, but because of a shared history of colonialism and conquest.

Representatives of the U.S. government, with their entrenched orientalist viewpoints, have used peace talks as opportunities to push their own values and preferences onto Palestinians. Khaled Elgindy describes how the Oslo Accords, for example, were intended not only to resolve the crisis in the Levant, but to transform "certain aspects of Palestinian politics in order to turn the Palestinians into a suitable partner." The United States, "along with donor countries and even the Israelis, had a direct say—and often an effective veto—over key aspects of Palestinian political life." The Palestinian Authority (PA), the governing body of Palestinians' day-to-day affairs in the territories, relied heavily on foreign aid and the goodwill of the Israeli military and its powerful friends and found itself subject to "an ever-widening assortment of conditions and restrictions regarding its security performance, internal governance, and even diplomatic activities."[9] To achieve its goals, the PA was forced to change its politics and institutions to suit American preferences.

Palestinians in the United States are living in a country that supports Israel's occupation of, and illegal expansion into, the Occupied Palestinian Territories and the politics that made refugees out of the Palestinian population in the first place. In addition, the United States takes political steps to deny cultural and heritage rights to Palestinians. Modern American politicians have embraced the anti-Semitic rhetoric surrounding Palestine and the Holocaust connection to Israel. These politicians sometimes represent Palestinian American constituents but seem not to deem their voices important or consider their experiences. Take comments by Senator Ted Cruz of Texas, who has said, "The suggestion that Israel has committed war crimes is particularly offensive given that the Jewish people suffered under the most horrific war crimes in the Holocaust."[10] The idea that victims of tragedy can never go on to perpetrate tragedy against others is a false dichotomy. This conflation of victimhood with innocence is an example of the ways in which the Jewish people's history of suffering is used to excuse the state of Israel's oppression of Palestinians.

Given its political and military power, how is it that the U.S. government is willing to overlook human rights violations and the denial of freedoms to maintain a fierce alliance with Israel? This chapter will examine the ways in which government policy has developed over time, and how structural political and legal precedents have created a culture of mandated oppression of Palestinian identity. It will examine the history of foreign policy in the United States toward Israel and Palestine and the influence of the September 11 terrorist attacks and lobbyists from Israel and within the United States, in particular from Christian Zionists, on that policy. It will examine the U.S. government's record as a member of the United Nations. Finally, it will consider federal, state, and municipal laws that codify support for Israel in American culture.

GOVERNMENT POLICY

U.S. foreign policy: A brief history

The United States has been, for decades, the "chief sponsor and sole mediator in the peace process between Israelis and Palestinians." While it's possible that the United States is the only country that could fill this role, since it is the only "global actor trusted enough by Israel's leaders to

INTENSIFICATION OF POLITICAL AND LEGAL BATTLES

guarantee Israel's security,"[11] and thus the only power Israel is willing to work with, the presence of Americans at the table brings an automatic tilt of power toward Israel's side. Washington's special relationship with Israel precludes their being a neutral party, and this fact, along with the inability of American politicians to recognize and address it, has made the negotiation of peace in the region incredibly ineffective. As Khaled Elgindy notes, "The United States has consistently put its thumb on the scale in Israel's favor while simultaneously discounting the importance of internal Palestinian political realities."[12] This friendly relationship between the United States and Israel goes back to the days of the British Mandate, before the state of Israel existed, but attitudes toward the dispossession of Palestinians in the region have certainly shifted. To fully understand the current state of the political relationship between the United States and Israel, it is important to have a rudimentary understanding of its history.

In 1919 a majority of members of Congress supported the creation of a Jewish state but maintained that the native population should not be harmed. There was considerable debate over the Balfour Declaration, and in the end they added a clause that "nothing shall be done which may prejudice the civil and religious rights of Christian and all other non-Jewish communities in Palestine."[13] Over time, American support for Israel and America's role in the pursuit of peace in the Middle East have changed, waxing and waning with each subsequent administration and the varying cultural and social temperatures of the day. Just over one hundred years after the lively and relatively even-handed debates over the Balfour Declaration, respect for the non-Jewish population in the area is nearly nonexistent in the U.S. government, but the seeds of this hostility were planted decades before.

In April 1922 the Foreign Affairs Committee of the U.S. House of Representatives convened a hearing to debate the Balfour Declaration. Selim Totah, a young American law student originally from Ramallah, spoke at the hearing, citing the American values of democracy and America's history to plead the case for Palestine.

> You gentlemen and your forefathers have fought for the idea, and that is taxation with representation. We are asking for the same principles. By the operation of the Balfour Declaration a majority of Jews will be established in Palestine, and after a while by their majority they will govern the native

people. Would you stand for things like that in California if the Japanese should come in and after 20 or 30 years become a majority and establish a republic of their own? Not for a moment. How would you expect 93 percent of the people in Palestine to stand for that?[14]

His speech was met with accusations of wanting to shut the Jewish people out of government, and his plea that the Arab majority be given a say in the policies that governed them was met with "hostility and derision."[15] A few months later, Congress voted in favor of the declaration and the creation of a home for the Jewish people in Mandatory Palestine.

Woodrow Wilson, who was president when the Balfour Declaration was being debated, was a proponent of Israel's bid for statehood. He was influenced by Zionist figures such as Louis Brandeis, "a close confidant whom he later appointed to the Supreme Court." Brandeis taught that Palestine was the original inheritance of the Israelites, having been given by God to their forefathers as far back as the biblical Abraham. Wilson, who was raised in a religious family, may also have been influenced by the British position, which was that a Jewish settlement in the region would be a way to "advance their own colonial ambitions in the region," as well as the "pioneering Zionist lobby" that was "already an established presence on Capitol Hill."[16]

The Balfour Declaration was controversial among American politicians, but after its passing it became the cornerstone of U.S. policy toward Israel and Palestine. It was also considered fundamental for officials and citizens to understand Palestine, the Zionist project, and the Arabs and Jews who lived in the region. By the time Israel declared itself a state in 1948, the basic tenets of American policy toward the conflict and the Palestinians were in place. Washington admired Israel's economic, political, and, particularly, military power, held strong doubts and reservations toward the often highly nationalistic Palestinian leadership, and was deeply divided over how to resolve the issues that continued to grow over time.[17]

In the 1940s, and especially after World War II, the United States took over Britain's role as the world's political powerhouse and the principal negotiator in Palestine. This coincided with the Zionist terror campaign of 1944–47, which enraged the British but did little to turn American sentiment from Israel.[18] By 1947, as noted by British foreign minister Ernest Bevin, it was "no secret that the terrorists in Palestine [here a reference to the Jewish population] have received the bulk of their financial and moral

INTENSIFICATION OF POLITICAL AND LEGAL BATTLES

support from the United States."[19] Despite this, support for an independent Jewish state was hardly unanimous in Washington. On May 11, 1948, the *New York Times* published a piece titled "Jews to Proclaim State Despite US," which stated, "Thus far, the United States delegation is continuing its efforts to bring about a truce, which, among other things, would require both Jews and Arabs to lay aside the idea of proclaiming independent states."[20]

It was at this time that Britain announced its plan to end the British Mandate of Palestine and turn the region over to the United Nations. With that decision, the fate of the "Jewish state" was in American hands, specifically those of President Harry Truman, who, despite his own State Department's stance that partition was "certain to undermine relations" with Arab and Muslim countries, took a number of steps to tip the scales in the Zionists' favor. Seeing that separate Jewish and Palestinian states were likely, the State Department suggested a plan to make partition equitable and just. This was forcefully resisted by the Jewish Agency and its lobby, the American Zionist Emergency Council, and Truman "pressed the State Department to withdraw the proposal."[21]

On November 29, 1947, the United Nations voted in favor of creating the Jewish nation, setting up the original partition plan which gave roughly 56 percent of the land of Palestine to the Jewish minority and inviting Jewish people from around the world to settle in the new nation of Israel. The remaining 44 percent of the land was given to the majority, who are Palestinian. This land division was protested by the Palestinian people but presented to the world as a peaceful solution and a safe harbor for the Jewish people, "a land without people for a people without land." Early propaganda films presented the area as in need of a new population to bring back its "long neglected fruitfulness."[22]

On May 14, 1948, the Jewish state announced the independent State of Israel. Eleven minutes later, President Truman announced that the United States "recognized the provisional government of Israel on a de facto basis. The news came as a shock to American diplomats, so much so that [Secretary of State George] Marshall had to send a State Department official to the United Nations to prevent the entire American delegation from resigning en masse."[23] In this way, the Zionists, led by President Truman, and against the judgment of many in Washington, legitimized the new nation and became its first and most important ally.

INTENSIFICATION OF POLITICAL AND LEGAL BATTLES

The original division, made official in 1948, lasted only briefly. By 1949 the nascent Israeli government had expanded to 78 percent of the land, uprooting 700,000 Palestinians and pushing them out of their homes.[24] This encroachment, while mildly protested, was largely ignored by the international community, and the state of Israel maintained its image of "little David" fighting Goliath for a place to exist. The rather disturbing trend of conflating Palestinians with all other Arabs and erasing their presence began during this period, when Washington dubbed the crisis the "Arab-Israeli Conflict." John Foster Dulles, secretary of state in the Eisenhower administration, visited Jordan in 1953 and met with Palestinian representatives to hear "impassioned pleas regarding the current situation, their rights, desire to return to their homes, and opposition to resettlement in the Arab countries." When he returned to the United States, Dulles did a radio broadcast but "did not mention meeting with the Palestinians and chose instead to emphasize resettlement combined with economic development over repatriation."[25]

The Suez Crisis clarified the possibilities of an Afro-Arab solidarity against the colonial dimensions of Israel/Palestine. When Egyptian premier Gamal Abdel Nasser seized control of the British and French–owned Suez Canal Company in 1956, he asserted himself as a leader willing to resist European colonial powers and take back control of assets belonging to his country. France, Britain, and Israel made a secret alliance and attempted together to take back control of the canal and depose Nasser. When the plan failed and the collusion was exposed, Nasser was left stronger than ever. The crisis had long-standing ramifications for U.S. involvement in the Middle East. As the historian Peter Hahn explains, "By undermining traditional Anglo-French hegemony, exacerbating the problems of revolutionary nationalism personified by Nasser, stoking Arab-Israeli conflict, and offering the Soviet Union a pretext for penetrating the region, the crisis drew the United States toward substantial, significant, and enduring involvement in the Middle East."[26]

In response to the shared French and British military support of Israel against the Egyptian nationalization of the Suez Canal in 1956, W. E. B. Du Bois wrote the poem "Suez." In the poem, Du Bois frames Israel's actions as typical of "the West," which "betrays its murdered, mocked, and damned," while depicting President Gamal Abdul Nasser as waving a "great black hand" that "grasps hard the concentrated hate of myriad million slaves."[27]

INTENSIFICATION OF POLITICAL AND LEGAL BATTLES

The David and Goliath image was challenged in 1967 when, in the aftermath of the Six-Day War, Israel occupied the West Bank and Gaza, effectively taking control of the remaining land belonging to the Palestinians. This land grab was recognized by the United Nations in Resolution 242, which called for "the withdrawal of Israeli troops from the occupied territories, acknowledges the claim of sovereignty, territorial integrity and political independence of every state in the region."[28] Despite this United Nations resolution (and subsequent resolutions that reinforced it), Israel has maintained military control over both regions to this day, and the censure by the UN did little to tarnish Israel's reputation in the eyes of American citizens and politicians.

After Israel's conquest of the West Bank, East Jerusalem, and the Gaza Strip, and the emergence of an autonomous Palestinian national movement, the United States was forced to accept and begin to grapple with the existence of the Palestinian people and the PLO that represented them. This fact is evidenced by a Brookings Institute report in 1975 that called for a "comprehensive peace settlement" and "some form of Palestinian self-determination."[29] In the fall of that year, hearings were held on the origins of the Israel/Palestine conflict, the nature of politics in the region, and the weaknesses of existing policy. Edward Said and Ibrahim Abu-Lughod spoke to Congress, the first Palestinians to do so in more than fifty years. Senator J. William Fulbright, chair of the Senate Foreign Relations Committee, "spoke openly for the first time about Palestinian rights and past suffering: 'Israel, I am convinced can and should survive as a peaceful, prosperous society—but within the essential borders of 1967. That much we owe them, but no more. We do not owe them our support of their continued occupation of Arab lands.... The Palestinian people have as much right to a homeland as do the Jewish people.'" In an unprecedented act of solidarity with Palestine, Senators James Abourezk of South Dakota and Howard Baker of Tennessee traveled to Beirut to meet with PLO leader Yasser Arafat.[30]

While Congress may have been tilting toward the Palestinians, the White House of the 1970s was firmly pro-Israel. A striking example of the way foreign policy is shaped by Orientalist attitudes is present in a speech President Gerald Ford gave to the National Security Council during that period. "I will tell you briefly about my record in Congress where Israel is concerned," he said. "It was so close that I have a black reputation with the

Arabs. I have always liked and respected the Israeli people. They are intelligent and dedicated to the causes in which they believe. They are dedicated to their religion, their country, their family and their high moral standards. I admire and respect them."[31] In this speech, Ford illustrates the dichotomy between Israel and the Arabs, makes sweeping positive generalizations about Israelis, and, by virtue of comparison, tacitly denigrates Arabs and Muslims. Ultimately, nothing changed in American policy toward the region. In 1978 Hamilton Jordan, chief of staff for President Jimmy Carter, prepared a document for the president outlining the power of the Jewish/Israeli block and urging him to consider it when making decisions. In the introduction to this document, he writes, "I would compare our present understanding of the American Jewish lobby (vis-a-vis Israel) to our understanding of the American Labor Movement four years ago. We are aware of its strength and influence, but don't understand the basis for that strength, nor the way it is used politically."[32] Jordan understood the political power behind the Israel lobby and sought to harness it for President Carter.

Jesse Jackson's presidential campaigns in 1984 and 1988 and the Rainbow Coalition made significant inroads in bringing the issue of Palestinian rights to the American public.[33] Jackson held a "principled position on the Israeli-Palestinian conflict that seeks to address Palestinian oppression and statelessness," a position that was unpopular with Jewish people in America and many conservatives.[34] Jackson was only the second African American to compete at a national level for the Democratic endorsement to run for president, and while he did not win the nomination, he "drew a historic level of support, including nearly 7 million votes in 1988."[35]

Under the pro-Israel Ronald Reagan administration, however, the U.S. relationship with Palestine deteriorated, and ties between the United States and Israel deepened. Secretary of State George Schultz, in a speech to the lobby in 1987, denounced Arafat and the PLO as "not qualified to be part of the peace process." As Shultz spoke, "he found himself unwittingly leading the audience in a chant of 'PLO? Hell, no!' The somewhat awkward moment was more than just a testament to the remarkable influence of the pro-Israel lobby in Washington."[36] Janice Terry says that "former President Reagan was described by Stuart Eizenstat, Carter's Assistant to the President for Domestic Affairs and an ardent Zionist supporter, as having a "particularly warm spot in his heart toward Israel, as did his Secretary of State George Shultz." According to Eizenstat, the relationship between the

United States and Israel "blossom[ed] into a strategic alliance" under Reagan.[37] The Reagan contribution to the culture of support for Israel is summed up nicely in an anecdote shared by Edward Said, who wrote, "The main contribution of the Reagan-Schultz era was to instill in all of Israel's supporters the discipline of 'not pressuring' Israel. On the very day in late 1987 that Ronald Reagan gently upbraided Israel for shooting unarmed Palestinian children, an additional $280 million was earmarked" for Israel.[38]

This stance led directly into the attempts in the 1990s to adjudicate peace in the region without offending or inconveniencing Israel. Elgindy describes how, "since the 1990s, American peacemaking in the Middle East has operated according to two interrelated and equally flawed assumptions: first, that a credible peace settlement could be achieved without addressing the vast imbalance of power between Israel and the Palestinians, and second, that it would be possible to ignore or bend internal Palestinian politics to the perceived needs of the peace process."[39] Palestinians were shut out of peace talks until the 1993 Oslo Accords, and while that agreement did include the involvement of Palestinian leadership, it did not place significant demands on Israel to restore justice. During the Clinton administration, the U.S. government had the opportunity to curb the building of new Israeli settlements in occupied areas but chose not to exert pressure on the Israeli government. In his book *Blind Spot: America and the Palestinians, from Balfour to Trump*, the scholar Khaled Elgindy recounts how "former Clinton peace team member Aaron David Miller stated, 'I don't recall a single tough, honest conversation in which we said to the Israelis, 'Look, settlements may not violate the letter of Oslo, but they're wreaking havoc with its spirit and compromising the logic of a gradual process of building trust and confidence.'"[40]

At the time of the Oslo Accords signing, Israel had to accept the legitimacy of the PLO and agreed to having the Palestinian Authority, a state-like institution, handle the day-to-day affairs of Palestinians in the Occupied Palestinian Territories. The State Department's public Office of the Historian account states that "Both sides agreed that a Palestinian Authority (PA) would be established and assume governing responsibilities in the West Bank and Gaza Strip over a five-year period. Then, permanent status talks on the issues of borders, refugees, and Jerusalem would be held."[41] Before the end of the five-year period, however, peace talks had dissolved, and Israel no longer recognized the authority of the PA. There is evidence that the accords were never going to be respected, including a leaked video in 2001 of Benjamin Netanyahu, current Israeli prime minister. The video shows him discussing his approach to the accords: "They asked me before the election if I would honor the Oslo Accords. I said I would but I am going to interpret the Accords in such a way that will allow me to put an end to this galloping forward to the 1967 borders. How do we do it? Nobody said what 'defined military zones' were. Defined military zones are security zones. As far as I'm concerned the entire Jordan Valley is a defined military zone." When a listener questioned whether this approach would bring censure from world leaders, Netanyahu responded, "I know what America is. America is a thing that can be moved very easily. Moved in the right direction."[42] In an interview in 2011 with President Barack Obama, Netanyahu repeated his stance, stating that in order for there to be peace, "the Palestinians will have to accept some basic realities. The first is that while Israel is prepared to make generous compromises for peace, it cannot go back to the 1967 lines."[43] In his speech to the joint session of Congress in 2015, Netanyahu received thunderous applause as he compared Israel and America. "America and Israel, we share a common destiny, the destiny of promised lands that cherish freedom and offer hope," he said. "Israel is grateful for the support of America—of America's people and of America's presidents, from Harry Truman to Barack Obama."[44]

In 2000, under the direction of President Bill Clinton, Israeli prime minister Ehud Barak and Palestinian leader Yasser Arafat met at Camp David to attempt a peace negotiation. After two weeks of talks, the summit ended without an agreement being reached. The blame for this failure was placed on Arafat and his unwillingness to compromise. One of Israel's principal negotiators at Camp David in 2000, Shlomo Ben-Ami, a former Israeli diplomat and historian, appeared to disprove this accusation in an interview by suggesting that he too would have rejected the offer if he were a Palestinian. Ben-Ami's perspective runs counter to the coverage in American media, which has consistently praised Ehud Barak for accepting the deal while blaming and demonizing Arafat for rejecting it.[45] The vilification continued when, in the lead-up to her Senate bid in 2000, Hillary Clinton returned a $50,000 donation from the Arab American Institute (AAI). According to her spokesman, Howard Wolfman, the donation was returned because the AAI had "made statements counter to the things that Hillary believes in." Clinton was accused of isolating Arab voters in New York. Jim Zogby, director of the Arab-American Institute in Washington, told *Salon*, "In an election as close as this, where everyone else is being courted, [Arab voters] are being told, 'We don't care how close it is, we don't need or want your support.'" During her Senate campaign, Clinton had not met with Arab leaders at all, despite a prominent Arab population in her district. Local American Muslim Alliance board member Ghazi Khankan said the race was "undeniably... the ugliest chapter in a hard-fought Senate race. 'It's a shame... Muslim Americans and Arab-Americans are being muddied and universally associated with acts of terrorism.'"[46]

The Bush administration was characterized by indecision and infighting between "two opposing camps with very different approaches to the Middle East and the world."[47] Some in the administration, like Secretary of State Colin Powell and CIA director George Tenet felt the United States should take an active role in the negotiations between Israel and Palestine and favored an approach that worked for both groups. In a keynote address at the American Task Force on Palestine inaugural gala, Secretary of State Condoleezza Rice had said, "I believe that there could be no greater legacy for America than to help to bring into being a Palestinian state for a people who have suffered too long, who have been humiliated too long, who have not reached their potential for too long, and who have so much to give to the international community and to all of us."[48] Vice President Dick Cheney and Defense Secretary Donald Rumsfeld disagreed, deferring to Israeli prime minister Ariel Sharon and following his lead. Condoleezza Rice later wrote, "The differences in the administration between the decidedly pro-Israel bent of the White House and the State Department's more traditional pro-Arab view percolated beneath the surface," and nothing was accomplished.[49]

By 2007 the prospect of a just agreement between Palestine and Israel had deteriorated to the point of being a nonstarter. Jimmy Carter, who remained active politically in regard to the issue, said, "I don't see any present prospect that any member of the US Congress, the House or Senate, would say, 'Let's take a balanced position between Israel and the Palestinians and negotiate a peace agreement.'... 'It's almost politically suicidal... for a member of the Congress who wants to seek reelection to take any stand that might be interpreted as anti-policy of the conservative Israeli government."[50] President Obama took a more active role in pursuing peace and justice for Palestinians, appointing a special envoy for Middle East peace and taking a tough stance on Israeli settlements, declaring that the United States would "not accept the legitimacy of continued Israeli settlements." Hamas leaders, encouraged by what they saw as a shift in the government's attitude toward Palestine, wrote to President Obama urging him to visit Gaza.[51] However, following the end of peace negotiations in 2010, Obama, appearing frustrated and disillusioned, disengaged from the process. He had tried to both restrain Israeli settlements and protect Israel from the United Nations after the Goldstone Report but was unsuccessful in changing much of the long-standing status quo, making him yet another American president yielding no change with regard to the Palestinian situation.

On May 19, 2011, Obama made a statement repeating official U.S. policy on Israel–Palestine relations, stating that "we believe the borders of Israel and Palestine should be based on the 1967 lines, with mutually agreed swaps, so that secure and recognized borders are established for both sides."[52] Although President Reagan had made similar remarks as far back as 1982, insisting that Israel had no need for further settlements, right-wing groups accused Obama of siding with Israel's enemies and setting up the Jewish people for a second holocaust. One ad put out by a pro-Israel advocacy group claimed that Obama had "moved sharply towards Israel's enemies. And the results could be disastrous."[53] The Christian Broadcasting Network produced a three-minute broadcast explaining that the 1967 borders were indefensible, and that it was necessary for Israel to control the entire Jordan Valley to protect it from countries in the East, such as Iran and Jordan. Neither Palestine nor the Palestinians living in the Jordan Valley were mentioned.[54] Obama was further demonized after remarks made to a small group of Democratic activists. He was quoted in the *Des Moines Register* as saying, "Nobody is suffering more than the Palestinian people." His comment inspired David Adelman, member of the American Israel Public Affairs Committee, to write a letter to Obama calling the comment "deeply troubling."[55] By 2016 the president had changed his position. He signed a $38 billion military aid agreement with Israel, "the largest single pledge of military assistance in U.S. history," and abstained from "a Security Council resolution condemning Israeli settlements as both illegal and a threat to Israeli-Palestinian peace."[56]

INTENSIFICATION OF POLITICAL AND LEGAL BATTLES

While little progress toward Palestinian self-determination was made under Obama, under the Donald Trump administration the situation for Palestinians under Israeli control quickly devolved into state-sanctioned apartheid. The U.S. approach to the Israel–Palestine conflict shifted entirely to one that backed Israel on ideological grounds. It has long been accepted practice for U.S. presidents to uphold the importance of international law as part of their diplomatic gestures. For example, the United States has routinely expressed "concerns" over violence against Palestinians, considered the West Bank and the Gaza Strip as occupied territories, and reiterated the importance of limiting Israeli settlement expansion. Marc Lamont Hill and Mitchell Plitnick point out that these "policy charades deployed by previous presidents . . . were simply abandoned." Hill and Plitnick also assess that "Trump's agenda was driven . . . not just by pro-Israel forces, but by the most radical of those forces: the religious-nationalist settler movement."[57] Trump's approach to Israeli settlements was more permissive; the White House issued a statement that it didn't "believe the existence of settlements is an impediment to peace."[58] Jared Kushner, Jason Greenblatt, and David Friedman, who made up the Middle East peace team, all had ties to the Israeli settler movement. Friedman, in particular, "alarmed Palestinians and much of the international community" with his frequent advocacy for Israeli settlers. The Charles and Seryl Kushner Foundation, run by Jared Kushner's parents, donated tens of thousands of dollars to Israeli causes, including the American Friends of Beit el Yeshiva and several charities that operate within the Gush Etzion settlement bloc. Jared Kushner sits on the board of the foundation, which has pledged to give far more in coming years, including a promise in 2014 to give $18 million to the Shaare Zedek Medical Center and a pledge of $315,000 to the Friends of the Israeli Defense League, on whose board Kushner also sits.[59] These entanglements not only were unethical but had material effects on the lives of Palestinians living under the oppression of an Israeli government propped up by sympathetic American power brokers.

In an example of how American support empowered Israel during the Trump administration, in 2014 Deputy Foreign Minister Ze'ev Elkin assured Israelis in a new settlement in the occupied city of Gitit in the Jordan Valley that they would not be forced to leave, despite the settlement being in direct conflict with the Geneva Convention and UN Resolution 242. "The

Jordan Valley must be under Israeli sovereignty forever," he said. "Now of all times, in a government headed by Likud, in a settlement built by Likud, we can say loud and clear: You will remain here forever and there will be Israeli sovereignty here."[60]

As noted by Shibley Telhami, "The Trump administration elevated Israel to unprecedented levels of importance in US foreign policy priorities, despite the absence of an immediate crisis or compelling strategic interest."[61] On December 6, 2017, Trump announced the official recognition by the United States of Jerusalem as Israel's capital.[62] This, along with the move of the U.S. Embassy to Jerusalem from Tel Aviv, had been a major campaign promise of Trump's. The decision infuriated Palestinian leaders as it went against seventy years of precedent in American's dealings with Palestine, and threatened the U.S. role in the peace process. "Not since Harry Truman defied the State Department and his intelligence community by recognizing Israel in May 1948 had a U.S. president decided such a weighty and consequential foreign policy matter almost entirely on the basis of domestic political considerations," says Elgindy.[63] Prime Minister Benjamin Netanyahu considered the announcement a victory for Israel, while Mahmoud Abbas, president of the State of Palestine, severed official ties with the United States. In response, Trump cut off U.S. assistance to the United Nations Relief Works Agency (UNRWA) for Palestine Refugees in the Near East, which was responsible for the care of five million Palestinian refugees. Up to that point, the United States had been UNRWA's largest donor. The new embassy in Jerusalem was opened on May 14, the anniversary of the Nakba, a choice that caused bitterness and disappointment among Palestinians. During the celebration in Jerusalem, Israeli soldiers killed sixty people in Gaza who were demonstrating. While international criticism of the event was high, the United States took Israel's side. Press Secretary Raj Shah declared that "the responsibility for these tragic deaths rests squarely with Hamas.... Hamas is intentionally and cynically provoking this response. And as the Secretary of State said, Israel has the right to defend itself."[64]

A few months later, the White House cut all $200 million in economic aid for the West Bank and Gaza. The administration chose to continue funding Palestinian security coordination with Israel, however, despite statements from the State Department that the money spent was "not in the best interests of the U.S. national interest" and "does not provide value to the U.S. taxpayer." Husam Zomlot, former Palestinian ambassador to the United States and later ambassador to the UK, "accused the Trump administration of 'weaponizing humanitarian and developmental aid as political blackmail' and of 'dismantling decades of US vision and engagement in Palestine.'"[65]

On March 25, 2019, President Trump legitimized Israel's occupation by recognizing its sovereignty over the Golan Heights. Trump's proclamation read:

> The State of Israel took control of the Golan Heights in 1967 to safeguard its security from external threats. Today, aggressive acts by Iran and terrorist groups, including Hizballah, in southern Syria continue to make the Golan Heights a potential launching ground for attacks on Israel. Any potential future peace agreement in the region must account for Israel's need to protect itself from Syria and other regional threats. Based on these unique circumstances, it is therefore appropriate to recognize Israeli sovereignty over the Golan Heights.
>
> NOW, THEREFORE, I, DONALD J. TRUMP, President of the United States of America, by virtue of the authority vested in me by the Constitution and the laws of the United States, do hereby proclaim that the United States recognizes that the Golan Heights are part of the State of Israel.[66]

Marc Lemont Hill and Mitchell Plitnick write that "with his statement, Trump undermined the most fundamental international law, which, as stated in the charter of the United Nations, forbids the acquisition of territory by force."[67] The same year, as reported in the *Jerusalem Post*, Prime Minister Netanyahu made remarks indicating he would never allow for Palestinian statehood and would continue to expand Israeli sovereignty. "Netanyahu spoke of a three-stage plan with regard to the West Bank, the third stage of which 'is to apply Israeli law to the communities in Judea and Samaria.'" Netanyahu's remarks were met with censure from leaders around the world, the *Post* continued: "PLO Secretary-General Saeb Erekat... strongly condemned Netanyahu's talk about annexation and the dangers of a Palestinian state." However, "[Erekat] was not surprised by Netanyahu's remarks. Israel, he said, 'will continue to brazenly violate international law for as long as the international community will continue to reward Israel with impunity, particularly with the Trump administration's support and endorsement of Israel's violation of the national and human rights of the people of Palestine.'" Turkish president Recep Tayyip Erdoğan's spokesman, Ibrahim Kalin, placed blame on world leaders: "'Will Western democracies react or will they keep appeasing? Shame on them all.'"[68]

Hill and Plitnick point out that while Trump may have been extreme in his treatment of Palestinians, his was not a new or extraordinary point of view. In fact, every U.S. president since Ronald Reagan had pledged to move the U.S. Embassy to Jerusalem, they write, and the move had been enshrined by the Jerusalem Embassy Act of 1995, which easily passed both the House and Senate. Up until Trump, presidents had simply signed waivers to delay the move.

> When Trump announced the recognition of Jerusalem as Israel's capital and, later, allowed the waiver to expire, he was not so much departing from long-standing U.S. policy as he was disregarding good sense in the execution of that policy.... It is tempting to view the ethical and political contradictions of American policy on Israel-Palestine as a result of the current political moment. Such an approach allows us to frame Donald Trump as a political outlier whose policies were out of step with both the global community and his political predecessors.... Rather than introducing a radically different policy agenda, Trump was simply the most aggressive and transparent articulation of long-standing bipartisan policies.

Hill and Plitnick go on to argue that "to truly produce justice in the region, progressives must absolutely challenge Donald Trump's policies. But we must also acknowledge that Trump was merely a dangerous extension, not the source, of deeply rooted and thoroughly bipartisan policies that have harmed the Palestinian people—and positioned Palestine as an exception to which core liberal American values are not applied."[69]

In fact, Trump's departure from the White House did not change the views of most in power in Washington. In June 2021 forty-seven members of Congress cosigned a letter to Defense Secretary Lloyd Austin urging him to "continue urgently engaging with Israel" on their request for aid in restocking the Iron Dome's interceptor missiles, and to "please report to Congress regarding Israel's needs as soon as possible." The letter cited the pledge of $3.8 billion a year in military assistance to Israel from fiscal year 2019 to 2028, and further requested "if Israel requests additional assistance,

INTENSIFICATION OF POLITICAL AND LEGAL BATTLES

as contemplated in the MOU, please work closely with Congress to expeditiously fulfill this request."[70]

Some, however, are pushing back. In 2021, in response to a decree signed by Israeli defense minister Benny Gantz that labeled six Palestinian human rights groups as terrorist organizations, a group of legislators, led by Representative Betty McCollum, chair of the House Defense Appropriations Subcommittee, introduced a resolution calling on the U.S. House of Representatives to condemn the move. McCollum's official statement read:

> Israel's decision to brand these prominent Palestinian civil society groups as terrorist organizations exposes the truth that Israel's occupation is violent, immoral, and unjust, and that peaceful efforts to defend the rights of Palestinian children, women, farmers, or prisoners must be declared illegal. The U.S. invests billions of our taxpayer dollars to support Israel's security, not Israel's system of occupation and repression of Palestinians. It is incumbent upon Democrats in the U.S. House and the Biden administration to condemn this Israeli decision and draw a clear line that anti-democratic repression of Palestinian civil society is not tolerated.[71]

The six organizations were the Defense for Children International—Palestine, Al-Haq, Addameer Prisoner Support and Human Rights Organization, Bisan Center for Research and Development, the Union of Agricultural Work Committees, and the Union of Palestinian Women's Committees.

Representative Rashida Tlaib made a speech in September 2022 in which she discussed the death of journalist Shireen Abu Akleh and the apartheid state of Israel. In her speech she said, "I want you all to know that among progressives it has become clear that you cannot claim to hold progressive values yet back Israel's apartheid government, and we will continue to push back and not accept this idea that you are progressive except for Palestine any longer." Her remarks angered some, including Rep. Debbie Wasserman-Schultz, who "denounced Tlaib's comments, labeling them 'antisemitic' and arguing that progressivism and support for Israel are not mutually exclusive."[72] Two months later, however, the FBI opened an investigation into the killing, an indication that the U.S. government is not satisfied with the internal investigation done by Israel. Israeli defense minister Benny Gantz has called the probe "a mistake" and said he would refuse to cooperate with it, but it may mark a turning point in relations between the two countries.[73]

In a speech to the United Nations in New York in September 2022, President Joe Biden spoke of the war between Russia and Ukraine. "This war is about extinguishing Ukraine's right to exist as a state, plain and simple, and Ukraine's right to exist as a people," he said. "Whoever you are, wherever you live, whatever you believe, that . . . should make your blood run cold."[74] One could replace "Ukraine" with "Palestine" and "Russia" with "Israel" and the sentiment ought to be, but often is not, identical. For decades, the United States has turned a blind eye to Israeli encroachment into Palestinian territory and denial of human rights of Palestinians. The Western world quickly rallied to the Ukrainian's defense, imposing sanctions on Vladimir Putin and supplying aid and arms to Ukrainians fighting to save their homeland. This kind of response has never been available to Palestinians, even during the unprecedented levels of violence against civilians and civilian infrastructure, which the International Court of Justice in the Hague labeled as "genocide" in January 2024. For them, according to KUVRD, "seeing the whole world quickly plaster the Ukrainian flag everywhere and collectively mobilize in celebration of resistance from a power hungry occupier when they're 'white, blonde, blue-eyed'" was a difficult juxtaposition in light of their own struggle.[75] Ukrainians who made homemade Molotov cocktails to throw at Russian tanks barreling down their streets were applauded; Palestinians who do the same are called terrorists.

President Biden did mention Palestine in this speech, however, indicating some changes. "We will continue to advocate for lasting negotiated peace between the Jewish and democratic state of Israel and the Palestinian people," he said. "The United States is committed to Israel's security, full stop. And a negotiated two-state solution remains, in our view, the best way to ensure Israel's security and prosperity for the future and give the Palestinians the state to which they are entitled."[76] Furthermore, in November 2022 "U.S. ambassador to Israel Tom Nides warned that the White House would "fight any attempt" by Israel to annex parts of the occupied West Bank." The United States "plans to work with a Netanyahu government, but 'we have to stand up for the things we believe in,' Nides said. 'We are a very strong ally, but there will be times we articulate our differences.'"[77]

As the war against Gaza continued, the images of death and destruction made their way to every corner of the globe. Coupled with the ruling of the

INTENSIFICATION OF POLITICAL AND LEGAL BATTLES

International Court of Justice describing Israeli violence against Palestinian civilians as genocide, U.S. public views changed drastically. This change happened in a relatively short period of time, as indicated in chapter 1.[78] President Biden's position, however, for the most part did not change. He doubled down on his support for Israel, directing billions of dollars in military aid to support Israel in its war against Gaza, even bypassing Congress to do so.[79] "Genocide Joe" emerged as an epithet referring to Biden's role in the Gaza genocide. Some believed that his support for Israel might affect the Democratic Party in election cycles.[80]

U.S. foreign policy toward Israel has remained staunchly supportive since the October 7 attacks and War against Gaza. In his initial address following the attack, Biden assured Israel that it was not alone and promised "to ask the United States Congress for an unprecedented support package for Israel's defense."[81] This support continued despite disagreements within the Democratic Party, as Biden's popularity among Israelis soared.[82] As the war and the number of civilian casualties in Palestine continued, the rhetoric being offered by the Biden administration changed, while in practice U.S. support remained constant. Reports said that President Biden was now pressing Israel to engage with Palestinians after the war is over, support their eventual independence, and reduce civilian casualties and increase aid to Gaza. Prime Minister Netanyahu resisted those calls, a January 2024 AP report claimed.[83]

Despite the U.S. administration's position, some elected officials started to feel the burden of unconditional support for Israel. In an unprecedented turn of events in February 2024, the House of Representatives failed to pass a bill aimed at providing Israel with an additional 17.6 billion dollars.[84] Along with Arab American community leaders, the mayor of Dearborn, Michigan, canceled a meeting with Biden's reelection campaign over the president's handling of the unfolding unprecedented violence against civilians.[85] In what seemed to be an effort to address deepening public relations fiasco, Biden issued an executive order targeting Israeli settler violence in the West Bank.[86]

THE ISRAEL LOBBY

How and why does Israel have such a strong influence on U.S. foreign and domestic policy? The answer lies in the multiplicity of well-funded pro-Israel lobby groups, which exert enormous sway over U.S. politicians and their staff. As Khaled Elgindy notes,

> U.S. administrations have largely avoided applying pressure on Israel to advance the goals of the peace process and have actively worked in the United Nations and other international forums to prevent such pressure being put on Israel. This preference stemmed from the theory, long espoused by the pro-Israel community, that Israeli leaders would be more willing to 'take risks for peace' if they felt secure politically and militarily. Most presidents have adhered to this logic, whether out of genuine conviction or simply to avoid running afoul of the powerful pro-Israel lobby and its supporters on Capitol Hill.[87]

Political scientist Robert Trice "described the pro-Israel lobby as 'comprised of at least 75 separate organizations—mainly Jewish—that actively support most of the actions and policy positions of the Israeli government.'"[88] These groups mobilize members not only to vote for pro-Israel candidates but also to write letters to politicians and news organizations, make financial contributions to pro-Israel candidates, and support the political aims of the organization through active involvement. In their book *The Israel Lobby and U.S. Foreign Policy*, Mearsheimer and Walt write:

> The influence of the Israel lobby on U.S. foreign policy merits the same scrutiny as the impact of energy interests on environmental regulations or the role of pharmaceutical companies in shaping policy on prescription drugs. We believe the activities of the groups and individuals who make up the lobby are the main reason why the United States pursues policies in the Middle East that make little sense on either strategic or moral grounds. Were it not for the lobby's efforts, the strategic and moral arguments that are commonly invoked to justify unconditional American support would be called into question more frequently and U.S. policy in the Middle East would be significantly different than it is today.[89]

While these pro-Israel lobby groups may not represent the sentiments of all Jewish Americans, the fact remains that Jewish Americans exert an enormous influence on elections. The *Washington Post* estimates that Democratic presidential candidates depend on Jewish supporters for at least

60 percent of campaign contributions, and despite comprising less than 3 percent of the population, Jewish Americans have high turnout rates in key states like California, Florida, and Illinois.[90] Thus they represent an important demographic for politicians to target and to gain support from.

AIPAC is undoubtedly the most influential pro-Israel lobby. It is consistently ranked the second-most powerful lobby in Washington, behind the AARP but ahead of other influential lobbies like the NRA and the AFL-CIO.[91] Although it began as a small, grassroots organization, AIPAC has grown substantially. The lobby's size, wealth, and influence grew tremendously after the Six-Day War in June 1967. According to Eizenstat, that conflict "galvanized the American Jewish public like no event since Israel's War of Independence.... The sense of pride in new Jews, proud, strong, capable of defending themselves, had an incalculable effect on American Jewry." In the early 1970s the organization had an annual budget of approximately $300,000; today it has "a staff of more than 150 employees and an annual budget (derived solely from private contributions) ... [of] an estimated $40–60 million."[92]

The purpose of the American Israel Public Affairs Committee (AIPAC) is to support Israel. In a statement, President Betsy Berns Korn and CEO Howard Kohr called for unity and solidarity in support for Israel: "The one thing that guarantees Israel's ability to defend itself is the enduring support of the United States. When we launched our political action committee last year, we decided that we would base decisions about political contributions on only one thing: whether a political candidate supports the U.S.-Israel relationship. Not on any other issue—just this one.... Our job today, as it has always been, is to bring more people to Israel's side and focus only on Israel's strength and ability to defend itself."[93] According to MJ Rosenberg, who worked not only in the House and the Senate but also for AIPAC itself, "AIPAC uses the same tactics as the NRA to ensure that the United States never deviates from support for whatever policy the Israeli government is pushing at the moment." AIPAC's goal, Rosenberg notes, is "to prevent *any* pressure on Israel to advance peace with the Palestinians despite the fact that the United States provides more aid to Israel than to any other country."[94] One former staffer said that "the theory was, no one is scared of you if they don't know about you." By the 1980s, notes Warren Bass, AIPAC was a "Washington powerhouse."[95]

According to the Center for Responsive Politics, pro-Israel individuals and PACs contributed a total of $33.1 million during the 2020 general elections cycle; $19.3 million went toward supporting Democrats, and $10.9 million went toward Republicans. Senate members or former members with the greatest contributions from pro-Israel PACs and individuals include Joe Biden ($4.3 million), Robert Menendez ($2.5 million), Hillary Clinton ($2.4 million), Joe Lieberman ($2.0 million) John McCain ($1.5 million), Mitch McConnell ($2 million), and Senator Chuck Schumer ($1.7 million). Current or former members of the House of Representatives with the greatest contributions include Mark Kirk ($2.3 million), Eric Cantor ($1.1 million), and Ron Wyden ($1.0 million).[96]

Mearsheimer and Walt note that "AIPAC President Howard Friedman told the organization's members in August 2006, 'AIPAC meets with every candidate running for Congress. These candidates receive in-depth briefings to help them completely understand the complexities of Israel's predicament and that of the Middle East as a whole. We even ask each candidate to author a "position paper" on their views of the U.S.-Israel relationship—so it's clear where they stand on the subject.'"[97] AIPAC also frequently provides direct assistance to legislators in analyzing issues, offering talking points and speeches, and supplying support staff to help on questions regarding Israel. A sister organization, American Israel Education Foundation, funds free trips to Israel for Congress members.[98]

AIPAC's stronghold on Washington politicians is notorious and "makes it dangerous for senators or representatives to utter even mild criticisms of Israel's conduct."[99] Rosenberg recalls watching his colleagues end the careers of politicians who strayed from AIPAC's policy desires. The intimidation techniques AIPAC uses to keep members of Congress in line, from funding opposing candidate's campaigns to derailing support for other, non-related bills, mean that Congress is unable to have frank conversations about U.S.-Israeli relations, despite the ramifications this alliance has on other aspects of foreign policy.[100] Mearsheimer and Walt contend that "the United States will not be able to deal with the vexing problems in the Middle East if it cannot have a serious and candid discussion of the role of the Israel lobby," which is currently impossible given AIPAC's tight control of debate in Congress.[101] Senator Ernest "Fritz" Hollings, a Democrat from South Carolina, was quoted as saying "you can't have an Israeli policy other than what AIPAC gives you around here."[102] It is worth noting that

INTENSIFICATION OF POLITICAL AND LEGAL BATTLES

Hollings was on his way out of office at the time of this statement; such a comment may have resulted in repercussions from AIPAC.

The extent to which AIPAC and other pro-Israel lobby groups control Congress is illustrated by the efforts to pass a bill criminalizing participation in boycotts against Israel by individuals in the United States. As Dima Khalidi, director of Palestine Legal, says,

> There has been a very concerted effort to get state legislators to pass this kind of legislation. There have been various investigative reports, various clues as to where this is coming from, but it's clear that the Israeli government is pushing it. It's clear that right wing groups like ALEC, the American Legislative Exchange Commission, have adopted this as a kind of policy initiative, so they push legislators to introduce such legislation and have copycat bills to pass around. And then you have a whole network of Israel advocacy groups, nonprofit organizations in the US that are putting a lot of weight and doing the lobbying and pushing legislatures to adopt this kind of legislation.[103]

Congress is not the only target of pro-Israel lobbyists; the White House is an equal, if not more important, target given the central role of the executive branch in shaping foreign policy. The State Department and the president leverage personal relationships with key foreign dignitaries and government leaders to broker deals; although a member of Congress must introduce legislation for debate, the executive branch may propose legislation. Furthermore, the president possesses the unique ability to issue executive orders that cannot be directly overturned by Congress. The best Congress can do if it opposes such an order is to pass a bill cutting funding for its implementation (subject to presidential veto). The pro-Israel lobby consistently applies pressure on the executive branch to stay in line with its policy perspectives. Mersheimer and Walt point out that this applies to executive stances that attempt to take the middle road with respect to Middle Eastern affairs: the pro-Israel lobby works diligently to ensure that the White House remains squarely biased toward Israel. In 2001, for instance, the Bush administration pressed Israel to cease building settlements in the Occupied Territories and called for the creation of a Palestinian state. These developments immediately raised alarm within the circle of Israeli leaders, who feared "that Washington might 'sell out' the Jewish state to win favor with the Arabs."[104]

Mersheimer and Walt report that "according to the political scientist Robert Trice, 'Most major Jewish groups are characterized by large memberships, well-trained professional staffs, adequately financed social, welfare and political programs, specialized working groups for particular problems and elaborate internal communications networks.'" Moreover, the existence of numerous organizations at the local and national level explains "the ability of the pro-Israel movement to mobilize rapidly and in a coordinated fashion on a national scale when important foreign policy issues arise." These efforts are facilitated by Israel's generally favorable image in the United States. As former senator Warren Rudman (R-NH) once commented, "They have a pretty good product to sell."[105]

In a *New York Times* opinion piece in 2019, Michelle Alexander wrote, "Our elected representatives, who operate in a political environment where Israel's political lobby holds well-documented power, have consistently minimized and deflected criticism of the State of Israel, even as it has grown more emboldened in its occupation of Palestinian territory and adopted some practices reminiscent of apartheid in South Africa and Jim Crow segregation in the United States."[106] It should be noted that the banner ad at the top of this article was for daily email updates from the *New York Times* on Ukrainian casualties as a result of Russian attacks, something the paper had never offered in relation to Palestinian casualties as a result of Israeli attacks. Although the coverage of the War on Gaza was prominent in U.S. mainstream media, analyses of the coverage showed pro-Israel bias.[107] As Benoît Bréville explains, the disparity and double standard in coverage between the invasion of Ukraine and the invasion of Palestine are staggering and offensive.[108]

CHRISTIAN ZIONISM

As we have seen, Christian Zionists have been instrumental in shaping American cultural perceptions of Israel. They have also worked as a voice to lobby the U.S. government and affect its policies toward the region. Though not as powerful or wealthy as the Jewish lobbying groups that have been covered, Christian Zionists, who share a religion with many American politicians, have a certain pull over their legislators. Some members of Congress are themselves Christian Zionists. Former House Speaker Richard Armey said in September 2002 that his "number one priority in foreign policy is to protect Israel," above, it would appear, even protecting his own country. Tom DeLay, who also held the position of House Speaker, was also known for his dedication to Zionist causes, calling himself "an Israeli at heart." Morton Klein, president of the Zionist Organization of America, said that DeLay "cared about Israel in every fiber of his being." Gary Ackerman (D-NY), who served as chair of the House Subcommittee on the Middle East and South Asia, was "another avid backer of Israel, while the chair of the larger Committee on Foreign Affairs [was] Tom Lantos (D-CA), who [had] no rival on Capitol Hill in his devotion to Israel. As one former AIPAC leader put it, Lantos was 'true blue and white.'"[109]

Several Christian Zionist groups have been formed to influence politics in favor of Israel. These include the National Christian Leadership Conference for Israel, the Unity Coalition for Israel, Christian Friends of Israeli Communities, the Christians' Israel Public Action Campaign, the International Christian Embassy Jerusalem, and Christians United for Israel (CUFI). CUFI was founded by John Hagee and intended as a "Christian Version of the American Israel Public Affairs Committee."[110] Hagee also authored a book, *Jerusalem Countdown: A Prelude to War*, which analyzes contemporary international and global affairs by placing them within broader interpretations of biblical prophecies and viewing them through the lens of Christian Zionism. The book makes the case that conflict with Iran is imperative. Hagee resolutely rejects coexistence with Islam. He claims, "Those who say that Christianity and Islam are sister faiths need to get their heads out of the sand. President George Bush has given moral clarity to this clash of civilizations saying, 'This nation is at war with Islamic fascists.'"[111] The "Islamic fascists," by default of ethnicity, include the Palestinians.

The International Fellowship of Christians and Jews and its American subsidiary, Stand for Israel, "aims to engage people both spiritually and politically on behalf of Israel and the Jewish people, by encouraging them to 'pray for the peace of Jerusalem' (Psalm 122:6) and providing them with the facts they need to advocate for the Jewish state and fight anti-Israel bias in the media."[112] Their website gives a list of "people we help," which includes Israeli soldiers and their families, the "persecuted and oppressed" and "victims of terror and war." Per the site, "When war breaks out in Israel, *IFCJ* acts quickly to meet the needs of Israelis in the line of fire. We provide emergency equipment for first responders, install and renovate bomb shelters in under-protected areas, provide resources for homebound elderly in need, offer free counseling to victims of trauma and fill other critical needs."[113] While help for Israelis in time of war is certainly laudable, the organization ignores the fact that Israel is often responsible for the ongoing conflict, and that Palestinians are inordinately affected; nor does it offer any aid to Palestinians involved in the same war.

Mearsheimer and Walt write about the value of Christian Zionists to pro-Israel groups: "Absent their support, settlers would be less numerous in Israel, and the U.S. and Israeli governments would be less constrained by their presence in the Occupied Territories as well as their political activities. Plus, Christian tourism (a substantial portion occurring under evangelical auspices) has become a lucrative source of income for Israel, reportedly generating revenues in the neighborhood of $1 billion each year."[114]

What is missing from the lobbying picture in regard to Israel and Palestine is any kind of advanced, coordinated effort for the Palestinians. The fact that a voice opposing the Israel lobby is nearly nonexistent increases the influence of voices for Zionism. The general public is exposed to one narrative decontextualized of historically factual events, resulting in politicians who act within a calculated political environment that caters to the dominant portrayal. As Paul Findley wrote in his autobiographical book *They Dare to Speak Out* of his time in Congress from 1960 to 1982, "Congressmen generally heard only the Israeli case. Arab American lobbies, fledgling forces even today, were nonexistent. Arab embassies, which even today hire public relations experts only with reluctance, then showed little interest in lobbying. Even if a Congressman had wanted to hear the Arab viewpoint, he would have had difficulty finding an Arab spokesman to explain it."[115]

SEPTEMBER 11 AND THE DELEGITIMIZATION OF PALESTINIANS' ACTIVISM

The 9/11 attacks had an enormous impact on the American psyche, including delegitimizing the Palestinian struggle. Orientalist cultural and political perceptions made their way into policy and federal law. Long before the attack, a torrent of news analyses depicting contemporary global relationships in Manichean terms of conflict between the civilized, rational West, led by the United States, and a fanatical, barbaric Muslim world opened the floodgates for a concerted attempt to polarize the world.[116] Palestinian

INTENSIFICATION OF POLITICAL AND LEGAL BATTLES

Americans were caught up in this fear and accused of being terrorists. The polarizing, racist trope of Arabs as evil and Europeans as good had massive policy and cultural impacts in the U.S., not least of which was the tighter relationship with Israel that came from the labeling of Israelis as "Western" and "European." The high emotion of the moment contributed to the passage of antiterrorist laws designed to "keep Americans safe," but which had the latent effect of being universally anti-Arab. As John Collins writes in *Global Palestine*, "the period following the September 11 attacks saw a sharp 'Israelization' of U.S. national security discourse as the categories, metaphors and justifications long employed in official Israeli discourse came to frame public debate in the US even more pervasive than they had in the past. Having already been ideologically constructed for over three decades as key purveyors of 'terrorism,' Palestinians found that 9/11 and the U.S. response only intensified the impact of this discourse."[117]

For a poignant example of the effect of this heightened discourse on Arab Americans, we can look to the experience of Sami Al-Arian, a tenured professor at the University of South Florida. Born in Kuwait to Palestinian refugees, Al-Arian had come to the United States to go to college and had studied electrical science and systems engineering.[118] An advocate for Palestine, he had been a guest at the White House during the Bush and Clinton administrations and had campaigned on behalf of President George W. Bush. This was not enough to save him from vicious attacks in the aftermath of September 11. On September 26, 2001, Al-Arian was invited to appear on the television show *The O'Reilly Factor*, to discuss the attacks. That discussion, however, never took place. Instead, host Bill O'Reilly accused Al-Arian of being a terrorist.

At the end of the segment, O'Reilly called on the CIA to investigate Al-Arian, who was no stranger to government scrutiny. Despite his impressive track record of academic achievement, excellence in teaching, and community involvement, Al-Arian was investigated in the mid-1990s for connection to terrorism related to his involvement with the World and Islamic Studies Enterprise (WISE), a think tank devoted to the promotion of dialogue between the West and the Middle East. As reported in the *St. Petersburg Times*, "In November 1995, federal agents investigating 'violations of perjury and immigration laws' searched Sami Al-Arian's home for six hours to seize bank statements dating as far back as 1986, airline passes, telephone bills, AAA travel maps, family videotapes, audiotapes, and computer disks."[119] By May 1996 the investigation concluded that there was no evidence tying Al-Arian or WISE to terrorism.[120] Al-Arian's brother-in-law was incarcerated in May 1997 on "secret charges" and not released until 2000, when "a judge ruled the government had no evidence to continue holding him" and that the court had violated his right to due process.[121]

Sami Al-Arian experienced the ways in which Palestinian Americans were under scrutiny in the United States, but to this point he had never been charged with any offense. Under the newly minted Patriot Act, however, he was indicted on seventeen charges, including racketeering for Palestine Islamic Jihad. At trial, he was acquitted of eight charges, and the jury was deadlocked on the other nine. His three codefendants were acquitted of all charges. "The verdict was seen as a major embarrassment to the U.S. government and to the Patriot Act,"[122] and eventually a plea deal was reached in which Al-Arian agreed to be deported in return for his freedom and the dropping of all but one charge. He had spent more than three years in prison, much of it in solitary confinement. He was also fired from his position at the University of South Florida. "Al-Arian labeled his arrest a consequence of post-9/11 hysteria at a public pronouncement in front of a courthouse rally by his supporters."[123]

The impact of 9/11 on how the United States addresses terrorism and security cannot be overstated. The Department of Homeland Security, formed in 2003, was given tremendous power, and security became focused on an approach that doesn't see individuals but profiles racialization and systems. The legalization and militarization of Homeland Security and the police in the aftermath of the attacks, not to mention the years of war in the Middle East, led in part to the polarization of America and the embrace of an "us versus them" ideology. Those who identified as American, white, and conservative agreed with narratives that portrayed foreigners as the enemy. Those in America who did not identify that way pushed back against the hardening of government response toward people it saw as threats, coalescing in protests against police violence and the BLM movement. All this social movement is made even more stark when considered in the light of a quote by Osama Bin Laden, the leader behind the September 11 attacks who, according to the U.S. 9/11 Commission, "explicitly sought to punish the United States for its policies in the Middle East, including its support for Israel."[124]

INTENSIFICATION OF POLITICAL AND LEGAL BATTLES

Israeli writer Miko Peled wrote his book *Injustice: The Story of the Holy Land Foundation Five* (2018) on the U.S. reaction to the 9/11 attacks. In a review of the book, Sami Al-Arian, now director and public affairs professor at the Center for Islam and Global Affairs, wrote, "Injustice is a must-read book for anyone who wants to know how after 9/11, the US criminal justice system has been undermined and become another tool utilized by the pro-Israeli camp to silence and intimidate Palestinian Americans. Peled thoroughly presents the decade long campaign to criminalize the giving of humanitarian aid to other Palestinians living in poor communities and squalid refugee camps, and how the US government has failed to uphold its ideals as these men came to the US for freedom, only to be ultimately denied their freedom."[125]

THE UNITED STATES IN THE UN: PROTECTING ISRAEL AS STANDARD OPERATING PROCEDURE

The United Nations exists as an organization devoted to peace, dignity, and equality and claims to be "the one place on Earth where all the world's nations can gather together, discuss common problems, and find shared solutions that benefit all of humanity."[126] The United States has been a member nation since its inception but has not always worked to find solutions that benefit all of humanity and has consistently worked against the interests of peace for the Palestinians. In 1974 Yasser Arafat, then chairman of the PLO, addressed the General Assembly of the United Nations with hope:

> The question of Palestine is being re-examined by the United Nations, and we consider that step to be a victory for the World Organization as much as a victory for the cause of our people. It indicates anew that the United Nations of today is not the United Nations of the past, just as today's world is not yesterday's world. Today's United Nations represents 138 nations, a number that more clearly reflects the will of the international community. Thus today's United Nations is more nearly capable of implementing the principles embodied in its Charter and in the Universal Declaration of Human Rights, as well as being more truly empowered to support causes of peace and justice."[127]

Despite Arafat's optimistic view, the United Nations has done little to support the Palestinian cause. This failure has largely been the result of U.S. efforts.

Since the inception of veto power in the United Nations, the United States has been a tight ally for Israel, vetoing more than fifty resolutions brought forth against Israel in as many years. The earliest of these vetoes was in 1972 regarding Israel's aggression in Lebanon. They have included resolutions "Deploring Israel's continued occupation of Palestinian territories," "Calling on Israel to uphold protection of holy places," and "Denouncing Israel's contravention of fourth Geneva Convention."[128] The United States has often been the only country to cast a negative vote for these resolutions. Because of this support for Israel, it was four decades before a resolution critical of Israel was passed. In 2017 President Barack Obama chose to abstain from a vote on Israeli settlements; the abstention allowed the resolution to pass.[129] U.S. ambassador to the UN Samantha Power said, "One cannot simultaneously champion expanding Israeli settlements and champion a viable two-state solution that would end the conflict. One had to make a choice between settlements and separation."[130]

Within the United Nations, the United States has also prevented measures that would benefit Palestine. Following its request to be admitted as a member of the United Nations, the PLO asked UNESCO for membership and for the protection of Bethlehem as a UNESCO World Heritage Site in 2011.[131] Jean Shaoul reports that the United States responded by blocking "nearly $200 million of humanitarian aid to the Palestinian people, intended for food, health care and development initiatives." Furthermore, the House Middle East Affairs Subcommittee suggested it would withhold the following year's $600 million allocation "if Abbas does not drop his bid for UN statehood recognition."[132] UNESCO's executive board gave initial approval to the Palestinian's request, despite opposition from the United States.

The United States also politically blocks other foreign powers from intervening on behalf of Palestinians. As a permanent seat holder in the UN Security Council, the United States holds veto power, and it has been cited numerous times for blocking international action that would penalize Israel for war crimes or support the Palestinian political agenda. The actions of the U.S. government exacerbate the exclusion and denial of Palestinians everywhere, reinforcing the common experience of being denied political and social equity at home and as refugees abroad. The transnational

INTENSIFICATION OF POLITICAL AND LEGAL BATTLES

identity of Palestinians is further unified each time another state or institution perpetrates harmful political and social discourse that affects Palestinians everywhere.

The election of President Trump saw an end to any hesitation on the part of the U.S. government in supporting Israel. His administration vetoed a resolution condemning his support of Israel moving its capital to Jerusalem, and in 2021, with a new president but an old playbook, and violence escalating between Israel and Palestine, "Washington blocked a joint statement calling for an immediate cease-fire between Israel and Hamas—the U.S.'s third such veto reportedly within a week."[133]

During the War on Gaza, the United States used its veto power to stop a United Nations Resolution calling for a cease-fire twice and finally abstained from voting for the resolution that was passed on December 22, 2023, even after it was significantly modified to avoid a third veto.[134] Cuba's UN ambassador, Gerardo Peñalver Portal, called it "deplorable" that the December 22 resolution didn't include a call for an immediate cessation of hostilities, saying a cease-fire is "a priority to halt the genocide against the Palestinian population."[135] The Russian ambassador, Vassily Nebenzia, similarly criticized the resolution, calling it "entirely toothless." Nebenzia also accused the United States of "'shameful, cynical, and irresponsible conduct' and of using 'gross pressure, blackmail and twisting arms' to change the content of the resolution."[136] The UN General Assembly voted "overwhelmingly" to finally pass the resolution, with 153 in favor.[137]

By January 2024, however, it appeared that the UN resolution hadn't had the desired effect. Pro-ceasefire groups, including Rabbis for Ceasefire, Jews for Racial and Economic Justice, Jewish Voice for Peace, and IfNotNow, organized a protest at the United Nations on January 9.[138] The protest included rabbis and rabbinical scholars who recited prayers in support of a ceasefire within the UN building while stressing that their issue was not with the United Nations itself, but with the United States and its blocking of resolutions. As Sophie Ellman-Golan, communications director for Jews for Racial and Economic Justice, explained to the *Huffington Post*, "Since the Biden administration is consistently, single-handedly blocking the UN from taking any meaningful action for a cease-fire, we are organizing 36 rabbis and rabbinical students from seven different states to come to the UN themselves, and say, 'We're speaking for the people, this is a moral call.'"[139]

While the Biden administration has responded to criticism over its support for Israel by using increasingly tough rhetoric regarding Israel's actions, analysts say it remains supportive in practice. National security analyst Joe Cirincione was harsh in his view of the administration's stance. "They have changed their rhetoric but not their policy," Cirincione, who initially praised Biden's handling of the crisis, told the *Guardian*. "They're emphasising that Israel must reduce civilian casualties, but when Israel doesn't reduce civilian casualties they don't do anything about it. It's not real—it's messaging. They are just providing cover for Netanyahu. They aren't changing his policy. I have great admiration for Blinken, but he looks pathetic at this point."[140]

Peter Beinart has also criticized the Biden response, saying:

There's something farcical about the Biden administration saying our policy is that we must keep a horizon open for a two-state solution. Our policy is that Israel should not expel people in Gaza to Egypt. Our policy is that Israel must limit humanitarian casualties. That's not really America's policy, right? It would be like me saying my policy is that I'm gonna run the New York marathon. But if I've never done a lick of running, and all I do is sit on my couch eating chocolate cake, that's not actually my policy, right? There's something called revealed preference. Revealed preference is not what you say, but what you do. And the Biden administration's revealed preference is Israel can do whatever it wants without consequence.[141]

In an interview on January 11, 2024, John Kirby, the National Security Council's strategic-communications coordinator, defended the administration's decision to remain supportive of the war and to twice bypass the legislature to make emergency weapons sales to Israel. "We want to make sure, as Israel prosecutes their operations, that they do so in the most precise, careful, deliberate way. We really are pushing hard to see if we can get a marked reduction in civilian casualties and in the damage to civilian infrastructure," Kirby said. Yet, when pressed as to whether Israel's actions were working to reduce civilian casualties or follow international law, his response was telling: "We're not going to hold a court of inquiry here to determine that. We're not going to armchair-quarterback every single operation and event that they conduct."[142]

INTENSIFICATION OF POLITICAL AND LEGAL BATTLES

FEDERAL POLITICS: LAWS AND CANDIDACIES

Foreign policy is only one way in which the U.S. government works to support Israel. It also passes and litigates laws that effectively legalize the oppression of Palestinian voices in American culture and promote pro-Israel activities and speech. The Israeli Anti-Boycott Act, mentioned earlier as a pet project of AIPAC, is one such law. It seeks to "bar U.S. persons from supporting boycotts against Israel, including its settlements in the Palestinian Occupied Territories, conducted by international governmental organizations, such as the United Nations and the European Union." Violations of the act would result in a minimum civil penalty of $250,000 and a maximum criminal penalty of $1 million.[143] Initially the act also included a penalty of up to twenty years in prison for violators, but pressure from the ACLU forced the bill's sponsors to introduce revisions.[144] In a letter addressed to members of the Senate, where the Israel Anti-Boycott Act was introduced, the ACLU's national policy director, Faiz Shakir, warned that the proposed bill "would impose civil and criminal punishment on individuals solely because of their political beliefs about Israel and its policies." He also criticized the bill's proposed purpose to prohibit discrimination, contrasting the bill with truly antidiscrimination measures such as the Civil Rights Act of 1964, which protects consumers from "discrimination based on race, color, religion, and national origin." This bill, he stated, "aims to punish people who support international boycotts that are meant to protest Israeli government policies, while leaving those who agree with Israeli government policies free from the threat of sanctions for engaging in the exact same behavior."[145]

In a separate statement condemning the Israel Anti-Boycott Act, ACLU representatives debunked the argument that the bill aimed to protect the economic interests of American businesses. The bill attempts to amend the Export Administration Act (EAA) of 1979, which was passed in response to the Arab League's boycott of Israel and subsequent pressure on American businesses to boycott Israel if they wished to do business with Arab League nations. The EAA bill, the ACLU notes, was passed to prevent "U.S. companies from entering into agreements with foreign governments to boycott countries friendly to the United States," while the Israel Anti-Boycott Act "seeks to dictate the political activities Americans can and can't engage in."[146] The distinction between the EAA and the Israel Anti-Boycott Act is crucial to understanding the aims of the pro-Israel lobby. While the former mandates how businesses can conduct their trade agreements, the latter goes a level deeper and punishes individuals for expressing critical views of Israel, limiting their First Amendment right to freedom of expression. The bill singles out individuals who criticize Israeli policies toward Palestinians and slaps punitive measures on them to prevent them from speaking out.

Dima Khalidi and her organization, Palestine Legal, track legislation aimed at curbing Palestinian activism and say they have seen an increase over time.

> We have tracked, since 2014, the introduction of waves of anti-boycott legislation. It really started in the wake of the ASA academic boycott ... at the end of 2013, I believe, where we saw state legislators proposing legislation that would cut the funds of public universities that in some way or another, participated or supported an academic boycott. Because those kinds of bills were so directly constitutionally problematic, they didn't really go anywhere, but then we saw the evolution of anti-boycott legislation targeting state investments and eventually targeting state contracting, prohibiting state contracts with entities that participate or support in boycotts of Israel. [There are] 31 states ... that have some kind of anti-boycott legislation and this doesn't even include states that have passed resolutions which are non-binding, the statement of the legislature condemning BDS and calling it all kinds of things, calling it anti-Semitism or even economic terrorism.

Khalidi sums things up in this way:

> It's been a primary tactic of the Israeli Government and its allies to label Palestinians and Palestinian resistance as terrorism and it doesn't matter what kind of resistance it is. I don't think it's necessary for me to say anything about the history of Israel's influence on the American political landscape when it comes to this issue, but there is a very strong hold on the part of Israel and its lobby on the narrative. And that narrative has been spun, not just in public relations but also legally. You look at the legal landscape; we have an entire regime of laws that criminalize Palestinian resistance, and a lot of that regime has been driven by Israel as well.[147]

These laws, and the bills that preceded them, tell a lot about the political leanings of legislators. While not all bills become law, a look at bills in process is informational. A bipartisan bill introduced by Senator Bob Casey (D-PA) and Senator Tim Scott (R-SC) called the Anti-Semitism Awareness Act was passed unanimously by the Senate in 2016 before stalling in the House of Representatives. According to a statement by Casey, the bill's purpose was to "'ensure the U.S. Department of Education (DOE) has the necessary statutory tools at their disposal to investigate anti-Jewish incidents' on college campuses."[148] The bill uses the broad definition that conflates criticism of Israel with anti-Semitism and was opposed by the ACLU, who said it "poses a serious threat to the First Amendment free speech rights of those on campus who may hold certain political views."[149] Journalist Anthony Fisher opined that while objectionable, "Holocaust denial is legal in the United States. Likewise, politically 'demonizing' Israel and unfairly holding Israel to a 'double standard' are thankfully legal, just as a pro-Israel speaker expressing an opinion blaming all of the tumult in the Middle East on Arab Muslims would be. That's how free speech works."[150] Similar bills made little progress through Congress, but in 2019 then-president Donald Trump signed an executive order essentially giving Judaism a racial and national component as well as a religious one, making it subject to Title VI antidiscrimination policies. Agencies charged with enforcing Title VI are instructed in the order to consider "the non-legally binding working definition of anti-Semitism adopted on May 26, 2016, by the International Holocaust Remembrance Alliance" and the "'Contemporary Examples of Anti-Semitism' identified by the IHRA."[151] Critics complained the policy "could be used to stifle free speech and legitimate opposition to Israel's policies toward Palestinians in the name of fighting anti-Semitism," but the order received broad bipartisan support.[152]

The first bill introduced in the Senate session in 2019 was one that addressed various Middle East policies, including a broad provision for states to pass anti-BDS legislation. At the time, twenty-six states had passed laws designed to punish companies that participated in anti-Israel boycotting. The bill was defeated, primarily due to the government shut down occurring at the time, but also because political opinion around Israel is changing. As *Vox* reporter Zach Beauchamp explains, "support for Israel, so long a bipartisan issue, is becoming polarized." The bill and others like it have been opposed as unconstitutional and interfering with free speech. The late Senator Dianne Feinstein, still in the Senate at the time, said, "Despite my strong support for Israel, I oppose this legislation because it clearly violates the Constitution."[153]

Not all members of Congress take the side of Israel, but those who don't suffer consequences. Representatives Rashida Tlaib and Ilhan Omar had planned a trip to visit Jerusalem and the West Bank but were denied entry by Israel. The denial may have been prompted by then-president Trump. The denial was especially cruel for Tlaib, whose grandmother and other relatives live in Beit Ur Al-Fauqa. *Reuters* reported that "Hanan Ashrawi, a senior Palestinian official with the Palestine Liberation Organization and founder of Miftah, a West Bank–based nongovernmental organization that is co-sponsoring the trip, called the decision to block it 'an affront to the American people and their representatives.'" The ban, Ashrawi told reporters, was "a clear case of discrimination and hostility based on political views and ethnic background, deserving of moral indignation and unequivocal condemnation in Palestine and the United States."[154]

LOCAL POLITICS: STATE LAW AND MUNICIPAL LAW

Federal laws are only one way in which the American legal system penalizes its citizens for being or supporting Palestinians. Anti-BDS laws have been passed or were being considered in forty-one states as of 2022. These laws have affected citizens across the country who attempt to exercise their First Amendment right to free speech and nonviolent protest. Boycotts have been an effective and highly regarded form of protest in the United States, and perhaps because of their effectiveness they have often been opposed by those in power. There are dozens of examples of laws to prohibit citizens from exercising their rights to protest. This section highlights only a few of them, but it is important to remember that they are just a small representation of the number of people whose lives are being affected by oppressive policies.

In Texas, anti-BDS laws were responsible for an elementary speech therapist losing her job, and her district losing its only Arabic-speaking speech pathologist. Bahia Amawi, a U.S. citizen and mother of four with a master's degree in speech pathology, had worked as an independent contractor for nine years when, in 2018, she was forced to sign an oath as part of her work contract "pledging that she 'does not currently boycott Israel,' that she 'will not boycott Israel during the term of the contract,' and that she shall refrain from any action 'that is intended to penalize, inflict economic harm on, or limit commercial relations with Israel, or with a person or entity

INTENSIFICATION OF POLITICAL AND LEGAL BATTLES

doing business in Israel or in an Israel-controlled territory.'" The clause was the only one of its kind in the contract, meaning that "in order to continue to work, Amawi would be perfectly free to engage in any political activism against her own country, participate in an economic boycott of any state or city within the U.S., or work against the policies of any other government in the world—except Israel."[155] She found herself unable to sign the contract in good faith because she had made a household decision not to purchase products from Israeli companies and was not offered an alternative. She is no longer employed with the district.

Also in Texas, residents of the town of Dickinson whose homes were destroyed by Hurricane Harvey in 2017 found that their ability to receive government relief was predicated on their agreement not to boycott Israel. As the journalist Rob Crilly reported in *The National*,

> City officials in Dickinson insist that they are bound by a Texas-wide law, introduced in May, that bans public money being spent on anti-Israel causes.... Andre Segura, Texas legal director of the American Civil Liberties Union, said the condition was reminiscent of the McCarthy witch hunts of the 1950s when prominent figures had to disavow membership of the Communist party and other "un-American activities. The First Amendment protects Americans' right to boycott, and the government cannot condition hurricane relief or any other public benefit on a commitment to refrain from protected political expression."[156]

Texas Governor Greg Abbot appeared to put the well-being of Israelis over even that of his own constituents and was quoted as saying, "Anti-Israel policies are anti-Texas policies, and we will not tolerate such actions against an important ally."[157] The City Council voted to remove the requirement for individuals to receive hurricane relief, although it interpreted the bill in such a way that businesses were still required to abstain from a boycott.[158]

The legislation in question was HB 89, a partisan bill that was sponsored by Representative (now Senator) Brandon Creighton and cosponsored by Representative (now Senator) Bryan Hughes, both Republicans.[159] In April 2019 a federal court blocked the law, "finding the plaintiffs were likely to succeed in showing that the law violates their First Amendment rights and that the state's continued enforcement of it would cause them irreparable harm." In response, the Texas legislature amended the law to exclude "sole proprietors, companies with fewer than 10 employees, and contracts worth less than $100,000" and passed it as HB 789. Further limitation of the statue was introduced in December 2022 and is currently pending as HB 1089. This bill would remove state contracts from the law, but leave in place the requirement for state investments to be restricted to organizations and companies that pledge not to boycott Israel.[160] HB 1089 was authored by a coalition of five Democratic representatives led by Jewish American Jon Rosenthal. In April 2019, as HB 789 was being debated, Rosenthal spoke to his fellow representatives about his love for both the state of Israel and the constitution. He later tweeted a video of those comments with the caption, "As a Jewish-American, I don't waiver when I say that I love Israel, just as I love the United States of America. I believe it is our right given to us by the First Amendment as Americans to express our opinions on a number of things, including how governments are run."[161] Rosenthal's comments are representative of a growing body of voices who refuse to equate the criticism of the state of Israel with criticism of Jewish people or anti-Semitic views.

In 2017 the Kansas legislature passed a law "requiring all parties contracting with the state to certify they were not engaged in a boycott of Israel."[162] This legislation, HB 2409, was sponsored by the bipartisan Committee on Appropriations.[163] Esther Koontz, a curriculum coach at a school in Wichita, decided to boycott Israeli businesses in May 2017 as a personal protest against conditions in Israel and Palestine. Koontz was "set to serve as a teacher trainer in a Math and Science Partnership program implemented by the Kansas State Department of Education," but before she could schedule any training sessions, "the program director asked Koontz to sign a certification that she was not involved in a boycott of Israel as required by the Kansas law." She refused. "As a result of Koontz's refusal to certify that she was not boycotting Israel, the Kansas Department of Education declined to pay or contract with Koontz." Koontz sued the state, and the court admitted that "forcing Koontz 'to disown her boycott is akin to forcing plaintiff to accommodate Kansas's message of support for Israel.'"[164] Koontz, who was engaging in the protest as a member of her Mennonite church, filed a challenge in the courts based on the law's violation of free speech rights. "In response, Kansas lawmakers amended the law so that it no longer applied to individuals like the plaintiff, rendering the case moot, but leaving the underlying constitutional issues unresolved."[165]

INTENSIFICATION OF POLITICAL AND LEGAL BATTLES

These laws have been quite common around the United States. Another example is the passage and challenge of SB1167 in Arizona, a law that mandates that all state contractors must declare that they would not engage in a boycott of Israel. A state contractor named Mikkel Jordahl declined to sign such an agreement, and so the state withheld payment. In 2019, Jordahl sued the state of Arizona. The court initially sided with Jordahl, ruling that, unlike other laws regulating state contractors that tended to be based "solely [on] economic interests," SB 1167 was incorrectly "being applied to plaintiffs whose actions were politically motivated, and therefore did not regulate only commercial speech."[166] However, the Arizona legislature then amended SB 1167, not to change how the law is applied, but to specifically exempt Jordahl's company from the requirement, and the suit was dismissed by the court of appeals. Adjustments similar to those seen in Kansas and Texas had been made to the Arizona law. "Arizona Republican State Sen. Paul Boyer, who sponsored the amended law, said in a statement when the amended law was passed through the state legislature in April [2019], 'Arizona's citizens not only stand with Israel because of the economic and practical benefits received, but as a matter of faith, principle, and as a point of American patriotism.'"[167]

In New York, Governor Andrew Cuomo signed an executive order in 2016 ordering by the commissioner of a list of institutions and companies that participate in BDS "either directly or through a parent or subsidiary." The order states that "all affected state agencies are directed to divest their money and assets from investment in any institution or company" on the list.[168] On June 4, 2016, Cuomo tweeted, "I am signing an Executive Order that says very clearly we are against the BDS movement. If you boycott Israel, New York will boycott you."[169] First Amendment activists pointed out that the order "seeks to punish people for criticizing Israel in a peaceful, effective manner."[170] The state of New York had more than a dozen bills proposed, some of which were enacted while others were defeated, and some are still pending. The bills were aimed at targeting several forms of boycott. They prohibit

> state investment in and state contracts with entities that engage in boycotts of Israel, . . . require the state to create a blacklist of corporations, non-profits, and groups engaged in prohibited boycotts, . . . direct the trustees of New York's public colleges and universities to prohibit funding for student groups that directly or indirectly promote or encourage boycotts of any allied nation

or companies based in an allied nation, including Israel and the territories it occupies, ... or prohibit the use of state funds by colleges and universities to fund or provide funds for membership in or travel to meetings of academic entities that engage in boycotts of countries that host New York state colleges, a short list that includes Israel.[171]

Laws that prohibit people from peacefully protesting, or threaten monetary sanctions for those who do, fundamentally inhibit the constitutionally protected right to free speech that is enjoyed by all Americans. These laws not only infringe on those rights but take a nearly traitorous position, putting the protection of and support for Israel over the rights and freedoms of Americans.

AMERICAN POLICE EXCHANGES WITH THE ISRAELI MILITARY

American police officers held their first official training expedition to Israel to learn about "counterterrorism" in 2002, just a few months after the 9/11 attacks. Since then, countless U.S. law enforcement agents have been trained in Israel. The collaboration between the U.S.-based state and national law enforcement at all levels with the Israeli military is exceptional.[172]

Such collaborations are often framed as sharing Israeli counterterrorism expertise and best practices, but that sharing has the consequence of reinforcing biased systems and upholding white supremacy.[173] Objections have been raised over the training by multiple organizations due to the fact that the trainings "facilitate an exchange of methods of state violence and control, including mass surveillance, racial profiling, and suppression of protest and dissent."[174]

One organization involved in these cross-cultural police trainings is the Jewish Institute for National Security of America. According to its website, JINSA

> is dedicated to advancing U.S. national security interests in the Middle East, of which a critical pillar is a robust U.S.-Israel security relationship. JINSA believes that Israel is the most capable and critical U.S. security partner in the 21st century and that a strong America is the best guarantor of Western civilization. JINSA advances its mission by conducting both educational programs that build ties among American, Israeli and other Middle Eastern

partner military leaders, along with in-depth research and actionable recommendations to influence U.S. policy.[175]

JINSA runs a number of exchange programs between the United States and Israel, including trips to bring active and retired military personnel to Israel and policy advising on Middle East issues with a priority on Israel's sovereignty in the region. The Homeland Security program, developed after 9/11, provides what it calls "best practices" training for police departments in cities across America.

The organization Demilitarize! Durham2Palestine originated in Durham, North Carolina, the first city in the United States to formally state it would not engage in police exchanges. In 2018 the City Council voted to oppose "international exchanges with any country in which Durham officers receive military-style training since such exchanges do not support the kind of policing we want here in the City of Durham."[176] The resolution was inspired by Demilitarize! Durham2Palestine and received criticism from pro-Israel groups, including a lawsuit filed by the North Carolina Coalition for Israel. Although the council statement opposed exchanges with any country that would offer military-style training, including Israel, the lawsuit alleged that the North Carolina Coalition and its officers were "personally aggrieved in that they live within the jurisdiction of the City of Durham or interact with same either as citizens, taxpayers or Jewish activists concerned with discrimination against the Jewish community and discrimination directed at that community."[177]

Durham mayor Steve Schewel, who is Jewish, "sided with proponents of the petition in agreeing that foreign military influence on local police was not in Durham's best interests, but he argued that the rhetoric in the petition falsely portrayed the police force as being heavily involved in Israeli training programs."[178] He accused both sides of distorting facts to stir up emotional reactions. The suit was eventually dismissed. Demilitarize! Durham2Palestine, which opposes "police/state militarization and racist state violence imposed through prisons, borders, military occupation, and war," has grown and keeps a heat map of Israel/U.S. police exchanges around the country. Its website highlights the need to cease police exchange programs with Israel, stating that "Israeli police operate under a de-facto shoot-to-kill policy as a first line of defense when dealing with Palestinian 'terror suspects,' mirroring practices of American police departments which treat people of color as deadly threats by default. 'Counter-terrorism' strategies of Israeli security forces amount to Islamophobia and racial profiling, arbitrary detentions, and disproportionate responses to non-violent or non-threatening protests."[179]

In her book *Freedom Is a Constant Struggle*, Angela Davis reflected on her experiences with police in the United States and abroad and the connection to the struggle in Palestine:

> I lived in London for ten years and every time you saw a cop in the street you got scared. They are technically "civil servants," but they do not fulfill this function. You talked about the U.S., the police being militarized—during the demonstrations for Gaza in France in Paris, it wasn't civil servants in the streets, it was riot police. Robocop-looking kind of people. This by itself creates and implies violence. Precisely. That was the whole point. And also it might be important to point out that the Israeli police have been involved in the training of U.S. police. So there is this connection between the U.S. military and the Israeli military. And therefore it means that when we try to organize campaigns in solidarity with Palestine, when we try to challenge the Israeli state, it's not simply about focusing our struggles elsewhere, in another place. It also has to do with what happens in U.S. communities.[180]

As police departments become more militarized and the relationship between American and Israeli security forces is strengthened, individuals respond with criticism and malice, and the actions that police hope will lead to fewer protests can actually encourage them.

ANTIDISCRIMINATION LAWSUITS

Discrimination against Palestinians is not always set down in policy and law; it occurs in everyday life, affecting Arab American citizens. According to its year-end report, advocacy group Palestine Legal "responded to 280 incidents of suppression of U.S.-based Palestine advocacy in 2021. This represents a 31 percent increase of incidents responded to from 2020, and a 13 percent increase from pre-pandemic numbers in 2019. Additionally, we responded to 67 legal questions from activists who were concerned their rights were threatened."[181] The Arab American News reported that workplace discrimination is on the rise in the United States, citing a report by

INTENSIFICATION OF POLITICAL AND LEGAL BATTLES

the Arab-American Anti-Discrimination Committee (ADC). The report, from 2021, explained that the number of calls to the ADC from employees who faced disciplinary action up to and including termination for posting or sharing pro-Palestinian images online was rising sharply. "'The constant volume of cases is troubling and has taken over the entirety of our legal work,' the ADC said in a press release. 'Our organization has been overwhelmed with the number of cases and are horrified with how individuals have been treated.'" The ADC has asked the House Education and Labor Committee to investigate "the discriminatory practices and hold the 'third-party entities' accountable for interfering with the employee-employer relationship."[182]

Palestine Legal, in its 2021 year-in-review report, published stories of individuals who had come to it for help after being fired over their support of Palestine. These stories are heartbreaking, and again, only a representative sample of a rising trend.

> In May, Michael Washburn, a head farmer at the luxury resort Blackberry Farms in Knoxville, Tennessee, posted a picture of a Palestinian poetry book on his private Instagram account. His caption asked when we will demand human rights for Palestinians, urged followers to "Please help bring peace to Palestine," and included the hashtags #endtheoccupation and #endZionism. After management received complaints about his post, Washburn was fired from his position of seven years. . . . In June, Phoenix-based pediatric radiologist Fidaa Wishah was targeted by an online mob for posting on social media about the Israeli government's efforts to suppress coverage of its attacks on Palestinians. Within two days of a smear campaign headed by StopAntisemitism.org, Phoenix Children's Hospital claimed that they had done a "thorough review of the facts related to this matter" and announced that Dr. Wishah was no longer providing care at the hospital. The Arizona chapter of the Council on American-Islamic Relations (CAIR) and several private law firms are representing Dr. Wishah in a wrongful termination case against the hospital.[183]

In 2021 Google announced a billion-dollar contract with the Israeli government called Project Nimbus. The contract to provide AI (artificial intelligence) and cloud services was met with backlash both from the general public and from employees of the company, who felt Google's dealings with the Israeli military went against the company's stated ethics, given the frequency with which the military broke international law and was accused of human rights violations. Dozens of employees spoke up, most anonymously, to report a culture of prejudice against Palestinians, Muslims, and Jewish people who support Palestinians who worked there. One employee, Ariel Koren, resigned in protest after years of complaints went unanswered by HR and executives. She went public with her story, asserting that her voice as a Jewish woman was ignored while pro-Zionist Jewish voices were given funding and a platform within Google leadership.[184] In her resignation letter, she outlined the "deeply ingrained cultural issues" she witnessed, including the "weaponization of antisemitism" to punish workers. She described coworkers being summoned by HR and disciplined for wearing a keffiyeh in a company ID photo, including the words "Free Palestine" in a company bio, and being given a formal warning for identifying as Palestinian.[185]

Palestine Legal also documented a number of incidents involving censorship at K–12 schools across the country in 2021:

> In May, a student club at a California high school was blocked from hosting an event on the history of settler-colonialism and apartheid in occupied Palestine. Administrators claimed that a picture of a young person holding a Palestinian flag used in a flier advertising the event was "inflammatory imagery." Relying on a letter from the ADL, the school also claimed that the language on the flyer, "From the river to the sea, Palestine will be free," "raises fear." The school immediately emailed families apologizing for the event and offering to connect offended students with school counselors. After months of pressure from students and community members, the school's principal stated in September that students would be allowed to reschedule the event.
>
> In June 2021, a Palestinian American high school student in California was forbidden from wearing a Palestinian stole at her graduation ceremony. Though the school allowed other students to wear Kente cloth stoles representing their heritage, the school claimed the Palestinian student's stole did not meet the criteria for cultural adornment. School administrators originally told the student she could wear the stole underneath her graduation gown, but on the night of graduation, administrators told her the rules had changed and she would not even be allowed to wear it under her gown.

INTENSIFICATION OF POLITICAL AND LEGAL BATTLES

[In the fall] a Palestinian sixth grader at a public school in California was removed from class by a counselor and told that a T-shirt bearing the words "Palestine" (in Arabic) and "Free Palestine" promoted violence and made other students feel unsafe. The T-shirt was a gift from the child's father, who grew up in a Palestinian refugee camp. The district apologized and conducted professional development with all school administrators regarding Palestinian cultural sensitivity, in addition to training with the staff involved in the incident. The district also recommitted to develop an ethnic studies curriculum that includes the history and experiences of Palestinian people.

An Illinois high school student of Palestinian descent was similarly censored in the fall of 2021 when she attempted to raise awareness about the dire humanitarian situation in the Gaza Strip. School administrators refused to approve a poster containing statistics about children's mental health and lack of clean water. On another occasion, the student was scrutinized for her club's poster advertising Palestinian culture and was restricted in the ways she was allowed to put up the posters.

Twenty-six-year-old teen educator Jesse Sander sued the Westchester Reform Temple in Scarsdale, N.Y., after she was fired in July 2021 over a blog post. The post, authored by Sander and a friend months before her employment began, criticized Israel's May 2021 bombardment of Gaza and called Israel an apartheid state. Sander's lawsuit, filed in January 2022, alleged that the Temple violated New York labor law and demanded compensatory and other damages, including lost wages.[186]

Abby Martin, a filmmaker and political activist, sued the state of Georgia over its requirement that she sign a pledge not to boycott Israel in order to speak at Georgia Southern University. She won her suit. The judge wrote in his finding, "The requirement contained in [the Georgia law] that parties seeking to contract with the state of Georgia sign a certification that they are not engaged in a boycott of Israel also is unconstitutional compelled speech."[187] Whether this will be the first of many victories is yet to be seen, but with thirty states enacting anti-BDS laws, it is reasonable to assume it will not be the last.

In the summer of 2019, U.S. ambassador to Israel David Friedman and President Trump's Middle East peace envoy Jason Greenblatt used sledgehammers to break through a wall during the inaugural ceremony of an ancient tourist site in East Jerusalem. They were opening a new archaeological site in Jerusalem's City of David, which lies underneath the Palestinian neighborhood of Silwan. Although Friedman insisted "no political message was intended,"[188] the event was symbolic of how the United States has traditionally dealt with situations that favor Israel: break through the Palestinian claims and use any means necessary to shield and legitimize Israeli policy and action, even when it stands against international law, norms, and covenants.

The question of Palestine/Israel has occupied a large portion of U.S. foreign policy. Although largely unchanged, its position has varied from administration to administration. The motivations of President Truman's support for Israel are very different from those of President Nixon. President George H. W. Bush's threat to withhold funds from Israel if it did not participate in the Madrid Peace Conference after the end of the Gulf War point to a more aggressive Israel strategy of expansion, while at the same time negotiations with Palestinians were taking place. These talks culminated in President Clinton's sponsorship of the signing of the Oslo Accords at the White House in 1993, paving the way for the establishment of a Palestinian state, which never materialized. Although the United States has seen itself as an impartial broker, it has long been understood that it has protected Israel since the beginning, even when engaged in "brokering" a deal between the Palestinians and Israelis. In more recent years, Trump and his special envoy/son-in-law Jared Kushner legitimized colonialism and military occupation. The idea of a Palestinian nation-state had long been dead but was certified by the Trump administration with the moving of the U.S. Embassy from Tel Aviv to Jerusalem, and by its recognition of Israeli sovereignty over the Syrian territory of the Golan Heights.

The basis of this support is political, cultural, and material and rests in large part on the success of large-scale lobbying efforts by pro-Israel groups, including Jewish Americans and Christian Zionists. Their actions, and the repercussions of the September 11 terrorist attack, affect public policy and foreign relations, influencing the way the United States uses its power in the United Nations and the types of laws that are passed domestically. This in turn affects state legislatures, who take up the call and pass laws of their own. Taken together, lobbying groups, foreign policy, and federal and state law all influence the policies of corporations and police departments,

INTENSIFICATION OF POLITICAL AND LEGAL BATTLES

culminating in policies that are discriminatory against Palestinians and those who support their cause.

On the other hand, there is a shift occurring as more and more people are willing to stand up to discrimination and speak out against oppression. There are signs that the reflexive charge of anti-Semitism is beginning to lose its power to stifle debate. Consider the perspective of Matt Duss, foreign policy advisor and expert on the Israel/Palestine conflict:

> More members of Congress have the courage to tell the truth. Bernie [Sanders] is one such person. You've got more.... Elizabeth Warren, she was being asked by If Not Now, if she supports ending the occupation. Just saying those words "end the occupation." Supporting the idea of conditioning aid, pushing through that taboo, conditioning aid was a very big deal. But now, having people like Rashida [Tlaib], having people like Ilhan Omar, obviously, who has, at key moments, stepped out on this. Jamaal Bowman beating [Jewish sixteen-term incumbent] Eliot Engel [for the congressional seat for New York's 16th district]. That was huge. If you listen, Jamaal is not making foreign policy his big thing, but ... what he showed is you can take a defensible, good, progressive position on this and ... win. I mean, he beat Eliot Engel among the Jewish voters in that. That's how this changes, is to show that you can take these good defensible positions and ... you'll get votes because they are consistent with your values. They are authentically progressive values, they're not anti-Jewish, you're not anti-Israel, they are humanitarian. Look at this past primary, the 2020 primary. How often did the issue come up of Palestinian rights? It came up quite a bit. This is something that democratic candidates for president have to have an answer for.[189]

Policy decisions over Palestine are made at different levels of U.S. political institutions, from local to state to federal. These decisions are made with little, if any, input from or consultations with Palestinians. Yet these decisions affect the lives of all Palestinians, whether living under Israeli occupation in the West Bank and the Gaza Strip, living inside Israel, or living as refugees in other countries in the Arab world and around the world. The way in which Palestinians are affected is very clear: ever since it was founded, Israel has received increasing U.S. funds and patronage. The sum of these funds is unparalleled in U.S. foreign policy yet has received little to no scrutiny. The funds, the political patronage, and the protection that Israel enjoys because of the United States directly disadvantage the Palestinian condition, reflecting the interconnectedness of the two people. The fate of Palestinians, in historical Palestine or transnationally, is connected to how the Zionist nationalist narrative around which Israel was created and is told, legitimated, made into policy, and implemented.

In recent years the transformation of the Palestinian narrative has been met with intensifying Zionist narratives, leading to sponsorship of laws equating critique of Israel to anti-Semitism. Almost all U.S. states either have passed laws or have bills in process that criminalize engaging in boycotting Israeli products or academic institutions. In July 2019 Representative Rashida Tlaib, the only current Palestinian American member of Congress and one of two Palestinian Americans to ever serve in this capacity, spoke on the House floor advocating against a bill condemning boycotting Israel. "I stand before you the daughter of Palestinian immigrants," Tlaib said the morning of the vote. "Parents who experienced being stripped of their human rights, the right to freedom of travel, equal treatment. So I can't stand by and watch this attack on our freedom of speech and the right to boycott the racist policies of the government and the state of Israel. I love our country's freedom of speech, Madam Speaker. Dissent is how we nurture democracy."[190]

And dissent among the American public, and among some politicians, is growing. Senator Bernie Sanders has pushed for a reconsideration of military aid to Israel. He introduced a resolution to condition Israeli aid on adherence to human rights guidelines, which was defeated.[191] As mentioned earlier, public support for Israel is fading. Increasingly, supporting Israel's war against Hamas is looking like supporting a war against civilians. The erosion of this support is bipartisan and may indicate a future change in the nature of the U.S. relationship with Israel.

Chapter Five

THE FIGHT FOR SOLIDARITY AND LEGITIMACY

I always felt that I had no choice.
I have to do this because it is the right thing to do.

—SARA ROY, MARCH 2021

As the struggle between Israel and Palestine intensifies and becomes more visible, it has taken on a transnational quality that transcends geographical barriers and a global importance that is outsized compared to the area in which it originates. The crisis is now arguably the most visible focus of global solidarity in the world. As John Collins notes, "The second Palestinian intifada has prompted the emergence of the International Solidarity Movement (ISM) and other groups committed to bringing the power of global solidarity to the on-the-ground struggle against Israeli colonization under the unofficial mantra, 'We are all Palestinians.' Meanwhile, Palestine continues to be a common theme at the World Social Forum and other gatherings associated with the global justice movement. All of this suggests that increasing numbers of people around the world feel they have a stake in the Palestinian struggle."[1] The movement is increasingly affiliated with other movements for rights and equality by other marginalized or dispossessed people. These groups are gaining popular support; examples include Black Lives Matter and the LGBTQ movement in the United States.

Lebanese scholar Saree Makdisi states that "the Palestinian flag is unique as a national symbol that has become affiliated with the cause of justice more generally: hence its prominence in protests such as Occupy Wall Street and environmental justice movements that might seem to have nothing to do with Palestine itself."[2] Edward Said has also commented on the transnational nature of the subject and puts it in context. "Remember the solidarity here and everywhere in Latin America, Africa, Europe, Asia and Australia, and remember also that there is a cause to which many people have committed themselves, difficulties and terrible obstacles notwithstanding," he says. He explains the reason Palestine has such frequent support in clear terms: "Why? Because it is a just cause, a noble ideal, a moral quest for equality and human rights."[3]

Palestinians are able to articulate and share their views to different populations in large part because of their global diaspora. Palestinians living in countries around the world interact with the people they live with, sharing their stories and experiences and becoming part of the fabric of the communities in which they live. In this way, solidarity increases and outside understanding of the struggle becomes more material and more articulated. According to Collins:

> Today's Palestinian revolutionaries operate in a context where the struggle has literally returned to its roots: land, trees, rocks and homes. It is no accident that more of the violence in Palestine in recent years has taken place in and around these basic elements of habitation. These conditions have given rise to new forms of popular struggle, particularly those associated with a robust movement of international solidarity that has arisen during the past decade, a movement that is now attracting significant participation from Israelis. This movement faces the difficult task of trying to defend the rights and the integrity of Palestinian communities while contributing as little oxygen as possible to the dromocratic war machine. It is precisely this challenge, however, that creates an increasingly strong basis from which to build bridges with wider movements that are facing the same dilemma, including movements for global justice, ecological sustainability, and indigenous rights.[4]

Palestine "has emerged as a focus of attention for activists connected with the broader global justice movement that has targeted a whole range of hierarchical, undemocratic and predatory structures associated with global capitalism and US imperialism."[5] As solidarity for Palestine increases, however, solidarity for Israel also increases. Every victory for the Palestinian cause creates pushback from those who side with Israel. This chapter examines the ways in which solidarity is increasing globally and within minority communities in the United States, and how that intensification is also seen on the "other side."

GLOBAL SOLIDARITY

Populations that have experienced colonial oppression have an innate empathy for Palestinians who are undergoing the same process. The Irish, for example, tend to take the side of Palestine, while the English typically identify with Israel. In 2021 Ireland's parliament voted unanimously to "condemn Israel's 'de facto annexation' of Palestinian land in the occupied territories."[6] Ireland was the first European Union member state to do so. The Irish flag was hoisted above Ramallah's city hall the next day, solidifying the relationship between the two countries and their shared status as oppressed peoples. Although Ireland initially supported Israel as an underdog fighting anti-Semitic oppression, its loyalty shifted overtime toward the Palestinian cause as it became clearer that Israel is a colonizing power.

Rory Miller notes in *Foreign Policy* that as the state of Israel was created and legitimized, "the Irish began to draw unflattering parallels between Israeli policies and their own divided existence. To many, the Jewish state now looked less like a besieged religious-national community struggling valiantly for its natural rights and more like a colony illegitimately established by British force of arms and intent on imposing itself on an indigenous population."[7] In 2010, in an act of both symbolic and material support, the Irish, in response to the May 31 assault on Gaza, sent the MV *Rachel Corrie* ship to aid the Palestinians.[8] Readers may recognize the name of the vessel as that of the American activist who was crushed to death by a bulldozer driven by an Israeli soldier. The British government, with its history of colonization, fully backs Israel, both in monetary and military support and through trade. According to the journalist Rafeef Ziadah, "While Britain has a particular legacy in the conflict, as the former colonial power in historical Palestine, support continues today with a thriving arms trade between the two states. Approved export licences for arms sales from the UK to Israel cover components for small arms, ammunition, night-sight technology and intelligence. The UK also imports Israeli-made weapons."[9]

Similarly, the people of Kashmir identify with and have a bond with Palestinians, while India is a strategic Israeli ally. In 2021, Kashmiris, who have been subject to oppression themselves, "extended solidarity with Palestine by wearing Palestinian flags on their shirts" on Eid al Fitr. As one Kashmiri individual wearing a Palestinian flag on his jacket told reporters Babrah Naikoo and Aaqib Fayez, "Today we're wearing these flags to show our solidarity with the people of Palestine. What India is doing in Kashmir is similar to Israeli atrocities imposed on Palestinians, and like our Palestinian brothers we too bear the consequence of Indian occupation."[10] Jawaharlal Nehru, the first prime minister of independent India, felt some sympathy for the Palestinian cause as well. Somdeep Sen describes how he insisted that "fundamentally the problem of Palestine is a nationalist one. The Arabs are struggling against imperialist control and domination. It is a pity, therefore, that the Jews of Palestine instead of aligning themselves with this struggle have thought it fit to take the side of British imperialism and to seek its protection against the inhabitants of the country." This stance did not last, however. Current Indian prime minister Narendra Modi has a close relationship with Israeli prime minister Netanyahu and visited Israel, the first Indian prime minister to do so. On Modi's arrival, according to Sen, Netanyahu said, "*Aapka swagat hai mere dost* [Welcome, my friend]. We love India. We admire your culture, history, democracy and commitment to progress. I am confident of the real mathematics of life, of success of our partnership for many reasons; talent of our people.' Celebrating the warming of diplomatic ties, Modi tweeted, 'I for I. Which means India for Israel and Israel for India.'" Today Israel is India's most reliable supplier of weapons.[11]

In France, government support for Israel and disdain for Palestine is apparent in the actions of President Emmanuel Macron, at whose request Interior Minister Gerald Dramanin announced in February 2022 that he would move to dissolve two pro-Palestinian groups, Palestine Vaincra (Palestine Will Win) and Comite Palestine Action (Palestine Action Committee), stating the groups "encourage hatred, violence, discrimination, and incitement to terrorist acts."[12] Tom Martin, spokesperson for Palestine Vaincra, announced the organization's intention to fight the dissolution legally. Three months later, the Conseil d'État, France's supreme court on government actions, "suspended the president's order banning two Palestine solidarity groups." The Conseil d'État said it "suspended the government orders after finding no evidence 'that the positions taken by these groups, although clear-cut and even virulent, constitute a call for discrimination, hatred or violence or a provocation to commit acts of terrorism.'"[13] The government was ordered to pay $3,000 to each group, and the decision cannot be appealed.

In Latin America, support for Palestinians began with waves of immigration starting in the late 1800s and has become more visible in the past twenty-five years, particularly in Chile and Bolivia, where, says Cecilia Baeza, "it is not unusual to see Palestine solidarity protests called by both Palestinian diaspora organizations and indigenous movements." Since the mid-2000s, "Palestinian and indigenous organizations in Latin America have begun to support each other by regularly staging joint events, including protests, informational events, exhibitions and music festivals." The increase in support for Palestine is concurrent with the emerging social movement in Latin America, in which common experiences and lack of historical animosity create dialogue between the two groups. Artists are joining activists in creating content that supports both Palestine and Latin American indigenous people. Chilean Anita Tijoux and Palestinian Shadia Mansour released a rap single in June 2014 called "Somos Sur" (We Are South). In it, the singers pressed the two demands for independent statehood. "In an interview with *Rolling Stone*, Tijoux said, 'The movements of global resistance, whether in Latin America, Africa or the Middle East, are fighting against the same patrons of violence who have repeated themselves throughout history. What this means is that many of these groups share similar demands. We are asking for a free Palestine in the same way as we are asking for an independent Wallmapu in Chile, without police control.'"[14]

Chile's president, Gabriel Boric, first spoke to the United Nations in 2022, calling out Israeli violations of human rights in regard to its occupation of Palestine. He "urged the world 'not to normalise the permanent violations of human rights against the Palestinian people and the law; international resolutions enacted by this Assembly must be adhered to year after year.'" Peruvian president Pedro Castillo Terrones added his voice to Boric's, denouncing "the crimes of the Israeli occupation" and asking "for the intervention of the international community to put an end to it."[15]

In Bolivia, where in 2006 Evo Morales was the first indigenous person elected president, Palestine has become a major part of foreign policy. Baeza reports that Bolivia has a small Palestinian population, but a strong devotion to the Palestinian cause. After the January 2009 bombardment of Gaza, Bolivia broke off diplomatic relations with Israel, and on December 17, 2010,

Morales announced Bolivia's recognition of Palestine as an independent state. "Since then, several agreements have been signed" between the two nations. "Within a century, relations between Palestinian immigrants and indigenous peoples in Latin America went from coexistence to active solidarity. The Palestinian cause echoes loudly in indigenous struggles in Latin America."[16] Diplomatic relations with Israel were re-established in 2020, only to be severed again in October 2023 in response to the genocide against Palestinians in Gaza.[17]

In Brazil the debate cuts a divide between the country's political actors. In the October 2022 election, Jair Bolsonaro, the incumbent president, was narrowly beaten by Luiz Inácio Lula da Silva, a member of the Workers Party. The two men have vastly different views on the Israel/Palestine struggle, as evidenced by photographs taken on the day of the election. Bolsonaro's wife, Michelle, wore a blue, short-sleeved Israel shirt when she went to vote, while da Silva wore a Kufiyyah (iconic Palestinian scarf).[18] The prominence of the emblems of another country on the day of Brazil's election are evidence of the importance of the conflict in Brazil.

Support for Israel is strong in Latin America, in large part due to Israel's support of dictatorial governments in South America. Guatemala's Efraín Ríos Montt, "who was convicted of genocide and crimes against humanity... for his role in the Guatemalan civil war, received support from Israel" and "Israel has armed and trained right-wing groups and regimes in Argentina, Bolivia, Brazil, Colombia, Costa Rica, Chile, the Dominican Republic, Ecuador, El Salvador, Haiti, Honduras, Nicaragua, Panama, Paraguay, Peru, and Venezuela according to investigative journalist Jeremy Bigwood."[19]

Colombia's relationship with Israel stretches back to at least the 1980s, when Israel sent soldiers to train what is now the *Autodefensas Unidas de Colombia* (AUC), a paramilitary arm of the Colombian government that is one of the worst human rights violators in the Americas. Fifty of the government's best soldiers were then sent to Israel for further training. Israel is also a major arms supplier for Colombia, and in May 2003 "GIRSA, an Israeli company associated with the Israeli Defence Forces and based in Guatemala was able to buy 3000 Kalashnikov assault rifles and 2.5 million rounds of ammunition that were then handed over to AUC paramilitaries in Colombia."[20]

THE FIGHT FOR SOLIDARITY AND LEGITIMACY

After the bombing of Gaza in 2021, the global community of Palestine supporters came out in force. Makdisi reports that "millions of people marched for Palestine in cities around the world, from Los Angeles and Santiago to Beirut and Aden, from Paris and Berlin (where authorities attempted to suppress such marches) to Johannesburg and Durban. Celebrities like Mark Ruffalo and even Paris Hilton—not previously known for her political pronouncements—expressed their condemnation of the savage Israeli bombardment of Gaza." In June 2021 more than sixteen thousand artists "signed a letter written by Palestinian artists connecting the dots between the scenes of Israel's violence against Palestinians ... linking the expulsions from Sheikh Jarrah, the mob violence and lynchings, the bombing of Gaza, and the overarching system of racial violence and racial privilege tying them all together. 'To frame this as a war between two equal sides is false and misleading' the letter states, 'Israel is the colonizing power. Palestine is colonized. This is not a conflict: this is apartheid.'"[21]

In some cases, global awareness of the Palestinian cause has led to legal action. In 2021 the International Criminal Court, an arm of the United Nations, launched an investigation into Israel after Fatou Bensouda, the court's prosecutor, found a "reasonable basis" to open it after a preliminary probe. Bensouda advised the investigation would also look at Hamas, a statement welcomed by Hamas leaders. Netanyahu, however, took a different stance, claiming that the court had no jurisdiction in Israel as they had already investigated themselves with a "world-class legal system." He also claimed the "biased international court in The Hague made a decision that is the essence of anti-Semitism and hypocrisy."[22] In January 2024 the International Court of Justice in The Hague found that Israel had committed genocide against the Palestinians in Gaza. If sanctions are to be introduced through the Security Council, the United States will most likely exercise its veto power.[23]

Ordinary citizens around the world are beginning to show solidarity with Palestinians. The 2022 FIFA World Cup in Qatar drew fans from around the world, many of whom were filmed showing their support for Palestine. American fans spoke on camera about their belief in Palestinians and their stories.[24] Fans from around the world refused to speak to Israeli reporters, with some reports saying that "the reporters [were] being told, live on air, that Israel 'doesn't exist.'"[25] Ayman Mohyeldin reported for MSNBC that the Moroccan team, in particular, used its winning streak to highlight the Palestinian cause, unfurling a Palestinian flag after their semifinal win in December 2022. Mohyeldin also noted the response of the Western press, which has "centered their commentary and reporting around the experiences of Israelis and Israeli reporters" and their feelings of being "unwelcome" at the World Cup, ignoring Arab experiences in their own country. "Once again, we see Western narratives that oversimplify Arab sentiments while omitting Israeli aggressions on neighboring Arab countries. They do so while promoting orientalist tropes of Arabs as angry and confrontational, while casting Israelis as victims."[26]

SOLIDARITY IN AMERICAN POLITICS

Writer and Stanford University professor Hilton Obenzinger writes that

> from the 1980s, with the Israeli invasion of Lebanon in 1982 and Jesse Jackson's second presidential campaign in 1988, the issue of Palestinian rights entered American political discourse in an unprecedented fashion. Arab and Palestinian Americans began to be involved in all aspects of American political life, including electoral politics, while a loose alliance of white New Left activists, African Americans, liberal Jewish groups, churches, and others began to create a consistent pro-Palestinian presence in the peace and anti-intervention movement, despite the fact that it was "arguably the most vilified peace and solidarity effort in the country."
>
> At the same time, several attempts to deepen intercommunal relations between the Arab American and African American communities were launched, and Jesse Jackson's Rainbow Coalition presidential campaigns of 1984 and 1988 brought the Palestinian issue into the public arena as never before.
>
> The task was to crack open the pro-Israel consensus that had dominated political life in the United States since at least 1967.[27]

Obenzinger notes that the November 29th Committee's bimonthly newspaper, *Palestine Focus*, regularly linked solidarity to antiracist politics, as in this article in 1983:

Israel is a "democracy" that is stamped with its own form of Jim Crow marked "for Jews only." . . . Palestinian youth, labeled by the Israelis as "terrorists," fight against illegal occupation and colonization with mere stones. There is, as well, a parallel with those young people who rode the Freedom Rides to challenge Jim Crow only to face terror and possible death. And those courageous Israelis who demonstrate for peace and justice for the Palestinians are cursed as "Arab lovers" just as whites who have come to the defense of Black people are attacked by racists.[28]

Obenzinger summarizes Jesse Jackson's position:

[His] attempt at an even-handed position was in line with the international consensus and was not particularly radical, although he had, as civil rights activist Frances Beai observed, a "built-in identification with Africans, Asians and Latin Americans." In his program on the Middle East, Jackson expressed his support for mutual recognition and Palestinian rights within the discourse of African American Christian tradition. This outlook grew logically from the Rainbow Coalition's sense of multiculturalism, the latest ideological framework for asserting equality as part of America's racial and ethnic tapestry.[29]

In July 2023 Representative Pramila Jayapal, a Democrat, made this remark to pro-Palestinian protestors at a Netroots Nation discussion: "I want you to know that we have been fighting to make it clear that Israel is a racist state, that the Palestinian people deserve self-determination and autonomy, that the dream of a two-state solution is slipping away from us—that it doesn't even feel possible." Her words were immediately condemned by her fellow Democrats, and Jayapal quickly recanted, saying, "Words do matter and so it is important that I clarify my statement. I do not believe the idea of Israel as a nation is racist. . . . I do, however, believe that Netanyahu's extreme right-wing government has engaged in discriminatory and outright racist policies and that there are extreme racists driving that policy within the leadership of the current government."[30] The incident was an interesting encapsulation of the tenor of conversation around Israel and Palestine today. More political leaders are coming to see the Palestinian cause as one worthy of support, while the greater political climate requires that they temper their expressions of that support.

BIPOC COMMUNITIES IN THE UNITED STATES AND PALESTINIAN SELF-DETERMINATION

Palestinians living in the United States have their own specific set of discriminatory experiences that reinforce their identity. Faida Abu-Ghazaleh notes that "the unfair treatment of the American government toward the Palestinian people in Palestine, the unlimited support of Israel and the one-sided way the American media views the conflict only serves to reinforce the Palestinian-American's sense of being Palestinian as they know they are the only ones, without international help, who could defend their rights and identity from being taken away."[31] In the United States, Palestinians experience discrimination in schools, in U.S. media, and when interacting with U.S. domestic and foreign politics. This directly affects the quality of life and the treatment of Palestinians in the United States.

Palestinian solidarity among African Americans

These experiences create shared values and goals between Palestinians and marginalized communities who have received unfair treatment in the United States. Ethnic and minority groups have taken note of the racialization of Palestinian Americans both historically and contemporarily. Organizers of the Civil Rights movement linked the dismantling of segregation and Black liberation to Palestinian liberation. James Baldwin, after a visit to Israel/Palestine, made the connection between Black Americans and Palestinians explicit: "'You have got to remember,' noted Baldwin, 'however bitter this may sound, no matter how bitter I may sound, that I have been, in America, the Arab at the hands of the Jews.'"[32] Baldwin's other writings implicitly connect the plight of Palestinians in the Occupied Territories to Black Americans living in segregated ghettos.

In "A Report from Occupied Territory," Baldwin observes how "the Negro's education, North and South, remains, almost totally, a segregated education, which is but another way of saying that he is taught the habits of inferiority every hour of every day that he lives. He will find it very difficult to overcome these habits. Furthermore, every attempt he makes to overcome them will be painfully complicated by the fact that the ways of being, the ways of life of the despised and rejected, nevertheless contain an incontestable vitality and authority."[33] In this passage, Baldwin concludes that any and all attempts by Black Americans to rise above the challenges facing their community, both internally (struggling with perceptions of inferiority) and externally (legal codification of segregation), will always attract the scorn of the oppressors. Rising above these struggles entails a balancing act between assimilating into the status quo of society and maintaining the unique characteristics of ethnic identity. For Palestinians, this also holds true. Any attempt to rise above the challenges posed by the Israeli occupation is immediately met with derision, and maintaining the core of Palestinian cultural identity while struggling against the erasure that would accompany full acceptance into mainstream society is another element of the liberation movement with which Palestinians must contend.

Baldwin also writes how Black children, "having seen the spectacular defeat of their fathers—having seen what happens to any bad nigger and, still more, what happens to the good ones—cannot listen to their fathers and certainly will not listen to the society which is responsible for their orphaned condition."[34] In other words, the struggle against injustice and inequality is passed down from generation to generation and does not die with the original victims of injustice. This sentiment is echoed in the experience of both Palestinians in the homeland and Palestinians abroad. The struggle for Palestinian liberation did not end with the passing of the Nakba generation but rather continued on with subsequent generations of Palestinians.

Exploited people tend to understand the struggles of others. As far back as 1967, the Student Nonviolent Coordination Committee (SNCC) linked Black liberation struggles in the United States to Palestinian liberation struggles abroad through a contestation of "racial violence endemic to U.S. imperial culture" and by "the fierce state repression of anti-colonial movements in the United States and abroad." SNCC condemned Israeli actions in the Occupied Palestinian Territories while simultaneously pointing out that this condemnation was not an expression of anti-Semitism, but rather a condemnation of state-sanctioned violence. SNCC's outspokenness with respect to the Palestinian-Israeli conflict "fashioned a conceptual bridge between the 'territorial colonies' of Black America and Palestine."[35]

In 1977 Peter Tosh, a Jamaican reggae musician, released a song called "Equal Rights." In it he mentions several African countries fighting for equality but also specifies Palestine. He was not the only Black liberationist who felt solidarity with the Palestinian cause. George Jackson, writer and

Black Panther, was murdered in prison by guards, and two poems were found in his cell. They were English translations of liberation poetry by the Palestinian Samih al Qasim.[36] Malcolm X wrote an article for the *Egyptian Gazette* titled "Zionist Logic" in which he argued that Zionism, rather being than a religious conflict, was a colonial and political project designed to insert Western powers into the Middle East. He also compared the oppression of Africans and Palestinians.[37]

Oppression is a common denominator between Palestinians and Black Americans. It is the violence they both face at the hands of the colonial state. When a police officer pulls over a vehicle driven by a black man in the United States, or when a soldier ushers a vehicle driven by a Palestinian on the streets of the West Bank, their respective humanity seems to be questioned. These very systems that perpetuate a social divide also create a world of privilege. A white man's privilege in the United States is like an Israeli's privilege of living in Palestine. African Americans and Palestinians are both "people of color," and their oppressors, conversely, are perceived as or identify as "white."[38] Many Israelis view themselves as a manifestation of European whiteness, a sentiment that, as historian Michael Fischbach points out, has been declared by Israeli officials themselves in contexts where they are trying to suggest kinship between Israel and its American and European allies. This whiteness is distinct from how Brown and Black people are seen in Israeli society and in the United States.[39]

Expressions of solidarity between the two communities, despite the distance, are reciprocal. For example, Palestinians have sent letters of solidarity and support to the leadership of the Black Lives Matter movement on multiple occasions, and shared remedies for tear gas to protectors in Ferguson, Missouri, and Black activists and leaders have expressed solidarity with the Palestinian people.[40]

Despite the geographic distances and cultural differences, the experience of being racialized unites communities across the world and creates deeper understanding of one another's struggle for equality and liberation. Many Black men and women, from intellectuals to laypeople, have spoken in support of Palestinian liberation.[41] Apartheid is understood by Black Americans because their conditions are products of apartheid-like systems, from segregation and redlining to job discrimination and incarceration. It should not come as a surprise that racialized communities comprehend the experiences of other racialized communities, both locally and transnationally.

Just like societies of the Global South, for example, understand the experiences of Palestinians, the African American community also sees the experiences of Palestinians as familiar, due to experiences of racialization, criminalization, and control that the Black community has endured for generations.

Similarly, when Palestinians living under Israeli occupation experience violence at the hands of Israeli soldiers, they understand the suffering experienced by the Black community in the United States and understand that the system is parallelly oppressive. Such connection is evident in a mural portraying Trayvon Martin on the apartheid/separation wall in the West Bank and in Palestinians' expressions of sympathy in a letter to Michel Brown's family.[42]

Art has served to reflect the experiences and connections between the two peoples. For example, rap artists in the United States and in Palestine expressed their views on liberation by evoking each other's suffering and the interconnectedness of their struggles for justice and liberation that transcend geographical boundaries and historical contexts.[43] As Michael Fischbach puts it, the color line dividing light and dark races theorized by W. E. B. Du Bois and Malcolm X in the twentieth century still exists, and or some African Americans, aligning with Palestinians situates them on the same side of that divide—a legacy that traces back to the Black Power movement of the 1960s.[44]

The Movement for Black Lives was criticized by some Jewish American organizations for calling out the military alliance between the United States and Israel on the basis that the military aid Israel receives from the United States "makes U.S. citizens complicit in the abuses committed by the Israeli government."[45] As early as 2016, the Movement for Black Lives labelled Israel's actions toward Palestinians as "genocide" and referred to Israel as an "apartheid state." It has been heavily criticized for using both terms by groups such as Boston JCRC, Truah: the Rabbinic Council for Human Rights, and the Union for Reform Judaism.[46] Janae Bonsu, the national public policy chair for Black Youth Project 100, one of the organizations that cosigned the Movement for Black Lives's demand statement, recognized the controversy surrounding the use of the term "genocide" to describe Israel's treatment of Palestinians but reaffirmed the movement's stance, noting that "we do believe that it is accurate from a legal perspective and a moral perspective."[47]

Of course, not all Jewish American organizations viewed the Movement for Black Lives's critique of Israeli policy in the same light. Intersectional Jewish groups such as Jews of Color Caucus affirmed their commitment to the Movement for Black Lives and its stance on Israeli policy toward Palestinians. The caucus published a statement likening Israeli state violence to U.S. police brutality, noting that "there are deep historical ties between Black and Palestinian struggle that go back to the Black Power Era. Any attempt to co-opt Black struggle while demeaning these connections is an act of anti-Black erasure." The caucus also condemns other Jewish groups' criticism of the movement, writing that such criticism sends "the message that the lives of Black Jews (along with Black gentiles), directly affected by U.S. police brutality are less important than protecting Israel from scrutiny." In a reversal in 2020, however, the group revised its statements, and the site no longer included any mention of Israel. It had also garnered considerable Jewish support. After the new platform was published, "a Jewish statement in support of Black Lives Matter appeared in a full-page *New York Times* ad, signed by more than 600 national and local Jewish groups and synagogues, including a major umbrella body and three of the four major Jewish religious movements."[48]

The Movement for Black Lives has aligned itself with the Palestinian struggle for human rights and self-determination over three overlapping issues: state-sanctioned violence, the mischaracterization of social justice movements, and the global struggle for decolonization. The movement, as well as Black Americans who have traveled to Israel/Palestine, have outlined clear parallels between the experiences of Black Americans and Palestinians, leveraging these parallels to defend themselves against accusations of anti-Semitism.

One parallel Black Lives Matter activists have identified between Israel and the United States is the similarity of U.S. police forces and the IDF racially profiling individuals in the name of the law. The Jews of Color Caucus notes that "police exchange programs with Israel are widespread in the United States, and can be tied to abusive tactics used against protesters in communities like St. Louis, New York City, and Oakland." The caucus finds the links between the U.S. police force and the Israeli military to be troubling and "cause for alarm to all those committed to racial justice."[49] Reflecting on state-sanctioned violence against Palestinians, rapper Vic Mensa writes that "as a Black man in America, being stereotyped as criminal is more than familiar to me, as is being unwanted on the streets of my own home and profiled by law enforcement."[50]

Specific tactics that the Black Lives Matter movement is concerned with are the "zero-tolerance policy" and the practice of "stop and frisk" at Israeli checkpoints, both of which were initiated by the New York Police Department and disproportionately used against people of color.[51] Israeli settlers are urging authorities to implement a zero-tolerance policy to quell Palestinian resistance; under such a policy, small acts of civil disobedience (such as throwing rocks) would result in severe disciplinary action, the reasoning being that deterring small crimes would prevent larger and more serious crimes from occurring. The result of zero-tolerance policies in New York, however, was an increase in the number of people of color being charged for crimes for acts of protest and civil disobedience. Mensa summarizes the parallels between the Black American experience with law enforcement and the Palestinian experience with law enforcement while pointing out the perils of a zero-tolerance policy. He writes, "Thinking of the young men I saw being detained by the roadside, my mind floats to the story of Kalief Browder, a 16-year-old boy incarcerated for three years without trial in Rikers Island for allegedly stealing a backpack."[52]

The mischaracterization of social justice movements is a common technique detractors use to smear the credibility or the intentions of the organizers, and the Black Lives Matter movement is no exception. BLM's alliance with Palestinian resistance has raised opposition from pro-Israel groups, some of whom claim that they can no longer support the movement because of its inclusion of a pro-Palestine stance. Such opposition, however, ignores the intersectional nature of both social movements and has left Jews of color in a particularly alienated position. Hamid Dabashi notes that this opposition essentially forces the Movement for Black Lives to "embrace the Zionist colonialisation of Palestine as all good and dandy" or risk being discredited.[53]

The Jews of Color Caucus, in their statement of solidarity with the Movement for Black Lives, expressed no regret for simultaneously backing the Palestinian movement. They condemned the characterization of Palestinian organizers as anti-Semitic for voicing opposition to Israeli occupation, and observed that such mischaracterization "amounts to a violent form of silencing."[54] The silencing of the Palestinian experience is problematic not only from the perspective of Palestinian activists, but also from the perspective of Jews of color, who feel that current Jewish identity is inseparable from white identity. In an interview with NPR, Yavilah McCoy, a Black Jewish teacher and activist, commented that moving "Jewish identity beyond just white identity" would be crucial for "comprehending what does racial justice and equity need to look like as an internal issue to the Jewish community."[55]

In a grander sense, the alliance between the Movement for Black Lives and Palestinian activism highlights the scale at which the movement hopes to achieve its goals: the movement is explicitly backing a "global struggle for liberation."[56] The inclusion of a transnational liberation movement element in the movement's platform shatters the perception that U.S. international policy affects only communities of color with direct ties to regions with U.S. involvement. The Movement for Black Lives counters that "American wars are unjust, destructive to Black communities globally, and do not keep Black people safe locally." The movement also calls out the ever-expanding U.S. military presence globally as responsible for the dwindling domestic resources toward infrastructure and social programs—by waging war globally, the U.S. is effectively ignoring the needs of its communities of color at home.[57]

Angela Davis, in an interview published in *Freedom Is a Constant Struggle*, says:

> Well, I think that we constantly have to make connections. So that when we are engaged in the struggle against racist violence, in relation to Ferguson, Michael Brown, and New York, Eric Garner, we can't forget the connections with Palestine. So in many ways I think we have to engage in an exercise of intersectionality. Of always foregrounding those connections so that people remember that nothing happens in isolation. That when we see the police repressing protests in Ferguson we also have to think about the Israeli police and the Israeli army repressing protests in occupied Palestine.[58]

This sentiment is echoed by other Black social activists, both well-known and relatively obscure. Prominent figures in the Black community like civil rights pioneer Stokely Carmichael and, and President Obama's former pastor Jeremiah Wright have linked Black and Palestinian struggles in the context of European colonization. Carmichael, in a speech at George

THE FIGHT FOR SOLIDARITY AND LEGITIMACY

Washington University in 1970, "declared today that the Palestinian Arabs were engaged in a 'just struggle' against an Israeli 'settler colony. . . . [He] described a 'settler colony' as one 'where Europeans leave their land, go to an area, and completely take it over.'"[59] At the twentieth anniversary of the Million Man March, Wright commented that "the youth in Ferguson and the youth in Palestine have united together to remind us that the dots need to be connected. And what Dr. King said, injustice anywhere is a threat to justice everywhere, has implications for us as we stand beside our Palestinian brothers and sisters, who have been done one of the most egregious injustices in the 20th and 21st centuries."[60]

Other Black social activists have linked the Black Lives Matter movement to a transnational struggle for self-determination. After traveling to Israel/Palestine with the Carter Foundation, artist and activist Ferrari Sheppard wrote a frank reflection piece in the *Huffington Post*, stating, "Currently, there is no 'conflict,' only the omnipresent power of the Israeli government and those who resist it." He linked the erasure of the Palestinian narrative to the early stages of colonialization: "In order for colonialism and occupation to be successful, previous inhabitants of a region must be dehumanized, labeled savages, and finally, their very existence denied. Once this paradigm has been established, any and all acts of horror can be inflicted upon them without recourse. Thus, the stories of the oppressed become irrelevant."[61]

Lesley Williams, a self-described "African-American Jew by choice," echoes Sheppard's sentiments in a post on Jewish Voice for Peace's website. She writes: "Here's the funny thing. African Americans such as myself, as well as indigenous people around the world, have an inexplicably stubborn prejudice against the 'inception' of states which dispossess local populations."[62]

Palestinian solidarity within the Latinx community

Latin Americans in South and Central America are pushing back against their dictatorial governments and Israel's influence in what they see as oppressive policies, and Latin Americans in the United States are taking note. Movimiento Estudiantil Chicano de Aztlán (MEChA), a Chicano student group, voted to affirm BDS in 2012, and "in a joint press release, Students for Justice in Palestine at Arizona State University and National

MEChA highlighted the growing trend of building 'cross-movement relationships' between Latino groups and Palestine solidarity organizations at universities across the country."[63] When Zionist groups such as the Anti-Defamation League and American Jewish Committee started taking Latino leaders on all-expenses-paid trips to Israel as a way to curry favor and support, activist Gabriel Camacho began organizing trips to Palestine. In 2010 he took a group of people of color to the West Bank to show them the other side of the story. As Adrian Maestas and Rania Khalek reported for *Electronic Intifada*, "Many of the participants recognized parallels between the oppression of Palestinians and their own oppression as colonized and marginalized people. 'A young Chicano from San Diego who was part of the delegation said, "Wow, this was just like home," and then he went on to describe how the border patrol asks for your ID and can stop you when you take a trolley to San Ysidro,' explained Camacho."[64]

On his return, Camacho developed a presentation called, "Two Walls, One Struggle," that highlighted the similarities between Israel's treatment of Palestine and the U.S. treatment of Hispanics, including the annexation of Mexican land in 1848. Some Hispanics, notably scholar Rudolfo Acuña, claim that "people of Mexican descent live under the domination of Anglo-American invaders," a claim that is the subject of his book, *Occupied America: A History of Chicanos*. Camacho also notes that Elbit Systems, the Israeli company that manages the border between Israel and Palestine, was also contracted by the United States to build sections of a proposed wall between the United States and Mexico.[65]

Puerto Ricans also identify with Palestinians as victims of colonization. Natasha Lycia Ora Bannan is a Puerto Rican lawyer who serves as executive vice president of the National Lawyers Guild, an association dedicated to human rights. The guild has long supported Palestine and organizes trips for individuals interested in an on-the-ground experience to gain better understanding of the situation. On those trips, there is a "focus on the conditions of detention for Palestinian political prisoners, an issue that has long affected Puerto Rico. Puerto Rico and Palestine have a shared history of fighting for their independence and sovereignty, leading to the imprisonment of many political prisoners."[66] Many Palestinians have fled to Puerto Rico.

Within the United States, pro-Israel groups contribute heavily to Latino campaigns for political office.[67] Whether their efforts are bearing fruit is another question. As Adrian Maestas and Rania Khalek report, "Curtis Marez, a professor of ethnic studies at the University of California, San Diego and [former] president of the American Studies Association, which has called for an academic boycott of Israeli universities, expressed doubts about the Israeli strategy to gain Latino political support. 'Focused on relatively elite Latinos such as politicians and Hollywood celebrities, I don't anticipate that Israel's marketing campaign will take hold among the vast majority of U.S. Latinos,'" he said.[68] According to a poll in 2011, more than half of Hispanic Americans felt the U.S. government was "too supportive" of Israel.[69]

Palestinian solidarity among the Asian American community

Another parallel that exists is the link between Palestinian American racialization and Asian American racialization. Asian Americans in the United States have experienced the "racial lumping" that Arab Americans have experienced. A hegemonic American definition of "Asians" presents all Asian Americans as the same.[70] Sunaina Maira of UC Davis and Magid Shihade of Birzeit University note that "linking Asian American and Arab American studies would challenge the arbitrary boundaries of ethnic and area studies that are tied to Cold War–era policy interests and current neocolonial ventures abroad as well as multiculturalist co-optation at home."[71] The racialization of Palestinian Americans based on political dissent mirrors the detainment of Japanese Americans during World War II due to suspicions that this subset of Americans were disloyal to U.S. national interests. While Palestinian Americans have not been detained, both groups have been represented by the media in the most negative forms of representation. Both groups suffered the consequences of being perceived as anti-American because of their backgrounds, which manifested itself through political opinions deemed contrary to U.S. imperialist interests.

As already noted, the Association for Asian American Studies was the first academic organization to sign a resolution in support of a boycott of Israeli academic institutions. More recently, some Asian Americans have begun to reframe the Middle East as "West Asia" and to identify with Palestinians as both Asians, victims of settler-colonialism, and Muslims, noting that more than 70 percent of the world's Muslims live in Asia, and that Islam is the most prevalent religion in the region.[72] The idea has been presented that Islamophobia is Asian hate: "Islamophobia is an issue for all Asian Americans. The Orientalist processes that motivate Islamophobia are symbiotic with the processes that underlie recent Asian hate incidents against those perceived to be of Far Eastern descent. There is no stopping one without stopping another. And there is no stopping all without the efforts, the solidarity of all."[73]

Israeli versus Palestinian solidarity within the Indigenous/Native American community

While Black Lives Matter has taken a stand with Palestine, Native American groups have tended to side with Israel. Chief Joseph RiverWind, leader of the Arawak Taino Nation, is a supporter of Israel and sees the occupation of Palestine as a success story that Native Americans would like to emulate. He and his wife traveled to Israel to meet with the head of the Samaria Regional Council and shared with him the story of Native American persecution as a parallel to Jewish persecution: "They took from us our language, our identity, our land, and here there is the story of returning to Israel. It is an honor for us to be in Samaria and to encourage people in America and overseas to support Israel, including Samaria, to speak against the BDS movement and to support any way to help Israel. . . . The Arab occupation must be stopped." The Seneca Nation offered its support as well, stating that "the Seneca Nation and the State of Israel share in common a passion for freedom and a willingness to fight for and defend our sovereignty and our shared right to be a free and independent people."[74]

The Crow Nation has formally expressed its solidarity with Israel. In a bill passed in 2013 with unanimous support by the Crow Tribal Legislature, officials declared that "the official policy of the Crow Tribe of Indians shall be to support the State of Israel, especially in its efforts to maintain economic, territorial and political integrity." The bill also states that "an official flag of the State of Israel is flown at the Veteran's Park in Crow Agency."[75] Navajo Nation president Jonathan Nez and his wife visited Israel on a "self-funded cultural exchange trip to learn more about the government of Israel's vision and efforts toward economic, infrastructure, and agricultural development."[76] During his visit, he expressed continued support for the relationship between Israel and the Navajo nation that was initiated by his predecessors. Former Navajo Nation president Ben Shelly also traveled to

Israel in 2012 to learn about agriculture and tourism.[77] Mvskoke (Muscogee Creek) Nation poet and author Joy Harjo accepted an invitation to perform at Tel Aviv University and has expressed publicly her opposition to the boycott of Israel.[78]

Support for Israel, however, is far from ubiquitous among Native Americans. Ms. Harjo's acceptance of the invitation was met with opposition from several of her peers. Robert Warrior, director of American Indian Studies at the University of Illinois at Urbana-Champaign, urged her to cancel her trip, saying that "opposing the occupation is among my most important causes." Playwright Richard Bracho implored her to "please cancel your Monday night event at Tel Aviv University. Do so to honor indigenous and anti-colonial practice and vision worldwide. Do so because Gaza is the world's largest open air prison." Native Hawaiian activist J. Kehaulani Kauanui "sent her a personal appeal asking her to not cross the picket line called by Palestinian civil society."[79]

Warrior has also expressed publicly his criticism of the Crow Nation and its support of Israel. When then-president Shelly visited Jerusalem, Warrior wrote an open letter on behalf of nine other prominent indigenous scholars expressing "'grave disappointment' over Shelly's ongoing public support of Israel. He wrote, 'As indigenous educators, we find your support for the state of Israel to be in complete contradiction to our values and sense of justice.'" He also expressed his confusion over the Native American identification with Israel rather than with Palestine. He pointed to the similarities between the Native American expulsion at the hands of the U.S. government and that of the Palestinian people, noting that the "Israeli demolition of the homes of Palestinian families is not all that different than the Long Walk your people endured in 1864. Your collusion with the Israeli government is a betrayal of that shared history and of the wisdom that has helped all Indigenous peoples survive for centuries." Kauanui posed the same dilemma to Native Americans who seek an alliance with Israel, saying: "The contested State of Israel perpetuates the violent domination and removal of the Palestinian people from their homeland, much like the U.S. settler colonial state's treatment of Native nations. Why any tribal leader would want to partner with Netanyahu is beyond curious; it is morally repugnant."[80]

The support of Israel by Native American leadership despite the shared experiences of Native Americans and Palestinians can be explained by a surge in Christian religious belief and an embrace of the "lost tribes" theology first put forward by Christopher Columbus after his voyages of the late 1400s. This is the idea that the Native Americans are descendants of the tribes of Israel and therefore share a theological and genetic heritage. Despite evidence refuting these claims, and the fact that the claim was originally and for many years put forward by nonnatives, many Native Americans have recently begun to embrace the concept. The Crow Nation's formal alliance with Israel included specifically biblical language in its explanation, such as: "Whereas, according to the King James Version of the Holy Bible, Book of Genesis, Chapter 12 ... the words of the Creator ('Akbaatatdia') to the nation of Israel provide that: 'I will make of thee a great nation, and I will bless thee, and make thy name great; and thou shalt be a blessing. And I will bless them that bless thee, and curse him that curseth thee, and in thee shall all families of the Earth be blessed.'"[81]

In *Thy Kingdom Come Thy Will be Done in Earth*, Crow pastor Jim Chosa teaches that the indigenous peoples of North America have the spiritual responsibility as the true owners of the land despite its theft by the U.S. government through the breaking of treaties. This responsibility was given to them by God, who "set forth relational principles, which would apply to all nations, through His relationship with the First Nation of the globe, Israel."[82] Therefore, "Native Americans are still the earthly host authority for the land of America, and the Native believers as new creatures of Christ restored to Heavenly authority in the Name of Jesus are the only ones who can righteously and permanently deal with any and all ancient issues of iniquity affecting the spiritual and natural landscape."[83] This appeal to the spiritual authority of Native Americans as given by God is the natural foundation for the particular strand of Zionism espoused by the Crow, Navajo, and Arawak Taino nations, among others, and the reason for their support of Israel over Palestine.

Warrior wrote in 2014 about the growing divide between Native American scholars and leaders who support Israel and those who support Palestine. Ryan Bellerose, a Metis from Canada who is active in Native American causes and a self-proclaimed Zionist, wrote a scathing indictment of Natives who support BDS and voicing support for the Jewish people as those truly indigenous to the Levant.[84] His critique was met with opposition from many, including Warrior, who wrote of the increasing urgency of the Palestinian cause, "while this brutality goes on unabated, Israel continues to build settlements on Palestinian lands, and those lands are typically the most resource-rich in Palestine. Those settlements are opposed by nearly every country in the United Nations. What makes all this possible is the protection of the United States, with its veto power in the UN Security Council."[85] Magid Shihade notes that "the argument that Jews are native and indigenous to Palestine was never a central, or even a partial, assertion among the leaders of the Zionist Movement.... All these Zionist leaders who have written about the prospects of the Zionist project in Palestine did not shy away from calling it a colonial one, and predicted that Native Palestinians would resist the colonization, something they saw as natural to any group that faces foreign domination."[86]

Salma abu Ayyash spoke on a podcast about meeting Mark Tilsen, an Oglala Lakota poet educator from the Pine Ridge Indian Reservation, in Palestine on a tour. While visiting a village that had been destroyed during the Nakba, Tilsen sang a native song, borrowed from the Cree people. He explained that the song commemorated a place one wanted to remember that no longer existed. This was the beginning of a friendship between the two. Abu Ayyash and a friend traveled to North Dakota to stand in solidarity with Tilsen at a protest against the Dakota Access Pipeline at Standing Rock. At the protest, Tilsen asked Abu Ayyash for a Palestinian flag, which he installed. Abu Ayyash also met Native Americans wearing keffiyehs. This experience of solidarity between the Native Americans and Palestinians is representative of the growing sense of unity between the two groups.[87] Abu Ayyash spoke of a shared sense of oppression and growing sense of shared destiny.

MUSLIM LEADERSHIP INITIATIVE: FAITHWASHING

For Zionism to survive, it must be able to propagate—and what better way than to normalize itself to some of the most vocal criticizers of Zionism: Muslims? The Muslim Leadership Initiative (MLI), is part of the Shalom Hartman Institute, the brainchild of Turkish American Abdullah Antepli, Duke's chaplain, and Yossi Klein Halavi, a former Jewish Defense League (JDL) activist turned author. The controversial program selects a cohort of Muslim Americans and, over the course of a year, provides educational programs and trips to Israel in the name of educating Muslims about Judaism, Zionism, and Israel. The official mission statement of MLI is "to expand participants' critical understanding of the complex religious, political, and socioeconomic issues facing people in Israel and Palestine. This is achieved through a rigorous academic curriculum and exposure to diverse narratives."[88]

While this mission statement sounds relatively innocuous, the reality of the MLI, as Hatem Bazian observes, is that it is "part of a new deal, in which ambitious American Muslim public figures will reap rewards for throwing Palestinians under the bus."[89] Criticism of the program, some of which comes directly from participants, centers around two themes: "faithwashing," or the practice of characterizing political conflicts as religious in nature, and the pro-Zionist bias of the MLI's purported "rigorous academic curriculum and exposure to diverse narratives." Sana Saeed defines faithwashing as "changing the cause of the Israeli-Palestinian conflict (or, rather, Israeli occupation and ethnic cleansing of Palestine) from a mid-20th century Euro-American settler-colonialist project (that brought anti-Semitism to the Muslim world) to a non-existent centuries long enmity between Jews and Muslims."[90]

Bazian echoes Saeed's observations. In a critique of Saud Anwar's *Huffington Post* piece describing his MLI experience, Bazian notes how Anwar propagates the falsehood of a centuries-long conflict between Jews and Muslims in the Middle East, playing "into an orientalist, Islamophobic and indeed anti-Jewish narrative in which Jews and Muslims are locked in mystical, ancient hatreds." The result, Bazian says, benefits Israel, since "unlike a political conflict, a religious one has no obvious solution."[91] Others have commented that the MLI conspicuously leaves out mention of Palestinian Christians, effectively erasing them from the narrative of the Palestinian-Israeli conflict. In his reflection piece, Anwar notes that "the 'bottom line' is that all of us—Muslim, Jewish, Israeli, Arab and American—want the same thing; peace," creating a dichotomy in the Israeli-Palestinian conflict that is split between religious and ethnic identification—between Muslim Arabs and Israeli Jews.[92] Sa'ed Atshan writes that the reduction of the conflict to Jewish-Muslim relations "further marginalizes the voices of Palestinian Christians, atheists and other segments of Palestinian society, diminishing the long and rich history of Palestinian Christians in their fight for freedom in Palestine."[93]

Furthermore, while the MLI claims to be a source of authority on religious conflict, it is funded heavily by Islamophobic groups in the United

States. The Shalom Hartman Institute, the parent organization of the MLI, receives funding from the Russell Berrie Foundation, which is linked to over $3 million worth of donations to anti-Muslim organizations.[94] As a program specifically targeted at Muslim Americans that receives funding from some of the largest anti-Islam organizations in the United States, MLI's intentions are questionable. While the MLI claims to represent a balanced and all-encompassing narrative of the Israeli-Palestinian issue, it really serves as an academy to convert Muslim Americans into pro-Zionist panderers. Part of the problem lies in the way the MLI has historically recruited participants: the majority of the participants have been South Asian Muslim Americans, as opposed to Arab Muslim Americans, and Palestinian Muslim Americans are almost unrepresented.

Kamal Abu-Shamsieh, possibly the only Palestinian Muslim American to have participated in the MLI (many of the participants' identities are not shared), ultimately concluded that the MLI provided no intellectual value that could not be gleaned from a simple internet source. He also discussed how his identity as a Palestinian, and his fellow peer's lack of identification as Palestinian, set them up for two very different experiences in the program. While Abu-Shamsieh "was an occupied man confronting his occupiers," his cohort participants "had had no firsthand experience and lacked context for the Palestinians' suffering." Abu-Shamsieh critiques the recruiting process of the MLI, noting that the program selects participants who are "naïve to the subtleties of the occupation." In addition to the problematic recruiting practices of the MLI, the leaders and experts tapped for the program are reluctant to address Palestinian concerns. Abu-Shamsieh notes that one of the speakers, Rabbi Donniel Hartmen, justified and defended Israel's actions in the 2014 Gaza war, without addressing the deaths of hundreds of Palestinians.[95] This anti-Palestinian sentiment is not an isolated incident: Hartman's annual report in 2013 discusses the organization's attempts to undermine Palestinian solidarity activism on college campuses, especially the BDS movement.[96]

The MLI is successful in converting its participants into mouthpieces for Zionism. After Palestinian Mazin Qumsiyeh called for a boycott of MLI, Haroon Moghul, an MLI participant, claimed that "Qumsiyeh, like other Palestinians, has no choice but to speak for boycott," a claim Atshan characterizes as a colonialist attempt to "deny the political agency of a leader in the Palestinian Christian community [Mazin Qumsiyeh], a former professor at Yale, and currently a professor at Bethlehem University and activist in the Palestinian nonviolent resistance movement."[97] This incident highlights MLI's unstated mission to foster relationships with key leaders in the United States who "can help normalize Zionism, legitimize Israel and thus delegitimize BDS."[98]

LGBTQ+ MOVEMENT ALLIES

BIPOC minorities are not the only groups taking a stand for Palestinian rights, nor are they the only groups being used to strengthen Israel's image. Israel has a relatively progressive stance on gay rights, a record that is promoted by "Brand Israel," a public relations campaign begun in 2005 to "portray Israel as hip, modern, and liberal to paper over its oppressive policies. They highlighted Israel's tech innovation, environmental sustainability, popular culture, and yes, gay rights," writes Liza Behrendt in *Haaretz*. The campaign contrasts Israel's treatment of sexual minorities with racist stereotypes about Palestinians and Arabs in general in an effort to "exaggerate homophobia in Palestine and downplay homophobia in Israel, encouraging liberals to excuse Israeli violence."[99] U.S.-based nonprofit A Wider Bridge was founded in 2010 to "provide opportunities for LGBTQ people in North America to build meaningful relationships with Israel and LGBTQ people in Israel" and to provide "LGBTQ people with the opportunity to engage with Israel in ways that matter to them personally, and to demonstrate that they have a stake in Israel and its future."[100] While A Wider Bridge has had a positive impact for queer Jewish Israelis, it has also prompted "harmful stereotypes of Palestinian, Muslim, and Arab queers," according to Behrendt. The effort to promote Israel's pro-LGBTQ policies and downplay its harsh treatment of Palestinians has been called 'Pinkwashing' and has become "so ubiquitous in LGBTQ spaces that queer Palestinian, Arab, and Muslim people often feel excluded."[101]

According to the BDS movement's website, "Israel's exploitation of LGBTQIA+ rights, known as pinkwashing, works to shift attention away from Israel's regime of occupation and apartheid. Israel's pinkwashing agenda seeks to portray itself as a fun-loving gay haven while using racist stereotypes to depict Palestinians as backward. Through lobby groups, often allied with right-wing homophobic organizations, Israel promotes its pinkwashing agenda around the world."[102] To counter this, a movement called

THE FIGHT FOR SOLIDARITY AND LEGITIMACY

#cancelpinkwashing has been growing. The coalition shut down a reception at gay activism conference Creating Change in Chicago in January 2016. A Wider Bridge denies its involvement in pinkwashing and stated its desire to "ensure that Creating Change can be a welcoming and safe space for LGBT people, Jews and non-Jews, who care about Israel."[103] Within Israel, some disagree that the government should get credit for the LGBTQ community. "They don't have the right to claim fame on that," says Mike Hamel, who is on the board of Israel's National LGBT Task Force, a private organization. "If Israel is a haven for the LGBT community, it's because of the community, the organizations that are working very hard to make it a good place for LGBT people to live. It's not because of the government policies. It's in spite of the government policies."[104]

Similarly, Israel has used feminist activism to forward its progressive image. After the murder of Mahsa Amini, an Iranian woman killed in police custody after being arrested for improper wearing of her hijab, Israel produced a video expressing solidarity with Iranian women who had begun protesting the oppressive and discriminatory regime under which they were living. As reported by Christians United for Israel, "'Israel loves you' was one of the messages published by Israel's Foreign Ministry this week. Other phrases included, 'We support Iranian women,' and 'All women deserve to live free.'"[105] The video presents Israel as a progressive country that stands against discrimination, while ignoring the oppression it exerts on Palestinians living within its borders. This allows the Israeli government to manage its image in the international community without actually meeting the standards it extols.

PALESTINIAN SOLIDARITY AMONG ENVIRONMENTALISTS

Israel prides itself in being environmentally focused and working to reverse climate change through the planting of forests. The planting is done primarily by two organizations: the Keren Kayemeth LeIsrael-Jewish National Fund (KKL-JNF) and Greening Israel. Over the past sixty years, the groups have planted millions of trees over thousands of acres. They insist they are reclaiming the desert, reducing flooding, and recapturing carbon dioxide in an effort to fight climate change. However, modern ecologists point out that the effort to plant forests in the desert has negatively affected the environment and that the trees "are obliterating grasslands that contain rare endemic species. There is also evidence that the new Israeli desert forests have so far caused more warming than cooling, as the dark mass of the Yatir Forest's trees is absorbing solar radiation."[106] The Society for the Protection of Nature in Israel sued the JNF in a contest that reached the Israeli Supreme Court after research found that "JNF's afforestation will harm the area's biodiversity. The High Court sided with the JNF."[107]

Besides the potentially negative environmental effects, the planting of trees has political consequences. On a Sunday in February 2022, activists gathered outside Israeli prime minister Naftali Bennett's office in Jerusalem to protest a tree-planting project in al-Naqab, claiming the forestation is "an attempt to displace the indigenous Bedouin population. . . . The JNF razed fruit trees and seeded fields in al-Naqab in January to 'make the desert bloom' with non-native plants. The purported environmental project has been met with fierce protest from the local villagers, with more than 60 Bedouin arrested."[108] The Bedouins are not the only group protesting the planting; Palestinians claim the project is less about saving the environment and more about claiming land for the Zionists. In fact, the KKL-JNF was not established as an environmental organization but was "created in 1901 to buy and develop land for the Zionist movement, and now owns around 13 percent of Israeli territory."[109] The preferred tree planted in Israel is the Aleppo pine, and native species such as pistachio, olive, and carob have been removed in order to bring them in, changing the landscape into the settlers' ideal image of Israel. According to Jessica Buxbaum, the greening project is a "cornerstone of the Zionist movement, in which Israel tries to paint Palestine as a desolate wasteland in need of a Jewish green thumb."[110] As one scientist described it, planting trees "is a way of saying we are here."[111]

As John Collins put it in *Global Palestine*, "the planting of trees has long served a dual purpose in Israel. First, it has provided a thin but powerful layer of ecological justification for the expropriation of land from non-Jewish owners and occupants. Equally important, however, it has provided ideological fuel for Zionism's entire settler colonial imaginary. Efforts to 'make the desert bloom,' after all, fit hand in glove with efforts to establish an indigenous identity for Jewish settlers by asserting their close connection to the land."[112]

It is also a way of covering up the atrocities of the Nakba and creating Israeli permanence where there were once Palestinian settlements. In August 2021 a wildfire burned 2,000 hectares west of Jerusalem, revealing

THE FIGHT FOR SOLIDARITY AND LEGITIMACY

"their underlying shape to become visible once more: their historic terraced slopes testifying to the work of Palestinian farmers over centuries, as they strove to cultivate the land and make it bear fruit for its inhabitants which go back more than 400 years."[113] Collins writes: "Despite the existence of powerful patriotic discourses that invoke the beauty of the land and the need to defend it, settler projects tend to be oriented toward the violent conquest of territory rather than the peaceful occupation of it."[114]

Take the village of Saffourieh. Once a rather sprawling hilltop village of stone homes, today the area is a pine forest. Its residents "languish in refugee camps in Lebanon," or in towns in the Galilee; "authorities call them 'present absentees.'" After the forced removal, Israeli forces demolished the town, then replanted the area with trees. There are perhaps hundreds of other examples. One can picnic among the ruins of Kar Bir'im. The Biriya Forest and Canada Park are billed to visitors as having groves, springs, hiking trails, and planted forests, but also an ancient synagogue, lime pit, and revered tombs. There is no mention in the marketing material of the eight villages over which these National Parks were planted. Yet these afforestation projects are globally lauded as ways to improve the landscape and as symbols of prosperity and peace. One cannot support new forests without acknowledging the reality of where they come from; as Saree Makdisi says, "the act of affirming the positive value of greening the land is inextricably bound up with the negative reality of ethnic cleansing and ecocidal disappearance in such a way that emphasizing the former makes the latter fade away into a carefully managed void: the absence *is* the trees."[115]

American Zionists have joined the effort. The Greening Israel Project, which is managed by HaYovel, a U.S. nonprofit organization, has been active for eighteen years planting trees with money raised in the United States and around the world. For $25, Americans can buy one tree to be planted under the Greening Israel Project's direction. Donors can also volunteer to go to Israel and plant trees. The group maintains the "barren land" trope on its website and uses biblical language to justify the occupation of Palestine. The site reads, "Just like the miracles that happened in Israel back in Bible times, there are miracles still happening today. Since the establishment of the modern state of Israel in 1948 and the return of Jewish people from around the world, the desolate, barren landscape of Israel is coming back to life, just as God promised in the pages of Scripture."[116] HaYovel is led by Tommy and Sherri Waller, "devout Christian Zionists committed to helping bring

Biblical prophecy to life in Israel." They see any opposition to their cause as antibiblical and use the derogatory term "sons of Ishmael" to describe Arabs.[117]

According to its website, the HaYovel project was hoping to plant three thousand trees in the West Bank, or what it calls the "Biblical heartland," by the end of 2022, and to plant twenty thousand trees on about 247 acres of land "every year at sites located throughout Israel's central mountain range in the regions of Judea and Samaria [the West Bank]." Nearly the entire area belongs to Palestinian farmers from the village of Burin and was intensively cultivated until the second intifada in the early 2000s. Since that time, Palestinian families "have been barred from their land." Judy Maltz, writing for *Haaretz*, reported that Burin resident Bashar Eid "was able to name several families, including his own, whose land he said had been appropriated for the forest." He told Maltz: "Twelve dunams out there is mine, but I have no way of getting to it anymore."[118]

When asked if he was aware that most of the plot near Har Bracha was privately owned by Palestinians from Burin, Tommy Waller admitted his organization doesn't own the land on which they plant trees but said, "From our perspective, [the Palestinians] don't have jurisdiction over that land." Spokespeople from the Civil Administration, which grants permits for tree planting, and for the settlement of Har Bracha denied having been approached by Hayovel for permission to plant. Dror Etkes, the founder of Kerem Navot, a nonprofit that monitors Israeli land policy in the West Bank, told Maltz, "In my 20 years of working in the West Bank, I have confronted innumerable instances of Jews stealing Palestinian land, but never before a case of Christians from the United States stealing Palestinian land."[119] The group seems to have some support from the Israeli military. In December 2020, when Waller's two security dogs went missing, Maltz reports that he was able to get Israeli soldiers to search for them.

Despite its history of human rights violations, the Jewish National Fund was given the opportunity to present on forestry at COP27, the climate change conference held in Egypt in November 2022.[120] In this way, the Israeli government has been successful in holding itself up as respectable and caring and has hidden its treatment of Palestinians literally behind trees.

As these examples increase, we notice that narrative is changing. Some very important changes have occurred in the Palestine struggle in the

United States, and globally, over the past several years. For far too long the issue of Palestinian freedom has been marginalized, so much so that many people in the United States have been progressive except for Palestine, yet this is changing. As Angela Davis says,

> The impact of the influence of Zionism, which used to be pervasive, is losing its force. On college and university campuses, Students for Justice in Palestine (SJP) has really grown and large numbers of people who are not necessarily Palestinian, who are not necessarily Arab or Muslim, have become active in the SJP groups.... The issue of Palestine is increasingly being incorporated into major social justice issues. And my own personal experience has been that in the past I could always expect resistance or challenges when talking about Palestine, but now this is [becoming] increasingly acceptable. And I think this has to do with what is happening in Palestine itself. It has to do with the rise of Palestine solidarity movements all over the world, not just in the U.S. It has to do specifically in the U.S. with increasing numbers of people associated with Black, and Native American, and Latino movements incorporating Palestine into the agenda. I think I spoke in the last interview about the tweets of Palestinian activists used to provide advice for protesters in Ferguson, on how to deal with the tear gas, so that direct connection that has been facilitated by social media has been important as well.[121]

Davis shared a further story of surprising support for Palestine. "Recently I had the opportunity to participate on a panel of the National Women's Studies Association (NWSA) conference, and the NWSA has never taken a position on Palestine due to Zionist influences, I would say. In a large plenary gathering with perhaps twenty-five hundred people, during a panel on Palestine, someone asked whether we could take a floor vote, whether people there wanted the NWSA to take a strong position in support of BDS, and virtually everyone in the audience stood up. This was so unprecedented."[122]

In 2022 the film *Boycott* was released, following "the stories of a news publisher, an attorney, and a speech therapist, who, when forced to choose between their jobs and their political beliefs, launch legal battles that expose an attack on freedom of speech across America."[123] While the film did receive pushback, it was an example of the ways that the Palestinian story is being told today. There were filmmakers willing to make the film, distribute it, and market it. It was widely praised and was an official selection at five film festivals, including SXSW and DOCNY. And it was done with an expert view toward the difficult politics surrounding the issue. *Boycott* has been praised for its focused narrative on the suffering of the Palestinian people and their experiences, moving away from the typical two-sidedness, which has dominated most conversations around Palestine and Israel in the United States.[124]

American progressives are moving toward solidarity with Palestine as well. In May 2021, Laura Kelly reported for *The Hill* that

> about 140 progressive groups . . . released a joint statement calling on the Biden administration to condemn the Israeli government over a host of policies they say amount to war crimes against Palestinians. . . . The statement was signed by prominent progressive groups like MoveOn, Justice Democrats, and the Sunrise Movement . . . that have maintained focus on the potential forced evictions of Palestinians in east Jerusalem and criticized claims by Jewish groups seeking legal justification to reclaim ownership. . . . Officials [in the United States] have refrained from criticizing the Israeli government outright and instead welcomed the move by the Israeli Supreme Court to delay a hearing over whether to enforce at least one eviction of a Palestinian family in east Jerusalem.

This reticence is less popular than it has been in the past, and the lack of effort by the government to protect innocent Palestinians has " 'more members of Congress than ever in history . . . scrutinizing the United States' relationship with Israel.' " As the activist Yasmine Taeb told Kelly, summing it up quite well: "This is unprecedented."[125]

The Palestinian rights movement has done an enormous job in building relationships with a whole range of other progressive activists and placing Palestine on the broader progressive agenda. These are all things we are going to show up for each other, because we have to fight all of these forms of oppression together, says Matt Duss. "One cannot claim to support equality in the United States and not support equality for Palestinians in Palestine/Israel."[126] Edward Said's open letter to Jewish intellectuals was a reminder to the supporters of human rights around the world that struggles for self-determination are universal. Commenting on this, John

Collins writes, "The Palestinian struggle, much like the anti-apartheid struggle in South Africa did in an earlier time, forms the hub of a global web that not only connects people of diverse experiences, but also provides an idiom within which to see important commonalities among those experiences."[127]

CONTEMPORARY NON-ZIONIST JEWISH VOICES

New historians: Recording an accurate history

For the Palestinian story to be heard and understood, it is important not only to have political and social allies, but to have an accurate history of the region. During the mid-twentieth century, the story of Israel was controlled primarily by Zionists. As mentioned in chapter 2, a group of historians is questioning that narrative and doing the work of reexamining that history. Edward Said, in his open letter, wrote, "You will surely have read or heard about the work of revisionist Israeli historians (Morris, Segev, Flapan, et al.) whose reconstructions of the ravages of 1948 and after mostly coincide with the testimony of Palestinian words and voices that were never heard in the US. Not heard because unpublished and undisseminated in media where, as several critics have shown in detail, fear of the Israeli lobby or outright suppression determined that we, our story, our deprivations were to be given no outlet, allowed no significant space."[128] These revisionist Israeli historians are now finding their voices and speaking out on behalf of Palestinians in ways they never have before.

It is important to note that the term "revisionist" used here has a different connotation than is sometimes used in American media. These revisionists are not changing history to fit their own agenda but are revising previous stories to more accurately reflect the truth of the matter. Their work has had an impact on contemporary reporting.

As observed by Peter Beinart, the evolving and shifting ideas around the question of Palestine both in the United States and in Israel have led to a dwindling number of Jewish American commentators defending Israel and its actions in leading progressive media outlets.[129] Peter Beinart described his first visit to the West Bank as a "shattering experience" akin to an American visiting the Jim Crow South and being astonished at the lack of rights enjoyed by Palestinians. "I have begun to wonder," he said, "for the first time in my life, whether the price of a state that favors Jews over Palestinians is too high."[130]

Over the past decade or so, Beinart has become a leading Jewish American voice in the intellectual struggle over the rights of Palestinians. He explains in an interview the different dynamic experienced by American Jews and Palestinians in their approach to politics. He says that the Jewish people in America,

> as a community that's been in the U.S. for a hundred years, roughly, [have] learned how to feel comfortable in the American political process and also [have] been assimilated to such a degree that Jews are not threatening. I think one of the dynamics of AIPAC is that many of those people who are now older in AIPAC are aware that their parents, in the 1940s, their parents' generation was not able to will political power in the way they would have liked during the Holocaust. Part of what their role is now, because they feel much more comfortable than their parents did, is to redeem that failure ... by making sure that there's not another Holocaust in Israel.[131]

This explanation helps us understand, if not excuse, the actions of Jewish Americans in their lobbying efforts.

In describing his own childhood, Beinart says, "Israel was very much there in the background because it's so bound up with this narrative of Jewish victimhood and fragility and safety. When the Intifada broke out in the late 1980s, as I was in my late teens, I think I became somewhat conscious of the way in which these tensions between human universal moral principles of human rights and the notion of Jewish self-preservation, of looking out for Jewish safety were coming into conflict." Yet this tension, and the choice to give primacy to a person's Jewishness above all else, is not universal. Instead, there is a division that is growing, of "people who you could call American Jews, which is to say that their Jewishness is the noun and Americanism is the adjective. And then, a whole lot of other people who better be described as Jewish Americans. You might ask a question of someone. 'Could you more easily imagine living as a Christian in the United States or a Jew in Australia?' If you ask that question, you will start to see the divide that exists." Because of this divide, some Jewish Americans are beginning to see ways in which they can be authentically, holistically Jewish and still support Palestinians.

THE FIGHT FOR SOLIDARITY AND LEGITIMACY

Beinart concisely illustrates the point in this way:

> The conservative movement has been in deep decline, so where you see the demographic growth is among orthodox Jews and among unaffiliated Jews. You also had another kind of identity, which was very strong, and this was the people who, for many generations, have run groups like AIPAC, people who are not particularly religiously observant but for whom Israel and the defense of the Jewish people was a kind of secular religion. Those are the people who really led the American Jewish establishment. There are parallels you may pick up between what's happening here and what's happening in Israel. But what you see among the younger generation is that the religious center and the political center was held by people who were democrats in the United States, fairly liberal, fairly progressive, not radically but fairly progressive, willing to support the Israeli government pretty much no matter what. That center has kind of collapsed. And what you have instead is an Orthodox community, which is growing demographically, a modern Orthodox community that's growing in numbers and self-confidence, more and more becoming the leadership of the American Jewish institutions.... The children of what I call in my book the secular tribalists really tend to be more secular universalists now, many of them express that universalism simply by not caring about Israel/Palestine much at all, it's just not a big thing for them. Their Jewish identity itself is not necessarily such a dominant force in their lives.[132]

Perhaps the most famous of the new historians is Ilan Pappé, an expatriate Israeli historian who has been called Israel's bravest historian.[133] Pappé was raised in Israel but began to question the morality of the IDF when he did his PhD degree at Oxford on the events of 1948. He has since worked to rewrite the history of Israel more accurately and has written several books, including *The Ethnic Cleansing of Palestine*, *Ten Myths about Israel*, and *The Biggest Prison on Earth*.

Dr. Gabor Maté, a Holocaust survivor whose grandparents died in Auschwitz, is now a physician. He has strong family ties to the Likud Party in Israel and, as a young man, was a Zionist who dreamed of a place of safety and freedom for the Jewish people. He found, however, that to make the Jewish dream a reality, one had to "visit a nightmare on the local population.... There was no land without a people. There was [sic] people living there who had been living there for hundreds of years or even longer."¹³⁴ In a video interview with Russell Brand, he promotes the new Israeli historians who have proven that the settling of Jewish people in Israel required the expulsion of Palestinians and describes his visit to Occupied Palestine during the first Intifada, during which he cried over the treatment of Palestinians at the hand of Israelis.

Soon after the outbreak of war in October 2023 and the subsequent unprecedented levels of violence and genocidal campaign against Gaza, Maté was interviewed by his daughter, Hannah Maté, and shared his thoughts about the Hamas attack on October 7 and Israeli attacks on Gaza. He described how context matters, and that for decades Palestinians have experienced extreme violence, and he shared several titles of books about the history of Palestine and Israel.¹³⁵

Shifting Jewish American and Israeli views on the question of Palestine

As discussed in chapter 2, Jewish Americans are increasingly becoming open to the idea that being critical of certain Israeli policies can, simultaneously, be compatible with a general sense of being pro-Israel. Examining polling data of Jewish Americans over the past decade, one can identify two trends: the first is around the generational difference, which follows a similar, larger, changing pattern in American views, signaling a shift in American cultural and political understanding of the question of Palestine. The second trend shows that the American Jewish community is changing from within, and a growing segment from within that defines their Jewishness through reclaiming the Jewish ideal of Tikkun Olam (Hebrew for "fixing the world")."¹³⁶ One of the latest polls (mentioned in chapter 2), conducted in November 2022, shows that "89% of Jewish voters agreed that 'someone can be critical of Israeli government policies and still be pro-Israel,' and 72% of Jewish voters disapproved of AIPAC endorsing and raising money for Members of Congress who support Israel but voted against certifying the 2020 Presidential election. . . . Only 4% of Jewish voters said that Israel was one of the their top two issues in deciding who they vote for Congress."¹³⁷ This noticeable Jewish American shift among younger generations is described by Atalia Omer in her book *Days of Awe: Reimagining Jewishness in Solidarity with Palestinians*. Omer examines how and why this shift is taking place, tracing its roots to the experiences of oppression felt by Jewish people themselves.[138]

As people who see themselves as members of an oppressed minority, Jewish Americans understand the significance of civil rights. But those who oppose Israel find their voices silenced by powerful pro-Israel groups. As Mearsheimer and Walt note, among Jewish Americans this community "has generally accepted the principle that on matters of fundamental security there ought to be no public criticism of Israel."[139] According to Steven Rosenthal, "For millions of American Jews, criticism of Israel was a worse sin than marrying out of the faith."[140]

Israelism is the title of a 2023 documentary that challenges how the relationship between Jewish Americans and Israel has long been framed: that the two are one and the same. The film directors, Erin Axelman and Sam Eilertsen, follow two Jewish Americans who were brought up to be indoctrinated that Judaism and Israel are conflated to be viewed as the same.[141] In his review of the film, "*Israelism* Review: The Dangers of Pro-Israel Indoctrination," Daniel Kushner describes how the documentary highlights the ways through which "Jewish institutions, such as the ADL, conflate valid criticism of Israel with antisemitism. So when politicians are tasked with confronting antisemitism, they can respond by touting support for Israel rather than denouncing the very real rise of antisemitism here in the United States." Kushner also explains how this film "functions as an effective conversation starter, drawing attention to the methodologies of pro-Israel indoctrination that we all must confront. Untangling the American Jewish population from the state of Israel continues to be a long and contentious process, one that leaves Jews who are critical of Israel feeling isolated. But this documentary demonstrates that those Jews are not alone. There is, in fact, a growing community of progressive Jews against Israel—one that holds the potential to enact great change."[142]

Criticism of Israel among Jewish Americans is not new. In 1973 a group of Jewish Americans formed Breira, which means "alternative" in Hebrew. Breira was "hailed by the *New York Times* and the *Washington Post* as a major political development, auguring a new willingness on the part of American Jews to criticize the state of Israel." The group, in its founding statements, wrote that "nothing is more important for the continued vitality of Jewish life than extensive discussion within the Jewish community about the State [of Israel], its problems, its policies, its relationship to us and our hopes for it." This open-ended statement allowed for discussion of various topics regarding Israel, but detractors were quick to demonize the group. Rael Jean Isaac, representing Americans for a Safe Israel, wrote that "the majority who join [it] are unaware of the purposes of the minority who shape the path of the organization."[143]

According to Zionist groups and major Jewish organizations like AIPAC, that purpose was an anti-Semitic one, to undermine the state of Israel. Mearsheimer and Walt document some of the backlash from other groups: "President of the Reform rabbinate, Arthur Lelyveld, said that groups like Breira 'gave aid and comfort . . . to those who would cut aid to Israel and leave it defenseless before murderers and terrorists.'" A Hadassah newsletter labeled Breira members "cheerleaders for defeatism" and warned its own members to "reject the advances of these organizations with their dogmas that run counter to Israeli security and Jewish survival." The president of the conservative Rabbinical Assembly declared that Breira was "fronting for the PLO," and forty-seven rabbis issued a statement terming Breira's positions "practically identical with the Arab point of view." The prosettlement group Americans for a Safe Israel distributed a thirty-page pamphlet smearing Breira's leaders for their involvement with other left-wing causes and referring to them as "Jews for Fatah."[144] Breira lasted five years before succumbing to pressure from pro-Israel groups and closing.

As mentioned earlier, the community of Israeli scholars, journalists, attorneys, and activists critical of Israeli policy and occupation is long and continues to grow. Similarly, in the United States, Jewish Americans critical of Israel are growing in numbers and influence. Their criticism is perceived to be more legitimate in the United States than, say, that of a Palestinian, due to their positionality as Jewish, which gives them the unique ability to distinguish between their identity and the exclusionary ideology of Zionism that has weaponized Jewish identity and manipulated definitions of speech critical to Israel as anti-Semitic. These individuals and groups play a significant role in battling these claims, especially since many of them are observant Jews and rabbis.

Remarkably, some Holocaust survivors are less likely than other Jewish Americans to support Zionism. Sara Roy describes how her parents, who survived Auschwitz, made a conscious choice not to go to Israel after the war. Growing up in the United States as a first-generation American, Roy

THE FIGHT FOR SOLIDARITY AND LEGITIMACY

noticed that her parents' views were not necessarily typical of the larger Jewish American community. "Jewish Americans had no experience with the Holocaust and, understandably, could not possibly comprehend what survivors had been through—no one could. It was also my impression growing up—and I could be wrong—that my parent's Jewish American friends didn't particularly want to know that much about what survivors had endured." Because of this, there was a marked disconnect between the survivor community and the Jewish American community, "at least in my experience" she says.[145]

Roy speaks of activist Hilda Silverman, a Bunting Peace Fellow dealing with Middle East issues, who found the disparity in perspective between Holocaust survivors and other Jews interesting. Silverman spent time in the early 1990s interviewing "about 100 Holocaust survivors and children of survivors on the issue of Palestinian human rights. She argued that within the Jewish community, many of the people who advocated for Palestinian rights and for a just solution for both Israelis and Palestinians were survivors and their children. This came as a shock to some people, but it made perfect sense to me."[146]

Roy continues her explanation into the new perspective many Jewish people have on the issue of Palestine: "While there is still strong and unquestioned support for Israel, there is also, undeniably, much more thoughtful and critical thinking on Israel and its repression of the Palestinian people, which is not only good for Palestinians, but also for Israel. Today, people both within and outside the Jewish community are far less fearful of dissenting from mainstream views, which appear increasingly insupportable against the harsh realities of Israel's occupation."[147]

It makes sense to many Jewish Americans, including attorney and UC Berkeley Law graduate Liz Jackson. After several Berkeley Law student groups voted not to invite speakers who hold Zionist views, they were derided for being anti-Semitic. Jackson responded with an op-ed describing her stance as a Jewish woman: "Zionism as an ideology supports a Jewish nation state which privileges the rights of Jewish people over others. In practice, Zionism entails theft, displacement and brutal violence against Palestinians. Anti-Zionism is core to my Jewish values. I believe that I am not free until all people are free, especially Palestinians who are imprisoned, assassinated and bombed under a flag with the Star of David on it."[148] Noam Chomsky, the celebrated academic who is also Jewish, has also been critical of Israel. In 2010 he was denied entry to Palestine when he tried to travel to Birzeit University and the Institute for Palestine Studies in Ramallah to give a series of lectures. In Chomsky's words, "the government of Israel doesn't like the kinds of things I say, which puts them into the same category as every other government in the world."[149]

Jewish Americans who are pro-Israel but also pro-Palestine have found a home in the political organization J Street. Peter Beinart, describing the organization, says,

> I think one of the fundamental difference in J Street [nonprofit advocacy group based in the United States whose stated aim is to promote American leadership to end the Arab–Israeli and Israeli–Palestinian conflicts peacefully and diplomatically] is that J Street fundamentally see this as a Palestinian struggle, and they see themselves as allies to the Palestinian struggle in the way that white Americans might be allies to black liberation in the United States, and so, for them, this is what the Palestinians have chosen to do, then their role is to support that, which is very different than the notion of Jews saving Israel.[150]

Sara Roy agrees:

> I can say there has been a dramatic change within the American Jewish community around the issue of Israel. Particularly after the 1967 war, Israel became a much more prominent feature of American Jewish life, at least in my own personal experience. Too much, in my view at least, that was about Judaism and Jewish history and culture increasingly seemed to be filtered through a Zionist lens. It was something that I felt very uncomfortable with . . . I rejected [it] because Zionism was one thing for me and Judaism was another. In my limited experience with organized religion in America as an adult, most synagogues that I've had interaction with tend to define one's Judaism, not only in terms of values and all the things we've been discussing, but also in political allegiance to Israel. You can find congregations that reject that but they're clearly in a minority. When I was growing up, the notion of questioning Israel or criticizing Israel or disagreeing with the standard understanding of what Israel is, what Israel is doing, why it's doing it was completely forbidden.[151]

THE FIGHT FOR SOLIDARITY AND LEGITIMACY

Roy continues her explanation into the new perspective many Jewish people have on the issue of Palestine: "So there are a whole combination of factors, but . . . my sense is that while, of course, there is still a lot of resistance and still a lot of support for Israel, there's much more thoughtful and critical thinking on this issue, which is not only good for Palestinians, it's good for Israel, it's to Israel's benefit. This kind of thinking and this kind of criticism is out there."[152] Illinois synagogue Tzedek Chicago declared itself officially "anti-Zionist" in December 2021. "The decision to add a statement decrying the creation of Israel as an 'injustice against the Palestinian people—an injustice that continues to this day' was taken by a vote." Seventy-three percent of the congregation's two hundred member families voted in favor.[153]

The move was criticized by some, including Daniel Koren, director of Hasbara Fellowships Canada, who wrote on Twitter, "I don't think they know what Judaism even is."[154] Rabbi Brant Rosen, who founded Tzedek Chicago, sees a growing movement of Jews who do not agree with Israeli strategy regarding Palestine. " 'There are increasing numbers of Jews out there, particularly young Jews, who don't identify as Zionist and resent the implication that somehow to be Jewish today one must be Zionist,' Rosen told Religion News Service in 2015." According to a Forward analysis, Tzedek Chicago is only one of more than a dozen synagogues to take such a position.[155] Jewish individuals are even more likely to hold either pro-Palestinian or sympathetic views than their synagogues might be. Pew data show that "five times as many American Jews between the ages of 18 and 29 think the United States is 'too supportive' of Israel as those over the age of 65," and that "only a third of Jews between the ages of 18 and 49 believe Israel's government is making a sincere attempt at peace with the Palestinians."[156]

Since October 2023, the intensification of violence against Palestinians civilians in the Gaza Strip and the West Bank has brought about a new phase of public discourse. Conversations around Palestine have shifted; encampments on college and university campuses all over the United States are clear evidence of an unstoppable generational transformation around justice and equality. As American society and politics views shift around the question of Palestine, and the relationship between the two nations, at the expense of Palestinian livelihood, the countercurrent to these forces intensifies, in a way that parallels the intensity of violence against Palestinians at the hands of the American-funded and -legitimized Israeli war machine. Over time, and to address the challenges emerging from its oppressive policies against Palestinians, Israel resorted to more violence and used new forms of control, introducing sophisticated surveillance technologies, and punished those who stand against its policies. Attempts to control have been met with new forms of activism that have transcended borders. Every action to silence these voices provides more reason for enhanced methods of activism on a global level. The pushback against the changing views of Americans, for example, is centered on certain spaces or domains. These spaces are where we find the intensifying fight taking place, from law, to education, to entertainment. The question of Palestine is at the heart of American society and politics, and it is here to stay.

Will pro-Israel voices be able to win the global fight against pro-Palestinian voices demanding justice and equal rights? Will they be able to keep the status quo? If history teaches us anything, it is that empires fall, and justice (or a form of it) prevails. It will become too costly, politically, for the U.S. government and elected officials to continue attempts to side with Israel right or wrong, as a calculated pragmatic approach to winning elections and avoiding the disapproval of the American public. The battle between the voices advocating for Palestinian rights and the voices attempting to preserve the status quo and the relationship between the United States and Israel is happening all around us. It's on the floors of state legislative bodies, in Congress, in court rooms, on college campuses, in corporate board meetings, in entertainment, in the streets, in synagogues, within communities, at dinner tables, and in virtual spaces.

One thing is for sure: the more Israel and its supporters in the United States push, the more pushback they will face. Escalating the violence against Palestinians has shown repeatedly that it will only create more solidarity with the Palestinian people, globally, and in the United States particularly. How long will members of Congress be able to continue being reelected if they ignore their constituents' demand for a just solution to Palestinian suffering?

CONCLUSION

> The Palestinian narrative is today more firmly anchored and more globally accepted than at any time in the past century.
>
> —RASHID KHALIDI, 2021

Israel has been able to control Palestinian lands since 1948 and to an extent succeeded in controlling the narrative surrounding its founding and the continuous portrayal of Palestinian claims as illegitimate. Although successful to a point over decades, the Israeli narrative is now being challenged not only by the global South or leftist groups around the world but also by countries that have traditionally supposed Israel "right or wrong" and by the mainstream of Western societies.

Times are changing. The Palestinian Nakba that started in 1948 might be seen as a form of Israeli control of time and space, but it also resembles the lack of control of times that have yet to come (i.e., the future), especially in spaces that it cannot control (i.e., exile). Every calamity creates opportunities, and the Palestinians have used theirs effectively. Control of a territory creates more spaces to challenge this control. Israeli control of the global narrative has been increasingly challenged, even in countries that have long been supportive of Israel, namely, the United States.

Americans have typically viewed Palestinians and advocacy of Palestinian equal rights with suspicion. Highly prejudiced, Orientalized views of Arabs or Middle Easterners have been prevalent in American society. Muslims have been seen as antithetical to Christians, and to modernity. The American political system has historically aligned closely with Israel, placing the United States as a country at odds with ideas of Palestinian liberation, because the United States is a settler-colonial state like Israel and is built around systems of oppression integral to its sociopolitical and economic structures. Aside from this larger comparison, American understanding of Palestine and Palestinians is a product of a larger context, which have been discussed in this book. Chapter 1, for example, examined the emergence of the American understanding of Palestine and how it was affected by Orientalism and Zionism. It considered the influence of misleading media narratives and fictional tropes and of the cultural Christianity of the United States, which conflates solidarity with the modern state of Israel with a historical sympathy for the ancient kingdom of biblical Israel.

Chapter 1 also looked at the close political relationship between the United States and Israel and the direct impact of that governmental friendship on the plight of Palestinians and struggle for liberation. The chapter reflected on the nature of education in the United States. While established to provide a free education for all, the U.S. public education system has also existed to promote nationalist American ideals and whitewashing its settler-colonial history, painting and promoting stereotypes of Black, Indigenous, and people of color (BIPOC). The entire social, political, and cultural fabric of American life, informed by the American history of colonialism and discrimination against Black and brown-skinned people, is tilted against solidarity with the Palestinian people and their struggle for freedom and self-determination.

This, however, is changing. Palestine has become at the heart of social justice in the United States. It highlights American prejudice, selective humanity, and the hypocrisy of American foreign policy. Palestine advocacy is at the forefront of free speech in the United States, and it is often dubbed as the litmus test of progressive politics in contemporary America.

Cultural shifts in American society and politics over the last twenty years have altered this dynamic. As discussed in chapter 2, a number of sociopolitical transformations have taken place in politics, media, society, and technology that have led to a more nuanced and equitable understanding of the Palestinian cause. The more recent Black Lives Matter movement has changed the landscape of civil rights conceptualization and action in the United States and globally, paving the way for other traditionally racialized communities to gain traction in larger society. BLM's use of social media,

CONCLUSION

its rallying of young people around the issue of minority rights, and its intentional solidarity with other oppressed groups have changed the strategy of social movements in the United States. The rise of BLM and the codification of other BIPOC rights and other underrepresented communities, such as gay marriage, are due in part to changes in media and an expanding cultural acceptance, due to declines in traditional institutions (like churches) that have maintained and reproduced the status quo. New forms of internet-based media have nearly eliminated the hold elites had on news production and distribution. The increasingly accessible technology, such as smartphones, has widened the audience for this new media. Concurrently, the American public sees itself less and less as religious, marking an ongoing decline in the influence of the Christian church in particular, which has historically favored Israel and taught and encouraged allegiance to it, even when Palestinian Christians, like all other Palestinians, suffer from the brutality of the Israeli military occupation. Together, these structural transformations have opened doors to the American imagination regarding Palestine and have altered the American perception of the struggle. It has been a slow process, as discussed in chapter 2. More and more people are embracing the idea of Palestinian self-determination and rejecting the oppression of innocent people everywhere.

The quest for legitimacy around the Palestinian narrative in politics and media for the hearts and minds of people has been intensifying and becoming a global phenomenon. It is this global approach that may finally be turning the tide for Palestine. The backlash from the establishment is also intensifying to counter the efforts fighting for justice and calling for boycotts and sanctions against Israel for its continuous colonization. The transnational fight for justice is taking place through investing in building solidarity networks, in formal education, and in advocating for BDS as pressure on Israel.

American politics and global diplomacy have played significant roles in protecting Israel from accountability and repercussions. The United States has served as the protector of Israel no matter the circumstances, even during indefensible situations like the murder of Palestinian children and journalists like Palestinian American Shireen Abu Akleh in 2021. Although there are countless violations of every international convention to protect journalists and civilian populations, the U.S. government tended to turn a blind eye and provided unfounded justifications.

CONCLUSION

The shift, however, is noticeable as well. Chapter 3 described the ways in which the U.S. government, institutions, and successive politicians have traditionally favored Israel above even their own interests. The chapter also explored the history of political policy in regard to Israel and the rise and reach of the Israel lobby and its powerful hold on Washington. Historically, foreign and domestic policy have held Israel as an ally, but current political measures have taken this friendship even further. Contemporary laws enforcing support of Israel through the banning of boycotts essentially makes opposition to Israeli policies of oppression or support for the Palestinian people and their suffering illegal. This shift is a response to the growing dissent in the United States over the preferential treatment received by Israel, whether by uninterrupted military and financial aid or through diplomatically sheltering Israel from the International Court of Justice, the United Nations, or even human rights organizations. At the same time, there is little measurable or meaningful American intervention to end the suffering of Palestinians living under military occupation.

The knowledge shift toward better understanding of the Palestinian cause is also noticeable outside of the United States. Chapter 4 relayed the rise in global solidarity, due in part to the transnational, diasporic nature of the Palestinian community. Palestinians living in countries around the world tend to relate to and find solidarity with other underrepresented groups. Their ability to connect with their adoptive communities has allowed them to share their stories with their new neighbors, coworkers, and social networks. Their stories are shared widely and to an increasingly diverse and receptive audience. Concurrently, the global West has become more progressive. Most Western countries have legalized gay marriage and LGBTQ and transgender protections against discriminatory practices and are more open to facing their own colonial pasts. An emergent, more progressive stance on race relations and racial politics is dominating global politics. Although Palestine has traditionally been neglected in these progressive viewpoints, it is slowly changing, and inevitably there has been a shift toward placing Palestine at the center of progressive politics. It is on the path toward greater sympathy for oppressed peoples everywhere.

Jewish American and Israeli dissent from the traditional narrative has also played a role in these changing views. Chapter 4 followed the rise within Jewish and Israeli dissent from oppressive tactics by the Israeli government,

CONCLUSION

asserting that not only is Zionism exclusionary but also not in line with Jewish values, and that criticism of some governmental policies does not equal anti-Semitism. These voices of Israeli historians and influential Jewish American figures are declaring that Jewish self-determination at the expense of continued settler-colonialism and violence directed at indigenous Palestinians is unethical and ought to stop.

The chapter looked at protests and boycotts as individuals and organizations put their newfound convictions into practice. The chapter also followed the rise of BDS and its commercial consequences and the solidarity shown by labor unions refusing to participate in the apartheid structures practiced by Israel. It took a look at artists, athletes, and celebrities who use their local and global influence to shed light on the atrocities being committed against the Palestinian people, willing to face potential financial loss for their ethical stances toward justice. The chapter considered the new forms of journalism made possible by technological advances and the ways traditional journalists are sometimes punished for reporting stories that are unfavorable to Israel. Finally, it discussed the U.S. education system, from the public K–12 program to universities, and the ways in which powerful voices work to control the image of Israel in curriculum and on college campuses, and how pro-Palestinian voices are fighting to take back control of their own stories.

Chapter 5 investigated how these cultural shifts have led to a larger social change in the United States and around the world. As shown in the chapter, these events started long before the post-October 2023 transformation in public opinion and views toward Palestine and Israel. Solidarities toward Palestinians are strengthening but are also challenged by different established elites interested in maintaining and preserving the status quo. Already, most of the international community, including the majority of members of the United Nations, acknowledge the illegal occupation of Palestine at least along the 1967 borders and have called the Israeli treatment of Palestinians apartheid. The United States is the last major holdout to censure Israel. Whether it will cease its funding and protection of Israel remains to be seen, but there are indications of such action on the horizon. There are also, however, signs of draconian and authoritarian measures meant to silence any critique of Israel from gaining traction.

Yet it is possible that the hyper-Zionism of Israeli leaders may, in itself, lead to the unraveling of apartheid and deliver its own destruction. In

CONCLUSION

December 2022 the Israeli people elected Benjamin Netanyahu as prime minister for the sixth time. Netanyahu's far-right political leanings may be a jolt to the international community, particularly the United States. As Gideon Levy writes,

> If we had a centrist government again, everyone would be so satisfied. Israelis would continue to believe they live in a democracy, the world would believe the occupation is temporary and stems from the security needs of the world's only Jewish state. After all, Israel has a government, and it believes that the 'conflict' must be resolved. There's even a solution on the shelf, two states, let's sing "Kumbaya." The new government will say "no" to all of these. There is no solution, no intention to end apartheid; the occupation is not related to security, but rather to the belief in Jewish exclusivity in this land and to messianic impulses. Annexation is already here, and now we will shove all of this into your surprised faces. The world is somewhat stunned by this government; it, like many good Israelis who thought everything was fine, doesn't know what to do with it.[1]

Between Arab, Jew, Palestinian, and Israeli, equality and justice have become subject to power and violence. These labels are ultimately constructed and defined, and they can be defined again and again. If anything, the stories are similar. The transnational Palestinian condition and exile parallels the conditions and the experiences of global Jewry. The Jewish people have been racialized, and so have Palestinians. Stereotypes and tropes about Jews and about Palestinians might seem different, but they have more in common than meets the eye. Jews were even referred to as "the Palestinians," as having earned a "reputation." In his *Anthropology from a Pragmatic Point of View* (1798), Immanuel Kant writes:

> The Palestinians, living among, us have, for the most part, earned a not unfounded reputation for being cheaters, because of their spirit of usury since their exile. Certainly, it seems strange to conceive of a nation of cheaters; but it is just as odd to think of a nation of merchants, the great majority of whom, bound by an ancient superstition that is recognized by the State they live in, seek no civil dignity and try to make up for this loss by the advantage of duping the people among whom they find refuge, and even

CONCLUSION

one another. The situation could not be otherwise, given a whole nation of merchants, as non-productive members of society.[2]

For us to begin to understand the question of Palestine and Israel, and be able to provide actual solutions, the global collective perception must disaggregate Judaism from Israel. Holding a Jewish identity does not mean accepting the colonial practices and human rights violations of Israel. Connecting Jewish identity to Zionism and Israel has significant consequences. This conflation perpetuates harmful stereotypes. Linking (and thus defining) Jewish identity exclusively to Israel ignores the long history and wide-ranging interpretations of Judaism. Judaism is a multifaceted religion with diverse beliefs, practices, and values. Reducing it solely to a political ideology is not only a misinterpretation of facts, but also misrepresenting the complexities of global Jewry and distinct cultural traditions. It is essential to recognize that Jewish identity encompasses a wide range of perspectives, including those critical of or unaffiliated with Zionism and the Israeli state. By equating Jewish identity with support for Israel, discussing or criticizing Israeli government actions can be misconstrued as an attack on Jews as a whole, evoking memories of extreme forms of violence and death that the Jewish people were subjugated to at the hands of Nazi Germany and Czarist Russia. This ethical conundrum is a product of conflating the two and only serves to prolong human rights violations as it stifles critical conversations and hinders efforts to address the everyday life of violence, subjugation, and mistreatment of Palestinians.

Palestinians in the West Bank and the Gaza Strip face perpetual systemic discrimination and human rights violations committed by the Israeli government, coupled with the adoption of discriminatory laws and policies that privilege Jews over non-Jews, all while Israel claims to be a beacon of democracy. Such hypocritical double standards within context of increasingly well-documented, intensified, and organized violence at the hands of the Israeli state and Israeli civilians against Palestinian civilians are bound to solicit a reaction, if not condemnation.

The International Court of Justice (ICJ) has called the unprecedented violence against Palestinians in Gaza and the bombing of hospitals, ambulances, schools, and homes genocide, yet Western leaders, particularly in the United States, have viewed calling for a cease-fire as a revolutionary act.

CONCLUSION

Far more children were killed in the first month of the Gaza war than in an entire year in the Ukraine.[3] More journalist have been killed in Gaza than in any other conflict in modern history.[4]

Those defending the actions of Israel have run out of justifications. Leading human rights organizations almost universally accept that Israel is committing crimes and, for some, war crimes against humanity. Labels like "apartheid" and "settler colonialism" are common descriptors of the brutality of Israel and daily realities of Palestinians living under Israeli occupation.

It is not surprising that these racist practices may ultimately lead to further isolation of Israel and ultimately the demise of the settler colonial project. Increasing international pressure, coupled with the call for the pursuit of a one-state scenario that centers on democratic participation, promoting equality regardless of religious or ethnic identity of the citizenry, presents new opportunities.

The prolonged occupation of the Palestinian Territories feeds into and strengthens the Israeli apartheid narrative because these actions not only deny Palestinians basic human rights but also further perpetuate the unequal power dynamic that favors Israeli settlers who reside on territories occupied in 1967, in clear and blatant violation of international law.

The intentional dismemberment of Palestinian society in 1948 led to unintentional forms of struggle beyond the control of the colonizers. The destruction of Palestinian villages and historical records of facts has not erased its existence but rather intensified it. The consequences of Israel's actions of separating Palestinians from the geography of Palestine provided a myriad of opportunities to resist Israeli crimes outside and well beyond the Palestinian geography it conquered. Palestinian resistance against Israeli injustice is uncontrollable. In other words, from their very own calamity emerge considerable opportunities for Palestinians.

It is inevitable for injustice to be confronted regardless of how long it takes. Discriminatory and unjust measures taken to ensure the persistence of injustice become the tools and the very reason for their reversal. The Palestinian disaster of displacement created the opportunity for continuity and ultimately increasing pressure on Israel. As Mahmoud Darwish, the late Palestinian poet, captured this idea in his words "Wa huboubu sunbulat-in tamount-u Satamla-u' al-Wadi Sanabel" (The seeds of a dying ear of wheat will fill the valley with ears of wheat), the Palestinian presence and

CONCLUSION

resistance is increasingly globally, and so is the confrontation of Israel and its human rights violations.

If Israel is able to violently control Palestinians in historic Palestine to follow its legalized apartheid discriminatory policies, then the fight will have no option but to move into different fronts that are beyond its geographic control. Today we are witnessing that Israel is increasingly unable to control voices that delegitimize its credibility, providing not only a competing but also a more accurate narrative to the story of Palestine and Israel. It is ironic that the attempts to rid the land of its people made the people and the idea of Palestine (even if not physically) even more imperishable. Despite all efforts to control any narrative around Palestine and Israel by ridding Palestinian claims of legitimacy, or even existence, Palestine resurfaces to become central in world and regional politics. When Palestine is not talked about, it becomes the elephant in the room with regard to human rights, double standards, and western hypocrisy. It is the exclusionary Zionist narrative itself that is contributing to how Palestine is becoming central to the conversations about equality and justice. Palestine has become imperishable.

The story of Palestine has been one of continued colonization, fragmentation, alienation, and social dismemberment, on the one hand, and a never-ending, sustained, resilient anticolonial struggle that adapts and evolves to different circumstances, spaces, and places, on the other. The clear and available path is obvious. A new vision centering restorative justice as a method has the potential of providing a decolonized future, where socially constructed meanings can be set aside to imagine a decolonized future of equity, freedom, and one state for all.

NOTES

INTRODUCTION

1. On the history of Palestine, see Nur Masalha, *Palestine: A Four Thousand Year History* (London: Zed, 2018).
2. Jason Lange and Matt Spetalnick, "US Public Support for Israel Drops; Majority Backs a Ceasfire, Reuters/Ipsos Shows," Reuters, November 15, 2023, https://www.reuters.com/world/us-public-support-israel-drops-majority-backs-ceasefire-reutersipsos-2023-11-15/.
3. See Human Rights Watch, "A Threshold-Crossed," April 2021, https://www.hrw.org/report/2021/04/27/threshold-crossed/israeli-authorities-and-crimes-apartheid-and-persecutionHuman; Amnesty International, "Israel's Apartheid Against Palestinians: Cruel System of Domination and Crime Against Humanity," February 2022; Jimmy Carter, *Palestine: Peace Not Apartheid* (New York, Simon and Schuster, 2005).
4. Ted Swedenburg, *Memories of Revolt: The 1936–1939 Rebellion and the Palestinian National Past* (Minneapolis: University of Minnesota Press, 1995), 3.
5. Ismat Zaidan, "Palestinian Diaspora in Transnational Worlds: Intergenerational Differences in Negotiating Identity, Belonging and Home," *SSRN Electronic Journal*, August 2012, https://doi:10.2139/ssrn.2009267.
6. Helena Lindholm Schulz, *The Palestinian Diaspora* (London: Routledge, 2003), 121.
7. Paolo Boccagni, "Rethinking Transnational Studies: Transnational Ties and the Transnationalism of Everyday Life," *European Journal of Social Theory* 15, no. 1 (2012): 126, https://doi:10.1177/1368431011423600.
8. Akhil Gupta and James Ferguson, *Culture, Power, Place: Explorations in Critical Anthropology* (Durham, NC: Duke University Press, 1997), 13–14.
9. Schulz, *The Palestinian Diaspora*, 1.

INTRODUCTION

10. Iyad Burghūthī, *Palestinian Americans: Socio-political Attitudes of Palestinian Americans Towards the Arab-Israeli Conflict*, Occasional Papers Series, no. 38 (Durham, UK: Centre for Middle Eastern & Islamic Studies, University of Durham, 1989), 8.
11. Lisa Majaj, "Arab Americans and the Meaning of Race," in *Postcolonial Theory and the United States: Race, Ethnicity, and Literature*, ed. Amritjit Singh and Peter Schmidt (Jackson: University Press of Mississippi, 2000); also Helen Hatab Samhan, "Not Quite White: Race Classification and the Arab-American Experience," in *Arabs in America Building a New Future*, ed. Michael W. Suleiman (Philadelphia: Temple University Press, 1999).
12. Rabab Abdulhadi, Evelyn Alsultany, and Nadine Christine Naber, eds., *Arab & Arab American Feminisms: Gender, Violence, & Belonging* (Syracuse, N.Y: Syracuse University Press, 2011), xxxiv.
13. Thea Renda Abu El-Haj, "'I Was Born Here, but My Home, It's Not Here': Educating for Democratic Citizenship in an Era of Transnational Migration and Global Conflict," *Harvard Educational Review* 77, no. 3 (2007): 287.
14. Abu El-Haj, 292.
15. Halleh Ghorashi, "How Dual Is Transnational Identity? A Debate on Dual Positioning of Diaspora Organizations," *Culture and Organization* 10, no. 4 (2004): abstract.
16. Faida Abu-Ghazaleh, *Ethnic Identity of Palestinian Immigrants in the United States: The Role of Material Cultural Artifacts* (El Paso, Tex.: LFB Scholarly, 2010), 21.
17. Abu-Ghazaleh, 22.
18. For more information about this survey and some of its findings, see Karam Dana, "The West Bank Apartheid/Separation Wall: Space, Punishment, and the Disruption of Social Continuity," *Geopolitics* 22, no. 4 (2017): 887–910; and Karam Dana, "Confronting Injustice Beyond Borders: Palestinian Identity and Nonviolent Resistance," *Politics, Groups, and Identities* 6, no. 4 (2018): 529–52.
19. José de Jesus Lopez Almejo, "Diasporas Lobbying the Host Government: Mexican Diaspora as a Third Actor of the Bilateral Relationship Between Mexico and the U.S.," *Migration and Diaspora: An Interdisciplinary Journal* 1, no. 1 (January–June 2018): 116.
20. Edward W. Said, *Orientalism* (New York: Vintage Books, 1979).
21. The idea of hegemony was introduced in Antonio Gramsci, Quintin Hoare, and Geoffrey Nowell-Smith, *Selections from the Prison Notebooks of Antonio Gramsci* (New York: International Publishers, 1972.)
22. Becky Little, "Arab Immigration to the United States: Timeline," *History*, March 23, 2022, https://www.history.com/news/arab-american-immigration-timeline.
23. Aihwa Ong et al., "Cultural Citizenship as Subject-Making: Immigrants Negotiate Racial and Cultural Boundaries in the United States [and Comments and Reply]," *Current Anthropology* 37, no. 5 (1996): 737–62, https://doi:10.1086/204560.
24. Marc Lamont Hill and Mitchell Plitnick, *Except for Palestine: The Limits of Progressive Politics* (New York: New Press, 2021).
25. Saree Makdisi, *Tolerance Is a Wasteland: Palestine and the Culture of Denial* (Oakland: University of California Press, 2022).
26. Keith P. Feldman, *A Shadow Over Palestine: The Imperial Life of Race in America* (Minneapolis: University of Minnesota Press, 2015).
27. John Collins, *Global Palestine* (London: Hurst, 2011).

1. PALESTINIANS IN THE AMERICAN IMAGINATION

28. Abu El-Haj, "'I Was Born Here,'" 285, 286.
29. For an in-depth discussion of this concept, see Paul Findley, *They Dare to Speak Out: People and Institutions Confront Israel's Lobby* (Chicago: Chicago Review Press, 2003); and John J. Mearsheimer and Stephen M. Walt, "The Israel Lobby and U.S. Foreign Policy," *Middle East Policy* 13, no. 3 (2006): 29–87, https://doi:10.1111/j.1475-4967.2006.00260.x.
30. Lizzy Ratner, "The War Between the Civilized Man and Pamela Geller," *Nation*, October 18, 2012, https://www.thenation.com/article/archive/war-between-civilized-man-and-pamela-geller/.
31. Joel Rose, "Controversial 'Anti-Jihad' Ads Posted in New York City," *NPR*, September 24, 2012, https://www.npr.org/2012/09/24/161706692/controversial-anti-jihad-ads-posted-in-new-york-city.
32. Theodore Sasson, "Mass Mobilization to Direct Engagement: American Jews' Changing Relationship to Israel," *Israel Studies* 15, no. 2 (2010): 173.
33. Several U.S. states have passed laws requiring state contractors to vow never to boycott Israel. For an in-depth look at this phenomenon, see chapter 4.
34. "Shatzi Weisberger Z"L, May Her Memory Be a Revolution," Jewish Voice for Peace, accessed December 12, 2022, https://www.jewishvoiceforpeace.org/zionism.
35. Gabriel Sheffer, "Integration Impacts on Diaspora–Homeland Relations," *Diaspora Studies* 6, no. 1 (2013): 17, https://doi:10.1163/09763457-00601002.
36. Miriyam Aouragh, *Palestine Online: Transnationalism, the Internet and the Construction of Identity* (London: Tauris, 2011), 44.
37. Sheffer, "Integration Impacts," 22.
38. Marguerite Casey Foundation, "2022 Freedom Scholars: Noura Erakat," YouTube, December 6, 2022, https://www.youtube.com/watch?v=v_69jPorRA0.

1. PALESTINIANS IN THE AMERICAN IMAGINATION

1. Despite the tumultuous relationship between the Britain and the United States during the American Revolution period, the British have been viewed favorably in the United States at least since the turn of the twentieth century.
2. Nadine Naber, "Ambiguous Insiders: An Investigation of Arab American Invisibility," *Ethnic and Racial Studies* 23, no. 1 (2000): 40–42.
3. Keith Feldman, *A Shadow Over Palestine: The Imperial Life of Race in America* (Minneapolis: University of Minnesota Press, 2015), 8.
4. AJ+, "Why Israel Matters to Americans," YouTube, November 4, 2022, https://www.youtube.com/watch?v=klXaDgmM8Fs.
5. Sunaina Maira, "'We Ain't Missing': Palestinian Hip Hop—a Transnational Youth Movement," *CR* 8, no. 2 (2008): 162, https://doi: 10.1353/ncr.0.0027.
6. Feldman, *A Shadow Over Palestine*, 43, 8.
7. Edward Said, *The Question of Palestine* (New York: Times Books, 1979), 40.
8. Peter Beinart, interview by author, April 19, 2021.
9. Arab.org, "What Is Orientalism?" accessed February 9, 2024, https://arab.org/blog/what-is-orientalism/#google_vignette.
10. Karam Dana, "Confronting Injustice Beyond Borders: Palestinian Identity and Nonviolent Resistance," *Politics, Groups, and Identities* 6, no. 4: (2018): 529–52.

1. PALESTINIANS IN THE AMERICAN IMAGINATION

11. Orientalism as a concept was introduced by Edward W. Said in *Orientalism* (New York: Vintage Books, 1979).
12. Norman Daniel, *Islam and the West: The Making of an Image* (London: Oneworld, 2009).
13. Janice Terry, *U.S. Foreign Policy in the Middle East the Role of Lobbies and Special Interest Groups* (London: Pluto Press, 2005), 17.
14. John Tehranian, *Whitewashed: America's Invisible Middle Eastern Minority* (New York: NYU Press, 2008), 73.
15. Kristine J. Ajrouch and Amaney Jamal, "Assimilating to a White Identity: The Case of Arab Americans," *International Migration Review* 41, no. 4 (2007): 862, http://www.jstor.org/stable/27645705.
16. Marc Lamont Hill and Mitchell Plitnick, *Except for Palestine: The Limits of Progressive Politics* (New York: New Press, 2021).
17. Feldman, *A Shadow Over Palestine*, 10.
18. Here Zarrugh relies on the work of Michael Omi and Howard Winant, *Racial Formation in the United States: From the 1960's to the 1990's*, 2d ed. (New York: Routledge, 1994).
19. Amina Zarrugh, "Racialized Political Shock: Arab American Racial Formation and the Impact of Political Events," *Ethnic and Racial Studies* 39, no. 15 (2016): 2722–39, https://doi:10.1080/01419870.2016.1171368.
20. Naber, "Ambiguous Insiders," 39.
21. Ian Haney Lopez, *White by Law: The Legal Construction of Race* (New York: NYU Press, 1997), 48.
22. Naber, "Ambiguous Insiders," 39.
23. Ajrouch and Jamal, "Assimilating to a White Identity," 861.
24. Naber, "Ambiguous Insiders."
25. Volha Charnysh, Christopher Lucas, and Prerna Singh, "The Ties That Bind: National Identity Salience and Pro-Social Behavior Towards the Ethnic Other," *Comparative Political Studies* 48, no. 3 (2015): 267–300, https://doi:10.1177/0010414014543103.
26. Sarah Song, "What Does It Mean to Be an American?" *Daedalus* 138, no. 2 (2009): 31–40, quote on 38.
27. Edward Said, "New History, Old Ideas," Miftah, May 28, 1998, http://www.miftah.org/PrinterF.cfm?DocId=2459.
28. Hill and Plitnick, *Except for Palestine*, 18.
29. Nisreen Eadeh, "Amal Clooney: A Figure of Hope for Everyone but the Palestinians," Arab America, April 14, 2016, https://www.arabamerica.com/amal-clooney-figure-hope-everyone-palestinians/.
30. Miko Peled, "In Nauseating Netanyahu Interview, Bill Maher Whitewashes a War Criminal," *Scheerpost*, October 26, 2022, https://scheerpost.com/2022/10/26/in-nauseating-netanyahu-interview-bill-maher-whitewashes-a-war-criminal/.
31. Marlow Stern, "Bill Maher Refuses to Ask Netanyahu About Corruption Charges, Wonders If Israel Will 'Retaliate' Against Kanye," *Daily Beast*, October 15, 2022, https://www.thedailybeast.com/bill-maher-asks-benjamin-netanyahu-if-israel-will-retaliate-against-kanye-west.
32. Stern.
33. U. Siddiqui and O. Zaheer. "Year of Occupation: A Sentiment and N-gram Analysis of US Mainstream Media Coverage of the Israeli Occupation of Palestine" 50:

1. PALESTINIANS IN THE AMERICAN IMAGINATION

1547246789711, https://vridar.org/wp-content/uploads/2019/01/416LABS_50_Years_of_Occupation.pdf.
34. Holly M. Jackson, "The New York Times Distorts the Palestinian Struggle: A Case Study of Anti-Palestinian Bias in US News Coverage of the First and Second Palestinian Intifadas," *Media, War & Conflict* (2023), https://doi:10.1177/17506352231178148.
35. Maha Nassar, "US Media Talks a Lot About Palestinians—Just Without Palestinians," 2020.
36. Jack G. Shaheen and William Greider, *Reel Bad Arabs: How Hollywood Vilifies a People* (New York: Olive Branch Press, 2001). See also Edward Said, "Permission to Narrate," *Journal of Palestine Studies* 13, no. 3 (1984): 27–48, https://doi:10.1525/jps.1984.13.3.00p0033m.
37. Sharif Nashashibi, "Obituary: Jack Shaheen, a Fighter Against Negative Arab Stereotypes," *Arab News*, July 13, 2017, https://www.arabnews.com/node/1128686/offbeat.
38. Matt Duss, interview by author, March 19, 2021.
39. James North, "How the New York Times Rigs News on Israel-Palestine," *Washington Report on Middle East Affairs* 38, no. 3 (2019): 31–37.
40. AJ+, "Why Israel Matters to Americans," YouTube, November 4, 2022, https://www.youtube.com/watch?v=klXaDgmM8Fs.
41. Edward Said, "An Open Letter to Jewish American Intellectuals," Jewish Currents, September 21, 2022, https://jewishcurrents.org/an-open-letter-to-american-jewish-intellectuals.
42. Steven Salaita, "Ethnic Identity and Imperative Patriotism: Arab Americans Before and After 9/11," *College Literature* 32, no. 2 (Spring 2005): 165.
43. PJ Grisar, "Who Is Sabra, Marvel's Israeli Superhero?" *Forward*, September 12, 2022, https://forward.com/culture/film-tv/517550/sabra-marvel-mcu-shira-haas-israeli-superhero-jewish-controversy/.
44. "Marvel Controversy: Israeli Heroine Sabra Outrages Arab World," *Algemeiner*, September 18, 2022, https://www.algemeiner.com/2022/09/18/marvel-controversy-israeli-heroine-sabra-outrages-arab-world/.
45. @paliroots, "A thread you need to read," Instagram, September 12, 2022, https://www.instagram.com/p/CibVnEcJe94/?igshid=N2NmMDY0OWE%3D.
46. "Marvel Controversy."
47. Laura Wray-Lake, Amy Syvertsen, and Constance Flanagan, "Contested Citizenship and Social Exclusion: Adolescent Arab American Immigrants' Views of the Social Contract," *Applied Developmental Science* 12, no. 2 (2008): 84–92.
48. "Edward Said on Palestinian Politics and the Search for Justice," Democracy Now, February 8, 2001, https://www.democracynow.org/2001/2/8/edward_said_on_palestinian_politics_and.
49. Najla Said, *Looking for Palestine: Growing Up Confused in an Arab-American Family* (New York: Riverhead Books, 2013), 2–3.
50. Karmah Elmusa, "I'm Longing for Palestine while Living the American Dream," *Elle*, October 30, 2015, https://www.elle.com/culture/career-politics/a31572/essay-on-being-palestinian-american/.
51. Edward Said, *Out of Place* (New York: Vintage Books, 2000), xiii.
52. Dean Obeidallah, "Do Palestinians Really Exist?," *Daily Beast*, April 14, 2017, https://www.thedailybeast.com/do-palestinians-really-exist.

1. PALESTINIANS IN THE AMERICAN IMAGINATION

53. Dean Obeidallah, "Stop the Anti-Semitism When Talking Gaza," *Daily Beast*, April 14, 2017, https://www.thedailybeast.com/stop-the-anti-semitism-when-talking-gaza.
54. Gigi Hadid, @gigihadid, Instagram, March 1, 2017, https://www.instagram.com/p/BRGnkZWAfeb.
55. Bella Hadid, @bellahadid, Instagram, December 7, 2017, https://www.instagram.com/p/BcaCVA-n3Yl.
56. Joe Coscarelli, "Newt Gingrich Says Palestinian People Are 'Invented,'" *Intelligencer*, December 9, 2011, https://nymag.com/intelligencer/2011/12/gingrich-says-palestinian-people-are-invented.html.
57. Meir Kahane, *They Must Go* (Israel: Grosset and Dunlap, 1981), 41.
58. Kahane, iv.
59. Mark Twain, *The Innocents Abroad* (New York: Harper and Brothers, 1911), 267, 392, 393.
60. Karl Sabbagh, *Palestine: A Personal History* (London: Atlantic, 2006), 73.
61. Twain, *The Innocents Abroad*, 233, 282.
62. Sabbagh, *Palestine*, 19.
63. Rob Eshman, "Can a Jew Cook Palestinian Food Without Being Disrespectful?," *Forward*, August 19, 2022, https://forward.com/food/515056/when-a-jew-cooks-palestinian-food/.
64. Nora Esther Murad, "Palestinian Erasure Starts in Preschool—with Sesame Street's Endorsement," Fair, September 30, 2022, https://fair.org/home/palestinian-erasure-starts-in-preschool-with-sesame-streets-endorsement/.
65. Murad.
66. Murad.
67. Murad.
68. Palestine Legal, "Palestine Children's Book: Threats & Censorship," February 20, 2018, https://palestinelegal.org/case-studies/2018/2/20/palestine-childrens-book-threats-censorship.
69. "New York's Muslims Push for Public Schools to Close for Eid Holidays," NPR, April 18, 2014, https://www.npr.org/2014/04/18/304526489/new-yorks-muslims-push-for-public-schools-to-close-for-eid-holidays.
70. Charlotte Hays, "Women's March Co-Chair Linda Sarsour: What Are Her Causes?," Independent Women's Forum, January 25, 2017, https://www.iwf.org/2017/01/25/womens-march-co-chair-linda-sarsour-what-are-her-causes/.
71. "Linda Sarsour Arrested at Paul Ryan's Office," *Al Jazeera*, March 6, 2018, https://www.aljazeera.com/news/2018/3/6/linda-sarsour-arrested-at-paul-ryans-office.
72. Alan Feuer, "Linda Sarsour Is a Brooklyn Homegirl in a Hijab," *New York Times*, August 7, 2015, https://www.nytimes.com/2015/08/09/nyregion/linda-sarsour-is-a-brooklyn-homegirl-in-a-hijab.html.
73. Laura Ingraham, "Linda Sarsour, Marc Lamont Hill and Anti-Semitism Hiding in Plain Sight," *Fox News*, November 30, 2018, https://www.foxnews.com/opinion/laura-ingraham-anti-semitism-hiding-in-plain-sight.
74. Nina Burleigh, "Rudy Giuliani's Flimsy Foreign Policy Credentials," *Newsweek*, November 15, 2016, https://www.newsweek.com/rudy-giuliani-flimsy-foreign-policy-credentials-521635.

1. PALESTINIANS IN THE AMERICAN IMAGINATION

75. Erik Skidrud, "Twenty Years Later, Still No Charges in Alex Odeh Assassination," *Electronic Intifada*, December 6, 2006, https://electronicintifada.net/content/twenty-years-later-still-no-charges-alex-odeh-assassination/6582.
76. Neve Gordon, "No Justice for Rachel Corrie," *Al Jazeera*, September 5, 2012, https://www.aljazeera.com/opinions/2012/9/5/no-justice-for-rachel-corrie/.
77. Amnesty International, "Rachel Corrie Verdict Highlights Impunity for Israeli Military," August 29, 2012, https://web.archive.org/web/20120902041711/http://www.amnesty.org/en/news/rachel-corrie-verdict-highlights-impunity-israeli-military-2012-08-28.
78. United States Court of Appeals for the Ninth Circuit, No. 05-36210 D.C. No. CV-05-05192-FDB; Opinion, September 17, 2007, https://web.archive.org/web/20071117111442/http://www.ca9.uscourts.gov/ca9/newopinions.nsf/6DFD4322CA06B5FA882573590 05660A6/%24file/0536210.pdf?openelement; Rory McCarthy, "Rachel Corrie's Family Bring Civil Suit Over Human Shield's Death in Gaza," *Guardian*, February 23, 2010, https://www.theguardian.com/world/2010/feb/23/corrie-death-law-case.
79. Nancy Stohlman and Laurieann Aladin, *Live from Palestine: International and Palestinian Direct Action Against the Israeli Occupation* (Cambridge, Mass: South End Press, 2003), 174.
80. Joseph Krauss, "Review Suggests Israeli Fire Killed Reporter, No Final Word," Associated Press, May 24, 2022, https://apnews.com/article/politics-west-bank-middle-east-israel-8df6c999627efcef2fe0ca2b401e7a2c?s=08.
81. Alice Speri, "Israeli Forces Deliberately Killed Palestinian American Journalist, Report Shows," *Intercept*, September 20, 2022, https://theintercept.com/2022/09/20/shireen-abu-akleh-killing-israel/.
82. Sahar Akbarzai et al., "Israel Reveals US Probe Into Shireen Abu Akleh's Death but Says It 'Will Not Cooperate,'" CNN, November 15, 2022, https://www.cnn.com/2022/11/15/middleeast/shireen-abu-akleh-israel-us-investigation-intl.
83. Matt Duss interview, March 19, 2021.
84. Peter Beinart, interview by author, April 19, 2021.
85. Not all pastors or denominations agree on the biblical stance on Judaism and modern Israel. Some, like the Reverend Jeremiah Wright of Trinity United Church of Christ in Chicago, have publicly called Israel an apartheid state. The Catholic Church has officially recognized Palestine as well. "Israeli Anger at Vatican Recognition of Palestine," Middle East Policy Council, accessed August 14, 2022.
86. Nur Masalha, *Palestine: A Four Thousand Year History* (London: Zed Books, 2020).
87. Candace Smith, "Jeb Bush Says US Should Allow Syrian Refugees Who Can Prove They're Christian," *ABC News*, November 17, 2015, https://abcnews.go.com/Politics/jeb-bush-us-syrian-refugees-prove-christian/story?id=35263074.
88. Hillary Kaell, "Pastors Wrapped in Torah: Why So Many Christians Are Appropriating Jewish Ritual," *Forward*, October 18, 2020, https://forward.com/news/456599/pastors-wrapped-in-torah-why-so-many-christians-are-appropriating-jewish/.
89. Hilary Kaell, "The Hebraic Style in Christian Nation-Building," Christian Nation Project, accessed August 13, 2022, https://thechristiannationproject.net/kaell-fullintro/.
90. Nur Masalha, *The Bible and Zionism: Invented Traditions, Archaeology, and Post-Colonialism in Israel-Palestine* (London: Zed Books, 2007), 119.

91. Diana Butler Bass, "Bad History," *Cottage*, September 8, 2022, https://dianabutler bass.substack.com/p/bad-history?r=45vbf&s=w&utm_campaign=post&utm_medium=web.
92. Umayyah Cable, "Compulsory Zionism and Palestinian Existence: A Genealogy," *Journal of Palestine Studies* 51, no. 2 (2022): 66–71, doi:10.1080/0377919X.2022.2040324.
93. Mohd Afandi Salleh and Mohd Fauzi Abu-Hussin, "The American Christians and the State of Israel," *Journal for the Study of Religions and Ideologies* 12, no. 34 (March 22, 2013): 154.
94. Carlo Aldrovandi, *Apocalyptic Movements in Contemporary Politics: Christian and Jewish Zionism* (London: Palgrave Macmillan, 2014).
95. Gerald R. McDermott, ed., *The New Christian Zionism: Fresh Perspectives on Israel and the Land* (Westmont, Ill.: IVP Academic, 2016), 79.
96. Ronald R. Stockton, "Christian Zionism: Prophecy and Public Opinion," *Middle East Journal* 41, no. 2 (1987): 234–53, http://www.jstor.org/stable/4327538.
97. Neale Adams, "Christian Zionism a 'Heresy' Says Anglican Priest," *Anglican Journal*, April 27, 2015, https://anglicanjournal.com/christian-zionism-a-heresy-says-anglican-priest/.
98. Stephen Sizer, "John Nelson Darby, the Father of Dispensationalism," Wordpress, accessed August 12, 2022, https://www.stephensizer.com/articles/darby1.html.
99. Rev. J. Logan Aikman, *Cyclopaedia of Christian Missions: Their Rise, Progress, and Present Position* (London: Richard Griffin, 1860), 196.
100. Albert Montefiore Hyamson, *British Projects for the Restoration of the Jews* (London: Petty & Sons, 1917), 6.
101. Victoria Clark, *Allies for Armageddon, the Rise of Christian Zionism* (New Haven, Conn.: Yale University Press, 2007), 67, 72.
102. Jerry Klinger, *Reverend William H. Hechler—the Christian Minister Who Legitimized Theodor Herzl*, accessed August 12, 2022, http://www.jewish-american-society-for-historic-preservation.org/images/Reverend_William_H.pdf.
103. Letter from John Adams to François Van der Kemp, February 16, 1809, National Archives' Founders Online, https://founders.archives.gov/documents/Adams/99-02-02-5302.
104. Richard Ned Lebow, "Woodrow Wilson and the Balfour Declaration," *Journal of Modern History* 40, no. 4 (1968): 501–23, http://www.jstor.org/stable/1878450.
105. Ronald R. Stockton, "Christian Zionism: Prophecy and Public Opinion," *Middle East Journal* 41, no. 2 (1987): 237.
106. Albert M. Hyamson, "British Projects for the Restoration of the Jews to Palestine," *Publications of the American Jewish Historical Society*, no. 26 (1918): 143, http://www.jstor.org/stable/43059305.
107. Paul Charles Merkley, *The Politics of Christian Zionism, 1891–1948* (London: Cass, 1998), 99.
108. Merkley, 101.
109. "Christian Council on Palestine Formed; Asks Admission of Refugees to America," Jewish Telegraphic Society Archive, accessed August 12, 2022, https://www.jta.org/archive/christian-council-on-palestine-formed-asks-admission-of-refugees-to-america.

1. PALESTINIANS IN THE AMERICAN IMAGINATION

110. National Archives, "Press Release Announcing U.S. Recognition of Israel (1948)," accessed August 12, 2022, https://www.archives.gov/milestone-documents/press-release-announcing-us-recognition-of-israel#.
111. Elizabeth Edwards Spalding, "We Must Put on the Armor of God: Harry Truman and the Cold War," in *Religion and the American Presidency*, ed. Mark J. Rosell and Gleaves Whitney (Cham, Switz.: Springer International, 2017), 109.
112. Clark, *Allies for Armageddon*, 222.
113. Clark, 154.
114. Philip Bump, "Half of Evangelicals Support Israel Because They Believe It Is Important for Fulfilling End-Times Prophecy," *Washington Post*, May 14, 2018, https://www.washingtonpost.com/news/politics/wp/2018/05/14/half-of-evangelicals-support-israel-because-they-believe-it-is-important-for-fulfilling-end-times-prophecy/.
115. Colin Shindler, "Likud and the Christian Dispensationalists: A Symbiotic Relationship," *Israel Studies* 5, no. 1 (2000): 165, http://www.jstor.org/stable/30245533.
116. Wajahat Ali et al., "Fear, Inc.: The Roots of the Islamophobia Network in America," Center for American Progress, August 2011, 71.
117. Shindler, "Likud and the Christian Dispensationalists," 165.
118. John Hagee, *Earth's Final Moments: Powerful Insights and Understanding of the Prophetic Signs That Surround Us* (Lake Mary, Fla.: Charisma House, 2011), 23.
119. Yaakov Ariel, "An Unexpected Alliance: Christian Zionism and Its Historical Significance," *Modern Judaism* 26, no. 1 (2006): 94, 74, http://www.jstor.org/stable/3526840.
120. Michael Lipka, "More White Evangelicals than American Jews Say God Gave Israel to the Jewish People," Pew Research Center, October 3, 2013, http://www.pewresearch.org/fact-tank/2013/10/03/more-white-evangelicals-than-american-jews-say-god-gave-israel-to-the-jewish-people/.
121. There is no standard definition of the area Zionists believe that God has decreed belongs to the Jewish people. Opinions include the inclusion of the 1967 territories only, the entire Levant as given to the "tribes of Israel" in the book of Joshua, and an area stretching from Egypt to Iraq as described in Genesis.
122. Clark, *Allies for Armageddon*, 3.
123. Stephen Spector, *Evangelicals and Israel: The Story of American Christian Zionism* (New York: Oxford University Press, 2009), 90.
124. Spector, 91.
125. Spector, 91–92.
126. Elizabeth Phillips, "Saying 'Peace' When There Is No Peace: An American Christian Zionist Congregation on Peace, Militarism, and Settlements," in *Comprehending Christian Zionism: Perspectives in Comparison*, ed. Gunner Göran and Robert O. Smith (Minneapolis: Augsburg Fortress, 2014), 19.
127. Adams, "Christian Zionism a 'Heresy.'"
128. Ronald Stockton, "Christian Zionism: Prophecy and Public Opinion," *Middle East Journal* 41, no. 2 (1987): 241, http://www.jstor.org/stable/4327538.
129. Stockton, 242.
130. Matt Duss interview, March 19, 2021.
131. Daniel Siryoti and Gideon Allon, "Palestinian Christians Reject Pence's Brand of Evangelical Christianity," *Israel Hayom*, January 23, 2018, https://www

.israelhayom.com/2018/01/23/palestinian-christians-reject-pences-brand-of-evangelical-christianity/.
132. Mitri Raheb, "Palestinian Christian Reflections on Christian Zionism," in *Comprehending Christian Zionism: Perspectives in Comparison*, ed. Gunner Göran and Robert O. Smith (Minneapolis: Augsburg Fortress, 2014), 191–98.
133. Stephen Robert Sizer, *Christian Zionists on the Road to Armageddon* (London: IVP Academic, 2004), 69.
134. Matt Duss interview, March 19, 2021.
135. Elizabeth Anne Oldmixon, *Uncompromising Positions: God, Sex, and the U.S. House of Representatives* (Washington, D.C.: Georgetown University Press, 2005), 182.
136. Pew Research Center, "Faith on the Hill," January 4, 2021, https://www.pewresearch.org/religion/2021/01/04/faith-on-the-hill-2021/.
137. William V. D'Antonio, Steven A. Tuch, and Josiah R. Baker, *Religion, Politics, and Polarization: How Religiopolitical Conflict Is Changing Congress and American Democracy* (New York: Rowman and Littlefield, 2013), 18.
138. Elizabeth Anne Oldmixon, Beth Rosenson, and Kenneth D. Wald, "Conflict Over Israel: The Role of Religion, Race, Party and Ideology in the U.S. House of Representatives, 1997–2002," *Terrorism and Political Violence* 17, no. 3 (2005): 407–26, https://doi:10.1080/09546550590929246.
139. Oldmixon, Rosenson, and Wald.
140. Pew Research Center, "Biden Is Only the Second Catholic President, but Nearly All Have Been Christians," January 4, 2021, http://www.pewresearch.org/fact-tank/2017/01/20/almost-all-presidents-have-been-christians/.
141. "U.S. Presidents & Israel: Quotes About Jewish Homeland & Israel," Jewish Virtual Library, accessed August 12, 2022, http://www.jewishvirtuallibrary.org/u-s-presidential-quotes-about-jewish-homeland-and-israel-jewish-virtual-library.
142. Eli E. Hertz, "Palestine Royal Commission Report, July 1937, Chapter II, p. 24," accessed August 12, 2022, http://www.mythsandfacts.org/conflict/mandate_for_palestine/mandate_for_palestine.htm#31.
143. Dwight D. Eisenhower, "Radio and Television Address to the American People on the Situation in the Middle East," February 20, 1957, *American Presidency Project*, https://www.presidency.ucsb.edu/documents/radio-and-television-address-the-american-people-the-situation-the-middle-east#.
144. Bernard Reich, *Securing the Covenant: United States–Israel Relations After the Cold War* (Westport, Conn.: Greenwood Press, 1995), 10.
145. Stephen Zunes, "Why the U.S. Supports Israel," *Foreign Policy in Focus*, May 1, 2002, http://fpif.org/why_the_us_supports_israel/.
146. Munther Isaac, *The Other Side of the Wall: A Palestinian Christian Narrative of Lament and Hope* (Westmont, Ill.: InterVarsity Press, 2020), 20.
147. Munther Isaac, "An Open Letter to U.S. Christians from a Palestinian Pastor," *Sojourners*, May 20, 2021, https://sojo.net/articles/open-letter-us-christians-palestinian-pastor.
148. F. Brinley Bruton, Lawahez Jabari, and Paul Goldman, "Holy Land Christians Feel Abandoned by U.S. Evangelicals," *NBC News*, May 5, 2018, https://www.nbcnews.com/news/world/holy-land-christians-feel-abandoned-u-s-evangelicals-n867371.
149. Bruton, Jabari, and Goldman.

1. PALESTINIANS IN THE AMERICAN IMAGINATION

150. Bruton, Jabari, and Goldman.
151. Noura Erakat, quoted in Marc Lamont Hill and Mitchell Plitnick, *Except for Palestine: The Limits of Progressive Politics* (New York: New Press, 2021), 25–26.
152. Sharon Basco, "Dissent in Pursuit of Equality, Life, Liberty and Happiness," HowardZinn.org, 2002, https://www.howardzinn.org/dissent-in-pursuit-of-equality-life-liberty-and-happiness/.
153. "Real Patriots Talk Back or, Why Dissent Can Be Patriotic, an Interview with Jonathan M. Hansen," University of Chicago Press, accessed August 12, 2022, http://press.uchicago.edu/Misc/Chicago/315843in.html.
154. Ali et al., "Fear, Inc.," 65, 66.
155. Bernard Lewis, "The Roots of Muslim Rage," *Atlantic*, September 1990, https://www.theatlantic.com/magazine/archive/1990/09/the-roots-of-muslim-rage/304643/.
156. Amy Kaplan, *Our American Israel: The Story of an Entangled Alliance* (Cambridge, Mass.: Harvard University Press, 2018), 5.
157. Kaplan, 80.
158. "The Lightning War in the Middle East," *Hearst Metrotone News*, Internet Archive, accessed December 12, 2022, https://archive.org/details/lightningwarinthemiddleeast.
159. Kaplan, *Our American Israel*, 166.
160. Kaplan, 275.
161. Feldman, *A Shadow Over Palestine*, 1.
162. John J. Mearsheimer and Stephen M. Walt, *The Israel Lobby and U.S. Foreign Policy* (New York: Farrar, Straus, and Giroux, 2008), 204–5, 208.
163. Mearsheimer and Walt, 208.
164. Mearsheimer and Walt, 87, 88.
165. Karam Dana. "Contextualizing Cynicism: Palestinian Public Opinion Towards Human Rights and Democracy," *Muslim World Journal of Human Rights* 14, no. 1 (2017): 113–44, https://doi:10.1515/mwjhr-2016-0023.
166. John J. Mearsheimer and Stephen M. Walt, "The Israel Lobby and U.S. Foreign Policy," *Middle East Policy* 13, no. 3 (2006): 31, https://doi:10.1111/j.1475-4967.2006.00260.x.
167. Morgan Rimmer, "Senate Passes Bipartisan Resolution Affirming Support for Israel," CNN, October 19, 2023, https://www.cnn.com/2023/10/19/politics/senate-passes-israel-bipartisan-resolution/index.html.
168. Allan Smith, "Sen. John Fetterman Faces a Left-Wing Backlash Over His Stance on Israel. He Isn't Budging," *NBC News*, November 1, 2023, https://www.nbcnews.com/politics/congress/sen-john-fetterman-faces-left-wing-backlash-israel-rcna122204.
169. Mearsheimer and Walt, "The Israel Lobby," 33.
170. Mearsheimer and Walt, 37.
171. Kathleen Christison, "The American Experience: Palestinians in the U.S.," *Journal of Palestine Studies* 18, no. 4 (1989): 18–36, https://doi:10.1525/jps.1989.18.4.00p0127c.
172. Hasan Minhaj, "Hasan Minhaj: Homecoming King | Official Trailer [HD] | Netflix," YouTube, 1:20, posted May 11, 2017, https://www.youtube.com/watch?v=Fu-u5VldxVY.

1. PALESTINIANS IN THE AMERICAN IMAGINATION

173. Christison, "The American Experience."
174. Christison.
175. Joshua Stewart, "Congressional Candidate Renounces Grandfather's Violent Legacy, Calls for Middle East Peace," *San Diego Union-Tribune*, February 21, 2018, http://www.sandiegouniontribune.com/news/politics/sd-me-ammar-grandfather-20180221-story.html.
176. "San Diego Rabbis Denounce Attacks Against Candidate with Palestinian Roots," *Times of Israel*, November 3, 2018, https://www.timesofisrael.com/san-diego-rabbis-denounce-attacks-against-candidate-with-palestinian-roots/.
177. Sarah Leah Whitson, Twitter, May 18, 2021, https://mobile.twitter.com/sarahleah1/status/1394606558802292742; Whitson, "The Israel-Palestine Narrative Has Evolved," *American Prospect*, May 18, 2021, https://prospect.org/world/israel-palestine-narrative-has-evolved/.
178. Shibley Telhami, "Arab and American Dimensions of the Israel/Palestine Issue: State Policies and Public Views on One State, Two States, and Beyond," in *The One State Reality: What Is Israel/Palestine?*, ed. Shibley Telhami et al. (Ithaca, N.Y.: Cornell University Press, 2023), 204.
179. Whitson, "The Israel-Palestine Narrative."
180. Matt Duss interview, March 19, 2021.
181. Asma Khalid, "Biden Faces Pushback Within His Own Party for His Unwavering Support of Israel," NPR, January 19, 2024, "https://www.npr.org/2024/01/19/1225573911/biden-faces-pushback-within-his-own-party-for-his-unwavering-support-of-israel.
182. Matt Duss interview, March 19, 2021.

2. STRUCTURAL TRANSFORMATIONS IN CULTURE, SOCIETY, AND POLITICS IN THE UNITED STATES

1. Frank Leon Roberts, "How Black Lives Matter Changed the Way Americans Fight for Freedom," *ACLU News and Commentary*, July 13, 2018, https://www.aclu.org/news/racial-justice/how-black-lives-matter-changed-way-americans-fight.
2. Char Adams, "A Movement, a Slogan, a Rallying Cry: How Black Lives Matter Changed America's View on Race," *NBC News*, December 29, 2020, https://www.nbcnews.com/news/nbcblk/movement-slogan-rallying-cry-how-black-lives-matter-changed-america-n1252434.
3. Zeeshan Aleem, "This One Chart Shows How Black Lives Matter Has Changed America," *Mic*, August 5, 2015, https://www.mic.com/articles/123445/this-one-chart-shows-how-black-lives-matter-has-changed-america.
4. Aleem.
5. Roberts, "How Black Lives Matter Changed."
6. Africa4Palestine, "Noura Erakat and Marc Lamont Hill: Black-Palestine Solidarity Is Not New, It's Historic," Instagram, November 7, 2022, https://www.instagram.com/reel/CkqX2YSK9U_/?igshid=MDJmNzVkMjY%3D.
7. Deadly Exchange, "About Deadly Exchange," accessed November 23, 2022, https://deadlyexchange.org/about-deadly-exchange/.

2. STRUCTURAL TRANSFORMATIONS IN U.S. CULTURE

8. Adeshina Emmanuel, "Spurred by Black Lives Matter, Coverage of Police Violence Is Changing," *Injustice Watch*, February 1, 2021, https://www.injusticewatch.org/longreads/2021/nieman-reports-police-violence-coverage-is-changing/.
9. Daoud Kuttab, "The 'Smartphone Intifada,'" *Al-Monitor*, October 13, 2015, https://www.al-monitor.com/originals/2015/10/west-bank-palestinian-protests-social-media.html.
10. Rebecca L. Stein, "Viral Occupation: Palestine and the Video Revolution," *Los Angeles Review of Books*, January 21, 2022, https://lareviewofbooks.org/article/viral-occupation-palestine-and-the-video-revolution/.
11. Stein.
12. Stein.
13. Janna Aladdin, "Israel's Systematic Surveillance of Palestinians," *Washington Report on Middle East Affairs*, December 17, 2021, https://www.wrmea.org/waging-peace/israels-systematic-surveillance-of-palestinians.html.
14. Roberts, "How Black Lives Matter Changed."
15. Maayan Jaffe-Hoffman, "TikTok Intifada Is 'Just the Tip of the Iceberg'—Analysis," *Jerusalem Post*, April 26, 2021, https://www.jpost.com/arab-israeli-conflict/tiktok-intifada-is-just-the-tip-of-the-iceberg-analysis-666403.
16. Yaron Steinbuch, "TikTok Used to Air Tensions, Incite Violence Between Israelis and Palestinians," *New York Post*, May 20, 2021, https://nypost.com/2021/05/20/tiktok-used-to-incite-violence-between-israel-palestine-reports/.
17. Thomas E. Patterson, "The Decline of Newspapers: The Local Story," *Nieman*, December 15, 2007, https://nieman.harvard.edu/articles/the-decline-of-newspapers-the-local-story/.
18. Dennis Dunleavy, "The Rise of Opinion Journalism: The FOX Is in the Hen House," March 21, 2005, https://ddunleavy.typepad.com/the_big_picture/2005/03/the_rise_of_opi.html.
19. Nico Carpentier, Peter Dahlgren, and Francesca Pasquali. "Waves of Media Democratization: A Brief History of Contemporary Participatory Practices in the Media Sphere," *Convergence* 19, no. 3 (August 1, 2013): 287–94, https://doi.org/10.1177/1354856513486529.
20. Jimmy Chan and Daniel F. Stone, "Media Proliferation and Partisan Selective Exposure," *Public Choice* 156, no. 3/4 (2013): 467–90.
21. John J. Mearsheimer and Stephen M. Walt, *The Israel Lobby and U.S. Foreign Policy* (New York: Farrar, Straus and Giroux, 2007), 80.
22. Michael Boulter, "In the Age of Memes, How Are Young People Getting Their News?," *PBS NewsHour*, January 23, 2020, https://www.pbs.org/newshour/nation/in-the-age-of-memes-how-are-young-people-getting-their-news.
23. Quoted in Entsu Abu Jahal, "TikTok Becomes Vital Weapon in Palestinians' Digital War," *Al-Monitor*, June 1, 2021, https://www.al-monitor.com/originals/2021/06/tiktok-becomes-vital-weapon-palestinians-digital-war.
24. Saree Makdisi, *Tolerance Is a Wasteland: Palestine and the Culture of Denial* (Oakland: University of California Press, 2022), 157.
25. "About the Electronic Intifada," *Electronic Intifada*, accessed November 11, 2022, https://electronicintifada.net/content/about-electronic-intifada/10159.
26. "e-Intifada: archief nrc.nl," Vorige.nrc.nl, July 25, 2006, https://en.wikipedia.org/wiki/The_Electronic_Intifada.

27. "About," *Palestine Chronicle*, accessed November 11, 2022, https://www.palestine chronicle.com/about/.
28. Gene Johnson, "Impact of WTO Protests in Seattle Still Felt 2 Decades Later," Associated Press, November 28, 2019, https://apnews.com/article/seattle-us-news-ap-top-news-wa-state-wire-environment-239fb5aca78345f0807fa4c9c505db9a.
29. Jared Morgan, "Post-9/11 Conflicts Increased Civilian Police Militarization, New Study Claims," *Military Times*, September 16, 2020, https://www.militarytimes.com/news/your-military/2020/09/16/post-911-conflicts-increased-civilian-police-militarization-new-study-claims/.
30. Scott W. Phillips, "Police Militarization," *Law Enforcement Bulletin*, August 14, 2017, https://leb.fbi.gov/articles/featured-articles/police-militarization.
31. Karam Dana and Matt Barreto, "American Muslims and the State: Contexts and Contentions," in *Understanding Muslim Political Life in America: Contested Citizenship in the Twenty-First Century*, ed. Brian Calfano, and Nazita Lajevardi (Philadelphia: Temple University Press, 2019). See also Angela X., Karam Dana, and Matt Barreto, "The American Muslim Voter: Community Belonging and Political Participation," *Social Science Research* 72 (2018): 84–99; Karam Dana, Matt Barreto, and Bryan Wilcox-Archuleta, "The Political Incorporation of Muslims in America: The Mobilizing Role of Religiosity in Islam," *Journal of Race, Ethnicity, and Politics* 2, no. 2 (2017): 170–200.
32. Farida Jalalzai, "The Politics of Muslims in America," *Politics and Religion* 2, no. 2 (2009): 163–99, https://doi.org:10.1017/S1755048309000194.
33. Christopher S. Parker and Matt A. Barreto, *Change They Can't Believe In: The Tea Party and Reactionary Politics in America—Updated Edition* (Princeton, N.J.: Princeton University Press, 2013), http://ebookcentral.proquest.com/lib/washington/detail.action?docID=1131671.
34. Wendy Hall, Ramine Tinati, and Will Jennings, "From Brexit to Trump: Social Media's Role in Democracy," *Computer* 51, no. 1 (2018): 18–27. doi:10.1109/MC.2018.1151005.
35. Steve Holland, "Obama Breaks Silence on Gaza, Voices Concern," Reuters, January 6, 2009, https://www.reuters.com/article/idUSN06437468.
36. Michael Corcoran, "Bernie Sanders and the Limits of Electoral Politics," TruthOut, December 10, 2015, https://truthout.org/articles/bernie-sanders-and-the-limits-of-electoral-politics/.
37. Green Papers, "Democratic Convention 2020," September 11, 2020, http://www.thegreenpapers.com/P20/D.
38. Matt Duss, interview by author, March 19, 2021.
39. Branko Marcetic, "Don't Look Now but Progressives Are About to Expand Their Ranks in Congress," *In These Times*, October 31, 2022, https://inthesetimes.com/article/progressives-dark-money-midterms-squad-democrats.
40. Akela Lacy, "Progressives, 'Massively Outgunned,' Ditched Nina Turner," *Intercept*, May 3, 2022, https://theintercept.com/2022/05/03/ohio-primary-elections-nina-turner-shontel-brown/.
41. Sam Adler-Bell, "Can DSA Go the Distance?" *Dissent* (Fall 2022), https://www.dissentmagazine.org/article/can-dsa-go-the-distance.
42. Michael Arria, "AIPAC Spent Over $4 Million Trying to Stop Summer Lee but She's Headed to Congress," *Mondoweiss*, November 9, 2022, https://mondoweiss

.net/2022/11/aipac-spent-over-4-million-trying-to-stop-summer-lee-but-shes-headed-to-congress/.
43. Adler-Bell, "Can DSA Go the Distance?"
44. Adler-Bell.
45. Willem Morris, "Centering Palestinian Liberation is Essential to Revitalizing the Labor Movement," Young Democratic Socialists of America, June 21, 2022, https://y.dsausa.org/the-activist/centering-palestinian-liberation-is-essential-to-revitalizing-the-labor-movement/.
46. WOLPalestine, "Palestine Is the Litmus Test," Instagram, November 8, 2022, https://www.instagram.com/p/CkrkZVoJnF6/?igshid=MDJmNzVkMjY%3D.
47. Hannah Frishberg, "American Church Attendance Hits Historic Low, Says Gallup Survey," *New York Post*, May 30, 2021, https://nypost.com/2021/03/30/american-church-attendance-hits-historic-low-survey/.
48. Tom Rosentiel, Scott Keeter, and Paul Taylor, "The Millennials," Pew Research Center, December 10, 2009, https://www.pewresearch.org/2009/12/10/the-millennials/.
49. Arthur Zuckerman, "60 Church Attendance Statistics: 2020/2021 Data, Trends, & Predictions," *Compare Camp*, May 8, 2020, https://comparecamp.com/church-attendance-statistics/.
50. Martyn Whittock, "The Strange Decline of US Evangelicalism," *Christianity Today*, July 28, 2021, https://www.christiantoday.com/article/the.strange.decline.of.us.evangelicalism/137169.htm.
51. Terry Johnson, "The Rise and Decline of Evangelicalism in the United States (1967–2017)," *Evangelical Times*, February 2, 2017, https://www.evangelical-times.org/the-rise-and-decline-of-evangelicalism-in-the-united-states-1967-2017/.
52. *Arab America*, "American Church Support for Palestine and Israel Is Schizophrenic," July 27, 2022, https://www.arabamerica.com/american-church-support-for-palestine-and-israel-is-schizophrenic/.
53. *Arab America*, "American Church Support."
54. *Arab America*.
55. J Street, "National Election Night Survey of Jewish Voters Finds Overwhelming Support for Democrats, Opposition to Trump and the Far-Right," November 10, 2022, https://jstreet.org/press-releases/national-election-night-survey-of-jewish-voters-finds-overwhelming-support-for-democrats-opposition-to-trump-and-the-far-right/#.Y26A33bMLe; Dov Waxman, @dovwaxman, "A post-election survey of American Jewish voters has some interesting findings about Jewish opinions," Twitter, November 10, 2022, https://twitter.com/dovwaxman/status/1590800150595006465?s=43&t=4lc_mFS0_QQyRAN9Kti36w.
56. Birthright Israel Foundation, "MythBuster: Common Misconceptions About Birthright Israel Trips," August 6, 2020, https://birthrightisrael.foundation/blog/mythbuster-common-misconceptions-about-birthright-israel-trips/.
57. NowThis Politics, "Birthright Participant Questions Israel Map That Erases Palestine," Facebook video, July 20, 2018, https://www.facebook.com/NowThisPolitics/videos/2178423775522434/.
58. Risa Nagel, "Why I Walked off My Birthright Israel Trip," *Huffpost*, July 23, 2018, https://www.huffpost.com/entry/opinion-nagel-birthright-israel-walkout_n_5b54f04fe4b0b15aba90107d.

59. International Women's Media Foundation, "Amira Haas," accessed November 11, 2022, https://www.iwmf.org/community/amira-haas/.
60. "Haaretz's Amira Hass Awarded Journalism Prize by Media Watchdog," *Huffpost*, March 18, 2010, https://www.huffpost.com/entry/haaretzs-amira-hass-award_n_377258.
61. American Friends Service Committee, "Profiles of Peace," https://afsc.org/sites/default/files/documents/Profiles of Peace Low Resolution.pdf.
62. Iwasaki Atsuko, "As Israelies, We Also Fight for Palestinians," Counterpunch, April 3, 2006, https://www.counterpunch.org/2006/04/03/quot-as-israelis-we-also-fight-for-palestinians-quot/.
63. Josh Reubner, "Envisioning a Post-colonial Palestine," *Electronic Intifada*, March 23, 2021, https://electronicintifada.net/content/envisioning-post-colonial-palestine/32596.
64. "Advocate," Home Made Docs, accessed November 11, 2022, https://www.homemadedocs.com/advocate.
65. Trilby Beresford, "Israeli Film 'Advocate' Wins Best Documentary Emmy," *Hollywood Reporter*, September 29, 2021, https://www.hollywoodreporter.com/tv/tv-news/advocate-documentary-emmy-winners-1235022667/.
66. "Palestinian Centre for Human Rights Wins France's Highest Award for Human Rights Endeavors," Palestinian Center for Human Rights, December 7, 1996, https://pchrgaza.org/en/palestinian-centre-for-human-rights-wins-frances-highest-award-for-human-rights-endeavours/.
67. Ilan Greilsammer, "The New Historians of Israel and Their Political Involvement," *Bulletin du Centre de recherche français à Jérusalem* [in English], January 20, 2013, http://journals.openedition.org/bcrfj/6868.
68. Greilsammer.
69. Greilsammer.
70. Bruce B. Lawrence, "Roy: Failing Peace: Gaza and the Palestinian-Israeli Conflict," *Journal of Palestine Studies* 37, no. 1 (Fall 2007): 111https://web.archive.org/web/20120213113623/http://www.palestine-studies.org/print.aspx?id=9678&jid=1&href=fulltext.
71. Sara Roy, "Living with the Holocaust: The Journey of a Child of Holocaust Survivors," *Journal of Palestine Studies* 32, no. 1 (2002): 5–12, https://doi:10.1525/jps.2002.32.1.5.
72. Peter Beinart, "The Failure of the American Jewish Establishment," *New York Review*, June 10, 2010, https://www.nybooks.com/articles/2010/06/10/failure-american-jewish-establishment/.
73. Jeffrey Goldberg, "Peter Beinart Is Right—or, a One-State Solution Is Inevitable If Settlements Continue," *Atlantic*, December 8, 2011, https://www.theatlantic.com/international/archive/2011/12/peter-beinart-is-right-or-a-one-state-solution-is-inevitable-if-settlements-continue/249608/.
74. Peter Beinart, "I No Longer Believe in a Jewish State," *New York Times*, July 8, 2020, https://www.nytimes.com/2020/07/08/opinion/israel-annexation-two-state-solution.html.
75. David Weinberg, "Peter Beinhart's Betrayal of Liberal Zionism and Israel," *Jerusalem Post*, July 9, 2020, https://www.jpost.com/opinion/peter-beinharts-betrayal-of-liberal-zionism-and-israel-634553; Shmuley Boteach, "The End of Israel and

2. STRUCTURAL TRANSFORMATIONS IN U.S. CULTURE

Peter Beinart as the Last Man," *Jerusalem Post*, July 21, 2020, https://www.jpost.com/opinion/the-end-of-israel-and-peter-beinart-as-the-last-man-635856.
76. Russell Brand, "Israel/Palestine—This Needs to Be Heard," YouTube, May 27, 2021, https://www.youtube.com/watch?v=WdPdslOTwJU.
77. B'tselem, "About B'Tselem," accessed November 11, 2022, https://www.btselem.org/about_btselem.
78. Americans for Peace Now, "About Us: Mission Statement," accessed November 11, 2022, https://peacenow.org/page.php?id=679.
79. Combatants for Peace, "Our Mission," accessed November 11, 2022, https://cfpeace.org/about/.
80. ICAHD, "Our Mission and Vision," accessed November 11, 2022, https://icahd.org/our-mission-and-vision/.
81. IfNotNow, "Why We Organize," accessed November 11, 2022, https://www.ifnotnowmovement.org/why-we-organize.
82. IfNotNow, "Learn More from Organizations in Israel/Palestine," accessed November 11, 2022, https://www.ifnotnowmovement.org/organizations-in-israel-palestine.
83. Dena Takruri and AJPlus, "How Israeli Apartheid Destroyed My Hometown," YouTube, October 27, 2022, https://www.youtube.com/watch?v=aEdGcej-6Do&list=PLZd3QRtSy5LOWaQBH1fLN2etOO9pCAxaJ.
84. Jewish Voice for Peace, "Why Is It Important That JVP Is a Jewish Group?" accessed November 11, 2022, https://www.jewishvoiceforpeace.org/faq/.
85. Jewish Voice for Peace, "How Is JVP Different from Other Major Jewish American Peace Groups?" accessed November 11, 2022, https://www.jewishvoiceforpeace.org/wp-content/uploads/2014/06/jvp-faq-page-2016.pdf.
86. Oliver Holmes, "Seth Rogen: 'I Was Fed a Huge Amount of Lies About Israel,'" *Guardian*, July 29, 2020, https://www.theguardian.com/world/2020/jul/29/seth-rogen-israel-palestinians-jewish-actor; Andrew Pulver, "Natalie Portman Pulls Out of Israel Award Due to 'Distressing Recent Events' There," *Guardian*, April 20, 2018, https://www.theguardian.com/film/2018/apr/20/natalie-portman-israel-genesis-prize.
87. Gideon Levy, "Gideon Levy: Americans 'Are Supporting the First Signs of Fascism in Israel,'" *Real News Network*, March 22, 2016, https://therealnews.com/thedges0318gideon.
88. Gabriel R. Sanchez and Edward D. Vargas, "Taking a Closer Look at Group Identity: The Link Between Theory and Measurement of Group Consciousness and Linked Fate," *Political Research Quarterly* 69, no. 1 (2016): 160–74, https://doi:10.1177/1065912915624571.
89. Kiana Cox, "Most U.S. Adults Feel What Happens to Their Own Racial or Ethnic Group Affects Them Personally," Pew Research Center, July 11, 2019, https://www.pewresearch.org/fact-tank/2019/07/11/linked-fate-connectedness-americans/.
90. Audrea Lim, ed., *The Case for Sanctions Against Israel* (London: Verso, 2012).
91. Gideon Levy, "Americans Are Supporting."
92. "Rising Spectre of Fascism in Israel," *Journal of Palestine Studies* 9, no. 3 (1980): 181–87, https://doi:10.1525/jps.1980.9.3.00p0240q.
93. "Israel: Upcoming Government 'Most Fascist' in History, Says MK," *Middle East Monitor*, November 14, 2022, https://www.middleeastmonitor.com/20221114-israel-upcoming-government-most-fascist-in-history-says-mk/.

94. Norman G. Finkelstein, *Beyond Chutzpah: On the Misuse of Anti-Semitism and the Abuse of History* (Berkeley: University of California Press, 2005), xxvii.

3. SOCIAL CHANGE AND SOUND BITES

1. David Feldman, *Boycotts Past and Present: From the American Revolution to the Campaign to Boycott Israel* (Cham, Switz.: Springer International, 2019), 1.
2. "Caterpillar Group Boycotted for Selling Bulldozers to Israel," *New Zealand Herald*, April 15, 2005, https://www.nzherald.co.nz/world/caterpillar-group-boycotted-for-selling-bulldozers-to-israel/P4GMHDBMSQ6R3GVTWOVPXDTBKI/.
3. Business and Human RIghts Resource Center, "Caterpillar Response Re Alleged Complicity in Human Rights Abuses in Israel & the Occupied Territories," January 23, 2012, https://www.business-humanrights.org/en/latest-news/caterpillar-response-re-alleged-complicity-in-human-rights-abuses-in-israel-the-occupied-territories/.
4. Susan Landau, "Say No to Settlement Products and Sabra Hummus," *Mondoweiss*, February 14, 2013, https://mondoweiss.net/2013/02/settlement-products-hummus/.
5. Ella L. Jones and Monique I. Vobecky, "Harvard Out of Occupied Palestine Protests Sabra Hummus in Harvard Yard," *Harvard Crimson*, February 9, 2022, https://www.thecrimson.com/article/2022/2/9/students-protest-sabra-hummus/.
6. Heddy Breuer Abromowitz, "Sabra Hummus Banned by Student Senate from Dickinson College Store," *Jerusalem Post*, December 24, 2019, https://www.jpost.com/Diaspora/Taking-a-swipe-at-Israel-A-tempest-in-a-hummus-bowl-611338; BDS University of Manchester, "BDS Triumph Over Sabra on Campus," February 6, 2018, https://bdsuom.com/2018/02/06/bds-triumph-over-sabra-on-campus/comment-page-1/.
7. Mark Muckenfuss, "UC Riverside Students Vote to Ban Sabra Hummus," *Press-Enterprise* (Riverside, Calif.), February 3, 2017, https://www.pe.com/2017/02/03/uc-riverside-students-vote-to-ban-sabra-hummus/.
8. Palestinian Solidarity Campaign, "Hewlett-Packard," February 13, 2020, https://www.palestinecampaign.org/psc-company/hewlett-packard-hp/.
9. BDS Movement, "Civil Society Organizations Around the World Urge HP Companies to End All Involvement in Violations of Palestinian Rights," March 29, 2018, https://bdsmovement.net/news/civil-society-organizations-around-world-urge-hp-companies-end-all-involvement-violations.
10. Charlie Pillsbury, "Why We Must Boycott Pillsbury," *Minnesota Star-Tribune*, April 28, 2021, https://www.startribune.com/why-we-must-boycott-pillsbury/600051334/.
11. American Friends Service Committee, "Pillsbury Family Calls for Boycott of Pillsbury Products," April 29, 2021, https://www.afsc.org/newsroom/pillsbury-family-calls-boycott-pillsbury-products.
12. "Ben and Jerry's Will End Sales of Our Ice Cream in the Occupied Palestinian Territory," press announcement, Ben and Jerry's, July 19, 2021, https://www.benjerry.com/about-us/media-center/opt-statement.
13. International Middle East Media Center, "U.S. Judge Forces Ben & Jerry's to Sell Ice Cream in Israeli Settlements," August 26, 2022, https://imemc.org/article/us

3. SOCIAL CHANGE AND SOUND BITES

-judge-forces-ben-jerrys-to-sell-ice-cream-in-israeli-settlements/; Reuters, "Judge Rejects Ben and Jerry's Bid to Halt Ice Cream Sales in the West Bank," *New York Post*, August 22, 2022, https://nypost.com/2022/08/22/ben-jerrys-loses-bid-to-halt-ice-cream-sales-in-west-bank/.

14. Kate Shuttleworth and Julia Carrie Wong, "Airbnb Lists Properties in Illegal Israeli Settlements," *Guardian*, January 13, 2016, https://www.theguardian.com/technology/2016/jan/12/airbnb-listings-illegal-settlements-israel-palestine-west-bank.
15. Sarah Ashley O'Brien, "Airbnb Will Allow Israeli Settlement Listings but Won't Profit Off Them," CNN Business, April 9, 2019, https://www.cnn.com/2019/04/09/tech/airbnb-reverses-israeli-settlement-stance/index.html.
16. "Palestinian Campaigners Call for Mass Boycott of Airbnb on May 15," *Al Jazeera*, May 14, 2019, https://www.aljazeera.com/economy/2019/5/14/palestinian-campaigners-call-for-mass-boycott-of-airbnb-on-may-15.
17. MEE Staff, "Booking.com to Put Warnings on Listings in Illegal Israeli Settlements," *Middle East Eye*, September 19, 2022, https://www.middleeasteye.net/news/bookingcom-israel-settlements-warnings-listings.
18. Court of Justice of the European Union, Press Release No. 140/19, "Foodstuffs Originating in Israel Territories Must Bear Indication of Their Territory of Origin," Luxembourg, November 12, 2019, https://curia.europa.eu/jcms/upload/docs/application/pdf/2019-11/cp190140en.pdf.
19. Jewish Voice for Peace, "Psagot Winery and Duty Free Stores," Instagram, November 7, 2022, accessed November 27, 2022, https://www.instagram.com/p/CkqvbJEuAjM/?igshid=MDJmNzVkMjY%3D; "US Duty Free Magnates Bankrolled Expansion of Israeli Settlement Vineyard Over Palestinian Land," *Independent*, November 12, 2019, https://www.independent.co.uk/news/world/middle-east/palestine-israel-land-us-falic-psagot-duty-free-land-a8989086.html.
20. Palestine Solidarity Campaign, "Boycott SodaStream," September 30, 2013, https://www.palestinecampaign.org/sodastream/.
21. Jewish Voice for Peace, "SodaStream," accessed August 26, 2022, https://www.jewishvoiceforpeace.org/boycott-divestment-and-sanctions/sodastream/.
22. BDS Movement, "SodaStream Is Still Subject to Boycott," August 22, 2018, https://bdsmovement.net/news/%E2%80%9Csodastream-still-subject-boycott%E2%80%9D.
23. Emily Harris, "When 500 Palestinians Lose Their Jobs at SodaStream, Who's to Blame?" NPR, March 27, 2016, https://www.npr.org/sections/parallels/2016/03/27/471885452/when-500-palestinians-lose-their-jobs-at-sodastream-whos-to-blame.
24. Gabe Fernandez, "Why Oakland Roots Fans Are Demanding the Team End Its Sponsorship Deal with Puma," *SFGate*, August 6, 2021, https://www.sfgate.com/sports/article/Oakland-Roots-supporters-group-Puma-Israel-protest-16367605.php.
25. Alexandra Ross, "Did Oakland Roots Football Team Drop Puma Over BDS?" *Local Today*, November 10, 2022, https://localtoday.news/ca/did-oakland-roots-football-team-drop-puma-over-bds-j-126508.html.
26. Debbie Reiss, "Balenciaga, Adidas Slammed for Hiring Anti-Israel Bella Hadid After Dropping Kanye," *World Israel News*, November 8, 2022, https://worldisraelnews.com/balenciaga-adidas-slammed-for-hiring-anti-israel-bella-hadid-after-dropping-kanye/.

27. "Protesters Seize Israel Weapons Manufacture in UK as Bombs Rain on Gaza," *Middle East Monitor*, May 19, 2021, https://www.middleeastmonitor.com/20210519-protesters-seize-israel-weapons-manufacture-in-uk-as-bombs-rain-on-gaza/.
28. Glen Murphy and Jack Power, "Thousands Attend Rallies in Irish Cities in Solidarity with Palestine," *Irish Times*, May 15, 2021, https://www.irishtimes.com/news/ireland/irish-news/thousands-attend-rallies-in-irish-cities-in-solidarity-with-palestine-1.4566435.
29. Alex N. Press, "Oakland Longshore Workers Say No to Israeli-Operated Cargo," *Jacobin*, June 8, 2021, https://jacobin.com/2021/06/palestine-zim-oakland-boycott-ship-ilwu-local-10.
30. "Italy: Workers Refuse to Load Arms Shipment to Israel," *Middle East Monitor*, May 17, 2021, https://www.middleeastmonitor.com/20210517-italy-workers-refuse-to-load-arms-shipment-to-israel/.
31. "Protests Against Israel in the USA Target Israeli Cargo," *Yeshiva World*, June 21, 2010, https://www.theyeshivaworld.com/news/israel-news/63063/protests-against-israel-in-the-usa-target-israeli-cargo.html.
32. "Swedish Longshoremen Boycott Israeli Vessels," *Yeshiva World*, June 24, 2010, https://www.theyeshivaworld.com/news/israel-news/63598/swedish-longshoremen-boycott-israeli-vessels.html..
33. Jewish News Syndicate, "San Francisco Teachers Union Becomes First to Pass Resolution Supporting BDS," May 28, 2021, https://www.jns.org/san-francisco-teachers-union-becomes-first-to-pass-resolution-supporting-bds/.
34. Isaac Scher, "AFL-CIO Leadership Tries to Block Affiliate's Vote on Endorsing BDS," *Intercept*, October 21, 2021, https://theintercept.com/2021/10/21/palestine-bds-san-francisco-labor-afl-cio/.
35. Jewish Labor Committee, "Statement of Opposition to Divestment from or Boycotts of Israel," July 2007, http://www.jewishlaborcommittee.org/2007/07/statement_of_opposition_to_div.html.
36. Scher, "AFL-CIO Leadership."
37. Darrin Hoop, "Seattle Educators Endorse BDS," *Tempest*, August 6, 2021, https://www.tempestmag.org/2021/08/seattle-educators-endorse-bds/.
38. "SF Teachers Union Votes to Support Palestinians Against Israeli Occupation," *San Francisco Independent Journal*, June 1, 2021, https://sfindependentjournal.com/sf-teachers-union-votes-to-support-palestinians-against-israeli-occupation/.
39. Neil Rubin, "Quaker Group Divests from Companies Working in Israel," Jewish Telegraphic Agency, September 28, 2012, https://www.jta.org/2012/09/28/israel/quaker-group-divests-from-companies-working-in-israel.
40. Anugrah Kumar, "Presbyterian Church USA Votes to Divest from Companies Israel Uses in West Bank; Jewish Group Denounces 'Radical, Prejudiced' Decision," *Christian Post*, June 23, 2014, https://www.christianpost.com/news/presbyterian-church-usa-votes-to-divest-from-companies-israel-uses-in-west-bank-jewish-group-denounces-radical-prejudiced-decision.html.
41. David Roach, "PCUSA's Israel Decision 'Tragic,'" *Baptist Press*, June 23, 2014, https://www.baptistpress.com/resource-library/news/pcusas-israel-decision-tragic/.
42. Kumar, "Presbyterian Church USA Votes to Divest."

3. SOCIAL CHANGE AND SOUND BITES

43. Roach, "PCUSA's Israel Decision 'Tragic.'"
44. "PCUSA Divestment Decision 'Threatens Presbyterian-Jewish Relations,'" *YNET News*, June 21, 2014, https://www.ynetnews.com/articles/0,7340,L-4532821,00.html.
45. Sean Savage, "Presbyterian Church Approves Israel Divestment, but Does Its Boycott Even Matter?" Jewish News Syndicate, June 20, 2014, https://www.jns.org/presbyterian-church-approves-israel-divestment-but-does-its-boycott-even-matter/.
46. Celine Hagbard, "United Church of Christ Divests from Israeli Occupation," *IMEMC News*, July 1, 2015, https://imemc.org/article/72119/.
47. Giulio Meotti, "Obama's Church to Divest from Israel," *Israel National News*, May 24, 2012, https://www.israelnationalnews.com/news/340280.
48. Jaweed Kaleem, "United Methodist Church Divests from Security Firm Targeted for Work in Palestinian Territories," *Huffington Post*, June 12, 2014, https://www.huffpost.com/entry/united-methodist-church-divestment_n_5489968.
49. Abra Forman, "In Rejection of Genesis 12:3, Methodist Church Divests from Israel," *Israel 365 News*, January 13, 2016, https://www.israel365news.com/58877/in-rejection-of-genesis-123-methodist-church-divests-from-israel-biblical-zionism/.
50. Hilary Rose and Stephen Rose, "Stephen Hawkings' Boycott Hits Israel Where It Hurts: Science," *Guardian*, May 13, 2013, https://www.theguardian.com/science/political-science/2013/may/13/stephen-hawking-boycott-israel-science.
51. Marcy Jane Knopf-Newman, "The Fallacy of Academic Freedom and the Academic Boycott of Israel," *CR: The New Centennial Review* 8, no. 2 (Fall 2008), Palestine Issue: 88.
52. Knopf-Newman, 88–89.
53. Raphael Ahren, "For First Time, U.S. Professors Call for Academic and Cultural Boycott of Israel," *Haaretz*, January 29, 2009, https://www.haaretz.com/2009-01-29/ty-article/for-first-time-u-s-professors-call-for-academic-and-cultural-boycott-of-israel/0000017f-e1b3-d75c-a7ff-fdbfaaaf0000.
54. US Campaign for the Academic and Cultural Boycott of Israel, "AAAS Votes in Historic Decision to Support Boycott of Israeli Academic Institutions," accessed September 19, 2022, https://usacbi.org/2013/04/aaas-votes-in-historic-decision-to-support-boycott-of-israeli-academic-institutions/; Maya Schwader, "134 Members of U.S. Congress Denounce ASA's Israel Boycott," *Jerusalem Post*, January 19, 2014, https://www.jpost.com/International/134-members-of-US-Congress-denounce-ASAs-Israel-boycott-338607.
55. Nick DeSantis, "Native American-Studies Group's Leadership Supports Israel Boycott," *Chronicle of Higher Education*, December 18, 2013, https://www.chronicle.com/blogs/ticker/native-american-studies-groups-leadership-supports-israel-boycott.
56. Elizabeth Redden, "Big Night for Boycott Movement," *Insider Higher Ed*, November 23, 2015, https://www.insidehighered.com/news/2015/11/23/anthropologists-overwhelmingly-vote-boycott-israeli-universities.
57. Elizabeth Redden, "Anthropology Group Won't Boycott Israel," *Insider Higher Ed*, June 7, 2016, https://www.insidehighered.com/news/2016/06/07/anthropology-group-rejects-resolution-boycott-israeli-academic-institutions.
58. Michael Arria, "Middle East Studies Scholars Overwhelmingly Vote to Endorse BDS," *Mondoweiss*, March 24, 2022, https://mondoweiss.net/2022/03/middle-east-studies-scholars-overwhelmingly-vote-to-endorse-bds/.

59. Phillip Weiss, "'Apartheid' Chorus Grows—60 Percent of Middle East Scholars Reach That Conclusion," *Mondoweiss*, April 25, 2022, https://mondoweiss.net/2022/04/apartheid-chorus-grows-60-percent-of-middle-east-scholars-reach-that-conclusion/.
60. David Lloyd and Malini Johar Schueller, "The Israeli State of Exception and the Case for Academic Boycott," *Journal of Academic Freedom* 4 (2013), https://www.aaup.org/JAF4/israeli-state-exception-and-case-academic-boycott#.Y1LpR3bMLe9.
61. Martin Kramer, "The Unspoken Purpose of the Academic Boycott," *Israel Affairs* 27, no. 1 (2021): 27–33, https://doi:10.1080/13537121.2021.1864846.
62. Evan Gerstmann, "Why an Academic Boycott of Israel Is Hypocritical," *Forbes*, February 21, 2019, https://www.forbes.com/sites/evangerstmann/2019/02/21/why-an-academic-boycott-of-israel-is-hypocritical/?sh=47b3d4f05f04.
63. Harriet Sherwood and Matthew Kalman, "Stephen Hawking Joins Academic Boycott of Israel," *Guardian*, May 7, 2013, https://www.theguardian.com/world/2013/may/08/stephen-hawking-israel-academic-boycott.
64. Tyler Jenke, "Lorde Labelled a 'Bigot' by U.S. Newspaper in Wake of Israel Controversy," *Tone Deaf*, February 1, 2018, https://tonedeaf.thebrag.com/lorde-bigot-israel-controversy/.
65. Shmuley Boteach, @rabbishmuley, "Pick up our full page ad against #Lorde," Twitter, December 31, 2017, https://twitter.com/RabbiShmuley/status/947529042537975808.
66. Jenke, "Lorde Labelled a 'Bigot.'"
67. World Values Network, "Mission and Values," accessed October 21, 2022, https://www.worldvalues.us/about-v2.
68. "Roger Waters and BDS Response," fundraiser organized by Shmuley Boteach, GoFundMe, accessed October 21, 2022, https://www.gofundme.com/f/end-of-year-giving-campaign.
69. Na'ama Carlin, "Are Israel Boycotts Really Anti-Semitic?," *Eureka Street*, February 14, 2018, https://www.eurekastreet.com.au/article/are-israel-boycotts-really-anti-semitic.
70. Itay Stern, "Lorde Fans Sue BDS Activists for 'Inciting' Her to Cancel Israel Show," *Haaretz*, February 1, 2018, https://www.haaretz.com/israel-news/2018-02-01/ty-article/.premium/israeli-lorde-fans-sue-bds-activists-for-inciting-her-to-cancel-show/0000017f-db25-d856-a37f-ffe51b1b0000.
71. Eleanor Ainge Roy, "Israel Fines New Zealand Women $18,000 for Urging Lorde Concert Boycott," *Guardian*, October 11, 2018, https://www.theguardian.com/music/2018/oct/12/israel-fines-new-zealand-teenagers-18000-for-urging-lorde-concert-boycott.
72. Open Letters, "Gaza Cultural Centers and Artists Call for a Boycott of Eurovision 2019," *Mondoweiss*, May 9, 2019, https://mondoweiss.net/2019/05/cultural-centers-eurovision/.
73. Letters, "Boycott Eurovision Song Contest hosted by Israel," *Guardian*, September 7, 2018, https://www.theguardian.com/tv-and-radio/2018/sep/07/boycott-eurovision-song-contest-hosted-by-israel.
74. Rob Picheta, "Iceland's Eurovision Entry Hatari Holds Up Palestinian Flag During Contest," CNN, May 18, 2019, https://www.cnn.com/2019/05/18/europe/iceland-eurovision-palestine-intl.

3. SOCIAL CHANGE AND SOUND BITES

75. Amy Spiro, "EBU Condemns Madonna, Iceland for Palestinian Flags at Eurovision," *Jerusalem Post*, May 20, 2019, https://www.jpost.com/israel-news/madonna-iceland-include-palestinian-flags-at-eurovision-590072.
76. Rachel Wolf, "Icelandic Broadcaster Fined Over Hatari's Palestinian Flag Waving," *Jerusalem Post*, September 21, 2019, https://www.jpost.com/breaking-news/icelandic-broadcaster-fined-over-hataris-palestinan-flag-waving-602402.
77. Spiro, "EBU Condemns Madonna."
78. PACBI, @pacbi, "Thank you Lana Del Rey for your principled decision to withdraw," Twitter, August 31, 2018, https://twitter.com/PACBI/status/1035578286225731584.
79. Chris Johnston, "Lana Del Rey Pulls Out of Israeli Festival After Backlash," *Guardian*, August 31, 2018, https://www.theguardian.com/music/2018/aug/31/lana-del-rey-pulls-out-of-israeli-festival-after-backlash.
80. Tia Goldenberg, "In Israel, Miss Universe Says Pageant No Place for Politics," *U.S. News*, November 17, 2021, https://www.usnews.com/news/world/articles/2021-11-17/in-israel-miss-universe-says-pageant-no-place-for-politics.
81. Associated Press, "Miss South Africa's Appearance in Miss Universe in Israel Ignites Controversy," *Fox News*, November 19, 2021, https://www.foxnews.com/world/miss-south-africa-pageant-israel.
82. Almog Ben Zikri and Hagar Shezef, "Burning Man Project Urges Israeli Organizers to Cancel West Bank Festival," *Haaretz*, March 9, 2020, https://www.haaretz.com/israel-news/2020-03-09/ty-article/.premium/burning-man-urges-israeli-organizers-to-cancel-controversial-west-bank-festival/0000017f-dbc7-d3a5-af7f-fbefe8d30000.
83. Tasnim News Agency, "'Musicians for Palestine' Campaign Urges Boycotting Israel," May 29, 2021, https://www.tasnimnews.com/en/news/2021/05/29/2511981/musicians-for-palestine-campaign-urges-boycotting-israel.
84. Danica Kirka, Menelaos Hadjicostis, and Fatima Hussein. "A Global Day of Protests Draws Thousands in Washington and Other Cities in Pro-Palestinian Marches," *AP News*, January 13, 2024, https://apnews.com/article/protest-gaza-israel-palestinians-london-29d5cd664c81654283344d1874691a4f.
85. KIW, "Finnish Musicians Threaten Eurovision Boycott If Israel's Participation Continues Amid Gaza Conflict," *essanews.com*, January 12, 2024, https://www.msn.com/en-us/news/world/finnish-musicians-threaten-eurovision-boycott-if-israel-s-participation-continues-amid-gaza-conflict/ar-AA1mSHk8.
86. *Al Jazeera*, "Pro-Palestine Protests Held Around the World as Gaza War Nears 100 Days," January 13, 2024, https://www.aljazeera.com/news/2024/1/13/pro-palestine-demonstrations-around-the-world-as-gaza-war-nears-100-days.
87. Democracy Now! "Pro-Palestine Protests Disrupt Rose Bowl & JFK Airport," January 2, 2024. https://www.democracynow.org/2024/1/2/headlines/pro_palestine_protests_disrupt_rose_bowl_jfk_airport.
88. Alaa Elassar and Emma Tucker, "At Least 320 Pro-Palestinian Protesters Arrested After Blocking Traffic Across New York City Bridges to Demand Gaza Ceasefire," CNN, January 8, 2024, https://www.cnn.com/2024/01/08/us/palestine-protest-nyc-gaza-ceasefire/index.html.
89. Nathaniel Meyersohn, "Starbucks' CEO Wants People to Stop Protesting Its Stores over Israel War in Gaza," CNN, December 21, 2023, https://www.cnn.com/2023/12/21/business/starbucks-israel-war-union/index.html.

90. "McDonald's Hit by Israel-Gaza 'Misinformation,'" *BBC*, January 4, 2024, https://www.bbc.com/news/business-67885910.
91. Nisha Anand, "'Boycott Mcdonald's' Trends as UK Unit Issues Statement on Israel-Hamas War," *Business Standard*, January 17, 2024, https://www.business-standard.com/world-news/boycott-mcdonald-s-trends-as-uk-unit-issues-statement-on-israel-hamas-war-124011800289_1.html.
92. Olivia Rosane, "Hundreds Block So-Called 'Genocide Boat' Carrying Weapons to Israel at Tacoma Port," *Common Dreams*, November 6, 2023, https://www.commondreams.org/news/hundreds-block-israel-boat-tacoma.
93. It's Going Down, "Oakland Rallies to Block Boat Carrying Israeli Arms Shipment," November 4, 2023. https://itsgoingdown.org/oakland-rallies-to-block-boat-carrying-israeli-arms-shipment/.
94. Lola Fadulu, "Zara Removes Campaign After Critics Call It Insensitive to Israel-Hamas War," *New York Times*, December 12, 2023, https://www.nytimes.com/2023/12/12/business/zara-campaign-israel-gaza-war.html.
95. Khaled Beydoun, "Khaled Beydoun on Instagram: 'Dear @Zara. . . .'" *Instagram*, June 15, 2021, https://www.instagram.com/p/CQHkHJZDSRT/.
96. Kenichi Serino, "Tens of Thousands Have Joined Pro-Palestinian Protests Across the United States. Experts Say They Are Growing." *PBS NewsHour*, published December 15, 2023, updated January 16, 2024, https://www.pbs.org/newshour/politics/tens-of-thousands-have-joined-pro-palestinian-protests-across-the-united-states-experts-say-they-are-growing.
97. "Largest Pro-Palestinian Mobilization in U.S. History," *Haaretz*.
98. Serino, "Tens of Thousands."
99. Serino.
100. Danielle Wallace, "Biden Interrupted by 'Cease-Fire Now Chants,' Vows He's Working to Get Israel 'Out of Gaza.'" *Fox News*, January 8, 2024, https://www.msn.com/en-us/news/politics/biden-interrupted-by-cease-fire-now-chants-vows-hes-working-to-get-israel-out-of-gaza/ar-AA1mElho.
101. Tim Craig and Clara Ence Morse, "Young U.S. Muslims Are Rising Up Against Israel in Unlikely Places," *Washington Post*, January 2, 2024, https://www.washingtonpost.com/nation/2023/12/25/palestinian-protests-muslim-american-activists/.
102. Sophia Barkoff, "Arab American Leaders Urge Michigan to Vote 'Uncommitted' and Send Message to Bided About Israel Policy," *CBS News*, February 3, 2024, https://www.cbsnews.com/news/michigan-vote-uncommitted-biden-israel-gaza/.
103. Craig and Morse, "Young U.S. Muslims Are Rising Up."
104. Craig and Morse.
105. Craig and Morse.
106. Giulia Carbonaro, "Pro-Palestinian Protests Break Out in Multiple U.S. Cities," *Newsweek*, October 9, 2023, https://www.newsweek.com/pro-palestinian-protests-break-out-multiple-american-cities-1833036.
107. Angelina Chapin, "When Posting About the Israel-Hamas War Costs You Your Job," *The Cut*, October 30, 2023, https://www.thecut.com/2023/10/israel-hamas-war-job-loss-social-media.html.

108. Mondoweiss Editors, "Roseanne Barr Talked Trash About Palestinians and Muslims for Years, Without Regrets," *Mondoweiss*, June 1, 2018, http://mondoweiss.net/2018/06/roseanne-palestinians-muslims/.
109. Zach Beauchamp, "How Natalie Portman Became the Latest Israel-Palestine Flashpoint," *Vox*, April 23, 2018, https://www.vox.com/world/2018/4/23/17270180/natalie-portman-israel-boycott.
110. Amir Bogan, "Roger Waters Pays Homage to Slain Palestinian Journalist in NYC Concert," *YNET News*, August 31, 2022, https://www.ynetnews.com/culture/article/s1dwahhko.
111. Rajaa Moini, "Roger Waters' Pro-Palestine Activism Is a Lesson for the West," *Express Tribune*, May 20, 2021, https://tribune.com.pk/story/2300850/roger-waters-pro-palestine-activism-is-a-lesson-for-the-west.
112. Amer Zahr, "Palestinians Bid Jon Stewart a Fond Farewell," *Al Jazeera*, August 6, 2015, https://www.aljazeera.com/opinions/2015/8/6/palestinians-bid-jon-stewart-a-fond-farewell/.
113. David Horovitz, "Jon Stewart—So Funny, So Wrong on Israel-Gaza," *Times of Israel*, July 16, 2014, https://www.timesofisrael.com/jon-stewart-so-funny-so-wrong-on-israel-gaza/.
114. "Mark Levin Slams Jon Stewart's 'Putrid' Criticism of Israel," *Fox News*, January 30, 2017, https://www.foxnews.com/transcript/mark-levin-slams-jon-stewarts-putrid-criticism-of-israel.
115. TOI Staff, "Jon Stewart: 'I'm Not Anti-Israel,'" *Times of Israel*, August 30, 2014, https://www.timesofisrael.com/jon-stewart-im-not-anti-israel/.
116. Chris Murphy, "Trevor Noah Asks Tough Questions About Israel and Palestine on *The Daily Show*," *Vanity Fair*, May 12, 2021, https://www.vanityfair.com/hollywood/2021/05/trevor-noah-asks-tough-questions-about-israel-and-palestine-on-the-daily-show.
117. Dean Obeidallah, "How Jon Stewart Made It Okay to Care About Palestinian Suffering," *Daily Beast*, April 14, 2017, https://www.thedailybeast.com/how-jon-stewart-made-it-okay-to-care-about-palestinian-suffering.
118. John Cusack, *Twitter*, July 18, 2014, https://twitter.com/johncusack/status/498874243756033.
119. Zach Beauchamp, "Rihanna and Dwight Howard Tweeted #FreePalestine and It Worked Out How You Would Expect," *Vox*, July 15, 2014, https://www.vox.com/2014/7/15/5901881/rihanna-tweets-freepalestine-immediately-deletes-it.
120. Obeidallah, "How Jon Stewart Made It Okay."
121. Selena Gomez, @selenagomez, "It's about humanity, pray for Gaza," Instagram, July 18, 2014, https://www.instagram.com/p/qnOKwBujA9/?modal=true.
122. "Selena Gomez: Pro-Humanity or Pro-Hamas?? We Don't Know... Does She?," *TMZ*, July 19, 2014, https://www.tmz.com/2014/07/19/selena-gomez-gaza-instsagram-israel/#ixzz387DyQqCH.
123. "Celtic Receive UEFA Fine for Flying Palestine Flags in UCL Match," *ESPN.com*, September 29, 2016, https://www.espn.com/soccer/celtic/story/2961926/celtic-receive-uefa-fine-for-flying-palestine-flags-in-ucl-match.
124. Steward Fisher, "Political Football: How UEFA and FIFA Changed Stance After Banning Celtic Palestine Display & Barcelona Flags to Allow Ukraine Emblems,"

125. Al Mayadeen, "Palestinian Armbands to Challenge FIFA Double Standards in World Cup," *Al Mayadeen*, October 1, 2022, https://english.almayadeen.net/in-pictures/palestinian-armbands-to-challenge-fifa-double-standards-in-w.
126. Africa4Palestine, "About the Organization," accessed September 9, 2022, https://africa4palestine.com/about-us/.
127. Africa4Palestine, #africa4palestine, Instagram, accessed October 21, 2022, https://www.instagram.com/africa4palestine/.
128. Africa4Palestine, #africa4palestine, "Here is a video of Vanessa Redgrave," Instagram, accessed October 21, 2022, https://www.instagram.com/reel/CiK8t9Cq5Ed/?igshid=N2NmMDY0OWE%3D.
129. Richard F. Shepard, "Redgrave Film on P.L.O. Stirs a Controversy," *New York Times*, November 10, 1977, https://www.nytimes.com/1977/11/10/archives/westchester-opinion-redgrave-film-on-plo-stirs-a-controversy.html.
130. Jessica Steinberg, "Israel, Unfiltered," *Times of Israel*, November 25, 2014, https://www.timesofisrael.com/israel-unfiltered/.
131. Podcast and Curious, "How BOBBY LEE Became Propaganda for the Israeli Government," YouTube, June 27, 2022, https://www.youtube.com/watch?v=vPiYpW6qp6A.
132. Alan McLeod, "Top Hollywood Producers Worked with Israel to Defend Its War Crimes," *Israel Palestine News*, September 27, 2022, https://israelpalestinenews.org/top-hollywood-producers-worked-with-israel-to-defend-its-war-crimes/.
133. McLeod.
134. Michael Arria, "Arizona Lawmakers Melt Down Over Movie Screening," *Mondoweiss Newsletters*, accessed October 21, 2022, https://newsletters.mondoweiss.net/emails/webview/59730/67610146069546407.
135. Arria.
136. Cherien Dabis, "For Cherien Dabis, the Emmy-Nominated Palestinian American Director of 'Only Murders in the Building,' Storytelling Is a Matter of Survival," *Variety*, August 16, 2022, https://variety.com/2022/tv/news/cherien-dabis-emmy-nominated-only-murders-in-the-building-boy-from-6b-1235341938/.
137. "Cherien Davis," *Emmys*, accessed October 7, 2022, https://www.emmys.com/bios/cherien-dabis.
138. Tea Kvetanadze, "Author Sally Rooney Turns Down Israeli Publisher In Solidarity with Palestinians," *Forbes*, October 12, 2021, https://www.forbes.com/sites/teakvetenadze/2021/10/12/author-sally-rooney-turns-down-israeli-publisher-in-solidarity-with-palestinians/?sh=30393ff03fod.
139. Against Apartheid, "A Letter Against Apartheid," accessed September 15, 2022, https://www.againstapartheid.com/.
140. Alison Flood, "Alice Walker Declines Request to Publish Israeli Edition of The Color Purple," *Guardian*, June 20, 2012, https://www.theguardian.com/books/2012/jun/20/alice-walker-declines-israeli-color-purple.
141. Stephen Kerschner, "Ta-Nehisi Coates' Case for Reparations & Spiritual Awakening," *Critique*, July 14, 2016, http://www.thecritique.com/articles/ta-nehisi-coates-case-for-reparations-spiritual-awakening/.

3. SOCIAL CHANGE AND SOUND BITES

142. Rania Khalek, "Ta-Nehisi Coates Sings of Zionism," *Electronic Intifada*, February 23, 2016, https://electronicintifada.net/content/ta-nehisi-coates-sings-of-zionism/15776.
143. Democracy Now, "Ta-Nehisi Coates Speaks Out Against Israel's 'Segregationist Apartheid Regime' After West Bank Visit," November 2, 2023, https://www.democracynow.org/2023/11/2/ta_nehisi_coates.
144. Elizabeth Gwoskin and Gerrit De Vynck, "Facebook's AI Treats Palestinian Activists Like It Treats American Black Activists. It Blocks Them," *Washington Post*, May 28, 2021, https://www.washingtonpost.com/technology/2021/05/28/facebook-palestinian-censorship/.
145. Gwoskin and De Vynck.
146. Ryan Mac, "Instagram Censored Posts About One of Islam's Holiest Mosques, Drawing Employee Ire," *Buzzfeed News*, May 12, 2021, https://www.buzzfeednews.com/article/ryanmac/instagram-facebook-censored-al-aqsa-mosque.
147. Mac.
148. Arwa Mahdawi, "Bella Hadid's Deleted Instagram Post Shows How Palestinians Are Silenced," *Guardian*, July 15. 2020, https://www.theguardian.com/commentisfree/2020/jul/15/bella-hadid-deleted-instagram-post-palestinians-silenced.
149. Associated Press in Jerusalem, "Facebook and Israel to Work to Monitor Posts That Incite Violence," *Guardian*, September 12, 2016, https://www.theguardian.com/technology/2016/sep/12/facebook-israel-monitor-posts-incite-violence-social-media?CMP=twt_gu.
150. Sam Biddle, "Facebook Report Concludes Company Censorship Violated Palestinian Human Rights," *Intercept*, September 21, 2022, https://theintercept.com/2022/09/21/facebook-censorship-palestine-israel-algorithm/.
151. Gwoskin and De Vynck, "Facebook's AI Treats Palestinian Activists."
152. Marcy Oster, "Amazon Slammed for Free Shipping to Israeli Settlements but Not to Palestinian Territories," *Haaretz*, February 16, 2020, https://www.haaretz.com/israel-news/2020-02-16/ty-article/amazon-slammed-for-free-shipping-to-israeli-settlements-but-not-palestinians/0000017f-db5a-db22-a17f-fffb03020000.
153. Palestine Lobby, "The Last Apartheid on Earth," Instagram, November 7, 2022, https://www.instagram.com/reel/CkqauzNNKV8/?igshid=MDJmNzVkMjY%3D.
154. Loretta Alper and Jeremy Earp, dirs., *The Occupation of the American Mind: Israel's Public Relations War in the United States*, documentary (Northampton, Mass: Media Education Foundation, 2016), https://www.occupationmovie.org/.
155. Alper and Earp.
156. Linda A. Malone, "The Kahan Report, Ariel Sharon and the Sabra-Shatilla Massacres in Lebanon: Responsibility Under International Law for Massacres of Civilian Populations," *Utah Law Review* 1985, no. 2 (1985): 373–433.
157. Alper and Earp, *The Occupation of the American Mind*.
158. Alper and Earp.
159. Alper and Earp.
160. John J. Mearsheimer and Stephen M. Walt, *The Israel Lobby and U.S. Foreign Policy* (New York: Farrar, Straus and Giroux, 2007), 173.
161. Janice Terry, *U.S. Foreign Policy in the Middle East the Role of Lobbies and Special Interest Groups* (London: Pluto Press, 2005), 15.
162. Alper and Earp, *The Occupation of the American Mind*.

163. Amer Mohammedwesam, "Critical Discourse Analysis of War Reporting in the International Press: The Case of the Gaza War of 2008–2009," *Palgrave Communications* 3, no. 1 (2017), https://doi:10.1057/s41599-017-0015-2.
164. Rod Such, "What's Behind the U.S. Media's Special Relationship with Israel?" *Electronic Intifada*, June 3, 2016, https://electronicintifada.net/content/whats-behind-us-medias-special-relationship-israel/16951.
165. Robert I. Friedman, "Selling Israel to America," *Journal of Palestine Studies* 16, no. 4 (1987): 169–79, https://doi.org/10.2307/2536739.
166. Debbie Schlussel, "Mike Wallace, RIH: No Tears for Anti-Israel, Anti-American Propagandist & Liar," debbieschlussel.com, April 9, 2012, https://www.debbieschlussel.com/48763/mike-wallace-rih-no-tears-for-anti-israel-anti-american-propagandist-fabricator/comment-page-1/#comments.
167. Surabhi Vaya, "Gaza War: How Bias Affects Coverage of Israel-Palestine Conflict," *Firstpost*, July 23, 2014, https://www.firstpost.com/world/gaza-how-bias-affects-coverage-of-israel-palestine-conflict-1628973.html.
168. Colin Campbell, "NBC Reportedly Pulls Reporter Who Witnessed Child Deaths from Gaza," *Business Insider*, July 17, 2014, https://www.businessinsider.com/nbc-reportedly-pulls-ayman-mohyeldin-from-gaza-strip-2014-7#.
169. Vaya, "Gaza War."
170. Caroline Frost, "BBC News Chief Fran Unsworth Says Jon Snow's Emotional Video About Gaza Children Would Have Failed BBC Impartiality," *Huffington Post*, September 9, 2014, https://www.huffingtonpost.co.uk/2014/09/09/jon-snow-gaza-video-channel4-bbc-news-sky-rts_n_5791204.html.
171. Jon Snow, "Gaza: Mark Regev Interviewed by Jon Snow About IDF Attacks," YouTube, posted August 24, 2018, https://www.youtube.com/watch?v=HGahJzFdqaY.
172. Philip Weiss, "Geraldo Rivera Regrets Not Backing Palestinians in Second Intifada," *Mondoweiss*, April 3, 2018, http://mondoweiss.net/2018/04/geraldo-palestinians-intifada/.
173. Chris Ariens, "Bob Simon Calls Out Israeli Ambassador to U.S. in '60 Minutes' Report," *TV Newser*, April 23, 2012, https://www.adweek.com/tvnewser/bob-simon-calls-out-israeli-ambassador-to-u-s-in-60-minutes-report/125018/.
174. Yisrael Medad, "Bob Simon & CBS Throw the Jews to the Lions," *Jerusalem Post*, April 24, 2012, https://www.jpost.com/Blogs/Green-Lined/Bob-Simon-and-CBS-throw-the-Jews-to-the-lions-365810.
175. Paul Bond, "CBS Shareholders Accuse '60 Minutes' of Anti-Semitism," *Hollywood Reporter*, May 23, 2013, https://www.hollywoodreporter.com/tv/tv-news/cbs-shareholders-accuse-60-minutes-555375/.
176. Debbie Schlussel, "Bob Simon, Anti-Israel Self-Hating Jew Who Also Lied About U.S. in Vietnam, RIH," debbieschlussel.com, February 12, 2015, https://www.debbieschlussel.com/77169/bob-simon-anti-israel-self-hating-jew-who-also-lied-about-us-in-vietnam-rih/.
177. Hosam Salem, @hosamsalemg, "My statement following my dismissal from the New York Times," Twitter, October 5, 2022, https://twitter.com/HosamSalemG/status/1577634451307339776/photo/3.
178. "Jewish American Journalist Fired for Calling Israel 'Apartheid' State," *Palestine Chronicle*, October 3, 2022, https://www.palestinechronicle.com/jewish-american-journalist-fired-for-calling-israel-apartheid-state/.

3. SOCIAL CHANGE AND SOUND BITES

179. "Marc Lamont Hill Apologizes for Urging 'Free Palestine from River to Sea,'" *Times of Israel*, December 3, 2018, https://www.timesofisrael.com/marc-lamont-hill-apologizes-for-urging-free-palestine-from-river-to-sea/.
180. Breakfast Club, "Marc Lamont Hill Discusses Israeli-Palestinian Conflict, the Limits of Progressive Politics + More," YouTube, posted March 1, 2021, https://www.youtube.com/watch?v=WERKhWjmoLw.
181. Federica Marsi, "'From the River to the Sea': What Does the Palestinian Slogan Really Mean?" *Al Jazeera*, November 2, 2023, https://www.aljazeera.com/news/2023/11/2/from-the-river-to-the-sea-what-does-the-palestinian-slogan-really-mean.
182. Palestine Legal, *2021 Year-in-Review: Palestinian Uprising Generates Record Solidarity—and Fierce Backlash*, https://palestinelegal.org/s/Pal-Legal-2022-Report.pdf.
183. Alper and Earp, *The Occupation of the American Mind*.
184. Siobhan O'Grady, "A Palestinian Medic Was Shot Dead in Gaza. Now Israel Says It Will Investigate," *Washington Post*, June 2, 2018, https://www.washingtonpost.com/news/worldviews/wp/2018/06/02/a-palestinian-medic-was-shot-dead-in-gaza-now-israel-says-it-will-launch-a-probe/?utm_term=.39c0193773b9.
185. Marlow Stern, "Bill Maher and Bari Weiss Cruelly Blame Palestinians for Gaza Massacre," *Daily Beast*, May 19, 2018, https://www.thedailybeast.com/bill-maher-and-bari-weiss-blame-palestinians-for-gaza-massacre.
186. Stern.
187. Shmuel Rosner, "Israel Needs to Protect Its Borders. By Whatever Means Necessary," *New York Times*, May 18, 2018, https://www.nytimes.com/2018/05/18/opinion/israel-defend-gaza-border.html.
188. Matt Duss, interview by author, March 19, 2022.
189. John J. Mearsheimer and Stephen M. Walt, *The Israel Lobby and U.S. Foreign Policy*, (New York: Farrar, Straus and Giroux, 2007), 171.
190. Mearsheimer and Walt, 171, 172.
191. Peter Beinart, "Learning from Ukraine," *Beinart Notebook*, October 9, 2022, https://peterbeinart.substack.com/p/learning-from-ukraine.
192. Wayne J. Urban and Jennings L. Wagoner, Jr., *American Education: A History* (New York: Taylor and Francis, 2013).
193. University of Minnesota Library, "A Brief History of Education in the United States," accessed August 14, 2022, https://open.lib.umn.edu/sociology/chapter/16-1-a-brief-history-of-education-in-the-united-states/.
194. University of Minnesota Library.
195. Howard Zinn, *A People's History of the United States* (London: Taylor and Francis, 2015), 685.
196. "A People's History of the United States: 1492—Present," HowardZinn.com, accessed August 14, 2022, https://www.howardzinn.org/collection/peoples-history/.
197. Marcy Jane Knopf-Newman, *The Politics of Teaching Palestine to Americans: Addressing Pedagogical Strategies* (New York: Palgrave Macmillan, 2011), 101, 32.
198. Knopf-Newman, 59.
199. Knopf-Newman, 195.
200. Grant F. Smith, "Preventing Israel Lobby Propaganda in Textbooks," *Washington Report on Middle East Affairs* 39, no. 5 (August–September 2020), https://link.gale.com/apps/doc/A632776894/AONE.
201. Smith.

3. SOCIAL CHANGE AND SOUND BITES

202. Gabi Kirk, "Authors of California Ethnic Studies Curriculum Decry Cuts to Arab Studies," *Jewish Currents*, February 3. 2021, https://jewishcurrents.org/authors-of-california-ethnic-studies-curriculum-decry-cuts-to-arab-studies.
203. Jeanne Trabulsi, "Jeanne Trabulsi: The Fight Against Israeli Propaganda in Virginia Textbooks," *Washington Report on Middle East Affairs*, May 2022, https://www.wrmea.org/transcending-the-israel-lobby-at-home-and-abroad/jeanne-trabulsi-the-fight-against-israeli-propaganda-in-virginia-textbooks.html.
204. Trabulsi.
205. Josh Kosman, "Students Howl as McGraw-Hill, Cengage Textbook Merger Nears DOJ Approval," *New York Post*, December 16, 2019, https://nypost.com/2019/12/16/students-howl-as-mcgraw-hill-pearson-textbook-merger-nears-doj-approval/.
206. Trabulsi, "Jeanne Trabulsi."
207. Aron Keller, "How British Pro-Israel Groups Are Rewriting Middle East History Textbooks," *+972 Magazine*, July 16, 2021, https://www.972mag.com/uk-pearson-books-anti-palestinian-bias/.
208. Anti-Defamation League, "What We Do," accessed November 18, 2022, https://www.adl.org/about/education.
209. Rebecca Shimoni-Stoil, "ADL: Trump's comments misinterpreted, not anti-Semitic," *Times of Israel*, December 4, 2015, https://www.timesofisrael.com/adl-trumps-comments-misinterpreted-not-anti-semitic/.
210. DropTheADL, "Support for Actual Anti-Semites, Donald Trump, and Other Right-wing, Racist Influencers," accessed November 18, 2022, https://droptheadl.org/the-adl-is-not-an-ally/#trump.
211. DropTheADL, "Islamophobia/Anti-Muslim Racism & Anti-Arab Racism," accessed November 20, 2022, https://droptheadl.org/the-adl-is-not-an-ally/#islamophobia.
212. Elly Bulkin and Donna Nevel, "Follow the Money: From Islamophobia to Israel Right or Wrong," AlterNet, October 3, 2012, https://www.alternet.org/2012/10/follow-money-islamophobia-israel-right-or-wrong/.
213. Thea Renda Abu El-Haj, *Unsettled Belonging: Educating Palestinian American Youth After 9/11* (Chicago: University of Chicago Press, 2015), 285, 286.
214. Ewan Palmer, "School Lesson Comparing Palestinian Plight to American Revolution Withdrawn," *Newsweek*, July 15, 2021, https://www.newsweek.com/israel-palestinians-school-question-washington-native-americans-1609998.
215. Jonah Cohen, "Washington State Removes Anti-Israel Lesson from K-12 Native American Curriculum," Jewish News Syndicate, July 8, 2021, https://www.jns.org/opinion/washington-state-removes-anti-israel-lesson-from-k-12-native-american-curriculum/.
216. Ari Hoffman, "Washington State Removes Anti-Semitic Material Curriculum on Native Americans, but Fails to Address Textbooks," *Post Millenial*, July 19, 2021, https://thepostmillennial.com/washington-state-removes-anti-semitic-material-curriculum-on-native-americans-but-fails-to-address-textbooks.
217. Palestine Legal, "Palestine Legal Urges Dept. of Education to End Extreme Delay into First-Ever Anti-Palestinian Discrimination Complaint," November 15, 2022, https://palestinelegal.org/news/2022/11/15/palestine-legal-urges-dept-of-education-to-end-extreme-delay-into-first-ever-anti-palestinian-discrimination-complaint.

3. SOCIAL CHANGE AND SOUND BITES

218. Dima Khalidi, interview by author, March 15, 2021.
219. Dima Khalidi interview.
220. Naomi Dann, "Criticism of Israel Is Not Anti-Semitism," *Jewish Voice for Peace*, May 4, 2015, https://www.jewishvoiceforpeace.org/2015/05/criticism-of-israel-is-not-anti-semitism/.
221. Times Editorial Board, "Editorial: Undermining Free Speech on Campus," *Los Angeles Times*, December 6, 2016, https://www.latimes.com/opinion/editorials/la-ed-senate-antisemitism-20161202-story.html.
222. Alex Emmons, "Senate Responds to Trump-Inspired Anti-Semitism by Targeting Students Who Criticize Israel," *Intercept*, December 2, 2016, https://theintercept.com/2016/12/02/senate-responds-to-post-trump-anti-semitism-by-targeting-students-who-criticize-israel/.
223. Murtaza Hussein, "Students in California Might Face Criminal Investigation for Protesting Film on Isreali Army," *Intercept*, June 23, 2016, https://theintercept.com/2016/06/23/students-in-california-might-face-criminal-investigation-for-protesting-film-on-israeli-army/.
224. Ehab Zahriyeh, "Report: Anti-Semitism Charges Used to Curb Pro-Palestinian Campus Speech," *Al Jazeera America*, September 30, 2015, http://america.aljazeera.com/articles/2015/9/30/anti-semitism-claims-used-to-crush-pro-palestinian-speech-on-campuses.html.
225. Peter Moskowitz, "The Campus Free Speech Battle You're Not Seeing," *Jezebel*, February 13, 2017, https://jezebel.com/the-campus-free-speech-battle-youre-not-seeing-1791631293.
226. Murtaza Hussain, "Professor Hopes to Return After Being Fired for "Disrespectful" Tweets Against Israel," *Intercept*, October 20, 2015, https://theintercept.com/2015/10/20/professor-hopes-to-return-after-being-fired-for-disrespectful-tweets-against-israel/.
227. Dima Khalidi interview.
228. "About Campus Watch," accessed September 19, 2022, https://www.meforum.org/campus-watch/about.
229. Tamar Lewin, "Web Site Fuels Debate on Campus Anti-Semitism," *New York Times*, September 27, 2002, https://www.nytimes.com/2002/09/27/us/web-site-fuels-debate-on-campus-anti-semitism.html.
230. Campus Watch, "Howler of the Month Archive," accessed September 19, 2022, https://www.meforum.org/campus-watch/howler-of-the-month/.
231. Canary Mission homepage, accessed September 27, 2022, https://canarymission.org/.
232. Paul Miller, "Exclusive: Sheldon Adelson Deploys Task Force to Combat Soaring Campus Anti-Semitism," *Observer*, August 9, 2016, https://observer.com/2016/08/exclusive-sheldon-adelson-deploys-task-force-to-combat-soaring-campus-anti-semitism/.
233. International Holocaust Remembrance Alliance, "What Is Antisemitism?" accessed September 8, 2022, https://www.holocaustremembrance.com/resources/working-definitions-charters/working-definition-antisemitism.
234. Maccabee Task Force homepage, accessed September 8, 2022, https://www.maccabeetaskforce.org/about/.

235. BDS Movement, "Portland State University Students Vote in Favour of Divestment in Support of Palestinian Human Rights," October 26, 2016, https://bdsmovement.net/news/portland-state-university-students-vote-favour-divestment-support-palestinian-human-rights.
236. Mike Anton, Nicole Santa Cruz, and Lauren Williams, "Students Guilty of Disrupting Speech in Irvine 11 Case," *Los Angeles Times*, September 24, 2011, http://articles.latimes.com/2011/sep/24/local/la-me-irvine-eleven-20110924.
237. Murtaza Hussain, "Students in California Might Face Criminal Investigation for Protesting Film on Israeli," *Intercept*, June 23, 2016, https://theintercept.com/2016/06/23/students-in-california-might-face-criminal-investigation-for-protesting-film-on-israeli-army/.
238. Erwin Chemerinsky, "Dean's Message: Our Community," Berkeley Law, October 21, 2022, https://www.law.berkeley.edu/article/deans-message-our-community-10-21-2022/.
239. Adam Sabes, "California, Berkeley University Law School Student Orgs Pledge to Boycott Zionist, Pro-Israel Speakers," *Fox News*, August 28, 2022, https://www.foxnews.com/us/california-berkeley-university-law-school-student-orgs-pledge-boycott-zionist-pro-israel-speakers.
240. "The Crimson's Anti-Palestinian Bias," *Harvard Political Review*, March 10, 2013, https://harvardpolitics.com/the-crimsons-anti-palestinian-bias/.
241. Crimson Editorial Board, "In Support of Boycott, Divest, Sanctions and a Free Palestine," *Harvard Crimson*, April 29, 2022, https://www.thecrimson.com/article/2022/4/29/editorial-bds/.
242. Miles J. Herszenshorn, "Anti-War Activists Protest Harvard Kennedy School Professor with Ties to Defense Contractor," *Harvard Crimson*, October 5, 2022, https://www.thecrimson.com/article/2022/10/5/hks-osullivan-class-protest/.
243. Jared Stone and Orli Epstein, "Caterpillar Referendum Peddles the Hate and Bigotry of the Global BDS Movement," *Daily Princetonian*, April 4, 2022, https://www.dailyprincetonian.com/article/2022/04/caterpillar-referendum-princeton-bds-hate.
244. Reid Zlotsky, "Caterpillar Referendum Supporters Avoid a Debate They Know They Can't Win," *Daily Princetonian*, April 7, 2022, https://www.dailyprincetonian.com/article/2022/04/princeton-bds-debate-caterpillar-referendum.
245. Alexandra Orbuch, "BDS-Aligned Referendum Fails to Win Majority Support," *Princeton Tory*, April 13, 2022, http://theprincetontory.com/princeton-bds-aligned-referendum-fails-to-win-majority-support/.
246. Jared Stone, "A Response to BDS at Princeton," *Jerusalem Post*, May 22, 2022, https://www.jpost.com/opinion/article-707403.
247. Alexandra Orbuch, "USG Approves BDS-Aligned Referendum," *Princeton Tory*, March 29, 2022, http://theprincetontory.com/usg-approves-bds-aligned-referendum-news/.
248. "Pro-Palestine Student Activists Targeted on College Campuses," *Washington Report on Middle East Affairs* 35, no. 1 (January/February 2016): 58, https://issuu.com/washreport/docs/volxxvno1-lo2.
249. Jessica Schulberg, "Student Felt 'Criminalized' After Campus Police Made Him Remove Palestinian Flag," *Huffington Post*, December 9, 2015, https://www.huffpost.com/entry/gw-palestinian-flag_n_5668bb47e4b080eddf56f7e2.

3. SOCIAL CHANGE AND SOUND BITES

250. Suhaib Khan and Rina Abd El Rahman, "Palestine Center Annual Conference Educates and Updates Attendees," *Washington Report on Middle East Affairs* 35, no. 1 (2016): 57–60.
251. Faida Abu-Ghazaleh, *Ethnic Identity of Palestinian Immigrants in the United States: The Role of Material Cultural Artifacts* (El Paso, Tex.: LFB Scholarly, 2010), 20.
252. Margaret Ferguson, "Former President of Modern Language Association Resigns Following Decision to Ban Debate on BDS," *Mondoweiss*, February 15, 2018, https://mondoweiss.net/2018/02/president-association-following/.
253. Mearsheimer and Walt, *The Israel Lobby*, 141.
254. Kenneth Marcus, "Berkeley Develops Jewish-Free Zones," *Jewish Journal*, September 28, 2022, https://jewishjournal.com/commentary/opinion/351854/berkeley-develops-jewish-free-zones/.
255. Ross E. Hassner and Ethan B. Katz, "UC Berkeley Has Many Jewish-Filled 'Zones.' If You Want to Support Campus Jews, Learn About Them," *Forward*, October 3, 2022, https://forward.com/opinion/520107/uc-berkeley-has-many-jewish-filled-zones/.
256. Rob Eshman, "Berkeley's 'Jew-Free Zones': Fake News That Does Real Damage," *Forward*, October 7, 2022, https://forward.com/opinion/520623/berkeleys-jew-free-zones-are-fake-news-that-do-real-damage/.
257. Eshman.
258. Edward Said, "My Encounter with Sartre," *London Review of Books* 22, no. 11 (June 1, 2000), https://www.lrb.co.uk/the-paper/v22/n11/edward-said/diary.
259. U.S. Department of Education, Office for Civil Rights, "Questions and Answers on Executive Order 13899 (Combating Anti-Semitism) and OCR's Enforcement of Title VI of the Civil Rights Act of 1964," January 19, 2021, https://www2.ed.gov/about/offices/list/ocr/docs/qa-titleix-anti-semitism-20210119.pdf.
260. Nora Barrows-Friedman, "Arizona University Forces Speakers to Sign Pledge They Don't Boycott Israel," *Electronic Intifada*, March 7, 2018, https://electronicintifada.net/blogs/nora-barrows-friedman/arizona-university-forces-speakers-sign-pledge-they-dont-boycott-israel.
261. Mearsheimer and Walt, *The Israel Lobby*, 183.
262. "Kennedy New UI Board of Trustees Chair," *Illinois Public Media*, September 10, 2009; *Loevy and Loevy*, "Settlement Reached in Case of Professor Fired for 'Uncivil' Tweets," November 12, 2015, https://www.loevy.com/blog/settlement-reached-in-case-of-professor-fired-for-uncivil-tweets/.
263. *Loevy and Loevy*.
264. Colleen Flaherty, "Steven Salaita Says He's Leaving Academe," *Inside Higher Ed*, July 24, 2017, https://www.insidehighered.com/quicktakes/2017/07/25/steven-salaita-says-hes-leaving-academe.
265. Matthew Abraham, *Out of Bounds: Academic Freedom and the Question of Palestine* (London: Bloomsbury, 2014), 86.
266. Yossi Melman, "Israel Denies Entry to High-Profile Critic Norman Finkelstein," *Haaretz*, May 24, 2008, https://www.haaretz.com/2008-05-24/ty-article/israel-denies-entry-to-high-profile-critic-norman-finkelstein/0000017f-e8bf-df5f-a17f-fbff95530000.
267. Ben Harris, "American Radical," Jewish Telegraphic Agency, November, 23, 2009, https://www.jta.org/2009/11/23/global/american-radical.

268. Alexander Nazaryan, "Dartmouth Dean Sparks Debate on the State of Israel and Anti-Semitism," *Newsweek*, May 21, 2017, http://www.newsweek.com/dartmouth-dean-accused-anti-israel-bias-colleague-611113.
269. Peter Moskowitz, "The Campus Free Speech Battle You're Not Seeing," *Jezebel*, February 13, 2016, https://jezebel.com/the-campus-free-speech-battle-youre-not-seeing-1791631293.
270. Mark G. Yudof and Ken Walzer, "Majoring in Anti-Semitism at Vassar," *Wall Street Journal*, February 17, 2016, https://www.wsj.com/articles/majoring-in-anti-semitism-at-vassar-1455751940.
271. Moskowitz, "The Campus Free Speech Battle."
272. Bernd Debusmann Jr., "Claudine Gay: Pressure Mounts on Harvard President to Step Down," BBC, December 11, 2023, https://www.bbc.com/news/world-us-canada-67684309.
273. Michael T. Nietzel, "College Presidents Issue Statement Supporting Israel and 'Moral Clarity' in War with Hamas," *Forbes*, October 18, 2023.
274. Khaleda Rahman. "Full List of US Universities Staging Pro-Palestinian Protests," *Newsweek*, October 11, 2023, https://www.newsweek.com/full-list-universities-staging-pro-palestinian-protests-1833807.
275. Sara Roy, interview by author, March 22, 2021.
276. Alice Rothchild, "When Donor Pressure Threatens to Erase Palestine from Academia," *Mondoweiss*, October 27, 2022, https://mondoweiss.net/2022/10/when-donor-pressure-threatens-to-erase-palestine-from-academia/.
277. Rothchild.
278. Rothchild.
279. Abigail Anthony, "Israeli Minister Asks Princeton to Remove 'Antisemitic Propaganda' from Course," *National Review*, August 17, 2023, https://www.nationalreview.com/news/israeli-minister-asks-princeton-to-remove-antisemitic-propaganda-from-course.
280. Michael Massing, "Why the Godfather of Human Rights Not Welcome at Harvard," *Nation*, January 5, 2023, https://www.thenation.com./article/society/hrw-harvard-israel-kennedy-school/.
281. Nadine Bahour and Shraddha Joshi, "Harvard Changes Its Mind on Ken Roth—Not on Allowing Free Speech About Palestine," *Nation*, January 24, 2023, https://www.thenation.com/article/activism/harvard-roth-palestine-free-speech/.
282. Timothy Nerozzi, "Pro-Palestinian Students Demand Israeli Prime Minister's Name Be Removed from Campus Library," *Fox News*, January 2024, https://www.msn.com/en-us/news/us/pro-palestinian-students-demand-israeli-prime-minister-s-name-be-removed-from-campus-library/ar-BB1gXsrL.
283. Benjamin Wallace-Wells, "Why a State Department Official Lost Hope in Israel," *New Yorker*, November 6, 2023, https://www.newyorker.com/news/the-political-scene/why-a-state-department-official-lost-hope-in-israel.
284. Asma Khalid, "Biden Faces Pushback Within His Own Party for His Unwavering Support of Israel," NPR, January 19, 2024, https://www.npr.org/2024/01/19/1225573911/biden-faces-pushback-within-his-own-party-for-his-unwavering-support-of-israel.
285. Sara Roy interview.

4. THE INTENSIFICATION OF POLITICAL AND LEGAL BATTLES IN THE UNITED STATES AND BEYOND

1. "Israel: Provide Vaccines to Occupied Palestinians," *Human Rights Watch*, January 17, 2021, https://www.hrw.org/news/2021/01/17/israel-provide-vaccines-occupied-palestinians.
2. Keith P. Feldman, *A Shadow Over Palestine: The Imperial Life of Race in America* (Minneapolis: University of Minnesota Press, 2015), 1.
3. "Trump Administration Issues Rule Further Watering Down Obamacare," Reuters, October 26, 2017, https://www.reuters.com/article/us-usa-healthcare-regulation/trump-administration-issues-rule-further-watering-down-obamacare-idUSKBN1HG384.
4. Saree Makdisi, *Tolerance Is a Wasteland: Palestine and the Culture of Denial*, (Oakland: University of California Press, 2022), 2.
5. Makdisi, *Tolerance Is a Wasteland*, 1–2.
6. Keith Peter Kiely, *U.S. Foreign Policy Discourse and the Israel Lobby: The Clinton Administration and the Israel-Palestine Peace Process* (Cham, Switz.: Springer International, 2017), 106.
7. Rawan Arar, Review of *A Shadow Over Palestine: The Imperial Life of Race in America*," *Ethnic and Racial Studies* 39, no. 8 (2016): 1490, https://doi:10.1080/01419870.2015.1131321.
8. Makdisi, *Tolerance Is a Wasteland*, 5.
9. Khaled Elgindy, *Blind Spot: America and the Palestinians, from Balfour to Trump*, (Washington, D.C: Brookings Institution Press, 2019), 21.
10. "Sen. Cruz Condemns Renewed Violence Against Israel," *Ted Cruz for Congress*, May 6, 2019, https://www.cruz.senate.gov/newsroom/press-releases/sen-cruz-condemns-renewed-violence-against-israel.
11. Elgindy, *Blind Spot*, 19.
12. Elgindy, 20.
13. Elgindy, 36.
14. Quoted in Elgindy, 32.
15. Elgindy, 33.
16. Elgindy, 35, 34, 36.
17. Elgindy, 33.
18. David A. Charters, "Jewish Terrorism and the Modern Middle East," *Journal of Conflict Studies* 27, no. 2 (2007), https://journals.lib.unb.ca/index.php/JCS/article/view/10538.
19. Elgindy, *Blind Spot*, 50.
20. Thomas J. Hamilton, "Jews to Proclaim State Despite US," *New York Times*, May 11, 1948, https://www.nytimes.com/1948/05/11/archives/jews-to-proclaim-state-despite-us-un-assembly-held-limited-to.html.
21. Elgindy, *Blind Spot*, 53.
22. Loretta Alper and Jeremy Earp, dirs., *The Occupation of the American Mind: Israel's Public Relations War in the United States* (Northampton, Mass: Media Education Foundation, 2016).
23. Elgindy, *Blind Spot*, 56.

4. INTENSIFICATION OF POLITICAL AND LEGAL BATTLES

24. Mohammed Haddad, "Nakba Day: What Happened in Palestine in 1948?," *Al Jazeera*, May 12, 2022, https://www.aljazeera.com/news/2022/5/15/nakba-mapping-palestinian-villages-destroyed-by-israel-in-1948.
25. Osama Khalil, "Pax Americana: The United States, the Palestinians, and the Peace Process, 1948–2008," *CR: The New Centennial Review* 8, no. 2 (Fall 2008): 1–41.
26. Peter Hahn, "The Suez Crisis (1956)," *Origins*, October 2021, https://origins.osu.edu/milestones/suez-crisis-1956.
27. W. E. B. Du Bois, "Suez," *AfroPoets Famous Writers*, accessed November 23, 2022, https://www.afropoets.net/webdubois1.html. See also Keith Feldman, "Representing Permanent War: Black Power's Palestine and the End(s) of Civil Rights," *CR: The New Centennial Review* 8, no. 2 (Fall 2008): 193–231.
28. "Security Council Resolution 242: The Situation in the Middle East," November 22, 1967, https://peacemaker.un.org/middle-east-resolution242.
29. Elgindy, *Blind Spot*, 95.
30. Elgindy, 95.
31. U.S. Department of State, *Foreign Relations of the United States: Diplomatic Papers* (Washington, D.C.: U.S. Government Printing Office, 1969), 581.
32. Office of the Chief of Staff Files, Hamilton Jordan's Confidential Files, Middle East, 1978, Container 35, Jimmy Carter Library, accessed November 9, 2022, https://www.jimmycarterlibrary.gov/digital_library/cos/142099/35/cos_142099_35_19-Middle_East_1977_2.pdf.
33. Hilton Obenzinger, "Palestine Solidarity, Political Discourse, and the Peace Movement, 1982–1988," *CR: The New Centennial Review* 8, no. 2 (Fall 2008): 233–52.
34. Martin Gouterman, "Toward a Jewish component of the Rainbow Coalition," *Monthly Review* (January 1988), https://link.gale.com/apps/doc/A6319805/AONE?u=seat57527&sid=googleScholar&xid=1add4440.
35. Sarah Pruitt, "How Jesse Jackson's Rainbow Coalition Championed Diversity," *History*, January 29, 2021, https://www.history.com/news/jesse-jackson-rainbow-coalition.
36. Elgindy, *Blind Spot*, 106.
37. Janice Terry, *U.S. Foreign Policy in the Middle East the Role of Lobbies and Special Interest Groups* (London: Pluto Press, 2005), 31.
38. Edward Said, "An Open Letter to Jewish American Intellectuals," *Jewish Currents*, September 21, 2022, https://jewishcurrents.org/an-open-letter-to-american-jewish-intellectuals.
39. Elgindy, *Blind Spot*, 13.
40. Elgindy, 149.
41. Office of the Historian, "The Oslo Accords and the Arab-Israeli Peace Process," accessed September 12, 2002, https://history.state.gov/milestones/1993-2000/oslo.
42. Alper and Earp, *The Occupation of the American Mind*.
43. Mark Memmott, "At White House, Netanyahu Calls '67 Border Lines 'Indefensible,'" NPR, May 20, 2011, https://www.npr.org/sections/thetwo-way/2011/05/24/136500693/at-white-house-netanyahu-calls-67-border-lines-indefensible.
44. Zeke Miller, "Transcript: Netanyahu Speech to Congress," *Time*, March 3, 2015, https://time.com/3730318/transcript-netanyahu-speech-to-congress/.
45. Shlomo Ben Ami and Norman Finkelstein, interview by Amy Goodman, "Fmr. Israeli Foreign Minister: 'If I were a Palestinian, I Would Have Rejected Camp

4. INTENSIFICATION OF POLITICAL AND LEGAL BATTLES

David,'" *Democracy Now*, February 14, 2006, https://www.democracynow.org/2006/2/14/fmr_israeli_foreign_minister_if_i.
46. Anthony York, "Muslims Charge They Are Being Scapegoated," *Salon*, November 2, 2000, https://www.salon.com/2000/11/02/ama/.
47. Elgindy, *Blind Spot*, 161.
48. Keynote Address by Secretary of State Condoleezza Rice at ATFP Inaugural Gala, American Task Force on Palestine, accessed October 3, 2022, http://www.americantaskforce.org/keynote_address_secretary_state_condoleezza_rice_atfp_inaugural_gala.
49. Elgindy, *Blind Spot*, 161.
50. John J. Mearsheimer and Stephen M. Walt, *The Israel Lobby and U.S. Foreign Policy* (New York: Farrar, Straus and Giroux, 2007), 176.
51. Elgindy, *Blind Spot*, 191.
52. White House Office of the Press Secretary, "Remarks by the President on the Middle East and North Africa," May 19, 2011, https://obamawhitehouse.archives.gov/the-press-office/2011/05/19/remarks-president-middle-east-and-north-africa%20.
53. Alper and Earp, *The Occupation of the American Mind*.
54. "Return to Israel's 1967 Borders National Suicide?," *Christian Broadcasting Network*, May 24, 2011, https://www.youtube.com/watch?v=hAZrKlRJZNw.
55. "Obama Under Fire for Comment on Palestinians," *NBC News*, March 15, 2007, https://www.nbcnews.com/id/wbna17631015.
56. Elgindy, *Blind Spot*, 222.
57. Marc Lamont Hill and Mitchell Plitnick, *Except for Palestine: The Limits of Progressive Politics* (New York: New Press, 2021), 7.
58. Julian Borger and Peter Beaumont, "US: Israeli Settlements No Impediment to Peace but May Not Be Helpful," *Guardian*, February 3, 2017, https://www.theguardian.com/world/2017/feb/03/trump-says-israeli-settlements-not-impediment-to-peace-but-expansion-unhelpful.
59. Jewish Telegraphic Agency, "Jared Kushner's Family Foundation Donated Tens of Thousands of Dollars to West Bank Groups," December 5, 2016, https://www.jta.org/2016/12/05/politics/foundation-of-jared-kushners-parents-donated-tens-of-thousands-of-dollars-to-west-bank-groups.
60. Barak Ravid, "Deputy Foreign Minister: 1967 Borders Are Auschwitz Borders," *Haaretz*, January 2, 2014, https://www.haaretz.com/2014-01-02/ty-article/1967-borders-are-auschwitz-borders/0000017f-dbc1-db22-a17f-fff146410000.
61. Shibley Telhami, "Arab and American Dimensions of the Israel/Palestine Issue: State Policies and Public Views on One State, Two States, and Beyond," in *The One State Reality: What Is Israel/Palestine?*, ed. Shibley Telhami et al. (Ithaca, N.Y.: Cornell University Press, 2023), 203.
62. Trump White House Archives, "President Donald J. Trump Keeps His Promise to Open U.S. Embassy in Jerusalem, Israel," May 14, 2018, https://trumpwhitehouse.archives.gov/briefings-statements/president-donald-j-trump-keeps-promise-open-u-s-embassy-jerusalem-israel/.
63. Elgindy, *Blind Spot*, 247.
64. Elgindy, 230, 249.
65. Elgindy, 249.

66. "Full Text: Trump's Proclamation Recognizing Israeli Sovereignty Over Golan Heights," *Haaretz*, March 25, 2019, https://www.haaretz.com/israel-news/2019-03-25/ty-article/full-text-trumps-proclamation-recognizing-israeli-sovereignty-over-golan-heights/0000017f-f80f-d887-a7ff-f8ef294b0000.
67. Hill and Plitnick, *Except for Palestine*, 70.
68. Tovah Lazaroff, "Netanyahu: A Palestinian State Won't Be Created," *Jerusalem Post*, April 8, 2019, https://www.jpost.com/arab-israeli-conflict/netanyahu-a-palestinian-state-wont-be-created-586017.
69. Hill and Plitnick, *Except for Palestine*, 90, 92, 6, 3–4, 92–93.
70. Omri Nahmias, "Bipartisan Letter Urges Austin to Provide Emergency Funding for Iron Dome," *Jerusalem Post*, June 2, 2021, https://www.jpost.com/american-politics/bipartisan-letter-urges-austin-to-provide-emergency-funding-for-iron-dome-669941.
71. "Mccollum Resolution Calls on U.S. House to Condemn Israel's Repressive Decision to Designate Six Prominent Palestinian Human Rights and Civil Society Groups as Terrorist Organizations," October 28, 2021, https://mccollum.house.gov/media/press-releases/mccollum-resolution-calls-us-house-condemn-israel-s-repressive-decision.
72. John Mason, "Rep. Tlaib's Remarks on 'Apartheid' Israel Misinterpreted as Anti-Semitic," *Arab America*, September 28, 2022, https://www.arabamerica.com/rep-tlaibs-remarks-on-apartheid-israel-misinterpreted-as-anti-semitic/.
73. Akbarzai et al., "Israel Reveals US Probe Into Shireen Abu Akleh's Death but Says It 'Will Not Cooperate,'" CNN, November 15, 2022, https://www.cnn.com/2022/11/15/middleeast/shireen-abu-akleh-israel-us-investigation-intl.
74. Olivia Land and Emily Crane, "Biden Rebukes Russia Over War with Ukraine at UN General Assembly," *New York Post*, September 21, 2022, https://nypost.com/2022/09/21/biden-to-rebuke-russia-over-ukraine-war-at-un/.
75. KUVRD Team, "Civilized vs Uncivilized: An Analysis of Ukraine, Palestine & Beyond," KUVRD, April 28, 2022, https://kuvrd.ca/blogs/blog/civilized-vs-uncivilized-humanity-divided.
76. Land and Crane, "Biden Rebukes Russia."
77. "US Will 'Fight' Any Israeli Annexation, Ambassador Says," *Middle East Eye*, November 10, 2022, https://www.middleeasteye.net/news/us-will-fight-any-israeli-annexation-ambassador-says.
78. Omar Suleiman, "Israel Has Lost the War of Public Opinion," *Al Jazeera*, November 30, 2023, https://www.aljazeera.com/opinions/2023/11/30/israel-has-lost-the-war-of-public-opinion; Jason Lange and Matt Spetalnick, "US Public Support for Israel Drops; Majority Backs a Ceasefire, Reuters/Ipsos Shows," Reutrs, November 15, 2023, https://www.reuters.com/world/us-public-support-israel-drops-majority-backs-ceasefire-reutersipsos-2023-11-15/; Shibley Telhami, "Is the Israel-Gaza War Changing US Public Attidues?," Brookings Institution, November 2, 2023, https://www.brookings.edu/articles/is-the-israel-gaza-war-changing-us-public-attitudes/.
79. Matthew Lee, "The Biden Administration Once Again Bypasses Congress on an Emergency Weapons Sale to Israel," AP, https://apnews.com/article/us-israel-gaza-arms-hamas-bypass-congress-1dc77f20aac4a797df6a2338b677da4f.
80. Ingrid Jacques, "Biden Tries to Shake Off 'Genocide Joe' Epithet, but It Could Be the Issue That Sinks Him," *USA Today*, February 7, 2024, https://www.usatoday

.com/story/opinion/columnist/2024/02/07/biden-israel-gaza-genocide-democrats-2024-election/72480021007/.
81. White House, "Remarks by President Biden on the October 7th Terrorist Attacks and the Resilience of the State of Israel and Its People," October 18, 2023, https://www.whitehouse.gov/briefing-room/speeches-remarks/2023/10/18/remarks-by-president-biden-on-the-october-7th-terrorist-attacks-and-the-resilience-of-the-state-of-israel-and-its-people-tel-aviv-israel/.
82. Dov Lieber, "Seeking Solace After Oct. 7 Attack, Many Israelis View Biden as Their Wartime Leader," *Wall Street Journal*, October 20, 2023, https://www.wsj.com/world/middle-east/seeking-solace-after-oct-7-attack-many-israelis-view-biden-as-their-wartime-leader-31705e37.
83. Julia Frankel, "Israel's Netanyahu Rejects Any Palestinian Sovereignty in Postwar Gaza, Rebuffing Biden," AP, January 20, 2024, https://apnews.com/article/israel-hamas-war-news-01-20-2024-ba66b165f3e5d1904d30b591199cface.
84. Ken Tran, "The House Rejected a Bill That Would Have Provided $17.6 Billion in Israel Aid. Here's Why," *USA Today*, February 6, 2024, https://www.usatoday.com/story/news/politics/2024/02/06/border-fight-house-rejects-bill-providing-17-6-billion-in-israel-aid/72484626007/.
85. Joey Cappelleti and Will Weissert, "Biden Reelection Campaign Team Gets Shunned by Some Arab American Leaders While Visiting Michigan," AP, January 26, 2024, https://apnews.com/article/biden-campaign-arab-american-support-israel-michigan-cf331a82f907fe70e22d5f0aa6d7346e.
86. Colleen Long, Zeke Miller, and Aamer Madhani, "Biden Sanctions Israeli Settlers Accused of Attacking Palestinians and Peace Activists in West Bank," AP, February 1, 2024, https://apnews.com/article/biden-west-bank-israeli-settlers-palestinians-80f9e6be6f6a7bb75dc86360ac2fa6ce.
87. Elgindy, *Blind Spot*, 21.
88. Mearsheimer and Walt, *The Israel Lobby*, 115.
89. Mearsheimer and Walt, 111.
90. John J. Mearsheimer, and Stephen M. Walt. "The Israel Lobby and U.S. Foreign Policy," *Middle East Policy* 13, no. 3 (2006): 29–87, https://doi:10.1111/j.1475-4967.2006.00260.x.
91. Feldman, *A Shadow Over Palestine*, 117.
92. Mearsheimer and Walt, *The Israel Lobby*, 134, 135.
93. "AIPAC Letter to Supporters," March 18, 2022, *Jewish Insider*, https://jewishinsider.nyc3.digitaloceanspaces.com/wp-content/uploads/2022/03/17214409/AIPAC-Letter-With-Watermark.pdf.
94. MJ Rosenberg, "Sorry, Democrats: Your NRA Is Spelled AIPAC," *Huffpost*, October 5, 2017, https://www.huffingtonpost.com/entry/sorry-democrats-your-nra-is-spelled-aipac_us_59d62c62e4b0666ad0c3cb12.
95. Mearsheimer and Walt, *The Israel Lobby*, 27, 28.
96. Open Secrets, "Pro-Israel Money to Congress," https://www.opensecrets.org/industries./totals.php?cycle=2018&ind=Q05 and https://www.opensecrets.org/industries/summary?cycle=All&ind=Q05&recipdetail=S.
97. Mearsheimer and Walt, *The Israel Lobby*, 170.
98. Hassan Abbas, "New Analysis Shows AIPAC Has Spent Millions to Fund U.S. Congressional Trips to Israel," *Arab American News*, June 27, 2019, https://www

.arabamericannews.com/2019/06/27/new-analysis-shows-aipac-has-spent-millions-to-fund-u-s-congressional-trips-to-israel/.
99. Mearsheimer and Walt, *The Israel Lobby*, 177.
100. Rosenberg, "Sorry, Democrats."
101. Mearsheimer and Walt, "The Israel Lobby."
102. Mearsheimer and Walt, *The Israel Lobby*, 178.
103. Dima Khalidi, interview by author, March 15, 2021.
104. Mearsheimer and Walt, *The Israel Lobby*, 204–5.
105. Mearsheimer and Walt, 141.
106. Michelle Alexander, "Time to Break the Silence on Palestine," *New York Times*, January 19, 2019, https://www.nytimes.com/2019/01/19/opinion/sunday/martin-luther-king-palestine-israel.html.
107. Adam Johnson and Ali Othman, "Coverage of Gaza War in the New York Times and Other Major Newspapers Heavily Favored Israel, Analysis Shows," *Intercept*, January 9, 2024, https://theintercept.com/2024/01/09/newspapers-israel-palestine-bias-new-york-times/.
108. Benoît Brévillé, "Ukraine and Gaza: Double Standards," *Le Monde diplomatique*, January 2024, https://mondediplo.com/2024/01/01editorial.
109. Mearsheimer and Walt, *The Israel Lobby*, 152, 153.
110. Mearsheimer and Walt, 134.
111. Hagee, *Jerusalem Countdown: A Prelude to War*, 3.
112. International Fellowship of Christians and Jews, "Stand for Israel," accessed October 3, 2022, https://www.ifcj.org/who-we-are/programs/stand-for-israel.
113. International Fellowship of Christians and Jews, "Victims of Terror and War" accessed October 3, 2022, https://www.ifcj.org/who-we-help/victims-of-terror-and-war.
114. Mearsheimer and Walt, *The Israel Lobby*, 138.
115. Paul Findley, *They Dare to Speak Out: People and Institutions Confront Israel's Lobby* (Chicago: Chicago Review Press, 2003), 1–2.
116. Terry, *U.S. Foreign Policy in the Middle East*, 16.
117. John Martin Collins, *Global Palestine* (London: Hurst, 2011), 7.
118. Bill Varian, "Al-Arian's Rise in U.S. Began in Academics," *Tampa Bay (Fla.) Times*, February 21, 2003, https://www.tampabay.com/archive/2003/02/21/al-arian-s-rise-in-u-s-began-in-academics/.
119. James Harper, "Professor's Home, Office Searched," *St. Petersburg (Fla.) Times*, November 21, 1995, https://www.tampabay.com/archive/1995/11/21/professor-s-home-office-searched/.
120. James Harper, "USF Ties to Islamic Group Cleared," *St. Petersburg (Fla.) Times*, May 30, 1996, https://www.tampabay.com/archive/1996/05/30/usf-ties-to-islamic-group-cleared/.
121. Vickie Chachere, "Freed Palestinian Vows to Be Activist for Others Being Held," *Deseret News*, December 18, 2000, https://www.deseret.com/2000/12/19/19545048/freed-palestinian-vows-to-aid-others.
122. Thomas Bartlett, "Al-Arian to Be Deported in Deal with Prosecutors," *Chronicle of Higher Education* 52, no. 34 (April 28, 2006), https://www.chronicle.com/article/al-arian-to-be-deported-in-deal-with-prosecutors/.

4. INTENSIFICATION OF POLITICAL AND LEGAL BATTLES

123. Rachel La Corte, "Al-Arian Calls Self 'Prisoner of Conscience,' Victim of Hysteria," Associated Press State & Local Wire, February 25, 2003, https://freerepublic.com/focus/news/851966/posts?page=2.
124. Mearsheimer and Walt, "The Israel Lobby," 33.
125. MikoPeled.com, "Published Books," accessed November 11, 2022, https://mikopeled.com/books/.
126. United Nations, "About Us," accessed October 28, 2022, https://www.un.org/en/about-us.
127. Jewish Virtual Library, "United Nations: Address by Yasser Arafat Before the General Assembly," November 13, 1974, https://www.jewishvirtuallibrary.org/address-by-yasser-arafat-before-the-un-general-assembly-november-1974.
128. Jewish Virtual Library, "U.N. Security Council: U.S. Vetoes of Resolutions Critical to Israel (1972—Present)," accessed October 10, 2022, https://www.jewishvirtuallibrary.org/u-s-vetoes-of-un-security-council-resolutions-critical-to-israel.
129. Steven Collinson, David Wright, and Elise Labott, "US Abstains as UN Demands End to Israeli Settlements," CNN, December 24, 2016, https://www.cnn.com/2016/12/23/politics/israel-official-rips-obama-un-settlements/index.html.
130. "The 43 Times US Has Used Veto Power Against UN Resolutions on Israel," *Middle East Eye*, December 19, 2017, https://www.middleeasteye.net/news/43-times-us-has-used-veto-power-against-un-resolutions-israel.
131. Institute for Middle East Understanding, "Fact Sheet on the PLO's Bid for UNESCO Membership," October 31, 2011, https://imeu.org/article/fact-sheet-on-the-plos-bid-for-unesco-membership.
132. Jean Shaoul, "US Congress Blocks Palestinian Aid After UN Statehood Bid," World Socialist website, October 5, 2011, https://www.wsws.org/en/articles/2011/10/isra-o05.html.
133. Creede Newton, "A History of the US Blocking UN Resolutions Against Israel," *Al Jazeera*, May 19, 2021, https://www.aljazeera.com/news/2021/5/19/a-history-of-the-us-blocking-un-resolutions-against-israel.
134. DW, "Israel-Hamas War: UN Security Council Passes Gaza Resolution," December 23, 2023, https://www.dw.com/en/israel-hamas-war-un-security-council-passes-gaza-resolution/live-67795998.
135. Edith M. Lederer, "UN Approves Watered-Down Resolution on Aid to Gaza Without Call for Suspension of Hostilities," AP, https://apnews.com/article/un-resolution-gaza-aid-palestinians-israel-a5bb32fb9f071689d231533a26beb838.
136. DW, "Israel-Hamas War."
137. Lederer, "UN Approves Watered-Down Resolution."
138. Matt Shuham, "Rabbis Stage Protest, Call for Cease-Fire Inside United Nations," *Huffpost*, January 2024, https://www.msn.com/en-us/news/world/rabbis-stage-protest-call-for-cease-fire-inside-united-nations/ar-AA1mHrus.
139. Julia Conley, " 'Stop Vetoing Pace,' Rabbis Tell Biden at UN Security Council Protest," Common Dreams, January 9, 2024, https://www.commondreams.org/news/rabbis-un-ceasefire.
140. Robert Tait, "The White House Is Changing Its Tune on Israel—but Does It Matter in Practice?," *Guardian*, December 6, 2023, https://www.theguardian.com/us-news/2023/dec/06/joe-biden-israel-gaza-rhetoric-analysis.

4. INTENSIFICATION OF POLITICAL AND LEGAL BATTLES

141. Peter Beinart, "American Words vs. American Deeds," Beinart Notebook, December 4, 2023, https://peterbeinart.substack.com/p/american-words-vs-american-deeds.
142. Isaac Chotiner, "How the Biden Administration Defends Its Israel Policy," *New Yorker*, January 11, 2024, https://www.newyorker.com/news/q-and-a/how-the-biden-administration-defends-its-israel-policy
143. "ACLU Letter to the Senate Opposing Israel Anti-Boycott Act," ACLU, July 17, 2017, https://www.aclu.org/letter/aclu-letter-senate-opposing-israel-anti-boycott-act.
144. Bryant Harris, "Israel Anti-Boycott Bill Inches Closer to Passing Senate After Revisions," *Al-Monitor*, March 6, 2018, https://www.al-monitor.com/pulse/originals/2018/03/israel-anti-boycott-bill-closer-passing-senate-revisions.html.
145. ACLU, "ACLU Letter to the Senate," July 17, 2017.
146. Brian Hauss, "The New Israel Anti-Boycott Act Is Still Unconstitutional," ACLU, March 7, 2018, https://www.aclu.org/blog/free-speech/rights-protesters/new-israel-anti-boycott-act-still-unconstitutional.
147. Dima Khalidi, interview by author, March 15, 2021.
148. Anthony Fisher, "Proposed 'Anti-Semitism Awareness Act' Is an Unconstitutional Mess," *Reason*, December 1, 2016, https://reason.com/2016/12/01/proposed-anti-semitism-awareness-act-is/.
149. ACLU, "Oppose H.R. 6421/S. 10, the Anti-Semitism Awareness Act of 2016," accessed September 19, 2022, https://www.aclu.org/letter/oppose-hr-6421s-10-anti-semitism-awareness-act-2016.
150. Fisher, "Proposed 'Anti-Semitism Awareness Act.'"
151. American Presidency Project, "Executive Order 13899—Combating Anti-Semitism," December 11, 2019, https://www.presidency.ucsb.edu/documents/executive-order-13899-combating-anti-semitism.
152. Peter Baker and Maggie Haberman, "Trump Targets Anti-Semitism and Israeli Boycotts on College Campuses," *New York Times*, December 10, 2019, https://www.nytimes.com/2019/12/10/us/politics/trump-antisemitism-executive-order.html.
153. Zach Beauchamp, "The Controversy Over Laws Punishing Israel Boycotts, Explained," *Vox*, January 9, 2019, https://www.vox.com/policy-and-politics/2019/1/9/18172826/bds-law-israel-boycott-states-explained.
154. Mayaan Lubell and Patricia Zengerle, "Israel Bars U.S. Democratic Lawmakers Ilhan Omar and Rashida Tlaib Under Pressure from Trump," Reuters, August 15, 2019, https://www.reuters.com/article/us-israel-palestinians-usa/israel-bars-u-s-democratic-lawmakers-ilhan-omar-and-rashida-tlaib-under-pressure-from-trump-idUSKCN1V50SF.
155. Glenn Greenwald, "A Texas Elementary School Speech Pathologist Refused to Sign a Pro-Israel Oath, Now Mandatory in Many States—So She Lost Her Job," *Intercept*, December 17, 2018, https://theintercept.com/2018/12/17/israel-texas-anti-bds-law/.
156. Rob Crilly, "No Hurricane Aid for Texas City Residents Who Boycott Israel," *National News*, October 21, 2017, https://www.thenationalnews.com/world/the-americas/no-hurricane-aid-for-texas-city-residents-who-boycott-israel-1.669094.
157. Crilly.

4. INTENSIFICATION OF POLITICAL AND LEGAL BATTLES

158. "Houston Suburb Cancels Hurricane Aid Requirement That Homeowners Must Denounce Israel Boycotts," *Arab America*, October 28, 2017, https://www.arabamerica.com/houston-suburb-cancels-hurricane-aid-requirement-homeowners-must-denounce-israel-boycotts/.
159. "Bill HB 89," *Texas Legislature Online*, accessed August 9, 2023, https://capitol.texas.gov/BillLookup/History.aspx?LegSess=85R&Bill=HB89.
160. Palestine Legal, Legislation, "Texas," accessed August 9, 2023, https://legislation.palestinelegal.org/location/texas.
161. Jon Rosenthal, @jon_rosenthaltx, "As a Jewish-American . . .," Twitter, April 12, 2019, https://twitter.com/Jon_RosenthalTX/status/1116790444933804032.
162. Koontz v. Watson, *Global Freedom of Expression: Columbia University*, accessed October 28, 2022, https://globalfreedomofexpression.columbia.edu/cases/koontz-v-watson/.
163. "HB 2409," Kansas 2017–2018 Legislative Sessions, accessed August 17, 2023, http://www.kslegislature.org/li_2018/b2017_18/measures/hb2409/.
164. Koontz v. Watson, *Global Freedom of Expression*.
165. Palestine Legal, "Legal Challenges to Anti Boycott Laws," accessed August 17, 2023, https://legislation.palestinelegal.org/location/kansas/#legislation-hb-2482.
166. Mikkel Jordahl v. Mark Brnovich, *Global Freedom of Expression: Columbia University*, accessed October 28, 2022, https://globalfreedomofexpression.columbia.edu/cases/mikkel-jordahl-v-mark-brnovich/. See also Jim Zanotti, Martin A. Weiss, Valerie C. Brannon, and Jennifer K Elsea, "Israel and the Boycott, Divestment, and Sanctions (BDS) Movement,". Congressional Research Service, December 3, 2019, https://www.everycrsreport.com/files/20191203_R44281_1c95dd528315abe4cb3528c526eae77488759f52.pdf.
167. Aaron Bandler, "Federal Court Upholds Amended Arizona Anti-BDS Law," *Jewish Journal*, January 10, 2020, https://jewishjournal.com/news/united-states/309422/federal-court-upholds-amended-arizona-anti-bds-law/.
168. Executive Order no. 157, accessed September 19, 2022, https://www.governor.ny.gov/sites/default/files/atoms/files/EO_157_new.pdf.
169. Archive, Governor Andrew Cuomo, @NYGovCuomo, "We are against the BDF boycott," *Twitter*, June 5, 2016, https://twitter.com/NYGovCuomo/status/739456398698909696.
170. True Activist, "New York Governor Signs Executive Order to Punish People Who Criticize Israel," *True Activist*, June 10, 2016, https://www.trueactivist.com/new-york-governor-signs-executive-order-to-punish-people-who-criticize-israel/.
171. Palestine Legal, "New York," accessed December 1, 2023, https://legislation.palestinelegal.org/location/new-york/.
172. Buki Domingos and George Majeed Khoury, "Commentary: It's time to end United States police training in Israel," *San Diego Union Tribune*, July 17, 2020, https://www.sandiegouniontribune.com/opinion/commentary/story/2020-07-17/commentary-time-to-end-police-training-in-israel.
173. Researching the American-Israeli Alliance (RAIA), in collaboration with Jewish Voice for Peace (JVP), "Deadly Exchange: The Dangerous Consequences of American Law Enforcement Trainings in Israel," 2019, https://deadlyexchange.org/wp-content/uploads/2019/07/Deadly-Exchange-Report.pdf

174. RAIA, in collaboration with JVP, "Deadly Exchange."
175. JINSA, "Our Mission," accessed October 24, 2022, https://jinsa.org/about/.
176. Jewish News Syndicate, "Durham, N.C., Becomes First American Vity to Ban Police Training with Israel," April 19, 2018, https://www.jns.org/durham-n-c-becomes-first-american-city-to-ban-police-training-with-israel/.
177. United States District Court for the Middle District of North Carolina, Civil Action No. 1:19-cv-00309, https://www.courthousenews.com/wp-content/uploads/2019/03/nc-israel.pdf.
178. Erika Williams, "NC City Council Accused of Stirring Anti-Semitism," *Courthouse News Service*, March 20, 2019, https://www.courthousenews.com/nc-city-council-accused-of-stirring-anti-semitism/.
179. Durham2Palestine.org, "Why Does It Matter If US Police Departments Participate in Exchange Programs with Israel?," accessed October 28, 2022, https://www.durham2palestine.org/learn.
180. Angela Y. Davis, Frank Barat, and Cornel West, *Freedom Is a Constant Struggle: Ferguson, Palestine, and the Foundations of a Movement* (Chicago: Haymarket Books, 2016), 14.
181. Palestine Legal, "2021 Year-in-Review: Palestinian Uprising Generates Record Solidarity—and Fierce Backlash," accessed October 10, 2022, https://palestinelegal.org/2021-report.
182. TRT World, @trtworld, "Workplace discrimination to silence pro-Palestinian voices on the rise," Instagram, June 17, 2021, https://www.instagram.com/p/CQPuOmDK6qo/?igshid=N2NmMDY0OWE%3D.
183. Palestine Legal, "Smear Campaigns Target Employment," accessed October 28, 2022, https://palestinelegal.org/2021-report#employment.
184. Ariel Koren, "Google's Complicity in Israeli Apartheid: How Google Weaponizes 'Diversity' to Silence Palestinians and Palestinian Human Rights Supporters," *Medium*, August 30, 2022, https://medium.com/@arielkoren/googles-complicity-in-israeli-apartheid-how-google-weaponizes-diversity-to-silence-palestinians-cb41b24ac423.
185. Institute for Middle East Understanding, "Podcast Episode: Google's Anti-Palestinian Racism and Project Nimbus," Facebook video, September 29, 2022, https://www.facebook.com/theIMEU/videos/631252611720508.
186. Palestine Legal, "Censorship at K-12 Schools," accessed October 28, 2022, https://palestinelegal.org/2021-report#k12.
187. Eric Stirgus, "Judge: Ga. Law Barring Contracts by Groups Boycotting Israel Unconstitutional," *Atlanta Journal Constitution*, May 25, 2021, https://www.ajc.com/education/judge-ga-law-barring-contracts-by-groups-boycotting-israel-unconstitutional/UO3WXWOHRBFUBHIX7DWGG4AEPA/.
188. Raphael Ahren, "US Envoy Friedman Defends Sledgehammering Open Controversial Archaeological Site," *Times of Israel*, July 1, 2019, https://www.timesofisrael.com/friedman-defends-sledgehammering-open-controversial-archaeological-site/.
189. Matt Duss, interview by author, March 19, 2021.
190. Pro-Israel America, "Jewish News Syndicate: US House Overwhelmingly Condemns the BDS Movement, Affirms Support for Israel," July 23, 2019, https://proisraelamerica.org/jewish-news-syndicate-july-24/.

191. Bernie Sanders, Press Release, "News: Senator Bernie Sanders Calls for No More U.S. Funding for Netanyahu's Illegal and Immoral War Against the Palestinian People," January 2, 2024, https://www.sanders.senate.gov/press-releases/news-senator-bernie-sanders-calls-for-no-more-u-s-funding-for-netanyahus-illegal-and-immoral-war-against-the-palestinian-people/#; Lauren Gambino, "Democrats Supporting Israel Oppose Bernie Sanders' Plan for Conditional Aid," *Guardian*, November 21, 2023, https://www.theguardian.com/us-news/2023/nov/21/bernie-sanders-israel-us-military-aid-democrat-backlash.

5. THE FIGHT FOR SOLIDARITY AND LEGITIMACY

1. John Martin Collins, "Global Palestine: A Collision for Our Time," *Critique* 16, no. 1 (2007): 3–18, https://doi:10.1080/10669920601148588.
2. Saree Makdisi, *Tolerance Is a Wasteland: Palestine and the Culture of Denial* (Oakland: University of California Press, 2022), 146.
3. Edward W. Said et al., *The Selected Works of Edward Said, 1966–2006*, ed. Moustafa Bayoumi and Andrew Rubin, 2d Vintage Books ed. (New York: Vintage Books, 2019), 523.
4. John Martin Collins, *Global Palestine* (London: Hurst, 2011), 114.
5. Steven Salaita, "Why American Indian Studies Should Be Important to Palestine Solidarity," *Inter/Nationalism: Decolonizing Native America and Palestine* (Minneapolis, 2016; Minnesota Scholarship Online, May 18, 2017), https://doi.org/10.5749/minnesota/9781517901417.003.0005.
6. Ruairi Casey, "What's Behind Ireland's Support for Palestine?," *Al Jazeera*, June 7, 2021, https://www.aljazeera.com/news/2021/6/7/whats-behind-irelands-support-for-palestine.
7. Rory Miller, "Why the Irish Support Palestine," *Foreign Policy*, June 23, 2010, https://foreignpolicy.com/2010/06/23/why-the-irish-support-palestine-2/.
8. Miller.
9. Rafeef Ziadah, "British Backing for Israel Helps to Sustain the Unbearable Status Quo," *Guardian*, June 13, 2021, https://www.theguardian.com/commentisfree/2021/jun/13/british-backing-israel-unbearable-status-quo-palestinians.
10. Babrah Naikoo and Aaqib Fayez, "Kashmiris Show Solidarity with Palestinians on Eid," *TRT*, May 14, 2021, https://www.trtworld.com/magazine/kashmiris-show-solidarity-with-palestinians-on-eid-46713.
11. Somdeep Sen, "India's Deepening Love Affair with Israel," *Al Jazeera*, September 9, 2021, https://www.aljazeera.com/opinions/2021/9/9/indias-deepening-love-affair-with-israel.
12. "France to Ban Two Palestine Solidarity Groups," *Middle East Monitor*, February 25, 2022, https://www.middleeastmonitor.com/20220225-france-to-ban-two-palestine-solidarity-groups/amp/.
13. Ali Abunimah, "Court Overturns French Ban on Palestine Solidarity Groups," *Electronic Intifada*, May 2, 2022, https://electronicintifada.net/blogs/ali-abunimah/court-overturns-french-ban-palestine-solidarity-groups.
14. Cecilia Baeza, "Palestinians and Latin America's Indigenous Peoples: Coexistence, Convergence, Solidarity," *Middle East Report*, no. 274 (2015): 34–37, https://merip.org/2015/04/palestinians-and-latin-americas-indigenous-peoples/.

5. THE FIGHT FOR SOLIDARITY AND LEGITIMACY

15. Eman Abusidu, "Latin America's Presidents Speak Loudly for Palestinian rights at the United Nations," *Middle East Monitor,* September 23, 2022, https://www.middleeastmonitor.com/20220923-latin-americas-presidents-speak-loudly-for-palestinian-rights-at-the-united-nations/.
16. Baeza, "Palestinians."
17. Daniel Ramos, "Bolivia Severs Ties with Israel, Others Recall Envoys Over Gaza," Reuters, October 3, 2023, https://www.reuters.com/world/americas/bolivia-severs-diplomatic-ties-with-israel-citing-crimes-against-humanity-2023-10-31/.
18. Africa4Palestine, @africa4palestine, "Our Leader Lula da Silva," Instagram, November 1, 2022, https://www.instagram.com/p/CkBcnhhaDt1Y/?igshid=MDJmNzVkMjY%3D.
19. Adrian Maestas and Rania Khalek, "How Latino Activists Are Standing Up to the Israel Lobby," *Electronic Intifada,* March 6, 2014, https://electronicintifada.net/content/how-latino-activists-are-standing-israel-lobby/13225.
20. "Israel's Latin American Trail of Terror," *Al Jazeera,* June 5, 2003, https://www.aljazeera.com/news/2003/6/5/israels-latin-american-trail-of-terror.
21. Makdisi, *Tolerance Is a Wasteland,* 154, 155.
22. "ICC Launches War Crimes Probe into Israeli Practices," PBS, March 3, 2021, https://www.pbs.org/newshour/world/icc-launches-war-crimes-probe-into-israeli-practices.
23. Alexander Smith, "What the U.N. Court Ordered Israel to Do and What It Didn't—and What It Means for the War in Gaza," *NBC News,* https://www.nbcnews.com/news/world/icj-genocide-ruling-israel-gaza-war-rcna135615.
24. Qudsnen, "American Fans Express their Solidarity," Instagram, December 1, 2022, https://www.instagram.com/reel/CllMDabMCAi/?igshid=OTRmMjhlYjM%3D.
25. James Brinford, "World Cup Fans Are Refusing to Speak to Israel TV Presenters: 'Not Welcome,'" *Newsweek,* November 29, 2022, https://www.msn.com/en-us/news/world/world-cup-fans-are-refusing-to-speak-to-israel-tv-presenters-not-welcome/ar-AA14G5jn.
26. Aydan Mohyeldin, "The Media Is Getting Pro-Palestinian Expression at the World Cup All Wrong," MSNBC, December 7, 2022, https://www.msnbc.com/opinion/msnbc-opinion/world-cup-2022-puts-palestinians-front-center-rcna60423.
27. Hilton Obenzinger, "Palestine Solidarity, Political Discourse, and the Peace Movement, 1982–1988," *CR: The New Centennial Review* 8, no. 2 (2008): 233–34, http://www.jstor.org/stable/41949600.
28. Obenzinger, 240, quoting "Reagan and Begin: Partners in Racism," *Palestine Focus,* 1983, 4.
29. Obenzinger, 244.
30. Barbara Sprunt, "Top House Democrats Reject Rep. Jayapal's Comments Calling Israel a 'Racist State,'" NPR, July 17, 2023, https://www.npr.org/2023/07/17/1188096678/jayapal-israel-racist-state-jeffries. Accessed August 23, 2023.
31. Faida Abu-Ghazaleh, *Ethnic Identity of Palestinian Immigrants in the United States: The Role of Material Cultural Artifacts* (El Paso, Tex.: LFB Scholarly, 2010), 22.
32. James Baldwin, "A Report from Occupied Territory," *Nation,* July 11, 1966, https://www.thenation.com/article/culture/report-occupied-territory/.
33. Baldwin.

5. THE FIGHT FOR SOLIDARITY AND LEGITIMACY

34. Baldwin.
35. Keith P. Feldman, *Shadow Over Palestine: The Imperial Life of Race in America* (Minneapolis: University of Minnesota Press, 2015), 60, 81.
36. Africa4Palestine, @africa4palestine, "There's no black liberation without Palestinian liberation," Instagram, September 5, 2022, https://www.instagram.com/reel/CiHlDcwKyzW/?igshid=N2NmMDY0OWE%3D.
37. "Malcolm X on Zionism: Zionism's Logic," *Colonial Karma*, June 28, 2020, https://churchills-karma.com/2020/06/28/malcolm-x-on-zionism-zionist-logic/.
38. Robert I. Friedman, "Selling Israel to America," *Journal of Palestine Studies* 16, no. 4 (1987): 169–79, https://doi:10.2307/2536739.
39. Michael R. Fischbach, *Black Power and Palestine: Transnational Countries of Color*, (Stanford, Calif.: Stanford University Press, 2019), 215; and Dana Weiler-Polack, "Israel Enacts Law Allowing Authorities to Detain Illegal Migrants for Up to 3 Years," *Haaretz*, June 3, 2012, https://www.haaretz.com/2012-06-03/ty-article/israels-new-infiltrators-law-comes-into-effect/0000017f-f08a-dc28-a17f-fcbfc6e70000.
40. Fischbach, *Black Power and Palestine*, 213.
41. Black for Palestine, "Over 1,100 Black Activists, Artists, Scholars, Students and Organizations Signed the 2015 Black Solidarity Statement with Palestine," accessed November 9, 2022, http://www.blackforpalestine.com/.
42. Fischbach, *Black Power and Palestine*, 213.
43. Benjamin Doherty, "WATCH: Hip Hop Artist Jasiri X Video 'Checkpoint,'" *Electronic Intifada*, January 28, 2014, https://electronicintifada.net/blogs/benjamin-doherty/watch-hip-hop-artist-jasiri-x-video-checkpoint. See also Sama'an Ashrawi, "Method Man: A Trailblazer of Hip-hop Solidarity with Palestine?," *Electronic Intifada*, March 16, 2015, https://electronicintifada.net/content/method-man-trailblazer-hip-hop-solidarity-palestine/14349.
44. Fischbach, *Black Power and Palestine*, 215.
45. Ben Ndugga-Kabuye and Rachel Gilmer, "A Cut in US Military Expenditures and a Reallocation of Those Funds to Invest in Domestic Infrastructure and Community Wellbeing," Movement for Black Lives, accessed November 25, 2022, https://m4bl.org/wp-content/uploads/2020/05/CutMilitaryExpendituresOnePager.pdf.
46. JOCSM, "Jews of Color Caucus Statement in Solidarity with the Movement for Black," August 5, 2016, http://jocsm.org/jews-of-color-caucus-statement-in-solidarity-with-the-movement-for-black-lives-matter/.
47. Emma Green, "Why Do Black Activists Care About Palestine?," *Atlantic*, August 18, 2016, https://www.theatlantic.com/politics/archive/2016/08/why-did-black-american-activists-start-caring-about-palestine/496088/.
48. Ben Sales, "New Movement for Black Lives Platform Contains No Mention of Israel," *Jerusalem Post*, August 29, 2020, https://www.jpost.com/diaspora/antisemitism/new-movement-for-black-lives-platform-contains-no-mention-of-israel-640351.
49. JOCSM, "Jews of Color Caucus Statement in Solidarity with the Movement for Black," August 5, 2016, http://jocsm.org/jews-of-color-caucus-statement-in-solidarity-with-the-movement-for-black-lives-matter/.
50. Vic Mensa, "Vic Mensa: What Palestine Taught Me About American Racism," *Time*, January 12, 2018, http://time.com/5095435/vic-mensa-palestine-israel-jerusalem/.

5. THE FIGHT FOR SOLIDARITY AND LEGITIMACY

51. Rebecca Pierce, "Israeli Settlers Want New York Police Tactics in Jerusalem," *Electronic Intifada*, October 21, 2015, https://electronicintifada.net/content/israeli-settlers-want-new-york-police-tactics-jerusalem/14939.
52. Mensa, "Vic Mensa."
53. Hamid Dabashi, "Black Lives Matter and Palestine: A Historic Alliance," *Al Jazeera*, September 6, 2016, https://www.aljazeera.com/indepth/opinion/2016/09/black-lives-matter-palestine-historic-alliance-160906074912307.html.
54. Jews of Color, "Jews of Color Caucus Statement in Solidarity with the Movement for Black Lives," August 5, 2016, http://jocsm.org/jews-of-color-caucus-statement-in-solidarity-with-the-movement-for-black-lives-matter/.
55. Quoted in Akinya Ochienga, "Black-Jewish Relations Intensified and Tested by Current Political Climate," NPR, April 23, 2017, https://www.npr.org/sections/codeswitch/2017/04/23/494790016/black-jewish-relations-intensified-and-tested-by-current-political-climate.
56. Emma Green, "Why Do Black Activists Care About Palestine?," *Atlantic*, August 18, 2016, https://www.theatlantic.com/politics/archive/2016/08/why-did-black-american-activists-start-caring-about-palestine/496088/.
57. Ndugga-Kabuye and Gilmer, "A Cut in US Military Expenditures."
58. Angela Y. Davis, Frank Barat, and Cornel West, *Freedom Is a Constant Struggle: Ferguson, Palestine, and the Foundations of a Movement* (Chicago: Haymarket Books, 2016), 45.
59. Jewish Telegraphic Agency, "Stokely Carmichael Contends Palestinian Arabs in Just Struggle Against Israel," April 10, 1970, https://www.jta.org/1970/04/10/archive/stokely-carmichael-contends-palestinian-arabs-in-just-struggle-against-israel.
60. Bradford Richardson, "Jeremiah Wright: 'Jesus Was a Palestinian,'" *Hill*, October 10, 2015, http://thehill.com/blogs/blog-briefing-room/256592-jeremiah-wright-jesus-was-a-palestinian.
61. Ferrari Sheppard, "I Traveled to Palestine-Israel and Discovered There Is No 'Palestinian-Israeli Conflict,'" *Huffpost*, February 10, 2014, https://www.huffpost.com/entry/i-traveled-to-palestine_b_4761896.
62. Leslie Williams, "The Anti-Defamation League Kills the Black/Jewish Alliance," Jewish Voice for Peace, August 26, 2016, https://jewishvoiceforpeace.org/the-anti-defamation-league-kills-the-blackjewish-alliance/.
63. Adrian Maestas and Rania Khalek, "How Latino Activists Are Standing Up to the Israel Lobby," *Electronic Intifada*, March 6, 2014, https://electronicintifada.net/content/how-latino-activists-are-standing-israel-lobby/13225.
64. Maestas and Khalek.
65. Maestas and Khalek.
66. Maestas and Khalek.
67. Open Secrets, "Pro-Israel Money to Congress, 2014," accessed November 7, 2022, https://www.opensecrets.org/industries/summary.php?cycle=2014&ind=Q05.
68. Maestas and Khalek, "How Latino Activists Are Standing Up."
69. Shlomo Shamir, "Poll: Nearly 50% of Hispanic Americans Believe U.S. Too Supportive of Israel," *Haaretz*, March 28, 2011, https://www.haaretz.com/jewish/2011-03-28/ty-article/poll-nearly-50-of-hispanic-americans-believe-u-s-too-supportive-of-israel/0000017f-db23-db22-a17f-ffb33f5b0001.

5. THE FIGHT FOR SOLIDARITY AND LEGITIMACY

70. David Lopez and Yen Espirito, "Panethnicity in the United States: A Theoretical Framework," *Ethnic and Racial Studies* 13, no. 2 (1990): 198–224, doi:10.1080/01419870.1990.9993669.
71. Sunaina Maira and Magid Shihade, "Meeting Asian/Arab American Studies," *Journal of Asian American Studies* 9, no. 2 (2006): 117.
72. JP, "Stopping Asian Hate Must Include Standing with Palestine," *Urbanity Magazine*, June 12, 2021, https://medium.com/urbanitymag/stopping-asian-hate-must-include-standing-with-palestine-739d0f96616e; Douglas P. Sjoquist. "The Demographics of Islam in Asia," *Association for Asian Studies* (Spring 2005), https://www.asianstudies.org/publications/eaa/archives/the-demographics-of-islam-in-asia/.
73. JP, "Stopping Asian Hate."
74. Liel Leibovitz, "Native American Chief Visits Israel," *Tablet Magazine*, April 23, 2018, https://www.tabletmag.com/sections/news/articles/native-american-chief-visits-israel.
75. Revealer, "Tribal Alliances: The State of Israel & Native American Christianity (Excerpt)," February 24, 2015, https://therevealer.org/tribal-alliances-the-state-of-israel-native-american-christianity-excerpt/.
76. "Nez Visits Jerusalem for Cultural Exchange, Seeks Vision for Navajo Nation," *Navajo-Hopi Observer*, February 18, 2020, https://www.nhonews.com/news/2020/feb/18/nez-visits-jerusalem-cultural-exchange-seeks-visio/.
77. JTA, "Navajo President, First Lady Visit Israel on Agricultural Tech Mission," *Times of Israel*, December 11, 2012, https://www.timesofisrael.com/navajo-president-first-lady-visit-israel-on-agricultural-tech-mission/.
78. Revealer, "Tribal Alliances."
79. Ali Abunimah, "Acclaimed Feminist Author, Musician Joy Harjo Lands in Tel Aviv to Find Boycott Calls from Native American Peers," *Electronic Intifada*, December 7, 2012, https://electronicintifada.net/blogs/ali-abunimah/acclaimed-feminist-author-musician-joy-harjo-lands-tel-aviv-find-boycott-calls.
80. Revealer, "Tribal Alliances."
81. Revealer.
82. James A. Chosa and Faith L. Chosa, *Thy Kingdom Come Thy Will Be Done in Earth: A First Nation Perspective on Strategic Keys for Territorial Deliverance and Transformation* (Yellowstone, Mont.: Day Chief Ministries, 2004), 98.
83. Revealer, "Tribal Alliances."
84. Ryan Bellerose, "Don't Mix Indigenous Fight with Palestinian Rights," *Indian Country Today*, September 12, 2018, https://indiancountrytoday.com/archive/dont-mix-indigenous-fight-with-palestinian-rights.
85. Robert Warrior, "Palestine Without Smears: Why Israel and Natives Aren't Natural Allies," *Indian Country Today*, January 29, 2014, https://ais.illinois.edu/news/2014-01-29/palestine-without-smears-why-israel-and-natives-arent-natural-allies.
86. Magid Shihade, "Beware of Misinformed Bloggers Regarding Palestine," *Indian Country Today*, September 12, 2018, https://indiancountrytoday.com/archive/beware-of-misinformed-bloggers-regarding-palestine.
87. "Salma, The Memory Song," Palestinians Podcast, episode 24, https://www.palestinianspodcast.com/episodes-1/2018/1/26/24-salma-the-memory-song, accessed August 20, 2023.

88. Muslim Leadership Initiative, "About," accessed November 4, 2022, https://www.hartman.org.il/program/muslim-leadership-initiative/#about-1.
89. Hatem Bazian, "American Muslims Must Not Become Tools of Israeli Propaganda," *Electronic Intifada*, September 2, 2015, https://electronicintifada.net/content/american-muslims-must-not-become-tools-israeli-propaganda/14818.
90. Sana Saeed, "An Interfaith Trojan Horse: Faithwashing Apartheid and Occupation," *Islamic Monthly*, July 1, 2014, http://www.theislamicmonthly.com/an-interfaith-trojan-horse-faithwashing-apartheid-and-occupation/.
91. Bazian, "American Muslims."
92. Saud Anwar, "Moving Beyond Our Comfort Zones: Seeking Signs of Peace in Israel and Palestine," *Huffpost*, August 26, 2015, https://www.huffingtonpost.com/dr-saud-anwar/moving-beyond-our-comfort_b_8045372.html.
93. Sa'ed Atshan, "Faithwashing: A Reflection on the Muslim Leadership Initiative," *New Arab*, April 7, 2015, https://www.alaraby.co.uk/english/amp/comment/2015/4/7/faithwashing-a-reflection-on-the-muslim-leadership-initiative.
94. Center for American Progress, "Fear, Inc. The Roots of Islamophobia in America," August 2011, https://docslib.org/doc/10511197/fear-inc-the-roots-of-the-islamophobia-network-in-america, pg. 20.
95. Kamal Abu-Shamsieh, "A Palestinian's Journey Towards Healing," *Huffpost*, May 22, 2015, https://www.huffingtonpost.com/entry/a-palestinians-journey-to_b_7339586.
96. Sa'ed Atshan, "Faithwashing."
97. Atshan.
98. Sana Saeed, "An Interfaith Trojan Horse: Faithwashing Apartheid and Occupation," *Islamic Monthly*, July 1, 2014, http://www.theislamicmonthly.com/an-interfaith-trojan-horse-faithwashing-apartheid-and-occupation/.
99. Liza Behrendt, "Shutting Down a Pinkwashing Event Is a Smart, Legitimate Protest Against Israel's Occupation," *Haaretz*, January 28, 2016, https://www.haaretz.com/opinion/2016-01-28/ty-article/.premium/shutting-down-pinkwashing-is-legitimate-protest-against-occupation/0000017f-db48-d856-a37f-ffc839fc0000.
100. A Wider Bridge, "History and Background," accessed September 15, 2022, https://awiderbridge.org/history-and-background/.
101. Behrendt, "Shutting Down a Pinkwashing Event."
102. BDS Movement, "Say No to Pinkwashing," accessed December 10, 2022, https://bdsmovement.net/pinkwashing.
103. JTA, "Hundreds of Protesters Disrupt Jewish Reception at Chicago LGBTQ Conference," *Haaretz*, January 24, 2016, https://www.haaretz.com/jewish/2016-01-24/ty-article/protesters-disrupt-jewish-reception-at-lgbtq-conference/0000017f-dbe1-d3a5-af7f-fbef33990000.
104. Lulu Garcia-Navarro, "Israel Presents Itself as Haven for Gay Community," NPR, June 4, 2012, https://www.wbur.org/npr/154279534/israel-presents-itself-as-haven-for-gay-community.
105. Christians United for Israel, "Israeli Women Stand with Iranian Women: 'Israel Loves You,'" September 30, 2022, https://www.cufi.org.uk/news/israeli-women-stand-with-iranian-women-israel-loves-you/.
106. Fred Pierce, "In Israel, Questions Are Raised About a Forest That Rises from the Desert," *Yale Environment 360*, September 9. 2019, https://e360.yale.edu/features/in-israel-questions-are-raised-about-a-forest-that-rises-from-the-desert.

5. THE FIGHT FOR SOLIDARITY AND LEGITIMACY

107. Jessica Buxbaum, "How Israel's Occupation of Palestine Intensifies Climate Change," *Monthly Review Online*, February 6, 2022, https://mronline.org/2022/02/06/how-israels-occupation-of-palestine-intensifies-climate-change/.
108. Buxbaum.
109. Pierce, "In Israel, Questions Are Raised."
110. Buxbaum, "Israel's Occupation of Palestine."
111. Pierce, "In Israel, Questions Are Raised."
112. Collins, *Global Palestine*, 122.
113. Nahed Dirbas, "Nature Is Fighting Back Against the Occupation," *New Arab*, August 31, 2021, https://www.newarab.com/features/jerusalem-wildfires-remind-lost-heritage.
114. Collins, *Global Palestine*, 116.
115. Makdisi, *Tolerance Is a Wasteland*, 26–27, 35.
116. "The Greening Israel Project," accessed September 14, 2022, https://greeningisrael.com/.
117. Adam Eliyahu Berkowitz, "Christians in Israel Fighting the Prophetic War for Trees," *Israel 365 News*, September 15, 2022, https://www.israel365news.com/268454/christians-in-israel-fighting-the-prophetic-war-for-trees/.
118. Judy Maltz, "'Biblical Mandate': The U.S. Evangelicals Behind the Latest West Bank Land Grab," *Haaretz*, August 22, 2022, https://www.haaretz.com/israel-news/2022-08-22/ty-article/.highlight/biblical-mandate-the-u-s-evangelicals-behind-the-latest-west-bank-land-grab/00000182-c64e-d6fa-abbe-d74f90570000.
119. Maltz.
120. USCPR, "Israel's Violent Colonialism," Instagram, November 9, 2022, https://www.instagram.com/p/CkwWiSCOx5Q/?igshid=MDJmNzVkMjY%3D.
121. Davis, Barat, and West, *Freedom Is a Constant Struggle*, 42.
122. Davis, Barat, and West, 44.
123. Email to the author, from Jen Marlow, communications assistant at Just Vision, September 20, 2022.
124. Mathew Monagle, "SXSW Film Review: *Boycott*," *Austin Chronicle*, March 22, 2022, https://www.austinchronicle.com/daily/screens/2022-03-22/sxsw-film-review-boycott/.
125. Laura Kelly, "Progressive Groups Call for Biden to Denounce Evictions of Palestinians as 'War Crimes,'" *Hill*, May 13, 2021, https://thehill.com/policy/international/553472-more-than-100-progressive-groups-call-for-biden-to-denounce-evictions-of/.
126. Matt Duss, interview by author, March 19, 2021.
127. Collins, *Global Palestine*, 127–28.
128. Edward Said, "An Open Letter to Jewish American Intellectuals," *Jewish Currents*, September 21, 2022, https://jewishcurrents.org/an-open-letter-to-american-jewish-intellectuals.
129. Peter Beinart, "Answering Said's Call," *Jewish Currents*, September 21, 2022, https://jewishcurrents.org/answering-saids-call.
130. Peter Beinart, "Yavne: A Jewish Case for Equality in Israel-Palestine," *Jewish Currents*, July 7, 2020, https://jewishcurrents.org/yavne-a-jewish-case-for-equality-in-israel-palestine#.
131. Peter Beinart, interview by author, April 19, 2021.

5. THE FIGHT FOR SOLIDARITY AND LEGITIMACY

132. Beinart interview.
133. Stefania Mauritzi, "Pappé: 'Since the Ukrainian War, Killing Palestinians Has Become a Daily Business,'" *Il Fatto Quotidiano*, October 28, 2022, https://www.ilfattoquotidiano.it/in-edicola/articoli/2022/10/28/pappe-since-the-ukrainian-war-killing-palestinians-has-become-a-daily-business/6854205/.
134. Russell Brand, "Israel/Palestine—This Needs to Be Heard," YouTube, May 27, 2021, https://www.youtube.com/watch?v=WdPdslOTwJU.
135. "Dr. Gabor Matté on Israel/Palestine," YoutTube, October 28, 2023, https://www.youtube.com/watch?v=SHDBw-wx6wo&t=148s.
136. For more on the history and context of Tikkun Olam in the United States, see J. Krasner, "The Place of Tikkun Olam in American Jewish Life," *Jewish Political Studies Review* 25, no. 3/4 (2013): 59–98.
137. J Street, "National Election Night Survey of Jewish Voters Finds Overwhelming Support for Democrats, Opposition to Trump and the Far-Right," November 10, 2022, https://jstreet.org/press-releases/national-election-night-survey-of-jewish-voters-finds-overwhelming-support-for-democrats-opposition-to-trump-and-the-far-right/#.Y26A33bMLe-; Dov Waxman, @dovwaxman, "A post-election survey of American Jewish voters has some interesting findings about Jewish opinions," Twitter, November 10, 2022, https://twitter.com/dovwaxman/status/1590800150595006465?s=43&t=4lc_mFSo_QQyRAN9Kti36w.
138. Atalia Omer, *Days of Awe: Reimagining Jewishness in Solidarity with Palestinians* (Chicago: University of Chicago Press, 2019).
139. John J. Mearsheimer and Stephen M. Walt. "The Israel Lobby and U.S. Foreign Policy," *Middle East Policy* 13, no. 3 (2006): 29–87, https://doi:10.1111/j.1475-4967.2006.00260.x.
140. John J. Mearsheimer and Stephen M. Walt, *The Israel Lobby and U.S. Foreign Policy* (New York: Farrar, Straus and Giroux, 2007), 41.
141. Erin Axelman and Sam Eilertsen, *Israelism*, documentary, 2023.
142. Daniel Kushner, "*Israelism* Review: The Dangers of Pro-Israel Indoctrination," New Voices, https://newvoices.org/2023/09/06/israelism-review-the-dangers-of-pro-israel-indoctrination/.
143. Joseph Shattan, "Why Brera?," *Commentary*, April 1977, https://www.commentary.org/articles/joseph-shattan/why-breira/.
144. Mearsheimer and Walt, *The Israel Lobby*, 123.
145. Sara Roy, interview by author, March 22, 2021.
146. Roy interview.
147. Roy interview.
148. Liz Jackson, "Palestine Liberation Is Core to My Jewish Beliefs," *Daily Californian*, November 7, 2022, https://dailycal.org/2022/10/25/anti-zionism.
149. Ed Pilkington, "Noam Chomsky Barred by Israelis from Lecturing in Palestinian West Bank," *Guardian*, May 16, 2010, https://www.theguardian.com/world/2010/may/16/israel-noam-chomsky-palestinian-west-bank.
150. Beinart interview.
151. Roy interview.
152. Roy interview.
153. Arno Rosenfeld, "Chicago Synagogue Officially Designates Itself 'Anti-Zionist,'" *Haaretz*, April 2, 2022, https://www.haaretz.com/jewish/2022-04-02/ty-article

/chicago-synagogue-officially-designates-itself-anti-zionist/00000180-5bc6-de8c-a1aa-dbeeb56b0000.
154. Rosenfeld.
155. Rosenfeld.
156. Pew Research Center, *A Portrait of Jewish Americans*, October 1, 2013, https://assets.pewresearch.org/wp-content/uploads/sites/11/2013/10/jewish-american-full-report-for-web.pdf.

CONCLUSION

1. Gideon Levy, "Netanyahu's Far-Right Gov't Will Usher in the End of Israeli Apartheid," *Haaretz*, December 11, 2022, https://www.haaretz.com/opinion/2022-12-11/ty-article-opinion/.premium/yearning-for-a-jolt-and-the-end-of-apartheid/00000184-fd67-d4c7-a786-fdf7a4ee0000.
2. Immanuel Kant, *Anthropology from a Pragmatic Point of View*, 1798 (Carbondale: Southern Illinois University Press, 1978), 10.
3. "Number of Gazan Children Killed in Under a Month Is 10 Times Higher than That of Ukrainian Children Killed in Entire First Year of Russia's Ongoing War," Euro-Med Human Rights Monitor, October 30, 2023, https://euromedmonitor.org/en/article/5903/Number-of-Gazan-children-killed-in-under-a-month-is-10-times-higher-than-that-of-Ukrainian-children-killed-in-entire-first-year-of-Russia%E2%80%99s-ongoing-war.
4 "Israel's War on Gaza Deadliest in Modern History for Journalists, CPJ Says," *Al Jazeera*, December 21, 2023, https://www.aljazeera.com/news/2023/12/21/israels-war-on-gaza-deadliest-in-modern-history-for-journalists-says-cpj.

BIBLIOGRAPHY

Abbas, Hassan. "New Analysis Shows AIPAC Has Spent Millions to Fund U.S. Congressional Trips to Israel." *Arab American News*, June 27, 2019. https://www.arabamericannews.com/2019/06/27/new-analysis-shows-aipac-has-spent-millions-to-fund-u-s-congressional-trips-to-israel/.

Abdulhadi, Rabab, Evelyn Alsultany, and Nadine Christine Naber, eds. *Arab & Arab American Feminisms: Gender, Violence, & Belonging*. Syracuse, N.Y: Syracuse University Press, 2011, xxiv.

Abraham, Matthew. *Out of Bounds: Academic Freedom and the Question of Palestine*. London: Bloomsbury, 2014.

Abromowitz, Heddy Breuer. "Sabra Hummus Banned by Student Senate from Dickinson College Store." *Jerusalem Post*, December 24, 2019. https://www.jpost.com/Diaspora/Taking-a-swipe-at-Israel-A-tempest-in-a-hummus-bowl-611338.

Abu El-Haj, Thea Renda. "'I Was Born Here, but My Home, It's Not Here': Educating for Democratic Citizenship in an Era of Transnational Migration and Global Conflict." *Harvard Educational Review* 77, no. 3 (2007): 285–316. https://doi.org/10.17763/haer.77.3.412l7m737q114h5m.

———. *Unsettled Belonging: Educating Palestinian American Youth After 9/11*. Chicago: University of Chicago Press, 2015.

Abu-Ghazaleh, Faida. *Ethnic Identity of Palestinian Immigrants in the United States: The Role of Material Cultural Artifacts*. El Paso, Tex.: LFB Scholarly, 2010.

Abu Jahal, Entsu. "TikTok Becomes Vital Weapon in Palestinians' Digital War." *Al-Monitor*, June 1, 2021. https://www.al-monitor.com/originals/2021/06/tiktok-becomes-vital-weapon-palestinians-digital-war.

Abunimah, Ali. "Acclaimed Feminist Author, Musician Joy Harjo Lands in Tel Aviv to Find Boycott Calls from Native American Peers." *Electronic Intifada*, December 7,

BIBLIOGRAPHY

2012. https://electronicintifada.net/blogs/ali-abunimah/acclaimed-feminist-author-musician-joy-harjo-lands-tel-aviv-find-boycott-calls.

———. "Court Overturns French Ban on Palestine Solidarity Groups." *Electronic Intifada*, May 2, 2022. https://electronicintifada.net/blogs/ali-abunimah/court-overturns-french-ban-palestine-solidarity-groups.

Abu-Shamsieh, Kamal. "A Palestinian's Journey Towards Healing." *Huffpost*, May 22, 2015. https://www.huffingtonpost.com/entry/a-palestinians-journey-to_b_7339586.

Abusidu, Eman. "Latin America's Presidents Speak Loudly for Palestinian Rights at the United Nations." *Middle East Monitor*, September 23, 2022. https://www.middleeastmonitor.com/20220923-latin-americas-presidents-speak-loudly-for-palestinian-rights-at-the-united-nations/.

ACLU. "ACLU Letter to the Senate Opposing Israel Anti-Boycott Act," July 17, 2017. https://www.aclu.org/letter/aclu-letter-senate-opposing-israel-anti-boycott-act.

———. "Oppose H.R. 6421/S. 10, The Anti-Semitism Awaremenss Act of 2016," accessed September 19, 2022. https://www.aclu.org/letter/oppose-hr-6421s-10-anti-semitism-awareness-act-2016.

Adams, Char. "A Movement, a Slogan, a Rallying Cry: How Black Lives Matter Changed America's View on Race." *NBC News*, December 29, 2020. https://www.nbcnews.com/news/nbcblk/movement-slogan-rallying-cry-how-black-lives-matter-changed-america-n1252434.

Adams, John, and Charles Francis Adams. *The Works of John Adams, Second President of the United States: With a Life of the Author, Notes and Illustrations*. Boston: Little, Brown, 1854.

Adams, Neale. "Christian Zionism a 'Heresy' Says Anglican Priest." *Anglican Journal*, April 27, 2015. https://anglicanjournal.com/christian-zionism-a-heresy-says-anglican-priest/.

Adler-Bell, Sam. "Can DSA Go the Distance?" *Dissent* (Fall 2022). https://www.dissentmagazine.org/article/can-dsa-go-the-distance.

Against Apartheid. "A Letter Against Apartheid," accessed September 15, 2022. https://www.againstapartheid.com/.

Ahren, Raphael. "For First Time, U.S. Professors Call for Academic and Cultural Boycott of Israel." *Haaretz*, January 29, 2009. https://www.haaretz.com/2009-01-29/ty-article/for-first-time-u-s-professors-call-for-academic-and-cultural-boycott-of-israel/0000017f-e1b3-d75c-a7ff-fdbfaaaf0000.

———. "US Envoy Friedman Defends Sledgehammering Open Controversial Archaeological Site." *Times of Israel*, July 1, 2019. https://www.timesofisrael.com/friedman-defends-sledgehammering-open-controversial-archaeological-site/.

Aikman, Rev. J. Logan. *Cyclopaedia of Christian Missions: Their Rise, Progress, and Present Position*. London: Richard Griffin, 1860.

AJ+. "Why Israel Matters to Americans." YouTube, November 4, 2022. https://www.youtube.com/watch?v=klXaDgmM8Fs.

Ajrouch, Kristine J., and Amaney Jamal. "Assimilating to a White Identity: The Case of Arab Americans." *International Migration Review* 41, no. 4 (2007): 860–79. https://doi.org/10.1111/j.1747-7379.2007.00103.x.

Akbarzai, Sahar, Xiaofei Xu, Hadas Gold, Michael Callahan and Evan Perez. "Israel Reveals US Probe Into Shireen Abu Akleh's Death but Says It 'Will Not Cooperate.'"

BIBLIOGRAPHY

CNN, November 15, 2022. https://www.cnn.com/2022/11/15/middleeast/shireen-abu-akleh-israel-us-investigation-intl.

Al Jazeera. "Pro-Palestine Protests Held Around the World as Gaza War Nears 100 Days," January 13, 2024. https://www.aljazeera.com/news/2024/1/13/pro-palestine-demonstrations-around-the-world-as-gaza-war-nears-100-days.

Aladdin, Janna. "Israel's Systematic Surveillance of Palestinians." *Washington Report on Middle East Affairs*, December 17, 2021. https://www.wrmea.org/waging-peace/israels-systematic-surveillance-of-palestinians.html.

Aldrovandi, Carlo. *Apocalyptic Movements in Contemporary Politics: Christian and Jewish Zionism*. London: Palgrave Macmillan UK, 2014.

Aleem, Zeeshan. "This One Chart Shows How Black Lives Matter Has Changed America." *Mic*, August 5, 2015. https://www.mic.com/articles/123445/this-one-chart-shows-how-black-lives-matter-has-changed-america.

Alexander, Michelle. "Time to Break the Silence on Palestine." *New York Times*, January 19, 2019. https://www.nytimes.com/2019/01/19/opinion/sunday/martin-luther-king-palestine-israel.html.

Ali, Wajahat, et al. "Fear, Inc. The Roots of Islamophobia in America." Center for American Progress, August 2011. https://docslib.org/doc/10511197/fear-inc-the-roots-of-the-islamophobia-network-in-america.

Alper, Loretta, and Jeremy Earp, dirs. *The Occupation of the American Mind: Israel's Public Relations War in the United States*. Documentary. Northampton, Mass: Media Education Foundation, 2016.

Amaney, Jamal, and Nadine Christine Naber. *Race and Arab Americans Before and After 9/11: From Invisible Citizens to Visible Subjects*. Syracuse, N.Y.: Syracuse University Press, 2008.

American Friends Service Committee. "Jeff Halper," March 30, 2010. https://www.afsc.org/story/jeff-halper.

——. "Pillsbury Family Calls for Boycott of Pillsbury Products," April 29, 2021. https://www.afsc.org/newsroom/pillsbury-family-calls-boycott-pillsbury-products.

American Presidency Project. "Executive Order 13899—Combating Anti-Semitism," December 11, 2019. https://www.presidency.ucsb.edu/documents/executive-order-13899-combating-anti-semitism.

Amnesty International. "Rachel Corrie Verdict Highlights Impunity for Israeli Military," August 29, 2012. https://web.archive.org/web/20120902041711/http://www.amnesty.org/en/news/rachel-corrie-verdict-highlights-impunity-israeli-military-2012-08-28.

Anand, Nisha. "'Boycott Mcdonald's' Trends as UK Unit Issues Statement on Israel-Hamas War," *Business Standard*, January 17, 2024. https://www.business-standard.com/world-news/boycott-mcdonald-s-trends-as-uk-unit-issues-statement-on-israel-hamas-war-124011800289_1.html.

Anthony, Abigail. "Israeli Minister Asks Princeton to Remove 'Antisemitic Propaganda' from Course." *National Review*, August 17, 2023. https://www.nationalreview.com/news/israeli-minister-asks-princeton-to-remove-antisemitic-propaganda-from-course.

Anton, Mike, Nicole Santa Cruz, and Lauren Williams. "Students Guilty of Disrupting Speech in Irvine 11 Case." *Los Angeles Times*, September 24, 2011. http://articles.latimes.com/2011/sep/24/local/la-me-irvine-eleven-20110924.

BIBLIOGRAPHY

Anwar, Saud. "Moving Beyond Our Comfort Zones: Seeking Signs of Peace in Israel and Palestine." *Huffpost*, August 26, 2015. https://www.huffingtonpost.com/dr-saud-anwar/moving-beyond-our-comfort_b_8045372.html.

Aouragh, Miriyam. *Palestine Online: Transnationalism, the Internet and the Construction of Identity*. London: Tauris, 2011.

Arab America. "American Church Support for Palestine and Israel is Schizophrenic," July 27, 2022. https://www.arabamerica.com/american-church-support-for-palestine-and-israel-is-schizophrenic/.

———. "Houston Suburb Cancels Hurricane Aid Requirement That Homeowners Must Denounce Israel Boycotts," October 28, 2017. https://www.arabamerica.com/houston-suburb-cancels-hurricane-aid-requirement-homeowners-must-denounce-israel-boycotts/.

Arab American National Museum. "What Is Orientalism?," accessed August 12, 2022. http://arabstereotypes.org/why-stereotypes/what-orientalism.

Arar, Rawan. Review of *A Shadow Over Palestine: The Imperial Life of Race in America*." *Ethnic and Racial Studies* 39, no. 8 (2016): 1489–91. https://doi.org/10.1080/01419870.2015.1131321.

Ariel, Yaakov S. (Yaakov Shalom). "An Unexpected Alliance: Christian Zionism and Its Historical Significance." *Modern Judaism* 26, no. 1 (2006): 74–100. https://doi.org/10.1093/mj/kjj005.

Ariens, Chris. "Bob Simon Calls Out Israeli Ambassador to U.S. in '60 Minutes' Report." *TV Newser*, April 23, 2012. https://www.adweek.com/tvnewser/bob-simon-calls-out-israeli-ambassador-to-u-s-in-60-minutes-report/125018/.

Arria, Michael. "AIPAC Spent Over $4 Million Trying to Stop Summer Lee but She's Headed to Congress." *Mondoweiss*, November 9, 2022. https://mondoweiss.net/2022/11/aipac-spent-over-4-Million-trying-to-stop-summer-lee-but-shes-headed-to-congress/.

———. "Arizona Lawmakers Melt Down Over Movie Screening." *Mondoweiss*, accessed October 21, 2022. https://newsletters.mondoweiss.net/emails/webview/59730/67610146069546407.

———. "Middle East Studies Scholars Overwhelmingly Vote to Endorse BDS." *Mondoweiss*, March 24, 2022. https://mondoweiss.net/2022/03/middle-east-studies-scholars-overwhelmingly-vote-to-endorse-bds/.

Associated Press. "Miss South Africa's Appearance in Miss Universe in Israel Ignites Controversy." *Fox News*, November 19, 2021. https://www.foxnews.com/world/miss-south-africa-pageant-israel.

Associated Press in Jerusalem. "Facebook and Israel to Work to Monitor Posts That Incite Violence." *Guardian*, September 12, 2016. https://www.theguardian.com/technology/2016/sep/12/facebook-israel-monitor-posts-incite-violence-social-media?CMP=twt_gu.

Atshan, Sa'ed. "Faithwashing: A Reflection on the Muslim Leadership Initiative." *New Arab*, April 7, 2015. https://www.alaraby.co.uk/english/amp/comment/2015/4/7/faithwashing-a-reflection-on-the-muslim-leadership-initiative.

Axelman, Erin, and Sam Eilertsen. *Israelism*. 2023. Documentary.

Baeza, Cecilia. "Palestinians and Latin America's Indigenous Peoples: Coexistence, Convergence, Solidarity." *Middle East Report* (New York, 1988), no. 274 (2015): 34–37.

BIBLIOGRAPHY

Bahour, Nadine, and Shraddha Joshi. "Harvard Changes Its Mind on Ken Roth—Not on Allowing Free Speech About Palestine." *Nation*, January 24, 2023. https://www.thenation.com/article/activism/harvard-roth-palestine-free-speech/.

Baker, Peter, and Maggie Haberman. "Trump Targets Anti-Semitism and Israeli Boycotts on College Campuses." *New York Times*, December 10, 2019. https://www.nytimes.com/2019/12/10/us/politics/trump-antisemitism-executive-order.html.

Bandler, Aaron. "Federal Court Upholds Amended Arizona Anti-BDS Law." *Jewish Journal*, January 10, 2020. https://jewishjournal.com/news/united-states/309422/federal-court-upholds-amended-arizona-anti-bds-law/.

Barkoff Sophia. "Arab American Leaders Urge Michigan to Vote 'Uncommitted' and Send Message to Bided About Israel Policy." *CBS News*, February 3, 2024. https://www.cbsnews.com/news/michigan-vote-uncommitted-biden-israel-gaza/.

Barrows-Friedman, Nora. "Arizona University Forces Speakers to Sign Pledge They Don't Boycott Israel." *Electronic Intifada*, March 7, 2018. https://electronicintifada.net/blogs/nora-barrows-friedman/arizona-university-forces-speakers-sign-pledge-they-dont-boycott-israel.

Bartlett, Thomas. "Al-Arian to Be Deported in Deal with Prosecutors." *Chronicle of Higher Education* 52, no. 34 (April 28, 2006). https://www.chronicle.com/article/al-arian-to-be-deported-in-deal-with-prosecutors/.

Basco, Sharon. "Dissent in Pursuit of Equality, Life, Liberty and Happiness." HowardZinn.org, 2002. https://www.howardzinn.org/dissent-in-pursuit-of-equality-life-liberty-and-happiness/.

Bazian, Hatem. "American Muslims Must Not Become Tools of Israeli Propaganda." *Electronic Intifada*, September 2, 2015. https://electronicintifada.net/content/american-muslims-must-not-become-tools-israeli-propaganda/14818.

BBC. "McDonald's Hit by Israel-Gaza 'Misinformation.'" January 4, 2024. https://www.bbc.com/news/business-67885910.

BDS Movement. "Civil Society Organizations Around the World Urge HP Companies to End All Involvement in Violations of Palestinian Rights," March 29, 2018. https://bdsmovement.net/news/civil-society-organizations-around-world-urge-hp-companies-end-all-involvement-violations.

———. "Portland State University Students Vote in Favour of Divestment in Support of Palestinian Human Rights," October 26, 2016. https://bdsmovement.net/news/Portland-state-university-students-vote-favour-divestment-support-palestinian-human-rights.

———. "Say No to Pinkwashing," accessed December 10, 2022. https://bdsmovement.net/pinkwashing.

———. "SodaStream Is Still Subject to Boycott," August 22, 2018. https://bdsmovement.net/news/%E2%80%9Csodastream-still-subject-boycott%E2%80%9D.

BDS University of Manchester. "BDS Triumph Over Sabra on Campus," February 6, 2018. https://bdsuom.com/2018/02/06/bds-triumph-over-sabra-on-campus/comment-page-1/.

Beauchamp, Zach. "The Controversy Over Laws Punishing Israel Boycotts, Explained." *Vox*, January 9, 2019. https://www.vox.com/policy-and-politics/2019/1/9/18172826/bds-law-israel-boycott-states-explained.

———. "How Natalie Portman Became the Latest Israel-Palestine Flashpoint." *Vox*, April 23, 2018. https://www.vox.com/world/2018/4/23/17270180/natalie-portman-israel-boycott.

———. "Rihanna and Dwight Howard Tweeted #FreePalestine and It Worked Out How You Would Expect." *Vox*, July 15, 2014. https://www.vox.com/2014/7/15/5901881/rihanna-tweets-freepalestine-immediately-deletes-it.

Behrendt, Liza. "Shutting Down a Pinkwashing Event Is a Smart, Legitimate Protest Against Israel's Occupation." *Haaretz*, January 28, 2016. https://www.haaretz.com/opinion/2016-01-28/ty-article/.premium/shutting-down-pinkwashing-is-legitimate-protest-against-occupation/0000017f-db48-d856-a37f-ffc839fc0000.

Beinart, Peter. "Answering Said's Call." *Jewish Current*, September 21, 2022. https://jewishcurrents.org/answering-saids-call.

———. "The Failure of the American Jewish Establishment." *New York Review*, June 10, 2010. https://www.nybooks.com/articles/2010/06/10/failure-american-jewish-establishment/.

———. "I No Longer Believe in a Jewish State." *New York Times*, July 8, 2020. https://www.nytimes.com/2020/07/08/opinion/israel-annexation-two-state-solution.html.

———. "Learning from Ukraine." *Beinart Notebook*, October 9, 2022. https://peterbeinart.substack.com/p/learning-from-ukraine.

———. "Yavne: A Jewish Case for Equality in Israel-Palestine." *Jewish Currents*, July 7, 2020. https://jewishcurrents.org/yavne-a-jewish-case-for-equality-in-israel-palestine#.

Bellerose, Ryan. "Don't Mix Indegenous Fight with Palestinian Rights." *Indian Country Today*, September 12, 2018. https://indiancountrytoday.com/archive/dont-mix-indigenous-fight-with-palestinian-rights.

Ben Ami, Shlomo, and Norman Finkelstein. Interview by Amy Goodman. "Fmr. Israeli Foreign Minister: 'If I were a Palestinian, I Would Have Rejected Camp David.'" Democracy Now, February 14, 2006. https://www.democracynow.org/2006/2/14/fmr_israeli_foreign_minister_if_i.

Ben Zikri, Almog, and Hagar Shezef. "Burning Man Project Urges Israeli Organizers to Cancel West Bank Festival." *Haaretz*, March 9, 2020. https://www.haaretz.com/israel-news/2020-03-09/ty-article/.premium/burning-man-urges-israeli-organizers-to-cancel-controversial-west-bank-festival/0000017f-dbc7-d3a5-af7f-fbefe8d30000.

Beresford, Trilby. "Israeli Film 'Advocate' Wins Best Documentary Emmy." *Hollywood Reporter*, September 29, 2021. https://www.hollywoodreporter.com/tv/tv-news/advocate-documentary-emmy-winners-1235022667/#!.

Berkowitz, Adam Eliyahu. "Christians in Israel Fighting the Prophetic War for Trees." *Israel 365 News*, September 15, 2022. https://www.israel365news.com/268454/christians-in-israel-fighting-the-prophetic-war-for-trees/.

Biddle, Sam. "Facebook Report Concludes Company Censorship Violated Palestinian Human Rights." *Intercept*. September 21, 2022. https://theintercept.com/2022/09/21/facebook-censorship-palestine-israel-algorithm/.

"Biden Is Only the Second Catholic President, but Nearly All Have Been Christians." Pew Research Center, January 4, 2021. http://www.pewresearch.org/fact-tank/2017/01/20/almost-all-presidents-have-been-christians/.

Birthright Israel Foundation. "MythBuster: Common Misconceptions About Birthright Israel Trips," August 6, 2020. https://birthrightisrael.foundation/blog/mythbuster-common-misconceptions-about-birthright-israel-trips/.

BIBLIOGRAPHY

Black for Palestine. "Over 1,100 Black Activists, Artists, Scholars, Students and Organizations Signed the 2015 Black Solidarity Statement with Palestine," accessed November 9, 2022. http://www.blackforpalestine.com/.

Boccagni, Paolo. "Rethinking Transnational Studies: Transnational Ties and the Transnationalism of Everyday Life." *European Journal of Social Theory* 15, no. 1 (2012): 117–32. https://doi:10.1177/1368431011423600.

Bogan, Amir. "Roger Waters Pays Homage to Slain Palestinian Journalist in NYC Concert." *YNET News*, August 31, 2022. https://www.ynetnews.com/culture/article/s1dwahhko.

Bond, Paul. "CBS Shareholders Accuse '60 Minutes' of Anti-Semitism." *Hollywood Reporter*, May 23, 2013. https://www.hollywoodreporter.com/tv/tv-news/cbs-shareholders-accuse-60-minutes-555375/.

Borger, Julian, and Peter Beaumont. "US: Israeli Settlements No Impediment to Peace but May Not Be Helpful." *Guardian*, February 3, 2017. https://www.theguardian.com/world/2017/feb/03/trump-says-israeli-settlements-not-impediment-to-peace-but-expansion-unhelpful.

Boteach, Shmuley. "The End of Israel and Peter Beinart as the Last Man." *Jerusalem Post*, July 21, 2020. https://www.jpost.com/opinion/the-end-of-israel-and-peter-beinart-as-the-last-man-635856.

Boulter, Michael. "In the Age of Memes, How Are Young People Getting Their News?" *PBS NewsHour*, January 23, 2020. https://www.pbs.org/newshour/nation/in-the-age-of-memes-how-are-young-people-getting-their-news.

Brand, Russell. "Israel/Palestine—This Needs to Be Heard." YouTube, May 27, 2021. https://www.youtube.com/watch?v=WdPdslOTwJU.

Breakfast Club. "Marc Lamont Hill Discusses Israeli-Palestinian Conflict, the Limits of Progressive Politics + More." YouTube, March 1, 2021. https://www.youtube.com/watch?v=WERKhWjmoLw.

Brinford, James. "World Cup Fans Are Refusing to Speak to Israel TV Presenters: 'Not Welcome.'" *Newsweek*, November 29, 2022. https://www.msn.com/en-us/news/world/world-cup-fans-are-refusing-to-speak-to-israel-tv-presenters-not-welcome/ar-AA14G5jn.

Brubaker, R. and F. Cooper. "Beyond 'Identity.'" *Theory and Society* 29, no. 1 (2000): 1–47. https://doi.org/10.1023/A/1007068714468.

Bruton, F. Brinley, Lawahez Jabari, and Paul Goldman. "Holy Land Christians Feel Abandoned by U.S. Evangelicals." *NBC News*, May 5, 2018. https://www.nbcnews.com/news/world/holy-land-christians-feel-abandoned-u-s-evangelicals-n867371.

Bulkin, Elly, and Donna Nevel. "Follow the Money: From Islamophobia to Israel Right or Wrong." *AlterNet*, October 3, 2012. https://www.alternet.org/2012/10/follow-money-islamophobia-israel-right-or-wrong/.

Burghūthī, Iyād. *Palestinian Americans: Socio-political Attitudes of Palestinian Americans Towards the Arab-Israeli Conflict*. Occasional Papers Series, no. 38. Durham, UK: Centre for Middle Eastern & Islamic Studies, University of Durham, 1989.

Burleigh, Nina. "Rudy Giuliani's Flimsy Foreign Policy Credentials." *Newsweek*, November 15, 2016. https://www.newsweek.com/rudy-giuliani-flimsy-foreign-policy-credentials-521635.

Business and Human Rights Resource Center. "Caterpillar Response Re Alleged Complicity in Human Rights Abuses in Israel & the Occupied Territories," January 23,

2012. https://www.business-humanrights.org/en/latest-news/caterpillar-response-re-alleged-complicity-in-human-rights-abuses-in-israel-the-occupied-territories/.

Butler Bass, Diana. "Bad History." *Cottage*, September 8, 2022. https://dianabutlerbass.substack.com/p/bad-history.

Buxbaum, Jessica. "How Israel's Occupation of Palestine Intensifies Climate Change." *Monthly Review Online*, February 6, 2022. https://mronline.org/2022/02/06/how-israels-occupation-of-palestine-intensifies-climate-change/.

Cable, Umayyah. "Compulsory Zionism and Palestinian Existence: A Genealogy." *Journal of Palestine Studies* 51, no. 2 (2022): 66–71. https://doi.org/10.1080/0377919X.2022.2040324.

Campbell, Colin. "NBC Reportedly Pulls Reporter Who Witnessed Child Deaths from Gaza." *Business Insider*, July 17, 2014. https://www.businessinsider.com/nbc-reportedly-pulls-ayman-mohyeldin-from-gaza-strip-2014-7#.

Carbonaro, Giulia. "Pro-Palestinian Protests Break Out in Multiple U.S. Cities." *Newsweek*, October 9, 2023, https://www.newsweek.com/pro-palestinian-protests-break-out-multiple-american-cities-1833036.

Carlin, Na'ama. "Are Israel Boycotts Really Anti-Semitic?" *Eureka Street*, February 14, 2018. https://www.eurekastreet.com.au/article/are-israel-boycotts-really-anti-semitic.

Carpentier, Nico, Peter Dahlgren, and Francesca Pasquali. "Waves of Media Democratization: A Brief History of Contemporary Participatory Practices in the Media Sphere." *Convergence* 19, no. 3 (August 1, 2013): 287–94. https://doi.org/10.1177/1354856513486529.

Casey, Ruairi. "What's Behind Ireland's Support for Palestine?" *Al Jazeera*, June 7, 2021. https://www.aljazeera.com/news/2021/6/7/whats-behind-irelands-support-for-palestine.

Chachere, Vickie. "Freed Palestinian Vows to Be Activist for Others Being Held." *Deseret News* (Salt Lake City, Utah), December 18, 2000. https://www.deseret.com/2000/12/19/19545048/freed-palestinian-vows-to-aid-others.

Chan, Jimmy, and Daniel F. Stone. "Media Proliferation and Partisan Selective Exposure." *Public Choice* 156, no. 3/4 (2013): 467–90.

Chapin, Angelina. "When Posting About the Israel-Hamas War Costs You Your Job." *The Cut*, October 30, 2023. https://www.thecut.com/2023/10/israel-hamas-war-job-loss-social-media.html.

Charnysh, Volha, Christopher Lucas, and Prerna Singh. "The Ties That Bind: National Identity Salience and Pro-Social Behavior Toward the Ethnic Other." *Comparative Political Studies* 48, no. 3 (2015): 267–300. https://doi.org/10.1177/0010414014543103.

Charters, David A. "Jewish Terrorism and the Modern Middle East." *Journal of Conflict Studies* 27, no. 2 (2007).

Chosa, James A., and Faith L. Chosa. *Thy Kingdom Come Thy Will Be Done in Earth: A First Nation Perspective on Strategic Keys for Territorial Deliverance and Transformation*. Yellowstone, Mont.: Day Chief Ministries, 2004.

Christian Broadcasting Network. "Return to Israel's 1967 Borders National Suicide?" YouTube, May 24, 2011. https://www.youtube.com/watch?v=hAZrKlRJZNw.

Christians United for Israel. "Israeli Women Stand with Iranian Women: 'Israel Loves You,'" September 30, 2022. https://www.cufi.org.uk/news/israeli-women-stand-with-iranian-women-israel-loves-you/.

BIBLIOGRAPHY

Clark, Victoria. *Allies for Armageddon: The Rise of Christian Zionism*. New Haven, Conn.: Yale University Press, 2007.

Cohen, Jonah. "Washington State Removes Anti-Israel Lesson from K-12 Native American Curriculum." *Jewish News Syndicate*, July 8, 2021. https://www.jns.org/opinion/washington-state-removes-anti-israel-lesson-from-k-12-native-american-curriculum/.

Collins, John Martin. *Global Palestine*. London: Hurst, 2011.

——. "Global Palestine: A Collision for Our Time." *Critique* 16, no. 1 (2007): 3–18. https://doi.org/10.1080/10669920601148588.

Collinson, Steven, David Wright, and Elise Labott. "US Abstains as UN Demands End to Israeli Settlements." CNN, December 24, 2016. https://www.cnn.com/2016/12/23/politics/israel-official-rips-obama-un-settlements/index.html.

Colonial Karma. "Malcolm X on Zionism: Zionism's Logic," June 28, 2020. https://churchills-karma.com/2020/06/28/malcolm-x-on-zionism-zionist-logic/.

Corcoran, Michael. "Bernie Sanders and the Limits of Electoral Politics." TruthOut, December 10, 2015. https://truthout.org/articles/bernie-sanders-and-the-limits-of-electoral-politics/.

Coscarelli, Joe. "Newt Gingrich Says Palestinian People Are 'Invented.'" *Intelligencer*, December 9, 2011. https://nymag.com/intelligencer/2011/12/gingrich-says-palestinian-people-are-invented.html.

Cox, Kiana. "Most U.S. Adults Feel What Happens to Their Own Racial or Ethnic Group Affects Them Personally." Pew Research Center, July 11, 2019. https://www.pewresearch.org/fact-tank/2019/07/11/linked-fate-connectedness-americans/.

Craig, Tim, and Clara Ence Morse. "Young U.S. Muslims Are Rising Up Against Israel in Unlikely Places." *Washington Post*, January 2, 2024.

Crilly, Rob. "No Hurricane Aid for Texas City Residents Who Boycott Israel." *National News*, October 21, 2017. https://www.thenationalnews.com/world/the-americas/no-hurricane-aid-for-texas-city-residents-who-boycott-israel-1.669094.

Crimson Editorial Board. "In Support of Boycott, Divest, Sanctions and a Free Palestine." *Harvard Crimson*, April 29, 2022. https://www.thecrimson.com/article/2022/4/29/editorial-bds/.

Dabashi, Hamid. "Black Lives Matter and Palestine: A Historic Alliance." *Al Jazeera*, September 6, 2016. https://www.aljazeera.com/indepth/opinion/2016/09/black-lives-matter-palestine-historic-alliance-160906074912307.html.

Dabis, Cherien. "For Cherien Dabis, the Emmy-Nominated Palestinian American Director of 'Only Murders in the Building,' Storytelling Is a Matter of Survival." *Variety*, August 16, 2022. https://variety.com/2022/tv/news/cherien-dabis-emmy-nominated-only-murders-in-the-building-boy-from-6b-1235341938/.

Dana, Karam. "Confronting Injustice Beyond Borders: Palestinian Identity and Nonviolent Resistance." *Politics, Groups, and Identities* 6, no. 4 (2018): 529–52.

——. "Contextualizing Cynicism: Palestinian Public Opinion Towards Human Rights and Democracy." *Muslim World Journal of Human Rights* 14, no. 1 (2017): 113–44. https://doi,org/10.1515/mwjhr-2016-0023.

——. "The West Bank Apartheid/Separation Wall: Space, Punishment, and the Disruption of Social Continuity." *Geopolitics* 22, no. 4 (2017): 887–910.

Dana, Karam, and Matt Barreto. "American Muslims and the State: Contexts and Contentions." In *Understanding Muslim Political Life in America: Contested Citizenship in the Twenty-First Century*, ed. Brian Calfano and Nazita Lajevardi. Philadelphia: Temple University Press, 2019.

Dana, Karam, Matt Barreto, and Bryan Wilcox-Archuleta. "The Political Incorporation of Muslims in America: The Mobilizing Role of Religiosity in Islam." *Journal of Race, Ethnicity, and Politics* 2, no. 2 (2017): 170–200.

Daniel, Norman. *Islam and the West: The Making of an Image*. London: Oneworld, 2009.

Dann, Naomi. "Criticism of Israel Is Not Anti-Semitism." Jewish Voice for Peace, May 4, 2015. https://www.jewishvoiceforpeace.org/2015/05/criticism-of-israel-is-not-anti-semitism/.

D'Antonio, William V., Steven A. Tuch, and Josiah R. Baker. *Religion, Politics, and Polarization: How Religiopolitical Conflict Is Changing Congress and American Democracy*. Lanham, Md.: Rowman and Littlefield, 2013.

Davis, Angela Y., Frank Barat, and Cornel West. *Freedom Is a Constant Struggle: Ferguson, Palestine, and the Foundations of a Movement*. Chicago: Haymarket Books, 2016.

Debusmann, Bernd, Jr. "Claudine Gay: Pressure Mounts on Harvard President to Step Down." BBC, December 11, 2023. https://www.bbc.com/news/world-us-canada-67684309.

Democracy Now. "Edward Said on Palestinian Politics and the Search for Justice," February 8, 2001. https://www.democracynow.org/2001/2/8/edward_said_on_palestinian_politics_and.

———. "Ta-Nehisi Coates Speaks Out Against Israel's 'Segregationist Apartheid Regime' After West Bank Visit," November 2, 2023. https://www.democracynow.org/2023/11/2/ta_nehisi_coates.

DeSantis, Nick. "Native American-Studies Group's Leadership Supports Israel Boycott." *Chronicle of Higher Education*, December 18, 2013. https://www.chronicle.com/blogs/ticker/native-american-studies-groups-leadership-supports-israel-boycott.

Doherty, Benjamin. "WATCH: Hip Hop Artist Jasiri X Video 'Checkpoint.'" *Electronic Intifada*, January 28, 2014. https://electronicintifada.net/blogs/benjamin-doherty/watch-hip-hop-Artist-jasiri-x-video-checkpoint.

Doumani, Beshara. *Rediscovering Palestine: Merchants and Peasants in Jabal Nablus, 1700–1900*. Berkeley: University of California Press, 1995.

DropTheADL. "Islamophobia/Anti-Muslim Racism & Anti-Arab Racism," accessed November 20, 2022. https://droptheadl.org/the-adl-is-not-an-ally/#islamophobia.

———. "Support for Actual Anti-Semites, Donald Trump, and Other Right-wing, Racist Influencers," accessed November 18, 2022. https://droptheadl.org/the-adl-is-not-an-ally/#trump.

Du Bois, W. E. B. *The Souls of Black Folk*. London: Random House, 1989.

———. "Suez." *AfroPoets Famous Writers*, accessed November 23, 2022. https://www.afropoets.net/webdubois1.html.

Dunleavy, Dennis. "The Rise of Opinion Journalism: The FOX Is in the Hen House," March 21, 2005. https://ddunleavy.typepad.com/the_big_picture/2005/03/the_rise_of_opi.html.

Durham2Palestine. "Why Does It Matter if US Police Departments Participate in Exchange Programs with Israel?," accessed October 28, 2022. https://www.durham2palestine.org/learn.

Dwoskin, Elizabeth. "Israel Escalates Surveillance of Palestinians with Facial Recognition Software." *Washington Post*, November 8, 2021. https://www.washingtonpost.com/world/middle_east/israel-palestinians-surveillance-facial-recognition/2021/11/05/3787bf42-26b2-11ec-8739-5cb6aba30a30_story.html.

Eadeh, Nisreen. "Amal Clooney: A Figure of Hope for Everyone but the Palestinians." Arab America, April 14, 2016. https://www.arabamerica.com/amal-clooney-figure-hope-everyone-palestinians/.

Editorial Board. "Editorial: Undermining Free Speech on Campus." *Los Angeles Times*, December 6, 2016. https://www.latimes.com/opinion/editorials/la-ed-senate-antisemitism-20161202-story.html.

Eisenhower, Dwight D. "Radio and Television Address to the American People on the Situation in the Middle East." Recorded February 20, 1957. *American Presidency Project*. https://www.presidency.ucsb.edu/documents/radio-and-television-address-the-american-people-the-situation-the-middle-east#.

Elassar, Alaa, and Emma Tucker. "At Least 320 Pro-Palestinian Protesters Arrested After Blocking Traffic Across New York City Bridges to Demand Gaza Ceasefire." CNN, January 8, 2024. https://www.cnn.com/2024/01/08/us/palestine-protest-nyc-gaza-ceasefire/index.html.

Elgindy, Khaled. *Blind Spot: America and the Palestinians, from Balfour to Trump*. Washington, D.C: Brookings Institution Press, 2019.

Elmusa, Karmah. "I'm Longing for Palestine While Living the American Dream." *Elle*, October 30, 2015. https://www.elle.com/culture/career-politics/a31572/essay-on-being-palestinian-american/.

Emmanuel, Adeshina. "Spurred by Black Lives Matter, Coverage of Police Violence Is Changing." Injustice Watch, February 1, 2021. https://www.injusticewatch.org/longreads/2021/nieman-reports-police-violence-coverage-is-changing/.

Emmons, Alex. "Senate Responds to Trump-Inspired Anti-semitism by Targeting Students Eho Criticize Israel." *Intercept*, December 2, 2016. https://theintercept.com/2016/12/02/senate-responds-to-post-trump-anti-semitism-by-targeting-students-who-criticize-israel/.

Eshman, Rob. "Berkeley's 'Jew-Free Zones': Fake News That Does Real Damage." *Forward*, October 7, 2022. https://forward.com/opinion/520623/berkeleys-jew-free-zones-are-fake-news-that-do-real-damage/.

———. "Can a Jew Cook Palestinian Food Without Being Disrespectful?" *Forward*, August 19, 2022. https://forward.com/food/515056/when-a-jew-cooks-palestinian-food/.

ESPN. "Celtic Receive UEFA Fine for Flying Palestine Flags in UCL Match." ESPN.com, September 29, 2016. https://www.espn.com/soccer/celtic/story/2961926/celtic-receive-uefa-fine-for-flying-palestine-flags-in-ucl-match.

Executive Order no. 157. Accessed September 19, 2022. https://www.governor.ny.gov/sites/default/files/atoms/files/EO_157_new.pdf.

Fadulu, Lola. "Zara Removes Campaign After Critics Call It Insensitive to Israel-Hamas War." *New York Times*, December 12, 2023. https://www.nytimes.com/2023/12/12/business/zara-campaign-israel-gaza-war.html.

Feldman, David. *Boycotts Past and Present: From the American Revolution to the Campaign to Boycott Israel*. Cham, Switz.: Springer International, 2019.

BIBLIOGRAPHY

Feldman, Keith P. "Representing Permanent War: Black Power's Palestine and the End(s) of Civil Rights." *CR* 8, no. 2 (2008): 193–231. https://doi.org/:10.1353/ncr.0.0035.

——. *A Shadow Over Palestine: The Imperial Life of Race in America*. Minneapolis: University of Minnesota Press, 2015.

Ferguson, Margaret. "Former President of Modern Language Association Resigns Following Decision to Ban Debate on BDS." *Mondoweiss*, February 15, 2018. https://mondoweiss.net/2018/02/president-association-following/.

Fernandez, Gabe. "Why Oakland Roots Fans Are Demanding the Team End Its Sponsorship Deal with Puma." *SFGate*, August 6, 2021. https://www.sfgate.com/sports/article/Oakland-Roots-supporters-group-Puma-Israel-protest-16367605.php.

Feuer, Alan. "Linda Sarsour Is a Brooklyn Homegirl in a Hijab." *New York Times*, August 7, 2015. https://www.nytimes.com/2015/08/09/nyregion/linda-sarsour-is-a-brooklyn-homegirl-In-a-hijab.html.

Findley, Paul. *They Dare to Speak Out: People and Institutions Confront Israel's Lobby*. Chicago: Chicago Review Press, 2003.

Finkelstein, Norman G. *Beyond Chutzpah: On the Misuse of Anti-Semitism and the Abuse of History*. Berkeley: University of California Press, 2005.

Fischbach, Michael R. *Black Power and Palestine: Transnational Countries of Color*. Stanford, Calif.: Stanford University Press, 2019.

Fisher, Anthony. "Proposed 'Anti-Semitism Awareness Act' Is an Unconstitutional Mess." *Reason*, December 1, 2016. https://reason.com/2016/12/01/proposed-anti-semitism-awareness-act-is/.

Fisher, Steward. "Political Football: How UEFA and FIFA Changed Stance After Banning Celtic Palestine Display & Barcelona Flags to Allow Ukraine Emblems." *Scottish Sun*, March 10, 2022. https://www.thescottishsun.co.uk/sport/football/8545538/uefa-fifa-changed-stance-celtic-palestine-display-barcelona-ukraine/.

Fishman, Andrew. "George Washington University Allows Flags to Fly from Dorm Rooms—Unless They're Palestinian." *Intercept*, December 9, 2015. https://theintercept.com/2015/12/09/gw-palestinian-flag/.

Flaherty, Colleen. "Steven Salaita Says He's Leaving Academe." *Inside Higher Ed*, July 24, 2017. https://www.insidehighered.com/quicktakes/2017/07/25/steven-salaita-says-hes-leaving-academe.

Flood, Alison. "Alice Walker Declines Request to Publish Israeli Edition of The Color Purple." *Guardian*, June 20, 2012. https://www.theguardian.com/books/2012/jun/20/alice-walker-declines-israeli-color-purple.

Forman, Abra. "In Rejection of Genesis 12:3, Methodist Church Divests from Israel." *Israel 365 News*, January 13, 2016. https://www.israel365news.com/58877/in-rejection-of-genesis-123-methodist-church-divests-from-israel-biblical-zionism/.

Fox News. "Mark Levin Slams Jon Stewart's 'Putrid' Criticism of Israel," January 30, 2017. https://www.foxnews.com/transcript/mark-levin-slams-jon-stewarts-putrid-criticism-of-israel.

——. "Transcript: O'Reilly Interviews Al-Arian in September 2001," January 13, 2015. https://www.foxnews.com/story/transcript-oreilly-interviews-al-arian-in-sepTember-2001.

French, Phoebe. "EU Court Rules on Israeli Wine Labelling Case." *Drinks Business*, November 13, 2019. https://www.thedrinksbusiness.com/2019/11/eu-court-rules-on-israeli-wine-labelling-case/.

BIBLIOGRAPHY

Friedman, Robert I. "Selling Israel to America." *Journal of Palestine Studies* 16, no. 4 (1987): 169–79. https://doi.org/10.2307/2536739.
Friel, Howard. *Chomsky and Dershowitz: On Endless War and the End of Civil Liberties*. Northampton, Mass.: Interlink Publishing, 2013.
Frishberg, Hannah. "American Church Attendance Hits Historic Low, Says Gallup Survey." *New York Post*, May 30, 2021. https://nypost.com/2021/03/30/american-church-attendance-hits-historic-low-survey/.
Frost, Caroline. "BBC News Chief Fran Unsworth Says Jon Snow's Emotional Video About Gaza Children Would Have Failed BBC Impartiality." *Huffington Post*, September 9, 2014. https://www.huffingtonpost.co.uk/2014/09/09/jon-snow-gaza-video-channel4-bbc-news-sky-rts_n_5791204.html.
Garcia-Navarro, Lulu. "Israel Presents Itself as Haven for Gay Community." NPR, June 4, 2012. https://www.npr.org/2012/06/04/154279534/israel-presents-itself-as-haven-for-gay-community.
Gatto, John Taylor. *Dumbing Us Down: The Hidden Curriculum of Compulsory Schooling*. Philadelphia: New Society, 1992.
Gerstmann, Evan. "Why an Academic Boycott of Israel Is Hypocritical." *Forbes*, February 21, 2019. https://www.forbes.com/sites/evangerstmann/2019/02/21/why-an-academic-boycott-of-israel-is-hypocritical/?sh=47b3d4f05f04.
Ghorashi, Halleh. "How Dual Is Transnational Identity? A Debate on Dual Positioning of Diaspora Organizations." *Culture and Organization* 10, no. 4 (2004): 329–40. https://doi.org/10.1080/1475955042000313768.
Goldberg, Jeffrey. "Peter Beinart Is Right—or, a One-State Solution Is Inevitable If Settlements Continue." *Atlantic*, December 8, 2011. https://www.theatlantic.com/international/archive/2011/12/peter-beinart-is-right-or-a-one-state-solution-is-inevitable-if-settlements-continue/249608/.
Goldenberg, Tia. "In Israel, Miss Universe Says Pageant No Place for Politics." *U.S. News*, November 17, 2021. https://www.usnews.com/news/world/articles/2021-11-17/in-israel-miss-universe-says-pageant-no-place-for-politics.
Gordon, Neve. "No justice for Rachel Corrie." *Al Jazeera*, September 5, 2012. https://www.aljazeera.com/opinions/2012/9/5/no-justice-for-rachel-corrie/.
Gouterman, Martin. "Toward a Jewish Component of the Rainbow Coalition." *Monthly Review* 39, no. 8 (1988).
Gramsci, Antonio, Quintin Hoare, and Geoffrey Nowell-Smith. *Selections from the Prison Notebooks of Antonio Gramsci*. New York: International Publishers, 1972.
Green, Emma. "Why Do Black Activists Care About Palestine?" *Atlantic*, August 18, 2016. https://www.theatlantic.com/politics/archive/2016/08/why-did-black-american-activists-start-caring-about-palestine/496088/.
Green, Rodney. *The Social and Political Implications of the 1984 Jesse Jackson Presidential Campaign*. London: Praeger, 1990.
Greening Israel. "The Greening Israel Project," accessed September 14, 2022. https://greeningisrael.com/.
Greenwald, Glenn. "A Texas Elementary School Speech Pathologist Refused to Sign a Pro-Israel Oath, Now Mandatory in Many States—So She Lost Her Job." *Intercept*, December 17, 2018. https://theintercept.com/2018/12/17/israel-texas-anti-bds-law/.

Greilsammer, Ilan. "The New Historians of Israel and Their Political Involvement." *Bulletin du Centre de recherche français à Jérusalem* [in English], January 20, 2013. http://journals.openedition.org/bcrfj/6868.

Grisar, PJ. "Who Is Sabra, Marvel's Israeli Superhero?" *Forward*, September 12, 2022. https://forward.com/culture/film-tv/517550/sabra-marvel-mcu-shira-haas-israeli-superhero-jewish-controversy/.

Gupta, Akhil, and James Ferguson. *Culture, Power, Place: Explorations in Critical Anthropology*. Durham, N.C.: Duke University Press, 1997.

Gwoskin, Elizabeth and Gerrit De Vynck. "Facebook's AI Treats Palestinian Activists Like It Treats American Black Activists. It Blocks Them." *Washington Post*, May 28, 2021. https://www.washingtonpost.com/technology/2021/05/28/facebook-palestinian-censorship/.

Haddad, Mohammed. "Nakba Day: What Happened in Palestine in 1948?" *Al Jazeera*, May 12, 2022. https://www.aljazeera.com/news/2022/5/15/nakba-mapping-palestinian-villages-destroyed-by-israel-in-1948.

Hagbard, Celine. "United Church of Christ Divests from Israeli Occupation." *IMEMC News*, July 1, 2015. https://imemc.org/article/72119/#.

Hagopian, Joachim. "The Dumbing Down of America—by Design." *Global Research*, January 30, 2018. https://www.globalresearch.ca/the-dumbing-down-of-america-by-design/5395928.

Hahn, Peter. "The Suez Crisis (1956)." *Origins*, accessed December 15, 2022. https://origins.osu.edu/milestones/suez-crisis-1956.

Hall, Wendy, Ramine Tinati, and Will Jennings. "From Brexit to Trump: Social Media's Role in Democracy." *Computer* 51, no. 1 (2018): 18–27. https://doi.org/10.1109/MC.2018.1151005.

Hamilton, Thomas J. "Jews to Proclaim State Despite US." *New York Times*, May 11, 1948. https://www.nytimes.com/1948/05/11/archives/jews-to-proclaim-state-despite-us-un-assembly-held-limited-to.html.

Harper, James. "Professor's Home, Office Searched." *St. Petersburg (Fla.) Times*, November 21, 1995. https://www.tampabay.com/archive/1995/11/21/professor-s-home-office-searched/.

——. "USF Ties to Islamic Group Cleared." *St. Petersburg (Fla.) Times*, May 30, 1996. https://www.tampabay.com/archive/1996/05/30/usf-ties-to-islamic-group-cleared/.

Harris, Ben. "American Radical." Jewish Telegraphic Agency, November, 23, 2009. https://www.jta.org/2009/11/23/global/american-radical.

Harris, Bryant. "Israel Anti-boycott Bill Inches Closer to Passing Senate After Revisions." *Al-Monitor*, March 6, 2018. https://www.al-monitor.com/pulse/originals/2018/03/israel-anti-boycott-bill-closer-passing-senate-revisions.html.

Harris, Emily. "When 500 Palestinians Lose Their Jobs at SodaStream, Who's to Blame?" NPR, March 27, 2016. https://www.npr.org/sections/parallels/2016/03/27/471885452/when-500-palestinians-lose-their-jobs-at-sodastream-whos-to-blame.

Harvard Political Review. "The Crimson's Anti-Palestinian Bias," March 10, 2013. https://harvardpolitics.com/the-crimsons-anti-palestinian-bias/.

Hassner, Ross E., and Ethan B. Katz. "UC Berkeley Has Many Jewish-Filled 'Zones.' If You Want to Support Campus Jews, Learn About Them." *Forward*, October 3, 2022. https://forward.com/opinion/520107/uc-berkeley-has-many-jewish-filled-zones/.

BIBLIOGRAPHY

Hauss, Brian. "The New Israel Anti-Boycott Act Is Still Unconstitutional." ACLU, March 7, 2018. https://www.aclu.org/blog/free-speech/rights-protesters/new-israel-anti-boycott-act-still-unconstitutional.

Hays, Charlotte. "Women's March Co-Chair Linda Sarsour: What Are Her Causes?" Independent Women's Forum, January 25, 2017. https://www.iwf.org/2017/01/25/womens-march-co-chair-linda-sarsour-what-are-her-causes/.

Hearst Metrotone News. "The Lightning War in the Middle East." Internet Archive, accessed December 12, 2022. https://archive.org/details/lightningwarinthemiddleeast.

Hebrew University of Jerusalem. "Hillel Cohen," accessed November 11, 2022. https://pluto.huji.ac.il/~hilcoh/.

Herszenshorn, Miles J. "Anti-War Activists Protest Harvard Kennedy School Professor with Ties to Defense Contractor." PopularResistance, October 5, 2022. https://popularresistance.org/anti-war-activists-protest-harvard-kennedy-school-professor-with-ties-to-defense-contractor/#.

Hertz, Eli E. "Palestine Royal Commission Report, July 1937, Chapter II, p. 24." Myth and Facts, accessed August 12, 2022. http://www.mythsandfacts.org/conflict/mandate_for_palestine/mandate_for_palestine.htm#31.

Hill, Marc Lamont, and Mitchell Plitnick. *Except for Palestine: The Limits of Progressive Politics*. New York: New Press, 2021.

Hoffman, Ari. "Washington State Removes Anti-Semitic Material Curriculum on Native Americans, but Fails to Address Textbooks." *Post Millenial*, July 19, 2021. https://thepostmillennial.com/washington-state-Removes-anti-semitic-material-curriculum-on-native-americans-but-fails-to-address-textbooks.

Holland, Steve. "Obama Breaks Silence on Gaza, Voices Concern." Reuters, January 6, 2009. https://www.reuters.com/article/idUSN06437468.

Holmes, Oliver. "Seth Rogen: 'I Was Fed a Huge Amount of Lies About Israel.'" *Guardian*, July 29, 2020. https://www.theguardian.com/world/2020/jul/29/seth-rogen-israel-palestinians-jewish-actor.

Home Made Docs. "Advocate," accessed November 11, 2022. https://www.homemadedocs.com/advocate.

Hoop, Darrin. "Seattle Educators Endorse BDS." *Tempest*, August 6, 2021. https://www.tempestmag.org/2021/08/seattle-educators-endorse-bds/.

Horovitz, David. "Jon Stewart—So Funny, So Wrong on Israel-Gaza." *Times of Israel*, July 16, 2014. https://www.timesofisrael.com/jon-stewart-so-funny-so-wrong-on-israel-gaza/.

HuffPost. "Haaretz's Amira Hass Awarded Journalism Prize by Media Watchdog," March 18, 2010. https://www.huffpost.com/entry/haaretzs-amira-hass-award_n_377258.

Human Rights Watch. "Israel: Provide Vaccines to Occupied Palestinians," January 17, 2021. https://www.hrw.org/news/2021/01/17/israel-provide-vaccines-occupied-palestinians.

Hussain, Murtaza. "Students in California Might Face Criminal Investigation for Protesting Film on Isreali Army." *Intercept*, June 23, 2016. https://theintercept.com/2016/06/23/Students-in-california-might-face-criminal-investigation-for-protesting-film-on-israeli-army/.

Hyamson, Albert Montefiore. *British Projects for the Restoration of the Jews*. London: Petty & Sons, 1917.

———. "British Projects for the Restoration of the Jews to Palestine." *Publications of the American Jewish Historical Society*, no. 26 (1918): 127–64. http://www.jstor.org/stable/43059305.

IfNotNow. "Learn More from Organizations in Israel/Palestine," accessed November 11, 2022. https://www.ifnotnowmovement.org/organizations-in-israel-palestine.

———. "Why We Organize," accessed November 11, 2022. https://www.ifnotnowmovement.org/about.

Ingraham, Laura. "Linda Sarsour, Marc Lamont Hill and Anti-Semitism Hiding in Plain Sight." *Fox News*, November 30, 2018. https://www.foxnews.com/opinion/laura-ingraham-anti-semitism-hiding-in-plain-sight.

Institute for Middle East Understanding. "Google's Anti-Palestinian Racism and Project Nimbus." Facebook video. Podcast episode, September 29, 2022. https://www.facebook.com/theIMEU/videos/631252611720508/.

International Fellowship of Christians and Jews. "Stand for Israel," accessed October 3, 2022. https://www.ifcj.org/who-we-are/programs/stand-for-israel.

———. "Victims of Terror and War," accessed October 3, 2022. https://www.ifcj.org/who-we-help/victims-of-terror-and-war.

International Holocaust Rememberance Alliance. "What Is Antisemitism?," accessed September 8, 2022. https://www.holocaustremembrance.com/resources/working-definitions-charters/working-definition-antisemitism.

International Middle East Media Center. "U.S. Judge Forces Ben & Jerry's to Sell Ice Cream in Israeli Settlements," August 26, 2022. https://imemc.org/article/us-judge-forces-ben-jerrys-to-sell-ice-cream-in-israeli-settlements/.

International Women's Media Foundation. "Amira Haas," accessed November 11, 2022. https://www.iwmf.org/community/amira-haas/.

Isaac, Munther. "An Open Letter to U.S. Christians from a Palestinian Pastor." *Sojourners*, May 20, 2021. https://sojo.net/articles/open-letter-us-christians-palestinian-pastor.

———. *The Other Side of the Wall: A Palestinian Christian Narrative of Lament and Hope*. Westmont, Ill.: InterVarsity Press, 2020.

It's Going Down. "Oakland Rallies to Block Boat Carrying Israeli Arms Shipment," November 4, 2023. https://itsgoingdown.org/oakland-rallies-to-block-boat-carrying-israeli-arms-shipment/.

Iwasaki, Atsuko. "As Israelies, We Also Fight for Palestinians," Counterpunch, April 3, 2006. https://www.counterpunch.org/2006/04/03/quot-as-israelis-we-also-fight-for-palestinians-quot/.

J Street. "National Election Night Survey of Jewish Voters Finds Overwhelming Support for Democrats, Opposition to Trump and the Far-Right," November 10, 2022. https://jstreet.org/press-releases/national-election-night-survey-of-jewish-voters-finds-overwhelming-support-for-democrats-opposition-to-trump-and-the-far-right/#.

Jackson, Holly M. "The New York Times Distorts the Palestinian Struggle: A Case Study of Anti-Palestinian Bias in US News Coverage of the First and Second Palestinian Intifadas." *Media, War & Conflict* (2023). https://doi.org/10.1177/17506352231178148.

BIBLIOGRAPHY

Jaffe-Hoffman, Maayan. "TikTok Intifada Is 'Just the Tip of the Iceberg'—Analysis." *Jerusalem Post*, April 26, 2021. https://www.jpost.com/arab-israeli-conflict/tiktok-intifada-is-just-the-tip-of-the-iceberg-analysis-666403.
Jalalzai, Farida. "The Politics of Muslims in America." *Politics and Religion* 2, no. 2 (2009): 163–99. https://doi.org/10.1017/S1755048309000194.
Jenke, Tyler. "Lorde Labelled a 'Bigot' by U.S. Newspaper in Wake of Israel Controversy." *Tone Deaf*, February 1, 2018. https://tonedeaf.thebrag.com/lorde-bigot-israel-controversy/.
Jewish Insider. "AIPAC Letter to Supporters," March 18, 2022. https://jewishinsider.nyc3.digitaloceanspaces.com/wp-content/uploads/2022/03/17214409/AIPAC-Letter-With-Watermark.pdf.
Jewish Labor Committee. "Statement of Opposition to Divestment From or Boycotts of Israel," July 2007. http://www.jewishlaborcommittee.org/2007/07/statement_of_opposition_to_div.html.
Jewish Telegraphic Agency. "Christian Council on Palestine Formed; Asks Admission of Refugees to America," accessed August 12, 2022. https://www.jta.org/archive/christian-council-on-palestine-formed-asks-admission-of-refugees-to-america.
———. "Stokely Carmichael Contends Palestinian Arabs in Just Struggle Against Israel," April 10, 1970. https://www.jta.org/1970/04/10/archive/stokely-carmichael-contends-palestinian-arabs-in-just-struggle-against-israel.
Jewish Virtual Library. "U.S. Presidents & Israel: Quotes About Jewish Homeland & Israel," accessed August 12, 2022. http://www.jewishvirtuallibrary.org/u-s-presidential-quotes-about-jewish-homeland-and-israel-jewish-virtual-library.
Jewish Voice for Peace. "Why Is It important That JVP Is a Jewish Group?," accessed November 11, 2022. https://www.jewishvoiceforpeace.org/faq/.
JOCSM. "Jews of Color Caucus Statement in Solidarity with the Movement for Black," August 5, 2016. http://jocsm.org/jews-of-color-caucus-statement-in-solidarity-with-the-movement-for-black-lives-matter/.
Johnson, Gene. "Impact of WTO Protests in Seattle Still Felt 2 Decades Later." Associated Press, November 28, 2019. https://apnews.com/article/seattle-us-news-ap-top-news-wa-state-wire-environment-239fb5aca78345f0807fa4c9c505db9a.
Johnson, Terry. "The Rise and Decline of Evangelicalism in the United States (1967–2017)." *Evangelical Times*, February 2, 2017. https://www.evangelical-times.org/the-rise-and-decline-of-evangelicalism-in-the-united-states-1967-2017/#.
Johnston, Chris. "Lana Del Rey Pulls Out of Israeli Festival After Backlash." *Guardian*, August 31, 2018. https://www.theguardian.com/music/2018/aug/31/lana-del-rey-pulls-out-of-israeli-festival-after-backlash.
Jones, Ella L., and Monique I. Vobecky. "Harvard Out of Occupied Palestine Protests Sabra Hummus in Harvard Yard." *Harvard Crimson*, February 9, 2022. https://www.thecrimson.com/article/2022/2/9/students-protest-sabra-hummus/.
"Jordahl v. Brnovich." *Global Freedom of Expression: Columbia University*, accessed October 28, 2022. https://globalfreedomofexpression.columbia.edu/cases/mikkel-jordahl-v-mark-brnovich/.
JP. "Stopping Asian Hate Must Include Standing with Palestine." *Urbanity Magazine*, June 12, 2021. https://medium.com/urbanitymag/stopping-asian-hate-must-include-standing-with-palestine-739d0f96616e.

JTA. "Hundreds of Protesters Disrupt Jewish Reception at Chicago LGBTQ Conference." *Haaretz*, January 24, 2016. https://www.haaretz.com/jewish/2016-01-24/ty-article/protesters-disrupt-jewish-reception-at-lgbtq-conference/0000017f-dbe1-d3a5-af7f-Fbef33990000.

——. "Navajo President, First Lady Visit Israel on Agricultural Tech Mission." *Times of Israel*, December 11, 2012. https://www.timesofisrael.com/navajo-president-first-lady-visit-israel-on-agricultural-tech-mission/.

Kaell, Hilary. "The Hebraic Style in Christian Nation-Building." Christian Nation Project, accessed August 13, 2022. https://thechristiannationproject.net/kaell-fullintro/.

——. "Pastors Wrapped in Torah: Why So Many Christians Are Appropriating Jewish Ritual." *Forward*, October 18, 2020. https://forward.com/news/456599/pastors-wrapped-in-torah-why-so-many-christians-are-appropriating-jewish/.

Kahane, Meir. *They Must Go*. Israel: Grosset and Dunlap, 1981.

Kaleem, Jaweed. "United Methodist Church Divests from Security Firm Targeted for Work in Palestinian Territories." *Huffington Post*, June 12, 2014. https://www.huffpost.com/entry/united-methodist-church-divestment_n_5489968.

Kansas Legislature. "HB 2409." *Kansas 2017-2018 Legislative Sessions*, accessed August 17, 2023. http://www.kslegislature.org/li_2018/b2017_18/measures/hb2409/.

Kant, Immanuel. 1798. *Anthropology from a Pragmatic Point of View*. Carbondale: Southern Illinois University Press, 1978.

Kaplan, Amy. *Our American Israel: The Story of an Entangled Alliance*. Cambridge, Mass.: Harvard University Press, 2018.

Keller, Aron. "How British Pro-Israel Groups Are Rewriting Middle East History Textbooks." *+972 Magazine*, July 16, 2021. https://www.972mag.com/uk-pearson-books-anti-palestinian-bias/.

Kelly, Laura. "Progressive Groups Call for Biden to Denounce Evictions of Palestinians as 'War Crimes.'" *Hill*, May 13, 2021. https://thehill.com/policy/international/553472-more-than-100-progressive-groups-call-for-biden-to-denounce-evictions-of/.

Kerschner, Stephen. "Ta-Nehisi Coates' Case for Reparations & Spiritual Awakening." *Critique*, July 14, 2016. http://www.thecritique.com/articles/ta-nehisi-coates-case-for-reparations-spiritual-awakening/.

Khalek, Rania. "Ta-Nehisi Coates Sings of Zionism." *Electronic Intifada*, February 23, 2016. https://electronicintifada.net/content/ta-nehisi-coates-sings-zionism/15776.

Khalid, Asma. "Biden Faces Pushback Within His Own Party for His Unwavering Support of Israel." NPR, January 19, 2024. https://www.npr.org/2024/01/19/1225573911/biden-faces-pushback-within-his-own-party-for-his-unwavering-support-of-israel.

Khalidi, Rashid. *Palestinian Identity: The Construction of Modern National Consciousness*. New York: Columbia University Press, 1997.

Khalil, Osamah. "Pax Americana: The United States, the Palestinians, and the Peace Process, 1948-2008." *CR* 8, no. 2 (2008): 1–41. https://doi.org/10.1353/ncr.0.0026.

Khan, Suhaib, and Rina Abd El Rahman. "Palestine Center Annual Conference Educates and Updates Attendees." *Washington Report on Middle East Affairs* 35, no. 1 (2016): 57–60.

Kiely, Keith Peter. *U.S. Foreign Policy Discourse and the Israel Lobby: The Clinton Administration and the Israel-Palestine Peace Process*. Cham, Switz.: Springer International, 2017.

Kiracofe, Clifford Attick. *Dark Crusade: Christian Zionism and US Foreign Policy*. London: Tauris, 2009.
Kirk, Gabi. "Authors of California Ethnic Studies Curriculum Decry Cuts to Arab Studies." *Jewish Currents*, February 3. 2021. https://jewishcurrents.org/authors-of-california-ethnic-studies-curriculum-decry-cuts-to-arab-studies.
Kirka, Danica, Menelaos Hadjicostis, and Fatima Hussein. "A Global Day of Protests Draws Thousands in Washington and Other Cities in Pro-Palestinian Marches." *AP News*, January 13, 2024. https://apnews.com/article/protest-gaza-israel-palestinians-london-29d5cd664c81654283344d1874691a4f.
KIW. "Finnish Musicians Threaten Eurovision Boycott If Israel's Participation Continues Amid Gaza Conflict." *essanews.com*, January 12, 2024. https://www.msn.com/en-us/news/world/finnish-musicians-threaten-eurovision-boycott-if-israel-s-participation-continues-amid-gaza-conflict/ar-AA1mSHk8.
Klinger, Jerry. *Reverend William H. Hechler—the Christian Minister Who Legitimized Theodor Herzl*, accessed August 12, 2022. http://www.jewish-american-society-for-historic-preservation.org/images/Reverend_William_H.pdf.
Knopf-Newman, Marcy Jane. "The Fallacy of Academic Freedom and the Academic Boycott of Israel." *CR: The New Centennial Review* 8, no. 2 (Fall 2008)..
———. *The Politics of Teaching Palestine to Americans: Addressing Pedagogical Strategies*. New York: Palgrave Macmillan, 2011.
"Koontz v. Watson." *Global Freedom of Expression: Columbia University*, accessed October 28, 2022. https://globalfreedomofexpression.columbia.edu/cases/koontz-v-watson/.
Koren, Ariel. "Google's Complicity in Israeli Apartheid: How Google Weaponizes 'Diversity' to Silence Palestinians and Palestinian Human Rights Supporters." *Medium*, August 30, 2022. https://medium.com/@arielkoren/googles-complicity-in-israeli-apartheid-how-google-weaponizes-diversity-to-silence-palestinians-cb41b24ac423.
Kosman, Josh. "Students Howl as McGraw-Hill, Cengage Textbook Merger Nears DOJ Approval." *New York Post*, December 16, 2019. https://nypost.com/2019/12/16/students-howl-as-mcgraw-hill-pearson-textbook-merger-nears-doj-approval/.
Kramer, Martin. "The Unspoken Purpose of the Academic Boycott." *Israel Affairs* 27, no. 1 (2021): 27–33. https://doi:10.1080/13537121.2021.1864846.
Kumar, Anugrah. "Presbyterian Church USA Votes to Divest from Companies Israel Uses in West Bank; Jewish Group Denounces 'Radical, Prejudiced' Decision." *Christian Post*, June 23, 2014. https://www.christianpost.com/news/presbyterian-church-usa-Votes-to-divest-from-companies-israel-uses-in-west-bank-jewish-group-denounces-radical-prejudiced-decision.html.
Kushner, Daniel. "'Israelism' Review: The Dangers of Pro-Israel Indoctrination." *New Voices*, September 6, 2023. https://newvoices.org/2023/09/06/israelism-review-the-dangers-of-pro-israel-indoctrination/.
Kuttab, Daoud. "The 'Smartphone Intifada.'" *Al-Monitor*, October 13, 2015. https://www.al-monitor.com/originals/2015/10/west-bank-palestinian-protests-social-media.html.
KUVRD Team. "Civilized vs Uncivilized: An Analysis of Ukraine, Palestine & Beyond." KUVRD, April 28, 2022. https://kuvrd.ca/blogs/blog/civilized-vs-uncivilized-humanity-divided.

Kvetanadze, Tea. "Author Sally Rooney Turns Down Israeli Publisher in Solidarity with Palestinians." *Forbes*, October 12, 2021. https://www.forbes.com/sites/teakvetenadze/2021/10/12/author-sally-rooney-turns-down-israeli-publisher-in-solidarity-with-palestinians/.

La Corte, Rachel. "Al-Arian Calls Self 'Prisoner of Conscience,' Victim of Hysteria." Associated Press State & Local Wire, February 25, 2003. https://freerepublic.com/focus/news/851966/posts.

Lacy, Akela. "Progressives, 'Massively Outgunned,' Ditched Nina Turner." *Intercept*, May 3, 2022. https://theintercept.com/2022/05/03/ohio-primary-elections-nina-turner-shontel-brown/.

Land, Olivia, and Emily Crane. "Biden Rebukes Russia Over War with Ukraine at UN General Assembly." *New York Post*, September 21, 2022. https://nypost.com/2022/09/21/biden-to-rebuke-russia-over-ukraine-war-at-un/.

Landau, Susan. "Say No to Settlement Products and Sabra Hummus." *Mondoweiss*, February 14, 2013. https://mondoweiss.net/2013/02/settlement-products-hummus/.

Lawrence, Bruce B. "Roy: Failing Peace: Gaza and the Palestinian-Israeli Conflict." *Journal of Palestine Studies* 37, no. 1 (Fall 2007): 111. https://web.archive.org/web/20120213113623/http://www.palestine-studies.org/print.aspx?id=9678&jid=1&href=fulltext.

Lazaroff, Tovah. "Netanyahu: A Palestinian State Won't Be Created." *Jerusalem Post*, April 8, 2019. https://www.jpost.com/arab-israeli-conflict/netanyahu-a-palestinian-state-wont-be-created-586017.

Lebow, Richard Ned. "Woodrow Wilson and the Balfour Declaration." *Journal of Modern History* 40, no. 4 (1968): 501–23. https://doi:10.1086/240237.

Leibovitz, Liel. "Native American Chief Visits Israel." *Tablet Magazine*, April 23, 2018. https://www.tabletmag.com/sections/news/articles/native-american-chief-visits-israel.

Levy, Gideon. "Gideon Levy: Americans 'Are Supporting the First Signs of Fascism in Israel.'" *Real News Network*, March 22, 2016. https://therealnews.com/thedgeso318gideon.

———. "Netanyahu's Far-Right Gov't Will Usher in the End of Israeli Apartheid." *Haaretz*, December 11, 2022. https://www.haaretz.com/opinion/2022-12-11/ty-article-opinion/.premium/yearning-for-a-jolt-and-the-end-of-apartheid/00000184-fd67-d4c7-a786-fdf7a4ee0000.

Lewin, Tamar. "Web Site Fuels Debate on Campus Anti-Semitism." *New York Times*, September 27, 2002. https://www.nytimes.com/2002/09/27/us/web-site-fuels-debate-on-campus-anti-semitism.html.

Lewis, Bernard. "The Roots of Muslim Rage." *Atlantic*, September 1990. Accessed August 13, 2022. https://www.theatlantic.com/magazine/archive/1990/09/the-roots-of-muslim-rage/304643/.

Lim, Audrea, ed. *The Case for Sanctions Against Israel*. London: Verso, 2012.

Lipka, Michael. "More White Evangelicals than American Jews Say God Gave Israel to the Jewish People." Pew Research Center, October 3, 2013. http://www.pewresearch.org/fact-tank/2013/10/03/more-white-evangelicals-than-american-jews-say-god-gave-israel-to-the-jewish-people/.

Lloyd, David, and Malini Johar Schueller. "The Israeli State of Exception and the Case for Academic Boycott." *Journal of Academic Freedom* 4 (2013). https://www.aaup.org/JAF4/israeli-state-exception-and-case-academic-boycott#.
Lopez, David, and Yen Espiritu. "Panethnicity in the United States: A Theoretical Framework." *Ethnic and Racial Studies* 13, no. 2 (1990): 198–224. https://doi:10.1080/01419870.1990.9993669.
Lopez, Ian Haney. *White by Law: The Legal Construction of Race*. New York: NYU Press, 1997.
Lopez Almejo, Jose de Jesus. "Diasporas Lobbying the Host Government: Mexican Diaspora as a Third Actor of the Bilateral Relationship Between Mexico and the U.S." *Migration and Diaspora: An Interdisciplinary Journal* 1, no. 1 (January–June 2018): 100–121.
Loevy and Loevy. "Settlement Reached in Case of Professor Fired for 'Uncivil' Tweets." November 12, 2015. https://www.loevy.com/blog/settlement-reached-in-case-of-professor-fired-for-uncivil-tweets/.
Lubell, Mayaan, and Patricia Zengerle. "Israel Bars U.S. Democratic Lawmakers Ilhan Omar and Rashida Tlaib Under Pressure from Trump." Reuters, August 15, 2019. https://www.reuters.com/article/us-israel-palestinians-usa/israel-bars-u-s-Democratic-lawmakers-ilhan-omar-and-rashida-tlaib-under-pressure-from-trump-idUSKCN1V50SF.
Mac, Ryan. "Instagram Censored Posts About One of Islam's Holiest Mosques, Drawing Employee Ire." *Buzzfeed News*, May 12, 2021. https://www.buzzfeednews.com/article/ryanmac/instagram-facebook-censored-al-aqsa-mosque.
Maestas, Adrian, and Rania Khalek. "How Latino Activists Are Standing Up to the Israel Lobby." *Electronic Intifada*, March 6, 2014. https://electronicintifada.net/content/how-latino-activists-are-standing-israel-lobby/13225.
Mahdawi, Arwa. "Bella Hadid's Deleted Instagram Post Shows How Palestinians Are Silenced." *Guardian*, July 15, 2020. https://www.theguardian.com/commentisfree/2020/jul/15/bella-hadid-deleted-instagram-post-palestinians-silenced.
Maira, Sunaina. "'We Ain't Missing': Palestinian Hip Hop—a Transnational Youth Movement." *CR* 8, no. 2 (2008): 161–92. https://doi:10.1353/ncr.0.0027.
Maira, Sunaina, and Magid Shihade. "Meeting Asian/Arab American Studies." *Journal of Asian American Studies* 9, no. 2 (2006).
Majaj, Lisa. "Arab Americans and the Meaning of Race." In *Postcolonial Theory and the United States: Race, Ethnicity, and Literature*, ed. Amritjit Singh and Peter Schmidt. Jackson: University Press of Mississippi, 2000.
Makdisi, Saree. *Tolerance Is a Wasteland: Palestine and the Culture of Denial*. Oakland: University of California Press, 2022.
Makhlouf, George. "No Room in My Luggage." In *Being Palestinian: Personal Reflections on Palestinian Identity in the Diaspora*, ed. Yasir Suleiman. Edinburgh: Edinburgh University Press, 2016.
Malone, Linda A. "The Kahan Report, Ariel Sharon and the Sabra-Shatilla Massacres in Lebanon: Responsibility Under International Law for Massacres of Civilian Populations." *Utah Law Review* 1985, no. 2 (1985): 373–433.
Maltz, Judy. "'Biblical Mandate': The U.S. Evangelicals Behind the Latest West Bank Land Grab." *Haaretz*, August 22, 2022. https://www.haaretz.com/israel-news/2022

-08-22/ty-article/.highlight/biblical-mandate-the-u-s-evangelicals-behind-the-latest-west-bank-land-grab/00000182-c64e-d6fa-abbe-d74f90570000.

Marcetic, Branko. "Don't Look Now but Progressives Are About to Expand Their Ranks in Congress." *In These Times*, October 31, 2022. https://inthesetimes.com/article/progressives-dark-money-midterms-squad-democrats.

Marcus, Kenneth. "Berkeley Develops Jewish-Free Zones." *Jewish Journal*, September 28, 2022. https://jewishjournal.com/commentary/opinion/351854/berkeley-develops-jewish-free-zones/.

Marguerite Casey Foundation. "2022 Freedom Scholars: Noura Erakat." YouTube, December 6, 2022. https://www.youtube.com/watch?v=v_69jPorRA0.

Marsi, Federica. "'From the River to the Sea': What Does the Palestinian Slogan Really Mean?" *Al Jazeera*, November 2, 2023. https://www.aljazeera.com/news/2023/11/2/from-the-river-to-the-sea-what-does-the-palestinian-slogan-really-mean.

Masalha, Nur. *The Bible and Zionism: Invented Traditions, Archaeology, and Post-Colonialism in Israel-Palestine*. London: Zed Books, 2007.

———. *Palestine: A Four Thousand Year History*. London: Zed Books, 2018.

Mason, John. "Rep. Tlaib's Remarks on 'Apartheid' Israel Misinterpreted as Anti-Semitic." *Arab America*, September 28, 2022. https://www.arabamerica.com/rep-tlaibs-remarks-on-apartheid-israel-misinterpreted-as-anti-semitic/.

Massing, Michael. "Why the Godfather of Human Rights Not Welcome at Harvard." *Nation*, January 5, 2023. https://www.thenation.com./article/society/hrw-harvard-israel-kennedy-school/.

Mauritzi, Stefania. "Pappé: 'Since the Ukrainian War, Killing Palestinians Has Become a Daily Business.'" *Il Fatto Quotidiano*, October 28, 2022. https://www.ilfattoquotidiano.it/in-edicola/articoli/2022/10/28/Pappe-since-the-ukrainian-war-killing-palestinians-has-become-a-daily-business/6854205/.

McCarthy, Rory. "Rachel Corrie's Family Bring Civil Suit Over Human Shield's Death in Gaza." *Guardian*, February 23, 2010. https://www.theguardian.com/world/2010/feb/23/corrie-death-law-case.

McCollum, Betty. "McCollum Resolution Calls on U.S. House ro Condemn Israel's Repressive Decision to Designate Six Prominent Palestinian Human Rights and Civil Society Groups as Terrorist Organizations." Press release, October 28, 2021. https://mccollum.house.gov/media/press-releases/mccollum-resolution-calls-us-house-condemn-israel-s-repressive-decision.

McDermott, Gerald R., ed. *The New Christian Zionism: Fresh Perspectives on Israel and the Land*. Westmont, Ill.: IVP Academic, 2016.

McLeod, Alan. "Top Hollywood Producers Worked with Israel to Defend Its War Crimes." *Israel Palestine News*, September 27, 2022. https://israelpalestinenews.org/top-hollywood-producers-worked-with-israel-to-defend-its-war-crimes/.

Mearsheimer, John J., and Stephen M. Walt. "The Israel Lobby and U.S. Foreign Policy." *Middle East Policy* 13, no. 3 (2006): 29–87. https://doi:10.1111/j.1475-4967.2006.00260.x.

———. *The Israel Lobby and U.S. Foreign Policy*. New York: Farrar, Straus and Giroux, 2008.

Medad, Yisrael. "Bob Simon & CBS Throw the Jews to the Lions." *Jerusalem Post*, April 24, 2012. https://www.jpost.com/Blogs/Green-Lined/Bob-Simon-and-CBS-throw-the-Jews-to-the-lions-365810.

BIBLIOGRAPHY

Melman, Yossi. "Israel Denies Entry to High-Profile Critic Norman Finkelstein." *Haaretz*, May 24, 2008. https://www.haaretz.com/2008-05-24/ty-article/israel-denies-entry-to-high-profile-critic-norman-finkelstein/0000017f-e8bf-df5f-a17f-fbff95530000.

Memmott, Mark. "At White House, Netanyahu Calls '67 Border Lines 'Indefensible.'" *NPR*, May 20, 2011. https://www.npr.org/sections/thetwo-way/2011/05/24/136500693/at-white-house-netanyahu-calls-67-border-lines-indefensible.

Mensa, Vic. "Vic Mensa: What Palestine Taught Me About American Racism." *Time*, January 12, 2018. http://time.com/5095435/vic-mensa-palestine-israel-jerusalem/.

Meotti, Giulio. "Obama's Church to Divest from Israel." *Israel National News*, May 24, 2012. https://www.israelnationalnews.com/news/340280.

Merkley, Paul Charles. *The Politics of Christian Zionism, 1891–1948*. London: Cass, 1998.

Meyersohn, Nathaniel. "Starbucks' CEO Wants People to Stop Protesting Its Stores Over Israel War in Gaza." CNN, December 21, 2023. https://www.cnn.com/2023/12/21/business/starbucks-israel-war-union/index.html.

Middle East Policy Council. "Israeli Anger at Vatican Recognition of Palestine," accessed August 14, 2022. https://mepc.org/commentary/israeli-anger-vatican-recognition-palestine.

Miller, Paul. "Exclusive: Sheldon Adelson Deploys Task Force to Combat Soaring Campus Anti-Semitism." *Observer*, August 9, 2016. https://observer.com/2016/08/exclusive-sheldon-adelson-deploys-task-force-to-combat-soaring-campus-anti-semitism/.

Miller, Rory. "Why the Irish Support Palestine." *Foreign Policy*, June 23, 2010. https://foreignpolicy.com/2010/06/23/why-the-irish-support-palestine-2/.

Miller, Zeke. "Transcript: Netanyahu Speech to Congress." *Time*, March 3, 2015. https://time.com/3730318/transcript-netanyahu-speech-to-congress/.

Minhaj, Hasan. "Hasan Minhaj: Homecoming King | Official Trailer [HD] | Netflix." YouTube, 1:20, May 11, 2017. https://www.youtube.com/watch?v=Fu-u5VldxVY.

Mohammedwesam, Amer. "Critical Discourse Analysis of War Reporting in the International Press: The Case of the Gaza War of 2008–2009." *Palgrave Communications* 3, no. 1 (2017). https://doi:10.1057/s41599-017-0015-2.

Mohyeldin, Aydan. "The Media Is Getting Pro-Palestinian Expression at the World Cup All Wrong." MSNBC, December 7, 2022. https://www.msnbc.com/opinion/msnbc-opinion/world-cup-2022-puts-palestinians-front-center-rcna60423.

Moini, Rajaa. "Roger Waters' Pro-Palestine Activism Is a Lesson for the West." *Express Tribune* (Pakistan), May 20, 2021. https://tribune.com.pk/story/2300850/roger-waters-pro-palestine-activism-is-a-lesson-for-the-west.

Monagle, Mathew. "SXSW Film Review: *Boycott*." *Austin (Tex.) Chronicle*, March 22, 2022. https://www.austinchronicle.com/daily/screens/2022-03-22/sxsw-film-review-boycott/.

Mondoweiss Editors. "Roseanne Barr Talked Trash About Palestinians and Muslims for Years, Without Regrets." *Mondoweiss*, June 1, 2018. http://mondoweiss.net/2018/06/roseanne-palestinians-muslims/.

Morgan, Jared. "Post-9/11 Conflicts Increased Civilian Police Militarization, New Study Claims." *Military Times*, September 16, 2020. https://www.militarytimes.com/news/your-military/2020/09/16/post-911-conflicts-increased-civilian-police-militarization-new-study-claims/.

Morris, Willem. "Centering Palestinian Liberation Is Essential to Revitalizing the Labor Movement." Young Democratic Socialists of America, June 21, 2022. https://y.dsausa.org/the-activist/centering-palestinian-liberation-is-essential-to-revitalizing-the-labor-movement/.

Moskowitz, Peter. "The Campus Free Speech Battle You're Not Seeing." *Jezebel*, February 13, 2017. https://jezebel.com/the-campus-free-speech-battle-youre-not-seeing-1791631293.

Muckenfuss, Mark. "UC Riverside Students Vote to Ban Sabra Hummus." *Press-Enterprise* (Riverside, Calif.), February 3, 2017. https://www.pe.com/2017/02/03/uc-riverside-students-vote-to-ban-sabra-hummus/.

Murad, Nora Esther. "Palestinian Erasure Starts in Preschool—with Sesame Street's Endorsement." Fair, September 30, 2022. https://fair.org/home/palestinian-erasure-starts-in-preschool-with-sesame-streets-endorsement/.

Murphy, Chris. "Trevor Noah Asks Tough Questions About Israel and Palestine on *The Daily Show*." *Vanity Fair*, May 12, 2021. https://www.vanityfair.com/hollywood/2021/05/trevor-noah-asks-tough-questions-about-israel-and-palestine-on-the-daily-show.

Murphy, Glen, and Jack Power. "Thousands Attend Rallies in Irish Cities in Solidarity with Palestine." *Irish Times*, May 15, 2021. https://www.irishtimes.com/news/ireland/irish-news/thousands-attend-rallies-in-irish-cities-in-solidarity-with-palestine-1.4566435.

Naber, Nadine. "Ambiguous Insiders: An Investigation of Arab American Invisibility." *Ethnic and Racial Studies* 23, no. 1 (2000): 37–61. https://doi:10.1080/014198700329123.

Nagel, Risa. "Why I Walked off My Birthright Israel Trip." *HuffPost*, July 23, 2018. https://www.huffpost.com/entry/opinion-nagel-birthright-israel-walkout_n_5b54f04fe4b0b15aba90107d.

Nahmias, Omri. "Bipartisan Letter Urges Austin to Provide Emergency Funding for Iron Dome." *Jerusalem Post*, June 2, 2021. https://www.jpost.com/american-politics/bipartisan-letter-urges-austin-to-provide-emergency-funding-for-iron-dome-669941.

Naikoo, Babrah, and Aaqib Fayez. "Kashmiris Show Solidarity with Palestinians on Eid." *TRT*, May 14, 2021. https://www.trtworld.com/magazine/kashmiris-show-solidarity-with-palestinians-on-eid-46713.

National Archives. "Press Release Announcing U.S. Recognition of Israel (1948)," accessed August 12, 2022. https://www.archives.gov/milestone-documents/press-release-announcing-us-recognition-of-israel#.

Nazaryan, Alexander. "Dartmouth Dean Sparks Debate on the State of Israel and Anti-Semitism." *Newsweek*, May 21, 2017. http://www.newsweek.com/dartmouth-dean-accused-anti-israel-bias-colleague-611113.

Ndugga-Kabuye, Ben, and Rachel Gilmer."A Cut in US Military Expenditures and a Reallocation of Those Funds to Invest in Domestic Infrastructure and Community Wellbeing," accessed November 25, 2022. https://m4bl.org/wp-content/uploads/2020/05/CutMilitaryExpendituresOnePager.pdf.

Newton, Creede. "A History of the US Blocking UN Resolutions Against Israel." *Al Jazeera*, May 19, 2021. https://www.aljazeera.com/news/2021/5/19/a-history-of-the-us-blocking-un-resolutions-against-israel.

BIBLIOGRAPHY

Nietzel, Michael T. "College Presidents Issue Statement Supporting Israel and 'Moral Clarity' in War with Hamas." *Forbes*, October 18, 2023.
North, James. "How the New York Times Rigs News on Israel-Palestine." *Washington Report on Middle East Affairs* 38, no. 3 (2019): 31–37.
Obama, Barack. "Remarks by the President on the Middle East and North Africa." White House, Office of The Press Secretary. May 19, 2011. https://obamawhitehouse.archives.gov/the-press-office/2011/05/19/remarks-president-middle-east-and-north-africa%20.
"Obama Under Fire for Comment on Palestinians." *NBC News*, March 15, 2007. https://www.nbcnews.com/id/wbna17631015.
Obeidallah, Dean. "Do Palestinians Really Exist?" *Daily Beast*, April 14, 2017. https://www.thedailybeast.com/do-palestinians-really-exist.
———. "How Jon Stewart Made It Okay to Care About Palestinian Suffering." *Daily Beast*, April 14, 2017. https://www.thedailybeast.com/how-jon-stewart-made-it-okay-to-care-about-palestinian-suffering.
———. "Stop the Anti-Semitism When Talking Gaza." *Daily Beast*, April 14, 2017. https://www.thedailybeast.com/stop-the-anti-semitism-when-talking-gaza.
Obenzinger, Hilton. "Palestine Solidarity, Political Discourse, and the Peace Movement, 1982–1988." *CR* 8, no. 2 (2008): 233–52. https://doi:10.1353/ncr.0.0033.
O'Brien, Sarah Ashley. "Airbnb Will Allow Israeli Settlement Listings but Won't Profit off Them." CNN Business, April 9, 2019. https://www.cnn.com/2019/04/09/tech/airbnb-reverses-israeli-settlement-stance/index.html.
Ochienga, Akinya. "Black-Jewish Relations Intensified and Tested by Current Political Climate." NPR, April 23, 2017. https://www.npr.org/sections/codeswitch/2017/04/23/494790016/black-jewish-relations-intensified-and-tested-by-current-political-climate.
Office of the Chief of Staff Files. Hamilton Jordan's Confidential Files. Middle East, 1978. Container 35, Jimmy Carter Library, accessed November 9, 2022. https://www.jimmycarterlibrary.gov/digital_library/cos/142099/35/cos_142099_35_19-Middle_East_1977_2.pdf.
O'Grady, Siobhan. "A Palestinian Medic Was Shot Dead in Gaza. Now Israel Says It Will Investigate." *Washington Post*, June 2, 2018. https://www.washingtonpost.com/news/worldviews/wp/2018/06/02/a-palestinian-medic-was-shot-dead-in-gaza-now-israel-says-it-will-launch-a-probe/.
Oldmixon, Elizabeth Anne. *Uncompromising Positions: God, Sex, and the U.S. House of Representatives*. Washington, D.C.: Georgetown University Press, 2005.
Oldmixon, Elizabeth Anne, Beth Rosenson, and Kenneth D. Wald. "Conflict Over Israel: The Role of Religion, Race, Party and Ideology in the U.S. House of Representatives, 1997–2002." *Terrorism and Political Violence* 17, no. 3 (2005): 407–26. https://doi:10.1080/09546550590929246.
Omer, Atalia. *Days of Awe : Reimagining Jewishness in Solidarity with Palestinians*. Chicago: University of Chicago Press, 2019.
Omi, Michael, and Howard Winant. *Racial Formation in the United States: From the 1960's to the 1990's*. 2d ed. New York: Routledge, 1994.
Ong, Aihwa, Virginia R. Dominguez, Jonathan Friedman, Nina Glick Schiller, Verena Stolcke, and Hu Ying. "Cultural Citizenship as Subject-Making: Immigrants Negotiate Racial and Cultural Boundaries in the United States." *Current Anthropology* 37, no. 5 (1996): 737–62. https://doi:10.1086/204560.

Orbuch, Alexandra. "BDS-Aligned Referendum Fails to Win Majority Support." *Princeton Tory*, April 13, 2022. http://theprincetontory.com/princeton-bds-aligned-referendum-fails-to-win-majority-support/.

———. "USG Approves BDS-Aligned Referendum." *Princeton Tory*, March 29, 2022. http://theprincetontory.com/usg-approves-bds-aligned-referendum-news/.

Oster, Marcy. "Amazon Slammed for Free Shipping to Israeli Settlements but Not to Palestinian Territories." *Haaretz*, February 16, 2020. https://www.haaretz.com/israel-news/2020-02-16/ty-article/amazon-slammed-for-free-shipping-to-israeli-settlements-but-not-palestinians/0000017f-db5a-db22-a17f-fffb03020000.

Palestine Legal. "Censorship at K-12 Schools," accessed October 28, 2022. https://palestinelegal.org/2021-report#k12.

———. "Legal Challenges to Anti Boycott Laws," accessed August 17, 2023. https://legislation.palestinelegal.org/legal-challenges-to-anti-boycott-laws/#Kansas.

———. "New York," accessed August 17, 2023. https://legislation.palestinelegal.org/location/new-york/.

———. "Palestine Children's Book: Threats & Censorship," February 20, 2018. https://palestinelegal.org/case-studies/2018/2/20/palestine-childrens-book-threats-censorship.

———. "Palestine Legal Urges Dept. of Education to End Extreme Delay Into First-Ever Anti-Palestinian Discrimination Complaint," November 15, 2022. https://palestinelegal.org/news/2022/11/15/palestine-legal-urges-dept-of-education-to-end-extreme-delay-into-first-ever-anti-palestinian-discrimination-complaint.

———. "Smear Campaigns Target Employment," accessed October 28, 2022. https://palestinelegal.org/2021-report#employment.

———. "2021 Year-in-Review: Palestinian Uprising Generates Record Solidarity—and Fierce Backlash," accessed October 10, 2022. https://palestinelegal.org/2021-report.

Palestine Solidarity Campaign. "Boycott SodaStream," September 30, 2013. https://www.palestinecampaign.org/sodastream/.

———. "Hewlett-Packard," February 13, 2020. https://www.palestinecampaign.org/psc-company/hewlett-packard-hp/.

Palestinian Center for Human Rights "Palestinian Centre for Human Rights Wins France's Highest Award for Human Rights Endeavours," December 7, 1996. https://pchrgaza.org/en/palestinian-centre-for-human-rights-wins-frances-highest-award-for-human-rights-endeavours/.

Palmer, Ewan. "School Lesson Comparing Palestinian Plight to American Revolution Withdrawn." *Newsweek*, July 15, 2021. https://www.newsweek.com/israel-palestinians-school-question-washington-native-americans-1609998.

Patterson, Thomas E. "The Decline of Newspapers: The Local Story." *Nieman*, December 15, 2007. https://nieman.harvard.edu/articles/the-decline-of-newspapers-the-local-story/.

PBS. "ICC Launches War Crimes Probe Into Israeli Practices," March 3, 2021. https://www.pbs.org/newshour/world/icc-launches-war-crimes-probe-into-israeli-practices.

Peled, Miko. "In Nauseating Netanyahu Interview, Bill Maher Whitewashes a War Criminal." *Scheerpost*, October 26, 2022. https://scheerpost.com/2022/10/26/in-nauseating-netanyahu-interview-bill-maher-whitewashes-a-war-criminal/.

BIBLIOGRAPHY

Pew Research Center. *Faith on the Hill*, January 4, 2021. https://www.pewresearch.org/religion/2021/01/04/faith-on-the-hill-2021/.

———. *A Portrait of Jewish Americans*, October 1, 2013. https://assets.pewresearch.org/wp-content/uploads/sites/11/2013/10/jewish-american-full-report-for-web.pdf.

Phillips, Elizabeth. "Saying 'Peace' When There Is No Peace: An American Christian Zionist Congregation on Peace, Militarism, and Settlements." In *Comprehending Christian Zionism: Perspectives in Comparison*, ed. Gunner Göran and Robert O. Smith. Minneapolis: Augsburg Fortress, 2014.

Phillips, Scott W. "Police Militarization." *Law Enforcement Bulletin*, August 14, 2017. https://leb.fbi.gov/articles/featured-articles/police-militarization.

Picheta, Rob. "Iceland's Eurovision Entry Hatari Holds Up Palestinian Flag During Contest." CNN, May 18, 2019. https://www.cnn.com/2019/05/18/europe/iceland-eurovision-palestine-intl.

Pierce, Fred. "In Israel, Questions Are Raised About a Forest That Rises from the Desert." *Yale Environment 360*, September 9. 2019. https://e360.yale.edu/features/in-israel-questions-are-raised-about-a-forest-that-rises-from-the-desert.

Pierce, Rebecca. "Israeli Settlers Want New York Police Tactics in Jerusalem." *Electronic Intifada*, October 21, 2015. https://electronicintifada.net/content/israeli-settlers-want-new-york-police-tactics-jerusalem/14939.

Pilkington, Ed. "Noam ChomskyBbarred by Israelis from Lecturing in Palestinian West Bank." *Guardian*, May 16, 2010. https://www.theguardian.com/world/2010/may/16/israel-Noam-chomsky-palestinian-west-bank.

Pillsbury, Charlie. "Why We Must Boycott Pillsbury." *Minnesota Star-Tribune*, April 28, 2021. https://www.startribune.com/why-we-must-boycott-pillsbury/600051334/.

Podcast and Curious. "How BOBBY LEE Became Propaganda for the Israeli Government." YouTube, June 27, 2022. https://www.youtube.com/watch?v=vPiYpW6qp6A.

Press, Alex N. "Oakland Longshore Workers Say No to Israeli-Operated Cargo." *Jacobin*, June 8, 2021. https://jacobin.com/2021/06/palestine-zim-oakland-boycott-ship-ilwu-local-10.

Pro-Israel America. "Jewish News Syndicate: US House Overwhelmingly Condemns the BDS Movement, Affirms Support for Israel," July 23, 2019. https://proisraelamerica.org/jewish-news-syndicate-july-24/.

"Pro-Palestine Student Activists Targeted on College Campuses." *Washington Report on Middle East Affairs* 35, no. 1 (January/February 2016). https://issuu.com/washreport/docs/volxxvno1-lo2.

"Protests Against Israel in the USA Target Israeli Cargo." *Yeshiva World*, June 21, 2010. https://www.theyeshivaworld.com/news/israel-news/63063/protests-against-israel-in-the-usa-target-israeli-cargo.html.

Pruitt, Sarah. "How Jesse Jackson's Rainbow Coalition Championed Diversity." *History*, January 29, 2021. https://www.history.com/news/jesse-jackson-rainbow-coalition.

Pulver, Andrew. "Natalie Portman Pulls Out of Israel Award Due to 'Distressing Recent Events' There." *Guardian*, April 20, 2018. https://www.theguardian.com/film/2018/apr/20/natalie-portman-israel-genesis-prize.

Raheb, Mitri. "Palestinian Christian Reflections on Christian Zionism." In *Comprehending Christian Zionism: Perspectives in Comparison*, ed. Gunner Göran and Robert O. Smith. Minneapolis: Augsburg Fortress, 2014.

BIBLIOGRAPHY

Rahman, Khaleda. "Full List of US Universities Staging Pro-Palestinian Protests." *Newsweek*, October 11, 2023. https://www.newsweek.com/full-list-universities-staging-pro-palestinian-protests-1833807.

"Rashida Tlaib Fights for Right to Boycott." Facebook video, July 24, 2019. https://www.facebook.com/ajplusenglish/videos/rashida-tlaib-fights-for-right-to-boycott/651366061935704/.

Ratner, Lizzy. "The War Between the Civilized Man and Pamela Geller." *Nation*, October 18, 2012. https://www.thenation.com/article/archive/war-between-civilized-man-and-pamela-geller/.

Ravid, Barak. "Deputy Foreign Minister: 1967 Borders Are Auschwitz Borders." *Haaretz*, January 2, 2014. https://www.haaretz.com/2014-01-02/ty-article/1967-borders-are-auschwitz-borders/0000017f-dbc1-db22-a17f-fff146410000.

Redden, Elizabeth. "Big Night for Boycott Movement." *Insider Higher Ed*, November 23, 2015. https://www.insidehighered.com/news/2015/11/23/anthropologists-overwhelmingly-vote-boycott-israeli-universities.

Reich, Bernard. *Securing the Covenant: United States-Israel Relations After the Cold War*. Westport, Conn.: Greenwood Press, 1995.

Reiss, Debbie. "Balenciaga, Adidas Slammed for Hiring Anti-Israel Bella Hadid After Dropping Kanye." *World Israel News*, November 8, 2022. https://worldisraelnews.com/balenciaga-adidas-slammed-for-hiring-anti-israel-bella-hadid-after-dropping-kanye/.

Reubner, Josh. "Envisioning a Post-colonial Palestine." *Electronic Intifada*, March 23, 2021. https://electronicintifada.net/content/envisioning-post-colonial-palestine/32596.

Reuters. "Judge Rejects Ben and Jerry's Bid to Halt Ice Cream Sales in the West Bank." *New York Post*, August 22, 2022. https://nypost.com/2022/08/22/ben-jerrys-loses-bid-to-halt-ice-cream-sales-in-west-bank/.

Rice, Condoleeza. Keynote Address by Secretary of State Condoleezza Rice at ATFP Inaugural Gala. American Task Force on Palestine, accessed October 3, 2022. http://www.americantaskforce.org/keynote_address_secretary_state_condoleezza_rice_atfp_inaugural_gala.

Richardson, Bradford. "Jeremiah Wright: 'Jesus Was a Palestinian.'" *Hill*, October 10, 2015. http://thehill.com/blogs/blog-briefing-room/256592-jeremiah-wright-jesus-was-a-palestinian.

"Rising Spectre of Fascism in Israel." *Journal of Palestine Studies* 9, no. 3 (April 1980): 181–87. https://doi.org/10.2307/2536567.

Roach, David. "PCUSA's Israel Decision 'Tragic.'" *Baptist Press*, June 23, 2014. https://www.baptistpress.com/resource-library/news/pcusas-israel-decision-tragic/.

Roberts, Frank Leon. "How Black Lives Matter Changed the Way Americans Fight for Freedom." *ACLU News and Commentary*, July 13, 2018. https://www.aclu.org/news/racial-justice/how-black-lives-matter-changed-way-americans-fight.

Rosane, Olivia. "Hundreds Block So-Called 'Genocide Boat' Carrying Weapons to Israel at Tacoma Port." Common Dreams, November 6, 2023. https://www.commondreams.org/news/hundreds-block-israel-boat-tacoma.

Rose, Joel. "Controversial 'Anti-Jihad' Ads Posted in New York City." NPR, September 24, 2012. https://www.npr.org/2012/09/24/161706692/controversial-anti-jihad-ads-posted-in-new-york-city.

BIBLIOGRAPHY

Rose, Hilary, and Stephen Rose. "Stephen Hawkings' Boycott Hits Israel Where It Hurts: Science." *Guardian*, May 13, 2013. https://www.theguardian.com/science/political-science/2013/may/13/stephen-hawking-boycott-israel-science.

Rosenberg, MJ. "Sorry, Democrats: Your NRA Is Spelled AIPAC." *Huffpost*, October 5, 2017. https://www.huffingtonpost.com/entry/sorry-democrats-your-nra-is-spelled-aipac_us_59d62c62e4b0666ad0c3cb12.

Rosenfeld, Arno. "Chicago Synagogue Officially Designates Itself 'Anti-Zionist.'" *Haaretz*, April 2, 2022. https://www.haaretz.com/jewish/2022-04-02/ty-article/chicago-synagogue-officially-designates-itself-anti-zionist/00000180-5bc6-de8c-a1aa-dbeeb56b0000.

Ross, Alexandra. "Did Oakland Roots Football Team Drop Puma Over BDS?" *Local Today*, November 10, 2022. https://localtoday.news/ca/did-oakland-roots-football-team-drop-puma-over-bds-j-126508.html.

Rosentiel, Tom, Scott Keeter, and Paul Taylor. "The Millennials." Pew Research Center, December 10, 2009. https://www.pewresearch.org/2009/12/10/the-millennials/.

Rosner, Shmuel. "Israel Needs to Protect Its Borders. By Whatever Means Necessary." *New York Times*, May 18, 2018. https://www.nytimes.com/2018/05/18/opinion/israel-defend-gaza-border.html.

Rothchild, Alice. "When Donor Pressure Threatens to Erase Palestine from Academia." *Mondoweiss*, October 27, 2022. https://mondoweiss.net/2022/10/when-donor-pressure-threatens-to-erase-palestine-from-academia/.

Roy, Eleanor Ainge. "Israel Fines New Zealand Women $18,000 for Urging Lorde Concert Boycott." *Guardian*, October 11, 2018. https://www.theguardian.com/music/2018/oct/12/israel-fines-new-zealand-teenagers-18000-for-urging-lorde-concert-boycott.

Roy, Sara. "Living with the Holocaust: The Journey of a Child of Holocaust Survivors." *Journal of Palestine Studies* 32, no. 1 (2002): 5–12. https://doi:10.1525/jps.2002.32.1.5.

Rubin, Neil. "Quaker Group Divests from Companies Working in Israel." Jewish Telegraphic Agency, September 28, 2012. https://www.jta.org/2012/09/28/israel/quaker-group-divests-from-companies-working-in-israel.

Sabbagh, Karl. *Palestine: A Personal History*. London: Atlantic, 2006.

Sabes, Adam. "California, Berkeley University Law School Student Orgs Pledge to Boycott Zionist, Pro-Israel Speakers." *Yahoo News*, August 28, 2022. https://www.law.berkeley.edu/article/deans-message-our-community-10-21-2022/.

Saeed, Sana. "An Interfaith Trojan Horse: Faithwashing Apartheid and Occupation." *Islamic Monthly*, July 1, 2014. http://www.theislamicmonthly.com/an-interfaith-trojan-horse-faithwashing-apartheid-and-occupation/.

Said, Edward W. "My Encounter with Sartre." *London Review of Books* 22, no. 11 (June 1, 2000). https://www.lrb.co.uk/the-paper/v22/n11/edward-said/diary.

———. "New History, Old Ideas." Miftah, May 28, 1998. http://www.miftah.org/PrinterF.cfm?DocId=2459.

———. "An Open Letter to Jewish American Intellectuals." Jewish Currents, September 21, 2022. https://jewishcurrents.org/an-open-letter-to-american-jewish-intellectuals.

———. *Orientalism*. New York: Vintage Books, 1979.

———. *Out of Place: A Memoir*. New York: Vintage Books, 2000.

———. "Permission to Narrate." *Journal of Palestine Studies* 13, no. 3 (1984): 27–48. https://doi:10.1525/jps.1984.13.3.00p0033m.

———. *The Question of Palestine*. New York: Times Books, 1979.

———. *The Selected Works of Edward Said, 1966–2006*, ed. Moustafa Bayoumi and Andrew Rubin. 2d ed. New York: Vintage Books, 2019.

Said, Najla. *Looking for Palestine: Growing Up Confused in an Arab-American Family.* New York: Riverhead Books, 2013.

Salaita, Steven. "Ethnic Identity and Imperative Patriotism: Arab Americans Before and After 9/11." *College Literature* 32, no. 2 (2005): 146–68. https://doi:10.1353/lit.2005.0033.

———. "Why American Indian Studies Should Be Important to Palestine Solidarity." In *Inter/Nationalism: Decolonizing Native America and Palestine.* Minneapolis: University of Minnesota Press, 2016. https://doi.org/10.5749/minnesota/9781517901417.003.0005.

Sales, Ben. "New Movement for Black Lives Platform Contains No Mention of Israel." *Jerusalem Post*, August 29, 2020. https://www.jpost.com/diaspora/antisemitism/new-movement-for-black-lives-platform-contains-no-mention-of-israel-640351.

Salleh, Mohd Afandi, and Mohd Fauzi Abu-Hussin. "The American Christians and the State of Israel." *Journal for the Study of Religions and Ideologies* 12, no. 34 (2013): 152–72.

Samhan, Helen Hatab. "Not Quite White: Race Classification and the Arab-American Experience." In *Arabs in America Building a New Future*, ed. Michael W. Suleiman. Philadelphia: Temple University Press, 1999.

Sanchez, Gabriel R., and Edward D. Vargas. "Taking a Closer Look at Group Identity: The Link Between Theory and Measurement of Group Consciousness and Linked Fate." *Political Research Quarterly* 69, no. 1 (2016): 160–74. https://doi:10.1177/1065912915624571.

Sasson, Theodore. "Mass Mobilization to Direct Engagement: American Jews' Changing Relationship to Israel." *Israel Studies* 15, no. 2 (2010): 173–95.

Savage, Sean. "Presbyterian Church Approves Israel Divestment, but Does Its Boycott Even Matter?" *Jewish News Syndicate*, June 20, 2014. https://www.jns.org/presbyterian-church-approves-israel-divestment-but-does-its-boycott-even-matter/.

Scher, Isaac. "AFL-CIO Leadership Tries to Block Affiliate's Vote on Endorsing BDS." *Intercept*, October 21, 2021. https://theintercept.com/2021/10/21/palestine-bds-san-francisco-labor-afl-cio/.

Schlussel, Debbie. "Bob Simon, Anti-Israel Self-Hating Jew Who Also Lied About U.S. in Vietnam, RIH." debbieschlussel.com, February 12, 2015. https://www.debbieschlussel.com/77169/bob-simon-anti-israel-self-hating-jew-who-also-lied-about-us-in-vietnam-rih/.

———. "Mike Wallace, RIH: No Tears for Anti-Israel, Anti-American Propagandist & Liar." debbieschlussel.com, April 9, 2012. https://www.debbieschlussel.com/48763/mike-wallace-rih-no-tears-for-anti-israel-anti-american-propagandist-fabricator/comment-page-1/#comments.

Schulberg, Jessica. "Student Felt 'Criminalized' After Campus Police Made Him Remove Palestinian Flag." *Huffington Post*, December 9, 2015. https://www.huffpost.com/entry/Gw-palestinian-flag_n_5668bb47e4b080eddf56f7e2.

Schulz, Helena Lindholm. *The Palestinian Diaspora.* London: Routledge, 2003.

BIBLIOGRAPHY

Schwader, Maya. "U.S. Scholars' Group Votes in Favor of Academic Boycott of Israel." *Jerusalem Post*, December 16, 2013. https://www.jpost.com/International/U.S.-scholars-group-votes-in-favor-of-academic-boycott-of-Israel-335178.

Sen, Somdeep. "India's Deepening Love Affair with Israel." *Al Jazeera*, September 9, 2021. https://www.aljazeera.com/opinions/2021/9/9/indias-deepening-love-affair-with-israel.

Serino, Kenichi. "Tens of Thousands Have Joined Pro-Palestinian Protests Across the United States. Experts Say They Are Growing." *PBS NewsHour*, December 15, 2023. https://www.pbs.org/newshour/politics/tens-of-thousands-have-joined-pro-palestinian-protests-across-the-united-states-experts-say-they-are-growing.

Shaheen, Jack G., and William Greider. *Reel Bad Arabs : How Hollywood Vilifies a People*. New York: Olive Branch Press, 2001.

Shamir, Shlomo. "Poll: Nearly 50% of Hispanic Americans Believe U.S. Too Supportive of Israel." *Haaretz*, March 28, 2011. https://www.haaretz.com/jewish/2011-03-28/ty-article/poll-nearly-50-of-hispanic-americans-believe-u-s-too-supportive-of-israel/0000017f-db23-db22-a17f-ffb33f5b0001.

Shaoul, Jean. "US Congress Blocks Palestinian Aid After UN Statehood Bid." *World Socialist*, October 5, 2011. https://www.wsws.org/en/articles/2011/10/isra-o05.html.

Shattan, Joseph. "Why Brera?" *Commentary*, April 1977. https://www.commentary.org/articles/joseph-shattan/why-breira/.

Sheffer, Gabriel. "Integration Impacts on Diaspora–Homeland Relations." *Diaspora Studies* 6, no. 1 (2013): 13–30. https://doi:10.1163/09763457-00601002.

Shepard, Richard F. "Redgrave Film on P.L.O. Stirs a Controversy." *New York Times*, November 10, 1977. https://www.nytimes.com/1977/11/10/archives/westchester-opinion-redgrave-film-on-plo-stirs-a-controversy.html.

Sheppard, Ferrari. "I Traveled to Palestine-Israel and Discovered There Is No 'Palestinian-Israeli Conflict.'" *HuffPost*, February 10, 2014. https://www.huffpost.com/entry/i-traveled-to-palestine_b_4761896.

Sherwood, Harriet, and Matthew Kalman. "Stephen Hawking Joins Academic Boycott of Israel." *Guardian*, May 7, 2013. https://www.theguardian.com/world/2013/may/08/stephen-hawking-israel-academic-boycott.

Shihade, Magid. "Beware of Misinformed Bloggers Regarding Palestine." *Indian Country Today*, September 12, 2018. https://indiancountrytoday.com/archive/beware-of-misinformed-bloggers-regarding-palestine.

Shimoni-Stoil, Rebecca. "ADL: Trump's Comments Misinterpreted, Not Anti-Semitic." *Times of Israel*, December 4, 2015. https://www.timesofisrael.com/adl-trumps-comments-misinterpreted-not-anti-semitic/.

Shindler, Colin. "Likud and the Christian Dispensationalists: A Symbiotic Relationship." *Israel Studies* 5, no. 1 (2000): 153–82. https://doi:10.2979/ISR.2000.5.1.153.

Shuttleworth, Kate, and Julia Carrie Wong. "Airbnb Lists Properties in Illegal Israeli Settlements." *Guardian*, January 13, 2016. https://www.theguardian.com/technology/2016/jan/12/airbnb-listings-illegal-settlements-israel-palestine-west-bank.

Siddiqui, U., and O. Zaheer. "Year of Occupation: A Sentiment and N-gram Analysis of US Mainstream Media Coverage of the Israeli Occupation of Palestine," 50: 1547246789711. 416Labs, 2018. https://vridar.org/wp-content/uploads/2019/01/416LABS_50_Years_of_Occupation.pdf.

Sizer, Stephen Robert. *Christian Zionists: On the Road to Armageddon*. London: IVP Academic, 2004.

———. "John Nelson Darby, the Father of Dispensationalism." Wordpress. Accessed August 12, 2022. https://www.stephensizer.com/articles/darby1.html.

Sjoquist, Douglas P. "The Demographics of Islam in Asia." Association for Asian Studies, Spring 2005. https://www.asianstudies.org/publications/eaa/archives/the-demographics-of-islam-in-asia/.

Skidrud, Erik. "Twenty Years Later, Still No Charges in Alex Odeh Assassination." *Electronic Intifada*, December 6, 2006. https://electronicintifada.net/content/twenty-years-later-still-no-charges-alex-odeh-assassination/6582.

Smith, Candace. "Jeb Bush Says US Should Allow Syrian Refugees Who Can Prove They're Christian." *ABC News*, November 17, 2015. https://abcnews.go.com/Politics/jeb-bush-us-syrian-refugees-prove-christian/story?id=35263074.

Smith, Grant F. "Preventing Israel Lobby Propaganda in Textbooks." *Washington Report on Middle East Affairs* 39, no. 5 (August–September 2020): 36+. https://link.gale.com/apps/doc/A632776894/AONE.

Snow, Jon. "Gaza: Mark Regev Interviewed by Jon Snow About IDF attacks." YouTube, August 24, 2018. https://www.youtube.com/watch?v=HGahJzFdqaY.

Song, Sarah. "What Does It Mean to Be an American ?" *Daedalus* 138, no. 2 (2009): 1–40.

Spalding, Elizabeth Edwards. "We Must Put on the Armor of God: History, Faith, and Peace in Truman's Thought." In *Religion and the American Presidency*, ed. Mark J. Rosell and Gleaves Whitney. Cham, Switz.: Springer International, 2017.

Spector, Stephen. *Evangelicals and Israel: The Story of American Christian Zionism*. New York: Oxford University Press, 2009.

Speri, Alice. "Israeli Forces Deliberately Killed Palestinian American Journalist, Report Shows." *Intercept*, September 20, 2022. https://theintercept.com/2022/09/20/shireen-abu-akleh-killing-israel/.

Spiro, Amy. "EBU Condemns Madonna, Iceland for Palestinian flags at Eurovision." *Jerusalem Post*, May 20, 2019. https://www.jpost.com/israel-news/madonna-iceland-include-palestinian-flags-at-eurovision-590072.

Sprunt, Barbara. "Top House Democrats Reject Rep. Jayapal's Comments Calling Israel a 'Racist State.'" NPR, July 17, 2023. https://www.npr.org/2023/07/17/1188096678/jayapal-israel-racist-state-jeffries.

Stein, Rebecca L. "Viral Occupation: Palestine and the Video Revolution." *Los Angeles Review of Books*, January 21, 2022. https://lareviewofbooks.org/article/viral-occupation-palestine-and-the-video-revolution/.

Steinberg, Jessica. "Israel, Unfiltered." *Times of Israel*, November 25, 2014. https://www.timesofisrael.com/israel-unfiltered/.

Steinbuch, Yaron. "TikTok Used to Air Tensions, Incite Violence Between Israelis and Palestinians." *New York Post*, May 20, 2021. https://nypost.com/2021/05/20/tiktok-used-to-incite-violence-between-israel-palestine-reports/.

Stern, Itay. "Lorde Fans Sue BDS Activists for 'Inciting' Her to Cancel Israel Show." *Haaretz*, February 1, 2018. https://www.haaretz.com/israel-news/2018-02-01/ty-article/.premium/israeli-lorde-fans-sue-bds-activists-for-inciting-her-to-cancel-show/0000017f-db25-d856-a37f-ffe51b1b0000.

BIBLIOGRAPHY

Stern, Marlow. "Bill Maher and Bari Weiss Cruelly Blame Palestinians for Gaza Massacre." *Daily Beast*, May 19, 2018. https://www.thedailybeast.com/bill-maher-and-bari-weiss-blame-palestinians-for-gaza-massacre.

———. "Bill Maher Refuses to Ask Netanyahu About Corruption Charges, Wonders If Israel Will 'Retaliate' Against Kanye." *Daily Beast*, October 15, 2022. https://www.thedailybeast.com/bill-maher-asks-benjamin-netanyahu-if-israel-will-retaliate-against-kanye-west.

Stewart, Joshua. "Congressional Candidate Renounces Grandfather's Violent Legacy, Calls for Middle East Peace." *San Diego Union-Tribune*, February 21, 2018. http://www.sandiegouniontribune.com/news/politics/sd-me-ammar-grandfather-20180221-story.html.

Stirgus, Eric. "Judge: Ga. Law Barring Contracts by Groups Boycotting Israel Unconstitutional." *Atlanta Journal Constitution*, May 25, 2021. https://www.ajc.com/education/judge-ga-law-barring-contracts-by-groups-boycotting-israel-unconstitutional/UO3WXWOHRBFUBHIX7DWGG4AEPA/.

Stockton, Ronald R. "Christian Zionism: Prophecy and Public Opinion." *Middle East Journal* 41, no. 2 (1987): 234–53.

Stohlman, Nancy, and Laurieann Aladin. *Live from Palestine: International and Palestinian Direct Action Against the Israeli Occupation*. Cambridge, Mass: South End Press, 2003.

Stone, Jared. "A Response to BDS at Princeton." *Jerusalem Post*, May 22, 2022. https://www.jpost.com/opinion/article-707403.

Stone, Jared, and Orli Epstein. "Caterpillar Referendum Peddles the Hate and Bigotry of the Global BDS Movement." *Daily Princetonian*, April 4, 2022. https://www.dailyprincetonian.com/article/2022/04/caterpillar-referendum-princeton-bds-hate.

Such, Rod. "What's Behind the U.S. Media's Special Relationship with Israel?" *Electronic Intifada*, June 3, 2016. https://electronicintifada.net/content/whats-behind-us-medias-special-relationship-israel/16951.

Takruri, Dena, and AJPlus. "How Israeli Apartheid Destroyed My Hometown." YouTube, October 27, 2022. https://www.youtube.com/watch?v=aEdGcej-6Do&list=PLZd3QRtSy5LOWaQBH1fLN2etOO9pCAxaJ.

Tasnim News Agency. "'Musicians for Palestine' Campaign Urges Boycotting Israel," May 29, 2021. https://www.tasnimnews.com/en/news/2021/05/29/2511981/musicians-for-palestine-campaign-urges-boycotting-israel.

Tehranian, John. *Whitewashed: America's Invisible Middle Eastern Minority*. New York: NYU Press, 2008.

Telhami, Shibley. "Arab and American Dimensions of the Israel/Palestine Issue: State Policies and Public Views on One State, Two States, and Beyond." In *The One State Reality: What Is Israel/Palestine?*, ed. Shibley Telhami, Michael Barnett, Nathan J. Brown, and Marc Lynch, 196–209. Ithaca, N.Y.: Cornell University Press, 2023. http://www.jstor.org/stable/10.7591/j.ctv2jhjx92.14.

Terry, Janice. *U.S. Foreign Policy in the Middle East the Role of Lobbies and Special Interest Groups*. London: Pluto Press, 2005.

Times of Israel Staff. "Jon Stewart: 'I'm Not Anti-Israel.'" *Times of Israel*, August 30, 2014. https://www.timesofisrael.com/jon-stewart-im-not-anti-israel/.

Trabulsi, Jeanne. "Jeanne Trabulsi: The Fight Against Israeli Propaganda in Virginia Textbooks." *Washington Report on Middle East Affairs*, May 2022. https://www.wrmea.org/transcending-the-israel-lobby-at-home-and-abroad/jeanne-trabulsi-the-fight-against-israeli-propaganda-in-virginia-textbooks.html.

"Tribal Alliances: The State of Israel & Native American Christianity (Excerpt)." *Revealer*, February 24, 2015. https://therevealer.org/tribal-alliances-the-state-of-israel-native-american-christianity-excerpt/.

True Activist. "New York Governor Signs Executive Order to Punish People Who Criticize Israel," June 10, 2016. https://www.trueactivist.com/new-york-governor-signs-executive-order-to-punish-people-who-criticize-israel/.

Trump White House Archives. "President Donald J. Trump Keeps His Promise to Open U.S. Embassy in Jerusalem, Israel," May 14, 2018. https://trumpwhitehouse.archives.gov/briefings-statements/president-donald-j-trump-keeps-promise-open-u-s-embassy-jerusalem-israel/.

United Nations. "Address by Yasser Arafat Before the General Assembly." *Jewish Virtual Library*, November 13, 1974. https://www.jewishvirtuallibrary.org/address-by-yasser-arafat-before-the-un-general-assembly-november-1974.

United Nations Security Council. "Security Council Resolution 242: The Situation in the Middle East," November 22, 1967. https://peacemaker.un.org/middle-east-resolution242.

———. "U.S. Vetoes of Resolutions Critical to Israel (1972—Present)." *Jewish Virtual Library*, accessed October 10, 2022. https://www.jewishvirtuallibrary.org/u-s-vetoes-of-un-security-council-resolutions-critical-to-israel.

United States Court of Appeals for the Ninth Circuit, No. 05-36210 D.C. No. CV-05-05192-FDB. Opinion, September 17, 2007. https://web.archive.org/web/20071117111442/http://www.ca9.uscourts.gov/ca9/newopinions.nsf/6DFD4322CA06B5FA882573590 05660A6/%24file/0536210.pdf?openelement.

United States Department of Education, Office for Civil Rights. "Questions and Answers on Executive Order 13899 (Combating Anti-Semitism) and OCR's Enforcement of Title VI of the Civil Rights Act of 1964," January 19, 2021. https://www2.ed.gov/about/offices/list/ocr/docs/qa-titleix-anti-semitism-20210119.pdf.

United States District Court for the Middle District of North Carolina. Civil Action No. 1:19-cv-00309, March 19, 2019. https://www.courthousenews.com/wp-content/uploads/2019/03/nc-israel.pdf.

University of Chicago Press. "Real Patriots Talk Back or, Why Dissent Can Be Patriotic, an Interview with Jonathan M. Hansen," accessed August 12, 2022. http://press.uchicago.edu/Misc/Chicago/315843in.html.

University of Minnesota Library. "A Brief History of Education in the United States," accessed August 14, 2022. https://open.lib.umn.edu/sociology/chapter/16-1-a-brief-history-of-education-in-the-united-states/.

Urban, Wayne J., and Jennings L. Wagoner, Jr. *American Education: A History*. New York: Taylor and Francis, 2013.

US Campaign for the Academic and Cultural Boycott of Israel. "AAAS Votes in Historic Decision to Support Boycott of Israeli Academic Institutions," accessed September 19, 2022. https://usacbi.org/2013/04/aaas-votes-in-historic-decision-to-support-boycott-of-israeli-academic-institutions/.

BIBLIOGRAPHY

U.S. Department of State. *Foreign Relations of the United States: Diplomatic Papers.* Washington, D.C.: U.S. Government Printing Office, 1969.

———. Office of the Historian. "The Oslo Accords and the Arab-Israeli Peace Process," accessed September 12, 2002. https://history.state.gov/milestones/1993-2000/oslo.

Varian, Bill. "Al-Arian's Rise in U.S. Began in Academics." *Tampa Bay Times*, February 21, 2003. https://www.tampabay.com/archive/2003/02/21/al-arian-s-rise-in-u-s-began-in-academics/.

Vaya, Surabhi. "Gaza War: How Bias Affects Coverage of Israel-Palestine Conflict." *Firstpost*, July 23, 2014. https://www.firstpost.com/world/gaza-how-bias-affects-coverage-of-israel-palestine-conflict-1628973.html.

Wajahat, Ali. "Pro-Israel Organizations, Donors and Islamophobia: Findings from Fear, Inc.: The Roots of the Islamophobia Network in America." *Washington Report on Middle East Affairs* 36, no. 3 (2017).

Wallace, Danielle. "Biden Interrupted by 'Cease-Fire Now Chants,' Vows He's Working to Get Israel 'Out of Gaza.'" *Fox News*, January 8, 2024. https://www.msn.com/en-us/news/politics/biden-interrupted-by-cease-fire-now-chants-vows-hes-working-to-get-israel-out-of-gaza/ar-AA1mElho.

Wallace-Wells, Benjamin. "Why a State Department Official Lost Hope in Israel." *New Yorker*, November 6, 2023. https://www.newyorker.com/news/the-political-scene/why-a-state-department-official-lost-hope-in-israel.

Warrior, Robert. "Palestine Without Smears: Why Israel and Natives Aren't Natural Allies." *Indian Country Today*, January 29, 2014. https://ais.illinois.edu/news/2014-01-29/palestine-without-smears-why-israel-and-natives-arent-natural-allies.

Wasow, Omar. "Agenda Seeding: How 1960s Black Protests Moved Elites, Public Opinion and Voting." *American Political Science Review* 114, no. 3 (2020): 638–59. https://doi:10.1017/S000305542000009X.

Weiler-Polack, Dana. "Israel Enacts Law Allowing Authorities to Detain Illegal Migrants for Up to 3 Years." *Haaretz*, June 3, 2012. https://www.haaretz.com/2012-06-03/ty-article/israels-new-infiltrators-law-comes-into-effect/0000017f-f08a-dc28-a17f-fcbfc6e70000.

Weinberg, David. "Peter Beinhart's betrayal of Liberal Zionism and Israel." *Jerusalem Post*, July 9, 2020. https://www.jpost.com/opinion/peter-beinharts-betrayal-of-liberal-zionism-and-israel-634553.

Weiss, Phillip. "'Apartheid' Chorus Grows—60 Percent of Middle East Scholars Reach That Conclusion." *Mondoweiss*, April 25, 2022. https://mondoweiss.net/2022/04/apartheid-chorus-grows-60-percent-of-middle-east-scholars-reach-that-conclusion/.

———. "Geraldo Rivera Regrets Not Backing Palestinians in Second Intifada." *Mondoweiss*, April 3, 2018. http://mondoweiss.net/2018/04/geraldo-palestinians-intifada/.

Whitson, Sarah Leah. "The Israel-Palestine Narrative Has Evolved." *American Prospect*, May 18, 2021. https://prospect.org/world/israel-palestine-narrative-has-evolved/.

Whittock, Martyn. "The Strange Decline of US Evangelicalism." *Christianity Today*, July 28, 2021. https://www.christiantoday.com/article/the.strange.decline.of.us.evangelicalism/137169.htm.

A Wider Bridge. "History and Background," accessed September 15, 2022. https://awiderbridge.org/history-and-background/.

BIBLIOGRAPHY

Williams, Erika. "NC City Council Accused of Stirring Anti-Semitism." *Courthouse News Service*, March 20, 2019. https://www.courthousenews.com/nc-city-council-accused-of-stirring-anti-semitism/.

Williams, Leslie. "The Anti-Defamation League Kills the Black/Jewish Alliance." *Jewish Voice for Peace*, August 26, 2016. https://jewishvoiceforpeace.org/the-anti-defamation-league-kills-the-blackjewish-alliance/.

Wolf, Rachel. "Icelandic Broadcaster Fined Over Hatari's Palestinian Flag Waving." *Jerusalem Post*, September 21, 2019. https://www.jpost.com/breaking-news/icelandic-broadcaster-fined-over-hataris-palestinan-flag-waving-602402.

Wray-Lake, Laura, Amy Syvertsen, and Constance Flanagan. "Contested Citizenship and Social Exclusion: Adolescent Arab American Immigrants' Views of the Social Contract." *Applied Developmental Science* 12, no. 2 (2008): 84–92.

X., Angela, Karam Dana, and Matt Barreto. "The American Muslim Voter: Community Belonging and Political Participation." *Social Science Research* 72 (2018): 84–99.

York, Anthony. "Muslims Charge They Are Being Scapegoated." *Salon*, November 2, 2000. https://www.salon.com/2000/11/02/ama/.

Yudof, Mark G., and Ken Walzer. "Majoring in Anti-Semitism at Vassar." *Wall Street Journal*, February 17, 2016. https://www.wsj.com/articles/majoring-in-anti-semitism-at-vassar-1455751940.

Zahr, Amer. "Palestinians Bid Jon Stewart a Fond Farewell." *Al Jazeera*, August 6, 2015. https://www.aljazeera.com/opinions/2015/8/6/palestinians-bid-jon-stewart-a-fond-farewell/.

Zahriyeh, Ehab. "Report: Anti-Semitism Charges Used to Curb Pro-Palestinian Campus Speech." *Al Jazeera America*, September 30, 2015. http://america.aljazeera.com/articles/2015/9/30/anti-semitism-claims-used-to-crush-pro-palestinian-speech-on-campuses.html.

Zaidan, Ismat. "Palestinian Diaspora in Transnational Worlds: Intergenerational Differences in Negotiating Identity, Belonging and Home." *SSRN Electronic Journal*, n.d. https://doi:10.2139/ssrn.2009267.

Zanotti, Jim, Martin A. Weiss, Kathleen Ann Ruane, and Jennifer K Elsea. "Israel and the Boycott, Divestment, and Sanctions (BDS) Movement." *Current Politics and Economics of the Middle East* 8, no. 3 (2017): 285–328.

Zarrugh, Amina. "Racialized Political Shock: Arab American Racial Formation and the Impact of Political Events." *Ethnic and Racial Studies* 39, no. 15 (2016): 2722–39. https://doi:10.1080/01419870.2016.1171368.

Ziadah, Rafeef. "British Backing for Israel Helps to Sustain the Unbearable Status Quo." *Guardian*, June 13, 2021. https://www.theguardian.com/commentisfree/2021/jun/13/british-backing-israel-unbearable-status-quo-palestinians.

Zinn, Howard. *A People's History of the United States*. London: Taylor and Francis, 2015.

———. "A People's History of the United States: 1492—Present." HowardZinn.org, accessed August 14, 2022. https://www.howardzinn.org/collection/peoples-history/.

Zlotsky, Reid. "Caterpillar Referendum Supporters Avoid a Debate They Know They Can't Win." *Daily Princetonian*, April 7, 2022. https://www.dailyprincetonian.com/article/2022/04/princeton-bds-debate-caterpillar-referendum.

Zuckerman, Arthur. "60 Church Attendance Statistics: 2020/2021 Data, Trends, & Predictions." *Compare Camp*, May 8, 2020. https://comparecamp.com/church-attendance-statistics/.

Zunes, Stephen. "Why the U.S. Supports Israel." Foreign Policy in Focus, May 1, 2002. http://fpif.org/why_the_us_supports_israel/.

Zuckerman, Arthur. "60 Church Attendance Statistics: 2020/2021 Data, Trends, & Predictions." *Compare Camp,* May 8, 2020. https://comparecamp.com/church-attendance-statistics/.

Zunes, Stephen. "Why the U.S. Supports Israel." Foreign Policy in Focus, May 1, 2002. http://fpif.org/why_the_us_supports_israel/.

INDEX

Abbas, Mahmoud, 200, 216
Abbot, Abiel, 72
Abbot, Greg, 223
ABC Nightline (news program), 137
Abd El Rahman, Rina, 172
Abounaja, Ramie, 172
Abourezk, James, 193
Abu Aker, Khaled, 84
Abu Akleh, Shireen, 49–50, 139, 203, 279
Abu Ayyash, Salma, 257
Abu El Haj, Nadia, 128
Abu El-Haj, Thea Renda, 9–10, 15, 163–164
Abu-Ghazaleh, Faida, 10–11, 173, 244
Abukhdeir, Sabrina, 85–86
Abu-Lughod, Ibrahim, 193
Abu-Shamsieh, Kamal, 259
Abu-Shanab, Nadia, 130
academic boycotts, 125–129, 171–172, 253
Access Now, 145
Ackerman, Gary, 211
ACT! for America, 70
acts of memory, 5
Acuña, Rudolfo, 252
Adams, Eric, 136
Adams, John, 56–57, 66

Addameer Prisoner Support and Human Rights Organization, 203
Adelman, David, 198
Adelson, Sheldon, 168
Adidas, 120
Adler-Bell, Sam, 96–97
Advocate (film), 104
Aeder, Sara Fredman, 174
Afghanistan, invasion of, 26
AFL-CIO, 122
Africa 4 Palestine, 141
Afro-Arab solidarity, 192
AIPAC. *See* American Israel Public Affairs Committee (AIPAC)
Airbnb, 118
Ajrouch, Kristine, 32–33, 35
Al-Akhras, Izz ad-Din, 84
Al-Aqsa mosque, 146
Al-Arian, Sami, 128, 213–215
Aldrovandi, Carlo, 55
Al-Durrah, Muhammad, 20
Aleem, Zeeshan, 81–82
Alexander, Michelle, 210
Al-Haq, 50, 203
All Around the World Israel (Spanier), 46
Allies for Armageddon (Clark), 60–61

INDEX

Allon, Gideon, 63
Al-Monitor (news website), 84
Al-Najjar, Muhammad Yusuf, 77
Al-Naqab, 262
Al-Qaeda, 75–76
Al Qasim, Samih, 246
Amawi, Bahia, 142, 222–223
Amazon, 147
AMCHA Initiative, 72
American Anthropological Association (AAA), 127
American Association of University Professors (AAUP), 127–128
American Christian Palestine Committee (ACPC), 58
American Civil Liberties Union (ACLU), 161, 219, 221
American Friends of Beit el Yeshiva, 199
American Friends Service Committee, 104, 117, 123
American Israel Education Foundation, 208
American Israel Public Affairs Committee (AIPAC), 63, 71–72, 96, 97, 102, 198, 207–209, 219, 272
American Jewish Committee, 252
American Jewish Congress, 151
American Jewish Council, 149
American Muslim Alliance, 197
American Muslims for Palestine, 175
American Palestine Committee, 58
American Radical (film), 177
American(s): exceptionalism, 30, 72, 96, 186; feelings towards different groups, 26; identity, 36; increasing support for Palestine, 78–79, 90–91, 133–137, 270–271; progressive, 93–98. See also Arab Americans; Jewish Americans; Palestinian Americans; United States
Americans for a Safe Israel, 272
Americans for Peace Now (APN), 108
American Studies Association (ASA), 126, 253
American Task Force on Palestine, 197
American Zionist Emergency Council, 191

American Zionist Organization, 57
Amin, 84
Amini, Mahsa, 261
Amnesty International, 3, 49, 154, 155
Amreeka (film), 143
Andoni, Ghassan, 104
Anglican London Society for Promoting Christianity, 56
Antepli, Abdullah, 257
Anthropologists for Dialogue on Israel/Palestine, 127
Anthropology from a Pragmatic Point of View (Kant), 282–283
anticolonialism, 11–12, 31, 285
Anti-Defamation League (ADL), 72, 123–124, 163, 252
antidiscrimination lawsuits, 228–231
antisemitism, 18, 28–29, 43, 62, 72, 105, 110, 120, 136, 163, 166–167, 168–169, 173–175, 234
Anti-Semitism Awareness Act (2016), 166, 221
antiterrorism, 20
Anti-War Committee, 168
anti-Zionism, 273–274
Anwar, Saud, 258
Aouragh, Miriyam, 22
apartheid, 3, 154, 186, 199, 203, 241, 246, 247, 281, 284. See also South Africa apartheid
Appalachian State University, 135
Apple, 145
Arab America (news website), 101
Arab-American Anti-Discrimination Committee (ADC), 27, 48, 229
Arab American Institute Foundation (AAI), 27, 28, 196–197
Arab American News, 228–229
Arab Americans: discrimination against, 143, 228–229; historical whitewashing of, 9, 29, 32, 34–35; identity of, 27; lobbies, 212; media biases against, 42; political erasure of, 27–28; selective racialization of, 32, 35, 93; socially constructed categorization of, 14

INDEX

Arab-American University Graduates (AAUG), 27
Arab Center for the Advancement of Social Media, 145
"Arab-Israeli Conflict," 192
Arab-Israeli War, 77, 105
Arab League, 219
Arab Revolts, 21, 85
Arab(s): anti-Arab racism, 137–138, 213; denigration of, 194; identity, 14; media biases against, 39, 77–78; stereotypes of, 31–32. *See also* Arab Americans
Arab Spring, 4
Arafat, Yasser, 48, 151, 193, 215–216
Arar, Rawan, 186
Arawak Taino Nation, 254
Ariel, Yaakov, 60
Arizona anti-BDS legislation, 225
Arizona State University, 251
Arkansas Times (periodical), 142
Armageddon, Oil, and the Middle East (Walvoord), 61
Armey, Richard, 210–212
Arria, Michael, 143
Ashrawi, Hanan, 222
Asian American solidarity, 253–254
Associated Press (AP), 50, 155
Association for Asian American Studies, 126, 253
Atarot Industrial Zone, 117
Ateek, Naim, 56, 62
Atlantic (periodical), 144
Atshan, Sa'ed, 258, 259–260
Atta, Mohamad, 155
Augustine, St., 56
Austin, Lloyd, 202
Australian solidarity, 121
Autodefensas Unidas de Colombia (AUC), 240
Avraham, Avner, 41
Axelman, Erin, 271

Backspace (news program), 28
Baeza, Cecilia, 239
Baker, Howard, 193
Baldwin, James, 244

Balenciaga, 120
Balfour Declaration, 57, 58, 66, 189–190
Bannan, Natasha Lycia Ora, 252
Barak, Ehud, 154, 196
Bardem, Javier, 142
Barr, Roseanne, 137–138
Barreto, Matt, 94
Bartley, Robert, 157
Barton, David, 54
Bashi, Golbarg, 47
Basic Law on Human Dignity and Liberty, 74
Bass, Warren, 207
Bazian, Hatem, 175, 258
BBC, 152
BDS. *See* Boycott, Divestment, and Sanctions (BDS) campaigns
BDS Africa, 141
Beauchamp, Zach, 138, 221
Beautiful World, Where Are You? (Rooney), 143–144
Bedouins, 46, 262
Begin, Menachem, 59
Behrendt, Liza, 260
Beinart, Peter, 30, 106–107, 157–158, 182, 218, 267–269, 274
Beit Ur Al-Fauqa, 222
Bellaiche, Phillippe, 104
Bellerose, Ryan, 256
Ben & Jerry's, 117–118
Ben-Ami, Shlmo, 196
Benaroya, Becky, 180
Beneath the Helmet (film), 170
Ben-Gurion, David, 72, 76, 160
Bennett, Naftali, 262
Ben-Shoshan, Yaron, 132
Bensouda, Fatou, 241
Berkeley Anti-Semitism Education Initiative (AEI), 174
Bethlehem, 67, 68
Between the World and Me (Coates), 144
Bevin, Ernest, 190–191
Biden, Joe, 79, 135, 208, 20205
Biden administration, 182, 217–218
Bin Laden, Osama, 75–76, 214
Biriya Forest, 263

Birth of the Palestinian Refugee Problem, 1947–1949, The (Morris), 105
Birthright Israel, 102
Bisan Center for Research and Development, 203
Black Americans: criminalization of, 247, 248–249; Jewish, 248, 249–250; in solidarity with Palestinians, 82–83, 244–251; treatment of, 139, 244–245
Black Lives Matter (BLM) movement, 4, 18, 21, 78, 81–85, 86, 90, 96, 114, 214, 235, 246, 248–251, 278–279
Black Youth Project 100, 247
Blaising, Craig, 55
Blind Spot (Elgindy), 195
BLM. *See* Black Lives Matter (BLM) movement
Blumenthal, Max, 111
Boccagni, Paolo, 6
Bolivian solidarity, 239–240
Bolsonaro, Jair, 240
Bolsonaro, Michelle, 240
Bonsu, Janae, 247
Book Culture, 47
Booking.com, 118
Boot, Max, 157
Boric, Gabriel, 239
Boteach, Shmuley, 129–130
Bowman, Jamaal, 97
Boycott (film), 142–143, 265–266
Boycott, Divestment, and Sanctions (BDS) campaigns: academic, 125–129, 171–172, 253; after October 2023, 133–137; anti-BDS legislation, 142–143, 209, 219–220, 221, 222–226, 231, 234; antisemitic claims against, 168–169; cultural, 129–133; DSA support for, 96–98; economic and commercial, 115–121; by labor unions, 121–123; longevity of, 112; as nonviolent protest, 111; perceived effectiveness of, 12; by religious organizations, 123–125; resistance to Israeli occupation via, 12; as a social movement, 114, 182–183
Boyer, Paul, 225
Bracho, Richard, 255

Brand, Russell, 107, 270
Brandeis, Louis, 190
"Brand Israel," 260
Brazilian solidarity, 240
Breaking the Silence, 85, 110, 173
Breira, 271–272
Breitbart, 48
Bréville, Benoit, 210
British Committee for the Universities of Palestine, 162
British Mandate, 189, 191
British Society for the Propagation of the Gospel Amongst the Jews, 56
British solidarity, 121, 237
Brodetsky, Selig, 57
Brog, David, 124
Brookings Institute, 193
Browder, Kalief, 249
Brown, Michael, 247
Brown Shonel, 96
B'Tselem, 49, 108, 154
Burning Man Project, 132
Bush, Cori, 97
Bush, George H. W., 232
Bush, George W., 59, 74, 93, 211, 213
Bush, Jeb, 53
Bush administration, 73, 171, 197, 209, 213
Butler Bass, Diana, 54
Buxbaum, Jessica, 262
Buzzfeed News (news website), 146
Bvaryahu, Avner, 85
Byrne, Steve, 141

Cable, Ummayah, 54
cable news viewership, 87, 88
Camacho, Gabriel, 252
Campa-Najjar, Ammar, 77
campus protests, 116, 135–137, 170–171, 275. *See also* academic boycotts
Campus Watch, 72, 168
Canada Park, 263
Canary Mission, 72, 168
#cancelpinkwashing, 261
Cannes Film Festival, 142
Canon, 40
Cantor, Eric, 208

INDEX

Carmichael, Stokely, 250–251
Carnie, Daniel, 170
Carpentier, Nico, 87
Carter, Andrew, 117–118
Carter, Jimmy, 3, 58, 94, 194, 197
Casablancas, Julian, 132
Case for Israel, The (Dershowitz), 177
Case for Sanctions Against Israel, The (Lim, ed.), 112
Casey, Bob, 221
Castile, Philando, 139
Caterpillar, 49, 116, 123, 171–172
Catholic University of America, 64
Cauce, Ana Mari, 180
CBS, 153
cease-fire, calls for, 217, 283–284
Celtic, 140
censorship, 145–147, 165–166, 230–231
Center for Constitutional Rights (CCR), 170, 172
Center for Islam and Global Affairs, 215
Center for Responsive Politics, 208
Ceylon Civil Service, 57
Chait, Jonathan, 157
Chan, Jimmy, 87–88
Change They Can't Believe In (Parker and Barreto), 94
Channel 4 (U.K.), 152
Chapin, Angelina, 137
Charles and Seryl Kushner Foundation, 199
Charnysh, Volha, 35
Chaudhry, Hammad, 135–136
Chemerinsky, Erwin, 169, 170, 174
Cheney, Dick, 74, 197
Chicago Sun-Times (periodical), 157
Chikli, Amichai, 181
children's books, erasure of Palestine from, 46–47
Chilean solidarity, 239
Chomsky, Noam, 273–274
Chosa, Jim, 256
Chosen People Ministries, 124
Christian Broadcasting Network, 198
Christian Council on Palestine (CCP), 58

Christian Friends of Israeli Communities, 211
Christianity Today (periodical), 99
Christian Right, 66–67, 69–70
Christians and Christianity: affiliation with Israel, 19, 30, 51–54, 98–99; Arabs, 35; in Congress, 64–66; divestment by, 115; influence of in U.S., 50–54; Israel tourism, 212; Jewish affinity, 53; "lost tribes" theology, 256; Orientalism, 13–14; Palestinians, 30, 52, 62–63, 67–69, 258; portrayals of Muslims, 53–54; presidents' affiliations, 66; support for Palestinians, 100–101; White Evangelicalism, 51–52, 59–61, 99, 100–101. *See also* Christian Zionism
Christians' Israel Public Action Campaign (CIPAC), 58, 211
Christians United for Israel (CUFI), 58, 59, 124, 174, 211, 261
Christian Zionism: Christian objections to, 62; defined, 54; development of, 56; dispensationalism beliefs, 55, 56, 60; Evangelicals and, 59–61, 67–68; impact on Palestinian Americans, 69–71; vs. Jewish affinity, 53; lobbying efforts, 210–212, 232–233; and Palestinian politics, 60–61; purpose of, 50–51; Restorationism beliefs, 61–62; U.S. manifestation of, 58–59; U.S. support for, 56–57, 66–69
Christison, Kathleen, 10, 76–77
Chung, Jamie, 141
church attendance, 19, 80, 99–100
Church of Scotland, 56
Church of the Holy Sepulcher, 67
Church of the Nativity, 67
Cirincione, Joe, 218
citizen journalism, 83–85, 86, 88–89, 112
citizenship, U.S., 9–10
Civil Rights Act (1964), 165, 219
Civil Rights movement, 90, 91, 112, 244
Clark, Victoria, 56, 60–61
Clinton, Bill, 94, 196, 232
Clinton, Hillary, 37, 196–197, 208

Clinton administration, 195, 213
Clooney, Amal, 37
Clooney, George, 37
CNN, 154
Coates, Ta-Nehisi, 144–145
Cohen, Hillel, 106
Çolakoğlu, Kaya, 98
Cole, Juan, 176
college campuses: academic boycotts, 125–129, 171–172; anti-Palestinian discrimination, 164–167; Middle East studies programs, 168; Palestinian activism, 167–175; protests, 116, 135–137, 275; repercussions and punishment for Palestinian activism, 175–179; as shifting landscapes for justice on Palestine, 179–184
Collins, John, 15, 213, 235, 236, 262–263, 266–267
Colombian solidarity, 240
colonialism, 16–17, 187, 192, 232, 278
colonization, 1, 4, 5, 31, 160, 235, 237, 250–251, 252
Color Purple, The (Walker), 144
Columbia University, 137
Columbus, Christopher, 256
Combatants for Peace, 108–109
Comite Palestine Action, 238
Commentary (periodical), 157
Committee for Accuracy in Middle East Reporting in America (CAMERA), 149, 153, 164
Committee to Protect Journalists, xii
Common Sense Media, 88
community, 7, 9–10
Congress, 64–66, 71, 92, 126, 166, 178–179, 189, 193, 202–203, 205, 208–209, 212, 222, 234, 270, 276
Congressional Record, 72
Conseil d'État, 238
Conservative Review, 48
Cooper, Anthony Ashley, 56
COP27, 264
Corcoran, Michael, 95
Corrie, Rachel, 49, 116
Costello, Elvis, 129
Cotton, Tom, 155

Council on American-Islamic Relations (CAIR), 136, 175
counterterrorism, 226, 228
Court of Justice of the European Union, 118–119
COVID-19 vaccination program, 185
Cox, Kiana, 112
Craig, Tim, 135–136
Creating Change, 261
Creighton, Brandon, 223
Crilly, Rob, 223
Crowd Counting Consortium, 134–135
Crow Nation, 254, 255, 256
Cruz, Penelope, 142
Cruz, Ted, 37, 188
cultural boycotts, 129–133
cultural citizenship, 14
Cuomo, Andrew, 225
Cusack, John, 140
Cut, The (news website), 137
Cypress Hill, 132

D., Hisham, 77
Dabashi, Hamid, 249
Dabis, Cherien, 143
Daily Beast (news website), 38
Daily Show (talk show), 110–111, 139
Daniel, Norman, 32
D'Antonio, William, 64
Daraldik, Ahmad, 164–165
Darby, John Nelson, 56
Dartmouth College, 98, 177
Dartmouth Radical (periodical), 98
Darwish, Mahmoud, 284
Da Silva, Luiz Inácio Lula, 240
Davis, Angela, 115, 228, 250, 265
Days of Awe (Omer), 270–271
Deadly Exchange, 82–83
Dead Sea Burn, 132
Dead Sea Reborn, 132
Declaration of Independence, 70, 72
Decolonizing Israel, Liberating Palestine (Halper), 104
Defense for Children International-Palestine, 203
DeLay, Tom, 211
Del Rey, Lana, 131

INDEX

Demilitarize! Durham2Palestine, 227–228
Democracy Now, 144–145
Democratic Majority for Israel, 96
Democratic Party, 90, 93–98
Democratic Socialists of America (DSA), 96–98
democratization of media, 19, 83–85, 87–89
Democrats for Israel, 96
DePaul University, 177
Dershowitz, Alan, 177
Des Moines Register (periodical), 198
diaspora, 2, 4–5, 7–10, 13, 22–23, 236
Dickerson, T. Sheri Amore, 81
Dickinson College, 116
discrimination, 7, 9, 13, 15–16, 143, 164–167, 228–231, 233, 244
dispensationalism, 55, 56, 60
dissent, 35–36, 69–70
divestment. *See* Boycott, Divestment, and Sanctions (BDS) campaigns
Doeden, Matt, 46
Dow, George, 35
Dramanin, Gerald, 238
Driver, Tom, 62
DropTheADL, 163
DSA. *See* Democratic Socialists of America (DSA)
Du Bois, W. E. B., 192, 247
Dugan, Daria, 157
Dulles, John Foster, 192
Duss, Matt, 39, 51, 62, 63, 78–79, 96, 156–157, 233, 266
Duthu, S. Bruce, 177

Eben, Abba, 151
Egyptian Gazette (periodical), 246
Eid, Bashar, 264
Eilertsen, Sam, 271
Eisenhower, Dwight, 66
Eisgruber, Christopher L., 181
Eizenstat, Stuart, 194–195, 207
Elbit Systems, 120–121, 252
elections, 208
Electronic Intifada (news website), 88, 89, 252

Elgindy, Khaled, 187, 189, 195, 200, 206
Elias, Chanan, 141
Elkin, Ze'ev, 199–200
El-Kurd, Mohammed, 84
Elle (periodical), 43
Ellman-Golan, Sophie, 217
Elmusa, Karmah, 43
Emmanuel, Adeshina, 83–84
Eno, Brian, 129
environmentalists, 114, 261–264
"Equal Rights" (song), 245
Erakat, Noura, 69, 82
Erdan, Gilad, 146–147
Erdoğan, Recep Tayyip, 202
Erekat, Noura, 23
Erekat, Saeb, 201
Eretz Ysrael, 45, 60–61
Eshman, Rob, 174
ethnicity, 7, 32, 35, 43, 74, 211, 253
Etkes, Dror, 264
European Broadcasting Union (EBU), 131
European Court, 118
European support for Israel, 15
Eurovision Song Contest, 130–131, 133
Evangelicals and Israel (Spector), 61
Evangelical Times (periodical), 100
Except for Palestine (Hill and Plitnick), 14–15, 37, 154
exceptionalism, 29, 30, 72, 96, 186–187
exile experience, 6–7, 11. *See also* diaspora
Export Administration Act (EAA) (1979), 219–220

Facebook, 94, 145–147
Face of Israel, 141
faithwashing, 257–260
Falic family, 119
Falwell, Jerry, 59, 74
fascism, 112–113
Fatah, 77
Fayez, Aaqib, 238
Federal Bureau of Investigation (FBI), 50, 146, 203
Feig, Glenn D., 141–142
Feinstein, Dianne, 221

INDEX

Feldman, Keith, 15, 28, 29, 33–34, 186
feminist activism, 261
Fenton, Martin, 149
Ferguson, James, 7
Fetterman, John, 75
FIFA World Cup, 140–141, 241–242
Findley, Paul, 212
Fink, Uri, 41–42
Finkelstein, Norman, 113, 128, 176–177
First Amendment rights, 142, 167, 220–225
Fischbach, Michael, 246, 247
Fisher, Anthony, 221
Five, The (talk show), 152
Fleischer, Ari, 74
Florida State University, 165
Floyd, George, 139
Fohrer, Mirit, 130
Ford, Gerald, 193–194
Foreign Policy (Miller), 237
foreign policy, U.S.: anti-American terrorism and, 75–76; history of, 188–205; influence of lobbying organizations, 12, 71–72; Israel-Palestine relations, 198–199, 204, 232–234; Middle East involvement, 192, 208, 214; military aid to Israel, 202–203, 205, 218, 234; Orientalist attitudes, 193–194; Palestinian American dissent from, 35–36, 69–70; Palestinian solidarity, 193, 197; peacemaking, 194–198; support for creation of Jewish state, 189–191; on Ukraine, 204; use of UN veto power, 215–218
Forensic Architecture, 50
Foundation for Middle East Peace, 39, 51
416Lab, 38
FOX News, 48, 87, 152
Frankel, Max, 157
Freedom Is a Constant Struggle (Davis), 228, 250
freedom of speech, 164–167, 168, 170, 221, 222, 278
French solidarity, 238
Friedman, David, 199, 231–232
Friedman, Howard, 208

Friedman, Robert, 150–151
Friends Fiduciary Corporation, 123
Friends of the Israeli Defense League, 199
"from the river to the sea," 154–155
Fuchs, Keith, 49
Fulbright, J. William, 193
fundamentalism, 51–52, 61

G4S, 124
Gabriel, Brigitte, 70–71
Galilee, 263
Gantz, Benny, 203–204
Garner, Eric, 139
Gay, Claudine, 178–179
Gaza, xi–xii, 2, 3, 21, 75, 78, 147, 150, 155, 178, 193, 195, 199, 210, 241, 283
Gazavision, 130
Geller, Pamela, 17
General Mills, 117
General's Son, The (Peled), 103
Geneva Convention, 74–75, 199
genocide, xi–xii, 21, 204, 205, 241, 247
George Washington University, 172
Georgia anti-BDS legislation, 231
Gerber, Haim, 46
Gerstmann, Evan, 128–129
Ghorashi, Halleh, 10
Gingrich, Newt, 44
Gisha, 110
Giuliani, Rudy, 48
Givati Brigade, 116
Glaser, Mitch, 124
Global Palestine (Collins), 15, 213, 262
Global War on Terror, 19–20
Globus, Yorum, 40–41
Golan, Menaham, 40–41
Golan Heights, 96, 201, 232
Golani Brigade, 116
Goldberg, Jeffrey, 107
Goldberg, Jonah, 157
Goldmann, Nahum, 76
Goldstone Report, 198
Gomez, Selena, 140
Google, 145, 147, 229–230
Gordon, Neve, 106
Gore, Al, 93

INDEX

Goselin, Peter, 137
Graham, Franklin, 59
Gramsci, Antonio, 13
Greek solidarity, 121
Green, Andy, 49
Greenblatt, Jonathan, 163, 199, 231–232
Greenburg, Bryan, 141
Greening Israel Project, 261, 263–264
Greenwald, Glenn, 151–152
Gregory, Tyler, 121
Greilsammer, Ilan, 105–106
Grinnell College, 98
group consciousness, 112
Guardian, The (periodical), 146, 218
Guatemalan solidarity, 240
Gulf War, 232
Gupta, Akhil, 7
Gush Etzion settlement, 199
Gustman, Alan, 177

Haaretz (periodical), 103, 135, 260, 264
Haas, Shira, 41–42
Habash, Tariq, 182
Hadid, Bella, 44, 120, 146
Hadid, Gigi, 44
Hadin, Shurat, 130
Hagee, John, 59–60, 211
Hahn, Peter, 192
Halavi, Yossi Klein, 257
Hall, Wendy, 94
Halper, Jeff, 104, 109
Halper, Katie, 154
Halperin, Liora, 180–181
Hamas, 75, 79, 136, 149, 155, 198, 200, 234, 241
Hamel, Mike, 261
Hannity, Sean, 139
Hansen, Johnatnan, 70
Hapoel Be'er Sheva, 140
Har Bracha, 264
Hardie, John, 152
Harjo, Joy, 255
Hartmen, Donniel, 259
Harvard Crimson, The (periodical), 170–171
Harvard Out of Occupied Palestine, 116

Harvard University, 116, 136, 137, 170–171, 178–179, 181–182
Harwitt, Cecily, 75
hasbara (explanation) campaign, 149
Hasbara Fellowships Canada, 275
hashtags, 145–146, 152, 261
Hass, Amira, 103
Hatari, 131
hate speech, 165–167, 168
Hawking, Stephen, 125, 129
Hayford, Jack, 61
HaYovel, 263–264
Hazan, Oren, 138
Hearst Metrotone News, 72
Hebraic style, 53
Hebrew University of Jerusalem, 46
Hechler, William Henry, 56
Heeb (periodical), 137
hegemony, 13
Hernandez, Alma, 142
Hertzberg, Arthur, 151
Hester, Bart, 143
Hewlett-Packard, 116–117, 123
higher education. *See* college campuses
Hill, Marc Lamont, 14–15, 37, 82, 154–155, 199, 201–202
Hill, The (news website), 154, 266
Hilton, Paris, 241
Hinn, Benny, 61
Hoagland, Jim, 157
Hollings, Ernest "Fritz," 208–209
Holocaust, 58, 176–177, 188, 272–273
Holocaust Industry, The (Finkelstein), 176–177
Homecoming King (film), 76
Horovitz, David, 139, 177
Howard, Dwight, 140
Huffington Post (news website), 102, 217, 251, 258
Hughes, Bryan, 223
human rights violations, 3, 16, 18, 76, 79, 81, 113, 116, 202, 264
Human Rights Watch, 3, 49, 154, 182; Middle East and North Africa Division, 78
Hunter, Duncan, 77

INDEX

Icelandic Broadcasting Union, 131
identity: Arab, 14; Arab-American, 27; community, 7; diaspora and, 6; erasure of Palestinian, 44–47, 161, 164; within Israel, 8; masking of, 8; Muslim, 14; nationality and, 7–8; pan-Arab, 27; politics, 11; racial (*see* race and racial identity); religious, 19, 35; role of in resisting Israel, 5–9; struggle as part of, 6; transnational nature of, 4, 164; wandering, 8
IfNotNow, 102, 109–110, 217
immigration policies, 14, 34–35
imperial culture, 28
In Context, 147
Incredible Hulk, The (comic), 41–42
Indian solidarity, 238
Indigenous/Native American solidarity, 254–257
Informed Comment (periodical), 176
Inhofe, James F., 45
Injustice (Peled), 215
Innocents Abroad, The (Twain), 45
Instagram, 19, 44, 140, 141, 145, 146, 154
Institute for Curriculum Services (ICS), 161–162
International Christian Embassy in Jerusalem (ICEJ), 60, 211
International Court of Justice, xii, 21, 204, 205, 241, 280, 283
International Criminal Court, 21, 50, 241
International Fellowship of Christians and Jews (IFCJ), 211–212
International Holocaust Remembrance Alliance (IHRA), 168–169, 175, 221
International Legal Forum, 120
International Longshore and Warehouse Union (ILWU), 121, 134
International Press Institute, 103
International Solidarity Movement (ISM), 235
internet. *See* democratization of media; social media
Irish solidarity, 121, 237
Isaac, Munther, 67–69
Isaac, Rael Jean, 272

Isaac, Rudaina, 63
Islam: Christian Zionism and, 61; negative depictions of, 32; Orientalist views of, 13–14
Islam and the West (Daniel), 32
Islamophobia, 138, 163, 228, 254, 258–259
Israel: as an apartheid state, 3, 154, 186, 199, 203, 241, 281; Boycott Law, 130; Christian affiliation with, 19, 30, 51–54, 98–99; compulsory Zionism, 54–55; condemnation of, 3; conflation of Judaism with, 128, 283; creation of, 1, 76, 86, 103, 185, 191, 234, 237; criticism of, 105–107, 271–276; European support for, 15; Evangelical support for, 65–66; fascism in, 112–113; human rights violations, 3, 16, 18, 76, 79, 81, 113, 116, 202; Jewish Americans and, 17; media portrayals of, 39–40; Palestinian identity within, 8; role of transnational identity in resistance to, 5–9; solidarity for, 236, 237, 238, 240, 254–257; U.S.-Israeli exceptionalism, 29, 186–187; U.S. support for, 3, 4, 13, 15, 16, 25, 64–66, 67, 71–79, 96, 148, 185–187, 205, 216 (*see also* foreign policy, U.S.); Zionism, xi, 16–17, 19–20, 40, 262
Israel ABCs (Schroeder), 46
Israel Anti-Boycott Act, 219–220
Israel Defense Forces (IDF), 49–50, 84–85, 116, 170, 240
Israeli Committee Against Home Demolitions (ICAHD), 104, 109
Israeli Genesis Prize, 138
Israelis: American feelings towards, 26; criticism of Israel, 105–107, 151; as "good guys," 148; organizations supporting Palestinians, 108–111; revisionists, 267–270; settler movement, 199; support for Palestine, 80, 90, 101–105, 270–276; "Western" labeling of, 213
Israelism (film), 271
Israeli Supreme Court, 49
Israel Lobby and US. Foreign Policy, The (Mearsheimer and Walt), 149, 206

INDEX

Israel on Campus Coalition (ICC), 173
ITN News, 152

Jackson, George, 245–246
Jackson, Jesse, 194, 243
Jackson, Liz, 273
Jamal, Amaney, 32–33, 35
Japanese Americans, 253
Jayapal, Pramila, 243
Jefferson, Thomas, 66
Jeffress, Robert, 68
Jerusalem Countdown (Hagee), 211
Jerusalem Embassy Act (1995), 202
Jerusalem Post (periodical), 105, 153, 172, 201
Jewish affinity, 53
Jewish Agency, 40, 191
Jewish Americans: Black, 248, 249–250; in Congress, 64–65; criticism of Israel, 101–102, 105–107, 271–276; intersectional organizations, 248; media support, 40; non-Zionist, 267–270; organizations supporting Palestinians, 108–111; pro-Israel lobby, 205–210, 232–233; relation to Israel, 17; support for Palestine, 19–20, 80, 90, 101–105, 138–140, 270–276; voters, 207, 270
Jewish Channel, 44
Jewish Community Relations Council (JCRC), 121, 162, 247
Jewish Institute for National Security of America (JINSA), 226–227
Jewish Journal (periodical), 173–174
Jewish National Fund, 264
Jewish News Syndicate, 124, 164
Jewish Voice for Peace (JVP), 19–20, 110, 155, 168, 170, 217
Jewish Week (periodical), 176
Jews for Racial and Economic Justice, 217
Jews of Color Caucus, 248–250
Jhally, Sut, 148
Johnson, Derek, 125
Johnson, Lyndon, 66
Johnson, Terry, 100
Jones, Rachel Lee, 104

Jordahl, Mikkel, 142, 225
Jordan, Hamilton, 194
journalists and journalism, 148–158; killed in Gaza, xii, 284
Journal of Palestine Studies (periodical), 112–113
J Street, 97, 274
Judaism, 52, 53, 128, 221, 283. *See also* Jewish Americans
Julia (film), 141
justice, 11, 89–90, 179–184, 282, 285

Kaell, Hillary, 53
Kagan, Robert, 157
Kahane, Meir, 44–45
Kairos Palestine document, 124
Kalin, Ibrahim, 202
Kansas anti-BDS legislation, 224
Kant, Immanuel, 282–283
Kaplan, Amy, 72, 73
Kar-Ben Publishing, 46
Kar Bir'im, 263
Kashmiri solidarity, 237–238
Katznelson, Avraham, 103
Kauanui, J. Kehaulani, 255
Kavanaugh, Ryan, 142
Keily, Keith Peter, 186
Kelly, Laura, 266
Kennedy, Christopher, 176
Kennedy, John F., 73, 185
Kennedy, Robert F., 31, 176
Keren Kayemeth LeIsrael-Jewish National Fund (KKL-JNF), 261–262
Kessler, Randy, 180
Khalek, Rania, 252–253
Khalid, Asma, 79
Khalidi, Dima, 165–166, 167–168, 220
Khalidi, Rashid, 155, 277
Khan, Suhaib, 172
Khankan, Ghazi, 197
King, Martin Luther, Jr., 251
Kirby, John, 218
Kirchwey, Freda, 40
Kirk, Mark, 208
Klarman, Seth, 179
Klein, David, 128
Klein, Morton, 149, 173, 211

Klinghoffer, Leon, 48
Knesset committee, 74
Knopf-Newman, Marcy Jane, 125–126, 159–160
Kohr, Howard, 207
Koontz Esther, 224
Koren, Ariel, 230
Koren, Daniel, 275
Korn, Betsy Berns, 207
Kramer, Martin, 128
Krauthammer, Charles, 157
Kristol, William, 157
Kushner, Daniel, 271
Kushner, Jared, 199, 232

labor union boycotts, 121–123
Labour Party (U.K.), 139
Landau, Susan, 116
Lantos, Tom, 211
Lara, Frank, 122
Larson, Satyel, 181
Late Great Planet Earth, The (Lindsey), 59
Latin American solidarity, 239–240
Latinx solidarity, 251–253
Lauder, Ronald, 181
Law, Bernard, 163
Lebanon, Israeli aggression against, 148–149
Lebzelter, Gisela, 54
Leding, Greg, 143
Lee, Bobby, 141
Lee, Summer, 97
legislation: anti-BDS, 142–143, 209, 219–220, 221, 222–226, 231, 234; anti-immigration, 160; against antisemitism, 166, 174, 175, 221; curbing Palestinian activism, 220–222; social media content regulation, 146–147
Leigh, Mike, 129
Leitner, Darshan, 130
Lelyveld, Arthur, 272
Lennox, Annie, 129
#LetAymanReport, 152
Leverett, Alan, 142
Levin, Mark, 139

Levy, Gideon, 111, 112, 282
Lewis, Bernard, 70
LexisNexis, 150
LGBTQ+ movement allies, 37, 114, 140, 235, 260–261, 280
Lieberman, Joseph, 93, 208
Light and the Glory, The (Marshall and Manuel), 54
Likud Party, 157, 269
Lincoln, Abraham, 66
Lindsey, Hal, 59
linked fate, 112
"Little Amal," 133
Lloyd, David, 127–128
Loach, Ken, 142
lobbying: Arab American, 212; Christian Zionist, 210–212; influence of on U.S. foreign policy, 71–72; perceived effectiveness of, 12; power of diasporic communities, 13; pro-Israel, 194, 205–210, 232–233; resistance to Israeli occupation via, 12
Looking for Palestine (Said), 42
Lopez Almejo, José de Jesus, 13
Lorde, 129–130
Los Angeles Times (periodical), 103, 157, 166
Lost Promise of Patriotism, The (Hansen), 70
"lost tribes" theology, 256
Lucas, Christopher, 35
L'Unione Sindacale di Base, 121

Mac, Ryan, 146
MacArthur Foundation, 144
Maccabee Task Force, 168–169
Macron, Emmanuel, 238
Maddow, Rachel, 150
Madonna, 131
Madrid Peace Conference, 232
Maestas, Adrian, 252–253
Magill, Liz, 178
Mahdawi, Arwa, 146
Maher, Bill, 37–38, 155–156
Maira, Sunaina, 28, 253
Makdisi, Saree, 15, 89, 186, 187, 235, 241, 263
Makhlouf, George, 63

INDEX

Malcolm X, 246, 247
Maltz, Judy, 264
Mandatory Palestine, 6, 127, 162, 190
Manning, Robert, 49
Mansour, Shadia, 239
Manuel, David, 54
Marcetic, Branco, 96
Marshall, George, 191
Marshall, Peter, 54
Martin, Abby, 231
Martin, Tom, 238
Martin, Trayvon, 247
Marvel, 41–42
Massing, Michael, 182
mass mobilization, 85–89
Maté, Gabor, 107, 269–270
Maté, Hannah, 270
May in the Summer (film), 143
McCain, John, 70, 208
McCollum, Betty, 203
McConnell, Mitch, 208
McCoy, Yavilah, 250
McDonald's, 134
McGarry, Greg, 122–123
McGraw Hill, 162
McVeigh, Timothy, 32
Mearsheimer, John J., 74, 75, 149, 157, 206, 208–210, 212, 271, 272
media: biases against Arabs, 39; biases against Muslims, 39; decline of traditional, 80, 84, 86–87; democratization of, 19, 83–85, 87–89; internet echo chambers, 94–95; journalists and journalism, xii, 148–158, 284; nontraditional channels, 88; portrayals of Israel, 39–40; portrayals of Palestine, 25, 33; portrayals of Palestinian Americans, 38–42
MediaBias/FactCheck, 89
Meir, Golda, 182
Menendez, Robert, 208
Mensa, Vic, 248–249
Merkley, Paul, 57
Meta, 147
Meza, Andrea, 132
Mic (periodical), 81–82
Michaelson, Wes, 62
Microsoft, 145
Midburn, 132
"Middle East Scholars Barometer" survey, 127
Middle East Studies Association (MESA), 127
Miftah, 222
millennials, 99
Miller, Aaron David, 195
Miller, Rory, 237
Minhaj, Hasan, 76
Minnesota Star-Tribune (periodical), 117
Mishor Adummim industrial zone, 119
missionaries, 56
Miss Universe Pageant, 131–132
Mitford, E. L., 57
Modern Language Association (MLA), 173
Modi, Narenda, 238
Moghul, Haroon, 259
Mohyeldin, Ayman, 151–152, 241–242
Mondoweiss, 88
Montt, Ríos, 240
Morales, Evo, 239–240
Moroccan solidarity, 242
Morris, Benny, 105, 160
Morse, Clara Ence, 135–136
Motorola Solutions, 123
Movement for Black Lives, 247–248, 249–250
Movimiento Estudiantil Chicano de Aztlán (MEChA), 251–252
Mullen, Bill, 178
Murad, Nora Esther, 46
Murdoch, Rupert, 163
Musicians for Palestine, 132–133
Muslim Leadership Initiative (MLI), 257–260
Muslim(s): American feelings towards, 26; in Asia, 253–254; Christian portrayals of, 53–54; Christian Zionism and, 61; identity, 14; media biases against, 39; selective racialization of, 32, 35, 39; stereotypes of, 31–32; support for Biden, 135; support for Palestine, 135–136; terrorist framing of, 212–215

Naber, Nadine, 35
Nagel, Risa, 102–103
Naikoo, Babrah, 238
Najour, Costa George, 34–35
Nakba, xi, 2, 3, 42, 160, 200, 262, 277
Nasir, Hanna, 126
Nassar, Maha, 38
Nasser, Gamal Abdel, 192
National Review (periodical), 181
Nation (periodical), 40, 182
National, The (periodical), 223
National Association of Arab Americans, 27
National Christian Leadership Conference for Israel, 211
nationalism, 8, 36
nationality, 7–8
National Lawyers Guild, 252
National Security Council, 193, 218
National Women's Studies Association (NWSA), 265
Native American and Indigenous Studies Association (NAISA), 126–127, 177
Native American/Indigenous solidarity, 254–257
Navajo Nation, 254
Navot, Kerem, 264
Nazzal, Rehab, 133
NBC, 151–152
NBC News, 68
Nebenzia, Vassily, 217
Nehru, Jawaharlal, 238
Netanyahu, Benjamin, 21, 37–38, 148, 149, 196, 200–201, 205, 238, 241, 243, 282
Netroots Nation, 243
Netta, 130
Neumann, Emanuel, 57–58
New Christian Zionism, The (Blaising), 55
new historian phenomenon, 105, 107, 267–270
New Republic (periodical), 157
newspaper circulation, 86–87
Newsweek (periodical), 136
Newton Public Schools, 161

New York anti-BDS legislation, 225–226
New York Police Department, 48, 249
New York Review of Books (periodical), 106
New York Sun (periodical), 157
New York Times (periodical), 38, 39, 48, 107, 153, 155, 156, 157, 191, 210, 248, 271
Nez, Jonathan, 254
Nides, Tom, 204
9/11 Commission, 75–76, 214
Nixon, Richard, 232
Noah, Mordecai Manuel, 66
Noah, Trevor, 139
North, James, 39
North Carolina Coalition for Israel, 227
Northeastern University, 172
November 29th Committee, 242
NowThis Politics, 102
NRC Handelsblad (periodical), 89

Oakland Roots, 120
Oakland Roots Radicals, 120
Obama, Barack, 73, 93–95, 124, 196, 197–199, 216
Obeidallah, Dean, 43, 139–140
Obenzinger, Hilton, 242–243
Obsession (film), 163
Ocasio-Cortez, Alexandria, 97
occupation, Israeli: BDS campaigns against, 12; challenging, 11–13; lobbying against, 12
Occupation of the American Mind (film), 139
Occupied America (Acuña), 252
Occupied Palestinian Territories (OPT), 3, 11, 16, 17, 20, 46, 49, 73, 103, 117–118, 185, 188, 195, 245
Occupy Wall Street, 4, 21, 235
October 7 Hamas attacks, xi, xii, 3, 75, 134, 270
Odeh, Alex, 48–49
Oklahoma City bombing, 32
Oldmixon, Elizabeth, 64–66
Omar, Ilhan, 97, 222
Omer, Atalia, 270–271
Only Murders in the Building (TV show), 143

INDEX

Operation Defense Shield, 73
oppression, 246
O'Reilly, Bill, 213–214
O'Reilly Factor, The (talk show), 213
Oren, Michael, 153, 169
Orientalism, 13–14, 17, 27, 29, 30, 31–32, 52, 92, 187, 212–213, 254
Orientalism (Said), 31
Oslo Accords, 11, 187, 195–196, 232
Ostrovsky, Arsen, 120
O'Sullivan, Meghan, 171
othering processes, 7, 32–36, 42
Other Side of the Wall, The (Isaac), 67
"our American Israel," 72–73
Our American Israel (Kaplan), 72
Out of Place (Said), 43
Oxfam, xii

Palestine: in the American imagination, 13–18, 27; American perceptions of, 25–27, 29–31; colonization of, 1, 4, 5; erasure of, 46–47, 102, 161; increasing U.S. support for, 78–79; Jewish settlements, 68–69, 74–75, 199; partition, 1, 160, 191; request for UN membership, 216; vilification of, 2
Palestine Action, 120–121
Palestine Chronicle (news website), 89
Palestine Focus (newsletter), 242
Palestine Islamic Jihad, 214
Palestine Israel Network, 124
Palestine Legal, 136, 165, 167, 170, 220, 228–230
Palestine Liberation Organization (PLO), 18, 148, 193, 194, 195, 216, 222
Palestine Solidarity Committee (PSC), 170–171
Palestine Vaincra, 238
Palestinian, The (film), 141
Palestinian Academic and Cultural Boycott of Israel, 125–126
Palestinian Americans: discrimination against, 228–231, 233, 244; hostility, intimidation, and violence towards, 47–50; identity, 36; impact of Christian Zionism on, 69–71; media portrayals of, 38–42; othering of, 35–36, 42; scrutiny faced by, 76–77; selective racialization of, 32–36, 39, 43–47, 71, 77, 253; terrorist framing of, 212–215; transnational identity of, 9–13, 43
Palestinian Authority (PA), 18, 50, 187, 195
Palestinian Campaign for the Academic and Cultural Boycott of Israel, 131, 173
Palestinian people: American perceptions of, 29–31; as "bad guys," 148; blame placed on, 156–157; Christians, 30, 52, 62–63, 67–69, 258; Christian support for, 100–101; discrimination against, 15–16; displacement of, 1–2, 8–9, 86, 284–285; erasure of identity of, 44–47, 161, 164; film depictions of, 40–41; lineage, 1; media portrayals of, 40–42, 77–78; narratives of, 17–18, 29; Orientalist discourse around, 27, 29, 30, 31–32, 52; as refugees, 188; terrorist framing of, 31, 39, 48, 155, 164; transnational support for, 2, 4; vilification of, 2, 4, 13; violence against, 275–276. *See also* Palestinian Americans
Pappé, Ilan, 106, 269
Parker, Christopher, 94
Parsons, Gradye, 123
Partition Plan (UN Resolution 181), 1, 160, 191
Patriot Act, 92, 93, 214
patriotism, 8, 36, 69–70, 158–159, 187
Patterson, Thomas E., 86
Paul, Josh, 182
PBS NewsHour, 88, 135
Peace Now, 108
peace talks, 11, 187, 188–189, 193, 194–198, 232
Pearson, 162
Peled, Matti, 103
Peled, Miko, 37–38, 103, 215
People's History of the United States, A (Zinn), 159
Pepsi, 116

Peres, Shimon, 111
Perilman, Vanessa, 134
Perry, Noam, 117
Peruvian solidarity, 239
Peterson, Christy, 46
Phillips, Elizabeth, 61
Phillips, Scott, 92
Pillsbury, 117
Pillsbury, Charlie, 117
Pink Floyd, 138–139
pinkwashing, 260–261
Pipes, Daniel, 168
P Is for Palestine (Bashi), 47
Pitzer College, 128–129
Plan Dalet, 160
Plitnick, Mitchell, 14–15, 37, 154, 199, 201–202
+972 Magazine, 88
police: American exchanges with Israeli military, 226–228, 248–249; militarization, 90, 91–93, 228; violence, 81–83, 90, 214, 248; WTO protests response, 91–92; zero-tolerance policies, 249
political action committees (PACs), 208
political racism, 28
politics: Democratic Party, 90, 93–98; federal, 219–222; influence of Christian Zionism on Palestinian, 60–61; influence of Zionism on U.S., 57–59, 63–69, 190; local, 222–226; polarization in, 93–98; political erasure of Arab Americans, 27–28; pro-Israel lobby, 194, 205–210; and racialization, 33–34; Republican Party, 93–94, 95–96; role of religion in, 64–66; solidarity in, 242–243. *See also* foreign policy, U.S.
Politics of Teaching Palestine, The (Knopf-Newman), 159–160
popular culture and solidarity, 137–143
Portal, Gerardo Peñalver, 217
Portland State University, 169
Portman, Natalie, 111, 138
Powell, Colin, 74, 197
Power, Samantha, 216
Power, Susan, 50

Presbyterian Church (USA) (PCUSA), 123–124
Pressley, Ayana, 97
Princeton University, 171–172, 181
"progressive except Palestine" phenomenon, xii, 14–15, 36–38, 75, 203, 265
progressive movements, 18–20, 93–98
Project for Excellence in Journalism, 86–87
propaganda, 149, 170, 191
protests: after October 2023, 133–137; campus, 113, 135–137, 170–171, 275; pro-ceasefire groups, 217; Standing Rock, 257; street demonstrations, 121. *See also* Boycott, Divestment, and Sanctions (BDS) campaigns
Psagot Winery, 118–119
Puar, Jasbir, 178, 181
public education: anti-Palestinian prejudice in, 163–164; censorship at K–12 schools, 230–231; as a moral force, 158–159; pro-Israel advocacy in, 161–163; school curricula, 15, 27, 114; textbooks, 158, 160; whitewashing history, 159–160. *See also* college campuses
Puerto Rican solidarity, 252
Puma, 120
Purdue University, 178
Putin, Vladimir, 204

Quakers, 104, 117, 123
Quds News Network, 84, 145
Question of Palestine, The (Said), 29
Qumsiyeh, Mazin, 259–260

Rabbinical Assembly, 272
Rabbinic Council for Human Rights, 247
Rabbis for Ceasefire, 217
race and racial identity: anti-Palestinian racism, 137–138; cultural impact of BLM, 81–83; racial profiling, 228; selective racialization, 32–36, 43–47, 246; in the U.S., 9–13; whiteness, 34–35
Rachel Corrie, MV (ship), 237

INDEX

radicalization of religion, 35
Radiohead, 131
Rage Against the Machine, 132
Raheb, Mitri, 63
Rah! Rah! Mujadara! (book), 46
Rainbow Coalition, 194
Ramadan/Yom Kippur War, 105
Raytheon Technologies, 171
Reagan, Ronald, 58–59, 194–195, 198, 202
Redgrave, Vanessa, 141
Reed, Ralph, 59
Reel Bad Arabs (Shaheen), 39, 49
Regev, Mark, 152
religion: BDS campaigns by religious organizations, 123–125; church attendance, 19, 80, 99–100; radicalization of, 35; religious affiliation, 19, 99–100; role of in politics, 64–66. *See also* Christians and Christianity
Religion News Service, 275
reparations, 144
Reporters Without Borders, 103
representation of minority voices, 18–20
Republican Party, 93–94, 95–96
Rest and Abolish the Military Industrial Complex, 171
Restorationism, 61–62
Reuters (news agency), 222
Rice, Condoleezza, 74, 197
Right to Maim, The (Puar), 181
Rihanna, 140
Riley, John, 152
Rivera, Geraldo, 152–153
RiverWind, Joseph, 254
Roberts, Frank Leon, 81, 82, 85
Robertson, Pat, 59
Robin, Corey, 135
Rodgers, Guy, 70
Rodney King riots, 91
Rogan, Seth, 111
Rolling Stone (periodical), 239
Romney, Mitt, 70
Rooney, Sally, 143–144
Roseanne (TV show), 138
Rose Bowl Parade, 133
Rosen, Brant, 105, 275

Rosenberg, MJ, 207, 208
Rosenthal, Jon, 224
Rosenthal, Steven, 271
Rosner, Schmuel, 156
Roth Kenneth, 182
Rotholz, Ron, 142
Roy, Sara, 106, 179–180, 183–184, 235, 272–275
Rudman, Warren, 210
Ruffalo, Mark, 241
Rumsfeld, Donald, 197
Russell Berrie Foundation, 259
Rutgers University, 178
Ryan, Paul, 48

Saban, Haim, 37
Sabra (comic-book character), 41–42
Sabra (hummus brand), 116
Sabra and Shatila massacre, 42
Sachs, Justine, 130
Saeed, Sana, 28, 258
Saffourieh, 263
Said, Edward, 13, 29, 31, 36–37, 40, 42, 43, 175, 193, 195, 235–236, 266, 267
Said, Najla, 42
Sainath, Radhika, 172–173
Salaita, Steven, 41, 167, 172, 176
Salamy, Jimmy, 121
Salem, Hosam, 153–154
Salon (news website), 197
Samaria Regional Council, 254
Samhan, Helen, 28
Sanchez, Gabriel, 112
Sanders, Bernie, 51, 95, 234
San Francisco Independent Journal (periodical), 123
San Francisco Labor Council (SFLC), 122
San Francisco Teacher's Union, 121–123
Sarsour, Linda, 47–48
Sartre, Jean-Paul, 175
Sasson, Theodore, 17
#savesheikhjarrah, 145
Schafer, Hannah, 170–171
Schewel, Steve, 227
Schlussel, Debbie, 151, 153

school curricula, 15, 27, 114, 158, 160, 161–162
Schroeder, Holly, 46
Schueller, Malini Johar, 127–128
Schultz, George, 194–195
Schumer, Chuck, 75, 208
Schusterman Family Foundation, 162
Schwartz, Edward, 153
Scott, Tim, 221
Seattle Education Association, 122
Segev, Tom, 106
selective racialization, 32–36
self-determination: American, 52; Israeli, 25; Jewish, 19, 26, 80; Palestinian, 19, 40, 48, 111, 199, 243; Palestinian American, 76; universalist beliefs in, 80
Sen, Somdeep, 238
Seneca Nation, 254
September 11 terror attacks, 14, 20, 26, 90, 92, 93, 212–215, 226
Serino, Kenichi, 135
settler colonialism, xi, xiii, 1, 64, 152–153, 251, 262, 278, 284
7amleh, 145
Shaare Zedek Medical Center, 199
Shabaik, Amr, 137
Shadow Over Palestine, A (Feldman), 15, 28, 186
Shah, Raj, 200
Shaheen, Jack, 39, 40, 49
Shaked, Ayelet, 146–147
Shakir, Faiz, 219
Shakir, Omar, 172
Shalom Hartman Institute, 257, 259
Shaoul, Jean, 216
Shapiro, Ben, 155
Sharon, Ariel, 73–74, 148, 160, 197
Sharoni, Simona, 166, 167, 177–178
Shatila Palestinian refugee camp, 148
Sheffer, Gabriel, 21–22
Sheikh Jarrah expulsion, 3–4, 21, 84, 88, 180, 241
Shelly Ben, 254–255
Sheppard, Ferrari, 251
Shihade, Magid, 253, 257
Shlaim, Avi, 106

Shoman, Samia, 161
Shorter, David, 128
Shugart, Paula, 131–132
Sidawi, Ramzi, 63
Silverman, Ben, 142
Silverman, Hilda, 273
Simon, Bob, 153
Singh, Prerna, 35
Sirhan, Sirhan, 31, 176
Siryoti, Daniel, 63
Six-Day War, 27, 193, 207
Sizer, Stephen Robert, 63
Sky News, 152
Slick, Chris, 70
Smith, Patti, 132
Snapchat, 19
Snow, Jon, 152
socialism, 95. *See also* Democratic Socialists of America (DSA)
social media, 19, 36, 44, 83–89, 94–95, 112, 114, 141, 145–147, 278–279
social movements, 4, 20–21, 90, 114, 182–183, 278–279
social revolution, 18, 91
societal transformations, 2
Society for the Protection of Nature in Israel, 262
SodaStream, 119
solidarity, Palestinian: African-American community, 244–251; in American politics, 242–243, 266–267; among Palestinians, 8–9; Asian American community, 253–254; by authors, 143–145; on college campuses, 116, 135–137, 167–175; environmentalist community, 261–264; global, 121, 237–242; Indigenous/Native American community, 254–257; International Solidarity Movement (ISM), 235; Latinx community, 251–253; LGBTQ+ movement, 260–261; in popular culture, 137–143; repercussions and punishment for in higher education, 175–179; repercussions for, 136–137; social media platforms, 145–147; transnational, 12–13; transnational

INDEX

nature of, 235–236. *See also* Boycott, Divestment, and Sanctions (BDS) campaigns; protests
Solomon, Norman, 148
"Somos Sur" ("We Are South") (song), 239
South Africa apartheid, 113, 115, 121, 122, 128, 130, 144
Southern Baptists, 124
Spalding, Elizabeth Edwards, 58
Spanier, Kristine, 46
Spector, Stephen, 61
Spielvogel, Carl, 149
Spy Legends, 41
Stand for Israel, 211
Standing Rock, 257
StandWithUs, 72, 167, 178, 180
Stanford College Republicans, 155
Starbucks, 134
Starbucks Workers United, 133–134
Stein, Rebecca, 84
Steinitz, Yuval, 138
stereotypes, 13, 24, 29, 31–33, 38–39, 143, 163, 248, 260, 278, 282–283
Stern, Marlow, 38
Stewart, Jon, 110–111, 139–140
Stockton, Ronald, 56, 57
Stone, Daniel, 87–88
Stoudemire, Amare, 140
St. Petersburg Times (periodical), 213
Strauss, 116
street demonstrations, 121
Strokes, The, 132
Student Nonviolent Coordination Committee (SNCC), 245
Students for Justice in Palestine, 155, 168, 170, 178, 251
"Suez" (Du Bois), 192
Suez Crisis, 192
SUNY Plattsburgh, 177–178
surveillance, 85, 90, 93
Swedenburg, Ted, 5
systemic racism, 81–83

Taeb, Yasmine, 266
Taha, Subhi, 44
Takruri, Dena, 110
Tankian, Serj, 132
Tea Party, 94
technology: and democratization of media, 19; social media platform operators, 145–147; surveillance, 85, 90; trans-state communication networks, 22–23
Tehranian, John, 32
Tel Aviv University, 255
Telhami, Shibley, 78, 200
Tenet, George, 197
Terrones, Pedro Castillo, 239
terrorism, 14, 17, 20, 29, 32, 75–76, 92, 212–215
Terry, Janice, 32, 150, 194
Texas anti-BDS legislation, 222–224
textbooks, 158, 160, 161–162
They Dare to Speak Out (Findley), 212
Third Jihad, The (film), 163
Thy Kingdom Come Thy Will be Done in Earth (Chosa), 256
Tibi, Ahmad, 113
Tijoux, Anita, 239
Tikkun Olam, 270
TikTok, 19, 85–86, 88, 141
Till, Emmett, 83
Tilsen, Mark, 257
Time (periodical), 157
Times of Israel (periodical), 139
Tintiangco-Cubales, Allyson, 161
Tlaib, Rashida, 97, 154, 203, 222, 234
TMZ (news website), 140
Tolerance Is a Wasteland (Makdisi), 15
Torres, Ritchie, 136
Tosh, Peter, 245
Totah, Selim, 189–190
Trabulsi, Jeanne, 162
transnationalism: duality experienced by, 10; identity and, 4, 164; role of in resisting Israel, 5–9; solidarity, 12–13, 235–236
Travel to Israel (Doeden), 46
tree-planting projects, 261–264
Trice, Robert, 206, 210
Trinity United Church of Christ, 124
Troutt Powell, Eve, 127
Truah, 247

Truman, Harry, 40, 58, 191, 232
Trumka, Richard, 122
Trump, Donald, 14, 37, 63, 73, 94, 95–96, 163, 175, 196, 200–202, 217, 221, 222, 232
Trump administration, 44, 48, 199–202, 232
Turner, Nina, 96
Tutu, Desmond, 124
Twain, Mark, 45
Twitter (X), 94, 140, 145, 153, 275
Tzedek Chicago, 105, 275
Tzemel, Leah, 104

UAV Tactical Systems, 120–121
Ukraine, support for, 140, 157–158, 204
Umm Al-Khair, 102–103
UN. *See* United Nations (UN)
Unilever, 117–118
union boycotts, 121–123
Union for European Football Associations (UEFA), 140
Union for Reform Judaism, 247
Union of Agricultural Work Committees, 203
Union of Palestinian Women's Committees, 203
Union of Progressive Zionists (UPZ), 173
United Against War and Militarism, 171
United Church of Christ, 124
United Methodist Church, 124–125
United Nations (UN): Biden's speech to, 204; Conference on the Exercise of the Inalienable Rights of the Palestinian People, 104; Hill's speech to, 154–155; International Criminal Court, 21, 50, 241; Partition Plan (UN Resolution 181), 1, 160, 191; Relief Works Agency (UNRWA), 200; Resolution 242, 193, 199–200; Resolution 3379, 186–187; Security Council, 16; UNESCO, 216; United States in, 215–218; urged to support Zionism, 40
United States: Christian influence, 50–54; citizenship, 9–10; compulsory education, 158–159; cultural citizenship, 14; cultural landscape, 91; discrimination against Palestinians, 7; elections, 93, 94, 135, 208; foreign policy (*see* foreign policy, U.S.); immigration policies, 14, 34–35; imperial culture, 28; labor union boycotts, 121–123; moving of embassy in Israel, 155–156, 200, 202, 232; Palestine in the American imagination, 13–18, 27; perceptions of Palestine, 25–27; racial identity in, 9–13; religious allegiance, 19; support for Israel, 3, 4, 13, 15, 16, 25, 64–66, 67, 71–79, 96, 148, 185–187, 205, 216 (*see also* foreign policy, U.S.); in the UN, 215–218; U.S.-Israeli exceptionalism, 29, 186–187; views of Palestinians, 2–3. *See also* American(s)
Unity Coalition for Israel, 211
University of Alabama, 136
University of California, Berkeley, 170, 173–174, 273
University of California, Irvine, 169–170
University of California, Riverside, 116
University of Illinois Urbana-Champaign, 176, 255
University of Manchester, 116
University of Maryland, 127
University of Pennsylvania, 178
University of South Florida, 213, 214
University of Washington, 180–181
University of Wisconsin-Milwaukee, 182
Unsworth, Fran, 152
U.S. Campaign for the Academic & Cultural Boycott of Israel, 126
U.S. Department of Education, 162, 165, 166, 182, 221
U.S. Department of Homeland Security, 214, 227
U.S. Foreign Policy Discourse and the Israel Lobby (Keily), 186
U.S. House of Representatives, 64, 65, 71, 126, 189–190, 202, 205, 208
U.S. Senate, 64, 71, 166, 193, 202, 208
U.S. State Department, 166, 182, 191, 195, 197, 200, 209

INDEX

Vanity Fair (periodical), 139
Vargas, Edward, 112
Vassar College, 178
Veolia Environment, 123
Virginia Coalition for Human Rights (VCHR), 162
Vogue Arabia (periodical), 44

Walker, Alice, 144
Wallace, Mike, 151
WallBuilders, 54
Waller, Sherri, 263–264
Waller, Tommy, 263–264
Wall Street Journal (periodical), 157, 176, 178
Walt, Stephen M., 74, 75, 149, 157, 206, 208–210, 212, 271, 272
Walvoord, John F., 61
wandering identity, 8
War on Gaza, 21, 75, 78, 155, 178, 210
War on Terror, 111
Warrior, Robert, 255, 256–257
Washington Post (periodical), 85, 129, 135, 157, 206, 271
Washington Report on Middle East Affairs, 161
Washington Times (periodical), 157, 176
Wasow, Omar, 111
Wasserman-Schultz, Debbie, 203
Waters, Roger, 129, 138–139
Weekly Standard (periodical), 157
Weiss, Bari, 155–156
Welcome to Israel with Sesame Street (Peterson), 46–47
West, Kanye, 120
West Bank, 74–75, 102, 118–119, 129, 147, 193, 195, 199, 283
Westerners: Israelis labeled as, 213; narratives of Palestinian solidarity, 242; views of Palestinians, 2
White Evangelicalism, 51–52, 59–61, 99, 100–101
whiteness, 9, 15, 34–35, 249
whitewashing, 28–29, 32, 63, 64, 90, 150–151, 159–160, 278
Whitson, Sara Leah, 78
Whittock, Martyn, 99–100

Wider Bridge, A, 260, 261
WikiLeaks, 142
Wilder, Emily, 155
Wildman, David, 125
Will, George, 157
Williams, Lesley, 251
Wilson, Woodrow, 57, 66, 190
WithinOurLifetime, 98
Wolfman, Howard, 196–197
Workman, Ryna, 136–137
work permit requirements, 119
workplace discrimination, 228–230
World and Islamic Studies Enterprise (WISE), 213–214
World Jewish Congress, 181
World Social Forum, 235
World Trade Organization (WTO) protests, 90, 91–92
World Values Network, 129
World War I, 52
World War II, 27, 55, 58, 72, 87, 190, 253
World Zionist Organization, 57
Wound of Dispossession (Christison), 76
Wray-Lake, Laura, 42
Wright, Jeremiah, 250–251
Wyden, Ron, 208

Yale University, 176
Yorke, Thom, 131
Young Democratic Socialists of America (YDSA), 98
YouTube, 44, 88, 110, 152, 154

Zahr, Amer, 139
Zaidan, Ismat, 5
Zaitar, Asmmaa, 136
Zara, 134
Zarrugh, Amina, 34
Zeitoon, Ashraf, 146
Ziadah, Rafeef, 237
ZIM, 121
Zinn, Howard, 70, 159
Zionism: anti-Zionism, 273–274; colonial efforts of, xi; compulsory, 54–55; exclusionary nature of, 69; influence of in U.S., 57–59; influence of on politics, 63–69, 190; Israeli narrative

Zionism (*continued*)
　　of, 16–17, 70; JVP's views on, 19–20; Malcolm X on, 246; Muslim Leadership Initiative and, 257; Native American/Indigenous, 256–257; promotion of, 40; in public education, 160; terror campaign (1944–47), 190; U.S. support for, 72. *See also* Christian Zionism

Zionist Congress, 56
Zionist Organization of America (ZOA), 149, 173, 211
Zlotsky, Reid, 171
Zogby, Jim, 197
Zomlot, Husam, 201
Zuckerberg, Mark, 145
Zunes, Stephen, 66–67

GPSR Authorized Representative: Easy Access System Europe, Mustamäe tee 50, 10621 Tallinn, Estonia, gpsr.requests@easproject.com

www.ingramcontent.com/pod-product-compliance
Lightning Source LLC
Chambersburg PA
CBHW022025290426
44109CB00014B/745